IMPORTANT

HERE IS YOUR REGISTRATION CODE TO ACCESS MCGRAW-HILL PREMIUM CONTENT AND MCGRAW-HILL ONLINE RESOURCES

For key premium online resources you need THIS CODE to gain access. Once the code is entered, you will be able to use the web resources for the length of your course.

Access is provided only if you have purchased a new book.

If the registration code is missing from this book, the registration screen on our website, and within your WebCT or Blackboard course will tell you how to obtain your new code. Your registration code can be used only once to establish access. It is not transferable

To gain access to these online resources

1. USE your web browser to go to: **www.mhhe.com/pattersonad7**

2. CLICK on "First Time User"

3. ENTER the Registration Code printed on the tear-off bookmark on the right

4. After you have entered your registration code, click on "Register"

5. FOLLOW the instructions to setup your personal UserID and Password

6. WRITE your UserID and Password down for future reference. Keep it in a safe place.

If your course is using WebCT or Blackboard, you'll be able to use this code to access the McGraw-Hill content within your instructor's online course.

To gain access to the McGraw-Hill content in your instructor's WebCT or Blackboard course simply log into the course with the user ID and Password provided by your instructor. Enter the registration code exactly as it appears to the right when prompted by the system. You will only need to use this code the first time you click on McGraw-Hill content.

These instructions are specifically for student access. Instructors are not required to register via the above instructions.

The McGraw·Hill Companies
McGraw Hill **Higher Education**

Thank you, and welcome to your McGraw-Hill Online Resources.

0-07-298321-3 t/a
Patterson
American Democracy, 7/e

Seventh Edition

The American
DEMOCRACY

Thomas E. Patterson

Bradlee Professor of Government and the Press
John F. Kennedy School of Government
Harvard University

Boston   Burr Ridge, IL   Dubuque, IA   Madison, WI   New York   San Francisco   St. Louis
Bangkok   Bogotá   Caracas   Kuala Lumpur   Lisbon   London   Madrid   Mexico City
Milan   Montreal   New Delhi   Santiago   Seoul   Singapore   Sydney   Taipei   Toronto

Higher Education

THE AMERICAN DEMOCRACY

Published by McGraw-Hill, a business unit of The McGraw-Hill Companies, Inc., 1221 Avenue of the Americas, New York, NY 10020. Copyright © 2005, 2003, 2001, 1999 by The McGraw-Hill Companies, Inc. All rights reserved. Previous editions © 1997, 1996, 1994, 1993, 1990 by Thomas E. Patterson. No part of this publication may be reproduced or distributed in any form or by any means, or stored in a database or retrieval system, without the prior written consent of The McGraw-Hill Companies, Inc., including, but not limited to, any network or other electronic storage or transmission, or broadcast for distance learning.

Some ancillaries, including electronic and print components, may not be available to customers outside the United States.

This book is printed on acid-free paper.

3 4 5 6 7 8 9 0 DOW/DOW 0 9 8 7 6 5

ISBN 0-07-286803-1

Editor-in-chief: *Emily Barrosse*
Publisher: *Lyn Uhl*
Sponsoring editor: *Monica Eckman*
Marketing manager: *Katherine Bates*
Director of development: *Lisa Pinto*
Development editors: *Jim Strandberg and Angela Kao*
Media producer: *Sean Crowley*
Media project manager: *Kate Boylan*
Supplements producer: *Louis Swaim*
Production supervisor: *Randy Hurst*
Project manager: *Christina Gimlin*
Design manager: *Preston Thomas*
Cover designer: *Belinda Fernandez*
Interior designer: *Jamie O'Neil*
Photo research coordinator: *Nora Agbayani*
Photo researcher: *Chris Hammond, PhotoFind, L.L.C.*
Composition: *10/12 Palatino by Cenveo*
Printing: *45# Mead Pub Matte, RR Donnelley, Willard*

Cover photo: © *Joseph Sohm/Corbis*

Because this page cannot legibly accommodate all the copyright notices, credits are listed on page C-1 and constitute a continuation of the copyright page.

Library of Congress Cataloging-in-Publication Data
Patterson, Thomas E.
   The American democracy / Thomas E. Patterson.—7th ed.
      p. cm.
   Includes bibliographical references and index.
   ISBN 0-07-286803-1 (acid-free paper)
   1. United States—Politics and government—Textbooks. I. Title.

JK276.P37 2005
320.473—dc22   2004059251

http://www.mhhe.com

ABOUT
THE AUTHOR

Thomas E. Patterson is Bradlee Professor of Government and the Press in the John F. Kennedy School of Government at Harvard University. He was previously Distinguished Professor of Political Science in the Maxwell School of Citizenship at Syracuse University. Raised in a small Minnesota town near the Iowa and South Dakota borders, he was educated at South Dakota State University and the University of Minnesota, where he received his Ph.D. in 1971.

He is the author of seven books and dozens of articles, which focus primarily on the media and elections. His book *The Vanishing Voter* (2002) describes and explains the long-term decline in Americans' electoral participation. An earlier book, *Out of Order* (1994), received national attention when President Clinton said every politician and journalist should be required to read it. In 2002, *Out of Order* received the American Political Science Association's Graber Award for the best book of the past decade in political communication. Another of Patterson's books, *The Mass Media Election* (1980), received a *Choice* award as Outstanding Academic Book, 1980–1981. Patterson's first book, *The Unseeing Eye* (1976), was selected by the American Association for Public Opinion Research as one of the fifty most influential books of the past half-century in the field of public opinion.

His research has been funded by major grants from the National Science Foundation, the Markle Foundation, the Smith-Richardson Foundation, the Ford Foundation, the Knight Foundation, and the Pew Charitable Trusts.

CONTENTS IN BRIEF

iv

CONTENTS

v

4 Civil Liberties: Protecting Individual Rights   104

7 Political Participation and Voting: Expressing the Popular Will 212

10 **The News Media: Communicating Political Images** 306

PART THREE   Governing Institutions   333

13   The Federal Bureaucracy: Administering the Government   412

14   The Federal Judicial System: Applying the Law   444

PART FOUR   Public Policy 479

15 Economic and Environmental Policy: Contributing to Prosperity 480

PREFACE for the Instructor

The past few decades have been a period of extraordinary change in America, raising new challenges to the practice of government. People in the millions from Asia and Latin America have joined the American community, bringing with them cultural traditions that have made our society richer and fuller but also more fragmented. Traditional institutions, from political parties to families, have weakened dramatically, straining the fabric of our politics but also creating the possibility of adaptive new arrangements. Minorities and women, long denied access to political and economic power, are seeking a fairer share—and sometimes getting it. America's workers and firms have built a highly productive economy but now face the risks and opportunities of the global marketplace. The cold war that dominated our attention in foreign policy for decades has been replaced by international terrorism and localized conflicts that raise troubling new issues of domestic and world insecurity.

Scholars are striving to keep pace with these developments. Never before has scholarship been so closely tied to the real world. If much of what political scientists study is arcane, we have increasingly tried to connect our work and our thinking to political realities. The result is a fuller understanding of how American government operates. I have tried in this book to convey this new understanding in an accurate and interesting way.

REACHING OUT TO THE STUDENT

Anyone who writes an introductory American government text faces the challenge of describing and explaining a vast amount of scholarship. One approach is to pile fact upon fact and list upon list. It's a common enough approach, but it turns politics into a pretty dry subject. Politics doesn't have to be dry, and it certainly doesn't have to be dull. Politics has all the elements of drama with the added feature of affecting the everyday lives of real people.

This is a narrative-based text, the opposite of a text that piles list upon list and that divides its material into discrete compartments. A narrative text provides plenty of information, but the information is always part of a larger discussion that ties the various elements together.

Research indicates that the narrative style is a superior method for teaching students a "soft" science such as political science. They learn more readily because a narrative makes the subject more readable, more accessible, and more interesting. Studies also indicate that students can read attentively for a longer period of time when a text is narrative in form.

A narrative text weaves together theory, information, and examples in order to bring out key facts and ideas. The goal is to draw the students into the subject, give them a contextual understanding of major concepts and issues, and encourage them to think about the implications. To quicken this process, I start each chapter by telling a story that addresses a basic issue. The chapter on civil liberties, for example, begins with the case of the Creighton family, whose home was raided in the middle of the night by gun-toting FBI agents who believed that the Creightons were harboring a relative suspected of bank robbery. The suspect was not found, and the Creightons, who were badly frightened by the intrusion, sued the FBI for wrongful search. Did the FBI have sufficient cause for a warrantless search, or did the FBI violate the Creightons' constitutional rights? Where should society draw the line between its public safety needs and the rights of the individual? Such questions in the context of a real-life situation immediately plunge students into the chapter's subject and into the process of thinking about its importance.

The narrative approach is part of a second pedagogical goal of this text: helping students think critically. Critical thinking is, I believe, the most important skill that a student can acquire from a social science education. Students do not learn to think critically by engaging in rote memorization. Rather, they acquire this skill by reflecting on what they read, by resolving challenges to their customary ways of thinking, and by confronting difficult issues. To this end, I have attempted to structure the discussion in ways that ask students to think more deeply and systematically about politics. In the first chapter, for example, I discuss the inexact meanings, conflicting implications, and unfulfilled promise of Americans' most cherished ideals, including liberty and equality. The discussion includes the "Chinese Exclusion," a grotesque and not well known chapter in our history that should lead students to think about what it means to be an American.

Finally, I have attempted in this book to present American government through the analytical lens of political science but in a way that captures the vivid world of real-life politics. I regularly reminded myself while writing this book that only a tiny percentage of introductory students are interested in an academic political science career. Most students take the course because it is required or because they like politics. I have sought to write a book that will kindle political interest in the first type of student and deepen the interest of the second type, while also giving students the systematic knowledge that a science of politics can provide. I had a model in mind for the kind of book that could achieve these goals: V. O. Key's absorbing *Politics, Parties, and Pressure Groups,* which I had read many years earlier as an undergraduate student. The late Professor Key was a masterful scholar who had a deep love of politics and who gently chided colleagues whose interest in political science was confined to the "science" part.

Few scholars can match Key's brilliance, but most political scientists share his fascination with politics. The result of their combined efforts is a body of knowledge about American government that is both precise and politically astute. This scholarship provides the text's unifying core. Political scientists have identified several major tendencies in the American political system that are a basis for a systematic understanding of how it operates, namely:

- Enduring ideals that are the basis of Americans' political identity and culture and that are a source of many of their beliefs, aspirations, and conflicts

- Extreme fragmentation of governing authority that is based on an elaborate system of checks and balances, which serves to protect against abuses of political power but also makes it difficult for political majorities to assert power when confronting an entrenched or intense political minority

- Many competing groups, which are a result of the nation's great size, population diversity, and economic complexity and which exercise considerable influence on public policy

- Strong emphasis on individual rights, which results in substantial benefits to the individual and places substantial restrictions on majorities

- Preference for the marketplace as a means of allocating resources, which has the effect of placing many economic issues beyond the reach of popular majorities

These tendencies are introduced in the first chapter and discussed in subsequent chapters. If students forget many of the points made in this book, they may at least take away from the course a knowledge of the deep underpinnings of the American political system.

FEATURES OF THIS EDITION

A noteworthy change from previous editions is a heightened emphasis on liberty, equality, and self-government as the three great principles of American democracy. The origin and nature of these ideals are discussed in the first chapter, which also points out the tension that can exist among them. Subsequent chapters have boxes titled "Liberty, Equality, and Self-Government" that ask students to grapple with issues related to these principles. These boxes help students recognize just how thoroughly these principles are embedded in American political practice and thought.

The boxes in the text are based on the same instructional philosophy that guided earlier editions. The boxes are not mere fillers or diversions. They are not meant to entertain in the way they do in some texts. Every student likes interesting or humorous anecdotes, and this text includes many such anecdotes. But what's different here is that such material is not featured. Rather, the boxes in this text are part of a broad pedagogical strategy of encouraging critical thinking and creating interest in politics. Once students' interest is aroused, they naturally want to learn more about politics and study it more enthusiastically.

In addition to the "Liberty, Equality, and Self-Government" boxes, each chapter has a "How the United States Compares" box and a "States in the Nation" box. The United States in many ways is the world's preeminent democracy, but it also has distinctive policies and practices. The American states, too, are quite different in their politics and policies, despite belonging to the same union. American students invariably gain a deeper understanding of their own communities when they recognize the ways in which their nation or state differs from others.

Encouraging students to compare states and nations is a natural way to foster critical thinking. When students discover, for example, that the United States has a higher child poverty rate than other Western democracies, they naturally ask why this is the case. Because comparative analysis stimulates critical thinking, this edition includes a large number of new cross-national tables and figures in addition to the "How the United States Compares" and the "States in the Nation" boxes. Many of these tables and figures involve comparisons of public opinion in the United States and elsewhere on major issues of our time, including immigration, church-state relations, economic globalization, and the fight against terrorism.

Critical thinking is also encouraged through the "Debating the Issues" and the "Why Should I Care?" boxes that appear in each chapter. The "Debating the Issues" boxes (called "Fighting Words" in the previous edition) present opposing opinions on current controversies, including Internet voting, the Kyoto accord on global warming, the Electoral College, same-sex marriage, and the Iraq conflict. The "Why Should I Care?" boxes ask students to use the material in the chapter to resolve, at least in their own minds, a difficult political issue. The "Why Should I Care?" box in the first chapter, for example, asks students to consider the meaning of the term *personal security* in the context of the USA Patriot Act, which expanded the government's search and seizure powers with respect to persons suspected of terrorist activities. The basic question, of course, is how far the student would allow the government to depart from normal due process procedures when terrorism is at issue.

Finally, three types of boxes are sprinkled throughout the book rather than appearing in each chapter. "Citizenship" boxes are designed to encourage students to participate in public life. "Political Culture" boxes address issues of diversity within the context of the idea that Americans are "one people out of many." "Global Perspective" boxes examine America's role in an increasingly interdependent world.

New to this edition is the Study Corner—a two-page study guide at the end of each chapter. Each Study Corner includes the chapter's key terms, a self-test, a critical-thinking exercise, and source references, as well as the suggestion of a civic or political activity in which the student can engage.

There is also much that is new in the body of the text. The chapters have been thoroughly updated to include the latest scholarship and most recent developments at home and abroad. The most substantial changes were occasioned by the 2004 presidential election and the conflict in Iraq, but many other changes are included, such as the latest Supreme Court rulings. The role of the Internet in American politics continues to feature prominently in the text's instructional content. Each chapter includes one or more World Wide Web icons (identified by a globe within which "WWW" appears). Each icon indicates relevant supplementary material (self-tests, simulations, and graphics) on the text's website. The chapters also include Historical Background icons, which identify key developments that helped shape the American political system.

Knowledge of history deepens students' understanding of U.S. politics, as does a critical perspective on events that are a vividly remembered part of their lives. For many students, Vietnam is ancient history and the Clinton-Lewinsky scandal a hazy middle-school memory. Students need to know about and learn from the past, but they also learn when they are asked to think deeply about events they believe they already know thoroughly. Every student is familiar with the war on terrorism. However, many students have not thought carefully about how, for example, it could affect civil liberties or foreign relations.

SUPPLEMENTS PACKAGE

This text is accompanied by supplementary materials. Please contact your local McGraw-Hill representative or McGraw-Hill Customer Service (800-338-3987) for details concerning policies, prices, and availability, as some restrictions may apply.

For Students and Instructors

OnLine Learning Center with PowerWeb

Visit our website at www.mhhe.com/pattersontad7

This website contains separate instructor and student areas. The instructor area contains the content of the Instructor's Resource CD-ROM, while the student area hosts a wealth of study materials such as additional Internet resources, concept lists, practice tests, essay questions, and thinking exercises. All chapter-by-chapter material has been updated for the new edition, and favorites such as the crossword puzzles, flashcards, video and audio indexes, and simulations have been retained.

New assets at this site also include:

- Updated participation suggestions dealing with constitutional foundations, institutions, political behavior, and policy. These suggestions were created to encourage students to become more involved in politics, to demonstrate how they can make a difference, and to give them advice on how to get started.
- Updated simulations accompanied by abstracts and learning goals.

PowerWeb for American Government

Now built into the *The American Democracy* Online Learning Center, this product offers daily news updates, weekly course updates, interactive activities, the best articles from the popular press, quizzes, instructor's manuals, student study material, and more.

Debate! Citizenship and Debate! Voting & Elections CD-ROMS

Political Science comes alive through **Debate!** McGraw-Hill's **Debate!** CD-ROM provides instant access to some of the most important and interesting documents, images, artifacts, audio recordings, and videos available on topics in political science. You can browse the collection across critical thinking questions, media types, subjects, or your own custom search criteria. Each source opens into our Source Window, packed with tools that provide rich scholarly contexts, interactive explorations, and access to a printable copy for each source.

While examining any of these sources, you can use our notebook feature to take notes, bookmark favorite sources, and save or print copies of all the sources for use outside of the archive (for example, inserting them into PowerPoint). After researching a particular theme or time period, you can use our **Debate!** outlining tool to walk you through the steps of composing a debate or presentation.

Through its browsing and inspection tool, **Debate!** helps you practice the art of political debate using a rich collection of multi-media evidence. This process of political science investigation follows three simple but engaging steps: **Ask** where you use our browsing panels to search and filter the sources, **research** where you use the Source Browser and Source Window's tools to examine the sources in detail, and **debate** where you can practice outlining arguments using selected sources from the collection.

For Instructors

Instructor's Manual/Test Bank

by Brian Fife of Indiana University–Purdue University Fort Wayne

For each chapter, the instructor's manual includes the following: learning objectives, focus points and main points, a chapter summary, a list of major concepts, a lecture outline, alternative lecture objectives, class discussion topics, and a list of Internet resources. The test bank consists of approximately twenty to twenty-five multiple-choice questions, fifteen to twenty true-false questions, and five suggested essay topics per chapter, with answers given alongside the questions and page references provided.

Test Bank CD-ROM

This test bank in CD-ROM format draws on questions from the Instructor's Manual/Test Bank to assist professors in generating tests.

Instructor's Resource CD-ROM

Tailored to the Table of Contents and format of the seventh edition, this CD integrates instructor's resources available in the Instructor's Manual/Test Bank with multimedia components, such as PowerPoint presentation, photographs, maps, and charts.

McGraw-Hill American Government Video Library

This new series of ten-minute video lecture-launchers was produced for McGraw-Hill by Ralph Baker and Joseph Losco of Ball State University.

Video #1: Devolution Within American Federalism: The Case of the Welfare System

0-07-303414-2

Video #2: Public Opinion and Participation: American Students Speak

0-07-229517-1

Video #3: Media and Politics in Presidential Campaigns

0-07-234442-3

Video #4: Women in Politics

0-07-242097-9

Video #5: Civil Liberties on the Internet

0-07-244205-0

Video #6: Affirmative Action and College Enrollment

0-07-244207-7

Video #7: The 2000 Campaign

0-07-250175-8

PageOut

At www.mhhe.com/pageout, instructors can create their own websites. PageOut requires no prior knowledge of HTML; simply plug the course information into a template and click on one of sixteen designs. The process leaves instructors with a professionally designed website.

PRIMIS Online

Instructors can use this textbook as a whole, or they can select specific chapters and customize this text to suit their specific classroom needs. The customized text can be created as a hardcopy or as an e-book. Also available in this format are custom chapters on **"California Government"** and **"Texas Government."**

For Students

Study Guide

by Brian Fife of Indiana University Purdue University Fort Wayne

Each chapter includes the following: learning objectives, focus and main points (to help direct students' attention to key material), chapter summary, major concepts (listed and defined), annotated Internet resources, analytical-thinking exercises, and test review questions—approximately 10 true-false, 15 multiple-choice, and 5 essay topics. The answers are provided at the end of each chapter.

2004 Presidential Election Update

by Richard Semiatin of American University

This supplement explores the 2004 presidential election campaign. Polls indicate that Americans saw the Bush-Kerry race as one of the most important elections of their lifetimes, and they responded by voting in unusually high numbers. Richard Semiatin analyzes the ups and downs of the election polls, and the determined efforts of the two campaigns to control the campaign agenda. This supplement examines the impact of partisanship and of the Iraq and economic issues on the vote. Also examined are, for example, media campaign, including some of the more controversial ads (including those of the Swift Boat Veterans for Truth); money and fundraising; the impact of the Electoral College on political strategy; and the televised presidential debates. Finally, Professor Semiatin examines the impact of the election on the direction of the nation's domestic and foreign policies. This booklet will be available in late spring of 2005.

Impeachment and Trial Supplement

by Richard Semiatin of American University

This 16-page supplement offers an overview of the impeachment and trial processes within a historical and constitutional context. It discusses the factors affecting the case of President Andrew Johnson in the 1860s and the vastly different, modern case of President Bill Clinton. This supplement also looks at alternatives to conviction and expulsion. This booklet can be shrink-wrapped free with the seventh edition of *The American Democracy.*

YOUR SUGGESTIONS ARE INVITED

The American Democracy has been in use in college classrooms for more than a dozen years. During that time, the text (including its concise edition, *We The People*) has been adopted at more than eight hundred colleges and universities. I am extremely grateful to all who have used it. I am particularly indebted to the many instructors and students over the years who have sent me recommendations or corrections. Professor James Chalmers of Wayne State University and Professor Richard Reiman of South Georgia College, for example, offered key ideas that were worked into this edition. Megan Reader, a Furman College undergraduate, was among the students who sent helpful suggestions. You can contact me at the John F. Kennedy School, Harvard University, Cambridge, MA 02138, or by e-mail: thomas_patterson@harvard.edu.

Thomas E. Patterson

PREFACE for the Student: A Guided Tour

This book describes the American political system, one of the most interesting and intricate systems in the world. The discussion is comprehensive; a lot of information is packed into the text. No student could possibly remember every tiny fact or observation that each chapter contains, but the main points of discussion are easily grasped if you make the effort.

The text has several features that will help you identify and understand the major points of discussion. For example, each chapter has an opening story that illustrates a central theme of the chapter, followed by a brief summary of the chapter's main ideas.

The guided tour presented here describes the organization and special features of your text.

Thomas E. Patterson

Opening Illustration

A narration of a compelling event introduces the chapter's main ideas.

Main Points

The chapter's three or four main ideas are summarized in the opening pages.

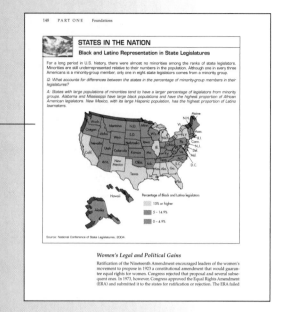

"States in the Nation" Boxes

Each chapter has a box that compares the fifty states on some aspect of politics.

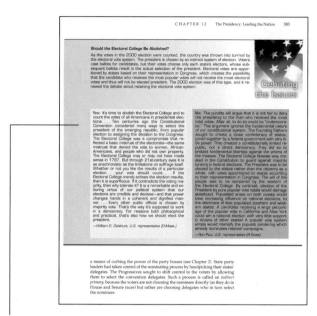

"Debating the Issues" Boxes

Each chapter has a box that introduces a current controversy and includes opposing opinions on the issue.

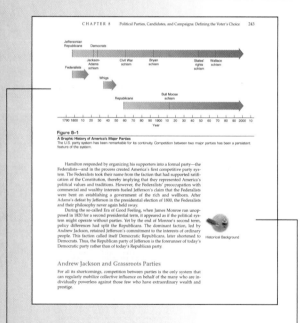

Figures and Tables

Each chapter has figures and tables that relate to points made in the discussion.

Reference Icons

These icons reference material that is of historical importance or available on the text's website.

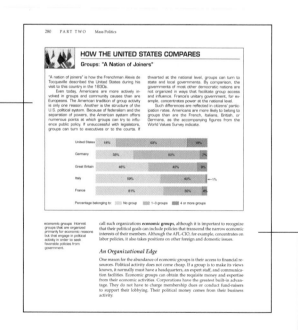

"How the United States Compares" Boxes

Each chapter has a box that compares the United States with other countries in regard to a major political feature.

Key Terms

Each key term is defined in the margin near its reference in the text.

"Liberty, Equality, and Self-Government" Boxes

Each chapter has a box that asks you to critically analyze and integrate material presented in the chapter that relates to America's founding principles.

"Why Should I Care?" Boxes

Each chapter has a box that addresses a persistent issue affecting Americans' lives.

"Political Culture" Boxes

Some chapters have a box that examines diversity topics relating to the notion that Americans are "one people out of many."

"Citizenship" Boxes

Some chapters have a box that provides advice and guidance for getting involved in civic and political activity.

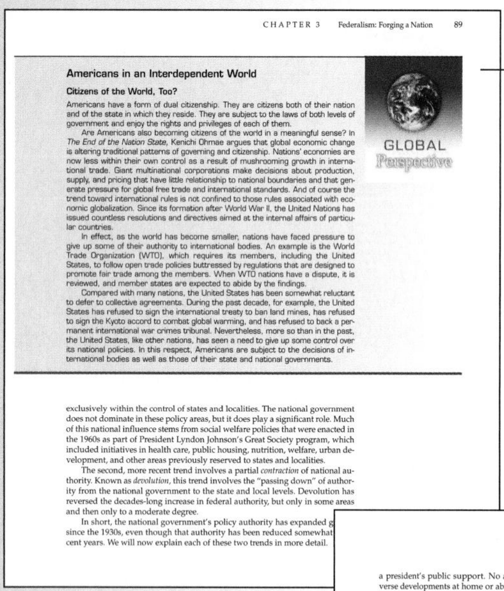

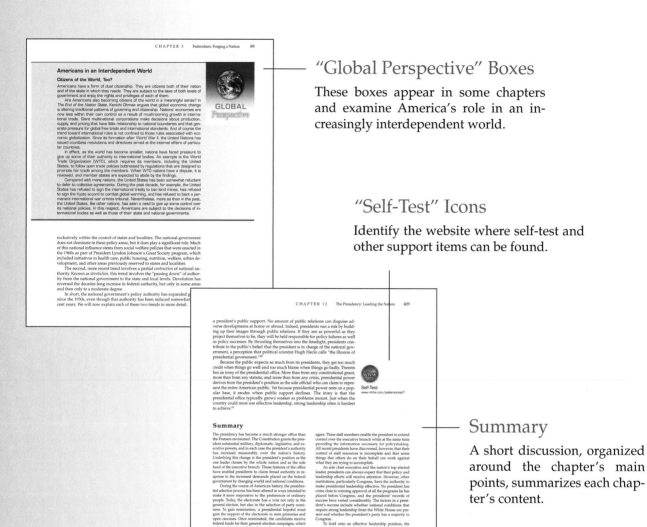

CHAPTER 3 Federalism: Forging a Nation 89

Americans in an Interdependent World

Citizens of the World, Too?

Americans have a form of dual citizenship. They are citizens both of their nation and of the state in which they reside. They are subject to the laws of both levels of government and enjoy the rights and privileges of each of them.

Are Americans also becoming citizens of the world in a meaningful sense? In *The End of the Nation State*, Kenichi Ohmae argues that global economic change is altering traditional patterns of governing and citizenship. Nations' economies are now less within their own control as a result of mushrooming growth in international trade. Giant multinational corporations make decisions about production, supply, and pricing that have little relationship to national boundaries and that generate pressure for global free trade and international standards. And of course the trend toward international rules is not confined to those rules associated with economic globalization. Since its formation after World War II, the United Nations has issued countless resolutions and directives aimed at the internal affairs of particular countries.

In effect, as the world has become smaller, nations have faced pressure to give up some of their authority to international bodies. An example is the World Trade Organization (WTO), which requires its members, including the United States, to follow open trade policies buttressed by regulations that are designed to promote fair trade among the members. When WTO nations have a dispute, it is reviewed, and member states are expected to abide by the findings.

Compared with many nations, the United States has been somewhat reluctant to defer to collective agreements. During the past decade, for example, the United States has refused to sign the international treaty to ban land mines, has refused to sign the Kyoto accord to combat global warming, and has refused to back a permanent international war crimes tribunal. Nevertheless, more so than in the past, the United States, like other nations, has seen a need to give up some control over its national policies. In this respect, Americans are subject to the decisions of international bodies as well as those of their state and national governments.

GLOBAL Perspective

exclusively within the control of states and localities. The national government does not dominate in these policy areas, but it does play a significant role. Much of this national influence stems from social welfare policies that were enacted in the 1960s as part of President Lyndon Johnson's Great Society program, which included initiatives in health care, public housing, nutrition, welfare, urban development, and other areas previously reserved to states and localities.

The second, more recent trend involves a partial *contraction* of national authority. Known as *devolution*, this trend involves the "passing down" of authority from the national government to the state and local levels. Devolution has reversed the decades-long increase in federal authority, but only in some areas and then only to a moderate degree.

In short, the national government's policy authority has expanded g[…] since the 1930s, even though that authority has been reduced somewhat […] cent years. We will now explain each of these two trends in more detail.

"Global Perspective" Boxes

These boxes appear in some chapters and examine America's role in an increasingly interdependent world.

"Self-Test" Icons

Identify the website where self-test and other support items can be found.

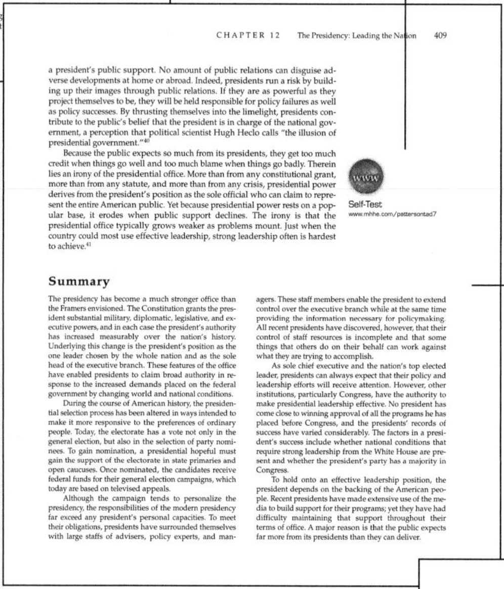

CHAPTER 12 The Presidency: Leading the Nation 409

a president's public support. No amount of public relations can disguise adverse developments at home or abroad. Indeed, presidents run a risk by building up their images through public relations. If they are as powerful as they project themselves to be, they will be held responsible for policy failures as well as policy successes. By thrusting themselves into the limelight, presidents contribute to the public's belief that the president is in charge of the national government, a perception that political scientist Hugh Heclo calls "the illusion of presidential government."[40]

Because the public expects so much from its presidents, they get too much credit when things go well and too much blame when things go badly. Therein lies an irony of the presidential office. More than from any constitutional grant, more than from any statute, and more than from any crisis, presidential power derives from the president's position as the sole official who can claim to represent the entire American public. Yet because presidential power rests on a popular base, it erodes when public support declines. The irony is that the presidential office typically grows weaker as problems mount. Just when the country could most use effective leadership, strong leadership often is hardest to achieve.[41]

WWW Self-Test www.mhhe.com/pattersonad7

Summary

The presidency has become a much stronger office than the Framers envisioned. The Constitution grants the president substantial military, diplomatic, legislative, and executive powers, and in each case the president's authority has increased measurably over the nation's history. Underlying this change is the president's position as the one leader chosen by the whole nation and as the sole head of the executive branch. These features of the office have enabled presidents to claim broad authority in response to the increased demands placed on the federal government by changing world and national conditions.

During the course of American history, the presidential selection process has been altered in ways intended to make it more responsive to the preferences of ordinary people. Today, the electorate has a vote not only in the general election, but also in the selection of party nominees. To gain nomination, a presidential hopeful must gain the support of the electorate in state primaries and open caucuses. Once nominated, the candidates receive federal funds for their general election campaigns, which today are based on televised appeals.

Although the campaign tends to personalize the presidency, the responsibilities of the modern presidency far exceed any president's personal capacities. To meet their obligations, presidents have surrounded themselves with large staffs of advisers, policy experts, and managers. These staff members enable the president to extend control over the executive branch while at the same time providing the information necessary for policymaking. All recent presidents have discovered, however, that their control of staff resources is incomplete and that some things that others do on their behalf can work against what they are trying to accomplish.

As sole chief executive and the nation's top elected leader, presidents can always expect that their policy and leadership efforts will receive attention. However, other institutions, particularly Congress, have the authority to make presidential leadership effective. No president has come close to winning approval of all the programs he has placed before Congress, and the presidents' records of success have varied considerably. The factors in a president's success include whether national conditions that require strong leadership from the White House are present and whether the president's party has a majority in Congress.

To hold onto an effective leadership position, the president depends on the backing of the American people. Recent presidents have made extensive use of the media to build support for their programs; yet they have had difficulty maintaining that support throughout their terms of office. A major reason is that the public expects far more from its presidents than they can deliver.

Summary

A short discussion, organized around the chapter's main points, summarizes each chapter's content.

Study Corner

A two-page section at the end of each chapter includes (as shown on the example page) key terms, a self-test, and a critical-thinking exercise; the second page (not shown) has suggested readings, annotated references to relevant websites, and a guide to civic and political participation.

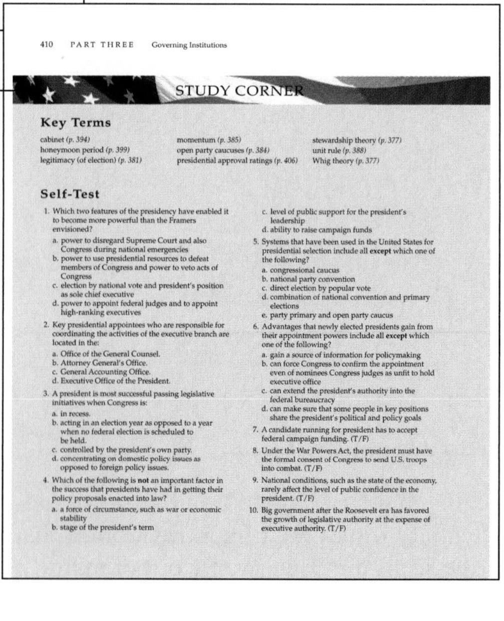

410 PART THREE Governing Institutions

STUDY CORNER

Key Terms

cabinet *(p. 394)*
honeymoon period *(p. 399)*
legitimacy (of election) *(p. 381)*
momentum *(p. 385)*
open party caucuses *(p. 384)*
presidential approval ratings *(p. 406)*
stewardship theory *(p. 377)*
unit rule *(p. 388)*
Whig theory *(p. 377)*

Self-Test

1. Which two features of the presidency have enabled it to become more powerful than the Framers envisioned?
   a. power to disregard Supreme Court and also Congress during national emergencies
   b. power to use presidential resources to defeat members of Congress and power to veto acts of Congress
   c. election by national vote and president's position as sole chief executive
   d. power to appoint federal judges and to appoint high-ranking executives
2. Key presidential appointees who are responsible for coordinating the activities of the executive branch are located in the:
   a. Office of the General Counsel.
   b. Attorney General's Office.
   c. General Accounting Office.
   d. Executive Office of the President.
3. A president is most successful passing legislative initiatives when Congress is:
   a. in recess.
   b. acting in an election year as opposed to a year when no federal election is scheduled to be held.
   c. controlled by the president's own party.
   d. concentrating on domestic policy issues as opposed to foreign policy issues.
4. Which of the following is **not** an important factor in the success that presidents have had in getting their policy proposals enacted into law?
   a. a force of circumstance, such as war or economic stability
   b. stage of the president's term
   c. level of public support for the president's leadership
   d. ability to raise campaign funds
5. Systems that have been used in the United States for presidential selection include all **except** which one of the following?
   a. congressional caucus
   b. national party convention
   c. direct election by popular vote
   d. combination of national convention and primary elections
   e. party primary and open party caucus
6. Advantages that newly elected presidents gain from their appointment powers include all **except** which one of the following?
   a. gain a source of information for policymaking
   b. can force Congress to confirm the appointment even of nominees Congress judges as unfit to hold executive office
   c. can extend the president's authority into the federal bureaucracy
   d. can make sure that some people in key positions share the president's political and policy goals
7. A candidate running for president has to accept federal campaign funding. (T/F)
8. Under the War Powers Act, the president must have the formal consent of Congress to send U.S. troops into combat. (T/F)
9. National conditions, such as the state of the economy, rarely affect the level of public confidence in the president. (T/F)
10. Big government after the Roosevelt era has favored the growth of legislative authority at the expense of executive authority. (T/F)

To my children,
Alex and Leigh

ACKNOWLEDGMENTS

Nearly two decades ago, when planning the first edition of *The American Democracy*, my editor and I concluded that it would be enormously helpful if a way could be found to bring into each chapter the judgment of those political scientists who teach the introductory course year in and year out. Thus, in addition to soliciting general reviews from a select number of expert scholars, we sent each chapter to a dozen or so faculty members at U.S. colleges and universities of all types—public and private, large and small, two-year and four-year. These political scientists, 213 in all, had well over a thousand years of combined experience in teaching the introductory course, and they provided countless good ideas.

Since then, scores of other political scientists have reviewed subsequent editions. These many reviewers will go unnamed here, but my debt to all of them remains undiminished by time.

For this new, seventh edition, I again received an enormous amount of sound advice. Reviewers are the lifeblood of a text, and I was fortunate to have the assistance of a skilled group of scholars. I am deeply grateful to each and all of them for their help:

Seymour Schwartz, Malcolm X College

Brian Reed, Ferris State University

Anthony Brown, Oklahoma State University

Michael Cobb, North Carolina State University

Brian Farmer, University of Wyoming

Geoff Peterson, University of Wisconsin, Eau Claire

Paul Parker, Truman State University

Kendra Stewart, Eastern Kentucky University

Russell Renka, Southeast Missouri State University

Kyle Smith, Western Texas College

Dina Krois, Lansing Community College

I also want to thank those at McGraw-Hill who contributed to the seventh edition. Monica Eckman, my editor, was again at the top of her game. Few authors have likely had the benefit of the extraordinary combination of professional skill and inspired direction that Monica has provided in the writing of the past few editions of *The American Democracy*. Angela Kao and Katherine Bates augmented Monica's contributions with critical inputs of their own for which I am deeply grateful. I also would like to thank a development editor and a project manager for their help: Jim Strandberg, who got the new edition off to a solid start, and Christina Gimlin, who brought it to a sound conclusion. Mary Roybal, a superb copyeditor, polished my clumsy phrases and improved my word selections. Others at McGraw-Hill, though not in direct contact with me, also made important contributions: Randy Hurst, production supervisor; Preston Thomas, designer; Nora Agbayani, photo research coordinator; and Louis Swaim, supplements producer.

At Harvard, I had the tireless, proficient, and cheerful support of my faculty assistant, Vanessa Schulz. She flawlessly updated many of the tables and figures, tracked down hard-to-find sources, copied endless draft pages, and prompted me to stay on schedule. I owe her deep thanks.

Thomas Patterson

PART
I

Foundations

The United States has the world's oldest constitution still in force. France has had fourteen constitutions during the same period in which the United States has had one. The British statesman William Gladstone in 1878 declared the U.S. Constitution to be "the most wonderful work ever struck off at a given time by the brain and purpose of man."

A reason why this remarkable system has endured is that the United States was founded on a set of common ideals that continue to serve as Americans' bond. Chapter 1 describes these ideals and their lasting influence on the nation's politics.

Chapters 2 and 3 examine how the writers of the Constitution resolved fundamental issues—liberty, self-government, and union. A central theme of these chapters is that basic constitutional issues are never fully settled. They are recurring sources of debate, and each generation is forced to find new answers.

Constitutional government is also a matter of individual rights, of a system in which people have basic freedoms that are constitutionally protected from infringement by government. Although these rights are rooted in principle, they are achieved through politics. Chapter 4 discusses how civil liberties—for example, free speech—are protected both from and through political action. Chapter 5 examines the degree to which Americans' rights are affected by characteristics such as gender and race.

PART ONE OUTLINE

1

American Political Culture:
Seeking a More Perfect Union

One hears people say that it is inherent in the habits and nature of democracies to change feelings and thoughts at every moment. . . . But I have never seen anything like that happening in the great democracy on the other side of the ocean. What struck me most in the United States was the difficulty experienced in getting an idea, once conceived, out of the head of the majority.

Alexis de Tocqueville[1]

At 8:47 A.M. on September 11, 2001, a hijacked American Airlines passenger jet slammed into one of the twin towers of New York City's World Trade Center. Twenty minutes later, a second hijacked passenger jet hit the other tower. A third hijacked jet then plowed into the Pentagon building in Washington, D.C. Within two hours, the World Trade Center towers collapsed, killing all still inside, including police and firefighters who had rushed bravely into the buildings to help in the evacuation. Three thousand Americans were murdered that September morning, the highest death toll ever from an attack on American soil by a foreign adversary. The toll would have been even higher if not for the bravery of passengers aboard United Airlines flight 93, who fought with its hijackers, causing the plane—which was aimed toward Washington, D.C.—to crash in a barren Pennsylvania field.

That evening, a somber George W. Bush addressed the nation. Urging Americans to stay calm and resolute, President Bush said: "America was targeted for an attack because we're the brightest beacon for freedom and opportunity in the world." Sprinkled throughout his speech were allusions to time-honored American ideals: liberty, the will of the people, justice, and the rule of law. "No one will keep that light from shining," said Bush.

The ideals that guided Bush's speech would have been familiar to any generation of Americans. These ideals have been invoked when Americans have gone to war, declared peace, celebrated national holidays, launched major policy initiatives, and asserted new rights.[2] The ideals contained in Bush's speech were the same ones that had punctuated the speeches of George Washington and Abraham Lincoln, Susan B. Anthony and Franklin D. Roosevelt, Dr. Martin Luther King Jr., and Ronald Reagan.

The ideals were also there at the nation's beginning, when they were put into words in the Declaration of Independence and the Constitution. Of course, the practical meaning of these words has changed greatly during the more than two centuries the United States has been a sovereign nation. When the writers of the Constitution began the document with the words "We the People," they did not have all Americans equally in mind. Black slaves, women, and men without property did not have the same rights as propertied white men.

When terrorists attacked the World Trade Center towers on September 11, 2001, America's political leaders, as they have done throughout the country's history, turned to time-honored ideals as a means of raising people's spirits. President George W. Bush described America as a beacon of liberty, saying, "No one will keep that light from shining."

Yet America's ideals have been remarkably enduring. Throughout their history Americans have embraced the same set of core values. They have quarreled over the meaning, practice, and fulfillment of these ideals, but they have never seriously questioned the principles themselves. As historian Clinton Rossiter concluded, "There has been in a doctrinal sense, only one America."[3]

This book is about contemporary American politics, not U.S. history or culture. Yet American politics today cannot be understood apart from the nation's heritage. Government does not begin anew with each generation; it builds on the past. In the United States, the most significant link between past and present lies in the nation's founding ideals. The Frenchman Alexis de Tocqueville was among the first to see that the main tendencies of American politics cannot be explained without taking into account the country's core beliefs. "Habits of the heart" was Tocqueville's description of Americans' ideals.[4]

This chapter briefly examines the principles that have helped shape American politics since the country's earliest years. The chapter also explains basic concepts—such as power, pluralism, and constitutionalism—that are important in the study of American government and politics. The main points made in this chapter are the following:

- *The American political culture centers on a set of core ideals—liberty, equality, self-government, individualism, diversity, and unity—that serve as the people's common bond.* These mythic principles have a substantial influence on what Americans will regard as reasonable and acceptable and on what they will try to achieve.

- *Politics is the process that determines whose values will prevail in society.* The play of politics in the United States takes place in the context of democratic procedures, constitutionalism, and capitalism and involves elements of majority, pluralist, bureaucratic, and elite rule.

- *Politics in the United States is characterized by a number of major patterns, including a highly fragmented governing system, a high degree of pluralism, an extraordinary emphasis on individual rights, and a pronounced separation of the political and economic spheres.*

POLITICAL CULTURE: THE CORE PRINCIPLES OF AMERICAN GOVERNMENT

The people of every nation have a few great ideals that characterize their political life, but as James Bryce observed, Americans are a special case.[5] Their ideals

U.S. politics is remarkable for its historical continuity, which is celebrated here in a ceremony at the Capitol in Washington, D.C.

are the basis of their national identity. Other people take their identity from the common ancestry that led them gradually to gather under one flag. Thus, long before there was a France or a Japan, there were French and Japanese people, each a kinship group united through blood. Even today, it is kinship that links them. There is no way to become fully Japanese except to be born of Japanese parents. Not so for Americans. They are a multitude of peoples linked by a political tradition. The United States is a nation that was abruptly founded in 1776 on a set of principles that became its people's common bond.[6]

A strong bond of some kind was a necessity. Nationalities that warred constantly in Europe had to find a way to live together in the New World. Americans' shared ideals contributed to a oneness, however uneasy, among nationalities that had never before trusted one another. Their effort to find common ground has been replayed many times during America's history. The United States is, and always has been, a nation of immigrants and of people struggling for a greater level of acceptance and unity. Today, the United States has a population of almost 300 million people, nearly all of whom can trace their ancestry to some other place (see Figure 1–1). Native Americans now make up about 1 percent of the population. They are outnumbered by Americans who have ancestral ties to Germany, Ireland, Africa, Poland, Mexico, or China, to name just a few places.

Yet Americans are also one people, brought together through allegiance to a set of commonly held ideals such as liberty and equality. These principles are habits of mind, a customary way of thinking about the world. They are part of what social scientists call **political culture,** a term that refers to the characteristic and deep-seated beliefs of a particular people about government and politics.[7]

political culture The characteristic and deep-seated beliefs of a particular people.

America's core ideals are rooted in the European heritage of the first white settlers. They arrived during the Enlightenment period, when people were awakening to the idea of human progress. These settlers wanted freedom to practice religion and hoped for a greater measure of self-government. They did not, as some Americans assume, invent an entirely new way of life. Their beliefs were shaped by European thought and practice, which in turn had been

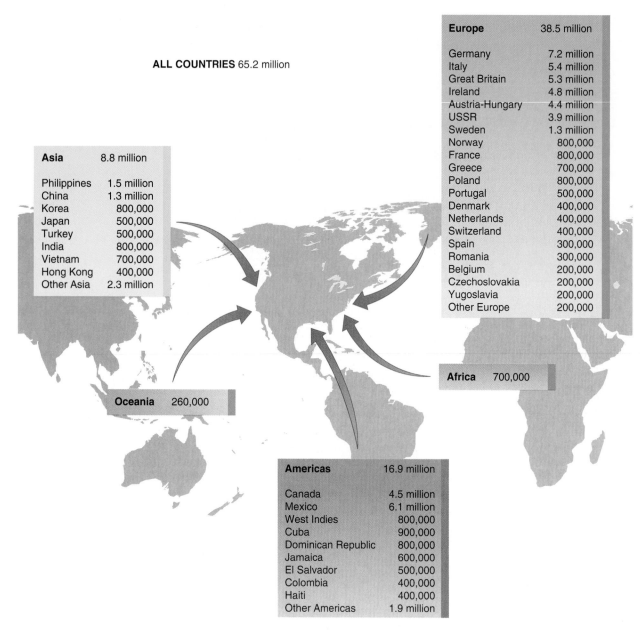

ALL COUNTRIES 65.2 million

Europe	38.5 million
Germany	7.2 million
Italy	5.4 million
Great Britain	5.3 million
Ireland	4.8 million
Austria-Hungary	4.4 million
USSR	3.9 million
Sweden	1.3 million
Norway	800,000
France	800,000
Greece	700,000
Poland	800,000
Portugal	500,000
Denmark	400,000
Netherlands	400,000
Switzerland	400,000
Spain	300,000
Romania	300,000
Belgium	200,000
Czechoslovakia	200,000
Yugoslavia	200,000
Other Europe	200,000

Asia	8.8 million
Philippines	1.5 million
China	1.3 million
Korea	800,000
Japan	500,000
Turkey	500,000
India	800,000
Vietnam	700,000
Hong Kong	400,000
Other Asia	2.3 million

Africa	700,000

Oceania	260,000

Americas	16.9 million
Canada	4.5 million
Mexico	6.1 million
West Indies	800,000
Cuba	900,000
Dominican Republic	800,000
Jamaica	600,000
El Salvador	500,000
Colombia	400,000
Haiti	400,000
Other Americas	1.9 million

Figure 1–1

Total Immigration to the United States, 1820–2000, by Continent and Country of Origin
Source: U.S. Immigration and Naturalization Service.

molded by Greco-Roman and Judeo-Christian traditions. As historian Paul Gagnon noted, "The first settlers did not sail into view out of a void, their minds as blank as the Atlantic Ocean. . . . Those who sailed west to America came in fact not to build a New World but to bring to life in a new setting what they had treasured most from the Old World."[8]

Colonial life expanded their vision, which then found expression in the Declaration of Independence and the Constitution. Ideals became the defining feature of the American political experience. Later immigrants adopted them while also leaving a distinctive mark on the practice of these ideals. As each new generation of Americans has discovered, there is no fixed way to live out these principles, and in practice these ideals have meant different things to different people even within the same generation. Few observers would argue, however, with the proposition that *a defining characteristic of the American political system is its enduring and powerful set of political ideals.*

 ## AMERICA'S CORE VALUES: LIBERTY, EQUALITY, AND SELF-GOVERNMENT

An understanding of America's ideals begins with a recognition that the individual comes first. Government is secondary. Its role is to serve the people, as opposed to a system in which government is at the pinnacle and people are expected to glorify it. No clearer statement of this principle exists than the reference in the Declaration of Independence to "unalienable rights"—freedoms that belong to each and every person and that cannot lawfully be denied by government.

Liberty, equality, and self-government are widely regarded as America's core political ideals. **Liberty** is the principle that individuals should be free to act and think as they choose, provided they do not infringe unreasonably on the freedom and well-being of others. The United States, as historian Louis Hartz said, was "born free."[9] The Declaration of Independence rings with the proclamation that people are entitled to "Life, Liberty and the Pursuit of Happiness." The preamble to the Constitution declares that the U.S. government is founded to secure "the Blessings of Liberty to ourselves and our Posterity." The Statue of Liberty stands in New York harbor as the symbol of the American nation, and the "Star-Spangled Banner" rings out with the words "land of the free."

At the time of the writing of the Constitution (1787), liberty was conceived as protection against unwarranted government interference in people's lives. The First Amendment, for example, defines a set of actions that government is forbidden to take: "Congress shall make no law respecting the establishment of religion, or prohibiting the free exercise thereof; or abridging the freedom of speech, or of the press; or the right of the people to peaceably assemble, and to petition the Government for a redress of grievances."

For a long period, America's vast wilderness and great distance from the Old World granted its white settlers extraordinary freedom. Ordinary people did not have to accept second-class treatment when greater personal liberty was as close as the next area of unsettled land. With time, however, this protection diminished and a new threat to personal liberty emerged. The Industrial Revolution spawned business trusts that gouged customers and forced laborers to work long hours at low pay in unsafe factories. It became harder to think about personal liberty as simply an issue of limits on government. Americans gradually looked to government for protection against powerful economic interests. Business regulation, social security, and minimum-wage laws were among the resulting policies.

liberty The principle that individuals should be free to act and think as they choose, provided they do not infringe unreasonably on the rights and freedoms of others.

Thomas Jefferson

(1743–1826)

Thomas Jefferson was the principal author of the Declaration of Independence. It was Jefferson who coined the renowned words "Life, Liberty and the Pursuit of Happiness." A powerful advocate of personal freedom, he also wrote the state of Virginia's Bill of Rights. Elected to the presidency in 1800, his purchase of the Louisiana Territory from the French Emperor Napoleon in 1803 doubled the size of the United States. After retiring to his Monticello estate, Jefferson designed and founded the University of Virginia, which he called his greatest achievement.

equality The notion that all individuals are equal in their moral worth, in their treatment under the law, and in their political voice.

A second American political ideal is **equality**—the notion that all individuals are equal in their moral worth and are entitled to equal treatment under the law. America provided its white settlers a new level of equality. Europe's rigid aristocratic system based on land ownership was unenforceable in frontier America. Almost any free citizen who wanted to own land could obtain it. It was this natural sense of equality that Thomas Jefferson expressed so forcefully in writing the Declaration of Independence: "We hold these truths to be self-evident, that all men are created equal."

Equality, however, has always been a less clearly defined concept than liberty. Even Jefferson professed not to know its exact meaning. A slave owner, Jefferson distinguished between free citizens, who were entitled to equal rights, and slaves, who were not. After slavery was abolished, Americans continued to argue over the meaning of equality, as they still do today. Does equality require that wealth and opportunity be widely shared? Or does it merely require that artificial barriers to advancement be removed? Despite differing opinions about such questions, the quest for equality is a distinctive feature of the American experience. Observers from Tocqueville to Bryce have seen fit to say that equality in America, as in no other country, is ingrained in people's thinking. Americans, said Bryce, reject "the very notion" that some people might be "better" than others merely because of birth or position.[10] And perhaps no ideal has so inspired Americans to political action as has their desire for fuller equality. The abolition and suffrage movements were rooted in this ideal. The more recent civil rights movements of black Americans, women, Hispanics, gays, and other groups are also testaments to the power of this ideal.

Of course, people differ in their wealth and talent, which means they are not equal in fact. Even today, for example, poor people accused of crime do not have access to the same quality of legal assistance that is available to the rich. In principle, however, Americans are equals, as expressed in phrases such as "equal justice under the law." These are not empty words. Although the poor have less access to legal assistance, no citizen can be tried for a felony offense without the opportunity for legal counsel, at government expense if necessary.

self-government The principle that the people are the ultimate source and proper beneficiary of governing authority; in practice, a government based on majority rule.

Self-government, America's third great political ideal, is the principle that people are the ultimate source of governing authority and must have a voice in how they are governed. "Governments," the Declaration of Independence proclaims, "deriv[e] their just powers from the consent of the governed." In his Gettysburg address, Lincoln extolled a government "of the people, by the people, for the people."

Americans' belief in self-government originated in colonial America. The Old World was an ocean away, and European governments had no option but to allow the American colonies a degree of self-determination. Out of this experience came the dream of a self-governing nation. It was an ideal that captured the imagination even of those in the lower ranks of society. Ordinary people willingly risked their lives to the cause of self-government during the American

---

America's Core Political Ideals

Liberty: The belief that individuals should be free to act and think as they choose, provided they do not infringe unreasonably on the freedom and well-being of others.

Equality: The belief that all individuals are equal in their moral worth and are entitled to equal treatment under the law.

Self-government: The belief that the people are the ultimate source of governing authority and must have a voice in how they are governed.

Revolution. The ensuing federal and state constitutions were based on the idea that government is properly founded on the will of the people. "We the People" is the opening phrase of the Constitution of the United States.

At no time in the nation's history has national leadership been conferred except through the vote. At various times and places elsewhere in the world, governing power has been seized by brute force. The United States has an unbroken history of free and open elections as the legitimate means of acquiring governmental power. Etched in a corridor of the nation's Capitol building are the words Alexander Hamilton spoke when asked about the foundation of the nation's government: "Here, sir, the people govern."

Although liberty, equality, and self-government are the core American political ideals, the American Creed—the set of core values that define the nation's political culture—also includes other principles. **Individualism** is a commitment to personal initiative, self-sufficiency, and material accumulation. It is related to the idea of liberty, which makes the individual the foundation of society, and is buttressed by the idea of equality, which holds that everyone should be given a fair chance to succeed. Individualism stems from the belief that people, if free to pursue their own path and not unfairly burdened, can attain their fullest potential. Individualism has roots in the country's origins as a wilderness society. The early Americans developed a pride in their "rugged individualism," and from this experience grew the idea that people ought to try to make it on their own.

individualism The idea that people should take the initiative, be self-sufficient, and accumulate the material advantages necessary for their well-being.

Unity and diversity are also part of the American creed. **Unity** is the principle that Americans are one people and form an indivisible union. **Diversity** holds that individual and group differences should be respected and that these differences are themselves a source of strength. These two principles acknowledge at once both the differences and the oneness that are part of the American experience. They are expressed in the phrase *E pluribus unum* ("One out of many").

unity The principle that Americans are one people and form an indivisible union.

diversity The principle that individual and group differences should be respected and are a source of national strength.

The Power of Ideals

Ideals serve to define the boundaries of action. They do not determine exactly what people will do, but they affect what people will regard as reasonable and desirable. Why, for example, does the United States spend relatively less money on government programs for the poor than do other fully industrialized democracies, including Germany, France, Switzerland, the Netherlands, Spain, Britain, Sweden, Italy, and Japan? Are Americans so much better off than these other

HOW THE UNITED STATES COMPARES

Capitalism, Self-Reliance, and Personal Success

The United States was labeled "the country of individualism *par excellence*" by William Watts and Lloyd Free in their book *State of the Nation*. They were referring to the emphasis that Americans place on self-reliance and the trust they have in the marketplace as a basis of economic security.

In European democracies, such views also prevail but are moderated by a greater acceptance of welfare programs. The difference between the American and European cultures reflects their differing political traditions. America was an open country ruled by a foreign power, and its revolution was fought largely over the issue of personal freedom. In European revolutions, equality was also at issue, because wealth was held by hereditary aristocracies. Europeans' concern with equality was gradually translated into a willingness to use government as a means of redistributing wealth. An example is government-paid medical care for all citizens.

Even today, Europeans are more likely than Americans to believe that personal success is determined largely by family background and other factors outside the individual's control, as indicated by these results from the 2002 Global Attitudes survey of the Pew Research Center for the People and the Press:

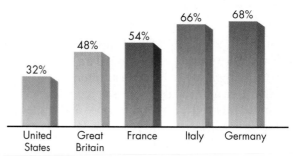

Percentage agreeing that "success in life is pretty much determined by forces outside our control."

people that they have less need for welfare programs? The answer is no. Of all these countries, the United States has the most poverty, in both relative and absolute terms. The United States spends less on social welfare chiefly because of its cultural emphasis on liberty and individualism. Americans have resisted giving government a larger social welfare role because of their deep-seated belief in self-reliance and limited government (see "How the United States Compares").

Of course, social welfare policy is not simply an issue of cultural differences. The welfare issue, like other issues, is part of the rough-and-tumble of everyday politics. There are always powerful interests aligned on both sides of important issues. In the United States, the Republican party, business groups, antitax groups, and others have resisted the expansion of the government's social welfare role, while the Democratic party, unions, minority groups, and others have from time to time argued for greater intervention. Nevertheless, Americans' belief in individualism, which has no exact equivalent in European society, has played a defining role in shaping U.S. welfare policy.

The distinctiveness of this cultural belief is clear from a 2002 survey that asked respondents in different countries whether it is more important "that everyone be free to pursue their life's goals without interference from government" or "that government play an active role in society so as to guarantee that nobody is in need." Two-thirds of Europeans, compared with only one-third of Americans, said that it is more important to ensure that "nobody is in need."[11]

The structure of U.S. society helps promote the American dream of success—for example, by encouraging young people to attend college.

Americans do not necessarily have less sympathy for the poor; rather, they place more emphasis on personal responsibility than Europeans do.[12]

The importance of individualism to American society is also evident in the emphasis on equal opportunity. If individuals are to be entrusted with their own welfare, they must be given a fair chance to succeed on their own. Nowhere is this philosophy more evident than in the country's elaborate system of higher education, which includes nearly three thousand two-year and four-year institutions and is designed to accommodate nearly every individual who wants to pursue a college education. More than a third of the nation's young people enter college, the world's highest rate. Western Europe has nothing comparable to the American system; fewer than one in five young people in these countries go to college. This difference is reflected in the number of citizens with college degrees (see "States in the Nation"). Even the American state that ranks lowest by this indicator—West Virginia, with its 15.3 percent of adults who are college graduates—has a higher percentage of residents with a bachelor's degree than does the average European country.

Of course, the idea that success is within equal reach of all Americans who strive for it is far from accurate. Young people who grow up in abject poverty and without adequate guidance know all too well the limits on opportunity. In some inner-city areas, teenage boys are more likely to spend time in jail than to spend time at college.

The Limits of Ideals

Cultural beliefs originate in a country's political and social practices, but they are not perfect representatives of these practices. They are mythic ideas—symbolic

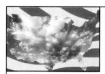

STATES IN THE NATION

A College Education

Reflecting their cultural beliefs of individualism and equality, Americans have developed the world's most extensive college system. Every state has at least eight colleges within its boundaries. No European democracy has as many colleges as either California (322) or New York (320). The extensive U.S. college system has enabled large numbers of Americans to earn a college degree. Even the states that rank low on this indicator have a higher percentage of college graduates than do most European countries.

Q: Why do the northeastern and western coastal states have a higher percentage of adults with college degrees?

A: The northeastern and western coastal states are more affluent and urbanized than most states. Thus, young people in these states can better afford the costs of college and are more likely to need a college degree for the work they intend to pursue.

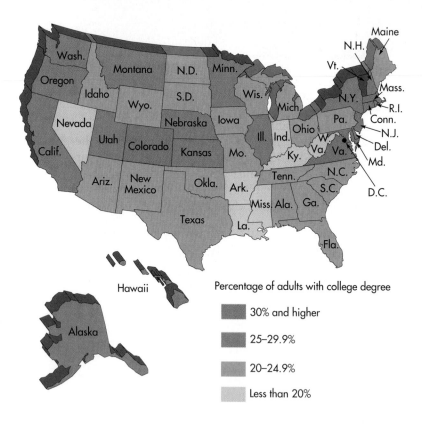

Percentage of adults with college degree

- 30% and higher
- 25–29.9%
- 20–24.9%
- Less than 20%

Source: U.S. Bureau of the Census, 2002. Based on percentage of adults twenty-five years of age or older with a college degree.

During the era of racial segregation in the South, this sign at the entrance to the Memphis public zoo meant that it was Tuesday—the only day black people were allowed to go to the zoo. On the other six days of the week, the sign excluded black people from entering.

positions taken by a people to justify and give meaning to their way of life.[13] Myths contain elements of truth, but they are far from the full truth.

High ideals do not come with a guarantee that a people will live up to them. The clearest proof of this failing in the American case is the human tragedy that began nearly four centuries ago and continues today. In 1619 the first black slaves were brought in chains to America. Slavery lasted 250 years. Slaves in the field worked from dawn to dark (from "can see, 'til can't"), in both the heat of summer and the cold of winter. The Civil War brought an end to slavery but not to racial oppression. Slavery was followed by the Jim Crow era of legal segregation: black people in the South were forbidden by law to use the same schools, hospitals, restaurants, and restrooms as white people. Those who spoke out against this system were subjected to beatings, firebombings, castrations, rapes, and worse—hundreds of African Americans were lynched by white vigilantes in the early 1900s. Today African Americans have equal rights under the law, but in fact they are far from equal. Compared with whites, blacks are twice as likely to live in poverty, twice as likely to be unable to find a job, and twice as likely to die in infancy.[14] There have always been at least two Americas, one for whites and one for blacks.

Despite the lofty claim that "all men are created equal," equality has never been an American birthright. In 1882 Congress suspended Chinese immigration on the assumption that the Chinese were an inferior people. Calvin Coolidge in 1923 asked Congress for a permanent ban on Chinese immigration, saying that people "who do not want to be partakers of the American spirit ought not to

Historical Background

www.mhhe.com/pattersontad7

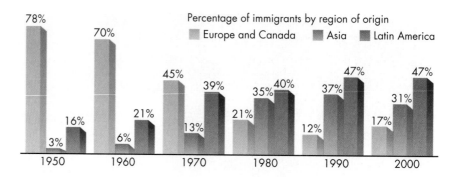

Figure 1-2

The Changing Face of Immigration
Until 1965, immigration laws were biased in favor of European immigrants. The laws enacted in 1965 increased the proportion of immigrants from Asia and Latin America.
Source: U.S. Immigration and Naturalization Service, 2003. Percentages are totals for each decade, e.g., the 2000 figures are for the 1991–2000 period.

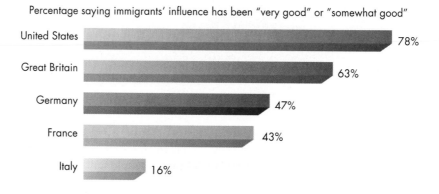

Figure 1-3

Opinion of the Influence on Society of Recent Immigrants
Americans are more likely than Europeans to believe that recent immigrants have had a positive influence on their society.
Source: The Pew Research Center for the People and the Press, Global Attitudes Survey, 2002. Respondents were asked whether a particular group has been a "very good, somewhat good, somewhat bad, or very bad" influence in their country. The question was asked in the following contexts: Hispanics (United States), black and Asian groups (Great Britain), Turks (Germany), North Africans (France), and Albanians (Italy).

settle in America."[15] Not until 1965 was discrimination against the Chinese and other Asians (and Hispanics, as well) effectively eliminated from U.S. immigration laws (Figure 1–2).

The claim that the United States is a gigantic melting pot is a blend of fact and fiction. No other nation has so fully opened its doors to groups from around the world. Even today, Americans are more likely than Europeans to support immigration. They also have a better opinion of recent immigrants (see Figure 1–3). For example, compared with French people's view of North African immigrants, Americans are nearly twice as likely to say that Hispanic immigrants are having a positive influence on society. Nevertheless, established groups in America have never fully embraced new arrivals. When Irish, Italian,

TABLE 1-1	**Telling the American Story to Children** Americans' values and myths are reflected in their preferences in teaching children about the nation's history.		
IN TEACHING THE AMERICAN STORY TO CHILDREN, HOW IMPORTANT IS THE FOLLOWING THEME?	**ESSENTIAL/VERY IMPORTANT**	**SOMEWHAT IMPORTANT**	**SOMEWHAT UNIMPORTANT/ VERY UNIMPORTANT/ LEAVE IT OUT OF THE STORY**
With hard work and perseverance, anyone can succeed in America.	83%	14%	4%
Our founders limited the power of government, so government would not intrude too much into the lives of its citizens.	74	19	8
America is the world's greatest melting pot in which people from different countries are united into one nation.	73	21	5
America's contribution is one of expanding freedom for more and more people.	71	22	6
Our nation betrayed its founding principles by cruel mistreatment of blacks and American Indians.	59	24	17
Our founders were part of a male-dominated culture that gave important roles to men while keeping women in the background.	38	28	35

Used by permission of the Survey of American Political Culture, James Davison Hunter and Carol Bowman, directors, Institute for Advanced Studies in Culture, University of Virginia.

and Eastern European immigrants reached this country's shores in large numbers in the nineteenth and early twentieth centuries, they encountered nativist elements that assailed their customs and religions. Many Americans, including some members of Congress, wanted Catholics and Jews completely barred from entry. During the last third of the twentieth century, Asian and Hispanic immigrants encountered stiff opposition in some parts of the country. After the September 11, 2001, terrorist attacks on the World Trade Center and the Pentagon, polls indicated that most Americans wanted Middle East immigration sharply reduced or stopped entirely.

Resistance to immigrant groups is not among the stories that Americans like to tell about themselves.[16] Such lapses of historical memory can be found among all peoples, but the tendency to rewrite history is perhaps exaggerated in the American case because Americans' beliefs are so idealistic (see Table 1–1). How could a nation that upholds the ideal of human equality have barred the Chinese, enslaved the blacks, betrayed the Indians, and subordinated women?

One reason America's ideals do not match reality is that they are general principles, not fixed rules of conduct. They derive from somewhat different experiences and philosophical traditions, and there are points at which they conflict. Equality, for instance, emphasizes fairness and the opportunity for all to partake of society's benefits, whereas liberty emphasizes personal freedom and threats posed to it by political power. Conflict between these ideals is inevitable. Take the issue of affirmative action. Proponents say that only through aggressive affirmative action programs will women and minorities receive the equal treatment in the job market to which they are entitled. Opponents say that aggressive affirmative action infringes unreasonably on the liberty of the employer and the initiative of the work force. Each side can say that it has America's ideals on its side, and no resort to logic can persuade either side that the opposing viewpoint should prevail.

Despite their inexact meanings, conflicting implications, and unfulfilled promise, Americans' ideals have had a strong impact on their politics. If racial, gender, ethnic, and other forms of intolerance constitute the sorriest chapter in the nation's history, the centuries-old struggle of Americans to create a more equal society is among the finest chapters. Few nations have battled so relentlessly against the insidious discrimination that stems from superficial human differences such as the color of one's skin. High ideals are more than mere abstractions. They are a source of human aspiration and, ultimately, of political and social change.

POLITICS: THE RESOLUTION OF CONFLICT

Cultural ideals help shape what people expect from politics and inspire people to work together for a collective purpose. Politics, however, is more than shared ideals and common efforts. Politics is also a struggle for power and advantage. Commenting on the competitive nature of politics, political scientist Harold Lasswell described it as the struggle over "who gets what, when, and how."[17] **Politics** is the process through which a society settles its conflicts.

> **politics** The process through which a society makes its governing decisions.

Political conflict has two primary sources. One is *scarcity*. Even the richest societies do not have enough wealth to satisfy everyone's desires. Conflict over the distribution of resources is the predictable result. Consider, for example, the issue of school funding. The quality of U.S. public schools varies widely. Affluent suburban districts have better schools than do poor inner-city districts. Lacking a strong local tax base, inner-city residents have pressured state governments to take over the financing of schools and to provide equal funding to all schools. Residents of suburban communities have fought this arrangement, fearing that it would increase their taxes and hurt their local schools.

Differences in values are the other main source of political conflict. People see issues differently as a result of differences in their beliefs, experiences, and interests. Abortion is an issue of freedom of choice for some and an issue of murder for others. People bring to politics a wide range of conflicting standards—about abortion, the environment, crime and punishment, the poor, the economy, and countless other issues.

Politics operates by a set of "rules" that determine whose voice will prevail when conflict arises over resources and values. Without such rules, people would be constantly at each other's throats, and society would dissolve into chaos and lawlessness.

The Social Contract

For a long period of world history, the rules of politics were stacked against ordinary people. They had no say in their governing and were at the mercy of those in authority. Government was controlled by absolute monarchs, whose

Should English Be Made America's Official Language?

America's ideals are broad principles that include conflicting elements. The principle of diversity extols Americans' differences. The principle of unity proclaims that Americans are one people and one nation. These principles have clashed whenever newly arrived immigrants have been at issue. A recent example is the question of whether English should be adopted as the language of government—meaning that official government business would be conducted in the English language only. Slightly more than half the states have laws to this effect, although these laws do provide for some exceptions.

Debating the Issues

Yes: English, the greatest unifier in our nation's history, is under assault in our schools, in our courts and by bureaucrats. Using scare tactics and divisive rhetoric, self-appointed leaders of immigrant groups are trying to prevent newcomers from learning our shared language. This vocal minority wrongly claims that an immigrant's culture and heritage will be lost if he or she agrees to have English as the official language. Let me be clear: Encouraging immigrants to learn English is not about bigotry or exclusion. On the contrary, teaching newcomers English is one of the strongest acts of inclusion to our society our government can provide. The whole notion of a melting pot culture is threatened if immigrants aren't encouraged to adopt the common language of this country. We're not suggesting that people give up their native languages. Bilingualism and multilingualism are quite advantageous in our fast-paced global economy. I, in fact, speak four languages. We believe it makes far more sense to funnel the money spent on translation services to providing newcomers with the most important instrument in their life's toolbox—the knowledge of English so they can go as far as their dreams take them.

—*Mauro E. Mujica, Chairman, U.S. English, Inc.*

No: At the time of the nation's founding, it was commonplace to hear as many as 20 languages spoken in daily life. . . . Even the Articles of Confederation were printed in German, as well as English. . . . Nonetheless, restrictive language laws have been enacted periodically since the late 19th century, usually in response to new waves of immigration. These laws, in practice if not in intent, have punished immigrants for their foreignness and violated their rights. In the early 1980s, again during a period of concern about new immigration, a movement arose that seeks the establishment of English as the nation's official language. The "English Only" movement promotes the enactment of legislation that restricts or prohibits the use of languages other than English by government agencies and, in some cases, by private businesses. . . . "English Only" laws . . . can abridge the rights of individuals who are not proficient in English, and . . . perpetuate false stereotypes of immigrants and non-English speakers. . . . An English Language Amendment to the Constitution would transform that document from being a charter of liberties and individual freedom into a charter of restrictions that limits, rather than protects, individual rights.

—*American Civil Liberties Union*

word was law. Some of these rulers were tyrants, and many of them taxed their subjects heavily to raise large armies and erect great palaces.

Roughly four centuries ago, ideas about the proper form of government began to change. Ironically, one of the theorists who contributed to this development was an advocate of absolute rule. In *Leviathan* (published in 1651), the English philosopher Thomas Hobbes argued that government rests on a **social contract** in which ordinary people surrender the freedom they would have in a state of nature in return for the protection that a sovereign ruler can provide. People give up their freedom, Hobbes said, because life in its natural state is

social contract A voluntary agreement by individuals to form government, which is then obliged to act within the confines of the agreement.

Politics includes conflict and consensus. Women have had to struggle to be treated as equals in the workplace, but their efforts have been supported by public opinion and public policies.

"nasty, brutish, and short"—the weak are constantly preyed upon by the strong. Thus, people seek the protection of a strong ruler whom they must obey, even if a particular ruler turns out to be cruel or capricious. The alternative—an endless "war of all against all"—is worse.

Forty years later, the English philosopher John Locke used Hobbes's idea of a social contract to argue *against* absolutism. In his *Second Treatise on Civil Government* (1690), Locke claimed that all individuals have certain natural (or inalienable) rights, including those of life, liberty, and property. Such rights, Locke wrote, belonged to people in their natural state before government was created. When people come together in order to have the protection that only organized government can provide, their natural rights are neither taken from them by government nor surrendered to them by government. People enter into the social contract—they agree to be governed—in order to safeguard their rights and property. Accordingly, government is obliged to provide this protection. If it fails to do so, Locke argued, the people can rightfully rebel against it and create a new government.

Three-quarters of a century later, the French philosopher Jean Jacques Rousseau extended the idea of a social contract to include popular sovereignty. Like Locke, Rousseau opposed absolute rule. "Man was born free, but everywhere he is in chains" are the opening words of Rousseau's *Social Contract* (1762). Rousseau claimed that people in the natural state are innocent and happy. Accordingly, the only government that people would willingly accept in its place is one that governs with their consent and for their benefit. The only legitimate government, Rousseau concluded, is one that serves the people's common interest or, as he called it, the "general will."

These ideas—that people have individual rights and must have a say in their government—sparked the American Revolution of 1776. The basic principle of contract theory—that the power of leaders is limited by a set of rules—was embodied in the Constitution of the United States, written in 1787.

Living Up to America's Founding Ideals

Author Theodore H. White described America as a nation "in search of itself." He was referring to the never-ending quest to fulfill the nation's promise. Liberty, equality, and self-government are daunting ideals that must be regularly adapted to fit new realities. Slavery, for example, could not long be maintained in a country that claimed to symbolize freedom and self-determination.

The disputed nature of America's ideals does not diminish White's claim. Indeed, because these ideals are not always self-evident in practice is a reason why they must be discovered through practice. They require constant redefinition and renewal. American history is in part a history of the ongoing struggle to attain a fuller realization of the nation's promise.

Signs of that struggle are all around you. They can be found in many young people's questioning of the responsiveness of their government. They can be found in the concern that many women and minority-group members have about their access to society's opportunities. They can be found in the effort of less affluent students to get through college so that they can attain a fuller measure of America's promise. They can be found in the fear of many Americans that global terrorism might somehow diminish freedom at home. The list could go on, but the point would be the same: as Theodore White said, America is a nation in search of itself.

This feature of American life can be a source of inspiration. American democracy is a work in progress, and each citizen has a part to play in it. What have you done, and what more might you do, to enhance America's founding ideals?

The Rules of American Politics

The major rules of American politics—democracy, constitutionalism, and capitalism—establish a political process that is intended to promote self-government, defend individual rights, and protect property.

Democracy

Democracy is a set of rules intended to give ordinary people a significant voice in government. The word *democracy* comes from the Greek words *demos*, meaning "the people," and *kratis*, meaning "to rule." In simple terms, **democracy** is a form of government in which the people govern, either directly or through elected representatives (see Chapter 2). A democracy thus is different from an **oligarchy** (in which control rests with a small group, such as top-ranking military officers or a few wealthy families) and from an **autocracy** (in which control rests with a single individual, such as a king or dictator).

Democratic government rests on the idea that legitimate authority stems from the consent of the governed, which in practice has come to mean majority rule through voting in elections—the Rousseauist principle that the views of the many should prevail over the views of the few. More direct forms of democracy exist, such as the town meeting in which citizens vote directly on issues affecting them, but the impracticality of such an arrangement at the national level has made majority rule through elections the operating principle of modern democracies.

Majority rule through the vote does not take the same form in all democracies. The U.S. electoral system was established in a period when the power of

democracy A form of government in which the people govern, either directly or through elected representatives.

oligarchy A form of government in which control rests with a few persons.

autocracy A form of government in which absolute control rests with a single person.

Democracy—the idea of a government of, for, and by the people—is an organizing principle of the American political system. In practice, democracy—and its accompanying feature, majoritarianism—is most clearly evident in elections when Americans through their votes choose their representatives.

government—whether it rested with a king or the majority—was greatly feared. To protect against abuses of power, the writers of the U.S. Constitution devised an elaborate system of checks and balances. Authority was divided among the executive, legislative, and judicial branches so that each branch could serve as a check on the power of the others and could balance their power with its own power (see Chapter 2). Indeed, *extreme fragmentation of governing authority is a defining characteristic of the American political system.* One result of this constitutional arrangement is that majority rule is less direct in the United States than in many democratic countries, including those of Europe. In the European democracies, a majority has the power in a single election to place executive and legislative power in the hands of a single group of representatives (see Chapter 2). In the United States, however, elections for the president, the Senate, and the House of Representatives are separate, and the terms of office for these officials are staggered. Thus, for a majority to exercise control in the United States, it must have enough strength and lasting power to dominate a series of elections.

Constitutionalism

The concept of democracy implies that the will of the majority should prevail over the wishes of the minority. If taken to the extreme, however, this principle would allow a majority to ride roughshod over the minority. Such action could deprive the minority even of its liberty, a clearly unacceptable outcome. Individuals have rights and freedoms that cannot lawfully be denied by the majority.

constitutionalism The idea that there are definable limits on the rightful power of a government over its citizens.

Constitutionalism is a set of rules that restricts the lawful uses of power. In its original sense, constitutionalism in Western society referred to a government based on laws and constitutional powers.[18] **Constitutionalism** has since come to refer specifically to the Lockean idea that there are limits to the rightful power of government over citizens. In a constitutional system, officials govern according to law, and citizens have basic rights that government cannot take away or deny.[19] Free speech is an example. Government is prohibited by the First Amendment from interfering with the lawful exercise of free speech. No right is absolute, which means that some restrictions are allowed. No student, for example, has a First Amendment right to shout loudly and disrupt a classroom. Nevertheless, free speech is broadly protected by the courts. During the buildup to war with Iraq in 2003, tens of thousands of antiwar demonstrators took to the streets. Despite instances where protesters were intimidated by police or arrested for disorderly conduct, those who opposed the government's pursuit of the war had the opportunity to express their views freely without threat of being sent to prison.

The constitutional tradition in the United States is at least as strong as the democratic tradition. In fact, *a defining characteristic of the American political system*

Free speech is a familiar aspect of constitutionalism. This anti–gun control rally took place in Austin, Texas.

is its extraordinary emphasis on individual rights. Issues that in other democracies would be resolved through elections and in legislative bodies are, in the United States, decided in courts of law as well. As Tocqueville noted, there is hardly a political issue in the United States that does not sooner or later become a judicial issue.[20] Abortion rights, nuclear power, busing, toxic waste disposal, and welfare services are among the scores of issues that in recent years have played out in part as questions of rights to be settled through the courts.

The war on terrorism has also been a subject of judicial action. After the terrorist attacks of September 11, 2001, Congress quickly enacted the USA Patriot Act, which granted law enforcement officials broad new powers, including the power in some circumstances to jail individuals without tangible evidence of wrongdoing (see "Liberty, Equality, and Self-Government"). The ink was barely dry on the Patriot Act before civil liberties groups went to court to challenge the constitutionality of certain provisions of the legislation (see Chapter 4).

Capitalism

Just as democracy and constitutionalism are systems of rules for allocating costs and benefits in American society, so too is capitalism. Societies have adopted alternative ways of organizing their economies. One way is **socialism,** which assigns government a large role in the ownership of the means of production, in regulating economic decisions, and in providing for the economic security of the individual. Under the form of socialism practiced in democratic countries, such as Sweden, the government does not attempt to manage the overall economy. Under **communism,** the government owns most or all major industries and also takes responsibility for overall management of the economy, including production quotas, supply points, and pricing.

socialism An economic system in which government owns and controls many of the major industries.

communism An economic system in which government owns most or all major industries and also takes responsibility for overall management of the economy.

Liberty, Equality, & Self-Government

What's Your Opinion?

Liberty and Security

The USA Patriot Act of 2001 was enacted less than two months after the September 11 terrorist attacks on the World Trade Center and the Pentagon. It was easily the most contentious domestic action taken by the U.S. government in the immediate aftermath of the bombings. Not all the provisions of the Patriot Act were controversial. For example, a provision that allowed for court-approved wiretaps of specific individuals as opposed to wiretaps of specific phone numbers was widely regarded as a necessary updating of wiretap procedures. However, the USA Patriot Act also allows government to examine medical, financial, and educational records on the basis of a minimal standard of suspicion; to detain individuals for short periods without tangible evidence of wrongdoing; to deport noncitizens who have even minimal association with suspected terrorist groups; and to secretly search homes and offices in some instances.

According to its supporters, the Patriot Act gave government the tools with which to combat terrorism and thereby protect the lives of Americans. Opponents argued that the bill included unwarranted incursions on individual rights.

This type of debate has occurred many times in the nation's history. After World War II, for example, Congress responded to a growing fear of the spread of communism by passing the Smith Act, which made it illegal for Americans to conspire to teach and advocate the violent overthrow of the U.S. government. Its proponents claimed that the legislation would protect the country against internal subversion, while opponents claimed it infringed on First Amendment rights. In the initial court cases, the Supreme Court upheld the restriction on free expression, but in later ones it declared that advocacy of the forceful overthrow of the government was lawful as long as it was "theoretical" and did not directly and substantially imperil the government.

What's your view on the USA Patriot Act? Do you feel more or less secure because of it? How, primarily, do you define your security? Do you worry about becoming the victim of a terrorist attack? Or do you worry more about having your rights abused by officials engaged in the war on terrorism? Would you have the same opinion if, say, your religion or ethnicity was different than it is? How far are you willing to let government depart from normal protections of individual rights in order to combat the terrorist threat?

capitalism An economic system based on the idea that government should interfere with economic transactions as little as possible. Free enterprise and self-reliance are the collective and individual principles that underpin capitalism.

Capitalism is an alternative method for distributing economic costs and benefits. **Capitalism** holds that the government should interfere with the economy as little as possible. Free enterprise, private property, and self-reliance are the principles of capitalism. Firms are allowed to operate in a free and open marketplace, and individuals are expected to rely on their own initiative to establish their economic security. Firms decide what they will produce and the price they will charge for their goods and services, while consumers decide what they will buy at what price. Meanwhile, following a Lockean principle, private property rights are vigorously protected and enforced through government action.

Like the rules of democracy and constitutionalism, the rules of capitalism are not neutral. Whereas democracy responds to numbers and constitutionalism responds to individual rights, capitalism responds to wealth. "Money talks" in a capitalist system, which means, among other things, that wealthier

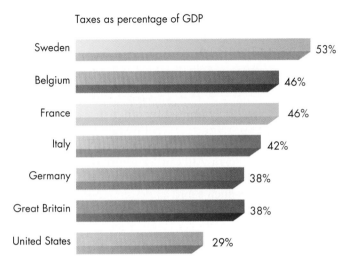

Taxes as percentage of GDP

Sweden	53%
Belgium	46%
France	46%
Italy	42%
Germany	38%
Great Britain	38%
United States	29%

Figure 1–4

Level of Taxation
Americans pay less in taxes than Europeans do.
Source: OECD. 2004. Percentages based on all taxes (national and subnational) relative to a country's Gross Domestic Product (GDP).

people will have by far the greater say not only in economic matters but in political ones as well. Most Americans see nothing wrong with this arrangement and, compared with Europeans, are more likely to accept limits on government action in the area of the economy.

For all practical purposes, this outlook places many kinds of choices that in other countries are decided collectively beyond the reach of political majorities in the United States. Although Americans complain that their taxes are too high, they are taxed at substantially lower rates than Europeans are (see Figure 1–4). This situation testifies to the extent to which Americans believe wealth to be more properly allocated through the economic marketplace than through government policy. *A major characteristic of the American system is a relatively sharp distinction between what is political, and therefore to be decided in the public arena, and what is economic, and therefore to be settled in the private realm.*

POLITICAL POWER: THE CONTROL OF POLICY

Rules are necessary in politics because the stakes are high. Individuals who decide how society will be governed have **power,** a term that refers to the ability of persons or institutions to control public policy.[21] **Public policy** is a decision by government to follow a course of action designed to produce a particular outcome. Persons or institutions with sufficient power can determine which side will prevail in policy disputes.

Some governments exercise absolute power. **Totalitarian governments** assert complete dominance over individuals and the institutions of society. They determine the culture, control the media, direct the economy, dictate what can and cannot be taught in schools, define family relations, and decide which religions—if any—can be practiced openly. In fact, virtually no area of life is beyond their sphere of control, which leads them to one-party rule and the use of fear, intimidation, and force to subdue the population. Germany under Adolf

power The ability of persons or institutions to control policy.

public policy A decision of government to pursue a course of action designed to produce an intended outcome.

totalitarian government A form of government in which the leaders claim complete dominance of all individuals and institutions.

Hitler and the Soviet Union under Josef Stalin were totalitarian regimes. Millions of people in both countries were deemed enemies of the state and were imprisoned, tortured, or murdered.

Harsh rule is also characteristic of **authoritarian governments.** Although authoritarian governments include totalitarian ones, it is useful to distinguish regimes such as Nazi Germany from regimes that, though they admit to no limits on their power, are effectively limited by other strong institutions in the society, such as churches, corporations, or wealthy families. The governments that have resulted periodically from military coups in Africa and South America usually are authoritarian in form. Although authoritarian regimes repress political opponents and restrict free expression, they refrain from asserting full authority, recognizing that any such claim could antagonize powerful institutions that might drive them out of office.

Unlike authoritarian governments, democratic governments are characterized by ongoing competition for power among a range of interests. This tendency is particulary pronounced in the case of the United States. The country's settlement by people of different lands and religions, its great size and geographical variation, and its economic complexity have made the United States a diverse nation. Perhaps no country has more competing interests than the United States. *Competition for power among a great many interests of all kinds is a major characteristic of American politics.* Indeed, America's great diversity helps explain why its political life is not a life-and-death struggle. In *Federalist* No. 10, James Madison argued that government is most dangerous when a single group is powerful enough to gain full political control. In such cases, the group will use government to further its interests at the expense of all others in society. Because the United States is so diverse, however, no single group can hope to achieve full control. This forces groups to work together to exercise power, a process that requires each group to accommodate the interests of the others.

authoritarian government A form of government in which leaders, though they admit to no limits on their powers, are effectively limited by other centers of power in the society.

Adolf Hitler's Nazi Germany was a brutal totalitarian regime responsible for the deaths of millions of people.

Nevertheless, as in every society, power in America is the means of controlling public policy. Americans who have enough power can levy or cut taxes, permit or prohibit abortions, protect or take away private property, provide or refuse health benefits, impose or relax trade barriers, make war or declare peace. With so much at stake, it is not surprising that Americans, like people elsewhere, seek power as a means of achieving their policy goals.

Authority

Political power can reside with private individuals and organizations as well as in the hands of those who occupy government positions. A case in point is the power exercised by the National Rifle Association (NRA) over gun control policy. NRA members are strongly opposed to restrictions on gun ownership and back up their position through the power of their votes and their money. Although Congress has the authority to enact stricter controls on guns, many of its members are reluctant to antagonize the NRA.

Nevertheless, U.S. officials do have a special kind of power as a result of the positions they hold. When government officials exercise power, it is called **authority,** defined as the recognized right of an individual, organization, or institution to make binding decisions. By this definition, government is not the only source of authority: parents have authority over their children; professors have authority over their students; firms have authority over their employees. However, government is a special case in that its authority is more encompassing in scope and more final in nature. Government's authority extends to all people within its geographical boundaries and can be used to redefine the authority of the parent, the professor, or the firm. Government's authority is also the most coercive. It includes the power to arrest and imprison, and even to legally punish by death those who violate its rules.

authority The recognized right of an individual or institution to exercise power.

Government needs coercive power to ensure that its laws will be obeyed. Without this power, lawlessness would prevail—as it does in Colombia, where drug lords control large areas of the country. Yet this power can itself be abused, as when government uses its coercive force to intimidate or repress opponents. The challenge, as Madison noted, is to grant government the authority necessary to prevent lawlessness while confining the uses of this authority to lawful purposes.

Theories of Power

Who has power in America? Who, in the end, decides the policies that the U.S. government pursues? Is it the people themselves who hold this power, or does it reside in the hands of a relatively small group of influential people, either within or outside of government?

This issue is compelling because the ultimate question of any political system is the question of who governs. Is power widely shared and used for the benefit of the many, or is it narrowly held and used to the advantage of the few? The issue is compelling for a second reason: power is easy to define but hard to identify. Consider, for example, the votes that members of Congress cast. Are

TABLE 1–2	**Theories of Power: Who Governs America?** There are four theories of power in America, each of which must be taken into account in any full explanation of the nation's policies.
THEORY	**DESCRIPTION**
Majoritarianism	Holds that numerical majorities determine issues of policy
Pluralism	Holds that policies are effectively decided through power wielded by special interests that dominate particular policy areas
Elitism	Holds that policy is controlled by a small number of well-positioned, highly influential individuals
Bureaucratic rule	Holds that policy is controlled by well-placed administrators within the government bureaucracy

these votes based on the members' own beliefs, or are they a response to pressure from various interests?

In fact, the pattern of political power has been found to differ substantially across individuals, institutions, and policy areas. As a result, there is no single theory of how power in America is held and exercised. Instead, four broad theories predominate (see Table 1–2). None of these theories describes every aspect of American politics, but each has some validity.

Majoritarianism: Government by the People

majoritarianism The idea that the majority prevails not only in elections but also in policy determination.

A basic principle of democracy is the idea of majority rule. **Majoritarianism** is the notion that the majority prevails not only in the counting of votes but also in the determination of public policy.

Majorities do sometimes rule in America. Their power is perhaps most evident in those states that offer voters the opportunity to decide directly on policy initiatives, which then become law if they receive a majority vote. The majority's influence is also felt indirectly through the decisions of elected representatives. When Congress in 1996 passed a welfare reform bill that included provisions requiring able-bodied welfare recipients to accept a job or job training after a two-year period or face the loss of their welfare benefits, it was acting in accord with the thinking of the majority of Americans who believe that employable individuals should be self-reliant. A more systematic assessment of the power of majorities is provided by Benjamin Page and Robert Shapiro's study of the relationship between majority opinions and more than three hundred policy issues. On major issues particularly, the researchers found that when majority opinion changed, policy tended to change in the same direction.[22]

Majorities do not always rule in America, however. In many policy areas, majority opinion is nonexistent or is ignored by policymakers. There are only a few issues at any moment that have the general public's attention and an even smaller number that the public really cares about. Thus, majoritarianism cannot account for most government policies. Other explanations are required.

Political Culture

One People out of Many

Hispanics: The New Largest "Minority"

Hispanic Americans were projected to surpass black Americans as the largest minority group early in the twenty-first century. Demographers were surprised when 2002 census data revealed that the change had already taken place. The Census Bureau estimated that there were 37 million Hispanics compared with 36 million African Americans.

The change came as some advocates were challenging the use of the term *minority* as a means of identifying a particular group of Americans. They contended that terms such as *people of color* were both more accurate and less stigmatizing. For the moment, however, *minority* remains an official designation for various government programs. America's five officially designated minorities are Hispanic Americans, African Americans, Asian Americans, Native Americans, and women (who, numerically, are a majority).

Although recent arrivals have helped make Hispanics the nation's largest minority group, Hispanics are one of the country's oldest ethnic groups. Some Hispanics are descendants of people who helped colonize the areas of California, Texas, Florida, New Mexico, and Arizona before those areas became part of the United States. The earliest Hispanics were here before the landing of the *Mayflower.*

As with all ethnic and racial groups, it is a mistake to use stereotypes with Hispanics that suggest its members have common backgrounds and characteristics. But Hispanics, like all other groups, have cultural tendencies that are somewhat distinctive. For example, the Hispanic culture is less individualistic and more community centered than is the northern European culture.

Hispanics are a growing political force in the American Southwest. Like all groups that include a lot of new citizens, Hispanics have relatively low voting rates. But as they become further assimilated into American society, their turnout is expected to approach the national average, at which point they will hold the balance of political power in a number of states, including California.

Pluralism: Government by Groups

One other explanation is provided by the theory of **pluralism,** which focuses on group activity and holds that many policies are effectively decided through power wielded by diverse (plural) interests.

Many policies are in fact more responsive to the interests of particular groups than to majority opinion. Agricultural subsidies, broadcast regulations, and corporate tax incentives are examples. For pluralists, the issue of whether interest-group politics serves the public good centers on whether it serves a diverse range of interests. Pluralists contend that it is misleading to view society only in terms of majorities that may or may not form around given issues. They see society as primarily a collection of separate interests. Farmers, broadcasters, college students, and multinational corporations have different needs and desires and, according to the pluralist view, should have a disproportionate say in policies that directly affect them. Thus, as long as many groups have influence in their own area of interest, government is responding to the interests of most

pluralism A theory of American politics that holds that society's interests are substantially represented through the activities of groups.

Americans. Pluralists such as Robert Dahl have argued that this is in fact the way the American political system operates most of the time.[23]

Critics argue that pluralists wrongly assume that the public interest is somehow represented in a system that allows special interests, each in its own sphere, to set public policy (see Chapter 9). Any such outcome, they say, represents the triumph of minority rule over majority rule. Critics also say that society's underprivileged groups are unable to compete effectively because of their lack of organization and money. They see a group system biased in favor of a small number of powerful interests.

Elitism: Government by a Few

elitism The view that the United States essentially is run by a tiny elite (composed of wealthy or well-connected individuals) who control public policy through both direct and indirect means.

Elite theory offers in varying degrees a pessimistic view of the U.S. political system. **Elitism** holds that power in America is held by a small number of well-positioned, highly influential individuals. A leading proponent of elite theory was sociologist C. Wright Mills, who argued that key policies are decided by an overlapping coalition of select leaders, including corporate executives, top military officers, and centrally placed public officials.[24] Other proponents of elite theory have defined the core group somewhat differently, but their contention is the same: America is governed not by majorities or a plurality of groups but by a small number of well-placed and privileged individuals.

Proponents of elite theory differ, however, in the extent to which they believe elites control policy for their own purposes. Some theorists, including G. William Domhoff, hold the view that elites operate behind the scenes in order to manipulate government for selfish ends.[25] Other theorists claim that elites, in part to protect their privileged positions and in part out of a sense of obligation, pursue policies that serve others' interests as well as their own. One such view holds that competing elites appeal to voters for support and, in the process, adopt policy positions favored by important blocs of voters.[26]

The Federal Reserve Board of Governors is a government body that through its interest-rate policies exerts a substantial influence on the American economy. The board meets in secrecy and is an example of the influence of political elites.

Unquestionably, certain policies are effectively controlled by a tiny circle of influential people. The nation's monetary policy, for example, is set by the decisions of the Federal Reserve Board ("the Fed"), which meets in secrecy and decides the interest rates that banks pay for the loans they receive from the Federal Reserve. These rates in turn affect the interest rates that banks charge their customers. The Fed is very responsive to the concerns of bankers. What is less clear is the Fed's responsiveness to the concerns of consumers.

Bureaucratic Rule: Government by Administrators

A fourth theory holds that power resides in the hands of career government bureaucrats. The leading proponent of the theory of **bureaucratic rule** was the German sociologist Max Weber, who argued that all large organizations tend toward the bureaucratic form, with the result that decision-making power devolves to career administrators whose experience and knowledge of policy issues exceed those of elected officials.[27] Another sociologist, Roberto Michels, propounded the "iron law of oligarchy," concluding that power inevitably gravitates toward experienced administrators at the top of large-scale organizations, even in the case of organizations that aim to be governed democratically.[28]

bureaucratic rule The tendency of large-scale organization to develop into the bureaucratic form, with the effect that administrators make key policy decisions.

Bureaucratic politics raises the possibility of a large, permanent government run by unaccountable administrators. Elections come and go, but the bureaucrats who staff executive agencies stay on. Government could not function without them, but in most cases they are not instruments of the majority. Bureaucrats, in fact, make many key policy decisions in areas as diverse as the environment, health, and law enforcement (see Chapter 13).

Who Does Govern?

The perspective of this book is that each of these theories—majoritarianism, pluralism, elitism, and bureaucratization—must be taken into account in any full explanation of politics and power in America. As subsequent chapters will demonstrate, some policies are decided by majority influence, whereas others reflect the influence of special interests, bureaucrats, or elites.

THE CONCEPT OF A POLITICAL SYSTEM AND THIS BOOK'S ORGANIZATION

As the foregoing discussion suggests, American government is based on a great many related parts. It is useful to regard these components as constituting a **political system.** The parts are separate, but they connect with one another, affecting how each performs. Political scientist David Easton, who was a pioneer in this conception of politics, said that it makes little sense to study political relations piecemeal when they are, in reality, "interrelated."[29]

political system The various components of American government. The parts are separate, but they connect with each other, affecting how each performs.

The complexity of government has kept political scientists from developing a fully explanatory model of the political system, but the concept of politics as a system is useful for instructional purposes. The concept emphasizes the actual workings of government rather than focusing on its institutional structures

Figure 1–5

The American Political System
This book's chapters are
organized within a political-
system framework.

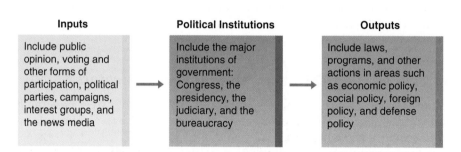

CONSTITUTIONAL FRAMEWORK

Includes provisions for limited government (e.g., checks and balances),
representative government, civil liberties, and civil rights

Inputs	Political Institutions	Outputs
Include public opinion, voting and other forms of participation, political parties, campaigns, interest groups, and the news media	Include the major institutions of government: Congress, the presidency, the judiciary, and the bureaucracy	Include laws, programs, and other actions in areas such as economic policy, social policy, foreign policy, and defense policy

alone. To view politics as a system is to emphasize the connections between the parts and how change in one area affects the others. It is a dynamic conception in that the political system is constantly changing in response to new conditions and to the interplay of its various parts—and all these changes take place for a purpose. The political system is the mechanism through which society is governed.

The political-system approach characterizes this book, beginning with the organization of its chapters (see Figure 1–5). The political system operates against the backdrop of a constitutional framework that defines how power is to be obtained and exercised. This structure is the focus of the opening chapters, which examine how the Constitution defines, in theory and practice, the institutions of government and the rights of individuals. Another part of the political system is *inputs:* the demands that people and organizations place on government and the support they provide for institutions, leaders, and policies. These inputs are explored in chapters on public opinion, political participation, political parties, interest groups, and the news media. The functioning of governing officials is addressed in chapters on the nation's *political institutions:* Congress, the presidency, the federal bureaucracy, and the federal courts. Some of the discussion in these chapters is devoted simply to describing these institutions, but most of the discussion explores their interrelationships and how their actions are affected by inputs and the constitutional system in which they operate. Throughout the book, but particularly in the closing chapters, attention is given to the political system's *outputs:* policy decisions that are binding on society. These decisions, which are made by political institutions in response to inputs, affect American life in many areas, including the economy, the environment, social welfare, education, foreign affairs, and national defense.

The chapters are collectively designed to convey a reliable body of knowledge that will enable the reader to think broadly and systematically about the nature of the American political system. To assist in this process, this opening chapter has identified five encompassing tendencies of American politics that will be examined further in later chapters:

- Enduring cultural ideals that are Americans' common bond and a source of their political goals
- Extreme fragmentation of governing authority that is based on an elaborate system of checks and balances
- Many competing interests, which are the result of the nation's great size, population diversity, and economic complexity
- Strong emphasis on individual rights, which is a consequence of the nation's political traditions
- A relatively sharp separation of the political and economic spheres, which has the effect of placing many economic issues outside the reach of political majorities

Underlying this book's concern with the broad patterns of the American political system is a question that must be asked of any democracy: what is the relationship of the people to their government? The answer to this question is the foundation not only of a reasonable assessment of the state of American democracy but also of good citizenship. Responsible citizenship depends finally on an informed perspective, on a recognition of how difficult it is to govern effectively and yet how important it is to try. It cannot be said too often that the issue of governing is the most difficult issue facing any society. Nor can it be said too often that governing is a quest and a search, not a resolved issue. The Constitution's opening phrase, "We the People," is a call to Americans to join that quest. E. E. Schattschneider said it clearly: "In the course of centuries, there has come a great deal of agreement about what democracy is, but nobody has a monopoly on it and the last word has not been spoken."[30]

Summary

Self-Test
www.mhhe.com/pattersontad7

The United States is a nation that was formed on a set of ideals. Liberty, equality, and self-government are foremost among these ideals, which also include the principles of individualism, diversity, and unity. These ideals became Americans' common bond and today are the basis of their political culture. Although they are mythic, inexact, and conflicting, these ideals have had a powerful effect on what generation after generation of Americans has tried to achieve politically for themselves and others.

Politics in the United States plays out through rules of the game that include democracy, constitutionalism, and capitalism. Democracy is rule by the people, which in practice refers to a representative system of government in which the people rule through their elected officials.

Constitutionalism refers to rules that limit the rightful power of government over citizens. Capitalism is an economic system based on a free-market principle that allows the government only a limited role in determining how economic costs and benefits will be allocated.

Politics is the process by which it is determined whose values will prevail in society. The basis of politics is conflict over scarce resources and competing values. Those who have power win out in this conflict and are able to control governing authority and policy choices. In the United States, no one faction controls all power and policy. Majorities govern on some issues, while groups, elites, and bureaucrats each govern on other issues.

STUDY CORNER

Key Terms

authoritarian government (*p. 26*)
authority (*p. 27*)
autocracy (*p. 21*)
bureaucratic rule (*p. 31*)
capitalism (*p. 24*)
communism (*p. 23*)
constitutionalism (*p. 22*)
democracy (*p. 21*)
diversity (*p. 4*)

elitism (*p. 30*)
equality (*p. 10*)
individualism (*p. 11*)
liberty (*p. 9*)
majoritarianism (*p. 28*)
oligarchy (*p. 21*)
pluralism (*p. 29*)
political culture (*p. 7*)
political system (*p. 31*)

politics (*p. 18*)
power (*p. 25*)
public policy (*p. 25*)
self-government (*p. 10*)
social contract (*p. 19*)
socialism (*p. 23*)
totalitarian government (*p. 25*)
unity (*p. 11*)

Self-Test

1. American political culture centers on a set of core ideals that includes all **except** which of the following?
   a. English as the official language
   b. liberty
   c. equality
   d. self-government

2. Compared with citizens in European democracies, Americans:
   a. emphasize individualism.
   b. feel that success in life is determined by forces outside their control.
   c. are willing to use government to redistribute economic resources.
   d. a and b.
   e. all of the above.

3. When people are able to control policy decisions and prevail in political conflicts, they are said to have:
   a. political authority.
   b. political power.
   c. pluralism.
   d. diversity.

4. America's commitment to the principle of constitutionalism means:
   a. the majority can decide all policy issues.
   b. there are limits on the rightful power of government over citizens.

   c. direct democracy will be favored over representative democracy.
   d. a "mixed economy" must be upheld at all costs.

5. Which one of the following is **not** among the four theories of power concerning who governs America mentioned in the text?
   a. majoritarianism
   b. pluralism
   c. aristocratic rule
   d. bureaucratic rule

6. Which of the following statements are true about American ideals?
   a. They do not fully match what happens in reality.
   b. There is inevitable conflict between these ideals.
   c. Americans have no interest in putting the ideals into practice.
   d. only a and b
   e. only b and c

7. Cultural beliefs are mythical in the sense that they are based on wishful thinking and serve no useful purpose for society (T/F)

8. Historically, America has been relatively free from racial and ethnic discrimination. (T/F)

9. Authority can be defined as the recognized right of an individual, organization, or institution to make binding decisions. (T/F)

10. Americans have the world's most extensive system of college education. (T/F)

Critical Thinking

How are Americans' beliefs about liberty, equality, and self-government related to their preference for constitutionalism? For capitalism? For democracy?

Suggested Readings

Dahl, Robert. *On Democracy*. New Haven, Conn.: Yale University Press, 1998. A handbook on democracy by a leading advocate of pluralism.

DeLaet, Debra L. *U.S. Immigration Policy in an Age of Rights*. Westport, Conn.: Praeger Publishers, 2000. Analysis of the impact of civil rights action on the changes in U.S. immigration policy in recent decades.

Domhoff, G. William. *Who Rules America? Power and Politics in the Year 2000*. Mountain View, Calif.: Mayfield Publishing, 1998. A critical assessment of American government by a leading proponent of elite theory.

Ferguson, Robert A. *Reading the Early Republic*. Cambridge, Mass.: Harvard University Press, 2004. Argues that America has always been a country trying to reach its ideals.

Lipset, Seymour Martin. *American Exceptionalism: A Double-Edged Sword*. New York: Norton, 1996. Argues that Americans' tendency to view society in idealized terms is a source of both alienation and progress.

Schmidt, Ronald. *Language Policy and Identity Politics in the United States*. Philadelphia: Temple University Press, 2000. A critical assessment of language policy and its role in Americans' identity.

Schuck, Peter H. *Diversity in America: Keeping Government at a Safe Distance*. Cambridge, Mass.: Belknap Press of Harvard, 2003. A far-reaching analysis of when diversity does and does not serve America's interests.

Stout, Jeffrey. *Democracy and Tradition*. Princeton, N.J.: Princeton University Press, 2004. An analysis of the moral claims associated with democracy.

List of Websites

http://www.conginst.org/
A site that provides up-to-date survey data on the American political culture.

http://www.loc.gov/
The Library of Congress website; it provides access to over seventy million historical and contemporary U.S. documents.

http://www.stateline.org/
A University of Richmond/Pew Charitable Trusts site dedicated to providing citizens with information on major policy issues.

http://www.tocqueville.org/
Includes biographical and other references to Alexis de Tocqueville and his writings.

Participate!

The American political culture includes a belief in liberty, equality, and self-government. As a prelude to getting involved in public affairs, reflect on what these ideals mean to you. What types of political activity are associated with each of these ideals? Thinking of your own experiences, what have you done to promote these ideals? What might you consider doing in the future to promote them?

Extra Credit

For up-to-the-minute *New York Times* articles, interactive simulations, graphics, study tools, and more links and quizzes, visit the text's Online Learning Center at www.mhhe.com/pattersontad7.

(Self-Test Answers: 1. a   2. a   3. b   4. b   5. c   6. d   7. F   8. F   9. T   10. T)

2

Constitutional Democracy:
Promoting Liberty and Self-Government

The people must be governed by a majority, with whom all power
resides. But how is the sense of this majority to be obtained?

Fisher Ames (1788)[1]

On the night of June 17, 1972, a security guard at the Watergate apartment-office complex in Washington, D.C., noticed that the latch on the door to the Democratic Party's national headquarters had been taped open. He called the police, who captured the five burglars inside. As it turned out, the men had links to Republican President Richard Nixon's Committee to Re-elect the President. Nixon called the incident "bizarre" and denied that anyone on his staff had had anything to do with the break-in.

The reality was that the Watergate break-in was part of an orchestrated campaign of "dirty tricks" designed to ensure Nixon's reelection. Funded by illegal contributions and conducted through the CIA, the IRS, the FBI, the Secret Service, and Nixon's own operatives (called the White House "plumbers"), the dirty-tricks campaign extended to wiretaps, tax audits, and burglaries of Nixon's political opponents (the "enemies list"), who included journalists and antiwar activists in addition to Democrats.

Although the Nixon White House managed for a time to hide the truth, the facts of the dirty-tricks campaign gradually became known. In early 1974 the House Judiciary Committee began impeachment proceedings, helped along, ironically, by Nixon's own words. During Senate hearings, a White House assistant revealed that Nixon had tape-recorded all his telephone calls and personal conversations in the Oval Office. Nixon at first refused to release the tapes but then made public what he claimed were "all the relevant" ones. The House Judiciary Committee demanded additional tapes, as did the special prosecutor who had been appointed to investigate criminal aspects of the Watergate affair. In late July the U.S. Supreme Court, which included four justices appointed by Nixon, unanimously ordered the president to supply sixty-four additional tapes. The tapes were incriminating, and two weeks later, on August 9, 1974, Richard Nixon resigned from office, the first president in U.S. history to do so.

Nixon's downfall was owed in no small measure to the handiwork two centuries earlier of the writers of the Constitution. They were well aware that power could never be entrusted to the goodwill of leaders. "If angels were to govern men," James Madison wrote in *Federalist* No. 51, "neither external nor internal controls on government would be necessary." Madison's point, of course, was that leaders are not angels and, as mere mortals, are subject to temptation and vice, including a lust for power—hence the Framers' insistence on constitutional checks on power, as when they gave Congress the authority to impeach and remove the president from office.

The Senate Judiciary Committee holds hearings on allegations of illegal acts by President Richard Nixon. The congressional investigation led to Nixon's resignation.

limited government A government that is subject to strict limits on its lawful uses of power, and hence on its ability to deprive people of their liberty.

self-government The principle that the people are the ultimate source and proper beneficiary of governing authority; in practice, a government based on majority rule.

The writers of the U.S. Constitution were intent on protecting *liberty* and therefore sought to restrain the use of political power. Their system of checks and balances was designed to limit what officials can do. At the same time, however, the writers of the Constitution wanted a government that was powerful enough to act on the people's behalf. The first objective was **limited government:** a government subject to strict limits on its lawful uses of power. The second objective was **self-government:** a government subject to the will of the people as expressed through the preferences of a majority. Self-government requires that the voters' preferences find their way into public policy in a substantial and timely way. However, limited government requires restraints on the majority as a way of protecting the rights and interests of the minority. These considerations resulted in a constitution that not only has provision for majority rule but also has built-in restrictions on the exercise of majority power.

This chapter describes how the principles of self-government and limited government are embodied in the Constitution and explains the tension between them. The chapter also indicates how these principles have been modified in practice in the course of American history. The main points of this chapter are the following:

- *America during the colonial period developed traditions of limited government and self-government.* These traditions were rooted in governing practices, philosophy, and cultural values.

- *The Constitution provides for limited government mainly by defining lawful powers and by dividing those powers among competing institutions.* The Constitution, with its Bill of Rights, also prohibits government from infringing on individual rights. Judicial review is an additional safeguard of limited government.

- *The Constitution in its original form provided for self-government mainly through indirect systems of popular election of representatives.* The Framers' theory of self-government was based on the notion that political power must be separated from immediate popular influences if sound policies are to result.

- *The idea of popular government—in which the majority's desires have a more direct and immediate impact on governing officials—has gained strength since the nation's beginning.* Originally, the House of Representatives was the only institution subject to direct vote of the people. This mechanism has been extended to other institutions and, through primary elections, even to the nomination of candidates for public office.

BEFORE THE CONSTITUTION: THE COLONIAL AND REVOLUTIONARY EXPERIENCES

Early Americans' admiration for limited government was based partly on their English heritage. Unlike other European nations of the eighteenth century, England did not have an absolute monarchy. British courts had developed a system of precedent known as "common law," which guaranteed trial by jury and due process of law as safeguards of life, liberty, and particularly property.

This tradition was evident in the American colonies. In each colony there was a right to trial by jury. There was also freedom of expression, although of a narrow kind. Religious freedom, for example, was not granted by all the colonies. There was also a degree of self-government in all the colonies. Each had an elected assembly, and although the assemblies were usually controlled by wealthier interests, they acted as representative bodies and grew increasingly powerful as the number of settlers increased.

"The Rights of Englishmen"

The Revolutionary War was partly a rebellion against England's failure to respect its own tradition of limited government in the colonies. Many of the colonial charters had conferred upon Americans "the rights of Englishmen," but Britain showed progressively less respect for this guarantee as time went on. The period after the French and Indian War (1755–1763) was a turning point in the relationship between the colonists and Britain. Until then the colonists had viewed themselves as loyal subjects of the Crown, and although occasional disputes had arisen, few voices argued for independence. In fact, colonists had fought alongside British soldiers to drive the French out of Canada and the Western territories.

Historical Background

At the end of the French and Indian War, however, Britain imposed burdensome taxes on the colonists. The war with France, which had also been waged in Europe, had created a severe financial crisis for the British government, which looked to the increasingly prosperous colonies for revenues. The colonies were not accustomed to paying taxes to the British. The practice was for Britain to raise its revenues from tariffs on the colonies' foreign trade while the colonists controlled and kept local taxes. But in 1765 the British Parliament levied a stamp tax on colonial newspapers and business documents. Because the colonists were not represented in the British Parliament that imposed the tax, the colonial pamphleteer James Otis declared that the Stamp Act violated the fundamental rights of the colonists as "British subjects and men." "No taxation without representation" became a rallying cry for the colonists.

This 1790s colored engraving by William Birch depicts a Philadelphia street scene. Philadelphia's role in the birth of the American nation is rivaled only by Boston's contribution.

Drafting the Declaration of Independence, a painting by J. L. Ferris. Benjamin Franklin, John Adams, and Thomas Jefferson (standing) drafted the historic document. Jefferson was the principal author; he inserted the inspirational words about liberty, equality, and self-government. Jealous of the attention that Jefferson later received, Adams declared that there wasn't anything in Jefferson's words that others hadn't already said.

Although Parliament backed down and repealed the Stamp Act, it then passed the Townshend Act, which imposed taxes on all paper, glass, lead, and tea. When the colonists protested, King George III sent additional British troops to America to enforce the new taxes. This action served only to further anger the colonists. Britain then tried to placate the Americans by repealing the Townshend duties except for a nominal tax on tea, which was retained in order to show the colonists that Britain was still in charge of their affairs. The colonists saw the tea tax as a petty insult, and in the "Boston Tea Party" of December 1773, a small band of patriots disguised as Native Americans boarded an English ship in Boston Harbor and dumped its cargo of tea overboard.

In 1774, the colonists met in Philadelphia at the First Continental Congress to decide what they would demand from Britain: They called for

Citizenship

Getting Involved, Making a Difference

Personal Commitment

Effective citizen action begins with a question: what goal do I care enough about to try to make it a reality?

The question is easy enough, but many people go through life without having asked and answered it. They are citizens in a constricted sense. They may vote. They may even donate money on occasion to a political cause. But they never get deeply enough involved in the life of the society to leave a lasting mark on it. The citizens who make a larger contribution to their community are those who commit themselves to action on a cause in which they believe. They are citizens in the fullest sense of the word.

These two types of citizenship were clearly evident when terrorists bombed the World Trade Center and the Pentagon on September 11, 2001. Some Americans rushed to help the victims. Many people donated blood. Others sent money and clothing to the victims' families. Thousands from around the country went to the site of the World Trade Center to offer their help in the rescue effort. Other Americans worked within their own communities to promote tolerance for those of Middle Eastern descent and of the Muslim faith. Still others helped local schools and organizations develop plans to prepare for and respond to future terrorist acts. Yet the war on terrorism for most Americans was something to be seen on television rather than something to be acted on directly, despite the great concern many of them felt about the issue.

So it goes, issue after issue. Most people sit on the sidelines, forgoing the opportunity to contribute substantially to public life. Because the United States has a federal system of government and a strong tradition of local government and free association, there are literally endless opportunities for people to get actively involved in politics and public affairs. Citizens interested in working on political campaigns can join local, congressional, statewide, and presidential campaigns. Volunteers interested in community affairs can choose among all sorts of local organizations, from churches to schools to community groups. The Internet offers countless national and international organizations in which to participate actively. For example, the international campaign to ban land mines, for which Jody Williams won the 1997 Nobel Peace Prize, began when she used the Internet from her home to organize the effort.

The difference that committed activists can make was never more in evidence than at the founding of the United States. Even though the Revolutionary War eventually enlisted a large number of participants, agitators such as Sam Adams in Boston and Patrick Henry in Virginia awakened other Americans to colonial injustices. Then, during the debate over ratification of the Constitution, the *Federalist* essays of Madison, Hamilton, and Jay helped sway opinion in favor of the proposed change in the nation's government.

Activists are the defining spirit of the community, whether that community consists of the people of the world, the citizens of a nation, the residents of a local community, or the students on a college campus. If you haven't been active to this point, what might you do now to get involved?

free assembly, an end to the British military occupation, their own councils for the imposition of taxes, and trial by local juries. (British authorities had resorted to shipping "troublemakers" back to London for trial.) King George III rejected their demands, and in 1775 British troops and colonial minutemen clashed at Lexington and Concord. Eight colonists died on the Lexington green in what became known as "the shot heard 'round the world." The American Revolution had begun.

The Declaration of Independence

Although grievances against Britain were the immediate cause of the American Revolution, ideas about the proper form of government were also on the colonists' minds.[2] The century-old theory of John Locke was particularly influential. Locke held that people have **inalienable rights** (or **natural rights**)—including those of life, liberty, and property—and can rebel against a ruler who tramples on these rights (see Chapter 1).

Thomas Jefferson declared that Locke "was one of the three greatest men that ever lived, without exception," and Jefferson paraphrased Locke's ideas in key passages of the Declaration of Independence:

> We hold these truths to be self-evident, that all men are created equal, that they are endowed by their Creator with certain unalienable rights, that among these are life, liberty and the pursuit of happiness.
>
> That to secure these rights, governments are instituted among men, deriving their just powers from the consent of the governed.

inalienable (natural) rights
Those rights that persons theoretically possessed in the state of nature, prior to the formation of governments. These rights, including those of life, liberty, and property, are considered inherent and, as such, are inalienable. Since government is established by people, government has the responsibility to preserve these rights.

This is a portion of Thomas Jefferson's handwritten draft of the Declaration of Independence, a formal expression of America's governing ideals.

> That whenever any form of government becomes destructive of these ends, it is the right of the people to alter or to abolish it, and to institute a new government.

The Declaration was a call to revolution rather than a framework for a new form of government, but the ideas it contained—liberty, equality, individual rights, self-government, lawful powers—became the basis, eleven years later, for the Constitution of the United States. (The Declaration of Independence and the Constitution are reprinted in their entirety in the appendixes of this book.)

The Articles of Confederation

The first government of the United States was based not on the Constitution but on the Articles of Confederation. The Articles, which were adopted during the Revolutionary War, created a very weak national government that was subordinate to the states. The colonies had always been governed separately, and their people considered themselves Virginians, New Yorkers, or Pennsylvanians as much as they thought of themselves as Americans. They naturally preferred a government that was constitutionally derived from the states. Moreover, they were leery of a powerful central government. The American Revolution was sparked by grievances against the arbitrary policies of King George III, and Americans were in no mood to replace him with a strong national authority of their own making.

Under the Articles of Confederation, each state retained its "sovereignty, freedom and independence." There was a national Congress, but its members were appointed and paid by their respective state governments. Each of the thirteen states had one vote in Congress, and the agreement of nine states was required to pass legislation. Moreover, any state could block constitutional change: the Articles of Confederation could be amended only by unanimous approval of the states.

Historical Background

The American union held together during the Revolutionary War out of necessity: the states had either to cooperate or to surrender to the British. But once the war ended, the states felt free to go their separate ways. Several states sent representatives abroad to negotiate their own separate trade agreements with foreign nations. New Hampshire, with its eighteen-mile coastline, even established its own navy. In a melancholy letter to Thomas Jefferson, George Washington wondered whether the United States deserved to be called a nation.

Congress was expected to provide for the nation's defense and establish the basis for a general economy, but the Articles of Confederation did not give it the powers necessary to achieve these goals. The Articles prohibited Congress from interfering in the states' commerce policies, and the states were soon engaged in ruinous trade wars. The Articles also denied to Congress the power to tax, and as a result it had no money with which to build a navy or hire an army.

Shays's Rebellion: A Nation Dissolving

By 1784, the nation was unraveling. Congress was so weak that its members often did not bother to attend its sessions.[3] Finally, in late 1786, a revolt in western

County courthouses in Massachusetts in 1786 were the scenes of brawls between angry farmers and citizens who supported the state's attempts to foreclose on farmers' property because of unpaid debts. The violence of Shays's Rebellion convinced many political leaders that anarchy was spreading and that a more powerful national government was required to stop it.

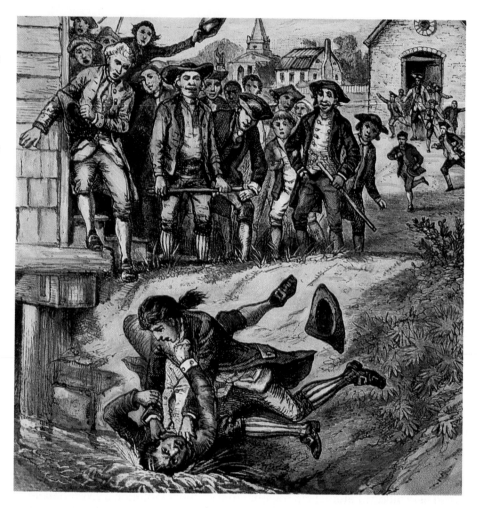

Massachusetts prompted leading Americans to conclude that the country's government had to be changed. A ragtag army of two thousand farmers armed with pitchforks marched on county courthouses to prevent foreclosures on their land and cattle. Many of the farmers were veterans of the Revolutionary War; their leader, Daniel Shays, had been a captain in the Revolutionary army. They had been given assurances during the Revolution that their land, which lay fallow because they were away at war, would not be confiscated for unpaid debts and taxes. They had also been told that they would get the back pay owed to them for their military service. (Congress had run out of money during the Revolution.) Instead, they received no back pay, and heavy new taxes were placed on their farms. Many farmers faced loss of their property and even jail because they could not pay their creditors.

Although many Americans, including Jefferson, sympathized with the farmers, Shays's Rebellion scared propertied interests, who called on the governor of Massachusetts to put down the revolt. He in turn asked Congress for help, but it had no army to send.[4] The governor finally raised enough money to hire a militia that put down the rebellion, but Shays's Rebellion made it clear that Congress and the army were weak and that mob action was increasing.

Fear that anarchy would overtake the country was widespread. At Virginia's urging, five states met at the Annapolis Convention in late 1786 to address the crisis. After inconclusive deliberations, they recommended that Congress authorize a constitutional convention of all the states to be held the following spring in Philadelphia. Congress authorized the convention but placed a restriction on it: the delegates were to meet for "the sole and express purpose of revising the Articles of Confederation."

NEGOTIATING TOWARD A CONSTITUTION

The delegates to the Philadelphia constitutional convention ignored the instructions of Congress. They drafted a plan for an entirely new form of government. Prominent delegates (among them George Washington, Benjamin Franklin, and James Madison) were determined from the outset to establish an American nation built on a strong central government.

The Great Compromise: A Two-Chamber Congress

Debate at the constitutional convention of 1787 began over a plan put forward by the Virginia delegation, which was dominated by strong nationalists. The **Virginia Plan** (also called the **large-state plan**) called for a two-chamber Congress that would have supreme authority in all areas "in which the separate states are incompetent," particularly defense and interstate trade. The Virginia Plan also provided that representation in both chambers would be based on size. Small states such as Delaware and Rhode Island would be allowed only one representative in the lower chamber, while large states such as Massachusetts and Virginia would have more than a dozen.

Not surprisingly, the Virginia Plan was roundly condemned by delegates from the smaller states. They rallied around a counterproposal made by New Jersey's William Paterson. The **New Jersey Plan** (also called the **small-state plan**) called for a stronger national government with the power to tax and to regulate commerce among the states; in most other respects, however, the Articles would remain in effect. Congress would have a single chamber in which each state, large or small, would have a single vote.

The debate over the New Jersey and Virginia Plans dragged on for weeks before the delegates reached what is now known as the **Great Compromise**. It provided for a bicameral (two-chamber) Congress: the House of Representatives would be apportioned among the states on the basis of population, and the Senate would be apportioned on the basis of an equal number of votes (two) for each state. The small states never would have agreed to join a union in which their vote was always weaker than that of large states,[5] a fact reflected in Article V of the Constitution: "No state, without its consent, shall be deprived of its equal suffrage in the Senate."

The North-South Compromise: The Issue of Slavery

The separate interests of the states were also the basis for a second major agreement: the **North-South Compromise** over economic issues. The South had a slave-based agricultural economy, and its delegates feared that the North,

Virginia (large-state) Plan A constitutional proposal for a strong Congress with two chambers, both of which would be based on numerical representation, thus granting more power to the larger states.

New Jersey (small-state) Plan A constitutional proposal for a strengthened Congress but one in which each state would have a single vote, thus granting a small state the same legislative power as a large state.

Great Compromise The agreement at the constitutional convention to create a two-chamber Congress with the House apportioned by population and the Senate apportioned equally by state.

North-South Compromise The agreement over economic and slavery issues that enabled northern and southern states to settle differences that threatened to defeat the effort to draft a new constitution.

which had a stronger manufacturing sector, would gain a numerical majority in Congress and then proceed to enact unfair tax policies. If Congress levied high import tariffs on finished goods from foreign nations in order to protect domestic manufacturers and placed heavy export tariffs on agricultural goods, the burden of financing the new government would fall mainly on the South. Its delegates also worried that northern representatives in Congress might tax or even bar the importation of slaves.

After extended debate, a compromise was reached. Congress was to be prohibited by the Constitution from taxing exports but could tax imports. In addition, Congress would be prohibited until 1808 from passing laws to end the slave trade. The South also gained a constitutional provision requiring each state to return runaway slaves to their state of origin.

The most controversial trade-off was the so-called "Three-Fifths Compromise." For purposes of apportionment of taxes and seats in the U.S. House of Representatives, each slave was to count as three-fifths of a person. Northern delegates had argued against the counting of slaves, since they were treated as property and held in bondage. Southern delegates wanted to count them as full persons for purposes of apportioning House seats (which would have the effect of increasing the number of southern representatives) and to count them as nonpersons for purposes of apportioning taxes (which would have the effect of decreasing the amount of federal taxes levied on the southern states). The delegates finally settled on a compromise that included both taxation and apportionment

Southern delegates at the constitutional convention sought assurances that Congress would not bar the importation and sale of slaves and that their slave-based agricultural economy would be protected. The photo shows a Civil War–era building in Atlanta that was a site of slave auctions.

but counted slaves as less than full persons. Although the southern states did not get all that they wanted, they got the better end of the bargain. If slaves had not been counted at all, the southern states would have had only slightly more than 35 percent of House seats. With the compromise, they held nearly 45 percent of the seats, giving them considerable power in matters of national legislation.

These compromises over the issue of slavery have led some observers to erroneously conclude that the Framers of the Constitution had no objections to the institution. In fact, most of the delegates were deeply troubled by slavery, recognizing the stark inconsistency between the practice of slavery and the Lockean ideals that all persons "are created equal" and are entitled to individual rights. "It is inconsistent with the principles of the Revolution," Maryland's Luther Martin stated, "and dishonorable to the American character to have such a feature in the constitution." George Mason, a Virginian and a slaveholder, said: "[Slaveholders] bring the judgment of heaven on a country."[6] Benjamin Franklin and Alexander Hamilton were among the delegates who were involved in antislavery organizations.

Yet the southern states' dependence on slavery was a reality that the delegates had to confront if there was to be a union of the states. The northern states had no economic use for forced labor and had few slaves, whereas the southern economies were based on slavery (see Figure 2–1). John Rutledge of South Carolina asked during the convention debate whether the North regarded southerners as "fools." Southern delegates declared that they would form their own union rather than join one that prohibited slavery or gave them little power in the Congress.

A Strategy for Ratification

The compromises over slavery and the structure of the Congress took up most of the four months that the convention was in session. Some of the other issues, such as the structure and powers of the federal judiciary, were the subject of surprisingly little debate.

There remained a final issue, however: would those Americans not attending the convention support the proposed Constitution? The delegates realized that ratification was not a sure thing. Congress had not authorized a wholesale restructuring of the federal government and had in fact created a barrier to any such plan. In authorizing the Philadelphia convention, Congress had stated that any proposed change in the Articles would have to be "agreed to in Congress" and then "confirmed by [all of] the states." The delegates recognized that if they followed this procedure, which required unanimity, the Constitution had no chance of ratification. Rhode Island had refused even to send a delegation to the convention. In a bold move, the delegates established their own ratification process. They instructed Congress to submit the document directly to the states, where it would become law after having been approved by at least nine states in special ratifying conventions of popularly elected delegates. It was a masterful strategy: there was little hope that all thirteen state legislatures would approve the Constitution, but nine states through conventions might be persuaded to ratify it. And indeed, North Carolina and Rhode Island were steadfastly opposed to the new union and did not ratify the Constitution until the eleven other states had ratified it and begun the process of establishing the new government.

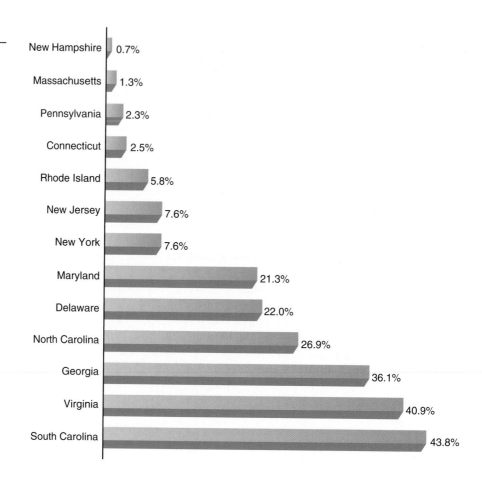

Figure 2–1

African Americans as a Percentage of State Population, 1790
At the writing of the Constitution, African Americans (most of whom were slaves) were concentrated in the southern states.
Source: U.S. Bureau of the Census.

The Ratification Debate

Anti-Federalists A term used to describe opponents of the Constitution during the debate over ratification.

The debate over ratification was a contentious one. The **Anti-Federalists** (as opponents of the Constitution were labeled) raised arguments that still echo in American politics. They claimed that the national government would be too powerful and would threaten the sovereignty of the separate states and the liberty of the people. Many Americans had an innate distrust of centralized power and worried that the people's liberty could be eclipsed as easily by a distant American government as it had been by the British king. The fact that the Constitution contained no bill of rights heightened this concern. Did its absence indicate that the central government would be free to define for itself what the people's rights would be?

The presidency was also a source of contention. No such office had existed under the Articles, and some worried that it would lead to the creation of an American monarchy. The fact that the president would be chosen by electors appointed by the states lessened but did not eliminate this concern.

Even the motives of the men who wrote the Constitution came under attack. They were men of wealth and education and had acted in response to debtors' riots. Would the Constitution become a tool by which the wealthy ruled over those with little or no money? And who would bear the burden of additional taxation? For Americans struggling with local and state tax payments, the creation of yet another tax agency was hardly an attractive proposal.

Most Anti-Federalists acknowledged a need to strengthen national commerce and defense. What they opposed was the creation of a powerful national government as the mechanism. They favored a revision of the Articles of Confederation, which in their opinion could accomplish these goals without the risk of establishing a government that could threaten their liberties, their livelihoods, and their local interests. (The Anti-Federalist argument is discussed further in Chapter 3.)

The **Federalists** (as the Constitution's supporters called themselves) responded with a persuasive case of their own. Their strongest arguments were set forth by James Madison and Alexander Hamilton, who along with John Jay wrote a series of essays during the New York ratification debate. The essays were published in a New York City newspaper under the pen name Publius and were titled "The Federalist." (The essays are collectively referred to as *The Federalist Papers* and are widely acknowledged as a brilliant political treatise.) Madison and Hamilton argued that the government of the Constitution would correct the defects of the Articles; it would have the power necessary to forge a secure and prosperous union. At the same time, because of restrictions on its powers, the new government would endanger neither the states nor personal liberty. In *Federalist* Nos. 47, 48, 49, 50, and 51, for example, Madison explained how the separation of national institutions was designed to both empower and restrict the federal government. (The Federalist argument is discussed further in Chapter 3.)

Whether the ratification debate changed many minds is unknown. Historical evidence suggests, however, that a majority of ordinary Americans opposed the Constitution's ratification. But their voice in the state ratifying conventions was smaller than that of wealthier interests, which in the main supported the change. The pro-ratification forces were also bolstered by the widespread assumption that George Washington would become the first president. He was far and away the most trusted and popular American leader. In the view of most historians, the fact that Washington had presided over the Philadelphia convention and the assumption that he would become the chief executive tipped the balance in favor of ratification.

Delaware was the first state to ratify the Constitution, and Connecticut, Georgia, and New Jersey followed, an indication that the Great Compromise had satisfied several of the small states. In the early summer of 1788, New Hampshire became the ninth state to ratify. The Constitution was law. But neither Virginia nor New York had ratified, and a stable union without these two major states was almost unthinkable. They were as large in area as many European countries and conceivably could survive as independent nations. They nearly did choose a separate course. In both states, the Constitution barely passed, and then only after the Federalists promised to support a bill of rights designed to protect individual freedoms from the power of the central government.

James Madison
(1751–1836)

James Madison is often called the "father of the Constitution" because he was instrumental in its writing and its ratification (through his *Federalist Papers* essays). He served as secretary of state during the Jefferson administration and in 1808 was elected the fourth U.S. president. He helped lead the nation to victory over the British in the War of 1812 and, after leaving the presidency in 1817, spoke out often against the growing movement toward states' rights that eventually led to the Civil War.

Federalists A term used to describe proponents of the Constitution during the debate over ratification.

www.mhhe.com/pattersontad7

TABLE 2–1	Major Goals of the Framers of the Constitution

1. To establish a government strong enough to meet the nation's needs—an objective sought through substantial grants of power to the federal government in areas such as defense and commerce (see Chapter 3).

2. To establish a government that would not threaten the existence of the separate states—an objective sought through federalism (see Chapter 3) and through a Congress connected to the states through elections.

3. To establish a government that would not threaten liberty—an objective sought through an elaborate system of checks and balances.

4. To establish a government based on popular consent—an objective sought through provisions for the direct and indirect election of public officials.

The Framers' Goals

constitution The fundamental law that defines how a government will legitimately operate.

A **constitution** is the fundamental law that defines how a government will legitimately operate: the method for choosing its leaders, the institutions through which these leaders will work, the procedures they must follow in making policy, and the powers they can lawfully exercise. The U.S. Constitution, which was written in Philadelphia in 1787, is exactly such a law. In theory, it is the highest law of the land: neither a popular majority nor a leader at the highest pinnacle of power stands above it. Its provisions define how power is to be acquired and how it can be used.

The Constitution reflected the Framers' vision of a proper government for the American people. Its provisions addressed four broad goals (see Table 2–1). One was the creation of a national government strong enough to meet the nation's needs, particularly in the areas of defense and commerce. Another goal was to preserve the states as governing entities. Accordingly, the Framers established a system of government (federalism) in which power is divided between the national government and the states. Federalism is discussed at length in Chapter 3, which also explains how the Constitution laid the foundation for a strong national government.

The Framers' other goals were to establish a national government that was restricted in its lawful uses of power (limited government) and that gave the people a voice in their governance (self-government). These two goals and how they were written into the Constitution are the focus of the rest of this chapter.

PROTECTING LIBERTY: LIMITED GOVERNMENT

A challenge facing the Framers of the Constitution was how to control the coercive force of government. Government's unique characteristic is that it alone can legally arrest, imprison, and even kill people who break its rules. Force is not the only basis of effective government, but government must be able to use force or lawless elements will take over society. The dilemma is that government itself can destroy civilized society by using its force to brutalize and intimidate its

Liberty, Equality, & Self-Government

What's Your Opinion?

Constitutionalism

Englishman James Bryce ranked America's written constitution as its greatest contribution to the practice of government. The Constitution offered the world a new model of government in which a written document defining the state's lawful powers was a higher authority than the actions of any political leader or institution.

The Framers' commitment to constitutionalism grew out of their recognition that although government must have coercive power in order to carry out the actions necessary to maintain a civil society, this same power can be used by unscrupulous leaders to strip others of their liberty.

Do you think these two considerations—the coercive power of government and the corruptibility of those in whom power is invested—lead almost inevitably to a belief in limited government and to the use of constitutional measures (such as checks and balances) as a means to control the uses of power? What historical examples, other than Watergate, can you think of that illustrate the significance of constitutional limitations on the exercise of power?

---

opponents. "It is a melancholy reflection," James Madison wrote to Thomas Jefferson shortly after the Constitution's ratification, "that liberty should be equally exposed to danger whether the government has too much or too little power."[7]

The men who wrote the Constitution sought to establish a government strong enough to enforce national interests, including defense and commerce among the states (see Chapter 3), but not so strong as to destroy liberty. Limited government was built into the Constitution through both grants and restrictions of political power.

Grants and Denials of Power

The Framers chose to limit the national government in part by confining its scope to constitutional **grants of power.** Congress's lawmaking powers are specifically listed in Article I, Section 8 of the Constitution. Seventeen in number, these listed powers include, for example, the powers to tax, to establish an army and navy, to declare war, to regulate commerce among the states, to create a national currency, and to borrow money. Authority *not* granted to the government by the Constitution is in theory denied to it. In a period when other governments had unrestricted powers, this limitation was remarkable.

The Framers also used **denials of power** as a means to limit government, prohibiting certain practices that European rulers had routinely used to intimidate political opponents. The French king, for example, could imprison a subject indefinitely without charge. The U.S. Constitution prohibits such action: individuals have the right to be brought before a court under a writ of habeas corpus for a judgment as to the legality of their confinement. The Constitution also forbids

grants of power The method of limiting the U.S. government by confining its scope of authority to those powers expressly granted in the Constitution.

denials of power A constitutional means of limiting government by listing those powers that government is expressly prohibited from using.

Congress and the states from passing ex post facto laws, under which citizens can be prosecuted for acts that were legal at the time they were committed.

As a further denial of power, the Framers made the Constitution difficult to amend, thereby making it hard for those in power to increase their lawful authority by changing the Constitution. An amendment could be proposed only by a two-thirds majority in both chambers of Congress or by a national constitutional convention called by two-thirds of the state legislatures. Such a proposal would then become law only if ratified by three-fourths of state legislatures or state conventions.

The Constitution grants Congress the power to decide whether state legislatures or state conventions will take part in the ratifying process. The Twenty-first Amendment is the only one for which Congress specified state conventions as the ratifying mechanism; in all other cases, state legislatures have done the ratifying. The Twenty-first Amendment repealed the Eighteenth Amendment, which had prohibited the manufacture, sale, and transportation of alcoholic beverages. Congress concluded that repeal was better addressed and more likely to occur in state conventions than in state legislatures. The national constitutional convention as a means of proposing amendments has never been used. All amendments have originated with Congress.

Using Power to Offset Power

Although the Framers believed that grants and denials of power could act as controls on government, they had no illusion that written words alone would restrain power. As a consequence, they sought to check power with power. The idea was to divide the authority of government so that no single institution could exercise great power without the agreement of other institutions.[8]

separation of powers The division of the powers of government among separate institutions or branches.

The idea that a **separation of powers** was necessary to the preservation of liberty had been proposed decades earlier by the French theorist Montesquieu. His argument was widely accepted in America, and when the states drafted new constitutions after the start of the Revolutionary War, they built their gov-

The Constitution was written in Philadelphia during the summer of 1787 in the East Room of the Old Pennsylvania State House, where the Declaration of Independence had been signed a decade earlier. George Washington presided over the Constitutional Convention, but in this role he was expected to remain neutral during the debate and thus he played a less active part in shaping the Constitution than did some other delegates.

ernments around the concept of a separation of powers. Pennsylvania was an exception, and its experience only seemed to prove the necessity of separated powers. Unrestrained by an independent judiciary or executive, Pennsylvania's all-powerful legislature systematically deprived minority groups of their basic rights and freedoms: Quakers were disenfranchised for their religious beliefs, conscientious objectors to the Revolutionary War were prosecuted, and the right of trial by jury was eliminated.

In *Federalist* No. 10, Madison asked why governments often act according to the interests of overbearing majorities rather than according to principles of justice. Why, he asked, has liberty suffered so mightily at the hands of majorities? He attributed the cause to "the mischiefs of faction." People, he argued, are divided into opposing religious, geographical, ethnic, economic, and other factions. These divisions are natural and desirable in that free people have a right to their personal opinions and interests. Yet factions can themselves be a source of oppressive government. If a faction gains full power, it will use government to advance itself at the expense of all others. (*Federalist* No. 10 is widely regarded as the finest political essay ever written by an American. It is reprinted at the back of this book.)

Out of this concern came the Framers' special contribution to the doctrine of the separation of powers. They did not believe that it would be enough, as Montesquieu had suggested, to divide the government's authority strictly along institutional lines, granting all legislative power to the legislature, all judicial power to the courts, and all executive power to the presidency. This total separation would make it too easy for a single faction to exploit a particular kind of political power. A faction that controlled the legislature, for example, could enact laws ruinous to other interests. A better system of divided government would be one in which political power could be applied forcibly only when institutions agreed on its use. This system would require separate but overlapping powers. Because no one faction could easily gain control over all institutions, factions would have to work together, a process that would require each to moderate its demands and thus would serve many interests rather than one or a few.[9]

Separated Institutions Sharing Power: Checks and Balances

The Framers' concept of divided powers has been described by political scientist Richard Neustadt as the principle of **separated institutions sharing power.**[10] The separate branches are interlocked in such a way that an elaborate system of **checks and balances** is created (see Figure 2–2). No institution can act decisively without the support or acquiescence of the other institutions. Legislative, executive, and judicial powers in the American system are divided in such a way that they overlap: each of the three branches of government checks the others' powers and balances those powers with powers of its own. As natural as this system now might seem to Americans, most democracies are of the parliamentary type, with executive and legislative power combined in a single institution rather than vested in separate ones. In a parliamentary system, the majority in the legislature selects the prime minister, who then serves as both the legislative leader and the chief executive (see "How the United States Compares.")

separated institutions sharing power The principle that, as a way to limit government, its powers should be divided among separate branches, each of which also shares in the power of the others as a means of checking and balancing them. The result is that no one branch can exercise power decisively without the support or acquiescence of the others.

checks and balances The elaborate system of divided spheres of authority provided by the U.S. Constitution as a means of controlling the power of government. The separation of powers among the branches of the national government, federalism, and the different methods of selecting national officers are all part of this system.

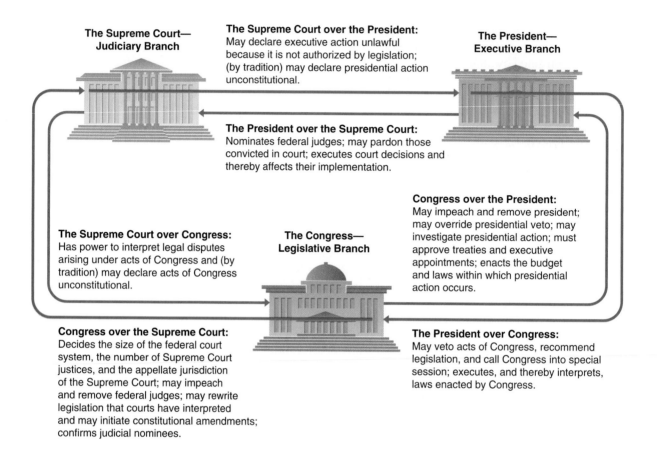

The Supreme Court—Judiciary Branch

The Supreme Court over the President: May declare executive action unlawful because it is not authorized by legislation; (by tradition) may declare presidential action unconstitutional.

The President—Executive Branch

The President over the Supreme Court: Nominates federal judges; may pardon those convicted in court; executes court decisions and thereby affects their implementation.

Congress over the President: May impeach and remove president; may override presidential veto; may investigate presidential action; must approve treaties and executive appointments; enacts the budget and laws within which presidential action occurs.

The Supreme Court over Congress: Has power to interpret legal disputes arising under acts of Congress and (by tradition) may declare acts of Congress unconstitutional.

The Congress—Legislative Branch

Congress over the Supreme Court: Decides the size of the federal court system, the number of Supreme Court justices, and the appellate jurisdiction of the Supreme Court; may impeach and remove federal judges; may rewrite legislation that courts have interpreted and may initiate constitutional amendments; confirms judicial nominees.

The President over Congress: May veto acts of Congress, recommend legislation, and call Congress into special session; executes, and thereby interprets, laws enacted by Congress.

Figure 2-2

The System of Checks and Balances

This elaborate system of divided spheres of authority was provided by the U.S. Constitution as a means of controlling the power of government. The separation of powers among the branches of the national government, federalism, and the different methods of selecting national officers are all part of this system.

Shared Legislative Powers

Under the Constitution, Congress has legislative authority, but that power is partly shared with the other branches and thus checked by them. The president can veto acts of Congress, recommend legislation, and call special sessions of Congress. The president also has the power to execute—and thereby interpret—the laws made by Congress.

The Supreme Court has the power to interpret acts of Congress that are disputed in legal cases. The Court also has the power of judicial review: it can declare laws of Congress void when it finds that they are not in accord with the Constitution.

Within Congress, there is a further check on legislative power: for legislation to be passed, a majority in each house of Congress is required. Thus, the Senate and the House of Representatives can block each other from acting.

HOW THE UNITED STATES COMPARES

Checks and Balances

All democracies place constitutional limits on the power of government. The concept of rule by law, for example, is characteristic of democratic governments but not of authoritarian regimes. Democracies differ, however, in the extent to which political power is restrained through constitutional mechanisms. The United States is an extreme case in that its government rests on an elaborate system of constitutional checks and balances. The system employs a separation of powers among the executive, legislative, and judicial branches. It also includes judicial review, the power of the courts to invalidate actions of the legislative or executive branch. These constitutional restrictions on power are not part of the governing structure of all democracies.

Most democracies have parliamentary systems, which invest both executive and legislative leadership in the office of prime minister. Britain is an example of this type of system. Parliament under the leadership of the prime minister is the supreme authority

in Britain. Its laws are not subject to override by Britain's high court, which has no power to review the constitutionality of parliamentary acts.

COUNTRY	SEPARATION OF EXECUTIVE & LEGISLATIVE POWERS?	JUDICIAL REVIEW?
Belgium	No	Yes
Canada	No	Yes
France	Yes	No
Germany	No	Yes
Great Britain	No	No
Italy	No	Yes
Japan	No	Yes
Mexico	Yes	Yes
United States	Yes	Yes

Shared Executive Powers

Executive power is vested in the president but is constrained by legislative and judicial checks. The president's power to make treaties and appoint high-ranking officials, for example, is subject to Senate approval. Congress also has the power to impeach and remove the president from office. In practical terms, Congress's greatest checks on executive action are its lawmaking and appropriations powers. The executive branch cannot act without laws that authorize its activities or without the money that pays for these programs.

The judiciary's major check on the presidency is its power to declare an action unlawful because it is not authorized by the legislation that the executive claims to be implementing.

Shared Judicial Powers

Judicial power rests with the Supreme Court and with lower federal courts, which are subject to checks by the other branches of the federal government. Congress is empowered to establish the size of the federal court system, to restrict the Supreme Court's appellate jurisdiction in some circumstances, and to impeach and remove federal judges from office. More important, Congress can rewrite legislation that the courts have misinterpreted and can initiate amendments when it disagrees with the courts' rulings on constitutional issues.

The president has the power to appoint federal judges with the consent of the Senate and to pardon persons convicted in the courts. The president is also responsible for executing court decisions, a function that provides opportunities to influence the way rulings are implemented.

The Bill of Rights

Although the delegates to the Philadelphia convention discussed the possibility of placing a list of individual rights (such as freedom of speech and the right to a fair trial) in the Constitution, they ultimately decided that such a list was unnecessary because of the doctrine of expressed powers: government could not lawfully engage in actions, such as the suppression of speech, that were not authorized by the Constitution. Moreover, the delegates concluded that a bill of rights was undesirable because government might feel free to disregard any right that was inadvertently left off the list or that emerged at some future time. These considerations did not allay the fears of leading Americans who believed that no possible safeguard of liberty should be omitted. "A bill of rights," Jefferson argued, "is what the people are entitled to against every government on earth, general or particular, and what no just government should refuse or rest on inference." Jefferson had included a bill of rights in the constitution he wrote for Virginia at the outbreak of the Revolutionary War, and all but four states had followed Virginia's example.

Bill of Rights The first ten amendments to the Constitution. They include such rights as freedom of speech.

Opposition to the absence of a bill of rights led to its addition to the Constitution. Madison himself introduced a series of amendments during the First Congress, ten of which were soon ratified by the states. These amendments, traditionally called the **Bill of Rights,** include such rights as freedom of speech and religion and due process protections (such as jury trial and legal counsel) for persons accused of crimes. (These rights, termed *civil liberties,* are discussed at length in Chapter 4.)

The Bill of Rights is a precise expression of the concept of limited government. In consenting to be governed, the people agree to accept the authority of government in certain areas but not in others; the people's constitutional rights cannot lawfully be denied by governing officials.

Judicial Review

The writers of the Constitution both empowered and limited government. But who was to decide whether officials were operating within the limits of their constitutionally authorized powers? The Framers did not specifically entrust this power to a particular branch of government, although they did grant the Supreme Court the authority to decide on "all cases arising under this Constitution." Moreover, at the ratifying conventions of at least eight of the thirteen states, it was claimed that the judiciary would have the power to nullify actions that violated the Constitution.[11]

Nevertheless, because the Constitution did not explicitly grant the judiciary this authority, the principle had to be established in practice. The opportunity arose with an incident that occurred after the election of 1800, in which John Adams lost his bid for a second presidential term after a bitter campaign against

Historical Background

The Bill of Rights: Why It Is Important to Your Liberty

The Bill of Rights was added to the Constitution despite the Framers' belief that it was unnecessary. In their view, the Constitution denied to the federal government any power not granted to it. From this perspective, there was no need, for example, for a guarantee of religious freedom because government was not authorized to deny people the right to worship as they pleased. The Framers feared, moreover, that any listing of rights would become a means of denying people rights that were not listed.

Other Americans in 1787 were not persuaded by this argument and said they would support ratification only if a bill of rights was added. To gain their backing, proponents of ratification promised that a bill of rights would be acted on in the first session of Congress. The first ten amendments to the Constitution—commonly called the Bill of Rights—were the result.

Can you think of any additional rights that you might have today if the Framers' position had prevailed? The Supreme Court has held, for example, that Americans are entitled to an "adequate" public school education but not an "equal" one because the Constitution does not list education as a basic individual right. If there were no Bill of Rights, do you think the courts would have concluded that all children have a right to an "equal" education?

Most constitutional scholars believe that, on balance, the Bill of Rights has enhanced personal liberty. It had the effect of transforming abstract rights (for example, "the right to life, liberty and the pursuit of happiness") into concrete legal rights, thus giving people a basis for judicial action should their legal rights be abridged or denied. If you speak your mind publicly or are charged with a criminal offense, for example, you have a specific constitutional provision under which to claim your right. The Sixth Amendment, for example, gives you a right to counsel if you are accused of a crime. Of course, authorities sometimes ignore restrictions in the Bill of Rights and often get away with it. Nevertheless, the fact that the Bill of Rights contains specific guarantees increases the likelihood that authorities will respect them. By refusing to allow a suspect to talk with an attorney, for example, authorities run the risk of having a judge dismiss the case because of a constitutional violation.

The Bill of Rights also protects you by narrowing legislative options. In the aftermath of the September 11, 2001, attacks on the World Trade Center and Pentagon, for example, Congress debated various means of combating terrorism. Some proposals (for example, unrestricted surveillance of people's e-mail messages) were rejected in part because of a recognition that they would likely be struck down by the courts as unconstitutional.

Jefferson. Between November 1800, when Jefferson was elected, and March 1801, when he was inaugurated, the Federalist-controlled Congress created fifty-nine additional lower-court judgeships, enabling Adams to appoint loyal Federalists to those positions before he left office. However, Adams's term expired before the secretary of state could deliver the judicial commissions to all the appointees. Without this formal authorization, an appointee could not take office. Knowing this, Jefferson told his secretary of state, James Madison, not to deliver the commissions. William Marbury was one of those who did not receive his commission, and he asked the Supreme Court to issue a writ of mandamus (a court order directing an official to perform a specific act) that would compel Madison to deliver it.

Marbury v. Madison (1803) became the foundation for judicial review by the federal courts. Chief Justice John Marshall wrote the *Marbury* opinion, which declared that Marbury had a legal right to his commission. The opinion also said,

Limits on Government in the U.S. Constitution

Grants of power: Powers granted to the national government by the Constitution; powers not granted it are denied it unless they are necessary and proper to the carrying out of granted powers.

Separated institutions sharing power: The division of the national government's power among three branches, each of which is to act as a check on the powers of the other two.

Federalism: The division of political authority between the national government and the states, enabling the people to appeal to one authority if their rights and interests are not respected by the other authority.

Denials of power: Powers expressly denied to the national and state governments by the Constitution.

Bill of Rights: The first ten amendments to the Constitution, which specify rights of citizens that the national government must respect.

Judicial review: The power of the courts to declare governmental action null and void when it is found to violate the Constitution.

Elections: The power of the voters to remove officials from office.

---

however, that the Supreme Court could not issue him a writ of mandamus because it lacked the constitutional authority to do so. Congress had passed ordinary legislation in 1789 that gave the Court this power, but Marshall noted that the Constitution prohibits Congress from expanding the Supreme Court's authority except through a constitutional amendment. That being the case, Marshall argued, the legislation that provided the authorization was constitutionally invalid.[12] In striking down this act of Congress on constitutional grounds, the Court asserted its power of **judicial review**—that is, the power of the judiciary to decide whether a government official or institution has acted within the limits of the Constitution and, if not, to declare its action null and void.

Marshall's decision was ingenious because it asserted the power of judicial review without creating the possibility of its rejection by either the executive or the legislative branch. In declaring that Marbury had a right to his commission, the Court in effect said that President Jefferson had failed in his constitutional duty to execute the laws faithfully. But because it did not order Jefferson to deliver the commission, he had no opportunity to refuse to comply with the Court's judgment. At the same time, the Court reprimanded Congress for passing legislation that exceeded its constitutional authority. Congress also had no way to retaliate. It could not force the Court to accept the power to issue writs of mandamus if the Court itself refused to do so.

judicial review The power of courts to decide whether a governmental institution has acted within its constitutional powers and, if not, to declare its action null and void.

 ## PROVIDING FOR SELF-GOVERNMENT

"We the People" is the opening phrase of the Constitution. It expresses the idea that in the United States the people will have the power to govern themselves. In a sense, there is no contradiction between this idea and the Constitution's provisions for limited government, because individual *liberty* is part of the process of *self-government*. If people cannot express themselves freely, they cannot be self-governing. In another sense, however, the contradiction is clear: restrictions on the power of the majority are a denial of its right to govern society as it chooses.

The Framers believed that the people deserved and required a voice in their government, but they also feared popular government. They worried that the people would become inflamed by a passionate issue or fiery demagogue and act without due regard for the interests of the minority. To the Framers, the great risk of popular government was **tyranny of the majority:** the people acting as an irrational mob that tramples on the rights of others. Their fear was not without foundation. The history of democracies was filled with examples of majority tyranny, and there were even examples from the nation's brief history. In 1786, for instance, debtors had gained control of Rhode Island's legislature and made paper money a legal means of paying debts, even though existing contracts called for payment in gold. Creditors were then hunted down and held captive in public places so that debtors could come and pay them in full with worthless paper money. A Boston newspaper wrote that Rhode Island should be renamed Rogue Island.

John Marshall

(1755–1835)

John Marshall forcefully expressed his nationalist views in important Supreme Court decisions during his thirty-four years as chief justice. Though a cousin of Thomas Jefferson, they were political opponents. Marshall was an ardent nationalist whereas Jefferson held that national power should not unduly intrude on the states. Marshall served for a time as John Adams's secretary of state before his appointment by Adams to the post of chief justice.

tyranny of the majority The potential of a majority to monopolize power for its own gain to the detriment of minority rights and interests.

Democracy versus Republic

No form of self-government could eliminate completely the threat to liberty of majority tyranny, but the Framers believed that the danger would be greatly diminished by properly structured institutions.[13] Madison summarized the Framers' intent when he said in *Federalist* No. 10 that the Constitution was "a republican remedy" for the excesses historically associated with "democratic" rule. Today the terms **democracy, republic,** and **representative democracy** are often used interchangeably to refer to a system of government in which ultimate political power rests with the majority through its capacity to choose representatives in free and open elections. To the writers of the Constitution, however, *democracy* and *republic* had different meanings. When the Framers complained about the risks of democracy, they were referring to a government subject to immediate popular influence, either because the public participated directly in policy decisions (pure or direct democracy, as in Ancient Greece or New England town meetings) or because lawmakers acted out of fear of the public (mobocracy). In their use of the term *republic,* the Framers were referring to *representative democracy* in which elected officials meet in representative institutions.[14]

The Framers' concept of a proper system of representation was similar to an idea put forth by the English theorist Edmund Burke (1729–1797). In his *Letter to the Sheriffs of Bristol,* Burke argued that representatives should act as public **trustees:** they are obliged to promote the interest of those who elected them, but the nature of this interest is for the representatives, not the voters, to decide. Burke was concerned about the ease with which society could degenerate into selfishness, and he thought it imperative for representatives to not surrender their judgment to popular whim.

democracy A form of government in which the people rule, either directly or through elected representatives.

republic Historically, the form of government in which representative officials met to decide on policy issues. These representatives were expected to serve the public interest but were not subject to the people's immediate control. Today, the term *republic* is used interchangeably with *democracy.*

representative democracy A system in which the people participate in the decision-making process of government not directly but indirectly, through the election of officials to represent their interests.

trustees Elected representatives whose obligation is to act in accordance with their own consciences as to what policies are in the best interests of the public.

Rhode Island was nicknamed "Rogue Island" for its disregard of property rights. Shown here is the Rhode Island three-dollar bank note, which came to be worth no more than the paper on which it was written and yet was used to pay off gold debts.

Electoral College An unofficial term that refers to the electors who cast the states' electoral votes.

electoral votes The method of voting that is used to choose the U.S. president. Each state has the same number of electoral votes as it has members in Congress (House and Senate combined). By tradition, electoral voting is tied to a state's popular voting. The candidate with the most popular votes in a state (or, in a few states, the most votes in a congressional district) receives its electoral votes.

Limited Popular Rule

The Constitution provided that all power would be exercised through representative institutions. There was no provision for any form of direct popular participation in the making of policy decisions. In view of the fact that the United States was much too large to be governed directly by the people in popular assemblies, a representative system was necessary. Moreover, the separation of powers meant that the majority's will, again by necessity, would be filtered through an institutional structure. The Framers went beyond what was necessary, however, and placed officials at a considerable distance from the people they represented (see Table 2–2).

The House of Representatives was the only institution that would be based on direct popular election—its members would be elected for two-year terms of office by a vote of the people. Frequent and direct election of House members was intended to make government sensitive to the concerns of popular majorities.

U.S. senators would be appointed by the legislatures of the states they represented. Because state legislators were popularly elected, the people would be choosing their senators indirectly. Every two years, a third of the senators would be appointed to six-year terms. The Senate was expected to check and balance the House, which, by virtue of the more frequent and direct election of its members, presumably would be more responsive to popular opinion.

Presidential selection was an issue of considerable debate at the Philadelphia convention. Direct election of the president was twice proposed and twice rejected because it linked executive power directly to popular majorities. The Framers finally chose to have the president selected by the votes of electors (the so-called **Electoral College**). Each state would have as many **electoral votes** as it had members in Congress and could select its electors by any method it chose. The president would serve four years and be eligible for reelection.

TABLE 2–2	**Methods of Choosing National Leaders** Fearing the concentration of political power, the Framers devised alternative methods of selection and terms of service for national officials.	
OFFICE	**METHOD OF SELECTION**	**TERM OF SERVICE**
President	Electoral College	4 years
U.S. senator	State legislature	6 years (one-third of senators' terms expire every 2 years)
U.S. representative	Popular election	2 years
Federal judge	Nominated by president, approved by Senate	Indefinite (subject to "good behavior")

Pictured here is the Old Senate Chamber, where the U.S. Senate met until 1859, when a new and larger chamber was constructed. The Old Senate Chamber was the scene of heated debates over slavery. Daniel Webster, Henry Clay, and John C. Calhoun gained national reputations here. After the Senate vacated the chamber, it was occupied by the U.S. Supreme Court until 1935, when the Court's own building across the street from the Capitol was completed. Not until 1914 were U.S. senators chosen by direct vote of the people.

The Framers decided that federal judges and justices would be appointed rather than elected. They would be nominated by the president and confirmed through approval by the Senate. Once confirmed, they would "hold their offices during good behavior." In effect, they would be allowed to hold office for life unless they committed a crime. Rather than being a representative institution, the judiciary was a "guardian" institution that would uphold the rule of law and serve as a check on the elected branches of government.[15]

These differing methods of selecting national officeholders would not prevent a determined majority from achieving unbridled power, but control could not be attained easily or quickly. Unlike the House of Representatives, institutions such as the Senate, presidency, and judiciary would not yield to an impassioned majority in a single election. The delay would reduce the probability that government would degenerate into mob rule driven by momentary whims.

Altering the Constitution: More Power to the People

The Constitution's provisions for limited government have stood the test of time. In its structure and formal powers, the national government today has nearly the same features as the government established in 1789. This is not true, however, of the provisions for self-government: several of the original provisions have been amended. In no other constitutional area have Americans shown a greater willingness to devise new arrangements.

A desire for change was evident nearly as soon as the Constitution was unveiled. The Framers' conception of self-government was at odds with what the average American in 1787 had come to expect. Every state but South Carolina held annual legislative elections, and several states also chose their governors through annual election. And it was not long after ratification of the Constitution that Americans sought a more substantial voice in their own governing.

Jeffersonian Democracy: A Revolution of the Spirit

Historical Background

Thomas Jefferson, who otherwise admired the Constitution, was among the prominent Americans who questioned its provisions for self-government—and it was Jefferson who may have spared the nation a bloody conflict over the issue of popular sovereignty. Under John Adams, the second president, the national government increasingly favored the nation's wealthy interests. Adams publicly suggested that the Constitution was designed for a governing elite, while Alexander Hamilton urged him to use force if necessary to suppress popular dissent.[16] Jefferson asked whether Adams, with the aid of a strong army, planned soon to deprive ordinary Americans of their liberty. Jefferson challenged Adams in the next presidential election and, upon defeating him, hailed his victory as the "Revolution of 1800."

Although Jefferson was a champion of the common people, he had no clear vision of how a popular government might work in practice. He believed that congressional majorities were the proper expression of popular majorities and accordingly was reluctant to use his presidency as the instrument of the people.[17] Jefferson also had no illusions about a largely illiterate population's readiness for playing a significant governing role and feared the ruinous consequences of inciting the masses to contest the moneyed class. But Jefferson did found the nation's first political party (the forerunner of today's Democratic party), which served to link like-minded leaders and thus act as a bridge across divided institutions of power. By and large, however, Jeffersonian democracy was a revolution of the spirit. Jefferson taught Americans to look upon the national government as belonging to all, not just to the privileged few.[18]

How the National Political System Was Made More Responsive to Popular Majorities

Earlier Situation	Subsequent Development
Separation of powers, as a means of dividing authority and blunting passionate majorities	Political parties, as a means of uniting authorities and linking them with popular majorities
Indirect election of all national officials except House members, as a means of buffering officials from popular influence	Direct election of U.S. senators and popular voting for president (linked to electoral votes), as means of increasing popular control of officials
Nomination of candidates for public office through political party organizations	Primary elections, as a means of selecting party nominees

Jacksonian Democracy: Linking the People and the Presidency

Not until Andrew Jackson was elected in 1828 did the country have a powerful president who was willing and able to involve the public more fully in government. Jackson carried out the constitutional revolution that Jeffersonian democracy had foreshadowed.

Jackson recognized that the president was the only official who could legitimately claim to represent the people as a whole. Unlike the president, members of Congress were elected from separate states and districts rather than from the entire country. Yet the president's claim to popular leadership was diminished by the existence of the Electoral College. Jackson persuaded the states to choose their presidential electors on the basis of a popular vote. Jackson's reform, which remains in effect today, basically places the selection of a president in the voters' hands. The winner of the popular vote in a state is awarded its electoral votes; hence, the candidate who wins most of the popular votes in the states is also most likely to receive a majority of the electoral votes. Since Jackson's time, only three candidates—Rutherford B. Hayes in 1876, Benjamin Harrison in 1888, and George W. Bush in 2000—have won the presidency after losing the popular vote. (The Electoral College is discussed further in Chapter 12.)

The Progressives: Senate and Primary Elections

The Progressive era of the early 1900s brought another wave of democratic reforms. The Progressives rejected the Burkean idea of representatives as trustees, instead embracing the idea of representatives as **delegates**—officeholders who are obligated to respond directly to the expressed opinions of the people they represent.

delegates Elected representatives whose obligation is to act in accordance with the expressed wishes of the people they represent.

The Progressives succeeded primarily in changing the way some state and local governments operate. Progressive reforms at these levels included the initiative and the referendum, which enable citizens to vote directly on legislative issues (see "States in the Nation"). Another Progressive reform was the recall election, which enables citizens through petition to require an officeholder to submit to reelection before the regular expiration of his or her term. (In 2003 a recall election in California resulted in the election of actor Arnold Schwarzenegger as the state's new governor.)

The Progressives also instigated two changes in federal elections. One was the direct election of U.S. senators, who before the Seventeenth Amendment was ratified in 1913 had been chosen by state legislatures and were widely perceived as agents of big business (the Senate was nicknamed the "Millionaires' Club"). Senators who stood to lose their seats in a direct popular vote had blocked earlier attempts to change the Constitution. Eventually, however, the Senate was persuaded to support an amendment by pressure from the Progressives and by revelations that corporate bribes had influenced the selection of several senators. The second change was the **primary election,** which gives rank-and-file voters the opportunity to select party nominees. In the early 1900s, nearly all states adopted the primary election as a means of choosing nominees for at least some federal and state offices. Before this change, nominees had been chosen by party leaders.

primary election A form of election in which voters choose a party's nominees for public office. In most states, eligibility to vote in a primary election is limited to voters who are registered members of the party.

STATES IN THE NATION

Direct Democracy: The Initiative and Referendum

In some states, citizens can exercise their power through the initiative and the referendum. The map identifies states that have the least restrictive forms of the initiative or referendum—that is, states where there is no substantial limit (except for judicial review) on what citizens can directly decide through their votes.

Q: Why are southern and northeastern states less likely to have the initiative and referendum than states in other areas?

A: The initiative and referendum were introduced in the early 1900s by the Progressives, who sought to weaken the power of political bosses. In the Northeast, party machines had enough strength in state legislatures to block their enactment. In the South, these devices were blocked by the white establishment, which feared that blacks and poor whites would make use of them.

Source: Compiled by author from multiple sources.

Should Congress Be Subject to Term Limits?

The public's control of its representatives was a topic of debate at the Philadelphia convention and has remained so. A current issue is "safe incumbency." Congressional incumbents have so many advantages over their election challengers that their reelection is often a sure thing. More than 95 percent of incumbents win reelection in congressional races. This situation has led some Americans to support term limits, which would restrict the number of terms that a member of Congress could serve. Opponents of term limits contend that the ballot is the proper method for deciding whether an official should be removed from office.

Debating the Issues

Yes: Term limitation will accomplish a number of positive things, but one stands out: it will improve the quality of leadership of our congressional public servants by a quantum amount, by replacing careerists whose primary motives are reelection, with citizen legislators whose motives are to serve the country. Only with citizen legislators can the Congress address all our problems from an honest perspective. The makeup of the Congress must be changed. We can no longer afford a Congress containing too many career politicians who put themselves and their careers first and the country last. It is time to let them know we put them there to serve the citizens of the country, and not themselves. . . . American citizens know this. Polls show that Americans want term limitation by margins as high as three-to-one, even four-to-one. This is an issue that separates American citizens, who want to recapture their government from a careerist-dominated Congress. . . . There is no other way to restore government to the people. There is no substitute for term limits. There are many second steps, depending upon where you sit, but there is only one first step toward turning the country around. It is congressional term limitation.

—Citizens for Term Limits Organization

No: [T]he voters themselves already have the power to impose term limits whenever they please, since Congressmen must face the voters every two years and Senators every six years. Unlike the proponents of term limits, I continue to have faith in the fundamental good judgment of the American voters. Denying voters the right to elect the person they believe best represents their interests would turn the very principle of democracy on its head. It is for these reasons that the founding fathers considered and unanimously rejected term limits. . . . One of the best safeguards we have against special interest abuse [is] Members who have served sufficiently long to fully understand the ramifications and implications of the various legislative issues which come before us. . . . [I]f the voters understood that the effect of term limits would be a massive transfer of power from elected Congressmen to the permanent bureaucracy of Congressional and Executive Branch staff as well as to corporate and foreign lobbyists, they would not be quite so enamored of the idea. Given a choice between an elected official beholden to the voters and an unelected bureaucrat, I think the voters would prefer to place their trust in the elected official.

—Congressman John Conyers, Jr. (D-Mich.)

The Progressive era spawned attacks on the Framers. A prominent criticism was laid out in historian Charles S. Beard's *An Economic Interpretation of the Constitution*.[19] Arguing that the Constitution grew out of wealthy Americans' fears of the debtor rebellions, and noting that many of the Framers were themselves wealthy men, Beard claimed that the Constitution's elaborate systems of power and representation were devices for keeping power in the hands of the rich. Beard's thesis was challenged by other historians, and he later acknowledged that he had not taken the Framers' full array of motives into account. Their conception of separation of powers, for example, was a time-honored governing principle that had previously been incorporated in state constitutions. Although the Framers did not have great trust in popular rule, to conclude they were foes of democracy would be a mistake. They were intent on balancing the demands of limited government with those of self-government and, in striking a balance, leaned toward the former, believing that the evil of unrestrained power was the greater danger to a civil society.

CONSTITUTIONAL DEMOCRACY TODAY

constitutional democracy A government that is democratic in its provisions for majority influence through elections, and constitutional in its provisions for minority rights and rule by law.

The type of government created in the United States in 1787 is today called a **constitutional democracy.** It is *democratic* in its provisions for majority influence through elections and *constitutional* in its requirement that power gained through elections be exercised in accordance with law and with due respect for individual rights.

By some standards, the American system of today is a model of *self-government*.[20] The United States schedules the election of its larger legislative chamber (the House of Representatives) and its chief executive more frequently than any other democracy. In addition, it is the only major democracy that relies extensively on primary elections rather than party organizations for the selection of party nominees. The principle of popular election to office, which the writers of the Constitution regarded as a prerequisite of popular sovereignty but a method to be used sparingly, has been extended further in the United States than anywhere else.

By other standards, however, the U.S. system is less democratic than many others. Popular majorities must work against the barriers to influence devised by the Framers—the elaborate system of divided powers, staggered terms of office, and separate constituencies. In fact, the link between an electoral majority and a governing majority is far less direct in the American system than in nearly all other democratic systems. In the European parliamentary democracies, for example, legislative and executive power are not separated, are not subject to close check by the judiciary, and are acquired through the winning of a legislative majority in national elections. The Framers' vision was a different one, dominated by a concern with *liberty* and therefore with controls on political power. It was a response to the experiences they brought with them to Philadelphia in the summer of 1787.

Summary Self-Test
www.mhhe.com/pattersontad7

The Constitution of the United States is a reflection of the colonial and revolutionary experiences of the early Americans. Freedom from abusive government was a reason for the colonies' revolt against British rule, but the English tradition also provided ideas about government, power, and freedom that were expressed in the Constitution and, earlier, in the Declaration of Independence.

The Constitution was designed in part to provide for a limited government in which political power would be confined to proper uses. The Framers wanted to ensure that the government they were creating would not itself be a threat to freedom. To this end, they confined the national government to expressly granted powers and also denied it certain specific powers. Other prohibitions on government were later added to the Constitution in the form of stated guarantees of individual liberties in the Bill of Rights. The most significant constitutional provision for limited government, however, was a separation of powers among the three branches. The powers given to each branch enable it to act as a check on the exercise of power by the other two, an arrangement that during the nation's history has in fact served as a barrier to abuses of power.

The Constitution, however, made no mention of how the powers and limits of government were to be judged in practice. In its historic ruling in *Marbury v. Madison*, the Supreme Court assumed the authority to review the constitutionality of legislative and executive actions and to declare them unconstitutional and thus invalid.

STUDY CORNER

Key Terms

Anti-Federalists *(p. 48)*
Bill of Rights *(p. 56)*
checks and balances *(p. 53)*
constitution *(p. 50)*
constitutional democracy *(p. 65)*
delegates *(p. 63)*
democracy *(p. 59)*
denials of power *(p. 51)*
Electoral College *(p. 60)*
electoral votes *(p. 60)*

Federalists *(p. 49)*
grants of power *(p. 51)*
Great Compromise *(p. 45)*
inalienable (natural) rights *(p. 42)*
judicial review *(p. 58)*
limited government *(p. 38)*
New Jersey (small-state) Plan *(p. 45)*
North-South Compromise *(p. 45)*
primary election *(p. 63)*
representative democracy *(p. 59)*

republic *(p. 59)*
self-government *(p. 38)*
separated institutions sharing
   power *(p. 53)*
separation of powers *(p. 52)*
trustees *(p. 59)*
tyranny of the majority *(p. 59)*
Virginia (large-state) Plan *(p. 45)*

Self-Test

1. The principle of checks and balances in the U.S. system of government:
   a. requires the federal budget to be a balanced budget.
   b. provides that checks cashed at U.S. banks will be honored as legal tender.
   c. was a principle invented by the Progressives.
   d. allows the majority's will to work through representative institutions but places checks on the power of those institutions.

2. The U.S. Constitution provides for limited government mainly:
   a. through direct election of representatives.
   b. through indirect systems of popular election of representatives.
   c. by defining lawful powers and by dividing those powers among competing institutions.
   d. by making state law superior to national law when the two conflict.

3. The U.S. Constitution provides for self-government mainly:
   a. through direct and indirect systems of popular election of representatives.
   b. by defining the lawful powers of government.
   c. by dividing governing powers among competing institutions.
   d. by giving the majority absolute power to govern as it pleases.

4. Shays's Rebellion called attention to:
   a. the lack of ability of Congress under the Articles of Confederation to put down popular rebellion.
   b. Americans' anger with Britain over "taxation without representation."
   c. inability of the states under the Articles to bring the American Revolution to a successful conclusion.
   d. the conditions that were leading to mutiny on U.S. naval vessels.

5. The addition of the Bill of Rights to the U.S. Constitution meant that:
   a. a list of individual rights would be protected by law.
   b. the Anti-Federalists no longer had any reason to oppose the adoption of the Constitution.
   c. the national government could infringe on the rights of the states.
   d. the state governments could infringe on the rights of the national government.

6. Of the issues taken up during the Constitutional Convention, which one consumed the most time and attention?
   a. structure of the presidency
   b. structure of Congress
   c. structure and powers of the federal judiciary
   d. ratification of the new Constitution

F 7. The Framers of the Constitution feared political apathy more than tyranny of the majority. (T/F)

T 8. The idea of popular government—in which the majority's desires have a more direct and immediate impact on public policy—has gained strength since the nation's beginning. (T/F)

T 9. The Supreme Court decision in *Marbury v. Madison* gave courts the power to declare governmental action null and void when it is found to violate the Constitution. (T/F)

F 10. The Virginia Plan (also known as the large-state plan) called for a Congress with equal representation of each state but with greatly strengthened powers. (T/F)

Critical Thinking

How does the division of power in the U.S. political system contribute to limited government? How do the provisions for representative government (the various methods of choosing national officials) contribute to limited government?

Suggested Readings

Beard, Charles S. *An Economic Interpretation of the Constitution.* New York: Macmillan, 1941. Argues that the Framers had selfish economic interests uppermost in their minds when they wrote the Constitution.

Edling, Max M.. *A Revolution in Favor of Government.* New York: Oxford University Press, 2003. Argues that the Framers intended the Constitution to create a strong government.

Ellis, Joseph J. *Founding Brothers: The Revolutionary Generation.* New York: Vintage, 2002. A riveting account of the lives of America's leading Founders.

Federalist Papers. Many editions, including a one-volume paperback version edited by Isaac Kramnick (New York: Penguin, 1987). A series of essays written by Alexander Hamilton, James Madison, and John Jay under the pseudonym Publius. The essays, published in a New York newspaper in 1787–88, explain the Constitution and support its ratification.

Hardin, Russell. *Liberalism, Constitutionalism, and Democracy.* New York: Oxford University Press, 1999. Analysis of the great ideas that underlie the Constitution.

Haskell, John. *Direct Democracy or Representative Government: Dispelling the Populist Myth.* Boulder, Colo.: Westview Press, 2001. Analysis of the two democratic philosophies that have affected American politics.

Holcombe, Randall G. *From Liberty to Democracy.* Ann Arbor: University of Michigan Press, 2002. An interpretive history of the transformation of American government.

Tocqueville, Alexis de. *Democracy in America,* vols. 1 and 2, ed. J. P. Mayer. New York: Doubleday/Anchor, 1969. A classic analysis (originally published 1835–40) of American democracy by an insightful French observer.

List of Websites

http://www.nara.gov/
The National Archives site; includes an in-depth look at the history of the Declaration of Independence.

http://odur.let.rug.nl/~usa/P/aj7/about/bio/jackxx.htm
A site that focuses on Andrew Jackson and his role in shaping U.S. politics.

http://www.yale.edu/lawweb/avalon/constpap.htm
Includes documents on the Constitution, the American Revolution, and the Constitutional Convention.

http://www.yale.edu/lawweb/avalon/presiden/jeffpap.htm
A site that includes the papers of Thomas Jefferson. His autobiography is among the available materials.

Participate!

In recent years, as a means of checking the power of elected officials, a number of states and localities have imposed a limit on the number of terms that representatives can serve. Although the term-limit movement has slowed, there are still opportunities to get involved on either side of the issue. If you favor term limits and want to get involved, you might start by examining the website of U.S. Term Limits (www.termlimits.org). If you oppose term limits, you could begin by looking at the Common Cause site (www.commoncause.org).

Extra Credit

For up-to-the-minute *New York Times* articles, interactive simulations, graphics, study tools, and more links and quizzes, visit the text's Online Learning Center at www.mhhe.com/pattersontad7.

(Self-Test Answers: 1. d   2. c   3. a   4. a   5. a   6. b   7. F   8. T   9. T   10. F)

3

Federalism:
Forging a Nation

The question of the relation of the states to the federal government is the cardinal question of our Constitutional system. It cannot be settled by the opinion of one generation, because it is a question of growth, and each successive stage of our political and economic development gives it a new aspect, makes it a new question.

—*Woodrow Wilson*[1]

In late 2001, Attorney General John Ashcroft directed federal agents to take action against Oregon physicians who prescribed federally controlled drugs to assist terminally ill patients in committing suicide. The physicians would lose their licenses to prescribe such drugs. Ashcroft's aim was to void the Oregon law that permits physician assistance in cases where a patient, in the judgment of at least two doctors, has less than six months to live, is suffering painfully, and is mentally competent to decide whether to end his or her life. Ashcroft's action was not the first federal attempt to nullify the Oregon law. Congress had twice initiated action—in one instance, a bill passed in the House but failed to come up for a vote in the Senate.

Oregon's voters had approved the assisted-suicide law in a statewide referendum, becoming the first state (and, as of 2004, the only state) to do so. A majority of Oregon's voters had been persuaded by the argument that no public benefit derives from requiring the dying to accept prolonged and painful suffering. Opponents had countered that society's interest in preserving life outweighs a patient's desire to die, that laws allowing doctors to assist a suicide would be abused, that doctors and relatives in some instances would persuade terminally ill patients to accept death against their will, and that depressed patients who asked to die would be granted their wish rather than be treated for their depression (after which they might choose to live). In filing suit against the Oregon law, the U.S. Department of Justice argued that "there are important medical, ethical and legal distinctions between intentionally causing a patient's death and providing sufficient dosages of pain medications to eliminate or alleviate pain."

Nevertheless, Oregon voters had twice—first in 1994 and again in 1997—approved the state's Death With Dignity Act. They prevailed again in 2002, when a federal district court judge halted the Justice Department's effort to nullify Oregon's physician-assisted suicide law. Ashcroft appealed the decision to the U.S. Court of Appeals for the Ninth Circuit, which ruled in Oregon's favor.

The controversy surrounding Oregon's Death With Dignity Act is one of thousands of disagreements during the course of American history that have hinged on whether national or state authority should prevail. Americans possess what amounts to dual citizenship: they are citizens both of the United States and of the state where they reside. The American political system is a *federal system*, in which constitutional authority is

A supporter of Oregon's Death with Dignity law holds a sign outside the federal courthouse in Portland, Oregon, where a hearing on the U.S. Justice Department's challenge to the law is being held. This type of struggle between the power of the federal government and the power of a state government has been repeated countless times in American history, a reflection of the U.S. federal system that vests sovereignty in both the national and state governments. In this particular case, the state, Oregon, prevailed. Federal courts upheld the Oregon law.

divided between a national government and state governments: each government is assumed to derive its powers directly from the people and therefore to have sovereignty (final authority) over the policy responsibilities assigned to it. The federal system consists of nation *and* states, indivisible yet separate.[2]

This chapter on American constitutionalism focuses on federalism. The nature of the relationship between the nation and the states was the most pressing issue when the Constitution was written in 1787. This chapter describes how that issue helped shape the Constitution. The chapter's closing sections discuss how federalism has changed throughout the nation's history and conclude with a brief overview of contemporary federalism. The main points presented in the chapter are the following:

- *The power of government must be equal to its responsibilities.* The Constitution was needed because the nation's preceding system (under the Articles of Confederation) was too weak to accomplish its expected goals, particularly those of a strong defense and an integrated economy.

- *Federalism—the Constitution's division of governing authority between two levels, nation and states—was the result of political bargaining.* Federalism was not a theoretical principle, but a compromise made necessary in 1787 by the prior existence of the states.

- *Federalism is not a fixed principle for allocating power between the national and state governments, but a principle that has changed over time in response to new political needs.* Federalism has passed through several distinct stages in the course of the nation's history.

- *Contemporary federalism tilts toward national authority, reflecting the increased interdependence of American society.* However, there is a current trend toward reducing the scope of federal authority.

FEDERALISM: NATIONAL AND STATE SOVEREIGNTY

Many of the nation's most prominent leaders, including George Washington and Benjamin Franklin, were delegates to the Philadelphia convention in 1787. Not all of America's top leaders were at the convention, however, and many of them were staunchly opposed to a strong national government. When rumors circulated that the delegates were planning to propose such a government, Patrick Henry, an ardent supporter of state-centered government, said that he "smelt a rat." After the convention had adjourned, he realized that his fears

Patrick Henry was a leading figure in the American Revolution ("Give me liberty or give me death!"). He later opposed ratification of the Constitution on grounds that the national government should be a union of states and not also of people.

were justified. "Who authorized them," he asked, "to speak the language of 'We, the People,' instead of 'We, the States'?"

The question—"people versus states"—was precipitated by the failure of the Articles of Confederation. The government under the Articles (see Chapter 2) was a union of states rather than also of people. The result was an inherently weak national government with no power to force the states to comply with its laws. Georgia and North Carolina, for example, contributed no money at all to the national treasury between 1781 and 1786, and the national government could do nothing more than beg them to pay their fair share of the costs of defense, diplomacy, and other national policies. The only realistic solution to this problem was a government based on the people. If ordered to pay taxes, individuals would either do so or face consequences—imprisonment or confiscation of property—that most of them would prefer to avoid.

Although the creation of a national government based directly on the people was therefore a goal of the writers of the Constitution, they also wanted to preserve the states as governing bodies. The states were already in existence, had their own constitutions, and enjoyed popular support. When Virginia's George Mason said he would never agree to a union that abolished the states, he was speaking for virtually all the delegates. The Philadelphia convention thereby devised a system of government that came to be known as **federalism.** Federalism is the division of **sovereignty,** or ultimate governing authority, between a national government and regional (that is, state) governments. Each directly governs the people and derives its powers from them.

American federalism is basically a system of divided authority (see Figure 3–1). The system gives states the power to address local issues in ways of their own choosing. At the same time, federalism gives the national government the

federalism A governmental system in which authority is divided between two sovereign levels of government: national and regional.

sovereignty The ultimate authority to govern within a certain geographical area.

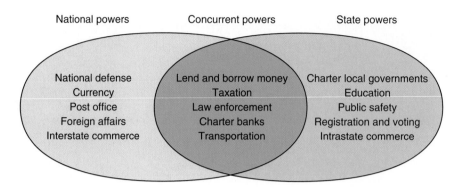

National powers   Concurrent powers   State powers

National defense   Lend and borrow money   Charter local governments
Currency   Taxation   Education
Post office   Law enforcement   Public safety
Foreign affairs   Charter banks   Registration and voting
Interstate commerce   Transportation   Intrastate commerce

Figure 3–1

Federalism as a Governing System: Examples of National, State, and Concurrent Powers

The American federal system divides sovereignty between a national government and the state governments. Each is constitutionally protected in its existence and authority, although their powers overlap somewhat even in areas granted to one level (for example, the federal government has a role in education policy).

power to decide matters of national scope. In practice, there is some overlap between state and national action, but there is also a division of responsibilities. The national government has primary responsibility for national defense and the currency, among other things, while the states have primary responsibility for policy areas such as public education and police protection. The national and state governments also have some concurrent powers (that is, powers exercised over the same areas of policy); for example, each has the power to raise taxes and borrow money.

A federal system is different from a **confederacy,** the type of government established by the Articles. A confederacy is a union in which the states alone are sovereign. The authority of the central government is derived from the states, which can, at will, redefine its authority. Federalism is also different from a **unitary system,** in which sovereignty is vested solely in the national government. Under a unitary system, the people are citizens or subjects only of the national government, and the other governments derive their authority from the national government, which can, in theory at least, abolish them or redefine their authority. By contrast, a federal system invests sovereignty in both the national and the state governments, thereby constitutionally guaranteeing the permanent existence of each level and protecting each level from unwarranted interference by the other.

Federalism was invented in America in 1787. It was different not only from a confederate or a unitary system but also from any form of government the world had known. The ancient Greek city-states and the medieval Hanseatic League were confederacies. The governments of Europe were unitary in form. The United States of America would be the first nation to be governed through a true federal system.

The Argument for Federalism

Unlike many other decisions made at the Philadelphia convention, the choice of federalism had no clear basis in political theory. Federalism was a practical

confederacy A governmental system in which sovereignty is vested entirely in subnational (state) governments.

unitary system A governmental system in which the national government alone has sovereign (ultimate) authority.

HOW THE UNITED STATES COMPARES

Federal Versus Unitary Governments

Federalism involves the division of sovereignty between a national government and subnational (such as state) governments. It was invented in 1787 in order to maintain the preexisting American states while establishing an effective central government. Since then a number of other countries have established a *federal* government, but most countries have a *unitary* government, in which all sovereignty is vested in the national government.

However, even within these alternative political systems there are important differences. In Germany's federal system, for example, the states have limited lawmaking powers but do have broad authority in determining how national laws are implemented. By comparison, the U.S. federal system grants substantial lawmaking powers to the states except in specified areas such as national defense and currency.

Unitary systems also differ. In Britain, the national government has delegated substantial authority to regions; Scotland, for example, has its own parliament, which exercises lawmaking powers. Political authority in France, on the other hand, is highly centralized.

In nearly all federal systems, the national legislature has two chambers—one apportioned by population (as in the case of the U.S. House of Representatives) and one apportioned by geographical area (as in the case of the U.S. Senate). Most unitary systems have but a single national legislative chamber, which is apportioned by population—there is no constitutional justification for a second chamber based on geography.

COUNTRY	FORM OF GOVERNMENT
Canada	Federal
France	Unitary
Germany	Federal
Great Britain	Modified unitary
Italy	Modified unitary
Japan	Unitary
Mexico	Modified federal
Sweden	Unitary
United States	Federal

necessity: there was a need for a stronger national government, and yet the states existed and were intent on retaining their sovereignty.

Nevertheless, the Framers developed arguments for the superiority of this type of political system. Federalism, they said, would protect liberty, moderate the power of government, and provide the foundation for an effective national government.

Protecting Liberty

Theorists such as Locke and Montesquieu had not proposed a division of power between national and local authorities as a means of protecting liberty. Nevertheless, the Framers came to look upon federalism as part of the Constitution's system of checks and balances (see Chapter 2). Alexander Hamilton argued in *Federalist* No. 28 that the American people could shift their loyalties back and forth between the national and state governments in order to keep each under control. "If [the people's] rights are invaded by either," Hamilton wrote, "they can make use of the other as the instrument of redress."

Alexander Hamilton

(1757–1804)

Alexander Hamilton was just thirty-two years old when he served as a delegate to the constitutional convention in Philadelphia. A strong nationalist, his *Federalist Papers* essays contributed to the ratification of the Constitution. George Washington appointed him to be the first secretary of the treasury, where he developed plans for the First Bank of the United States and for placing the federal government on a sound financial footing. He was fatally wounded in a duel with Aaron Burr, a political and personal foe.

Moderating the Power of Government

To the Anti-Federalists (opponents of the Constitution), the sacrifice of the states' power to the nation was as unwise as it was unnecessary. They argued that a distant national government could never serve the people's interests as well as the states could. In support of their contention, the Anti-Federalists turned to Montesquieu, who had concluded that a small republic is more likely than a large one to respect and respond to the people it governs. When government encompasses a small area, he argued, its leaders are in closer touch with the people and have a greater concern for their interests.

James Madison took issue with this claim. In *Federalist* No. 10, Madison argued that whether a government serves the common good is a function not of its size but of the range of interests that share political power. The problem with a smaller republic, Madison claimed, is that it is likely to have a dominant faction—whether it be large landholders, financiers, an impoverished majority, or some other group—that is strong enough to take full control of government and to use this power to advance its selfish interests. A large republic is less likely to have such an all-powerful faction. If financiers are strong in one area of a large republic, they are likely to be weaker elsewhere. The same will be true of other interests. A large republic, Madison concluded, would impede the efforts of any single group to gain control and would force groups to compromise and work together. "Extend the sphere," said Madison, "and you take in a greater variety of parties and interests; you make it less probable that a majority of the whole will have a common motive to invade the rights of other citizens."

Strengthening the Union

The most telling argument in 1787 for a federal system, however, was that it would overcome the deficiencies of the Articles. The Articles had numerous flaws (including a very weak executive and a judiciary subservient to the state courts), and two of them were fatal: the government had neither the power to tax nor the power to regulate commerce.

Historical Background

Under the Articles, Congress was given responsibility for national defense but was not granted the power to tax, so it had to rely on the states for the money to maintain an army and navy. During the first six years under the Articles, Congress asked the states for $12 million but received only $3 million—not even enough to pay the interest on Revolutionary War debts. By 1786 the national government was so desperate for funds that it sold the navy's ships and had fewer than a thousand soldiers in uniform—this at a time when England had an army in Canada and Spain occupied Florida.

Congress was also expected to shape a national economy, yet it was powerless to do so because the Articles prohibited it from interfering with the states' commerce policies. States were free to do whatever they wanted, and they took

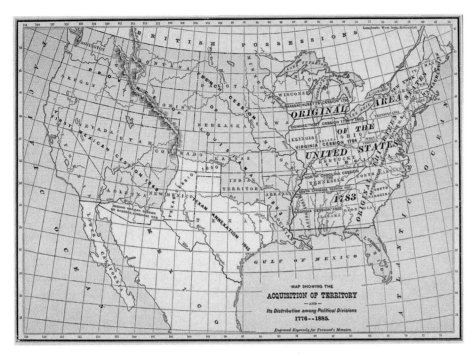

It could take weeks to travel overland or by ship from the most distant points in the American states. The great size of America compared with European countries was used as an argument by both those who favored a strong union and those who opposed it.

advantage of the situation by imposing trade barriers on each other. Connecticut, for example, placed a higher tariff on manufactured goods from its trading rival Massachusetts than it did on the same goods shipped from England.

The Articles of Confederation showed the fallacy of the adage "That government is best which governs least." The consequences of an overly weak authority were abundantly clear: public disorder, economic chaos, and inadequate defense.

The Powers of the Nation

The Philadelphia convention met to decide the powers of the national government. The delegates had not been sent to determine how state government should be structured. Accordingly, the U.S. Constitution focuses on the lawful authority of the national government, which is provided through *enumerated* and *implied powers*. Authority that is not in this way granted to the national government is left—or "reserved"—to the states. Thus, the states have *reserved powers*.

Enumerated Powers

Article I of the Constitution grants to Congress seventeen **enumerated (expressed) powers.** These powers were intended by the Framers to be the basis for a government strong enough to forge a union that was secure in its defense and stable in its commerce. Congress's powers to regulate commerce among the states, to create a national currency, and to borrow money, for example, would

enumerated (expressed) powers The seventeen powers granted to the national government under Article I, Section 8 of the Constitution. These powers include taxation and the regulation of commerce as well as the authority to provide for the national defense.

provide a foundation for a sound national economy. Its power to tax, combined with its authority to declare war and establish an army and navy, would enable it to provide for the common defense. In addition, the Constitution prohibits the states from actions that would interfere with the national government's exercise of its lawful powers. Article I, Section 10 forbids the states to make treaties with other nations, raise armies, wage war, print money, or make commercial agreements with other states without the approval of Congress.

The writers of the Constitution recognized that the lawful exercise of national authority would at times conflict with the actions of the states. In such instances, national law was intended to prevail. Article VI of the Constitution grants this dominance in the so-called **supremacy clause,** which provides that "the laws of the United States . . . shall be the supreme law of the land."

supremacy clause Article VI of the Constitution, which makes national law supreme over state law when the national government is acting within its constitutional limits.

Implied Powers

The Framers of the Constitution also recognized that an overly narrow definition of national authority would result in a government incapable of adapting to change. Under the Articles of Confederation, Congress was strictly confined to those powers expressly granted to it, limiting its ability to respond effectively to the country's changing needs after the Revolutionary War. Concerned that the enumerated powers by themselves might be too restrictive of national authority, the Framers added the **"necessary and proper" clause** or, as it later came to be known, the **elastic clause.** Article I, Section 8 gives Congress the power "to make all laws which shall be necessary and proper for carrying into execution the foregoing [enumerated] powers." This grant gave the national government **implied powers:** the authority to take action that is not expressly authorized by the Constitution but that supports actions that are so authorized.

"necessary and proper" clause (elastic clause) The authority granted Congress in Article I, Section 8 of the Constitution "to make all laws which shall be necessary and proper" for the implementation of its enumerated powers.

implied powers The federal government's constitutional authority (through the "necessary and proper" clause) to take action that is not expressly authorized by the Constitution but that supports actions that are so authorized.

The Powers of the States

The Framers' preference for a sovereign national government was not shared in 1787 by all Americans. Although Anti-Federalists recognized a need to strengthen defense and interstate commerce, they feared the consequences of a strong central government. The interests of the people of New Hampshire were not identical to those of Georgians or Pennsylvanians, and the Anti-Federalists argued that only state-centered government would protect and preserve the differences.

The Federalists responded by claiming that the national government would have no interest in dominating the states.[3] The national government would take responsibility for establishing a strong defense and for promoting a sound economy, while the states would retain nearly all other governing functions, including oversight of public morals, education, and safety.

This argument did not alleviate the Anti-Federalists' fear of a powerful national government. The supremacy and "necessary and proper" clauses were particularly worrisome, because they provided a constitutional basis for future expansions of national authority. Such concerns led to demands for a constitutional amendment that would protect the states against encroachment by the national government. Ratified in 1791 as the Tenth Amendment to the

Federalism: Who Governs Affects You

When Americans think about the question "Who governs?" they usually think in terms of whether the Republicans or the Democrats are in power. For much of America's history, however, the question evoked thoughts of federalism. Would the nation decide? Or would the states decide?

Even though Americans are governed more uniformly today than in the past, the issue of state or nation is still a critical one. Abortion is perhaps the preeminent example. The Supreme Court's *Roe v. Wade* (1973) decision made the choice of an abortion a constitutionally protected right in some circumstances. Before then, abortion was governed strictly by state laws, and most states banned it entirely. States still have some authority in the area (for example, they can impose a parental-consent requirement on mi-

nors in some circumstances), but they are prevented by federal law from outlawing it entirely.

Federal power has lost out to state power in some policy areas. For example, two federal acts—the Age Discrimination Act and the Americans with Disabilities Act—have recently been judged not to apply to the actions of state governments. State governments have broad discretion in their treatment, for example, of elderly and disabled employees and job seekers.

The list of examples could be extended, but the point would be the same: how you are governed depends to a degree on who does the governing. Policy issues are not determined solely by whether the Republicans or the Democrats are in charge. They are also affected by whether the decisions are made in Washington or in the state capital. For that reason, every American has a stake in how power is divided between the national and state governments.

Constitution, it reads: "The powers not delegated to the United States by the Constitution, nor prohibited by it to the States, are reserved to the States." The states' powers under the U.S. Constitution are thus called **reserved powers.**

reserved powers The powers granted to the states under the Tenth Amendment to the Constitution.

FEDERALISM IN HISTORICAL PERSPECTIVE

Since ratification of the Constitution over two centuries ago, no aspect of it has provoked more frequent or bitter conflict than federalism. By establishing two levels of sovereign authority, the Constitution created competing centers of power and ambition, each of which was sure to claim disputed areas as belonging within its realm of authority.

Conflict between national and state authority was also ensured by the brevity of the Constitution. The Framers deliberately avoided detailed provisions, recognizing that brief phrases would lend flexibility to the government they were creating. The document does not define, for example, the difference between *inter*state commerce (which the national government is empowered to regulate) and *intra*state commerce (which is reserved for regulation by the states).

Not surprisingly, federalism has been a contentious and dynamic system, its development determined less by constitutional language than by the strength of contending interests and by the country's changing needs. Federalism can be viewed as having progressed through three historical eras, each of which has involved a different relationship between the nation and the states.

A first dispute over federalism was whether the Constitution allowed the creation of a Bank of the United States (shown here in an early nineteenth-century painting). The Constitution had a clause authorizing the printing of currency but not the establishment of a bank itself.

An Indestructible Union (1789–1865)

The issue during the first era, which lasted from the Constitution's beginnings in 1789 through the end of the Civil War in 1865, was the Union's survival. Given the state-centered history of America before the Constitution, it was inevitable that the states would dispute national policies that threatened their particular interests.

The Nationalist View: McCulloch v. Maryland

A first dispute over federalism arose when President George Washington's secretary of the treasury, Alexander Hamilton, proposed that Congress establish a national bank. Thomas Jefferson, Washington's secretary of state, opposed the bank on the grounds that its activities would benefit the interests of the rich at the expense of the interests of ordinary people. Jefferson claimed that the bank was unlawful because the Constitution did not explicitly authorize the creation of a national bank. Hamilton and his supporters claimed that because the federal government had constitutional authority to regulate currency, it had the "implied power" to establish a national bank.

Hamilton's view prevailed when Congress in 1791 established the First Bank of the United States, granting it a twenty-year charter. When the bank's charter expired in 1811, Congress did not renew it. However, Congress in 1816 established the Second Bank of the United States over the objections of state and local bankers. Responding to the bankers' complaints, several states, including Maryland, attempted to drive the Second Bank of the United States out of existence by levying taxes on its operations within their borders. Edwin McCulloch, who was head cashier of the Maryland branch of the U.S. Bank, refused to pay the Maryland tax, and the resulting dispute reached the Supreme Court.

Historical Background

John Marshall, the chief justice of the Supreme Court, was, like Hamilton, a strong nationalist, and in *McCulloch v. Maryland* (1819) the Court ruled decisively in favor of national authority. It was reasonable, Marshall concluded, to infer that a government with powers to tax, borrow money, and regulate commerce could establish a bank in order to exercise those powers properly. Marshall's argument was a clear statement of *implied powers*—the idea that through the "necessary and proper" clause the national government's powers extend beyond a narrow reading of its enumerated powers.

Marshall also addressed the meaning of the Constitution's supremacy clause. The state of Maryland argued that it had the sovereign authority to tax the national bank even if the bank was a legal entity. The Supreme Court rejected Maryland's position, concluding that valid national law prevailed over conflicting state law. Because the national government had the power to create the bank, it could also protect the bank against actions by the states, such as taxation, that might destroy it.[4]

The *McCulloch* decision served as precedent for future assertions of national authority, including a second landmark decision by the Marshall Court. In *Gibbons v. Ogden* (1824), the Court ruled on the power of Congress to regulate commerce. The state of New York had granted a monopoly to Aaron Ogden to operate a ferry between New York and New Jersey. When Thomas Gibbons set up a competing ferry under a federal coastal licensing agreement, Ogden tried to prevent Gibbons from operating it. Marshall invalidated the New York monopoly, saying it intruded on Congress's power to regulate commerce among the states. Going further, Marshall ruled that Congress's power extended *into* a state when commerce between two or more states was at issue.[5]

Marshall's opinions asserted that legitimate uses of national power took precedence over state authority and that the "necessary and proper" clause and the commerce clause were broad grants of national power. As a nationalist, Marshall was providing the U.S. government the legal justification for expanding its power in ways that fostered the development of the nation as a nation rather than as a collection of states. This constitutional vision was of utmost significance. As Justice Oliver Wendell Holmes Jr. noted a century later, the Union could not have survived if each state had been allowed to determine for itself the extent to which it would accept national authority.[6]

John C. Calhoun

(1782–1850)

John C. Calhoun was a champion of states' rights and of slaveholding. He was Andrew Jackson's first vice president, but he resigned that post after Jackson came out strongly against Calhoun's doctrine of nullification. Calhoun then returned to the U.S. Senate to fight for his proposal. Calhoun later secured passage of a gag rule that for a period prohibited the discussion of slavery in the Senate.

The States'-Rights View: The Dred Scott Decision

Although John Marshall's rulings helped strengthen national authority, the issue of slavery posed a growing threat to the Union's survival. Fearing that northern members of Congress might move to abolish slavery, southern leaders did what others have done throughout American history: they devised a constitutional argument to fit their political desires. John C. Calhoun of South Carolina argued that the Constitution had created "a government of states . . . not a government of individuals."[7] This line of reasoning led Calhoun to his

www.mhhe.com/pattersontad7

famed "doctrine of nullification," which declared that each state had the constitutional right to nullify a national law.

In 1832 South Carolina invoked this doctrine, declaring "null and void" a tariff law that favored northern interests. President Andrew Jackson retorted that South Carolina's action was "incompatible with the existence of the Union," a position that was strengthened when Congress authorized Jackson to use military force against South Carolina. The state backed down when Congress agreed to amend the tariff act slightly.

The clash foreshadowed a confrontation of far greater scope and consequence: the Civil War. War between the states would not break out for another thirty years, but in the interim, conflicts over states' rights intensified.[8] Westward expansion and immigration into the northern states were tilting power in Congress toward the free states, which increasingly signaled their determination to outlaw slavery in the United States at some future time. Attempts to find a compromise acceptable to both the North and the South were fruitless.

The Supreme Court's infamous *Dred Scott* decision (1857), written by Chief Justice Roger Taney, an ardent states'-rights advocate, intensified the conflict. Dred Scott, a slave, applied for his freedom when his master died, citing a federal law—the Missouri Compromise of 1820—that made slavery illegal in a free state or territory. Scott had lived in the North for four years, but the Supreme Court in a 7-2 decision ruled that slaves were "property" and that persons of African descent were barred from citizenship and thereby could not sue for their freedom in federal courts. The Court also invalidated the Missouri Compromise, declaring that, because slaves were property and because U.S. citizens could take their property into any state or territory, Congress could not outlaw slavery in any part of the United States.[9]

Taney's outrageous argument in the *Dred Scott* case inflamed many northerners and contributed to a sectional split in the majority Democratic party (the northern and southern wings nominated separate candidates) that enabled Republican Abraham Lincoln to win the presidency in 1860 with only 40 percent of the popular vote. Lincoln had campaigned for the gradual, compensated abolition of slavery. By the time he assumed office, seven southern states had already seceded from the Union. In justifying his decision to wage civil war on these states, Lincoln said, "The Union is older than the states." In 1865 the superior strength of the Union army settled by force the question of whether national authority would be binding on the states.

Dual Federalism and Laissez-Faire Capitalism (1865–1937)

Although the Civil War preserved the Union, new challenges to federalism were surfacing. Constitutional doctrine held that certain policy areas, such as interstate commerce and defense, belonged exclusively to the national government, whereas other policy areas, such as public health and intrastate commerce, belonged exclusively to the states. This doctrine, known as **dual federalism,** was based on the idea that a precise separation of national and state authority was both possible and desirable. "The power which one possesses," said the Supreme Court, "the other does not."[10]

dual federalism A doctrine based on the idea that a precise separation of national power and state power is both possible and desirable.

The American Civil War was the bloodiest conflict the world had yet known. Ten percent of fighting-age males died in the four-year war, and uncounted others were wounded. The death toll—618,000 (360,000 from the North, 258,000 from the South)—exceeded that of the American war dead in World War I, World War II, the Korean War, and the Vietnam War combined. This death toll was in a nation with a population only one-ninth the size it is today.

American society, however, was in the midst of changes that raised questions about the suitability of dual federalism as a governing concept. The Industrial Revolution had given rise to large business firms, which were using their economic power to dominate markets and exploit workers. Government was the logical counterforce to this economic power. Which level of government—state or national—would regulate business?

There was also the issue of the former slaves. The white South had lost the war but was hardly of a mind to share power with newly freed slaves. Would the federal government be allowed to intervene in state affairs to ensure the fair treatment of African Americans?

Dual federalism became a barrier to an effective response to these issues. From the 1860s through the 1930s, the Supreme Court held firm to the idea that there was a sharp line between national and state authority and, in both areas, a high wall of separation between government and the economy. This era of federalism was characterized by state supremacy in racial policy and by business supremacy in commerce policy.

The Fourteenth Amendment and State Discretion

Ratified after the Civil War, the Fourteenth Amendment was intended to protect citizens (especially black Americans) from discriminatory actions by state governments.[11] A state was prohibited from depriving "any person of life, liberty, or property without due process of law," from denying "any person within its jurisdiction the equal protection of the laws," and from abridging "the privileges or immunities of citizens of the United States."

Historical Background

Liberty, Equality, & Self-Government

What's Your Opinion?

Large Versus Small Republics

During the debate over ratification of the Constitution, Americans argued over whether liberty, equality, and self-government would be better protected by the states or by the nation. The Anti-Federalists argued that a small republic was closer to the people and therefore would do more to protect their rights. James Madison countered by saying that a large republic was preferable because it would have such a diversity of interests that compromise and tolerance among various groups would be required.

Was Madison correct? Or were the Anti-Federalists correct? In your view, which level of government—national or state—is more likely to protect and enhance America's core ideals? Does the broad sweep of American history support your view? Which level of government has been more likely to promote the interests of the American people generally? Which level of government has been more likely to promote the interests of a particular group at the expense of another group?

Supreme Court rulings during subsequent decades, however, helped to undermine the Fourteenth Amendment's promise. The Court held, for example, that the Fourteenth Amendment did not substantially limit the power of the states to determine the rights to which their residents were entitled.[12] Then, in *Plessy v. Ferguson* (1896), the Court issued its infamous "separate but equal" ruling. A black man, Homer Adolph Plessy, had been convicted of violating a Louisiana law that required white and black citizens to ride in separate railroad cars. The Supreme Court upheld his conviction, concluding that state governments could require blacks to use separate railroad cars and other accommodations as long as those facilities were "equal" in quality to those reserved for use by whites. "If one race be inferior to the other socially," the Court concluded, "the Constitution of the United States cannot put them on the same plane." The lone dissenting justice in the case, John Marshall Harlan, had harsh words for his colleagues: "Our Constitution is color-blind and neither knows nor tolerates classes among citizens. . . . The thin disguise of 'equal' accommodations . . . will not mislead anyone nor atone for the wrong this day done."[13]

With its *Plessy* decision, the Court undercut the Fourteenth Amendment and allowed southern states to segregate the races. Black children were forced into separate schools that seldom had libraries and usually had few teachers, most of whom had no formal training. Hospitals for blacks had few doctors and nurses and almost no medical supplies and equipment. Legal challenges to these discriminatory practices were generally unsuccessful. The *Plessy* ruling had become a justification for the separate and *unequal* treatment of black Americans.

Judicial Protection of Business

Through its rulings after the Civil War, the Supreme Court also provided a constitutional basis for uncontrolled private power. The Supreme Court was dom-

After the Civil War Reconstruction, the white majority in the South used the power of government to enforce creation of a two-race society in which the public schools and other public facilities for blacks were vastly inferior to those for whites.

inated by adherents of the doctrine of laissez-faire capitalism (which holds that business should be "allowed to act" without interference), and they interpreted the Constitution in ways that frustrated government's attempts to regulate business activity. In 1886, for example, the Court decided that corporations were "persons" within the meaning of the Fourteenth Amendment, and thus their property rights were protected from substantial regulation by the states.[14] The irony was inescapable. A constitutional amendment that had been enacted to protect the newly freed slaves was ignored for this purpose but was used instead to protect fictitious persons—business corporations.

The Court also weakened the national government's regulatory power by narrowly interpreting its commerce power. The Constitution's **commerce clause** says that Congress shall have the power "to regulate commerce" among the states but does not spell out the economic activities included in the grant of power. When the federal government invoked the Sherman Antitrust Act (1890) in an attempt to break up a monopoly on the manufacture of sugar, the Supreme Court blocked the action, claiming that interstate commerce covered only the "transportation" of goods, not their "manufacture."[15] Manufacturing was deemed part of intrastate commerce and thus, according to the dual federalism doctrine, subject to state regulation only. However, because the Court had previously decided that the states' regulatory powers were restricted by the Fourteenth Amendment, the states were relatively powerless to control manufacturing activity.

commerce clause The clause of the Constitution (Article I, Section 8) that empowers the federal government to regulate commerce among the states and with other nations.

Although the national government subsequently made some headway in business regulation, the Supreme Court remained an obstacle. An example is the case of *Hammer v. Dagenhart* (1918), which arose from a 1916 federal act that prohibited the interstate shipment of goods produced by child labor. The act was popular because factory owners were exploiting children, working them for long hours at low pay. Citing the Tenth Amendment, the Court invalidated the law, ruling that factory practices could be regulated only by the states.[16]

Between 1865 and 1937, the Supreme Court's rulings severely restricted national power. Narrowly interpreting Congress's constitutional power to regulate commerce, the Court forbade Congress to regulate child labor and other aspects of manufacturing.

However, in an earlier case, *Lochner v. New York* (1905), the Court had prevented a state from regulating labor practices, concluding that such action was a violation of firms' property rights.[17]

In effect, the Supreme Court had denied both Congress and the states the authority to decide economic issues. As the constitutional scholars Alfred Kelly, Winifred Harbison, and Herman Belz concluded, "No more complete perversion of the principles of effective federal government can be imagined."[18]

National Authority Prevails

Historical Background

Judicial supremacy in the economic sphere ended abruptly in 1937. For nearly a decade, the United States had been mired in the Great Depression, which President Franklin D. Roosevelt's New Deal was designed to alleviate. The Supreme Court, however, had ruled much of the New Deal's economic recovery legislation unconstitutional. A constitutional crisis of historic proportions seemed inevitable until the Court suddenly reversed its position. In the process, American federalism was fundamentally and forever changed.

The Great Depression revealed clearly that Americans had become a national community with national economic needs. By the 1930s, more than half the population lived in cities (compared to a fifth in 1860), and more than ten million workers were employed by industry (compared to one million in 1860). Urban workers were typically dependent on landlords for their housing, on farmers and grocers for their food, and on corporations for their jobs. Farmers were more independent, but they too were increasingly a part of a larger economic network. Their income depended on market prices and shipping and equipment costs.[19]

This economic interdependence meant that no area of the economy was immune if things went wrong. When the depression hit in 1929, its effects could

During the Great Depression, shantytowns were erected in most cities by people who had lost their jobs and homes. State and local governments could not cope with the enormous problems created by the Great Depression, so the federal government stepped in with its New Deal programs, greatly changing the nature of federal-state relations.

not be contained. A decline in spending was followed by a drop in production, a loss of jobs, unpaid rents and grocery bills, and a shrinking market for food-stuffs, which led to a further decline in spending, and so on, creating a relentless downward spiral. At the depths of the Great Depression, one-fourth of the nation's work force was unemployed.

The states by tradition had responsibility for welfare, but they were nearly penniless because of declining tax revenues and the growing ranks of poor people. The New Deal programs offered a way out of the crisis; for example, the National Industry Recovery Act (NIRA) of 1933 called for a massive public works program to create jobs and for coordinated action by major industries. However, the New Deal was opposed by economic conservatives (who accused Roosevelt of leading the nation down the road to communism) and by justices of the Supreme Court. In *Schechter v. United States* (1935), the Court invalidated the Recovery Act by a 5-4 vote, ruling that it usurped powers reserved to the states.[20]

Frustrated by the Court, Roosevelt in 1937 proposed his famed Court-packing plan. Roosevelt recommended that Congress enact legislation that would permit an additional justice to be appointed to the Court whenever a seated member passed the age of seventy. The number of justices would in-crease, and Roosevelt's appointees presumably would be more sympathetic to his programs. Roosevelt's scheme was resisted by Congress, but the controversy ended with "the switch in time that saved nine," when, for reasons that have never become fully clear, Justice Owen Roberts abandoned his opposition to Roosevelt's policies and thus gave the president a 5-4 majority on the Court.

Within months, the Court upheld the 1935 National Labor Relations Act, which gave employees the right to organize and bargain collectively.[21] In pass-ing the act, Congress had argued that labor-management disputes disrupt the nation's economy and therefore could be regulated through the commerce clause. In upholding the act, the Supreme Court in effect granted Congress the authority to apply its commerce powers broadly.[22] During this same period, the Court also loosened its restrictions on Congress's use of its taxing and spending powers.[23] These decisions removed the constitutional barrier to increased federal authority, a change that the Court later acknowledged when it said that Congress's commerce power is "as broad as the needs of the nation."[24]

In effect, the Supreme Court had finally recognized the obvious: that an industrial economy is not confined by state boundaries and must be subject to national regulation. It was a principle that business itself also increasingly accepted. The nation's banking industry, for example, was saved in the 1930s from almost complete collapse by the creation of a federal regulatory agency, the Federal Deposit Insurance Corporation (FDIC). By insuring depositors' savings against loss, the FDIC gave depositors the confidence to keep their money in banks, enabling many banks to remain solvent during the depression.

Toward National Citizenship

The fundamental change in the constitutional doctrine of federalism as applied to economic issues that took place in the 1930s was paralleled by similar changes in other areas. One example is the area of civil rights. As we will discuss in Chapter 5, federal authority has compelled states and localities to eliminate government-sponsored discrimination and, in some cases, to create compensatory opportunities for minorities and women. In 1954, for example, the Supreme Court held that racial segregation in public schools was unconstitutional on grounds that it violated the Fourteenth Amendment.[25]

The idea that Americans are equal in their rights regardless of where they reside has also been applied in other areas. As Chapter 4 discusses, states have been required to broaden individual rights of free expression and fair trial. An example is the Supreme Court's *Miranda* ruling, which requires police officers to inform crime suspects of their rights at the time of arrest.[26]

Of course, important differences remain in the rights and privileges of the residents of the separate states, as could be expected in a federal system. The death penalty, for example, is legal in some states but not others, and states differ greatly in terms of their services, such as the quality of their public schools. Nevertheless, national citizenship—the notion that Americans should be equal in their rights and opportunities regardless of the state in which they live—is a more encompassing idea today than in the past.

 **FEDERALISM TODAY**

Since the 1930s, the relation of the nation to the states has changed so fundamentally that dual federalism is no longer even a roughly accurate description of the American situation.

An understanding of the nature of federalism today requires a recognition of two countervailing trends. The first trend is a long-term *expansion* of national authority that began in the 1930s and continued for the next half century. The national government now operates in many policy areas that were once almost

Americans in an Interdependent World

Citizens of the World, Too?

Americans have a form of dual citizenship. They are citizens both of their nation and of the state in which they reside. They are subject to the laws of both levels of government and enjoy the rights and privileges of each of them.

Are Americans also becoming citizens of the world in a meaningful sense? In *The End of the Nation State*, Kenichi Ohmae argues that global economic change is altering traditional patterns of governing and citizenship. Nations' economies are now less within their own control as a result of mushrooming growth in international trade. Giant multinational corporations make decisions about production, supply, and pricing that have little relationship to national boundaries and that generate pressure for global free trade and international standards. And of course the trend toward international rules is not confined to those rules associated with economic globalization. Since its formation after World War II, the United Nations has issued countless resolutions and directives aimed at the internal affairs of particular countries.

In effect, as the world has become smaller, nations have faced pressure to give up some of their authority to international bodies. An example is the World Trade Organization (WTO), which requires its members, including the United States, to follow open trade policies buttressed by regulations that are designed to promote fair trade among the members. When WTO nations have a dispute, it is reviewed, and member states are expected to abide by the findings.

Compared with many nations, the United States has been somewhat reluctant to defer to collective agreements. During the past decade, for example, the United States has refused to sign the international treaty to ban land mines, has refused to sign the Kyoto accord to combat global warming, and has refused to back a permanent international war crimes tribunal. Nevertheless, more so than in the past, the United States, like other nations, has seen a need to give up some control over its national policies. In this respect, Americans are subject to the decisions of international bodies as well as those of their state and national governments.

GLOBAL Perspective

exclusively within the control of states and localities. The national government does not dominate in these policy areas, but it does play a significant role. Much of this national influence stems from social welfare policies that were enacted in the 1960s as part of President Lyndon Johnson's Great Society program, which included initiatives in health care, public housing, nutrition, welfare, urban development, and other areas previously reserved to states and localities.

The second, more recent trend involves a partial *contraction* of national authority. Known as *devolution*, this trend involves the "passing down" of authority from the national government to the state and local levels. Devolution has reversed the decades-long increase in federal authority, but only in some areas and then only to a moderate degree.

In short, the national government's policy authority has expanded greatly since the 1930s, even though that authority has been reduced somewhat in recent years. We will now explain each of these two trends in more detail.

Interdependency and Intergovernmental Relations

Interdependency is a primary reason why national authority increased dramatically in the twentieth century. Modern systems of transportation, commerce, and communication transcend local and state boundaries. These systems are national, and even international, in scope, which means that problems affecting Americans in one part of the country are likely to affect Americans living elsewhere. This situation has required Washington to assume a larger policy role. National problems ordinarily require national solutions.

Interdependency has also encouraged national, state, and local policymakers to work together to solve policy problems. This collaborative effort has been described as **cooperative federalism**.[27] The difference between this system of federalism and the older dual federalism has been likened to the difference between a marble cake, whose levels flow together, and a layer cake, whose levels are separate.[28]

cooperative federalism The situation in which the national, state, and local levels work together to solve problems.

Cooperative federalism is based on shared policy responsibilities rather than sharply divided ones. An example is the Medicaid program, which was created in 1965 as part of Johnson's Great Society initiative and provides health care for the poor. The Medicaid program is jointly funded by the national and state governments, operates within eligibility standards set by the national government, and gives states some latitude in determining the benefits that recipients receive. The Medicaid program is not an isolated example. Literally hundreds of policy programs today are run jointly by the national and state governments. In many cases, local governments are also involved. The following characteristics describe these programs:

- Jointly funded by the national and state governments (and sometimes by local governments)

- Jointly administered, with the states and localities providing most of the direct service to recipients and a national agency providing general administration

- Jointly determined, with both the state and national governments (and sometimes the local governments) having a say in eligibility and benefit levels, and with federal regulations, such as those prohibiting discrimination, providing an element of uniformity to the various state and local efforts

Cooperative federalism should not be interpreted to mean that the states are powerless and dependent. States have retained most of their traditional authority. In fact, the states have a larger influence in many policy areas than Washington does (see Figure 3–2). Nearly 95 percent of the funding for public schools, for example, is provided by states and localities, which also set most of the education standards, from teachers' qualifications to course requirements to the length of the school day. Moreover, the policy areas dominated by the states—such as education, law enforcement, and transportation—tend to be those that have the greatest impact on people's daily lives. Finally, contrary to what many Americans might think, state and local governments have nearly six times as many employees as the federal government.

Nevertheless, the federal government's involvement in policy areas traditionally reserved for the states has increased its influence on policy and diminished state-to-state policy differences.[29] Before the enactment of the federal Medicaid program in 1965, for example, poor people in many states were not

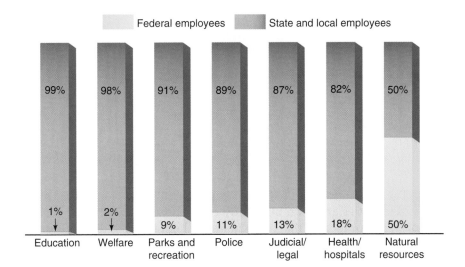

Federal employees   State and local employees

99%	98%	91%	89%	87%	82%	50%
1%	2%	9%	11%	13%	18%	50%
Education	Welfare	Parks and recreation	Police	Judicial/ legal	Health/ hospitals	Natural resources

Figure 3–2

Federal and State/Local Government Employees, as Percentage of All Government Employees Who Work in Selected Policy Areas
Although federal authority has reached into areas traditionally dominated by the state governments, state and local governments still dominate many policy areas. One indicator is the high percentage of government employees in selected areas who work for state or local governments.
Source: U.S. Bureau of the Census, 2004.

John Cornyn, attorney general of Texas (and subsequently U.S. Senator), speaks at a gathering of federal, state, and local law enforcement officials. Cooperative federalism brings together officials from all levels of government in joint efforts to solve common problems.

entitled to government-paid health care. Now most poor people are eligible regardless of where in the United States they live.

Government Revenues and Intergovernmental Relations

The interdependency of American society—the fact that developments in one area affect what happens elsewhere—is one of two major reasons why the federal government's policy role has expanded greatly since the early twentieth

Figure 3–3

Federal, State, and Local Shares of Government Tax Revenue
The federal government raises more tax revenues than all state and local governments combined.
Source: U.S. Department of Commerce, 2003.

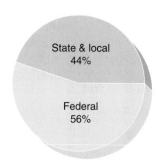

State & local
44%

Federal
56%

century. The other reason is the federal government's superior taxing capacity. States and localities are in an inherently competitive situation with regard to taxation. A state or locality that raises taxes too high will lose residents or firms to a location where taxes are lower. People and businesses are much less likely to move to another country in search of a lower tax rate. The result is that the federal government raises more tax revenues than do all fifty states and the thousands of local governments combined (see Figure 3–3).

Fiscal Federalism

fiscal federalism A term that refers to the expenditure of federal funds on programs run in part through states and localities.

grants-in-aid Federal cash payments to states and localities for programs they administer.

The federal government's revenue-raising advantage has helped make money the basis for many of the relations between the national government and the states and localities. **Fiscal federalism** refers to the expenditure of federal funds on programs run in part through state and local governments.[30] The federal government provides some or all of the money for a program through **grants-in-aid** (cash payments) to states and localities, which then administer the program.

The pattern of federal assistance to states and localities during the last half-century is shown in Figure 3–4. Federal grants-in-aid increased dramatically during this period. A sharp rise occurred in the late 1960s and early 1970s as a result of President Johnson's Great Society programs. Roughly one in every five dollars spent by local and state governments in recent decades has been raised not by them, but by the government in Washington (see "States in the Nation").

Cash grants to states and localities have extended Washington's influence on policy decisions. State and local governments can reject a grant-in-aid, but if they accept it they must spend it in the way specified by Congress. Also, because most grants require states to contribute matching funds, the federal programs in effect determine how states will allocate some of their own tax dollars. Federal grants have also pressured state and local officials to accept broad national goals, such as the elimination of racial and other forms of discrimination. A building constructed with the help of federal funds, for example, must be accessible to persons with disabilities.

Nevertheless, federal grants-in-aid also serve the policy interests of state and local officials. These officials have often complained that federal grants contain too many restrictions and infringe too much on their authority, but they have been eager to obtain the money because it permits them to offer services they could not otherwise provide. An example is a 1994 federal grant program that enabled local governments to put seventy-five thousand additional police officers on the streets.

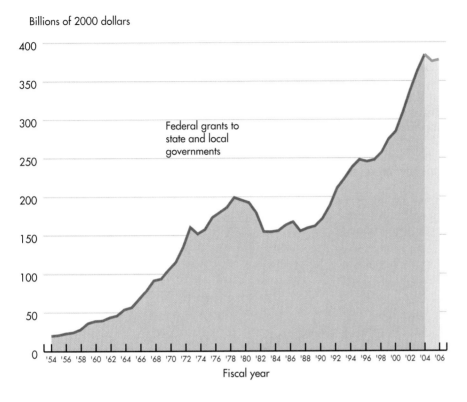

Billions of 2000 dollars

Federal grants to
state and local
governments

Fiscal year

Figure 3–4

Federal Grants to State and Local Governments
Federal aid to states and localities has increased dramatically since the 1950s.

Source: Office of Management and Budget, 2004. Figure is based on constant (2000) dollars in order to control for the effect of inflation.

Categorical and Block Grants

State and local governments receive two major types of assistance, categorical grants and block grants. These differ in the extent to which Washington defines the conditions of their use.

Categorical grants are the more restrictive. They can be used only for a designated activity. An example is funds directed for use in school lunch programs. These funds can be used only in support of school lunches; they cannot be diverted for other school purposes, such as the purchase of textbooks or the hiring of teachers. **Block grants** are less restrictive. The federal government specifies the general area in which the funds must be used, but state and local officials select the specific projects. A block grant targeted for the health area, for example, might give state and local officials leeway in deciding whether to use the money for hospital construction, medical equipment, or some other health care activity.

State and local officials naturally have preferred federal money that comes with fewer strings attached and thus have favored block grants. On the other hand, members of Congress have at times preferred categorical grants, because this form of assistance gives them more control over how state and local officials spend federal funds. Recently, however, officials at all levels have looked to block grants as the key to a more workable form of federalism. This tendency is part of a larger trend—devolution.

categorical grants Federal grants-in-aid to states and localities that can be used only for designated projects.

block grants Federal grants-in-aid that permit state and local officials to decide how the money will be spent within a general area, such as education or health.

STATES IN THE NATION

Federal Grants-in-Aid to the States

Federal assistance accounts for a significant share of state revenue, but the variation is considerable. Louisiana (with a third of its total revenue coming from federal grants-in-aid) is at one extreme. Nevada (a seventh of its revenue) is at the other extreme.

Q: Why do states in the South, where anti-Washington sentiment is relatively high, get more of their revenue from the federal government than most other states?

A: Many federal grant programs are designed to assist low-income people, and poverty is more widespread in the South. Moreover, southern states have traditionally provided fewer government services, and federal grants therefore constitute a larger proportion of their budgets.

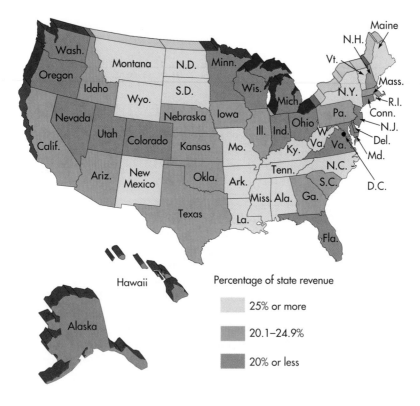

Percentage of state revenue

- 25% or more
- 20.1–24.9%
- 20% or less

Source: U.S. Bureau of the Census, 2003.

When the 1994 elections were over, Newt Gingrich declared that "1960s-style federalism is dead." As Speaker of the House of Representatives, Gingrich helped enact major changes in federal-state relations. Gingrich (on the left) is shown with Senate majority leader Robert Dole.

A New Federalism: Devolution

Devolution embodies the idea that American federalism will be improved by a shift in authority from the federal government to the state and local governments. Devolution, which is reshaping American federalism, is attributable to both practical and political developments.

devolution The passing down of authority from the national government to the state and local governments.

Budgetary Pressures and Public Opinion

As a practical matter, the growth in federal assistance had slowed by the early 1980s. The federal government was facing huge budget deficits, and awarding large new grants-in-aid to states and localities was not feasible.

As budgetary pressures intensified, relations among national, state, and local officials became increasingly strained. A slowdown in the annual increase in federal assistance had forced states and localities to pay an increasingly larger share of the costs of joint programs. As state and local governments raised taxes or cut other services to meet the costs of joint programs, taxpayer anger intensified. Some grant programs, such as food stamps and public housing, had not been very popular before the budget crunch and now came under even heavier criticism.

By the early 1990s, American federalism was positioned for a change. Two decades earlier, three-fourths of Americans had expressed confidence in Washington's ability to govern effectively. Less than half the public now held this view. A 1993 CBS News/New York Times survey indicated that 69 percent of Americans believed that "the federal government creates more problems than it solves."

The Republican Revolution

When the Republican party scored a decisive victory in the 1994 congressional elections, Newt Gingrich declared that "1960s-style federalism is dead." Republican lawmakers proposed to cut some programs, but, even more, they sought to increase state and local control.

That Republicans would lead the move to a more decentralized form of federalism was no surprise. Although members of both parties had supported expansions of federal authority, Republicans had more often questioned the overall result. Republican presidents Richard Nixon and Ronald Reagan, for example, proposed versions of a "new federalism" in which some areas of public policy for which the federal government had assumed responsibility would be returned to states and localities.[31]

Upon taking control of Congress in 1995, Republican lawmakers acted to reduce *unfunded mandates,* federal programs that require action by states or localities but provide no or insufficient funds to pay for it. For example, states and localities are required by federal law to make their buildings accessible to the physically handicapped, but Washington pays only part of the cost of these accommodations. In the Unfunded Mandates Reform Act of 1995, Congress eliminated some of these mandates, although under threat of a presidential veto it exempted those that deal with civil rights and liberties. The GOP-controlled Congress also took action to lump additional categorical grants into block grants, thereby giving states more control over how federal money would be spent.

The most significant legislative change came a year later, when the Republican Congress enacted the sweeping 1996 Welfare Reform Act. Its key element, the Temporary Assistance for Needy Families block grant (TANF), ended the decades-old program that granted cash assistance to every poor family with children. TANF restricts a family's eligibility for federal assistance to five years, and after two years a family head normally has to go to work for the benefits to continue. Moreover, TANF gives states wide latitude in setting benefit levels, eligibility criteria, and other regulations affecting aid to poor families. Ironically, TANF actually increased the level of federal grant spending because Washington picked up a larger share of welfare costs, but states gained more control over how the funds would be spent. (TANF and other aspects of the 1996 welfare reform legislation are discussed further in later chapters.)

After passage of the 1996 Welfare Reform Act, congressional efforts to reduce federal authority declined sharply. Devolution had hardly rolled back a half century of Washington-centered federalism, nor had it blunted new federal assistance programs. Among the federal initiatives enacted recently are grants for classroom modernization and the hiring of additional teachers. The war on terrorism has also expanded Washington's power. The federal Department of Homeland Security was created in 2002 to coordinate governmental efforts to deal with the terrorist threat. State and local agencies will be on the front lines of any response to a terrorist attack on U.S. soil, just as they were in New York City on September 11, 2001, but the coordination of their efforts as well as most of the investigative and intelligence work will be centered in Washington.

Devolution has resulted in a modification of fiscal and cooperative federalism rather than their demise. States and localities have recaptured some of their authority, but there are limits on how far the process can go. Because of the complexity of modern policy issues and the interdependency of American society, the states will never again have the level of autonomy that they enjoyed early in the twentieth century.

Devolution, Judicial Style

In the five decades after the 1930s, the Supreme Court granted Congress broad discretion in the enactment of policies affecting state and local governments. In *Garcia v. San Antonio Authority* (1985), for example, the Court held that federal minimum wage standards apply even to employees of state and local governments.[32] States and localities are prohibited from paying their employees less than the federally mandated minimum wage.

William H. Rehnquist

(1924–)

William H. Rehnquist graduated at the top of his Stanford Law School class and almost immediately got involved in politics, which led eventually to his appointment to the U.S. Supreme Court in 1971 as an associate justice. President Reagan appointed him chief justice when Warren Burger retired from that post in 1986. Rehnquist's major contribution to federalism has been a series of decisions that have limited Congress's authority to enact laws binding on the states.

In recent years, however, the Supreme Court has restricted congressional authority somewhat. Chief Justice William Rehnquist and some of the other Republican appointees on the Supreme Court believe that Congress in some instances has encroached on powers properly belonging to state governments. In *United States v. Lopez* (1995), for example, the Court cited the Tenth Amendment in striking down a federal law that prohibited the possession of guns within one thousand feet of a school. Congress had justified the law as an exercise of its commerce power, but the Court stated that the ban had "nothing to do with commerce, or any sort of economic activity."[33] Two years later, in *Printz v. United States* (1997), the Court struck down that part of the federal Handgun Violence Prevention Act (the so-called Brady bill) that required local law-enforcement officers to conduct background checks on prospective handgun buyers. The Court concluded that the provision violated the Tenth Amendment in that it ordered state officials, in this case police officers, to "enforce a federal regulatory program."[34] Congress can force federal officials to take such action, but it cannot require state officials to do so.

The Supreme Court has also limited federal authority over how state governments treat their own employees. In *Kimel v. Florida Board of Regents* (2000), for example, the Supreme Court held that states do not have to abide by a recent federal law that prohibits discrimination against older workers. Because age discrimination is not among the types of discrimination prohibited by the Fourteenth Amendment, the Court concluded that a state could decide for itself the age-related policies that will apply to its own employees.[35] In *Board of Trustees of the University of Alabama v. Garrett* (2002), the Court extended this principle to include people with disabilities, saying they cannot sue a state for violations of the Americans with Disabilities Act. In rejecting a lawsuit for monetary damages against the state of Alabama filed by a cancer patient who had been demoted after returning to her job with the state, the Supreme Court held that Alabama was immune from the suit because of the Eleventh Amendment, which protects a nonconsenting state from being sued by private individuals in a federal court. An exception occurs when a state is in violation of the Fourteenth Amendment. The Supreme Court held that disability discrimination

Debating the Issues

Does Congress Have Authority to Prevent States from Legalizing Marijuana Use for Medical Purposes?

Federalism has been a source of uncounted disputes between states and the national government. One of the more unusual is the current controversy over the medical use of marijuana and whether states have authority to create exceptions to a federal ban on marijuana. California is among a small number of states that in recent years have enacted laws approving the use of marijuana to relieve pain and other symptoms of illness. These laws, however, contradict the federal Controlled Substances Act, which prohibits the manufacture, distribution, and use of various drugs, including marijuana. In 2001, the Supreme Court ruled in *United States v. Oakland Cannabis Buyers' Cooperative* that Congress has the authority to prohibit a state from legalizing the use of marijuana for medical purposes.

Yes: There is no medical necessity exception to the Controlled Substances Act's prohibitions on manufacturing and distributing marijuana. Because that Act classifies marijuana as a schedule I controlled substance, it provides only one express exception to the prohibitions on manufacturing and distributing the drug: Government-approved research projects. . . . [T]he Act reflects a determination that marijuana has no medical benefits worthy of an exception (other than Government-approved research). Whereas other drugs can be dispensed and prescribed for medical use, the same is not true for marijuana, which has "no currently accepted medical use" at all. . . . Also rejected is the Cooperative's argument that a drug may be found medically necessary for a particular patient or class even when it has not achieved general acceptance as a medical treatment. It is clear from the text of the Act that Congress determined that marijuana has no medical benefits worthy of an exception granted to other drugs. The statute expressly contemplates that many drugs have a useful medical purpose, but it includes no exception at all for any medical use of marijuana. This Court is unwilling to view that omission as an accident and is unable, in any event, to override a legislative determination manifest in the statute.

—*Majority Opinion, Supreme Court of the United States*

No: Clearly, this is a blatant effort by the federal government to impose a national policy on the people in the states in question, people who have already elected a contrary policy. Federal officials do not agree with the policy the people have elected; they mean to override it, local rule notwithstanding. That effort cannot be justified under the 14th Amendment, for the states have not enacted a policy that runs roughshod over the privileges or immunities of their citizens or denies them due process or equal protection of the laws. No one in the states is complaining that the state government is violating his rights, which might require federal intervention. On the contrary, state policy in the states in question has been changed to recover rights, the rights of those who might want to prescribe or use medicinal marihuana. . . . If we want the federal government to exercise more power than it is authorized to exercise under our Constitution, there is a legitimate way to bring that about. We turn to Article V, where the Framers provided a method for amending the Constitution. Otherwise, we live within its limits, and leave the American people free to plan and live their own lives.

—*Roger Pilon, Cato Institute*

is not among the forms of discrimination expressly protected by the Fourteenth Amendment and, accordingly, that states cannot be sued without their consent in such cases.[36]

Although these court rulings limit federal authority, they do not constitute a radical change in federalism.[37] The rulings apply only to state employees, not to employees who work for private firms within a state. The latter are protected by federal age and disability laws. Furthermore, the Supreme Court has not always sided with the states on issues of employee protection. In *Nevada*

Department of Human Resources v. Hibbs (2003), for example, the Court rejected Nevada's claim to immunity from lawsuits filed under the federal Family and Medical Leave Act, which provides unpaid leave and a guarantee of job retention to employees who have a newborn baby or a seriously ill family member.[38]

Most important, the Supreme Court has not retreated from the principle that Congress's commerce and spending powers are broad and substantial. This principle, established in the 1930s, has enabled the federal government, through its grants-in-aid and business regulatory policies, to thrust its authority into policy areas once reserved for the states. In *Reno v. Condon* (2000), for example, the Supreme Court held that state governments, as well as private firms, had to comply with a federal law barring the selling of databases containing personal information obtained from automobile license applicants; the Court ruled that such databases are "an article of commerce" and thus subject to regulation through Congress's commerce power.[39] In short, American federalism, even with devolution, is a far different governing system today than it was prior to the 1930s.[40]

THE PUBLIC'S INFLUENCE: SETTING THE BOUNDARIES OF FEDERAL-STATE POWER

The ebb and flow in Washington's power in the twentieth century coincided closely with public opinion. The American people have had a decisive voice in determining the relationship between the federal and the state governments.

During the Great Depression, when it was clear that the states would be unable to help, Americans turned to Washington for relief. For people without jobs, the fine points of the Constitution were of little consequence. President Roosevelt's programs, though a radical departure from the past, quickly gained public favor. A 1936 Gallup Poll indicated, for example, that 61 percent of Americans supported Roosevelt's social security program, whereas only 27 opposed it. This support reflected a new public attitude: the federal government, not the states, was expected to take the lead in protecting Americans from economic hardship.[41]

The second great wave of federal social programs—Lyndon Johnson's Great Society—was also driven by public demands. Income and education levels had risen dramatically after the Second World War, and Americans wanted more and better services from government.[42] When the states were slow to respond, Americans pressured federal officials to act. The Medicare and Medicaid programs, which were created in 1965 and provide health care for the elderly and the poor respectively, are examples of Washington's response. So, too, was increased federal aid in areas such as education, housing, and transportation.

Public opinion was also behind the rollback in federal authority in the 1990s. Americans' dissatisfaction with federal deficits and policies provided the springboard for the Republican takeover of Congress in the 1994 midterm election, which led to policies aimed at devolving power to the states.[43] The capstone program was the widely popular 1996 Welfare Reform Act.

The continuing effect of public opinion on federalism can be seen in recent debates in the health care area. More than forty million Americans have no health insurance. They do not receive it through their employer and have either too much income to qualify for Medicaid or do not have enough income to afford health insurance on their own. The result has been growing pressure on government to develop programs that will reduce the ranks of the uninsured. Because most working-age Americans get their health insurance through employers and because commerce in today's world is mainly a national issue, the uninsured have looked to Washington rather than the states for an answer to their problem. Republican and Democratic leaders alike have responded. At all levels of government, their assumption has been that the health-insurance problem will have to be solved through action by Washington. In the 2004 presidential election campaign, for example, both John Kerry and George W. Bush proposed major new *federal* programs for helping the uninsured. Bush's program emphasized tax credits for lower-income Americans and tax-deductible health care savings accounts for the more affluent. Kerry proposed an expansion of Medicaid by raising the income level for eligibility and an expansion of employer-based insurance through increased tax credits to business firms. Both candidates pledged to make health insurance a top priority of their administration. Kerry said that, if the choice came down to an expansion of health insurance or an increase in the budget deficit, he would choose the health insurance option.

The public's role in defining the boundaries between federal and state power would come as no surprise to the Framers of the Constitution. For them, federalism was a pragmatic issue, one to be decided by the nation's needs rather than by inflexible rules. James Madison predicted as much when he said Americans would look to whichever level of government was more responsive to their interests. Indeed, each succeeding generation of Americans has seen fit to devise a balance of federal and state power that would serve its needs. Historian Daniel Boorstin said the true genius of the American people is their pragmatism, their willingness to try new ways when the old ones stop working.[44] In few areas of governing has Americans' ingenuity been more apparent than in their approach to federalism.

Summary   Self-Test
www.mhhe.com/pattersontad7

A foremost characteristic of the American political system is its division of authority between a national government and state governments. The first U.S. government, established by the Articles of Confederation, was essentially a union of the states.

In establishing the basis for a stronger national government, the U.S. Constitution also made provision for safeguarding state interests. The result was the creation of a federal system in which sovereignty was vested in both national and state governments. The Constitution enumerates the general powers of the national government and grants it implied powers through the "necessary and proper" clause. Other powers are reserved to the states by the Tenth Amendment.

From 1789 to 1865, the nation's survival was at issue. The states found it convenient at times to argue that their sovereignty took precedence over national authority. In the end, it took the Civil War to cement the idea that the United States was a union of people, not of states. From 1865 to 1937, federalism reflected the doctrine that certain policy areas were the exclusive responsibility of the national government, whereas responsibility in other policy areas belonged exclusively to the states. This constitutional position permitted the laissez-faire doctrine that big business was largely beyond governmental control. It also allowed the states to discriminate against African Americans in their public policies. Federalism in a form recognizable today began to emerge in the late 1930s.

In the areas of commerce, taxation, spending, civil rights, and civil liberties, among others, the federal government now plays an important role, one that is the inevitable consequence of the increasing complexity of American society and the interdependence of its people. National, state, and local officials now work closely together to solve the country's problems, a situation described as cooperative federalism. Grants-in-aid from Washington to the states and localities have been the chief instrument of national influence. States and localities have received billions in federal assistance; in accepting federal money, they have also accepted both federal restrictions on its use and the national policy priorities that underlie the granting of the money.

In recent years, the issue of the relationship between the nation and the states has again become a priority. Power has shifted downward to the states, and a new balance in the ever-evolving system of U.S. federalism is being achieved. This change, like changes throughout U.S. history, has sprung from the demands of the American people.

STUDY CORNER

Key Terms

block grants *(p. 93)*

categorical grants *(p. 93)*

commerce clause *(p. 85)*

confederacy *(p. 74)*

cooperative federalism *(p. 90)*

devolution *(p. 95)*

dual federalism *(p. 82)*

enumerated (expressed) powers *(p. 77)*

federalism *(p. 73)*

fiscal federalism *(p. 92)*

grants-in-aid *(p. 92)*

implied powers *(p. 78)*

"necessary and proper" clause (elastic clause) *(p. 78)*

reserved powers *(p. 79)*

sovereignty *(p. 73)*

supremacy clause *(p. 78)*

unitary system *(p. 74)*

Self-Test

1. Describing the United States as having a federal system of government means that:
   a. the states are not included in the power arrangement.
   b. constitutional authority for governing is divided between a national government on the one hand and the state governments on the other.
   c. the states are not bound by the rules and regulations of the national government.
   d. constitutional authority for governing is placed entirely in the hands of the states rather than the national government.
   e. America set up the exact same type of governing structure as England except for the establishment of a monarchy.

2. The significance of the Preamble of the Constitution reading "We the People" rather than "We the States" is that:
   a. there was to be no change in the power relationship between the states and nation in the new Constitution.
   b. the new Constitution symbolically recognized the people for winning the Revolutionary War.
   c. the states would not have to pay their war debts.
   d. the national government under the Constitution would have direct power over the people, which it did not have under the Articles of Confederation.

3. Which type of power was given to the states under the Constitution?
   a. the power to declare war
   b. supremacy over the national government
   c. reserved power
   d. necessary and proper power

4. The Supreme Court's opinion in *McCulloch v. Maryland*:
   a. ruled in favor of state-centered federalism.
   b. affirmed that national law is supreme over conflicting state law.
   c. established the principle of judicial review.
   d. declared the "necessary and proper" clause unconstitutional.

5. All **except** which one of the following describe trends in government revenues and intergovernmental relations in the United States?
   a. The federal government raises more revenues than all state and local governments combined.
   b. Unlike states and localities, the federal government controls the American dollar and has a nearly unlimited ability to borrow money to cover its deficits.
   c. The states possess the organizational resources to make fiscal federalism a workable arrangement.
   d. Financial assistance from the federal government to the states is gradually being eliminated.

6. The concept of devolution is used to explain:
   a. the current trend to shift authority from the federal government to state and local governments.
   b. the necessity for keeping federal and state spheres of responsibility absolutely separate from each other.
   c. a failed political revolution.
   d. increased recognition that the industrial economy is not confined by state boundaries and must be subject to national regulation.

F 7. Categorical grants allow the states more flexibility and discretion in the expenditure of funds than block grants do. (T/F)

T 8. The primary goal of the writers of the Constitution was to establish a national government strong enough to forge a union secure in its defense and open in its commerce. (T/F)

T 9. Dual federalism is the idea that the national and state governments should not interfere in each other's activities. (T/F)

F 10. Fiscal federalism involves the states raising money for programs and the federal government administering the programs. (T/F)

Critical Thinking

How have interdependency and the federal government's superior taxing power contributed to a larger policy role for the national government? Do you think these factors will increase or decrease in importance in the future? What will this trend mean for the future of American federalism? (You might find it helpful to think about these questions in the context of a specific policy area, such as the terrorist threat facing the country.)

Suggested Readings

Beer, Samuel H. *To Make a Nation: The Rediscovery of American Federalism.* Cambridge, Mass.: The Belknap Press of Harvard University, 1993. An innovative interpretive framework for understanding the impact of federalism and nationalism on the nation's development.

Cornell, Saul. *The Other Founders: Anti-Federalism and the Dissenting Tradition in America.* Chapel Hill: University of North Carolina Press, 1999. An analysis of Anti-Federalist thought, its origins, and its legacy.

Elkins, Stanley, and Eric McKitrick. *The Age of Federalism: The Early American Republic, 1788–1800.* New York: Oxford University Press, 1993. An award-winning book on the earliest period of American federalism.

Ross, William G. *A Muted Fury: Populists, Progressives, and Labor Unions Confront the Courts, 1890–1937.* Princeton, N.J.: Princeton University Press, 1993. A valuable study of the political conflict surrounding the judiciary's laissez-faire doctrine in the 1890–1937 period.

Teaford, John. *The Rise of the States: Evolution of American State Government.* Baltimore, Maryland: Johns Hopkins University Press, 2002. A historical assessment of state government that spans the past century.

Walker, David B. *The Rebirth of Federalism,* 2d ed. Chatham, N.J.: Chatham House Publishers, 2000. An optimistic assessment of the state of today's federalism.

Yarbrough, Tinsley. *The Rehnquist Court and the Constitution.* New York: Oxford University Press, 2000. A penetrating analysis of the Rehnquist Court, including its doctrine of federalism.

List of Websites

http://lcweb2.loc.gov/ammem/amlaw/lawhome.html

A site containing congressional documents and debates from 1774 to 1873.

http://www.csg.org/

The site of the Council of State Governments; includes current news from each of the states and basic information about their governments.

http://www.temple.edu/federalism

The site of the Center for the Study of Federalism, located at Temple University; offers information and publications on the federal system of government.

http://www.yale.edu/lawweb/avalon/federal/fed.htm

A documentary record of the Federalist Papers, the Annapolis Convention, the Articles of Confederation, the Madison Debates, and the U.S. Constitution.

Participate!

Federalism can be a contentious system in that a policy outcome may depend on whether the issue is settled at the national or the state level. Oregon's physician-assisted suicide law (see the chapter's opening example) is a case in point. Consider writing a letter expressing your view of what ought to be done in this case to the attorney general of the United States (U.S. Department of Justice, 950 Pennsylvania Avenue NW, Washington DC 20530-0001, or AskDOJ@usdoj.gov). In preparing your letter, you will need to address two questions: What is your opinion on the issue of physician-assisted suicide? What is your opinion on the question of whether an issue of this type should be properly decided at the state or the federal level? Note that your opinion on the issue may be at odds with your opinion on whether state or federal authority should prevail—for example, you may conclude that the issue should be decided by Oregon even though you personally oppose physician-assisted suicide.

Extra Credit

For up-to-the-minute *New York Times* articles, interactive simulations, graphics, study tools, and more links and quizzes, visit the text's Online Learning Center at www.mhhe.com/pattersontad7.

(Self-Test Answers: 1. b   2. d   3. c   4. b   5. d   6. a   7. F   8. T   9. T   10. F)

4

Civil Liberties:
Protecting Individual Rights

> A bill of rights is what the people are entitled to against every
> government on earth, general or particular, and what no just
> government should refuse, or rest on inference.
>
> —*Thomas Jefferson*[1]

R obert and Sarisse Creighton and their three children were asleep when FBI agents and local police broke into their home in the middle of the night. Brandishing guns, the officers searched the house for a relative of the Creightons who was suspected of bank robbery. When asked to show a search warrant, the officers said, "You watch too much TV." The suspect was not there, and the officers left as abruptly as they had entered. The Creightons sued the FBI agent in charge, Russell Anderson, for violating their Fourth Amendment right against unlawful search.

The Creightons won a temporary victory when the U.S. Circuit Court of Appeals for the Eighth Circuit—noting that individuals are constitutionally protected against warrantless searches unless officers have good reason ("probable cause") for a search and unless they have good reason ("exigent circumstances") for conducting that search without a warrant—concluded that Anderson had been derelict in his duty. In the judgment of the appellate court, Anderson should have sought a warrant from a judge, who would have decided whether a search of the Creightons' home was justified.

The Supreme Court of the United States overturned the lower court's ruling. The Court's majority opinion stated: "We have recognized that it is inevitable that law enforcement officials will in some cases reasonably but mistakenly conclude that probable cause is present, and we have indicated that in such cases those officials . . . should not be held personally liable." Justice John Paul Stevens and two other justices sharply dissented. Stevens accused the Court's majority of showing "remarkably little fidelity" to the Fourth Amendment.[2] Civil liberties groups claimed that the Court's decision gave police an open invitation to invade people's homes on the slightest pretext. On the other hand, law enforcement officials praised the decision, saying that a ruling in the Creightons' favor would have made them hesitant to pursue suspects for fear of a lawsuit whenever the search failed to produce the culprit.

As this case illustrates, issues of individual rights are complex and political. No right is absolute. For example, the Fourth Amendment protects Americans not from *all* searches but from *unreasonable* searches. The public would be unsafe if law officials could never pursue a suspect into a home. Yet the public would also be unsafe if police could invade homes anytime they wanted. The challenge for a civil society is to establish a level of police authority that balances the demands of public safety with those of personal freedom. The balance point, however, is always subject to dispute. Did FBI agent Anderson have sufficient cause for a warrantless search of the Creightons' home?

civil liberties The fundamental individual rights of a free society, such as freedom of speech and the right to a jury trial, which in the United States are protected by the Bill of Rights.

Bill of Rights The first ten amendments to the Constitution, which set forth basic protections for individual rights to free expression, fair trial, and property.

Or was his evidence so weak that his forcible entry constituted an unreasonable search? Law enforcement officials and civil liberties groups had widely different opinions on these questions. Nor did the justices of the Supreme Court hold a uniform view. Six justices sided with Anderson, and three backed the Creightons' position.

This chapter examines issues of **civil liberties**: specific individual rights, such as freedom of speech and protection against self-incrimination, that are constitutionally protected against infringement by government. As seen in Chapter 2, the Constitution's failure to enumerate individual freedoms led to demands for the **Bill of Rights.** Enacted in 1791, these first ten amendments to the Constitution specify certain rights of life, liberty, and property that the national government is obliged to respect. A later amendment, the Fourteenth, became the basis for protecting these rights from actions by state and local governments.

Rights have full meaning only as they are protected in law. A constitutional guarantee of free speech, for example, is worth no more than the paper on which it is written if authorities are able to stop people from speaking freely. Judicial action is important in defining what people's rights mean in practice and in setting and enforcing limits on official action that may infringe on these rights. In some areas, the judiciary devises a specific test to determine whether government action is lawful. A test applied in the area of free speech, for example, is whether general rules (such as restrictions on the time and place of a public gathering) are applied fairly to all groups. Government officials do not meet this test if they apply one set of rules for groups that they like and a harsher set of rules for those they dislike.

Issues of individual rights have become increasingly complex and important. The writers of the Constitution could not possibly have foreseen the United States of the early twenty-first century, with its huge national government, enormous corporations, pervasive mass media, urban crowding, and vulnerability to terrorist acts. These developments are potential threats to individual liberty, and the judiciary in recent decades has seen fit to expand the rights to which individuals are entitled. However, these rights are constantly being balanced against competing individual rights and society's collective interests. The Bill of Rights operates in an untidy world where people's highest aspirations collide with their worst passions, and it is at this juncture that issues of civil liberties arise. Should an admitted murderer be entitled to recant a confession? Should the press be allowed to print military secrets whose publication might jeopardize national security? Should prayer be allowed in the public schools? Should extremist groups be allowed to publicize their messages of prejudice and hate? Such questions are among the subjects of this chapter, which focuses on the following major points:

- *Freedom of expression is the most basic of democratic rights, but like all rights, it is not unlimited.* Free expression recently has been strongly supported by the Supreme Court.

- *"Due process of law" refers to legal protections (primarily procedural safeguards) designed to ensure that individual rights are respected by government.*

- *During the last half-century particularly, the civil liberties of individual Americans have been substantially broadened in law and given greater judicial protection from*

Protesters in San Francisco demonstrate against the possibility of war with Iraq. Freedom of expression is widely regarded as the most basic of rights because other aspects of a free society, such as open and fair elections, are dependent on it.

action by all levels of government. Of special significance has been the Supreme Court's use of the Fourteenth Amendment to protect these individual rights from action by state and local governments.

- *Individual rights are constantly being weighed against the demands of majorities and the collective needs of society.* All political institutions are involved in this process, as is public opinion, but the judiciary plays the central role in it and is the institution that is most partial to the protection of civil liberties.

 FREEDOM OF EXPRESSION

Freedom of political expression is the most basic of democratic rights. Unless citizens can openly express their political opinions, they cannot properly influence their government or act to protect their other rights. As the Supreme Court concluded in 1984, "The freedom to speak one's mind is not only an aspect of individual liberty—and thus a good unto itself—but also is essential to the common quest for truth and the vitality of society as a whole."[3]

It is for such reasons that the First Amendment provides the foundation for **freedom of expression**—the right of individual Americans to hold and communicate views of their choosing. For many reasons, such as a desire to conform to social pressure or a fear of harassment, Americans do not always choose to express themselves freely. Moreover, freedom of expression, like other rights,

freedom of expression
Americans' freedom to communicate their views, the foundation of which is the First Amendment rights of freedom of conscience, speech, press, assembly, and petition.

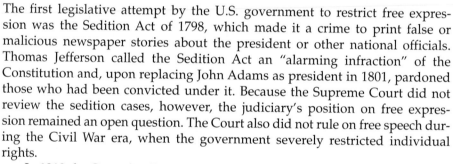

Oliver Wendell Holmes Jr.

(1841–1935)

Oliver Wendell Holmes Jr. was nominated for the Supreme Court in 1901 by President Theodore Roosevelt and served for more than three decades. The son of a famous writer and physician, Holmes was a leading intellectual force on the Court. An advocate of judicial restraint, he nonetheless argued that the law had to keep pace with society. He helped lay the foundation for an interpretation of the First Amendment that limited government's ability to restrict free expression.

is not absolute. It does not entitle individuals to say or do whatever they want, to whomever they want, whenever they want. Free expression can be denied, for example, if it endangers national security, wrongly damages the reputations of others, or deprives others of their basic freedoms. Nevertheless, the First Amendment provides for freedom of expression by prohibiting laws that would abridge the freedoms of conscience, speech, press, assembly, and petition.

In recent decades, free expression has been vigorously protected by the courts. Today, under most circumstances, Americans can freely express their political views without fear of governmental interference. In earlier times, however, Americans were less free to express their opinions.

The Early Period: The Uncertain Status of the Right of Free Expression

Historical Background

The first legislative attempt by the U.S. government to restrict free expression was the Sedition Act of 1798, which made it a crime to print false or malicious newspaper stories about the president or other national officials. Thomas Jefferson called the Sedition Act an "alarming infraction" of the Constitution and, upon replacing John Adams as president in 1801, pardoned those who had been convicted under it. Because the Supreme Court did not review the sedition cases, however, the judiciary's position on free expression remained an open question. The Court also did not rule on free speech during the Civil War era, when the government severely restricted individual rights.

In 1919 the Court finally ruled on a case that challenged the national government's authority to restrict free expression. The defendant had been convicted under the 1917 Espionage Act, which prohibited forms of dissent, including the distribution of antiwar leaflets, that could harm the nation's effort in World War I. In *Schenck v. United States* (1919), the Court unanimously ruled that the Espionage Act was constitutional. In the opinion written by Justice Oliver Wendell Holmes, the Court said that Congress could restrict speech that was "of such a nature as to create a clear and present danger" to the nation's security. In a famous passage, Holmes argued that not even the First Amendment would permit a person to falsely yell "Fire!" in a crowded theater and create a panic that could kill or injure innocent people.[4]

clear-and-present-danger test A test devised by the Supreme Court in 1919 in order to define the limits of free speech in the context of national security. According to the test, government cannot abridge political expression unless it presents a clear and present danger to the nation's security.

Although the *Schenck* decision upheld a law that limited free expression, it also established a standard—the **clear-and-present-danger test**—for determining when government had exceeded its constitutional authority to restrict speech. Political speech that was not a clear and present danger could not be banned by government. (The clear-and-present-danger test was later replaced by an even more stringent standard—the imminent-lawless-action test—that is discussed later in the chapter.)

Civil Liberties and National Security

At the writing of the Constitution, Alexander Hamilton claimed that war is always a threat to civil liberties. The freedoms that people enjoy in peacetime are restricted in wartime. The current war on terrorism is an example. After September 11, 2001, for example, Congress gave the Central Intelligence Agency (CIA) authority to engage in certain types of clandestine domestic surveillance. The CIA may, for instance, read secret grand jury testimony without first seeking a judge's approval to do so.

When the CIA was created in 1947 as part of America's effort at containing the spread of communism, President Harry Truman insisted that the CIA's surveillance activities be limited to foreign soil. Fascist and communist governments, said Truman, spy on their citizens. Democratic governments do not. Accordingly, the CIA was prohibited from conducting surveillance operations within the United States. Two decades later, Congress discovered that the CIA had violated its mandate. The CIA had tapped Americans' phones, opened their mail, and burglarized their homes and offices. Congress responded with new restrictions on and closer oversight of the CIA. This action, however, had the effect of limiting coordination between the CIA and the FBI, which, according to some analysts, contributed to the failure of U.S. officials to uncover plans for the terrorist attacks on the World Trade Center and Pentagon on September 11, 2001. Although both agencies had information that indicated a major terrorist act was in the offing, they did not closely coordinate the intelligence reports they had gathered.

Nearly every analyst now agrees that domestic surveillance will have to increase if America is to be made safe from terrorism. Many analysts also believe that the CIA should be part of that effort, although they disagree on the extent of that authority. The CIA itself would like extensive powers. In 2002, for example, it requested authority to intercept e-mail messages routed to the United States from abroad without having to obtain a warrant from a judge.

Where do you stand on the issue of domestic surveillance? What trade-offs between personal freedom and physical security are you willing to make in the context of the war on terrorism? How far would you let the CIA go in conducting surveillance on American citizens? Would you make a distinction between American citizens and the noncitizens who live here, granting the CIA more leeway in the case of the latter group?

John Ashcroft, the attorney general of the United States, has said that people who oppose greatly expanded surveillance and detention as tools in the war on terrorism are, in effect, choosing to side with the terrorists. *New York Times* columnist Anthony Lewis argues that, if the war on terrorism is waged at the expense of civil liberties, Americans will have lost sight of what they are fighting to protect. Which view comes closer to your own?

The Modern Period: Protecting Free Expression

Until the twentieth century, the tension between national security interests and free expression was not a pressing dilemma for the United States. The country's great size and ocean barriers provided protection from potential enemies, minimizing concerns about internal subversion. World War I, however, intruded on America's isolation, and World War II brought it to an abrupt end. Since then, Americans' rights of free expression have been defined largely in the context of national security concerns.

This tendency is clearly evident in recent government actions in the war on terrorism, including the USA Patriot Act of 2001 (see Chapter 1). The government's powers of surveillance and detention have been expanded, narrowing the legal protections provided to people even remotely suspected of having ties to terrorist activity. Some of these new powers have been reviewed by the judiciary; others are sure to be tested in future cases.

Free Speech and Assembly

During the cold war that developed after World War II, many Americans perceived the Soviet Union as bent on destroying the United States, and the Supreme Court allowed government to place substantial limits on free expression. In 1951, for example, the Court upheld the convictions of eleven members of the U.S. Communist party who had been prosecuted under a law that made it illegal to express support for the forceful overthrow of the U.S. government.[5]

Historical Background

By the late 1950s, however, fear of internal communist subversion was subsiding, and the Supreme Court expanded the scope of permissible speech.[6] The Court implicitly embraced a legal doctrine first outlined by Justice Harlan Fiske Stone in 1938. Stone argued that First Amendment rights of free expression are the basis of Americans' liberty and ought to have a "preferred position" in the law. If government can control what people know and say, it can manipulate their opinions and thereby deprive them of the right to decide for themselves how they will be governed. Therefore, government should be broadly prohibited from restricting free expression.[7]

This philosophy has led the Supreme Court to rule that government officials must show that national security is directly and substantially imperiled before they can lawfully prohibit citizens from speaking out or assembling. For example, during the Vietnam era, despite the largest sustained protest movement in America's history, not a single individual was convicted solely for speaking out against the government's war policy. (Some dissenters were found guilty on other grounds, such as inciting riots and assaulting the police.)

symbolic speech Action (for example, the waving or burning of a flag) for the purpose of expressing a political opinion.

The Supreme Court's protection of **symbolic speech** has been less substantial than its protection of verbal speech. For example, the Court in 1968 upheld the conviction of a Vietnam protester who had burned his draft registration card. The Court said that government can prohibit action that threatens a legitimate public interest as long as the main purpose of the policy is not to restrict free expression. The Court concluded that the federal law prohibiting the destruction of draft cards was designed primarily to protect the military's need for soldiers, not to prevent people from criticizing government policy.[8]

The Supreme Court, however, has not granted the government broad power to restrict symbolic speech. In 1989, for example, the Court ruled that the burning of the American flag is a protected form of free expression. The ruling came in the case of Gregory Lee Johnson, a member of the Communist Youth Brigade, who had set fire to a U.S. flag outside the hall in Dallas where the 1984 Republican National Convention was being held. The Supreme Court rejected the state of Texas's argument that flag burning is, in every instance, an imminent danger to public safety. "If there is a bedrock principle underlying the First Amendment," the Court ruled in the *Johnson* case, "it is that the Government may not prohibit the expression of an idea simply because society finds the idea itself offensive or disagreeable."[9] (A year later the Court struck down a new federal statute that made it a federal crime to burn or deface the flag.[10])

After the terrorist attacks on the World Trade Center and the Pentagon, the American flag suddenly appeared on offices, homes, and vehicles throughout the country. Kevin Sabia of Kent, Connecticut, chose to paint his house like a flag. Americans can also choose to burn the flag. In 1989, the Supreme Court declared flag burning to be a constitutionally protected right of free expression.

Press Freedom and Prior Restraint

Freedom of the press has also received strong judicial support in recent decades. In *New York Times Co. v. United States* (1971), the Court ruled that the *Times*'s publication of the "Pentagon papers" (secret government documents revealing official deception about the success of the Vietnam war policy) could not be blocked by the Department of Justice, which claimed that publication would hurt the war effort. The documents had been illegally obtained by antiwar activists, who had turned them over to the *Times* for publication. The Court ruled that "any system of prior restraints" on the press is unconstitutional unless the government can clearly justify the restriction.[11]

The unacceptability of **prior restraint**—government prohibition of speech or publication before the fact—is basic to the current doctrine of free expression. The Supreme Court has said that any attempt by government to prevent expression carries "a 'heavy presumption' against its constitutionality."[12] News organizations and individuals are legally responsible after the fact for what they report or say (for example, they can be sued by an individual whose reputation is wrongly damaged by their words), but generally government cannot stop them in advance from expressing their views. One exception is the reporting on U.S. military operations during wartime. The courts have allowed the government to censor reports filed by journalists who are granted access to the battlefront. The courts have also upheld the government's authority to ban uncensored publications by certain past and present government employees, such as CIA agents, who have taken part in classified national security activities.

prior restraint Government prohibition of speech or publication before the fact, which is presumed by the courts to be unconstitutional unless the justification for it is overwhelming.

Free Expression and State Governments

In 1790 Congress rejected a proposed amendment to the Constitution that would have applied the Bill of Rights to the states. Thus, the freedoms guaranteed in the Bill of Rights were initially protected only from action by the national government, a constitutional arrangement that the Supreme Court upheld in *Barron v. Baltimore* (1833).[13] The effect was that the Bill of Rights had little practical meaning in the lives of ordinary Americans because state and local governments carry out most of the activities, such as law enforcement, in which people's rights are at issue.

Not until the twentieth century did the Supreme Court begin to protect individual rights from infringement by state and local governments. The vehicle for this change was the **due process clause of the Fourteenth Amendment** to the Constitution.

The Fourteenth Amendment and Selective Incorporation

The Fourteenth Amendment, ratified in 1868, includes a clause that forbids a state from depriving any person of life, liberty, or property without due process of law (due process refers to the legal procedures that have been established as a means of protecting individuals' rights). Six decades later, the Supreme Court in *Gitlow v. New York* (1925) decided that the Fourteenth Amendment applied to state action in the area of freedom of expression. Although the Court upheld Benjamin Gitlow's conviction for violating a New York law making it illegal to advocate the violent overthrow of the U.S. government, the Court said that the states were not completely free to limit expression:

> For present purposes we may and do assume that freedom of speech and of the press—which are protected by the First Amendment from abridgement by Congress—are among the fundamental personal rights and "liberties" protected by the due process clause of the Fourteenth Amendment from impairment by the states.[14]

There is no indication that Congress, when it passed the Fourteenth Amendment after the Civil War, meant it to protect First Amendment rights from state action. The Supreme Court justified its new interpretation in the *Gitlow* case by referring to **selective incorporation**—the incorporation into the Fourteenth Amendment of certain provisions of the Bill of Rights, particularly freedom of speech and press, so that these rights can be protected from infringement by the states. The Court reasoned that the Fourteenth Amendment's due process clause would be largely meaningless if states had the power to stop their residents from speaking openly.

This interpretation of the Fourteenth Amendment provided the Court with a legal basis for striking down state laws that infringed unreasonably on free expression. But the Supreme Court acts only in the context of specific cases; it does not have the authority to issue blanket rulings. Accordingly, further action by the Court did not occur until appropriate cases arose and reached the Court on appeal from lower courts. Within a dozen years (see Table 4–1), the Court had received four cases that enabled it to invalidate state laws restricting expression in the areas of speech (*Fiske v. Kansas*), press (*Near v. Minnesota*), religion (*Hamilton v. Regents, University of California*), and assembly and petition (*DeJonge v. Oregon*).[15] The *Near* decision is the most famous of these rulings. Jay Near was the publisher of a Minneapolis weekly newspaper that regularly made scurrilous attacks on blacks, Jews, Catholics, and labor union leaders. His paper was

TABLE 4–1	**Selective Incorporation of Rights of Free Expression** In the 1920s and 1930s, the Supreme Court selectively incorporated the free-expression provisions of the First Amendment into the Fourteenth Amendment so that these rights would be protected from infringement by the states.	

SUPREME COURT CASE	YEAR	CONSTITUTIONAL RIGHT AT ISSUE
Gitlow v. New York	1925	Fourteenth Amendment protection of free expression
Fiske v. Kansas	1927	Free speech
Near v. Minnesota	1931	Free press
Hamilton v. Regents, U. of California	1934	Religious freedom
DeJonge v. Oregon	1937	Freedom of assembly and of petition

closed down on authority of a state law banning "malicious, scandalous, or defamatory" publications. Near appealed the shutdown, and the Supreme Court ruled in his favor, saying that the Minnesota law was "the essence of censorship."[16]

Limiting the Authority of States to Restrict Expression

Since the 1930s, the Supreme Court has broadly protected freedom of expression from action by the states and by local governments, which derive their authority from the states. The Court has held that the states cannot restrict free expression except when it is almost certain to lead directly to lawless action. A leading free speech case was *Brandenburg v. Ohio* (1969). The appellant was a Ku Klux Klan member who, in a speech delivered at a Klan rally, said that "revenge" might have to be taken if the national government "continues to suppress the white Caucasian race." He was convicted of advocating force under an Ohio law prohibiting criminal syndicalism, but the Supreme Court reversed the conviction, saying that the First Amendment prohibits a state from suppressing speech that advocates the unlawful use of force "except where such advocacy is directed to inciting or producing imminent lawless action, and is likely to produce such action."[17]

This test—the likelihood of **imminent lawless action**—is a strong limit on the government's power to restrict expression. It is rare for words alone to incite others to resort to immediate unlawful action. In effect, Americans are free to say almost anything they want on political issues.

The Court has broadly held that hate speech cannot be silenced. In a unanimous 1992 opinion, the Court struck down a St. Paul, Minnesota, ordinance making it a crime to engage in speech likely to arouse "anger or alarm" on the basis of "race, color, creed, religion or gender." The Court said that the First Amendment prohibits government from "silencing speech on the basis of its content."[18] This protection of violent *speech* does not, however, extend to violent *crimes*, such as assault, motivated by racial or other forms of prejudice. A Wisconsin law that provided for increased sentences for such crimes was

imminent lawless action test
A legal test that says government cannot lawfully suppress advocacy that promotes lawless action unless such advocacy is aimed at producing, and is likely to produce, imminent lawless action.

Exercising their right of free expression, antiabortion protesters gather outside a government building. Individuals do not have a constitutional right to demonstrate in any place at any time, but government is required to accommodate requests for marches and other displays of free expression.

challenged as a violation of the First Amendment. In a unanimous 1993 opinion, the Court said that the law was aimed at "conduct unprotected by the First Amendment" rather than the defendant's speech.[19]

In a key case involving freedom of assembly, the U.S. Supreme Court in 1977 upheld a lower-court ruling against local ordinances of Skokie, Illinois, that had been invoked to prevent a parade there by the American Nazi party.[20] Skokie had a large Jewish population, including many survivors of Nazi Germany's concentration camps. The Supreme Court held that the right of free expression takes precedence over the mere *possibility* that exercising the right may have undesirable consequences. Before government can lawfully prevent a speech or rally, it must offer persuasive evidence that an evil will almost certainly result from the event and must also demonstrate the lack of alternative ways (such as assigning police officers to control the crowd) to prevent the evil from happening.

The Supreme Court has recognized that freedom of speech and assembly may conflict with the routines of daily life. Accordingly, individuals do not have the right to hold a public rally in the middle of a busy intersection during rush hour, nor do they have the right to command immediate access to a public auditorium. The Court has held that public officials can regulate the time, place, and conditions of public assembly, provided that these regulations are reasonable and are applied evenhandedly to all groups, including those that hold unpopular views.[21]

In general, the Supreme Court's position is that the First Amendment makes any government effort to regulate the *content* of a message highly suspect. In the flag-burning case, Texas was regulating the content of the message—contempt for the flag and the principles it represents. Texas could not have been regulating the act itself, for the Texas government's own method of disposing of worn-out flags is to burn them. But a content-neutral regulation (no public rally can be held in the middle of a busy intersection at rush hour) is acceptable as long as it is reasonable and does not discriminate against certain groups or ideas.

Libel and Slander

The constitutional right of free expression is not a legal license to avoid responsibility for the consequences of what is said or written. If false information that greatly harms a person's reputation is published (**libel**) or spoken (**slander**), the injured party can sue for damages. The ease of winning such suits has obvious implications for free expression. Individuals and organizations are less likely to express themselves openly if they stand a good chance of subsequently losing a libel or slander suit.

libel Publication of material that falsely damages a person's reputation.

slander Spoken words that falsely damage a person's reputation.

Libel is the more compelling issue for the political process because it affects the news media's ability to criticize public officials. A leading decision in this area was *New York Times Co. v. Sullivan* (1964), in which the Court overruled an Alabama state court that had found the *Times* guilty of libel for printing an advertisement criticizing Alabama officials for physically assaulting black civil rights demonstrators. The Court ruled that libel of a public official requires proof of actual malice, which was defined as a knowing or reckless disregard for the truth.[22] It is very difficult to prove that a publication has acted with reckless or deliberate disregard for the truth. In fact, no federal official has won a libel judgment against a news organization in the four decades since the *Sullivan* ruling. (The press has less protection against a libel judgment when its target is a private person rather than a public official. The courts regard the communication of information about private individuals as less basic to the democratic process than information about public officials, and therefore the press must take greater care in ascertaining the validity of claims made about an ordinary citizen.)

The *Sullivan* decision notwithstanding, the greatest protection against a libel judgment is truthfulness. As long as what is printed or broadcast is true, however damaging it might be to someone's reputation, the news organization is normally protected against a libel judgment. The Court has held that expressions of opinion deserve "full constitutional protection" against the charge of libel as long as they do not contain "a provably false factual connotation."[23]

Obscenity

Obscenity is a form of expression that is not protected by the First Amendment. However, the Supreme Court has found it difficult to define which publicly disseminated sexual materials are obscene and which are not. The Court has struggled to develop a standard that gives predictability to the law without endangering First Amendment rights.

The Court's first test was established in *Roth v. United States* (1957), when the Court defined obscenity as material that "taken as a whole" appealed to

Congress has attempted to regulate sexually explicit material on the Internet in an effort to prevent it from reaching children. The Supreme Court has held that portions of this legislation infringe on the free-speech rights of adults and has urged lawmakers to devise less restrictive ways of regulating sexually explicit content on the Internet.

"prurient interest" and had no "redeeming social significance." The perspective was to be that of "the average person, applying contemporary community standards."[24] This test proved unworkable. Even the justices, when personally examining allegedly obscene material, would argue over whether it appealed to prurient interest and was without redeeming social value. In the end, they usually concluded that it had at least some social significance.

In *Miller v. California* (1973), the Court narrowed the "contemporary community standards" to the local level. The Court said that what might offend residents of "Mississippi might be found tolerable in Las Vegas."[25] But even this test proved too restrictive. The Court subsequently ruled that material cannot be judged obscene simply because the "average" local resident might object to it. "Community standards" were to be judged in the context of a "reasonable person"—someone whose outlook is broad enough to evaluate the material on its overall merit rather than its most objectionable feature. The Court later also modified its content standard, saying that the material must be of a "particularly offensive type."[26] These efforts illustrate the difficulty of defining obscenity and, even more, of developing a legal standard that can be applied evenhandedly by courts when an obscenity case arises.

The Supreme Court has distinguished between obscene materials in public places and those in the home. A unanimous ruling in 1969 held that what adults read and watch in the privacy of their homes cannot be made a crime.[27] The Court created an exception to this rule in 1990 by upholding an Ohio law making it a crime to possess pornographic photographs of children.[28] The Court reasoned that the purchase of such material encouraged producers to use children in the making of pornographic materials, which is a crime. Consistent with this reasoning, the Court in *Ashcroft v. Free Speech Coalition* (2002) held that pictures of adults digitally altered to look like children cannot be banned because children are not used in the production of this type of material.[29]

The shielding of children from the effects of the demand for sexually explicit material has also affected cable television policy. In 1996 the Supreme Court held that although cable operators are not required to scramble the signal of channels that provide adult programming, they must do so for individual subscribers who request that the signal be scrambled.[30]

The Internet can also be a source of indecent material. To prevent such material from reaching children, Congress in 1996 passed the Communications Decency Act, which made it a federal crime to use the Internet to transmit obscene material to someone under eighteen years of age or to post obscene material in a way that made it available to minors. In a 1997 ruling, *Reno v. American Civil Liberties Union*, the Supreme Court declared the Decency Act unconstitutional on the grounds that its restrictions were so broad that they had the effect of suppressing material intended for adults.[31] Congress responded with the

Child Online Protection Act (COPA) of 1998, which defines indecency according to "contemporary community standards." In *Ashcroft v. American Civil Liberties Union* (2004), the Supreme Court blocked enforcement of the 1998 law, saying that it "likely violates the First Amendment." The case was returned to a lower court, which was asked to decide in trial whether less restrictive measures, such as filtering software, would be equally effective in keeping indecent material beyond the reach of children.[32]

FREEDOM OF RELIGION

Free religious expression is the precursor of free political expression, at least within the English tradition of limited government. England's Glorious, or Bloodless, Revolution of 1689 centered on the issue of religion and resulted in the Act of Toleration, which gave members of all Protestant sects the right to worship freely and publicly. The English philosopher John Locke (1632–1704) extended this principle, arguing that legitimate government could not inhibit free expression, religious or otherwise. The First Amendment reflects this tradition, providing for freedom of religion along with freedom of speech, press, assembly, and petition.

Historical Background

In regard to religion, the First Amendment reads: "Congress shall make no law respecting an establishment of religion, or prohibiting the free exercise thereof." The prohibition on laws aimed at "establishment of religion" (the establishment clause) and its "free exercise" (the free-exercise clause) applies to states and localities through the Fourteenth Amendment.

The Establishment Clause

The **establishment clause** has been interpreted by the courts to mean that government may not favor one religion over another or support religion over no religion. (This position contrasts with that of a country such as England, where Anglicanism is the official, or "established," state religion, though no religion is prohibited.) The Supreme Court's interpretation of the establishment clause has been described as maintaining a "wall of separation" between church and state that includes a prohibition on nondenominational support for religion.[33] The Court has taken a pragmatic approach, however, by permitting some establishment activities but disallowing others. The Court has permitted states to provide secular textbooks for use by church-affiliated schools,[34] for instance, but has forbidden states to pay part of the salaries of teachers in church-affiliated schools.[35] Such distinctions follow no strict logic but are based on judgments of whether government action involves "*excessive* entanglement with religion."[36] In allowing public funds to be used by religious schools for secular textbooks but not for teachers' salaries, the courts have indicated that, whereas it is relatively easy to ascertain whether the content of a particular textbook promotes religion, it would be much harder to determine whether a particular teacher was promoting religion in the classroom.[37]

In a key 2002 decision, however, the Supreme Court upheld an Ohio law that allows students in Cleveland's failing public schools to receive a tax-supported voucher to attend private or parochial school. The Court's majority

establishment clause The First Amendment provision stating that government may not favor one religion over another or favor religion over no religion, and prohibiting Congress from passing laws respecting the establishment of religion.

Should "Under God" Be Removed from the Pledge of Allegiance?

The Pledge of Allegiance originally did not contain the words "under God." They were added by Congress in 1954 when fear of communism was high. In 2004 the Supreme Court heard a case that addressed the issue of whether the words "under God" in the Pledge of Allegiance violate the Constitution's establishment clause. Michael Newdow, an atheist, had sued his daughter's school (California's Elk Grove United School District), claiming that the school-required Pledge of Allegiance violates her religious liberty. Neither sides' position in the case prevailed. The Supreme Court declined to rule on the substance of the arguments, concluding that Newdow, as a non-custodial parent, did not have the legal standing required to bring suit on his daughter's behalf. The school district argued that the words are ceremonial rather than religious.

Yes: Every morning . . . tax-paid teachers lead impressionable children in joint recitations claiming that the United States is "one Nation under God." For those who do not share the majority's belief that there exists a God—and who wish to instill non-Monotheistic values in their children—this intrudes into their rights of parenthood. It is also . . . contrary to the Establishment Clause's principles. This is best realized by considering the constitutionally equivalent phrase, "one Nation under Jesus." Every justification given for "God" can be matched by a similar justification for "Jesus." Yet no one would deem that version permissible. . . . Here, purely religious dogma is injected into the nation's sole Pledge of Allegiance, with government agents leading small children in repeating that dogma every day. This violates religious neutrality, endorses disputed religious claims, was instituted for a religious purpose, turns citizens into "outsiders" on the basis of their religious beliefs, and—especially in the public school environment—is coercive. . . . "Under God" in the Pledge is an example of the majority using the machinery of the state to enforce its preferred religious orthodoxy.

—*Michael Newdow, respondent and parent*

No: The Pledge [is not coercive] because it does not result in students being subjected to a religious act or statement of religious belief. The Pledge is simply a patriotic expression, that includes a long-standing philosophy of government. . . . A statute or policy violates the Establishment Clause if it is wholly motivated by religious considerations. . . . Instead, the policy was adopted to promote patriotism. . . . Likewise, the policy neither advances nor inhibits religion. Instead, it merely requires willing students to recite the Pledge each day. The effect of the policy is that students recite or hear others recite the Pledge which in turn promotes unity and patriotism. . . . The preferred method of teaching elementary-age children ideas such as liberty and citizenship is through the study and recognition of symbols, customs, and landmarks, such as the Pledge. . . . The Pledge is not a supplication to God, nor is it an "earnest request or wish." It is not delivered in any manner that is consistent with the way a prayer would be physically delivered. . . . Prayer is a religious activity while recitation of the Pledge is no more than a patriotic activity.

—*Elk Grove Unified School District, petitioner*

argued in *Zelman v. Simmons-Harris* that the program did not violate the establishment clause because students had a choice between secular and religious education. Four members of the Court dissented sharply with the majority's reasoning. Justice Stevens said the ruling had removed a "brick from the wall that was once designed to separate religion from government."[38]

Yet the Court has held firm in its position, first announced in *Engel v. Vitale* (1962), that the establishment clause prohibits the reciting of prayers in public

The First Amendment's protection of free expression includes religious freedom, which has led the courts to hold that government cannot in most instances promote or interfere with religious practices.

schools.[39] A year later the Court struck down Bible readings in public schools.[40] Religion is a powerful force in American life, and the Supreme Court's school-prayer position has evoked strong opposition. An Alabama law attempted to circumvent the prayer ruling by permitting public schools to set aside one minute each day for silent prayer or meditation. In 1985 the Court declared the law unconstitutional, ruling that "government must pursue a course of complete neutrality toward religion."[41] The Court in 2000 reaffirmed the ban by extending it to include organized student-led prayer at public school football games.[42]

The Free-Exercise Clause

The First and Fourteenth Amendments also prohibit governmental interference with the free exercise of religion. The idea underlying the **free-exercise clause** is clear: Americans are free to hold any religious belief they choose.

Although people are free to believe what they want, they are not always free to act on their beliefs. The courts have allowed government interference in the exercise of religious beliefs when such interference is the secondary result of an overriding social goal. An example is the legal protection of children with life-threatening illnesses whose parents refuse to permit medical treatment on religious grounds. A court may order that such children be given medical assistance because the social good of saving their lives overrides their parents' free-exercise rights.

In some circumstances, exceptions to certain laws have been permitted on free-exercise grounds. The Supreme Court ruled in 1972 that Wisconsin could not compel Amish parents to send their children to school beyond the eighth grade because this policy violates a centuries-old Amish religious practice of having children leave school and begin work at an early age.[43] In upholding free exercise in such cases, the Court may be said to have violated the establishment clause by granting preferred treatment to people who hold a particular religious belief. The Court has recognized the potential conflict between the free-exercise and establishment clauses and, as in other such situations, has tried to strike a reasonable balance between the competing claims.

free-exercise clause A First Amendment provision that prohibits the government from interfering with the practice of religion or prohibiting the free exercise of religion.

GLOBAL Perspective

Americans in an Interdependent World

Universal Human Rights

In his 2002 State of the Union Address, President George W. Bush declared that certain values are universal and that it was the responsibility of the United States to ensure their permanence and observance. Said Bush: "America will lead by defending liberty and justice because they are right and true and unchanging for all people everywhere. No nation owns these aspirations, and no nation is exempt from them. We have no intention of imposing our culture—but America will always stand firm for the nonnegotiable demands of human dignity: the rule of law, limits on the power of the state, respect for women, private property, free speech, equal justice, and religious tolerance."

Commentators praised Bush's statement but noted the apparent contradiction between his claim that these rights are "nonnegotiable" and his claim that the United States has no intention of "imposing our culture" on other nations. The rights listed by Bush coincide with American values. Other cultures take exception to some of these rights. Some cultures, for example, make sharp distinctions between the roles, rights, and privileges of men and those of women and have embedded these distinctions in law. Some cultures hold that there is only one true God and have embedded this belief in their constitutions. Some cultures as a matter of law believe that property, or at least much of it, should be held in common rather than privately owned.

Where would you draw the line between what is properly "universal" and what is properly "cultural"? Even if you accept the notion of "universal" rights, how much latitude should nations have in balancing these rights against their cultural traditions?

What do you make of the fact that the world community itself has given some recognition to the notion of universal rights? In 1948, the United Nations General Assembly adopted the Universal Declaration of Human Rights. The Declaration recognizes that the "inherent dignity of all members of the human family is the foundation of freedom, justice and peace in the world." Among its list of rights are life and liberty, property ownership, freedom of expression, religious freedom, and freedom from abusive treatment by law enforcement and security officials.

What about the United States itself? Should it be held to widely accepted human-rights standards? In a 2002 decision, the U.S. Supreme Court invalidated a Virginia law that permitted the death penalty for the mentally retarded convicted of a capital offense. In its ruling, the Court noted that nearly all countries in the world prohibit the execution of the mentally retarded. Should U.S. courts be guided by global standards on certain human-rights issues?

When the free-exercise and establishment clauses cannot be balanced, the Supreme Court has been forced to make a choice. In 1987 the Court overturned a Louisiana law requiring that creationism (the Bible's account of how the world was created) be taught along with the theory of evolution in public school science courses. Creationism, the Court concluded, is a religious doctrine, not a scientific theory; thus, its inclusion in public school curricula violates the establishment clause by promoting a religious belief.[44] Creationists viewed the Court's decision as a violation of their right to the free exercise of religion; they argued that their children were being forced to study a theory of evolution that contradicts their religious beliefs.

Abortion rights activists demonstrate outside the Supreme Court while the justices inside hear arguments on Pennsylvania's controversial abortion law. By a 5-4 vote, the Court narrowly reaffirmed the principle that a woman has the right to choose an abortion during the early months of pregnancy.

 ## THE RIGHT OF PRIVACY

Until the 1960s, Americans' constitutional rights were confined largely to those enumerated in the Bill of Rights. This situation prevailed despite the Ninth Amendment, which reads: "The enumeration in the Constitution, of certain rights, shall not be construed to deny or disparage others retained by the people."

In 1965, however, the Supreme Court added to the list of individual rights, declaring that Americans have "a right of privacy." This judgment arose from the case of *Griswold v. Connecticut*, which challenged a state law prohibiting the use of birth control devices, even by married couples. The Supreme Court invalidated the statute, concluding that a state had no business interfering with a married couple's decision regarding contraception. The Court did not base its decision on the Ninth Amendment but reasoned instead that the freedoms in the Bill of Rights imply an underlying right of privacy. Individuals have, said the Court, a "zone of [personal] privacy" that government cannot lawfully infringe upon.[45]

Abortion

The right of privacy was the basis for the Supreme Court's ruling in *Roe v. Wade* (1973), which gave women full freedom to choose abortion during the first three months of pregnancy.[46] In overturning a Texas law prohibiting abortion except to save the life of the mother, the Supreme Court said that the right to privacy is "broad enough to encompass a woman's decision whether or not to terminate her pregnancy."

After *Roe*, antiabortion activists sought to reverse or weaken the Court's ruling. Attempts at a constitutional amendment that would ban abortions were unsuccessful, but abortion foes succeeded in a campaign to prohibit the use of government funds to pay for abortions for poor women. Then, in *Webster v. Reproductive Health Services* (1989), the Supreme Court upheld a Missouri law that prohibits abortions from being performed in Missouri's public hospitals and by its public employees.[47]

The *Webster* decision was followed in 1992 by a judgment in the Pennsylvania abortion case *Planned Parenthood v. Casey*, which antiabortion advocates saw as an opportunity for the Supreme Court to overturn the *Roe* precedent. The Court did not do so. By a 5-4 margin, the Court embraced the principle that a woman has a right to abortion in the earliest months of pregnancy. The Court said that "the essential holding of *Roe v. Wade* should be retained and once again reaffirmed."[48] However, the Court also ruled that a state can impose regulations that do not place an "undue burden" on women seeking an abortion. In this vein, the Court upheld, for example, a provision of the Pennsylvania law that requires a minor to have parental or judicial consent before obtaining an abortion.

After this ruling, antiabortion advocates sought other ways to limit the practice. The Nebraska legislature passed a law banning so-called partial birth abortion (in which the fetus's life is terminated during delivery). In *Stenberg v. Carhart* (2000), the Supreme Court struck down the Nebraska law, saying that abortion at delivery is sometimes the most appropriate medical procedure for protecting the life or health of the mother.[49] This ruling did not stop Congress from passing a federal law in 2003 that banned partial birth abortion and made doctors criminally liable if they performed the procedure, even if the woman's health was at risk. The ban has been challenged in lower federal courts and is expected to be reviewed by the U.S. Supreme Court.

Sexual Relations Among Consenting Adults

Although it was widely claimed that the Supreme Court's *Griswold (1965)* ruling on contraceptive use took "government out of people's bedrooms," a clear exception remained. All states at the time prohibited sexual relations between consenting adults of the same sex. A number of states abolished this prohibition over the next two decades, and others stopped enforcing it. Nevertheless, in a 1986 Georgia case, *Bowers v. Hardwick*, the Supreme Court ruled that states could prohibit sodomy, saying that the right of privacy did not extend to homosexual acts among consenting adults.[50]

In 2003, however, the Court reversed itself and in the process invalidated the sodomy laws of the thirteen states that still had them. The ruling came in response to a Texas law prohibiting consensual sex between adults of the same sex. In *Lawrence and Garner v. Texas*, the Court in a 6-3 vote concluded that the Texas sodomy law violated privacy rights protected by the due process clause of the Fourteenth Amendment. The Court said: "The petitioners are entitled to respect for their private lives. The State cannot demean their existence or control their destiny by making their private sexual conduct a crime."[51] The decision was hailed by gay and lesbian rights groups but condemned by some religious leaders, who said that it would open the door to same-sex marriage (see Chapter 5).

The Continuing Issue of Privacy Rights

The right of privacy is a broad issue that extends into many areas, including but not limited to personal medical and financial records and the government's war on terrorism (see the section "Rights and the War on Terrorism" later in this chapter).

In most of these areas, the "zone of privacy" that is constitutionally protected has yet to be defined and likely will be subject to adjustment as technology and lifestyles change. The Supreme Court undoubtedly will extend privacy protection into new areas and deny it in other areas, as it did with the issue of "the right to die." In a ruling involving New York and Washington state laws that prohibit physician-assisted suicide, the Court held that "liberty" in the Fourteenth Amendment does not include the constitutional right to doctor-assisted suicide.[52] At the same time, the Court hinted that states have the authority to permit physician-assisted suicide if they should decide to do so. Oregon has such a law.

Privacy questions are among the most contentious in American politics because of the moral and ethical issues they raise. The abortion issue, for example, has provoked intense debate for three decades, and there is no end in sight to the controversy. The American public is divided on the issue (see Figure 4–1), and there are many deeply committed activists on both sides. As with other rights, the abortion issue is not only, or even primarily, fought out in the courts. Abortion opponents have waged demonstrations outside clinics in an effort to stop the practice. Some of these protests have erupted in violent acts against women trying to enter the clinics. In 1994, Congress made it unlawful to block the entrance to abortion clinics or otherwise prevent people from entering. (The Supreme Court upheld the law, concluding that it regulated abortion protesters' actions as opposed to their words and thus did not violate their right to free speech.)[53]

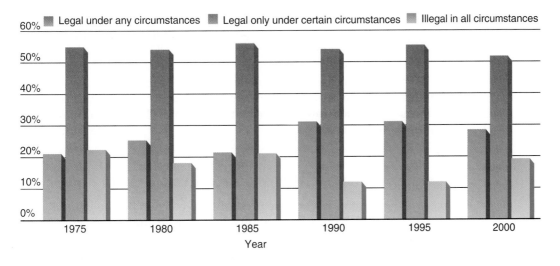

Figure 4–1

Americans' Opinions on Abortion

Since abortion was judged a constitutional right in 1973, public opinion on the issue has not changed greatly.

Source: Gallup polls, various dates.

RIGHTS OF PERSONS ACCUSED OF CRIMES

Due process refers to legal protections that have been established to preserve the rights of individuals. The most significant form of these protections is **procedural due process;** the term refers primarily to procedures that authorities must follow before a person can legitimately be punished for an offense.

procedural due process The constitutional requirement that government must follow proper legal procedures before a person can be legitimately punished for an alleged offense.

The U.S. Constitution provides for several procedures designed to protect a person from wrongful arrest, conviction, and punishment. According to Article I, Section 9, any person taken into police custody is entitled to seek a writ of habeas corpus, which requires law enforcement officials to bring the suspect into court and to specify the legal reason for the detention. The Fifth and Fourteenth Amendments provide generally that no person can be deprived of life, liberty, or property without due process of law. Specific procedural protections for the accused are spelled out in the Fourth, Fifth, Sixth, and Eighth Amendments:

- *The Fourth Amendment* forbids the police to conduct searches and seizures unless they have probable cause to believe that a crime has been committed.
- *The Fifth Amendment* protects against double jeopardy (being prosecuted twice for the same offense); self-incrimination (being compelled to testify against oneself); indictment for a crime except through grand jury proceedings; and loss of life, liberty, and property without due process of law.
- *The Sixth Amendment* provides the right to have legal counsel, to confront witnesses, to receive a speedy trial, and to have a trial by jury in criminal proceedings.
- *The Eighth Amendment* protects against excessive bail or fines and prohibits the infliction of cruel and unusual punishment on those convicted of crimes.

These procedural protections have been subject to interpretation. The Sixth Amendment, for example, provides the right to have legal counsel. But what if a person cannot afford a lawyer? For most of the nation's history, poor people had almost no choice but to act as their own attorneys. They had a right to counsel but could avail themselves of it only if they had the money to hire a lawyer. Today, if a person is accused of a serious crime and cannot afford a lawyer, the government must provide one. This change came about not through a constitutional amendment but through Supreme Court rulings that gave new meaning in practice to the Sixth Amendment.

Selective Incorporation of Procedural Rights

For most of the nation's history, the procedural protections in the Bill of Rights applied only to the actions of the national government. States in their criminal proceedings were not bound by them. There were limited exceptions, such as a 1932 Supreme Court ruling that a defendant charged in a state court with a crime carrying the death penalty had to be provided with an attorney.[54] Nevertheless, even as the Court was moving to protect free-expression rights from state action in the 1930s, it held back on doing the same for the rights of

Liberty, Equality & Self-Government

What's Your Opinion?

Procedural Due Process

"The history of liberty has largely been the history of the observance of procedural guarantees," said Justice Felix Frankfurter in *McNabb v. United States* (1943). No system of justice is foolproof. Even in the most honest systems, innocent people have been wrongly accused, convicted, and punished with imprisonment or death. But the scrupulous application of procedural safeguards, such as a defendant's right to legal counsel, greatly increases the likelihood that justice will prevail.

However, as recent police scandals in Dallas, Los Angeles, New York, and several other cities would indicate, constitutional guarantees are no assurance that people will be treated justly. In Dallas, dozens of people,

many of them Hispanics, were accused of peddling drugs after having been set up by police officers, who planted fake evidence while arresting them. Some were held in jail for months before they were cleared of wrongdoing. Wrongful arrests and cooked-up evidence are not by any means the norm in U.S. law enforcement, but they occur with enough frequency to be a cause of concern to anyone committed to the principle of legal justice.

What do you think can be done to safeguard individuals' due process rights? Do you share the view of social theorists who say that when procedural due process is violated, the fault lies more with a public that is willing to tolerate abuses than with the few errant law enforcement officials who commit these abuses?

the accused. The Court claimed that free-expression rights were more deserving of federal protection because they are more "fundamental" to the preservation of liberty. Such rights, the Court said in a 1937 ruling, are "the indispensable condition of nearly every other form of freedom."[55]

This view changed abruptly in the 1960s when the Supreme Court broadly required states also to safeguard procedural rights. Changes in public education and communication made Americans more aware of their rights, and the civil rights movement dramatized the fact that rights were administered very unequally: the poor and minority group members had many fewer rights in practice than other Americans did. In response, the Supreme Court in the 1960s "incorporated" Bill of Rights protections for the accused by ruling that these rights are protected against state action by the Fourteenth Amendment's guarantee of due process of law (see Table 4–2).

This selective incorporation process began with *Mapp v. Ohio* (1961). Dollree Mapp's home had been entered by Cleveland police, who, though they failed to find what they were looking for, happened to discover some pornographic material. Mapp's conviction for its possession was overturned by the Supreme Court on the grounds that she had been subjected to unreasonable search and seizure.[56] The Court ruled that illegally obtained evidence could not be used in state courts.

Two years later, the Court's decision in *Gideon v. Wainwright* (1963) required the states to furnish attorneys for poor defendants in all felony cases. Clarence Gideon, an indigent drifter, had been convicted and sentenced to prison in

TABLE 4–2	Selective Incorporation of Rights of the Accused In the 1960s, the Supreme Court selectively incorporated the fair-trial provisions of the Fourth through Eighth Amendments into the Fourteenth Amendment so that these rights would be protected from infringement by the states.	
SUPREME COURT CASE	**YEAR**	**CONSTITUTIONAL RIGHT (AMENDMENT) AT ISSUE**
Mapp v. Ohio	1961	Unreasonable search and seizure (Fourth)
Robinson v. California	1962	Cruel and unusual punishment (Eighth)
Gideon v. Wainwright	1963	Right to counsel (Sixth)
Malloy v. Hogan	1964	Self-incrimination (Fifth)
Pointer v. Texas	1965	Right to confront witnesses (Sixth)
Miranda v. Arizona	1966	Self-incrimination and right to counsel (Fifth and Sixth)
Klopfer v. North Carolina	1967	Speedy trial (Sixth)
Duncan v. Louisiana	1968	Jury trial in criminal cases (Sixth)
Benton v. Maryland	1969	Double jeopardy (Fifth)

Florida for breaking into a poolroom. He successfully appealed on the grounds that he had been denied due process because he could not afford to pay an attorney.[57]

During the 1960s, the Court also ruled that defendants in state criminal proceedings cannot be compelled to testify against themselves,[58] have the right to remain silent and to have legal counsel when arrested,[59] have the right to confront witnesses who testify against them,[60] must be granted a speedy trial,[61] have the right to a jury trial,[62] and cannot be subjected to double jeopardy.[63] The best known of these cases is *Miranda v. Arizona* (1966), which arose when Ernesto Miranda confessed during police interrogation to kidnap and rape. The Supreme Court overturned his conviction on the grounds that he had not been informed of his rights to remain silent and to have legal assistance, which led to the development of the "Miranda warning" that police are now required to read to suspects: "You have the right to remain silent. . . . Anything you say can and will be used against you in a court of law. . . . You have the right to an attorney."

In a 2000 case, *Dickerson v. United States*, the Supreme Court reaffirmed the *Miranda* decision, saying that because it had established "a constitutional rule," it was not subject to change by legislative action. The Court further strengthened the Miranda precedent in *Missouri v. Siebert* (2004). This ruling came in response to a police strategy of questioning suspects first and then reading them their Miranda rights, followed by a second round of questioning. In such instances, suspects who admitted wrongdoing in the first round of questioning tended also to do so in the second round. The Court concluded that the strategy was intended "to undermine the Miranda warnings" and was not permissible.[64]

Limits on Defendants' Rights

In the courtroom, the rights to counsel, to confront witnesses, and to remain silent are of paramount importance. Before the courtroom phase in a criminal

The Bill of Rights: A Selected List of Constitutional Protections

First Amendment

Speech: You are free to say almost anything except that which is obscene, slanders another person, or has a high probability of inciting others to take imminent lawless action.

Assembly: You are free to assemble, although government may regulate the time and place for reasons of public convenience and safety, provided such regulations are applied evenhandedly to all groups.

Religion: You are protected from having the religious beliefs of others imposed on you, and you are free to believe what you like.

Fourth Amendment

Search and seizure: You are protected from unreasonable searches and seizures, although you forfeit that right if you knowingly waive it.

Arrest: You are protected from arrest unless authorities have probable cause to believe you have committed a crime.

Fifth Amendment

Self-incrimination: You are protected against self-incrimination, which means that you have the right to remain silent and to be protected against coercion by law enforcement officials.

Double jeopardy: You cannot be tried twice for the same crime if the first trial results in a verdict of innocence.

Due process: You cannot be deprived of life, liberty, or property without proper legal proceedings.

Sixth Amendment

Counsel: You have a right to be represented by an attorney and can demand to speak first with an attorney before responding to questions from law enforcement officials.

Prompt and reasonable proceedings: You have a right to be arraigned promptly, to be informed of the charges, to confront witnesses, and to have a speedy and open trial by an impartial jury.

Eighth Amendment

Bail: You are protected against excessive bail or fines.

Cruel and unusual punishment: You are protected from cruel and unusual punishment, although this provision does not protect you from the death penalty or from a long prison term for a minor offense.

---

proceeding, the key protection is the Fourth Amendment's restriction on illegal search and seizure. This restriction holds that police must have suspicion of wrongdoing (and, sometimes, a judge's permission) before they can search your person, your car, or your residence, although involvement in an offense can lead to a permissible search that uncovers wrongdoing of another kind. Without search and seizure protection, individuals could be subject to unrestricted police harassment and intimidation, characteristics of a totalitarian state, not a free society.

The Fourth Amendment, however, does not provide blanket protection against searches. In 1990, for example, the Supreme Court held that roadside checkpoints at which police stop drivers to check them for signs of intoxication are legal as long as the action is systematic and not arbitrary (for example, stopping only young drivers would be unconstitutional). The Court justified its decision by saying that roadblocks serve a public safety purpose.[65] However, the Court does not allow the same types of roadblocks to check for drugs in the car. In *Indianapolis v. Edmund* (2001), the Court held that narcotics roadblocks, because they serve a general law enforcement purpose rather than one specific to highway safety, violate the Fourth Amendment's requirement that police have suspicion of wrongdoing before they can search an individual's auto.[66]

The Court also ruled in 2001 (*Kyllo v. United States*) that police may not use a thermal-imaging device in order to detect whether unusual heat sources are located in a home. The Court held that police cannot enter a home without a warrant based on suspicion of wrongdoing and that searches based on modern technology must meet the same standard.[67]

The Fourth Amendment protects individuals in their persons as well as in their homes and vehicles. The police cannot arbitrarily stop and search someone on the street or in other settings. In *Ferguson vs. Charleston* (2001), for example, the Court held that patients in public hospitals cannot be forced to take a test for illegal drugs if the purpose is to turn over to the police those patients who test positive. Such action, said the Court, constitutes an illegal search of the person.[68] Yet the Court in *Board of Education of Independent School District No. 92 of Pottawatomie County v. Earls* (2002) held that random drug testing of high school students involved in extracurricular activities does not violate the ban on unreasonable searches.[69]

The Exclusionary Rule

exclusionary rule The legal principle that government is prohibited from using in trials evidence that was obtained by unconstitutional means (for example, illegal search and seizure).

In general, the Supreme Court in recent decades has reduced but not eliminated the protections afforded to the accused by *Mapp* and other 1960s rulings. This reduction can be seen in the application of the **exclusionary rule,** which bars the use in trials of evidence obtained in violation of a person's constitutional rights. The rule was formulated in a 1914 Supreme Court decision,[70] and its application was expanded in federal cases. The *Mapp* decision extended the exclusionary rule to state trial proceedings. Subsequent decisions of the Supreme Court broadened its application to the point where almost any type of illegally obtained evidence was considered inadmissible in a criminal trial. In the 1980s, the Supreme Court reversed the trend by placing restrictions on the rule's application, concluding that illegally obtained evidence can sometimes be admitted in trials if the procedural errors are inadvertent or if the prosecution can show that it would have discovered the evidence anyway.[71]

Recent decisions have also lowered the standard that must be met for a lawful search and seizure to occur. In the 1960s, the Court developed the principle that police had to have a solid basis ("probable cause") for believing that an individual was involved in a specific crime before they could stop a person and engage in search-and-seizure activity. This principle has been modified, as illustrated by *Whren v. United States* (1996), which upheld the conviction of an individual who had been found with drugs in the front seat of his car. The police had no evidence (no "probable cause") indicating that drugs were in the car, but they suspected that the driver was involved in drug dealing and they used a minor traffic infraction as a pretext to stop and check him. The Supreme Court accepted defense arguments that the police had no clear evidence for their suspicion, that the traffic infraction was not the real reason the individual was stopped, and that police usually do not stop a person for the infraction in question (turning a corner without signaling). However, the Court concluded that the officers' motive was irrelevant, as long as an officer in some situations

In recent decades, the Supreme Court has restricted the scope of the exclusionary rule. This rule excludes from use in court proceedings any evidence that is illegally obtained by law enforcement officials.

might reasonably stop a car for the infraction that occurred. Thus, the stop-and-search action was deemed to meet the Fourth Amendment's reasonableness standard.[72]

The Court's objective has been to weaken the exclusionary rule without giving police unlimited discretion. In *U.S. v. Drayton et al.* (2002), for example, the Court upheld the conviction of two bus passengers who had been found with cocaine after voluntarily agreeing to a police search. They were not told of their right to refuse the search, and their attorneys argued that the evidence was therefore inadmissible. The Supreme Court said that police are not required by the Fourth Amendment "to advise bus passengers of their right . . . to refuse consent to searches." However, the Court also said that police cannot tell passengers they must submit to a search and cannot threaten them into permitting one.[73]

Habeas Corpus Appeals

Legal protection for the accused has also been reduced by a restriction on habeas corpus appeals to federal courts by individuals who have been convicted of crimes in state courts. (Habeas corpus gives defendants access to federal courts in order to argue that their rights under the Constitution of the United States were violated when they were convicted in a state court.) A 1960s Supreme Court precedent had assured prisoners of the right to have their petitions heard in federal court unless they had "deliberately bypassed" the opportunity to first make their appeal in state courts.[74]

This precedent was overturned in 1992 when the Court held that inmates can lose the right to a federal hearing even if a lawyer's mistake is the reason they failed to first present their appeal properly in state courts.[75] Another significant habeas corpus setback for inmates occurred in 1993 when the Supreme Court held that federal courts cannot overturn a state conviction on the basis of constitutional error unless the prisoner can demonstrate that the error contributed to the conviction.[76] Previously, the burden of proof had been on the state: it had to prove that the error did not affect the case's outcome. Then, in *Felker v. Turpin* (1996), the Court upheld a recently enacted federal law that prohibited in most

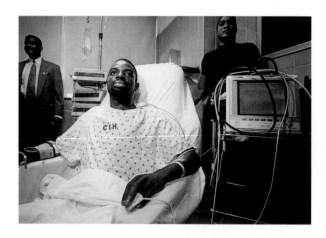

Abner Louima was sodomized with a wooden handle by a New York City police officer after having been taken into custody. Louima's case focused national attention on the issue of police brutality and dramatized the difference that can exist between the theory and the reality of constitutional rights.

cases federal habeas corpus appeals by state prison inmates who have already filed one.[77]

Through these decisions, the Supreme Court has sought to prevent frivolous and multiple federal court appeals. At the same time, the Court has taken steps to ensure that meritorious appeals are heard. In two 2003 cases, for example, the Court expressed concern that lower federal courts in some instances were not being sufficiently careful in identifying legitimate appeals.[78] Yet the trend has been toward raising the threshold for appeals that will be heard in federal court. State prisoners have used habeas corpus appeals to contest even small issues, and some—particularly those on death row—have filed appeal after appeal. An effect is the clogging of the federal courts and a delay in hearing other cases. A majority of Supreme Court justices concluded that a more restrictive policy toward these appeals is required. They have held that it is fair to ask inmates to first pursue their options in state courts and then, except in unusual cases,[79] to confine themselves to a single federal appeal. Civil liberties groups have objected to the change, arguing that no procedure that would protect the innocent from wrongful punishment—particularly when the death penalty is at issue—is too big a burden to place on the courts.

Nevertheless, no one claims that recent decisions mark a return to the lower procedural standards that prevailed before the 1960s. Many of the vital precedents set in that decade remain in effect, including the most important one of all: the principle that procedural protections guaranteed to the accused by the Bill of Rights must be observed by the states as well as by the federal government.

Crime, Punishment, and Police Practices

www.mhhe.com/pattersontad7

The theory and practice of procedural guarantees are often two quite different things, as Adrienne Cureton discovered on January 2, 1995. She is a plainclothes police officer who, with a uniformed partner, was called to the scene of a domestic dispute. A struggle ensued, and her partner radioed for help. When the officers arrived, Cureton and her partner had already handcuffed the homeowner. The officers barged in and mistook Cureton, an African American, for the other person involved in the dispute. They grabbed her by the collar, dragged her by the hair onto the porch, and clubbed her repeatedly with flashlights, despite her screams that she was a police officer.[80]

There is no reliable estimate of how often Americans' rights are violated in practice, but infringements of one sort or another are commonplace. Minorities and the poor are the more likely victims. *Racial profiling* (the assumption that certain groups are more likely to commit particular crimes) is a common police practice and results in the unequal treatment of minorities. A 1999 American Civil Liberties Union study found that although minority and white motorists were about equally likely to commit traffic infractions, 80 percent of the

STATES IN THE NATION

The Death Penalty

Most crimes and punishments in the United States are defined by state law. Nowhere is this arrangement more obvious than in the application of the death penalty. Some states prohibit it, and others apply it liberally. Texas, Florida, and Virginia are far and away the leaders in its application. Roughly a third of all executions in the past quarter-century have taken place in Texas alone.

Q: What do many of the states that prohibit capital punishment have in common?

A: States without the death penalty are concentrated in the North. Most of these states are relatively affluent, rank high on indicators of educational attainment, and have a small minority-group population.

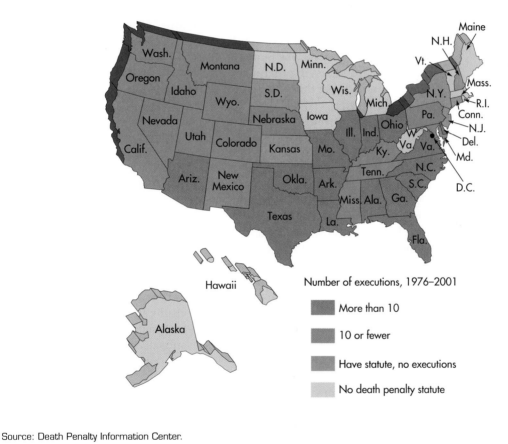

Source: Death Penalty Information Center.

motorists stopped and searched by Maryland State Police on Interstate 95 were minorities and only 20 percent were white, despite the fact that white motorists constituted 75 percent of all drivers. A 1999 report by the New Jersey Attorney General's Office revealed a similar pattern in that state.

Profiling of a different kind came to the forefront after the terrorist attacks of September 11, 2001, when males of Middle Eastern descent were stopped and searched for reasons of appearance alone in airports and other places where further attacks were feared. Sixty-eight percent of Americans in one poll said they favored allowing police to stop and search people who might fit a terrorist profile.[81]

Another issue of justice in America is whether adherence to proper legal procedures produces reasonable outcomes. The Eighth Amendment prohibits "cruel and unusual punishment" of those convicted of crime, but judgments in this area are subjective. Although the Supreme Court has ordered officials to relieve inmate overcrowding and to improve prison facilities in a few instances, it has concluded that inmates cannot sue over prison conditions unless prison officials show "deliberate indifference" to the conditions.[82] The severity of a sentence can also be an Eighth Amendment issue.[83] A divided Supreme Court in 2003 upheld California's "three-strikes" law that resulted in life imprisonment for a thrice-convicted felon who, the third time, was convicted of shoplifting videotapes worth $100.[84] In general, the Court has shied away from Eighth Amendment decisions, preferring to leave those decisions to legislative bodies. In *Atkins v. Virginia* (2002), however, the Supreme Court outlawed the death penalty for the mentally retarded, saying that it constitutes "cruel and unusual punishment." The Court noted that thirty states and nearly all countries in the world prohibit such executions.[85]

The Supreme Court has limited judges' discretion in deciding upon the punishment of those convicted of crime. In *Ring v. Arizona*, the Court held that the Sixth Amendment right to a jury trial prohibits judges—as opposed to juries—from deciding whether the death penalty will be imposed. Then, in a 2004 decision (*Blakely v. Washington*) that some analysts predicted would create turmoil in the justice system, the Supreme Court ruled that any factor that would result in a longer prison sentence, except prior convictions, had to be proven to a jury. The Court held that the Sixth Amendment right to trial by jury includes a determination by a jury, not a judge, as to whether aggravating factors, such as the cruelty of the crime, justify a longer sentence than the law ordinarily allows. Justice Sandra Day O'Connor dissented from the ruling, saying it would create "havoc" for trial courts by forcing them to employ juries not only to determine guilt or innocence but also to decide whether other considerations that might result in a stiffer sentence had been proven beyond a reasonable doubt. O'Connor envisioned increasingly lengthy trials and thousands of appeals from inmates who had been given a stiff sentence because a judge had decided the crime was of such a nature as to warrant an extended sentence.[86]

Nevertheless, most efforts to lengthen sentences have come from legislators rather than judges. In the past decade or so, Congress along with most states have mandated stiffer sentences for a wide range of crimes and have limited the ability of judges to reduce sentences because of extenuating circumstances, such as when the accused has no prior conviction. As a result, the number of federal and state prisoners has more than doubled since 1990. The United States now has a larger proportion of its people behind bars than any country in the world (see "How the United States Compares").

As the prison population has increased and sentencing has become more severe, debate over America's criminal justice system has intensified. The severest criticisms have been directed at the death penalty and the incarceration of nonviolent drug users. In these areas, U.S. policies are at odds with those of

HOW THE UNITED STATES COMPARES

Law and Order

Individual rights are a cornerstone of the American governing system and receive strong protection from the courts. The government's ability to restrict free expression is severely limited, and the individual's right to a fair trial is protected through elaborate due process guarantees.

According to Amnesty International, a watchdog group that monitors human rights achievements and violations around the world, the United States has a good record in terms of its constitutional protection of civil liberties. A number of countries in Asia, Africa, Eastern Europe, the Middle East, and Latin America are accused by Amnesty International of "appalling human rights catastrophes" that include the execution, torture, and rape of persons accused of crime or regarded as opponents of the government. Amnesty International does not rank the United States as high as the countries of northern Europe in terms of respect for human rights. Among other problems, Amnesty International faults police in

the United States for "excessive force" in their treatment of prisoners and faults U.S. immigration officials for the forcible return of asylum seekers to their country of origin without granting them a hearing.

Although human rights groups admire America's elaborate procedural protections for those accused of crime, they are critical of its sentencing and incarceration policies. The United States is the world leader in the number of people it places behind bars and in the length of sentences for various categories of crime. Defenders of U.S. policy say that although overall crime rates are about the same here as elsewhere, there is more violent crime in America. Critics reply that although the murder rate is high in the United States, it is also true that more than half of the people in prison were convicted of nonviolent offenses, such as drug use or a crime against property. Whatever the reasons, the United States is rivaled only by Russia in the proportion of its people who are in prisons.

Incarceration rates (per 100,000 inhabitants)

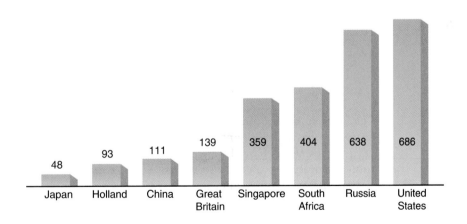

Japan	Holland	China	Great Britain	Singapore	South Africa	Russia	United States
48	93	111	139	359	404	638	686

Source: The Sentencing Project, 2004.

other industrialized countries, nearly all of which have outlawed the death penalty and nearly all of which rely more heavily on treatment programs than on prisons in dealing with drug users. Critics have also cited studies that indicate minorities and the poor are punished more severely than are middle-class white Americans who commit the same crimes. In 2003, outgoing Illinois governor George Ryan acted on his belief that the justice system is flawed. Claiming that the death penalty process is "arbitrary and capricious, and therefore immoral," Ryan pardoned four Illinois death-row inmates who had been convicted on false evidence, and he commuted to life in prison the sentences of the other 167 death-row inmates. Ryan's unprecedented action was applauded by some observers but swiftly condemned by others, including prosecutors and some of the victims' relatives.

RIGHTS AND THE WAR ON TERRORISM

When the nation has been at war, the courts typically have allowed government to exercise authority that would not be permitted in peacetime. After the Japanese attack on Pearl Harbor in 1941, for example, President Franklin D. Roosevelt ordered the forced evacuation of tens of thousands of Japanese Americans living on the West Coast. They were relocated to detention camps in Arizona, Utah, and other inland locations. Congress endorsed the policy, and the Supreme Court upheld it.[87] Another Supreme Court ruling during World War II denied a U.S. citizen arrested as a Nazi collaborator a court trial after the government decided to try him before a military tribunal. In yet another case, a federal appeals court upheld the imprisonment without charge or trial of an Italian American captured while fighting as a soldier in the Italian army.[88]

After the terrorist attacks of September 11, 2001, precedents such as these were invoked by the Bush administration, which declared that customary legal protections must be altered if the war on terrorism was to be waged successfully. "[There is] the necessity for certain types of action . . . when we are in danger," said Solicitor General Theodore Olson.

Detention of Enemy Combatants

The Bush administration soon announced its policy for handling "enemy combatants"—individuals judged to be engaged in terrorism directed at the United States. They were to be detained without access to lawyers or family members until the president decided to release them. The Administration also claimed the authority to round up and hold in secret any individuals living in the United States who are suspected of terrorist activities. Noncitizens suspected of terrorist ties could be deported without benefit of a hearing to determine their guilt or innocence.

Hundreds of individuals, nearly all of Middle Eastern descent, were taken into custody after the terrorist attacks of September 11, 2001. Many were held for months, and, though nearly all these detainees were eventually cleared of wrongdoing by the FBI, some were deported for immigration violations. This action brought protests from Arab-American groups and civil rights activists, who claimed that people had been detained simply because of their Middle

In the aftermath of the September 11, 2001, terrorist attacks, Arab Americans were subject to ethnic profiling at airports and other locations. Shown here is an Arab American protesting the practice of profiling.

Eastern background. A lawsuit that would have forced the Administration to release information on why these individuals were taken into custody was turned down by the Supreme Court in 2004. The Administration had argued that release of the information would enable terrorists to discover the methods by which the government identifies suspected terrorists.[89]

Two other issues relating to detainees were heard by the Supreme Court in 2004. One involved the status of six hundred prisoners held at the U.S. Naval Base at Guantanamo Bay, Cuba. They had been captured during the fighting in Afghanistan and flown to Guantanamo Bay, where they were being held without access to lawyers and without the right to a hearing that might lead to their release. (Many denied being involved in terrorist activities, claiming that they were ordinary soldiers serving in Afghanistan when it was attacked by U.S. forces.) Lawyers acting on the prisoners' behalf filed suit, arguing that the prisoners were being housed on territory controlled by the United States and therefore should have access to American courts.

The Supreme Court held that, though the United States has authority to hold the detainees, they have the right to challenge their detention in federal court. The Court said that though the base is in Cuba, it is on land leased to the United States, and therefore not beyond the reach of the American courts.

The second issue facing the Court in 2004 involved the legal rights of enemy combatants who are U.S. citizens. This issue was addressed by two separate cases.[90] One involved a soldier captured in Afghanistan who had been born in the United States but raised in Saudi Arabia. The other involved a U.S. citizen arrested in Chicago on suspicion of involvement in a terrorist plot to detonate a radioactive bomb.

The Supreme Court sidestepped the second case, ruling that the lawsuit had been filed against the wrong authority and would have to be refiled before it could be heard. However, in the first case, *Hamdi v. Rumsfeld* (2004), the Court came down strongly on behalf of the suspect. The Court said that, though the government could hold the prisoner as an enemy combatant, he had the constitutional right to use the U.S. courts to challenge his detention. The Court said that a citizen was entitled to a "fair opportunity to rebut the government's factual assertions before a neutral [judge]" and that "essential constitutional promises may not be eroded" because of the security situation. The Court went on to say: "As critical as the government's interest may be in detaining those who actually pose an immediate threat to the national security of the United States during ongoing international conflict, history and common sense teach us that an unchecked system of detention carries the potential to become a means of oppression and abuse of others who do not present that sort of threat."[91]

The ruling was criticized by Bush administration officials and drew a sharp dissent from Justice Clarence Thomas who wrote: "This detention falls squarely within the federal government's war powers, and we lack the expertise and capacity to second-guess that decision." On the other hand, civil liberties groups applauded the decision, as did some members of Congress. "The Supreme Court's verdict shows," said Senator Charles Schumer (D-New York), "that, contrary to what the administration believes, we can have both security and liberty."

Surveillance of Suspected Terrorists

After the September 11 terrorist attacks, the Bush administration requested legislation that would expand the government's surveillance powers. Congress responded with the USA Patriot Act (see Chapter 1). The law included a relaxing of the wiretapping standards that would apply if a suspected criminal were the target. Authorities were granted more discretion and a lower burden of proof when seeking to wiretap a suspected terrorist. The law also specified that any information about ordinary criminal activity that was gathered through intelligence investigations of terrorist activity could be shared with criminal investigators. Previously, such information could be shared only if it was obtained by the legal standards that apply in criminal proceedings.

The new rules also gave government enhanced investigative powers. The government could examine medical, financial, and student records on the basis of a minimal standard of suspicion of terrorist activity and, in some instances, could secretly search homes and offices.

Critics claimed that the reduction of America's constitutional protections was a moral victory for the terrorists. "No one is questioning the government's authority to prosecute spies and terrorists," said Ann Beeson of the American Civil Liberties Union. "But we do not need to waive the Constitution to do so."[92] Some abuses have occurred. For example, although the FBI's Terrorist Unit eventually backed down, it authorized the delivery of subpoenas in 2004 to Drake University administrators ordering them to turn over documents relating to an antiwar conference that had been held on the Drake campus and then imposed a gag order prohibiting discussion of the subpoenas.

For their part, officials have claimed that the expanded authority granted by the USA Patriot Act is a necessary weapon in the war on terrorism. "The danger that darkened the United States of America and the civilized world on September 11 did not pass with the atrocities committed that day," said Attorney General John Ashcroft. "It requires that we provide law enforcement with the tools necessary to identify, dismantle, disrupt and punish terrorist organizations." Ashcroft promised restraint in the exercise of the new powers, and congressional oversight committees have been largely satisfied with the executive branch's use of them; however, some criticisms have been expressed.[93]

Aspects of the Patriot Act are certain to be reviewed by the Supreme Court. Lower-court decisions so far have been mixed.[94] One ruling, for example, held that crime-related information obtained in domestic intelligence operations could be shared with law-enforcement officials. However, another ruling held that government without judicial consent cannot require Internet or telephone companies to turn over customer records and then block them from revealing publicly that they have done so.

 ## THE COURTS AND A FREE SOCIETY

A free and democratic nation has a vital stake in maintaining individual freedoms. The United States was founded on the belief that individuals have an innate right to personal liberty—to speak their minds, to worship as they choose, to be free of police intimidation. Yet a majority of Americans have sometimes

"Should someone who says that terrorism is the fault of how our country behaves in the world be allowed to make a speech at a college?"

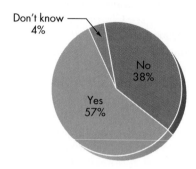

Figure 4–2

Opinions on Speech About Terrorism Causes on College Campuses
Two-fifths of Americans would deny a college speaking opportunity to someone who claims terrorism is the result of U.S. policies abroad.
Source: National Public Radio/Kaiser Family Foundation/Kennedy School of Government Poll, Oct. 31–Nov. 12, 2001.

preferred policies that would diminish the freedom of those who hold minority views, have unconventional lifestyles, or simply "look different" than they do.

Americans are very supportive of rights and freedoms in the abstract but are much less supportive—and in some cases antagonistic—when confronted with these same rights in concrete situations. For example, after the terrorist attacks of September 11, 2001, polls indicated that a third of Americans would favor putting Arab Americans under special surveillance, half said they would favor requiring Arab Americans to carry special identification cards, and a fourth said they would approve of special detention facilities for members of suspect groups.[95] Two-fifths even said they would not allow someone who says that terrorism is the result of U.S. foreign policy to give a speech at a college (see Figure 4–2).

Support for individual rights is stronger among the political elite, who are also better positioned than ordinary citizens to act on their beliefs. However, they are not always willing to support what they believe. Often, the exercise of rights involves society's least savory characters—its murderers, rapists, drug dealers, and hate peddlers. These are not the type of people who engender public support at any level.

The courts are not isolated from the public mood. They inevitably balance society's demand for safety and order against the rights of the individual. Nevertheless, the judicial branch can normally be expected to grant more consideration to the rights of the individual, however unpopular his or her views or actions, than will the general public or elected officials. How far the courts will go in protecting a person's rights depends on the facts of the case, the existing status of the law, prevailing social needs, and the personal views of the judges. Nevertheless, the courts regard the protection of individual rights as one of their most significant responsibilities. The Bill of Rights transformed the inalienable rights of life, liberty, and property into legal rights, thus granting them judicial protection.[96]

The judiciary alone, however, cannot provide adequate protection for individual rights. A civil society rests also on open-minded representatives and a tolerant citizenry. If, for example, politicians and the public encourage police to infringe on the rights of vaguely threatening minorities or nonconformists, the judiciary's protection of persons accused of crimes will not ensure justice. It may be said that the test of a truly civil society is not its treatment of popular ideas and of its best citizens but its willingness to tolerate ideas that the majority detests and to respect equally the rights of its least popular citizens.

Summary Self-Test
www.mhhe.com/pattersontad7

In their search for personal liberty, Americans added the Bill of Rights to the Constitution shortly after its ratification. These amendments guarantee certain political, procedural, and property rights against infringement by the national government. Freedom of expression is the most basic of democratic rights. People are not free unless they can freely express their views. Nevertheless, free expression may conflict with the nation's security needs during times of war and insurrection. The courts at times have allowed government to limit expression substantially for purposes of national security. In recent decades, however, the courts have protected a very wide range of free expression in the areas of speech, press, and religion.

The guarantees embodied in the Bill of Rights originally applied only to the national government. Under the principle of selective incorporation of these guarantees into the Fourteenth Amendment, the courts extended them to state governments, though the process was slow and uneven. In the 1920s and 1930s, First Amendment guarantees of freedom of expression were given protection from infringement by the states. The states continued to have wide discretion in criminal proceedings until the early 1960s, when most of the fair-trial rights in the Bill of Rights were given federal protection.

Due process of law refers to legal protections that have been established to preserve individual rights. The most significant form of these protections consists of procedures or methods (for example, the right of an accused person to have an attorney present during police interrogation) designed to ensure that an individual's rights are upheld. A major controversy in this area is the breadth of the exclusionary rule, which bars the use in trials of illegally obtained evidence. The right of privacy, particularly as it applies to the abortion issue, is also a source of controversy, as is the issue of constitutional rights in the pursuit of the war on terrorism.

Civil liberties are not absolute but must be balanced against other considerations (such as national security or public safety) and against one another when different rights conflict. The judicial branch of government, particularly the Supreme Court, has taken on much of the responsibility for protecting and interpreting individual rights. The Court's positions have changed with time and conditions, but the Court has generally been more protective of and sensitive to civil liberties than have elected officials or popular majorities.

STUDY CORNER

Key Terms

Bill of Rights *(p. 106)*

civil liberties *(p. 106)*

clear-and-present-danger test *(p. 108)*

due process clause (of the Fourteenth Amendment) *(p. 112)*

establishment clause *(p. 117)*

exclusionary rule *(p. 128)*

freedom of expression *(p. 107)*

free-exercise clause *(p. 119)*

imminent lawless action test *(p. 113)*

libel *(p. 115)*

prior restraint *(p. 111)*

procedural due process *(p. 124)*

selective incorporation *(p. 112)*

slander *(p. 115)*

symbolic speech *(p. 110)*

Self-Test

1. The _____ Amendment, as interpreted by the Supreme Court after 1925, provides protection of individual rights from the actions of a repressive state government.
   a. Fourteenth
   b. Tenth
   c. Fifth
   d. Fourth
   e. First

2. The exclusionary rule holds that:
   a. people who are biased against the defendant may be excluded from serving on a jury.
   b. a court can order or constrain an action by an individual.
   c. evidence obtained from an illegal search and seizure cannot be used in a trial.
   d. "fighting words" can be excluded from constitutional protection.

3. The U.S. Bill of Rights as originally approved and interpreted protected individual liberties from violation by:
   a. state government only.
   b. the national government only.
   c. both national and state governments.
   d. all levels of government in the United States.

4. The establishment clause prohibits government from:
   a. establishing exceptions to the Bill of Rights.
   b. interfering in any matters where the church and the state conflict.
   c. favoring one religion over another or supporting religion over no religion.
   d. interfering with a person's practice of religion.

5. The right to privacy was the basis for the Supreme Court ruling in:
   a. *Roe v. Wade.*
   b. *Mapp v. Ohio.*
   c. *Miranda v. Arizona.*
   d. *Schenck v. United States.*

6. The term that refers primarily to procedures that authorities must follow before a person can legitimately be punished for an offense is:
   a. the three-point test.
   b. the right to privacy.
   c. procedural due process.
   d. substantive due process.
   e. suspension of the write of habeas corpus.

7. Sexual material that is offensive to any one individual in society is automatically deemed obscene and is not protected under the First Amendment. (T/F)

8. Modern Americans' rights of free expression have been defined largely in the context of national security concerns. (T/F)

9. In order to win a libel suit, public officials must prove that a news organization or journalist acted with knowing or reckless disregard for the truth. (T/F)

10. The Supreme Court supported the effort of the state of Texas to outlaw the burning of the U.S. flag. (T/F)

Critical Thinking

What is the process of selective incorporation, and why is it important to the rights you possess today?

Suggested Readings

Abraham, Henry J. *Freedom and the Court.* New York: Oxford University Press, 2003. A comprehensive analysis of the Supreme Court's work on civil rights and civil liberties.

Epstein, Lee, and Thomas G. Walker. *Constitutional Law for a Changing America,* 5th ed. Washington, D.C.: Congressional Quarterly Press, 2004. An accessible introduction to U.S. constitutional law.

Hull, N. E. H., and Peter Charles Hoffer. *Roe v. Wade: The Abortion Rights Controversy in American History.* Lawrence: University Press of Kansas, 2001. A thorough assessment of both sides of the abortion conflict, beginning with the *Roe v. Wade* decision.

Nagel, Robert F. *Judicial Power and American Character.* New York: Oxford University Press, 1996. Concludes that the real protection for legal rights resides in political action rather than judicial decisions.

Perry, Michael J. *Religion in Politics: Constitutional and Moral Perspectives.* New York: Oxford University Press, 1997. A legal and philosophical analysis of the role of religion in politics.

Vestal, Theodore H. *The Eisenhower Court and Civil Liberties.* Westport, Conn.: Praeger, 1993. A look at the Supreme Court that greatly expanded the rights of the criminally accused.

Wirenius, John F. *First Amendment, First Principles.* New York: Holmes and Meier, 2000. Analysis of verbal acts and freedom of speech.

List of Websites

http://www.fepproject.org/

Includes information and opinions on a wide range of free-expression policy issues.

http://www.aclu.org/

The American Civil Liberties Union site; it provides information on current civil liberties and civil rights issues, including information on recent and pending Supreme Court cases.

http://www.findlaw.com/casecode/supreme.html

An excellent source of information on Supreme Court and lower-court rulings.

http://www.ncjrs.org/

The site of the National Criminal Justice Reference Service, a federally funded organization that compiles information on a wide range of criminal-justice issues.

Participate!

Although their right of free expression is protected by law, Americans often choose not to exercise this right for fear of social pressure or official reprisal. Yet constitutional rights tend to wither when people fail to exercise them. Think of an issue that you favor but that is unpopular on your campus or in your community. Consider writing a letter expressing your opinion to the editor of your college or local newspaper. (Practical advice: Keep the letter short and to the point; write a lead sentence that will get readers' attention; provide a convincing argument for your position; and be sure to sign the letter and provide a return address so the editor can contact you if there are questions.)

Extra Credit

For up-to-the-minute *New York Times* articles, interactive simulations, graphics, study tools, and more links and quizzes, visit the text's Online Learning Center at www.mhhe.com/pattersontad7.

(Self-Test Answers: 1. a   2. c   3. b   4. c   5. a   6. c   7. F   8. T   9. T   10. F)

Equal Rights:
Struggling Toward Fairness

*I have a dream that one day this nation will rise up and live out the
true meaning of its creed: "We hold these truths to be self-evident:
that all men are created equal."*

Martin Luther King Jr.[1]

The producers of ABC television's *PrimeTime Live* put hidden cameras on two young men, equally well dressed and groomed, and then sent them on different routes to do the same things—search for an apartment, shop for a car, look at albums in a record store. The cameras recorded the reactions the two men received. One was greeted with smiles and was provided with quick service. The other man was often greeted with suspicious looks and was sometimes made to wait. Why the difference? The explanation was simple: the young man who was routinely well received was white; the young man who was sometimes treated poorly was an African American.

The Urban Institute conducted a similar experiment. The experiment used pairs of specially trained white and black male college students who were the same in all respects—education, work experience, speech patterns, physical builds—except for their race. The students responded individually to nearly five hundred classified job advertisements in Chicago and Washington, D.C. The black applicants got fewer interviews, had shorter interviews, and received fewer job offers than the white applicants. An Urban Institute spokesperson said, "The level of reverse discrimination [favoring blacks over whites] that we found was limited, was certainly far lower than many might have been led to fear, and was swamped by the extent of discrimination against black job applicants."[2]

These two experiments suggest why some Americans are still struggling to achieve equal rights. In theory, Americans are equal in their rights, but in reality, they are not now equal nor have they ever been. African Americans, women, Hispanic Americans, the disabled, Jews, Native Americans, Catholics, Asian Americans, gays and lesbians, and members of nearly every other minority group have been victims of discrimination in fact and in law. The nation's creed—"all men are created equal"—has encouraged minorities to demand equal treatment. But inequality is built into almost every aspect of U.S. society. For example, compared with whites, African Americans with correctable health problems are significantly less likely to receive coronary-artery bypass surgery, to receive a kidney transplant, or to undergo surgery for early-stage lung cancer.[3]

civil rights, or **equal rights**
The right of every person to equal protection under the laws and equal access to society's opportunities and public facilities.

This chapter focuses on **equal rights,** or **civil rights**—terms that refer to the right of every person to equal protection under the laws and equal access to society's opportunities and public facilities. Chapter 4 explained that civil liberties refer to specific *individual* rights, such as freedom of speech, that are protected from infringement by government. Equal rights, or civil rights, have to do with whether individual members of differing *groups*—racial, sexual, and the like—are treated equally by government and, in some areas, by private parties. To oversimplify, civil liberties deal with issues of personal freedom, and civil rights deal with issues of equality.

Although the law refers to the rights of individuals first and to those of groups in a secondary and derivative way, this chapter concentrates on groups because the history of civil rights has been largely one of group claims to equality. The chapter emphasizes the following main points:

* *Disadvantaged groups have had to struggle for equal rights.* African Americans, women, Native Americans, Hispanic Americans, Asian Americans, and others have all had to fight for their rights in order to come closer to equality with white males.

* *Americans have attained substantial equality under the law.* They have, in legal terms, equal protection of the laws, equal access to accommodations and housing, and an equal right to vote. Discrimination by law against persons because of race, sex, religion, or ethnicity is now almost nonexistent.

* *Legal equality for all Americans has not resulted in de facto equality.* African Americans, women, Hispanic Americans, and other traditionally disadvantaged groups have a disproportionately small share of America's opportunities and benefits. Existing inequalities, discriminatory practices, and political pressures are still major barriers to their full equality. Affirmative action and busing are policies designed to help the disadvantaged achieve full equality.

THE STRUGGLE FOR EQUALITY

Equality has always been the least fully developed of America's founding concepts. Not even Thomas Jefferson, who had a deep admiration for the "common man," believed that a precise meaning could be given to the claim of the Declaration of Independence that "all men are created equal."[4]

The history of America shows that disadvantaged groups have rarely achieved a greater measure of justice without a struggle.[5] Their gains have nearly always followed intense and sustained political action, such as the civil rights movement of the 1960s, that has forced entrenched interests to relinquish or share their privileged status (see Chapter 7).

Disadvantaged groups have a shared history of political exclusion, struggles for empowerment, and policy triumphs, but they each have distinctive histories as well, as is evident by a brief review of the equal rights efforts of African Americans, women, Native Americans, Hispanic Americans, Asian Americans, and other groups.

Two police dogs attack a black civil rights activist (*center left*) during the 1963 Birmingham demonstrations. Such images of hatred and violence shook many white Americans out of their complacency regarding race relations.

African Americans

No Americans have faced greater hardship than have black Americans. Their ancestors came to this country as slaves after having been captured in Africa, shipped in chains across the Atlantic, and sold in open markets in Charleston, Boston, and other seaports.

The Civil War brought slavery, but not racism, to an end. When federal troops withdrew from the South in 1877, the region's whites regained power and enacted laws that prohibited black citizens from using the same public facilities as whites.[6] In *Plessy v. Ferguson* (1896), the Supreme Court endorsed these laws, ruling that "separate" facilities for the two races did not violate the Constitution as long as the facilities were "equal." "If one race be inferior to the other socially," the Court argued, "the Constitution of the United States cannot put them on the same plane."[7] The *Plessy* decision became a justification for the separate and *unequal* treatment of African Americans. For example, black children were forced into separate schools that rarely had libraries and had few teachers; they were given worn-out books that had been used previously in white schools.

Black Americans challenged these discriminatory policies through legal action, but not until the late 1930s did the Supreme Court begin to acknowledge their plight. The Court began modestly by ruling that where no separate public facilities existed for African Americans, they must be allowed to use those reserved for whites.[8] When Oklahoma, which had no law school for blacks, was ordered to admit Ada Sipuel as a law student in 1949, it created a separate law school for her—she sat alone in a roped-off corridor of the state capitol building. The white students, meanwhile, continued to meet at the University of Oklahoma's law school in Norman, twenty miles away.

Martin Luther King Jr.

(1929–1968)

Martin Luther King Jr. is the only American of the twentieth century to be honored with a national holiday. The civil rights leader was the pivotal figure in the movement to gain legal and political rights for black Americans. The son of a Baptist minister, King used rhetorical skills and nonviolent protest to sweep aside a century of governmental discrimination and to inspire other groups, including women and Hispanics, to assert their rights. The recipient of the Nobel Peace Prize in 1964 (the youngest person ever to receive that honor), King was assassinated in Memphis in 1968.

The Brown Decision

Substantial judicial relief for African Americans was finally achieved in 1954 with *Brown v. Board of Education of Topeka,* arguably the most significant ruling in Supreme Court history. The case began when Linda Carol Brown, a black child in Topeka, Kansas, was denied admission to an all-white elementary school that she passed every day on her way to her all-black school, which was twelve blocks farther. In its decision, the Court reversed its *Plessy* doctrine by declaring that racial segregation of public schools "generates [among black children] a feeling of inferiority as to their status in the community that may affect their hearts and minds in a way unlikely ever to be undone. . . . Separate educational facilities are inherently unequal."[9]

A 1954 Gallup poll indicated that a substantial majority of southern whites opposed the *Brown* decision. The same poll found that a slim majority of whites outside the South agreed with the decision.

The Black Civil Rights Movement

After *Brown,* the struggle of African Americans for their rights became a political movement. Perhaps no single event turned national public opinion so dramatically against segregation as a 1963 march led by Dr. Martin Luther King Jr. in Birmingham, Alabama. As the nation watched on television in disbelief, police officers led by Birmingham's sheriff, Eugene "Bull" Connor, attacked King and his followers with dogs, cattle prods, and fire hoses.

The modern civil rights movement peaked with the triumphant March on Washington for Jobs and Freedom of August 2, 1963. Organized by Dr. King and other civil rights leaders, it attracted 250,000 marchers, one of the largest gatherings in the history of the nation's capital. "I have a dream," the Reverend King told the gathering, "that my four little children will one day live in a nation where they will not be judged by the color of their skin but by the content of their character."

A year later, after a months-long fight in Congress marked by every parliamentary obstacle that racial conservatives could muster, the Civil Rights Act of 1964 was enacted. The legislation provided African Americans and other minorities with equal access to public facilities and prohibited job discrimination. President Lyndon Johnson, who had been a decisive force in the battle to pass the Civil Rights Act, called for new legislation that would also end racial barriers to voting. Congress answered with the 1965 Voting Rights Act.

The Aftermath of the Civil Rights Movement

Although the most significant progress in history toward the legal equality of all Americans occurred during the 1960s, Dr. King's dream of a color-blind society has remained elusive.[10] Even the legal rights of African Americans do

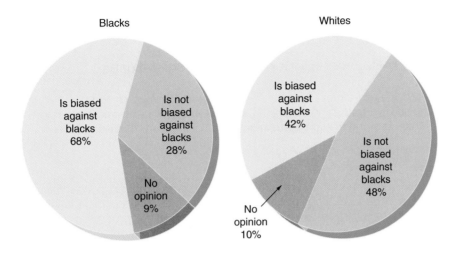

Blacks

Is biased against blacks 68%

Is not biased against blacks 28%

No opinion 9%

Whites

Is biased against blacks 42%

Is not biased against blacks 48%

No opinion 10%

Figure 5–1

Opinions on Racial Bias in the Justice System

African Americans are much more likely than white Americans to believe that the courts are biased against black people.

Source: National Center for State Courts, 1999.

not, in practice, match the promise of the civil rights movement. Studies have found, for example, that African Americans accused of crime are more likely to be convicted and to receive stiff sentences than are white Americans on trial for comparable offenses. Federal statistics indicate, for example, that black Americans account for more than 75 percent of crack cocaine convictions but only about 35 percent of crack cocaine users.[11] It is hardly surprising that many African Americans believe that the nation has two standards of justice, with a tougher one for blacks than for whites (see Figure 5–1).

One area in which African Americans have made substantial progress since the 1960s is elective office (see "States in the Nation"). Although the percentage of black elected officials is still far below the proportion of African Americans in the population, it has risen sharply over recent decades.[12] As of 2004, there were more than twenty black members of Congress and four hundred black mayors—including the mayors of some of this country's largest cities.

Women

The United States carried over from English common law a political disregard for women, forbidding them to vote, hold public office, or serve on juries.[13] Upon marriage, a woman essentially lost her identity as an individual and could not own and dispose of property without her husband's consent. Even a wife's body was not fully hers. A wife's adultery was declared by the Supreme Court to be a violation of the husband's property rights![14]

The first women's rights convention in America was held in 1848 in Seneca Falls, New York, after Lucretia Mott and Elizabeth Cady Stanton had been barred from the main floor of an antislavery convention. Thereafter, the struggle for women's rights became closely aligned with the abolitionist movement, but the passage of the post–Civil War constitutional amendments proved to be a setback for the women's movement.[15] The Fifteenth Amendment, for example, said that the right to vote could not be abridged on account of race or color but said nothing about sex. It was not until passage of the Nineteenth Amendment in 1920 that women gained the right to vote.

STATES IN THE NATION

Black and Latino Representation in State Legislatures

For a long period in U.S. history, there were almost no minorities among the ranks of state legislators. Minorities are still underrepresented relative to their numbers in the population. Although one in every three Americans is a minority-group member, only one in eight state legislators comes from a minority group.

Q: What accounts for differences between the states in the percentage of minority-group members in their legislatures?

A: States with large populations of minorities tend to have a larger percentage of legislators from minority groups. Alabama and Mississippi have large black populations and have the highest proportion of African American legislators. New Mexico, with its large Hispanic population, has the highest proportion of Latino lawmakers.

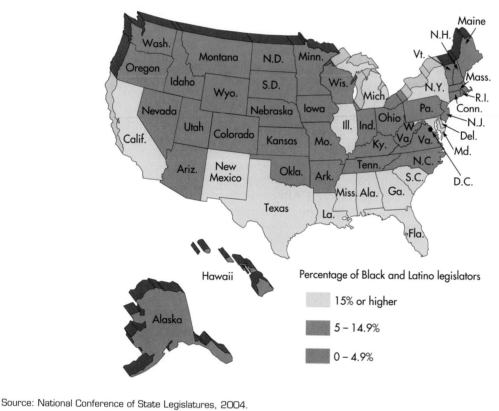

Source: National Conference of State Legislatures, 2004.

Women's Legal and Political Gains

Ratification of the Nineteenth Amendment encouraged leaders of the women's movement to propose in 1923 a constitutional amendment that would guarantee equal rights for women. Congress rejected that proposal and several subsequent ones. In 1973, however, Congress approved the Equal Rights Amendment (ERA) and submitted it to the states for ratification or rejection. The ERA failed by three states to receive the three-fourths majority required for ratification.[16]

Although the ERA did not become part of the Constitution, it helped bring women's rights to the forefront at a time when developments in Congress and the courts were contributing significantly to legal equality for women.[17] Among the congressional initiatives were the Equal Pay Act of 1963, which prohibits sex discrimination in salary and wages by some categories of employers; the Civil Rights Act of 1964, which prohibits sex discrimination in federally funded programs; Title IX of the Education Amendment of 1972, which prohibits sex discrimination in education; and the Equal Credit Act of 1974, as amended in 1976, which prohibits sex discrimination in the granting of financial credit.

Women have made substantial gains in the area of appointive and elective offices.[18] In 1981, President Reagan appointed the first woman to serve on the Supreme Court, Sandra Day O'Connor. When the Democratic party in 1984 chose Geraldine Ferraro as its vice presidential nominee, she became the first woman to run on the national ticket of a major political party. The elections of California's Dianne Feinstein and Barbara Boxer in 1992 marked the first time that women occupied both U.S. Senate seats from a state.

Despite such signs of progress, women are still a long way from political equality with men.[19] Women occupy fewer than 15 percent of congressional seats and only 20 percent of statewide and city council offices (see "How the United States Compares").

Although women are underrepresented in political office, their vote is becoming increasingly powerful. Until the 1970s, there was almost no difference in the voting patterns of women and men. Today, there is a substantial **gender gap:** women and men differ in their opinions and their votes. Women are more supportive than men of government programs for the poor, minorities, children, and the elderly. They also have a greater tendency to cast their votes for Democratic candidates (see Figure 5–2). The gender gap is discussed further in Chapter 6.

> ### *Susan B. Anthony* (1820–1906)
>
> Susan B. Anthony was a pioneer in the women's suffrage movement. She was twice arrested and fined in her adopted hometown of Rochester, New York, for organizing election day protests against laws denying women the vote. Anthony, who was also active in the temperance movement, served for a decade as president of the American Women Suffrage Association. She died before her dream of women's suffrage was fulfilled.

gender gap The tendency of women and men to differ in their political attitudes and voting preferences.

Job-Related Issues: Family Leave, Comparable Worth, and Sexual Harassment

In recent decades, increasing numbers of women have sought employment outside the home. Government statistics indicate that more than two-thirds of employment-age women work outside the home compared with only one in eight a half-century ago. Women have made gains in many traditionally male-dominated fields. For example, women now make up more than a third of the new lawyers and physicians trained each year. The change in women's work status is also reflected in education statistics. A few decades ago, more white, black, and Hispanic men than women were enrolled in college. Throughout the past decade, the reverse has been true: more women than men of each group were enrolled.

HOW THE UNITED STATES COMPARES

Inequality and Women

The one form of inequality common to all nations is that of gender: nowhere are women equal to men in law or in fact. But there are large differences between countries. A study by the Population Crisis Committee ranked the United States third overall in women's equality, behind only Sweden and Finland. Based on five measures—jobs, education, social relations, marriage and family, and health—the study rated the status of U.S. women at 82.5 percent that of men.

The inequality of women is underscored by their underrepresentation in public office. In no country do women comprise as many as half the members of the national legislature. The Scandinavian countries rank highest in terms of the percentage of female lawmakers. Other northern European countries have lower levels, but their levels are higher than in the United States. The accompanying figure indicates the approximate percentage of seats held by women in the largest chamber of each country's national legislature.

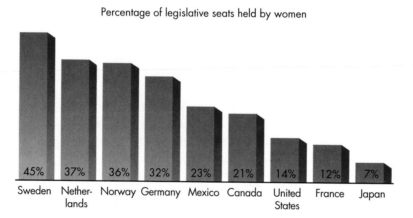

Percentage of legislative seats held by women

Sweden	Nether-lands	Norway	Germany	Mexico	Canada	United States	France	Japan
45%	37%	36%	32%	23%	21%	14%	12%	7%

Source: For non–U.S. countries, Inter-Parliamentary Union, 2001; for U.S., U.S. House of Representatives, 2004.

Figure 5–2

The Gender Gap in Congressional Voting
Women and men differ, on average, in their political behavior. For example, women are more likely than men to vote Democratic, as shown by the difference between the women's vote and the men's vote for Democratic candidates in U.S. House races.

Source: National Election Studies (1988–1998); estimated from multiple polls (2000–2004).

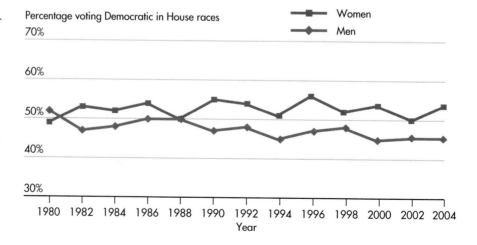

Percentage voting Democratic in House races

— Women
— Men

The majority of women with preschool children work outside the home, a situation that has created demands for government support of day care centers, parental leave, and other programs and services.

The increased presence of women in the workplace has created demands for the expansion of programs such as day care centers and parental leave. In 1993, Congress passed the Family and Medical Leave Act, which provides up to twelve weeks of unpaid leave for employees, male or female, to care for a new baby or a seriously ill family member. Upon their return from leave, employees ordinarily must be restored to their original or equivalent positions with equivalent pay, benefits, and other employment terms.

Nevertheless, women are less than equal to men when it comes to job opportunities. Although women increasingly hold managerial positions, they are less likely than men to be appointed to the top positions. The term *glass ceiling* refers to the invisible but nonetheless real barrier to advancement that talented women encounter after they have reached the middle-management level. Women employees also are paid less. Although the disparity is decreasing, the average pay for full-time female employees is only about three-fourths that of full-time male employees. This situation has led women to propose equal pay for work that is of similar difficulty and that requires similar training—a concept called *comparable worth*. Women have asked, for example, why female secretaries routinely receive lower pay than male truck drivers, even though they often have as much or more education, experience, and responsibility.[20] Advocates of comparable worth gained an early but rare victory in 1981 when the Supreme Court held that female prison guards had to be paid the same wages as male guards, even if their work assignments differed.[21]

Workplace discrimination against women includes sexual harassment. Lewd comments and unwelcome advances are a part of everyday life for many working women, and the courts have increasingly held business firms and government agencies liable if they tolerate this type of behavior.[22]

Figure 5–3

Opinions on Women's Role in Marriage

Americans are more likely than Western Europeans to believe that the "more satisfying" marriage is one where "the wife takes care of the house and children" rather than one where "the husband and wife both have jobs."

Source: Global Attitudes Survey (2002) by the Pew Research Center for the People and the Press.

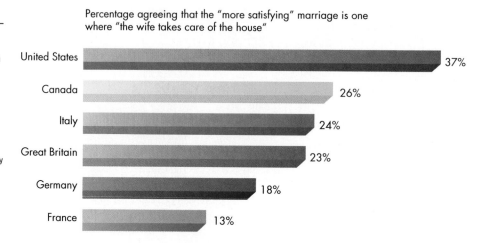

Percentage agreeing that the "more satisfying" marriage is one where "the wife takes care of the house"

- United States 37%
- Canada 26%
- Italy 24%
- Great Britain 23%
- Germany 18%
- France 13%

The obstacles to fuller advances for women in the workplace include traditional attitudes about a woman's role. Although attitudes have changed markedly in recent decades, many Americans continue to hold to the idea that a woman's proper place is in the home. This view is more prevalent in the United States than in Europe (see Figure 5–3), even though women's legal gains in the United States have been at least as substantial as those in Europe.

Native Americans

When white settlers began arriving in America in large numbers during the seventeenth century, an estimated ten million Native Americans were living in the territory that would become the United States. By 1900, the Native American population had plummeted to less than a million. No people in human history suffered a sharper decline. Diseases brought by white settlers took the largest toll on the various Indian tribes, but wars and massacres contributed. "The only good Indian is a dead Indian" is not simply a hackneyed expression from cowboy movies. It was part of a strategy of westward expansion, as settlers and U.S. troops alike mercilessly drove the eastern Indians from their ancestral lands to the Great Plains and later took those lands as well. Even well-intentioned policies failed. Reservation lands in some instances were divided into farming plots in the naive belief that Native Americans would readily adjust to an agricultural life based on private property rights.

Today Native Americans number more than one million, about half of whom live on or close to reservations set aside for them by the federal government. Reservations are governed by treaties signed when they were established. State governments have no direct authority over federal reservations, and the federal government's authority is limited by the terms of a particular treaty. Although U.S. policy toward the reservations has changed over time, the current policy is to promote self-government and economic self-sufficiency.[23] Preservation of Native American cultures is also a policy goal. For example, Native American children can now be taught in their own languages; at an earlier time in schools run by the Bureau of Indian Affairs, children were required to use English.

Members of the American Indian Movement stand watch in 1973 at Wounded Knee on the Oglala Sioux reservation in South Dakota. They had seized the hamlet in protest against federal policies toward Native Americans. The site of the armed protest was not a coincidence. In 1890, the U.S. cavalry massacred 146 Indians, including women and children, at this location.

Native Americans are less than half as likely to attend college as other Americans, their life expectancy is more than ten years lower than the national average, and their infant mortality rate is more than three times higher than that of white Americans. In recent years, some Native American tribes have erected gaming casinos on reservation land. The casinos have brought jobs and income to the reservations but have also brought controversy—traditionalists argue that the casinos are destroying their tribal cultures.

The civil rights movement of the 1960s at first did not include Native Americans. Then, in the early 1970s, militant Native Americans occupied the Bureau of Indian Affairs in Washington, D.C., and later seized control of the village of Wounded Knee on a Sioux reservation in southwestern South Dakota, exchanging gunfire with U.S. marshals. These episodes brought attention to the grievances of Native Americans and may have contributed to the passage in 1974 of legislation that granted Native Americans on reservations a greater measure of control over federal programs that affected them. Native Americans had already benefited from the legislative climate created by the 1960s civil rights movement: in 1968, Congress enacted the Indian Bill of Rights, which gives Native Americans on reservations constitutional guarantees similar to those held by other Americans.

In recent years Native Americans have filed suit to reclaim lost ancestral lands and have won a few settlements. But they stand no realistic chance of getting back even those lands that had been granted to them by federal treaty but were later sold off or seized forcibly by federal authorities. Native Americans were not even official citizens of the United States until passage of an act of Congress in 1924. This status came too late to be of much help; their traditional way of life had already been destroyed.

Cesar Estrada Chavez

(1927–1993)

Cesar Chavez led the first successful farm workers' strike in U.S. history. Founder of the United Farm Workers of America, Chavez was called "one of the heroic figures of our time" by Robert F. Kennedy and is widely regarded as the most influential Latino leader in modern U.S. history. A migrant worker as a child, Chavez knew firsthand the deprivations suffered by farm laborers. Like Martin Luther King Jr., Chavez was an advocate of nonviolent protest, and he organized food boycotts that eventually caused agricultural firms to improve wages and working conditions for farm workers. In 1994, Chavez was posthumously awarded the Presidential Medal of Freedom, the highest civilian honor that an American can receive.

Hispanic Americans

The fastest-growing minority in the United States is that of Hispanic Americans, that is, people of Spanish-speaking background. Hispanics are also one of the country's oldest ethnic groups. Some Hispanics are descendants of people who helped colonize the areas of California, Texas, Florida, New Mexico, and Arizona before those areas were annexed by the United States. But most Hispanics are recent immigrants or their descendants.

Hispanics recently surpassed African Americans as the nation's largest racial or ethnic minority group. There are more than 35 million Hispanics living in the United States, an increase of 40 percent over the 1990 census. They have emigrated to the United States primarily from Mexico and the Caribbean islands, mainly Cuba and Puerto Rico. About half of all Hispanics in the United States were born in Mexico or claim a Mexican ancestry. Hispanics are concentrated in their states of entry; thus Florida, New York, and New Jersey have large numbers of Caribbean Hispanics, while California, Texas, Arizona, and New Mexico have many immigrants from Mexico. More than half the population of Los Angeles is of Hispanic—mostly Mexican—descent.

Legal and Political Action

Hispanic Americans have benefited from laws and court rulings aimed primarily at protecting other groups. Thus, although the Civil Rights Act of 1964 was largely a response to the condition of black people, its provisions against discrimination apply broadly to other groups as well.

Nevertheless, Hispanics had their own civil rights movement. Its most publicized actions were the farm workers' strikes of the late 1960s and the 1970s that aimed at achieving basic labor rights for migrant workers. Migrants were working long hours for low pay, were living in shacks without electricity or plumbing, and were unwelcome in many local schools as well as in some local hospitals. Farm owners at first refused to bargain with the workers, but a well-organized national boycott of California grapes and lettuce forced that state to pass a law giving migrant workers the right to bargain collectively. The strikes were led in California by Cesar Chavez, who himself grew up in a Mexican American migrant family. Chavez's tactics were copied in other states, particularly Texas, but the results were less successful.

Hispanics face some distinctive problems. The fact that many do not speak English led to a 1968 amendment to the 1964 Civil Rights Act funding public school programs that offer English instruction in the language of children for whom English is a second language. In addition, many Hispanics are illegal aliens and do not have the full rights of citizens. In *De Canas v. Bica* (1976), for example, the Supreme Court upheld a state law barring illegal aliens from employment.[24]

U.S. Congresswoman Loretta Sanchez (D-Calif.) represents a part of Orange County, California. Hispanic Americans are growing in political and cultural influence as their numbers increase in California, Arizona, New Mexico, Texas, and other states.

The issue of illegal aliens was also addressed through California's controversial Proposition 187. Placed on the state's ballot in 1994 through a citizen petition, Proposition 187 received the votes of a majority of Californians even though most of the state's Mexican Americans voted against it. The initiative aimed to cut off public services to illegal immigrants, the great majority of whom are Mexicans. They would no longer receive state-funded food stamps, welfare, and medical care except in life-threatening circumstances, and they would no longer be eligible for public schooling at any level. To many of California's Mexican Americans, the initiative was a thinly disguised attempt to discourage additional people from Mexico from entering the state. The implementation of Proposition 187 was delayed pending a court ruling on its constitutionality, and most of its key provisions were subsequently judged to be unconstitutional.

Of the various initiatives of recent years, none would likely match the impact of President George Bush's 2004 proposal to establish a guest worker program. Under the plan, workers who are in the country illegally could enroll in the guest worker program, which would guarantee them a three-year stay, possibly with a chance of renewal. Other workers could enter the country under the program provided they have a job waiting for them. With ten million or more illegal workers—mostly Hispanics—already in the United States, the program would address the nation's labor needs while shutting off the flow and subsequent employment of illegal workers. Bush's proposal has been strongly endorsed by business leaders who see the program as an answer to their labor needs. However, some conservatives have argued that the program is a bad idea because it would reward people who have broken the law by entering the country illegally. Liberals have also spoken out against it, claiming that the program should have an automatic provision for eventual citizenship for those workers who hold onto their jobs and have no criminal record.[25]

Figure 5–4

Hispanics' Party Identification
Hispanics' party loyalties lean heavily toward the Democratic party.
Source: CBS News/New York Times poll, August 2003.

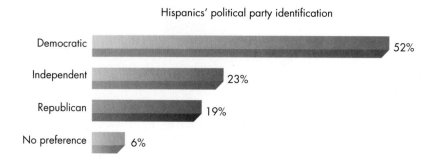

Hispanics' political party identification

- Democratic — 52%
- Independent — 23%
- Republican — 19%
- No preference — 6%

Growing Political Power

More than four thousand Hispanic Americans nationwide hold public office. Hispanics have been elected to statewide office in several states, including New Mexico and Arizona. About twenty Hispanic Americans currently serve in the House of Representatives.

Hispanic Americans are an important political force in several states and communities, and their influence is likely to increase substantially in the future. By the middle of the century, Hispanics are projected to become the largest racial or ethnic group in California. Their political involvement, like that of other immigrant groups, can be expected to increase as they become more firmly rooted in society. At present, about half of all Hispanics are not registered to vote, and only about a third actually vote, limiting the group's political power. Nevertheless, the sheer size of the Hispanic population in states such as Texas and California makes the group a potent political force, as was evident in the 2004 election when both the Republican party and the Democratic party mounted massive efforts to woo Hispanic voters.

With the exception of the conservative Republican–leaning Cuban Americans of southern Florida, Hispanics lean toward the Democratic party (see Figure 5–4). However, Hispanics are not a cohesive voting bloc in the same way that African Americans are. Blacks of all income levels are solidly Democratic, while among Hispanics, Democratic support is concentrated among those of lower income. Opinion surveys show that Hispanics tend to be relatively liberal on economic issues and relatively conservative on social issues. These tendencies suggest that the Democratic party will benefit in the short term from the Hispanic vote but that, over a longer period and as Hispanics become more affluent, the Hispanic vote will divide more evenly between the parties.[27]

Asian Americans

Chinese and Japanese laborers were brought into western states during the late 1800s to work in mines and to build railroads. When the need for this labor declined, Congress in 1892 ordered a temporary halt to Asian immigration. Over the next three decades, informal agreements kept all but a few Asians from entering the country. In 1930, Congress completely blocked the entry of Japanese. Japan had protested a California law that prohibited persons of Japanese descent from buying property in the state. Rather than finesse what was called "the

California problem," Congress bluntly told Japan that its people were not wanted in the United States.[28]

Discrimination against Asians did not ease substantially until 1965, when Congress enacted legislation that adjusted the immigration quotas to favor those who had previously been assigned very small numbers. This change in the law was a product of the 1960s civil rights movement, which increased public awareness of all forms of discrimination. About half a million people now emigrate to the United States each year, and a majority come from Asian and Latin American countries. Asian Americans numbered about twelve million in the 2000 census, or roughly 4 percent of the total U.S. population. Most Asian Americans live on the West Coast, particularly in California. China, Japan, Korea, India, Vietnam, and the Philippines are the ancestral homes of most Asian Americans.

Asian Americans studying in a high school classroom. Many Asian American families emphasize academic achievement as a basis of personal advancement.

The rights of Asian Americans have been expanded primarily by court rulings and legislation, such as the Civil Rights Act of 1964, that were responses to the problems of other minorities. In some instances, however, the actions of Asian Americans have strengthened the rights of other minorities. In *Lau v. Nichols* (1974), a case initiated by a Chinese American family, the Supreme court ruled unanimously that placing public school children for whom English is a second language in regular classrooms without special assistance is a violation of the Fourteenth Amendment's equal protection clause, because it denies them an equal educational opportunity.[29] Although the Court did not mandate bilingual instruction as the form of that assistance and later held that bilingual courses are not required, the *Lau* decision did lead many schools to establish bilingual instruction. Since the, some states have restricted its use. In California, the limitation was enacted in 1998 through Proposition 227, which requires children for whom English is a second language to take their courses in English after their first year in school, though other forms of assistance and waivers are permitted in some cases. Proposition 227 was opposed by teachers' organizations and by many within California's Asian and Hispanic communities, but its advocates argued that English immersion was a necessary step in the full integration of students into schools and the larger society.

Asian Americans are an upwardly mobile group. The values of most Asian cultures include a commitment to hard work, which, in the American context, has included an emphasis on academic achievement. For example, Asians make up a disproportionate share of the students at California's leading public universities, which base admission primarily on high school grades and standardized test scores. However, Asian Americans are still underrepresented in certain areas of the workplace. According to U.S. government figures, Asian Americans account for about 5 percent of professionals and technicians, slightly more than their percentage of the total population. Yet they hold less than 2 percent of managerial jobs; past and present discrimination has kept them from obtaining their fair share of top business positions. They are also underrepresented politically.[30] It was not until 1996, for example, that the first Asian American was elected governor of a state other than Hawaii.

Other Groups and Their Rights

The 1964 Civil Rights Act (discussed further later in the chapter) prohibits discrimination by sex, race, or national origin. This act classified women and racial and ethnic minorities as legally protected groups, enabling them to vigorously pursue their rights. As these minority groups gained success, other groups began to make their own claims for protection. They have sought to prevent discrimination that is rooted in prejudicial attitudes or assumptions.

Older Americans

Older Americans are one such group. The Age Discrimination Act of 1975 and the Age Discrimination in Employment Act of 1967 prohibit discrimination against older workers in hiring for jobs in which age is not clearly a crucial factor in job performance. More recently, mandatory retirement ages for most jobs have been eliminated by law. Forced retirement for reasons of age is permissible only if it is justified by the nature of a particular job or by the performance of a particular employee.

However, older Americans are not as fully protected in law as some other groups. As explained in Chapter 3, the Supreme Court has held that Congress cannot require state governments to comply with federal laws banning discrimination against older workers. The Court holds that, because age discrimination is not among the forms of discrimination expressly prohibited by the U.S. Constitution, states have the power to decide for themselves the age-related policies that will apply to their own employees.[31] (Most states do provide substantial legal protections for older residents.)

Disabled Americans

Disabled Americans are also protected from discrimination. Roughly 40 million Americans have a physical or mental disability that prevents them from performing a critical function, such as seeing, hearing, or walking. A goal of the disabled is equal access to society's opportunities. This was facilitated by the 1990 Americans with Disabilities Act, which grants the disabled the same employment and other protections enjoyed by other disadvantaged groups. In addition, the Education for All Handicapped Children Act of 1975 mandates that all children, however severe their disability, receive a free, appropriate education. Before the legislation, 4 million children with disabilities were getting either no education or an inappropriate one (as in the case of a blind child who is not taught Braille).

The Supreme Court has held that state governments are not bound by the 1990 Americans with Disabilities Act in the treatment of their own employees but are required to take reasonable steps to provide the disabled with access to state-provided public services and facilities.[32]

Gays and Lesbians

A group that until very recently has not received substantial legal protection is gays and lesbians. In 2000, for example, the Supreme Court ruled that the Boy

Equality: The American Birthright

In his acceptance speech at the 1996 Republican National Convention, Robert Dole said that any delegate who didn't believe in racial equality should leave through the nearest exit. If the country itself had exit doors, Dole's instructions would still make sense. Superficial differences in skin color, religion, gender, and the like should never be a basis for discriminatory words or actions.

Equality has always been America's most unrealized ideal. Since the introduction of slavery four hundred years ago, Americans have struggled to create a more equal society. Disadvantaged groups have had to fight to achieve a fuller measure of recognition and justice. It is not surprising that they would choose to make the fight. No people in human history have thought that second-class status is preferable to equal treatment. What is somewhat surprising, however, is the resistance of dominant groups to the more equal treatment of others. If the economic self-interest of the slaveowner somehow made slavery understandable, though no less abominable, what could possibly underlie discrimination today except blatant prejudice?

The negative aspects of inequality have long been part of the American experience. Less attention has been paid to the positive aspects of equality. In the absence of discrimination, people are more productive and more sociable in every phase of life. The economy, the society, and the polity all benefit from the more equal treatment of all citizens. There is wider affluence, less crime, and more civic trust. The effect can be compared to an upswing in the economic cycle. When the economy expands, employment and production expand, improving the position of everyone. So it is with a more equal society. Few are worse off, and society as a whole is better off.

The American experience has always been in part a grand experiment to see whether diverse peoples can live together in harmony and mutual respect. It is justifiably called an experiment because, in the history of the world, peaceful relations between different peoples within the same national boundaries have been difficult to achieve.

Scouts, as a private organization that has a right to freedom of association, can ban gays because the Scout creed prohibits homosexuality.[33]

Research has not identified the full extent of discrimination against gays and lesbians, but fragmentary evidence indicates that it is substantial. A disproportionate number of hate crimes—including assaults—are directed at gay men. A poll found that nearly 40 percent of the members of the Los Angeles Bar Association had witnessed overt discrimination in their firm and that more than 50 percent thought their firm's work environment was antagonistic to lawyers who were gay or lesbian. A survey of New York State gays and lesbians found that half had experienced gender-based discrimination at a restaurant, store, hotel, or other public place.[34]

Historically, gays and lesbians fought discrimination by trying to keep their sexual orientation a secret. Many still do so, but gays and lesbians now also comprise a powerful political group. One of the first indications was when Democratic presidential nominee Bill Clinton in 1992 promised to change the military's ban on homosexuals. The resulting "don't ask, don't tell" policy allows gays and lesbians to remain in the military as long as they do not by words or actions openly reveal their sexual preference. Nevertheless, the "don't ask, don't tell" policy was a hollow victory to many gays and lesbians, who had wanted the ban to be lifted completely.

Debating the Issues

Should Same-Sex Marriage Be Legalized?

The Massachusetts Supreme Judicial Court in 2003 declared that the state's constitution required that same-sex couples be given the same opportunity to marry as opposite-sex couples. The court ordered the state legislature to enact a law to that effect within six months. In 2004, Massachusetts became the first state to allow same-sex marriage. Four years earlier, Vermont had authorized civil unions for same-sex couples, which provided them with many of the same legal rights enjoyed by opposite-sex married couples. Widespread public debate accompanied these policy developments, particularly same-sex marriage.

Yes: The Massachusetts Supreme Judicial Court ruled that the rights, protections, and responsibilities afforded by civil marriage should not be denied to any resident of that state. It is a great victory for the seven couples represented by the Gay & Lesbian Advocates & Defenders, for every gay and lesbian couple in Massachusetts—and for all fair-minded people who believe every American deserves equal treatment under the law. The opening statement of the court's decision says it all: "The exclusive commitment of two individuals to each other nurtures love and mutual support; it brings stability to our society." This decision affirms the inherent value and social benefit that committed, loving relationships between gay and lesbian people bring to society at large—and utterly dismisses the claims made by the anti-gay industry that granting basic protections and rights to same-sex families somehow threatens the fabric of our society. My partner of 22 years and I have experienced firsthand the benefits a loving, mutually supportive relationship has had on our three children. It's gratifying to see the Massachusetts court acknowledge relationships like ours—and we look forward to a day when every state recognizes the benefit of treating relationships like ours equally under the law.

—Joan Garry, Executive Director, Gay and Lesbian Alliance Against Defamation

No: Across times, cultures, and very different religious beliefs, marriage is the foundation of the family. The family, in turn, is the basic unit of society. Thus, marriage is a personal relationship with public significance. Marriage is the fundamental pattern for male-female relationships. It contributes to society because it models the way in which women and men live interdependently and commit, for the whole of life, to seek the good of each other. The marital union also provides the best conditions for raising children: namely, the stable, loving relationship of a mother and father present only in marriage. The state rightly recognizes this relationship as a public institution in its laws because the relationship makes a unique and essential contribution to the common good. Laws play an education role insofar as they shape patterns of thought and behavior, particularly about what is socially permissible and acceptable. . . . When marriage is redefined so as to make other relationships equivalent to it, the institution of marriage is devalued and further weakened. The weakening of this basic institution at all levels and by various forces has already exacted too high a social cost.

—U.S. Conference of Catholic Bishops

Gays and lesbians gained a significant legal victory when the Supreme Court in *Romer v. Evans* (1996) struck down a Colorado constitutional amendment that nullified all existing and any new legal protections for homosexuals. In a 6-3 ruling, the Court said that the Colorado law violated the Constitution's guarantee of equal protection because it subjected individuals to employment and other forms of discrimination simply because of their sexual preference. The Court concluded that the law had no reasonable purpose but was instead motivated by hostility toward homosexuals.[35] In *Lawrence v. Texas* (2003), the Court handed gays and lesbians another victory by invalidating state laws that prohibit sexual relations between consenting adults of the same sex (see Chapter 4.[36]

Recently, a major issue for gays and lesbians has been securing the same legal status that the law extends to married opposite-sex couples. During the past decade or so, same-sex couples have succeeded in getting some states and many cities and firms to extend employee benefits, such as health care, to employees' same-sex partners.[37] These arrangements, however, do not apply to things such as inheritance and hospital visitation rights, which are granted by state law to married couples and their families. There is also the issue of the social validation accorded to couples who are married as opposed to those who are not. For these reasons, gay and lesbian couples have pressed for legal recognition of their relationships. In 2000, the state of Vermont legalized the civil union of same-sex couples, thereby granting them the same legal rights as those held by opposite-sex married couples. In 2004, upon order of the state's high court, Massachusetts instituted same-sex marriage, giving same-sex married couples the same social and legal status as opposite-sex married couples.

This issue spilled over to the 2004 presidential campaign when President George W. Bush reacted to the Massachusetts high court decision by claiming that marriage should be reserved for "a man and a woman." The Democratic party's nominee, John Kerry, also came out against same-sex marriage, but, unlike Bush, he endorsed civil unions.

For their part, a majority of Americans oppose same-sex marriage, although they are divided almost evenly on the issue of civil unions.[38] Nevertheless, attitudes toward same-sex relationships have moderated substantially in recent decades. Most Americans, for example, now believe that partners in same-sex relationships should receive the same employee health benefits as spouses.[39] Yet Americans, perhaps because of their deeper religious beliefs (see Chapter 6), are less supportive of gay and lesbian lifestyles than are Europeans (see Figure 5–5). One thing is sure: issues of gay and lesbian rights, including same-sex marriage and civil union, will be a focus of political action and controversy for the foreseeable future.

Percentage agreeing that "homosexuality is a way of life that should be accepted by society."

Germany 83%
France 77%
Great Britain 74%
Italy 71%
Canada 69%
United States 51%

Figure 5–5

Opinions on Gay and Lesbian Lifestyles
Americans are less likely than Western Europeans to believe that society should accept gay and lesbian lifestyles.
Source: Global Attitudes Survey (2002) by the Pew Research Center for the People and the Press.

EQUALITY UNDER THE LAW

The catchphrase of nearly every group's claim to a more equal standing in American society has been "equality under the law." Once they are secure in their legal rights, people are in a stronger position to insist that their rights be respected and find it easier to pursue equality in other arenas, such as the economic sector. Americans' claims to legal equality are embodied in a great many laws, a few of which are particularly noteworthy.

Equal Protection: The Fourteenth Amendment

The Fourteenth Amendment, which was ratified in 1868, declares in part that no state shall "deny to any person within its jurisdiction the equal protection of the laws." Through this **equal-protection clause,** the courts have protected such groups as African Americans and women from discrimination by state and local governments.

The Fourteenth Amendment's equal-protection clause does not require government to treat all groups or classes of people the same way in all circumstances. By law, for example, twenty-one-year-olds can drink alcohol but twenty-year-olds cannot. The judiciary allows such inequalities because they are held to be "reasonably" related to a legitimate government interest. In applying this **reasonable-basis test,** the courts require government only to show that a particular law has a sound basis. For example, the courts have held that the goal of reducing fatalities from alcohol-related accidents involving young drivers is a valid reason for imposing a twenty-one-year minimum age requirement for the purchase of alcohol.

The reasonable-basis test does not apply, however, to racial or ethnic classifications, particularly when these categories serve to discriminate against minority group members (see Table 5–1). Any law that treats people differently because of race or ethnicity is subject to the **strict-scrutiny test,** under which

> **equal-protection clause** A clause of the Fourteenth Amendment that forbids any state to deny equal protection of the laws to any individual within its jurisdiction.

> **reasonable-basis test** A test applied by courts to laws that treat individuals unequally. Such a law may be deemed constitutional if its purpose is held to be "reasonably" related to a legitimate government interest.

> **strict-scrutiny test** A test applied by courts to laws that attempt a racial or ethnic classification. In effect, the strict scrutiny test eliminates race or ethnicity as a legal classification when it places minority group members at a disadvantage.

TABLE 5–1	**Levels of Court Review for Laws That Treat Americans Differently**	
TEST	**APPLIES TO**	**STANDARD USED**
Strict scrutiny	Race, ethnicity	Suspect category—assumed unconstitutional in the absence of an overwhelming justification
Intermediate scrutiny	Gender	Almost suspect category—assumed unconstitutional unless the law serves a clearly compelling and justified purpose
Reasonable basis	Other categories (such as age and income)	Not suspect category—assumed constitutional unless no sound rationale for the law can be provided

such a law is unconstitutional in the absence of an overwhelmingly convincing argument that it is necessary. The strict-scrutiny test has virtually eliminated race and ethnicity as permissible classifications when the effect is to place a hardship on members of a minority group. The Supreme Court's position is that race and national origin are **suspect classifications**—in other words, that legal classifications based on race and ethnicity are assumed to have discrimination as their purpose and are presumed unconstitutional.

Although women are excluded by law from having to register for the draft, they serve with distinction in the U.S. military.

The strict-scrutiny test emerged after the 1954 *Brown* ruling and became a basis for invalidating laws that discriminated against black people. As other groups, especially women, began to organize and assert their rights in the late 1960s and early 1970s, the Supreme Court gave early signs that it might expand the scope of suspect classifications to include gender. In the end, however, the Court announced in *Craig v. Boren* (1976) that sex classifications were permissible if they served "important governmental objectives" and were "substantially" related to the achievement of those objectives.[40] The Court thus placed sex distinctions in an intermediate (or almost suspect) category, to be scrutinized more closely than some other classifications (for example, income or age level) but, unlike racial classifications, justifiable in some instances. In *Rostker v. Goldberg* (1980), for example, the policy of male-only registration for the military draft was upheld on grounds that the exclusion of women from *involuntary* combat duty serves a legitimate and important purpose.[41]

suspect classifications Legal classifications, such as race and national origin, that have invidious discrimination as their purpose and are therefore unconstitutional.

The inexactness of the **intermediate-scrutiny test** has led some scholars to question its usefulness as a legal principle. Nevertheless, when evaluating claims of sex discrimination, the judiciary applies a stricter level of scrutiny than is required by the reasonable-basis test. Rather than giving government broad leeway to treat men and women differently, the Supreme Court has invalidated most of the laws it has recently reviewed that contain sex classifications. A leading case is *United States v. Virginia* (1996), in which the Supreme Court determined that the male-only admissions policy of Virginia Military Institute (VMI), a 157-year-old state-supported college, was unconstitutional. The state had developed an alternative program for women at another college, but the Court concluded that it was no substitute for the unique education and other opportunities that attendance at VMI could provide. (The VMI decision also had the effect of ending the all-male admissions policy of the Citadel, a state-supported military college in South Carolina.)[42]

intermediate-scrutiny test A test applied by courts to laws that attempt a gender classification. In effect, the test eliminates gender as a legal classification unless it serves an important objective and is substantially related to the objective's achievement.

Equal Access: The Civil Rights Acts of 1964 and 1968

The Fourteenth Amendment applies only to action by government. It does not prohibit discrimination by private parties. As a result, for a long period in the nation's history, owners could legally bar black people from restaurants, hotels, and other accommodations, and employers could freely discriminate in their

Liberty, Equality & Self-Government

What's Your Opinion?

Private Discrimination

The courts have ruled that private organizations are often within their rights in discriminating against individuals because of color, gender, creed, national origin, or other characteristics. The Fifth and Fourteenth Amendments only prohibit discrimination by government bodies.

Jews, Catholics, and blacks are among the groups that historically have been denied membership in private clubs and organizations. The most celebrated recent incident was the decision of the Boy Scouts of America (BSA) to revoke the membership of Scoutmaster James Dale. Dale is gay, and the BSA excludes homosexuals

from membership. Dale's suit against the BSA went to the Supreme Court, which ruled in 2000 that the BSA, as a private organization, had the right to deny membership to gays.

Issues of liberty and equality are at the forefront of such cases. Liberty is enhanced when private organizations are free to pick their members. But equality is diminished when people are denied opportunities because of their physical characteristics or lifestyles.

What's your opinion on the Dale–BSA dispute? What general limits, if any, would you impose on the discriminatory acts of private organizations?

job practices. Since the 1960s, private firms have had much less freedom to discriminate for reasons of race, sex, ethnicity, or religion.

Accommodations and Jobs

The Civil Rights Act of 1964 entitles all persons to equal access to restaurants, bars, theaters, hotels, gasoline stations, and similar establishments serving the general public. The legislation also bars discrimination in the hiring, promotion, and wages of employees of medium-size and large firms. A few forms of job discrimination are still lawful under the Civil Rights Act. For example, an owner-operator of a small business can discriminate in hiring his or her coworkers, and a religious school can take the religion of a prospective teacher into account.

The Civil Rights Act of 1964 has nearly eliminated the most overt forms of discrimination in the area of public accommodations. Some restaurants and hotels may provide better service to white customers, but outright refusal to serve African Americans or other minority group members is rare. Such a refusal is a violation of the law and could easily be proved in many instances. It is harder to prove discrimination in job decisions; accordingly, the act has been less effective in rooting out employment discrimination— a subject that we will discuss in detail later in this chapter.

Housing

In 1968, Congress passed civil rights legislation designed to prohibit discrimination in housing. A building owner cannot refuse to sell or rent housing because of a person's race, religion, ethnicity, or sex. An exception is allowed for owners of small multifamily dwellings who reside on the premises.

Despite legal prohibitions on discrimination, housing in America remains highly segregated. Less than a third of all African Americans live in a neighborhood that is mostly white. One reason is that the annual income of most black families is substantially below that of most white families. Another reason is banking practices. At one time, banks contributed to housing segregation by redlining—refusing to grant mortgage loans in certain neighborhoods. This practice drove down the selling prices of homes in these neighborhoods, which led to an influx of African Americans and an exodus of whites. Redlining is prohibited by the 1968 Civil Rights Act, but many of the segregated neighborhoods that it helped create still exist.

Recent studies indicate that minority status is still a factor in the lending practices of some banks.[43] A report of the U.S. Conference of Mayors indicated that, among applicants with average or slightly higher incomes relative to their community, Hispanics and African Americans were twice as likely as whites to be denied a mortgage.[44]

Equal Ballots: The Voting Rights Act of 1965, as Amended

Free elections are perhaps the foremost symbol of American democracy, yet the right to vote has only recently become a reality for many Americans, particularly African Americans.

The Nineteenth Amendment, which in 1920 gave women the right to vote, effectively ended resistance to women's suffrage; paradoxically, resistance to black suffrage was intensified by the Fifteenth Amendment, which in 1870 gave black persons the right to vote. Southern whites invented a series of devices, including whites-only primaries, poll taxes, and rigged literacy tests to keep African Americans from registering and voting. For example, almost no votes were cast by African Americans in North Carolina between the years 1920 and 1946.[45]

Barriers to black participation in elections began to crumble in the mid-1940s, when the Supreme Court declared that whites-only primary elections were unconstitutional.[46] Two decades later, the Twenty-fourth Amendment outlawed poll taxes.

The major step toward equal voting rights for African Americans was passage of the Voting Rights Act of 1965, which forbids discrimination in voting and registration.[47] The legislation empowers federal agents to register voters and to oversee participation in elections. The Voting Rights Act, as interpreted by the courts, also eliminates literacy tests; local officials can no longer deny registration and voting for reasons of illiteracy. Although civil rights legislation has seldom had a large and immediate impact on people's behavior, the Voting Rights Act was an exception. In the 1960 presidential election, voter turnout among African Americans was barely 30 percent nationwide (see Figure 5–6). In 1968, three years after passage of the legislation, the turnout rate exceeded 40 percent.

Congress renewed the Voting Rights Act in 1970, 1975, and 1982. The 1982 extension is noteworthy because it renewed the act for twenty years and

Figure 5-6

Voter Turnout in Presidential Campaigns Among Black and White Americans, 1960–2004

Voter turnout among black Americans rose dramatically during the 1960s as legal obstacles to their voting were removed.

Source: U.S. Bureau of the Census. The 2004 figures based on preliminary estimates.

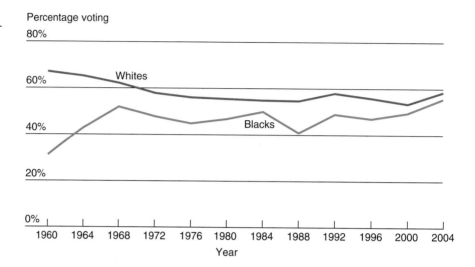

requires states and localities to clear with federal officials any electoral change that has the effect, intended or not, of reducing the voting power of a minority group. One way to reduce the power of a group's votes is to spread members of the group across election districts so that their number in any given district is too small to constitute a voting majority. When congressional district boundaries were redrawn after the 1990 census (see Chapter 11), the 1982 extension became the basis for the creation of districts that included a majority of Hispanic or African American voters. The result was the election of an unprecedented number of minority group members to Congress in 1992, when the number of Hispanic and African American representatives jumped from 27 to 63.

However, in three separate cases that were each decided by a 5–4 margin, the Supreme Court ruled that the redistricting of several congressional districts in Texas, North Carolina, and Georgia was unconstitutional because race had been the "dominant" factor in their creation. The Court held that the redistricting violated the rights of white voters under the Fourteenth Amendment's equal-protection clause, and the states were ordered to redraw the districts. Three of the justices voting with the majority indicated, however, that there *might* be instances in which race, along with other factors, could be taken into account in redistricting decisions. But the Court's majority was insistent in its claim that race cannot be the *deciding* factor in redistricting arrangements.[48]

In a 2001 decision, *Easley v. Cromartie,* the Court granted states considerably more flexibility in drawing district lines. The Court held that as long as a district's boundaries were based on partisan considerations, the fact that a large number of minority group members were concentrated in a district did not violate the equal-protection clause. State legislatures routinely draw district boundaries in ways designed to increase the likelihood that the congressional seat will be won by a particular party. The Court has long held that this action is permissible. In *Easley v. Cromartie,* the Court said that even though the North Carolina district in question contained a large proportion of black Americans, it was drawn with the goal of creating a safe Democratic seat and, as such, did not violate the Fourteenth Amendment.[49]

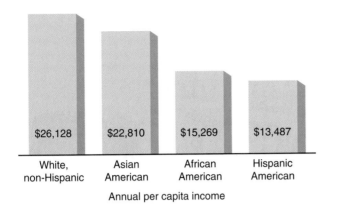

Figure 5–7

**U.S. per Capita Income, by
Race and Ethnicity**
The average income of white
Americans is substantially
higher than that of most other
Americans.
Source: U.S. Bureau of the Census,
2004.

 ## EQUALITY OF RESULT

America's disadvantaged groups have made significant progress toward equal rights, particularly during the past few decades. Through acts of Congress and rulings of the Supreme Court, most forms of government-sponsored discrimination—from racially segregated public schools to gender-based pension plans—have been banned.

However, civil rights problems involve deeply rooted conditions, habits, and prejudices and affect whole categories of people. For these reasons, a new civil rights policy rarely produces a sudden and dramatic change in society. Despite their greater equality in law, America's traditionally disadvantaged groups are still substantially unequal in their daily lives. Consider the issue of income disparity (see Figure 5–7). The average Hispanic or African American's income is less than 60 percent of the average white person's income.

Such figures reflect **de facto discrimination,** which is discrimination that is a consequence of social, economic, and cultural biases and conditions. This type of discrimination is different from **de jure discrimination,** which is discrimination based on law, as in the case of segregation in southern public schools during the pre-*Brown* period. De facto discrimination is difficult to root out because it is embedded not in the law but in the very structure of society. **Equality of result** is the aim of policies intended to reduce or eliminate de facto discriminatory effects. Such policies are inherently more controversial because many Americans believe that government's responsibility extends no further than the removal of legal barriers to equality. This attitude reflects the culture's emphasis on personal *liberty*—the freedom to choose one's associates, employees, neighbors, and classmates. This cultural belief helps explain public resistance to any large-scale government effort to reduce the economic and social gaps between Americans of varying racial and ethnic backgrounds. Nevertheless, a few policies—notably affirmative action and busing—have been implemented to achieve equality of result.

de facto discrimination
Discrimination on the basis of
race, sex, religion, ethnicity,
and the like that results from
social, economic, and cultural
biases and conditions.

de jure discrimination
Discrimination on the basis of
race, sex, religion, ethnicity,
and the like that results from a
law.

equality of result The objective
of policies intended to reduce
or eliminate the effects of
discrimination so that
members of traditionally
disadvantaged groups will have
the same benefits of society as
do members of advantaged
groups.

Affirmative Action: Workplace Integration

The difficulty of converting newly acquired legal rights into everyday realities is illustrated by the 1964 Civil Rights Act. Although the legislation prohibited

Since its inception in the 1960s, affirmative action policy has been a source of contentious debate but also a source of progress for women and minorities.

discrimination in employment, women and minorities did not suddenly obtain jobs for which they were qualified. Many employers maintained a deliberate though unwritten preference for white male employees. Other employers adhered to established employment procedures that continued to keep women and minorities at a disadvantage; membership in many union locals, for example, was handed down from father to son. Moreover, the Civil Rights Act did not require employers to prove that their hiring practices were not discriminatory. Instead, the burden of proof was on the woman or minority group member who had been denied a particular job. It was costly and often difficult for individuals to prove in court that their sex or race was the reason they had not been hired. In addition, a victory in court helped only the individual in question; these case-by-case settlements did not affect the millions of other women and minorities facing job discrimination.

A broader remedy was obviously required, and the result was the emergence during the late 1960s of affirmative action programs. **Affirmative action** is a deliberate effort to provide full and equal opportunities in employment, education, and other areas for members of traditionally disadvantaged groups. Affirmative action requires corporations, universities, and other organizations to establish programs designed to ensure that all applicants are treated fairly. Affirmative action also places the burden of proof on the providers of opportunities, who, to some extent, must be able to demonstrate that any disproportionate granting of opportunities to white males is not the result of discriminatory practices.

Few issues in recent years have provoked more controversy than has affirmative action.[50] Although most Americans say they believe that minorities and women deserve a truly equal chance at jobs and other opportunities, they also say they worry that aggressive affirmative action programs will discriminate against more qualified males, an outcome that is called *reverse discrimination* (see Figure 5–8).

affirmative action A term that refers to programs designed to ensure that women, minorities, and other traditionally disadvantaged groups have full and equal opportunities in employment, education, and other areas of life.

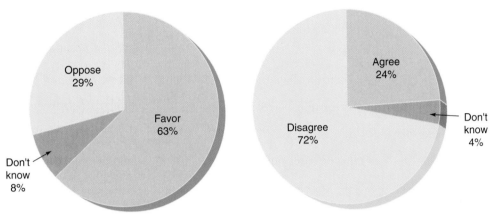

"In order to overcome past discrimination, do you favor or oppose affirmative action programs designed to help blacks, women, and other minorities get better jobs and education?"

Oppose
29%

Favor
63%

Don't know
8%

"We should make every possible effort to improve the position of blacks and other minorities, even if it means giving them preferential treatment."

Agree
24%

Don't know
4%

Disagree
72%

Figure 5–8

Opinions on Affirmative Action

Most Americans support affirmative action when it comes to programs that will give women and minorities an equal chance at opportunities but oppose it when it comes to programs that will give them preferential treatment.

Source: The Pew Research Center for the People and the Press, March 14, 2003.

Affirmative Action in the Law

Most issues that pit individuals against each other in a struggle over society's benefits eventually end up in the courts, and affirmative action is no exception (see Table 5–2). The policy was first tested before the Supreme Court in *University of California Regents v. Bakke* (1978). Alan Bakke, a white man, had twice been denied admission to a University of California medical school, even though his admission test scores were higher than those of several minority-group students who had been accepted. Bakke sued, claiming the school had a quota system for minorities that discriminated against white males. The Court ruled in Bakke's favor but did not invalidate affirmative action per se. The Court said only that rigid racial quotas could not be used in determining medical school admissions.[51]

Bakke was followed by two rulings in favor of affirmative action programs, one of which—*Fullilove v. Klutnick* (1980)—upheld a quota system that required 10 percent of federal public works funds to be set aside for minority-owned firms.[52]

In the 1980s, the appointment of more conservative justices to the Supreme Court narrowed the scope of affirmative action policy. The Court held, for example, that preferential treatment of minorities normally could be justified only in cases where discrimination had been severe and that affirmative action could be applied only in a way that did not infringe on the rights of white employees to keep their jobs (thus restricting the use of race as a basis for determining which employees would be terminated in the case of job layoffs).[53]

TABLE 5–2	Key Decisions in the History of Affirmative Action Policy

YEAR	ACTION
1969	Nixon administration's Department of Labor initiates affirmative action policy
1978	Supreme Court in *Bakke* invalidates rigid quotas for medical school admissions but does not invalidate affirmative action
1980	Supreme Court in *Fullilove* upholds a quota system for minority-owned firms in granting of federal contracts
1980s	Supreme Court in a series of decisions narrows situations in which preferential treatment of minorities will be permitted
1991	In Civil Rights Act of 1991, Congress places burden of proof on business in situations where there is a pattern of white male dominance
1995	Supreme Court in *Adarand* eliminates fixed quotas in the granting of government contracts, reversing the *Fullilove* (1980) precedent
1996	California voters enact Proposition 209, which bans public employment, education, and contracting programs based on race, ethnicity, or sex
2003	Supreme Court in *Gratz v. Bollinger* and *Grutter v. Bollinger* upholds affirmative action but invalidates formula-based (quota-like) programs.

Proponents of affirmative action succeeded, however, in shifting some of the burden of proof about discrimination from employees to employers. After the Supreme Court in the 1980s allowed business firms more latitude in defending their hiring practices,[54] Congress responded with the Civil Rights Act of 1991, which requires larger firms in some instances to prove why their overwhelmingly male or white workforce is the result of business necessity (such as the nature of the work or the locally available labor pool) and not the result of systematic discrimination against women or minorities.

In a key 1995 decision, *Adarand v. Pena,* the Supreme Court sharply curtailed the federal government's affirmative action authority. The case arose when Adarand Constructors filed suit over a federal contract that had been awarded to a Hispanic-owned company even though Adarand had submitted a lower bid. The Court in a 5-4 ruling said that the government had to prove that a preference program for minorities was a response to specific past acts of discrimination, not just historical discrimination in a general sense. In reversing its *Fullilove* precedent, the Supreme Court held that set-aside contracts for minority applicants are lawful only in situations where it can be conclusively shown that such applicants have been discriminated against. Even in such situations, the remedy must be "narrowly tailored" to the situation—that is, it must be designed specifically to fix the problem at issue.[55] In other words, the government cannot issue general requirements (such as an automatic 10 percent set-aside of contracts for minority firms) as a means of remedying past discrimination.

Even supporters of affirmative action concluded that the *Adarand* decision likely marked the end of the era of extensive racial and gender preferences. By holding that affirmative action must be narrowly tailored and based on specific past acts of discrimination, the Court substantially restricted the authority of federal officials to mandate broad affirmative action remedies. Earlier, the Court

The University of Michigan was the focus of national attention in 2003 as a result of its affirmative action admissions programs. The Supreme Court upheld the use of race as a factor in admissions but rejected the use of a "point system" as the method of applying it.

had restricted the authority of state and local governments to institute such requirements.

Another blow to affirmative action proponents was the California Civil Rights Initiative, which bans in California any public employment, education, or contracting program that is based on race, ethnicity, or sex. Known as Proposition 209, the initiative was placed on the 1996 ballot by citizen petition and was approved 54 percent to 46 percent by California voters. The vote divided along racial, ethnic, and gender lines, with white males most strongly in favor and blacks and Hispanics most strongly opposed. The constitutionality of Proposition 209 was challenged by opponents, but the Supreme Court upheld it in 1997. Black and Hispanic enrollment in the entering classes at University of California campuses fell by more than 30 percent in 1998.

In 1998, the state of Texas devised an innovative response to the problem of equal opportunity. Recognizing the disparity in the quality of its public schools and other factors that result in lower average scores on standardized tests for minorities, the state established a policy that guarantees admission at the public university campus of his or her choice to any Texas high school student who graduates in the top 10 percent of the class. This approach initially faced little opposition from even critics of affirmative action[56] but opposition has increased as a result of growing enrollment pressure at Texas's flagship universities and the widening perception that students at weaker high schools have an undue advantage.

A major affirmative action ruling—one that many observers saw as the most important decision since the Supreme Court's *Bakke* ruling three decades earlier—was handed down in 2003. At issue were two University of Michigan affirmative action admission policies: Michigan's point system for undergraduate admission, which granted twenty points (out of a total of one hundred fifty possible points) to minority applicants, and its law school admission process, in which race (along with other factors such as work experience and extracurricular activities) was taken into account in admission decisions. The case attracted national attention, including the involvement of major U.S. corporations, which argued that programs such as those at the University of Michigan were necessary to achieving their goal of finding well-educated minorities to fill managerial positions.

Opponents of affirmative action hoped that the Court would strike down the Michigan policies, effectively ending the use of race as a factor in college admissions. Indeed, by a 6-3 vote in *Gratz v. Bollinger,* the Supreme Court did strike down Michigan's undergraduate admissions policy because its point system assigned a specific weight to race.[57] However, by a 5-4 vote in *Grutter v. Bollinger,* the Court upheld the law school's program, concluding that it was being applied in a limited and sensible manner and furthered Michigan's "compelling interest in obtaining the educational benefits that flow from a diverse student body." The Court's majority opinion said further that the law school's policy "promotes 'cross-racial understanding,' helps to break down racial stereotypes, and enables [a] better understand[ing of] persons of different races."[58]

Thus, affirmative action remains a part of national education policy. Advocates of affirmative action recognize, however, that the Supreme Court's narrow 5-4 majority in the 2003 case means that the issue will almost certainly resurface at some future time.

School Integration: Busing

The 1954 *Brown* ruling mandated an end to *forced segregation* of public schools. Government would no longer be permitted to prevent minorities from enrolling in white schools. *Brown* did not, however, mandate school *integration.* Government was not required by *Brown* to take action to require that white and minority children attend school together, and *Brown* did little to change the face of America's schools. Ten years after *Brown,* because of neighborhood segregation, less than 3 percent of black children were attending schools that were predominantly white. This situation set the stage for one of the few public policies to force whites into close regular contact with blacks: the busing of children out of their neighborhoods for the purpose of achieving greater racial balance in schools.

The Swann Decision and Its Aftermath

In 1971, affirming a lower-court decision, the Supreme Court held in *Swann v. Charlotte-Mecklenburg County Board of Education* that the busing of children from one neighborhood to another was a permissible way for courts to compel the integration of public schools that remained segregated due to residential patterns created by past years of official segregation.[59]

Few policies of recent times provoked as much controversy as the introduction of forced busing. Surveys indicated that more than 80 percent of white Americans and a majority in Congress disapproved of forced busing. Angry demonstrations lasting weeks took place in Charlotte, Detroit, Boston, and other cities. Unlike *Brown,* which affected mainly the South, *Swann* also applied to northern communities in which African Americans and whites lived apart as a result of economic and cultural differences as well as discriminatory real estate practices and local housing ordinances.

Despite the widespread protests, busing became a part of national policy. Its application was narrowed, however, by court-imposed restrictions on its use. The Supreme Court in 1974—perhaps in response to the protests over busing—

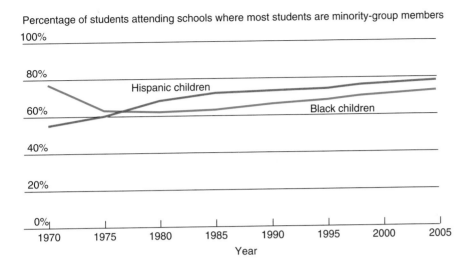

Percentage of students attending schools where most students are minority-group members

Figure 5-9

Segregation in Public Schools Has Been Increasing
In the past two decades, racial and ethnic segregation in America's public schools has increased. More than two-thirds of black and Hispanic children today attend a school in which most of the students are members of a minority group. An increase in the number of white non-Hispanic students attending private schools and a decrease in racial busing are factors in the trend.
Source: U.S. Department of Education, 2004.

held that it could be applied *across* school districts only in situations where it could be shown that district boundaries were purposely drawn so as to segregate the races.[60] Because school districts in most states coincide with community boundaries, the ruling meant that most suburbs would not be affected by busing.

Does Busing Work?

Studies indicate that busing has contributed to more positive racial attitudes among children. Studies also show that the performance of black children on standardized tests improves when they attend white-majority schools and that the test performance of the white children is not adversely affected.[61]

However, busing has contributed to whites' departure from public schools, which, along with population and residential shifts, has made it increasingly difficult to achieve diversity in city schools. In Boston, for example, less than 20 percent of public school children today are white, compared with more than 50 percent when busing began there in 1974.

Busing also fragmented neighborhoods and forced children into taking long bus rides to and from school. Many black and white families alike were affected by what came to be called "busing fatigue." Parents asked, in effect, whether busing was worth the costs. That debate led the Prince George's County (Maryland) school board, which had a black majority, to abandon busing in 1998 and replace it with improved funding for neighborhood schools. Alvin Thornton, chair of the Prince George's County school board and a Howard University professor, argued that the change would increase "the sense of community" among the county's African Americans.[62]

Diversity and America's Schools

Prince George's County is among dozens of communities—including Seattle, Jacksonville, Minneapolis, Mobile, and Boston—that have cut back or eliminated their school busing programs in recent years. In 1999, the school district where busing policy began—Charlotte-Mecklenburg—joined the list. The trend is consistent with Supreme Court rulings in the 1990s that held that busing was

Citizenship

Getting Involved, Making a Difference

Moral Action

In *Moral Man and Immoral Society,* Reinhold Niebuhr puzzled over how to reconcile morality and strategy when confronting official injustice. The citizen has a moral obligation to obey the law. But what if the law itself is immoral? Is it moral to disobey such a law, perhaps even through violent means? Niebuhr concluded that, although a strategy of violent opposition would be immoral, nonviolent resistance would not be. This tactic, he argued, involved a "harmonious joining" of the moral and strategic dimensions of political action. Refusal to obey an unjust law would be a moral act, as long as the refusal was nonviolent and the person was willing to accept the legal consequences.

Martin Luther King Jr. described himself as "transformed" by Niebuhr's argument, and he dedicated himself to a campaign of nonviolent resistance against laws that forcibly segregated the races. To prepare for the campaign, King went to India to study Gandhi's nonviolent tactics and then set up instructional workshops to teach others what he had learned. (One of these lessons focused on self-protection when being attacked by the police; the proper technique is to look the attacker in the eyes while using arms and legs to protect vital organs.) King also recruited a select group of young African American men with physical strength and personal character to absorb a savage beating without fighting back. As it happened, television images of brutal police attacks on passive demonstrators were instrumental in turning public opinion against the South's system of racial segregation.

The civil rights movement is an exceptional moment in the history of citizen action, but every activist should ask the same question that Niebuhr asked: what constitutes moral action? Political advocacy can be a severe test of moral character. It is tempting for the activist to slip into unethical practices—to fudge facts to strengthen an argument, to twist the meaning of an opponent's position, to appeal to people's irrational impulses. And the pressures to use these techniques mount when an opponent employs them.

Indeed, the line between moral and immoral action can be breached. Whatever the momentary gain, the loss is greater. The purpose of citizen action is to elevate public life. Immoral action saps the community's strength by corrupting the process through which collective decisions are made. Immoral action also corrupts those who engage in it by diminishing their sensitivity to the difference between private ambition and public purpose.

intended as a temporary, not permanent, solution to the problem of segregated schools[63] and that communities can devise alternative programs to replace their busing programs.[64]

The cutback in busing has contributed to an increase in racial segregation in schools. Nationwide, desegregation peaked in the late 1980s, but segregation has increased steadily since then (see Figure 5–9). Only about one in three black children today attends a predominantly white school, about the same proportion as in 1970, before busing began. The proportion is even lower for Hispanic children, only about one in four of whom attends a predominantly white school.

The trend is unlikely to be reversed anytime soon through public policy, because *diversity,* unlike *equality,* has no explicit constitutional status. Government is compelled by the Constitution to treat people equally; it is not required to promote diversity.[65]

As busing recedes, the focus has shifted to parity in school financing. In comparison with predominantly white schools, schools with mostly minority students have significantly larger classroom sizes, fewer certified teachers, and fewer resources, including library materials, computers, and science laboratories.[66] In Prince George's County and other communities that have dismantled busing programs, local and state governments have promised to increase funding for predominantly minority schools.

PERSISTENT DISCRIMINATION: SUPERFICIAL DIFFERENCES, DEEP DIVISIONS

In 1944, Swedish sociologist Gunnar Myrdal gained fame for his book *An American Dilemma,* whose title referred to deep-rooted racism in a country that idealized equality.[67] Since then, legal obstacles to the mixing of the races have been nearly eliminated, and public opinion has softened significantly. In the early 1940s, a majority of white Americans believed that black children should not be allowed to go to school with white children; today less than 5 percent of white Americans express this belief. There are also visible signs of black progress. In the past two decades, increasing numbers of African Americans have attended college, earned undergraduate degrees, obtained jobs as professionals and managers, and moved into suburban neighborhoods.

Nevertheless, true equality for all Americans has remained elusive. The realities of everyday American life are still very different for its white and black citizens. For example, a black child born in the United States has more than twice the chance of dying before reaching his or her first birthday than a white child does. The difference in the infant mortality rates of whites and African Americans reflects differences in their nutrition, medical care, and education—in other words, differences in their access to the most basic resources of a modern society.

The history of equality in America is one of progress and of setbacks and, always, of new challenges. The latest challenge is the treatment of Arab Americans and Muslims in the aftermath of the terrorist attacks of September 11, 2001. Shortly afterward, a radio talk-show host suggested that all recent immigrants from the Middle East should be deported, a message eerily reminiscent of what some people once said about black Americans and Irish Americans and, more recently, about Hispanics. Other Americans took direct action. Many Middle Eastern Americans were cursed as they walked the streets. Some were beaten and at least three were murdered. The Los Angeles Police Department alone recorded more than 150 hate-crime incidents directed against Americans of Middle Eastern origin. Mosques in many U.S. cities were defaced. There was even a bizarre case of malicious misidentification. A Sikh spiritual center in upstate New York was set ablaze by four hooligans because they thought the Sikhs were Arabs who supported Osama bin Laden and his terrorist network. The Sikh spiritual center was named Gobind Sadan, which they thought stood for "go bin Laden."

Churches, synagogues, mosques, and other houses of worship have long been targets of hate crime. The ugliness of racial segregation in America was seldom more evident than on September 15, 1963 when member of the Ku Klux Klan set off a bomb at the Sixteenth Street Baptist Church in Birmingham, Alabama. It killed four young African American girls who were in the church basement changing into their choir robes. Twenty others were injured in the blast. An all-white jury acquitted the Klansmen accused of the crime. Such incidents are hardly a relic of times long past. In the late 1990s, there was a rash of church bombings in the South. The Rising Star Baptist Church in Greensboro, Alabama was one of several dozen predominately black churches that were torched by arsonists in 1996 alone.

Although the great majority of Americans have a lot more sense than is displayed by a violent few, many of them do not necessarily embrace fully the notion that the United States is "one people and one nation." They accept the idea in the abstract but often find it difficult to apply in everyday life. The color of a person's skin or the accent in a person's voice can lead them to respond differently to someone they meet, whether on the street, in a store, on the job, or in the house next door. A recent NBC special report told of what happened when middle-class black Americans began moving to the Chicago suburb of Matteson. Their educational attainment and on-the-job success mattered less to some of their white neighbors than their skin color. For-sale signs began popping up in front of white residences.

Equality is a difficult idea in practice because it requires people to shed preconceived and often deeply embedded notions about how other people think, behave, and feel. Nearly everyone has difficulty seeing beyond superficial differences—whether those differences relate to skin color, national origin, religious preference, sex, or lifestyle—to the shared humanity that unites people of all backgrounds. Myrdal called discrimination "America's curse." He could have broadened the generalization. Discrimination is civilization's curse, as is evident in the scores of ethnic, national, and religious conflicts that have marred human history. But America is a special case because, as Lincoln said in his Gettysburg address, it is a nation founded "on the proposition that all men are created equal." No greater challenge faces America, today as throughout its history, than the challenge of living out the full meaning of its most imposing ideal.

Summary Self-Test
www.mhhe.com/pattersontad7

During the past few decades, the United States has undergone a revolution in the legal status of its traditionally disadvantaged groups, including African Americans, women, Native Americans, Hispanic Americans, and Asian Americans. Such groups are now provided equal protection under the law in areas such as education, employment, and voting. Discrimination by race, sex, and ethnicity has not been eliminated from American life, but it is no longer substantially backed by the force of law.

Traditionally disadvantaged Americans have achieved fuller equality primarily as a result of their struggle for greater rights. The Supreme Court has been an important instrument of change for minority groups. Its ruling in *Brown v. Board of Education* (1954), which declared racial segregation in public schools to be an unconstitutional violation of the Fourteenth Amendment's equal-protection clause, was a major breakthrough in equal rights. Through its busing, affirmative action, and other rulings, the Court has also mandated the active promotion of integration and equal opportunities.

However, because civil rights policy involves large issues of social values and the distribution of society's resources, questions of civil rights are politically explosive. For this reason, legislatures and executives as well as the courts have been deeply involved in such issues, at times siding with established groups and sometimes backing the claims of underprivileged groups.

In recent years, affirmative action programs—programs designed to achieve equality of result for African Americans, women, Hispanic Americans, and other disadvantaged groups—have become a civil rights battleground. Affirmative action has had the strong support of civil rights groups and has won the qualified endorsement of the Supreme Court, but it has been opposed by those who claim that it unfairly discriminates against white males. Busing is another issue that has provoked deep divisions within American society.

STUDY CORNER

Key Terms

affirmative action *(p. 168)*
civil rights *(p. 144)*
de facto discrimination *(p. 167)*
de jure discrimination *(p. 167)*

equality of result *(p. 167)*
equal-protection clause *(p. 162)*
equal rights *(p. 144)*
gender gap *(p. 149)*

intermediate-scrutiny test *(p. 163)*
reasonable-basis test *(p. 162)*
strict-scrutiny test *(p. 162)*
suspect classifications *(p. 163)*

Self-Test

1. The term *civil rights* refers to:
   a. treating groups equally under the law.
   b. protecting an individual's right to religious belief.
   c. protecting public safety.
   d. permitting marriage by justices of the peace.

2. The Supreme Court of the United States:
   a. has never tolerated discriminating against people on the basis of their race.
   b. outlawed discrimination based on race in the *Plessy* case.
   c. refused to hear the law case involving school segregation in Topeka, Kansas, because Kansas was not considered part of the South.
   d. in *Brown v. Board of Education* prohibited the practice of separate public schools for the purposes of racial segregation.

3. The legal test that in some cases (such as the legal consumption of alcohol) allows government to treat people differently based on their characteristics (such as age) is called:
   a. reasonable-basis test.
   b. strict-scrutiny test.
   c. suspect classification standard.
   d. none of the above.

4. Government policies that have been implemented to eliminate discrimination with the goal of achieving "equality of result" include:
   a. redlining.
   b. affirmative action.
   c. busing.
   d. a and b only.
   e. b and c only.

5. Regarding job-related issues, women:
   a. have made gains in many traditionally male-dominated fields.
   b. have achieved gains in the workplace through such programs as day care and parental leave.
   c. are less likely than men to be promoted to top-level corporate jobs.
   d. hold a disproportionate number of the lower-wage jobs in society.
   e. all of the above.

6. Regarding affirmative action, Supreme Court decisions in the 1980s and 1990s have:
   a. moved to outlaw it entirely.
   b. moved to narrow its application to specific past acts of discrimination.
   c. asked Congress to clarify the policy.
   d. asked the president to clarify the policy.

7. De facto discrimination is much harder to overcome than de jure discrimination. (T/F)

8. The history of discrimination against Hispanics is virtually the same as the history of discrimination against African Americans, which helps account for the similarity of their political and economic situations. (T/F)

9. In recent years, the struggle for equal rights has been extended to the elderly but not to the disabled or to children. (T/F)

10. Asian Americans have made such great progress in overcoming discrimination that the percentage of Asian Americans in top managerial positions and elected political offices is greater than the percentage of Asian Americans in the U.S. population. (T/F)

Critical Thinking

What role have political movements played in securing the legal rights of disadvantaged groups? How has the resulting legislation contributed to a furtherance of these groups' rights?

Suggested Readings

Armor, David. *Forced Justice: School Desegregation and the Law*. New York: Oxford University Press, 1996. An evaluation that concludes that the federal courts have overstretched their legal mandate by requiring school integration rather than simply school desegregation.

Bergmann, Barbara A. *In Defense of Affirmative Action*. New York: Basic Books, 1996. An economist's analysis of affirmative action that concludes that the policy is necessary for women and broadly beneficial to society.

Chang, Gordon H., ed. *Asian Americans and Politics*. Stanford, Calif.: Stanford University Press, 2001. A broad look at the political engagement of Asian Americans.

Howard, John R. *The Shifting Wind*. Albany: State University of New York Press, 1999. A review of the Supreme Court and civil rights from Reconstruction to the *Brown* decision.

Nagel, Joane. *American Indian Ethnic Renewal: Red Power and the Resurgence of Identity and Culture*. New York: Oxford University Press, 1997. Explores the meaning of activism for Native Americans' ethnic identification.

Pinello, Daniel R. *Gay Rights and American Law*. New York: Cambridge University Press, 2003. A careful study of recent appellate-court decisions dealing with gay rights issues.

Reeves, Keith. *Voting Hopes or Fears? White Voters, Black Candidates, and Racial Politics in America*. New York: Oxford University Press, 1997. A critical assessment of race and politics in American society.

Skrentny, John David. *The Ironies of Affirmative Action: Politics, Culture, and Justice in America*. Chicago: University of Chicago Press, 1996. An empirical analysis of affirmative action and its impact.

Stavans, Ilan. *The Hispanic Condition: Reflections on Culture and Identity in America*. New York: HarperPerennial, 1996. An analysis of the behavioral and cultural differences and similarities among the major Hispanic groups.

Willingham, Alex. *Beyond the Color Line?* New York: Brennan Center for Justice, 2002. A set of articles on race and representation.

List of Websites

http://www.airpi.org/

The website of the American Indian Policy Center, which was established by Native Americans in 1992; includes a political and legal history of Native Americans and examines current issues affecting them.

http://www.naacp.org/

The website of the National Association for the Advancement of Colored People (NAACP); includes historical and current information on the struggle of African Americans for equal rights.

http://www.nclr.org/

The website of the National Council of La Raza (NCLR), an organization dedicated to improving the lives of Hispanics; contains information on public policy, immigration, citizenship, and other subjects.

http://www.rci.rutgers.edu/~cawp

The website of the Center for the American Woman and Politics (CAWP) at Rutgers University's Eagleton Institute of Politics.

Participate!

Think of a disadvantaged group that you would like to assist. It could be one of the federal government's designated groups (such as Hispanics), one of the other groups mentioned in the chapter (such as the disabled), or some other group (such as the homeless). Contact a college, community, national, or international organization that seeks to help this group and volunteer your assistance. (The Internet provides the names of thousands of organizations, such as Habitat for Humanity, that are involved in helping the disadvantaged.)

Extra Credit

For up-to-the-minute *New York Times* articles, interactive simulations, graphics, study tools, and more links and quizzes, visit the text's Online Learning Center at www.mhhe.com/pattersontad7.

(Self-Test Answers: 1. a   2. d   3. a   4. e   5. e   6 b.   7. T   8. F   9. F   10. F)

PART
II

Mass Politics

We are concerned about public affairs, but preoccupied with our private lives, Walter Lippmann wrote. Nevertheless, the integrity of the democratic process requires that citizens have significant opportunities to make their voices heard.

Citizens individually participate in public affairs. Their influence is greatest, however, when they join together in common purpose. This joining together comes during elections and through intermediaries such as political parties, interest groups, and the media.

The chapters in Part Two explore these avenues of citizen politics. Chapter 6 examines the way Americans think politically and the effect of their opinions on government. Chapter 7 describes the nature and impact of citizen participation. Chapter 8 looks at parties, candidates, elections, and campaigns. Interest groups are the subject of Chapter 9, and the news media are addressed in Chapter 10.

All democracies depend on these instruments of popular influence, but the United States does so in relatively unique ways. For example, America's political parties are among the weakest in the world, while its interest groups and media are among the strongest. The consequences are significant. Political action enables Americans to make their voices heard, but the precise nature of this activity determines whose voices will be heard the loudest.

PART TWO OUTLINE

6

Public Opinion and Political Socialization:

Shaping the People's Voice

To speak with precision of public opinion is a task not unlike coming
to grips with the Holy Ghost.

—V. O. Key Jr.[1]

As the U.S. troop buildup in the Persian Gulf region continued into 2003, most Americans were unsure of the best course of action. They had been hearing about Saddam Hussein for years and had concluded that he was a brutal and dangerous tyrant and a terrorist threat. A majority expressed a willingness to support a war in Iraq if President George W. Bush deemed it necessary. But Americans had differing opinions on how to decide when and if war would occur. Some wanted to give United Nations inspectors ample time to discover and dismantle Iraq's weapons program before a final decision on war was made. Others preferred to hold off on making the decision until the United States could line up international support for a war in Iraq. Still others supported more immediate action but preferred a bombing campaign to the launching of a ground war that could result in high casualties among U.S. forces.

Once the bombs started dropping on Iraq and U.S. ground troops poured into Iraq from their staging base in Kuwait, however, Americans strongly supported the action. Polls indicated that roughly 70 percent backed the decision to use military force against Iraq, with 20 percent opposed and 10 percent undecided.

The unfolding of public opinion toward the Iraq war is a revealing example of the influence of public opinion on government: public opinion rarely forces officials to take a particular course of action. If President Bush had decided that the Iraq situation could have been resolved through UN weapons inspectors, public opinion would have supported that policy. A majority of Americans would also have supported the president if he had decided that war made sense only if it had broad international support or was limited to an air war.

Although public opinion has a central place in democratic societies because of a belief that public policy should reflect the will of the people, public opinion is seldom an exact guide when it comes to questions about how best to deal with policy issues. Political leaders ordinarily enjoy wide leeway in choosing a course of action. Rather than fighting a war against Iraq, for example, President Bush could have decided to concentrate on finishing the war begun earlier in Afghanistan. Concentrations of Al Qaeda and Taliban fighters were still operating in Afghanistan, and terrorist leader Osama bin Laden was still at large. Bush also had the option of a law-enforcement response to the terrorist threat: he could have decided to pump resources into a worldwide police and intelligence effort aimed at finding and eliminating terrorist cells. The September 11, 2001, terrorist attacks on the World Trade Center and the Pentagon had created an expectation among Americans that the Bush administration would act decisively to

In 2003, the United States invaded Iraq. In taking this action, President Bush had majority support, even though a majority of Americans would also have backed other ways of containing the regime of Saddam Hussein.

counter the terrorist threat. But the precise nature of the response was largely up to the president and his advisers to decide.

This chapter discusses public opinion and its influence on the U.S. political system. A major theme is that public opinion is a powerful and yet inexact force in American politics. The policies of the U.S. government cannot be understood apart from public opinion; at the same time, as stated above, public opinion is not a precise determinant of public policy. This apparent paradox is explained by the fact that *self-government* in a large and complex country involves a division of influence between the public and its representatives. The public ordinarily affects only the general direction of government, whereas the lawmakers decide the specific actions. The main points made in this chapter are the following:

- *Public opinion consists of those views held by ordinary citizens that are openly expressed.* Public officials have many means of gauging public opinion but increasingly have relied on public opinion polls to make this determination.

- *The process by which individuals acquire their political opinions is called political socialization.* This process begins during childhood, when, through family and school, Americans acquire many of their basic political values and beliefs. Socialization continues into adulthood, during which peers, political institutions and leaders, and the news media are major influences.

- *Americans' political opinions are shaped by several frames of reference. Four of the most important are ideology, group attachments, partisanship, and political culture.* These frames of reference form the basis of political consensus and conflict among the general public.

- *Public opinion has an important influence on government but ordinarily does not directly determine what officials will do.* Public opinion works primarily to place limits on the choices made by officials.

THE NATURE OF PUBLIC OPINION

Public opinion is a relatively new concept in the history of political thought. Not until pressures began to mount in the 1700s for representative government was there a need for a term to refer to what ordinary people thought about politics. The first English-speaking philosopher to write at length about public opinion was Jeremy Bentham (1748–1832).[2] Originally an advocate of government by enlightened leaders, Bentham came to believe that the public's views had to be taken into account if leaders were to govern properly.

Public opinion is now a widely used term. It is typically applied in ways that suggest that the public has a common set of concerns. Ordinarily, however, it is not very meaningful to lump all citizens together as if they constituted a coherent whole. There is, to be sure, an occasional issue of such power and breadth

that it captures the attention of nearly all citizens. The large majority of issues, however, do not attract the attention of most citizens.
Agricultural conservation programs, for example, are of intense interest to some farmers, hunters, and environmentalists but of little
interest to other people. This pattern is so pervasive that opinion analysts have described America as a nation of *many* publics.[3]

On numerous issues, there is literally no majority opinion. On
issues such as agricultural conservation programs, a form of *pluralist* democracy usually prevails. Government responds to the views
of an intense minority. In other cases, *elitist* opinion prevails. On the
question of U.S. relations with Finland, for example, there is little
likelihood that ordinary citizens would know or care what the U.S.
government does. In such instances, the policy opinions of an elite
group of business and policy leaders ordinarily prevail. *Majority*
opinion also can be decisive, but its influence is normally confined
to a few broad issues that elicit widespread attention and concern,
such as social security and employment. This situation may suggest
a limited role for popular majorities, but such issues, though few in
number, typically have the greatest impact on society as a whole.

Hence, any definition of the term *public opinion* cannot be based
on the assumption that all citizens, or even a majority, are actively interested in and hold a preference about all aspects of political life.
Public opinion can be defined as the politically relevant opinions
held by ordinary citizens that they are willing to express openly.[4] This
expression need not be verbal. It could also take the form, for example, of a protest demonstration or a vote for one candidate rather than
another. The crucial point is that a person's private thoughts on an issue become public opinion when they are expressed openly.

Dressed in his own clothes and as he
requested, the remains (with wax head) of
Jeremy Bentham are on display at
University College, London. Bentham
(1748–1832), who was the first English-
speaking theorist to write at length on
public opinion, is best known as a founder
of utilitarian philosophy. He developed the
principle of utility, which holds that action is
acceptable if it promotes an increased
amount of pleasure and unacceptable if it
promotes an increased amount of pain.

How Informed Is Public Opinion?

A practical obstacle to government by public opinion is that people have differing opinions; in responding to one side of an issue, government is compelled to
reject other preferences. Public opinion is also contradictory in many cases.
Polls indicate, for example, that Americans would like better schools, health
care, and other public services while also favoring a reduction in taxes (see
Figure 6–1). A significant increase in the quantity and quality of social services
cannot be accomplished without additional taxes. Which opinion of the people
should govern—their desire for more services or their desire for lower taxes?

Another limitation is that people's opinions, even on issues of great importance, are often misinformed. In the buildup to the U.S. invasion of Iraq in 2003,
for example, polls revealed that more than half of the American public incor-
rectly believed that Iraq had close ties to the terrorist network Al Qaeda and
that Iraqis were among the nineteen terrorists who had flown airplanes into the
World Trade Center and the Pentagon on September 11, 2001. Moreover, despite
opposition to the war on the part of most European, Asian, Arab, South
American, and African governments, one-fourth of Americans believed that
world opinion favored the war. Americans who held such views were more
supportive of the Iraq war than were other Americans.[5]

public opinion The politically
relevant opinions held by
ordinary citizens that they
express openly.

Figure 6–1

Opinions on Taxing and Spending

People's opinions can be contradictory. Americans say, for example, that taxes are too high and yet also say, when asked about specific policy areas, that government is spending too little.

Used by permission of National Opinion Research Center, University of Chicago.

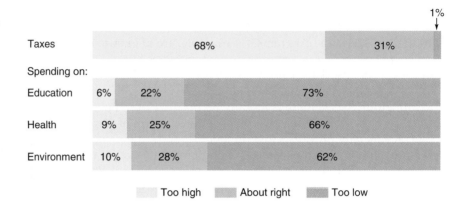

Taxes	68%	31%	1%
Spending on:		
Education	6%	22%	73%
Health	9%	25%	66%
Environment	10%	28%	62%

☐ Too high   ☐ About right   ☐ Too low

The public's relatively low level of information is due partly to what is called "the will to believe." People like to think that their opinions are supported by the "facts." However, they sometimes form their opinions first and then devise "facts" that support those opinions.

Moreover, most Americans are not closely attentive to politics and therefore do not have a lot of factual information about it. Over 80 percent of Americans, for example, are unable to recall the name of the chief justice of the U.S. Supreme Court. Americans are not unique in this respect, but in some areas they are less informed than citizens of most other Western democracies. In a seven-country survey, Americans ranked next to last (ahead of only Spaniards) in their ability to respond correctly to five factual questions about prominent world leaders and developments.[6] Despite America's leading role in the world, Americans are less knowledgeable about international affairs than are Europeans.

Even many college-educated Americans lack basic information about public affairs. A survey of Ivy League students found that one-third could not identify the British prime minister, half could not name both U.S. senators from their state, and three-fourths could not identify Abraham Lincoln as the author of the phrase "a government of the people, by the people, and for the people."[7]

The public's lack of information is not as significant a factor as it might seem. Citizens do not necessarily have to be well informed about a situation to have a reasonable opinion about it. Opinions stem more from people's general beliefs, values, and policy orientations than from precise information about specific policy alternatives. It is in the context of these orientations that most citizens judge matters of public affairs.[8] Many people's opinions on the abortion issue, for example, derive from

Public opinion includes contradictory elements. According to surveys, for example, most Americans say they want lower taxes but also say they want more public services. At a Boston rally, this demonstrator expresses anger with President Clinton's tax-increase legislation while also demanding that government provide free health care.

The World: The Importance of Informed Opinion

When Americans after September 11, 2001, began to hear about Afghanistan, the Taliban, Islam, and Al Qaeda, it was new information to most of them. Even though some of the information had been available previously through the news media, most Americans had not paid much attention to it.

Americans are generally uninformed about global affairs. The war on terrorism has increased their understanding of some parts of the world, but Americans typically have had less interest in what is occurring elsewhere than have comparably educated people in other countries. Analysts suggest that America's "ocean isolation" is a reason why its citizens are insular. Unlike Europeans, Americans are not surrounded by many other countries. But ocean isolation is not a complete explanation. Americans share a border with Canadians and Mexicans, for example, but know much less about Canada and Mexico than Canadians and Mexicans know about the United States.

International terrorism and the increasing globalization of the economy suggest that Americans should pay more attention to the larger world in which they live. Many Americans, for example, were mystified that their country had been targeted for the terrorist attacks. Their initial impulse was to say that the country had been attacked because it represents freedom. As Americans discovered, however, that explanation was incomplete. The terrorists had specific grievances with the United States, including its policies in the Middle East. The terrorists' decision to target innocent civilians to express their discontent was cowardly and despicable, but as Americans came to understand during the months after the attacks, it was not rooted in envy.

Americans can no longer afford to be comfortable with their ocean isolation. An informed public is better positioned to participate in the making of policies that affect it. As the world shrinks, an expanded horizon is required. For good and ill, developments elsewhere increasingly affect Americans' lives. If Americans are to be in a position to help shape that world rather than being forced to respond to crises thrust on them by that world, they need to be more curious about it. You could start by paying attention to the international coverage in your local newspaper or on a news website.

deep-seated religious beliefs. The fact that most individuals have only a foggy notion of Supreme Court rulings on the abortion issue does not make their opinions any less relevant. Similarly, people can have a considered view of how the United States should respond to foreign aggression without having detailed knowledge of global affairs.

Nevertheless, the public's lack of information restricts the role it can play in policy formation. The choice of one policy over another requires knowledge of the likely consequences of the various alternatives. Citizens typically lack this knowledge.

The Measurement of Public Opinion

Woodrow Wilson once said he had spent nearly all his adult life in government and yet had never seen a "government." What Wilson was saying, in effect, was that government is a system of relationships. A government is not a building or a person; it is not tangible in the way that a car or a bottle of soda is. So it is with public opinion. No one has ever seen a "public opinion," and thus it cannot be measured directly. It must be assessed indirectly.

Debating the Issues

Should Representatives Lead on the Basis of Opinion Polls?

A fundamental principle of democracy is that public opinion ought to be the foundation of government. However, the role that public opinion should play in specific policy decisions is, and always has been, a subject of dispute. James Madison distinguished between the public's momentary passions and its enduring concerns, arguing that government is obliged to represent only the latter. In contrast, the Jacksonians and Progressives had a strong faith in the judgment of ordinary citizens and a distrust of entrenched elites. With the advent of the public opinion poll, it became possible to measure citizens' policy views more directly. Should policymakers follow the polls in making their decisions? Some analysts have held that leaders should act in close accord with the polls. Other analysts have argued that polls measure fleeting opinions about topical issues and that leaders in any event are obliged only to respond to the people's deep and enduring beliefs.

Yes: Sixty-eight percent of Americans think they should have a great deal of influence on the decisions of elected and government officials in Washington, but fewer than one in ten (9%) believe they do. . . . Who instead do Americans think bends the ears of the politicians and officials in the Capitol? According to the public, money talks. Nearly six in ten [say] that politicians pay a great deal of attention to their campaign contributors when making decisions about important issues. . . . Fifty-four percent of Americans expect their officials to follow what the majority wants, even if it goes against the officials' knowledge and judgment. Fewer (42%) want officials to use their own judgment if it goes against the wishes of the majority. . . . If we all lived in small New England towns, then perhaps town hall meetings would be a realistic means of injecting public opinion into the national debate. However, when it takes one western senator a whole year to travel to every single county in his or her home state, it is clear that the limits imposed by geography and time necessitate a continuing place for polling in public policy.

—*Bill McInturff and Lori Weigel, pollsters*

No: True statesmen are not merely mouthpieces for opinion polls. British historian Lord Acton recognized that the will of the majority could be and often is just as tyrannical as the will of a monarch, and in some cases more dangerous because the error has the support of the masses. Thus he observes, "It is bad to be oppressed by a minority, but it is worse to be oppressed by a majority," and "The will of the people cannot make just that which is unjust." . . . In the United States we have compelling historical and contemporary examples of the majority siding with what were, in retrospect, clear-cut cases of injustice. The legalization and promotion of slavery by governments are a prime example, and stand as a stark rebuke to elected officials who think they ought to represent the people without regard to their own conscience. Today, there are a number of hotly contested issues—such as abortion, stem cell research, and, now, marriage—whose partisans often make appeals based on poll data. Our elected officials follow the shifting temper of the electorate with rapt attention. But is this how we ask our elected officials to lead? . . . [T]oo many political leaders have settled on an inadequate answer: the will of the people (and the pollsters).

—*Jordon J. Ballor, Acton Institute*

A time-honored method of interpreting public opinion is election returns. The vote is routinely interpreted by the press and politicians as an indicator of the public's mood—whether liberal or conservative, angry or satisfied, quiet or intense. Letters to the editor in newspapers, e-mail messages to elected officials, and the size of crowds at mass demonstrations are other means of judging public opinion. Yet another device is the activity of lobbyists, who bring the concerns of their constituents to government's attention.

All these indicators are important and receive attention from those in power. As a guide to what is on people's minds, however, each of these indicators has shortcomings. Elections offer citizens only a yes-or-no choice between candidates, and different voters will make the same choice for quite different reasons. The winning candidate may claim that the public has based its choice on a particular issue or inclination, but election returns mask a more complex reality. As for letter writers and demonstrators, they are not at all representative of the general population. Less than 1 percent of Americans participate each year in a mass demonstration, and fewer than 10 percent write to the president or a member of Congress. The opinions of demonstrators and letter writers tend to be less moderate than those of other citizens.[9]

Public Opinion Polls

In an earlier day, indicators such as elections and letters to the editor were the only means by which public officials could gauge what the public was thinking. Today, they can also rely on polls or surveys, which provide a more systematic method of estimating public sentiment.[10]

In a **public opinion poll**, a relatively few individuals—the **sample**—are interviewed in order to estimate the opinions of a whole **population**, such as the students of a college, the residents of a city, or the citizens of a country. If a sufficient number of individuals are chosen at random, their views will tend to be representative—that is, roughly the same as the views held by the population as a whole.

How is it possible to measure the thinking of a large population on the basis of a relatively small sample? How can interviews with, say, one thousand Americans provide a reliable estimate of what 300 million are thinking? The answer is found in the theory of probability. Opinion sampling is based on the mathematical laws of probability, which can be illustrated by the hypothetical example of a huge jar filled with a million marbles, half of them red and half of them blue. If a blindfolded person reaches into the jar, the likelihood of selecting a marble of a given color is fifty-fifty. And if one thousand marbles are chosen in this random way, it is likely that about half of them will be red and half will be blue. Opinion sampling works in the same way. If respondents are chosen at random from a population, their opinions will be approximately the same as those of the population as a whole.

Many people assume that a poll of the United States, with its nearly 300 million people, must utilize a much larger sample to achieve the same level of accuracy as, say, a poll of Massachusetts or Arizona. In fact, the mathematics of polling are such that sample size is the critical factor. A sample of one thousand people will have nearly the same level of accuracy whether the population is that of the nation, a state, or a large city. Consider again the example of a huge jar filled with marbles, half of them red and half of them blue. If one thousand marbles were randomly selected, about half would be red and half would be blue, regardless of whether the jar held 3 million or 300 million marbles.

The accuracy of a poll is usually expressed in terms of **sampling error,** which indicates the likelihood that the responses of the sample accurately represent the view of the population. As would be expected, the larger the size of the sample, the greater the likelihood that the sample's opinions will accurately reflect those of the population. Thus, the larger the sample, the smaller the sampling error.

public opinion poll A device for measuring public opinion whereby a relatively small number of individuals (the sample) are interviewed for the purpose of estimating the opinions of a whole community (the population).

sample In a public opinion poll, the relatively small number of individuals who are interviewed for the purpose of estimating the opinions of an entire population.

population In a public opinion poll, the people (for example, the citizens of a nation) whose opinions are being estimated through interviews with a sample of these people.

sampling error A measure of the accuracy of a public opinion poll. The sampling error is mainly a function of sample size and is usually expressed in percentage terms.

President Harry Truman holds up the early edition *Chicago Tribune* with the headline "Dewey Defeats Truman." The *Tribune* was responding to analysts' predictions that Dewey would win the 1948 election.

A properly drawn sample of one thousand individuals has a sampling error of about plus or minus 3 percent, which is to say that the proportions of the various opinions expressed by the people in the sample are likely to be within 3 percent of those of the whole population. For example, if 55 percent of a sample of one thousand respondents say that they intend to vote for the Republican candidate for president, then the chances are high that 52 to 58 percent (55 percent plus or minus 3 percent) of the whole population plan to vote for the Republican.

The impressive record of the Gallup poll in predicting the outcomes of presidential elections indicates that the theoretical accuracy of polls can be matched in practice. The Gallup organization has polled voters in every presidential election since 1936 (eighteen elections in all) and has erred badly only once: it stopped polling several weeks before the 1948 election and missed a late shift that carried Harry Truman to victory.

Problems with Polls

probability sample A sample for a poll in which each individual in the population has a known probability of being selected randomly for inclusion in the sample.

Mathematical estimations of poll accuracy require a **probability sample**—a sample in which each individual in the population has a known probability of being selected at random for inclusion. In practice, pollsters can only approximate this ideal. Because pollsters rarely have a list of all individuals in a population from which to draw a random sample, they usually base their sample on telephones. Pollsters use computers to randomly pick telephone numbers, which are then dialed by interviewers to reach respondents. Because the computer is as likely to pick one telephone number as any other and because 95 percent of U.S. homes have a telephone, a sample selected in this way is usually assumed to be reasonably representative of the population. Even this assumption, however, is problematic in that Americans increasingly refuse to participate in telephone polls. Pollsters often get a refusal rate of 50 percent or more. Although pollsters are still able to predict election outcomes accurately, it cannot be assumed for every issue that the opinions of those who respond are similar to those of the people who refuse to participate.

Nevertheless, such polls are superior to those that are not based on probability sampling. For example, news reporters sometimes conduct "people-in-the-street" interviews to obtain individual responses to political questions. Although a reporter may say that the opinions of those interviewed reflect the views of the general public, this claim is faulty. For example, interviews conducted on a downtown street at the noon hour will include a disproportionate number of business employees taking their lunch breaks. Housewives, teachers, and factory workers—not to mention farmers—are among the many groups that would be underrepresented in such a sample.

Polls are also affected by how questions are worded and whether they ask about unfamiliar topics. Consider, for example, the issue of federal funding for research on human embryonic stem cells. This issue was in the news in 2001, as President George W. Bush weighed the question of whether to support or oppose such funding. An NBC News/Wall Street Journal poll reported that 69 percent of Americans favored such funding. In contrast, a survey sponsored by the Conference of Catholic Bishops found that only 24 percent supported it. The difference can be explained partly by the wording of the questions asked in the two surveys. The NBC News/Wall Street Journal poll focused on the research issue, while the Conference of Catholic Bishops poll emphasized the fact that stem cells are taken from human embryos. The huge difference in the outcome of the two polls is also attributable to the fact that many people had not thought or talked much about the stem-cell issue. If they had, they would have had firmer opinions and their responses would have been less affected by the questions' wording. For these respondents, pollsters were measuring what scholars call "nonopinions" or "nonattitudes." These respondents expressed an opinion only because a polling organization contacted them.[11]

Despite these and other sources of error, the poll or survey is the most relied-upon method of measuring public opinion. More than one hundred organizations are in the business of conducting public opinion polls. Some, like the Gallup Organization, conduct polls that are then released to the news media by syndication. Most large news organizations also have their own in-house polls; one of the foremost of these is the CBS News/New York Times poll. Some polling firms specialize in conducting surveys for candidates and officeholders.

www.mhhe.com/pattersontad7

POLITICAL SOCIALIZATION: HOW AMERICANS LEARN THEIR POLITICS

Analysts have long been interested in the process by which public opinion is formed. The learning process by which people acquire their political opinions, beliefs, and values is called **political socialization.** Just as a language, a religion, or an athletic skill is acquired through a learning process, so too are people's political orientations. Political beliefs are not ingrained; they are acquired. Americans believe that free elections are the proper method of choosing leaders. People in some parts of the world find other methods perfectly natural.

For most Americans, the socialization process starts in the family with exposure to the political loyalties and opinions of their parents. The schools later

political socialization The learning process by which people acquire their political opinions, beliefs, and values.

Political Culture

One People out of Many

National Pride

Americans are justifiably proud of their nation. It is the oldest continuous democracy in the world, an economic powerhouse, and a diverse yet peaceful society.

What Americans may not recognize, because it is so much a part of everyday life in America, is the degree to which they are bombarded with messages and symbols of their nation's greatness. Political socialization in the United States is not the rigid program of indoctrination that some societies impose on their people. Nevertheless, Americans receive a thorough political education. Their country's values are impressed on them by every medium of communication: newspapers, daily conversations, television, movies, books. After the terrorist attacks of September 11, 2001, these tendencies reached new heights. The NBC television network outfitted its peacock logo with stars and stripes, and computer-generated flags festooned the other networks' broadcasts.

The words and symbols that regularly tell Americans of their country's greatness are important to its unity. In the absence of a common ancestral heritage to bind them, Americans need other methods to instill and reinforce the idea that they are one people. As discussed in Chapter 1, America's political ideals have this effect. So too do everyday reminders, such as the flying of the flag on homes and private buildings, a practice that is almost uniquely American. (Elsewhere, flags are rarely displayed except on public buildings.)

One indicator of Americans' political socialization is their high level of national pride. Harvard University's

Pippa Norris (in Marian Sawer's edited volume *The People's Choice*) constructed an index of national pride based on people's admiration for their country's political, economic, artistic, sporting, scientific, and other achievements. Americans ranked at the top, as shown by the following chart, which is based on Norris's index:

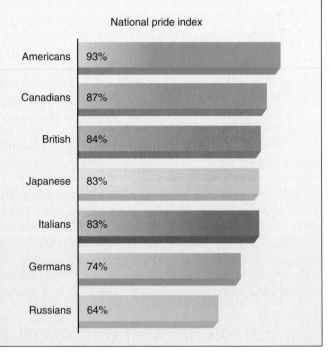

National pride index

Americans	93%
Canadians	87%
British	84%
Japanese	83%
Italians	83%
Germans	74%
Russians	64%

contribute to the process, as do the mass media, friends, work associates, and other agents. Political socialization is a lifelong process.

The Process of Political Socialization

The process of political socialization in the United States has several major characteristics. First, although socialization continues throughout life, most people's political outlook is substantially influenced by their childhood learning. That which is learned first is often lodged most firmly in a person's mind. Basic ideas about race, gender, and political party, for example, are often formed uncritically in childhood, much in the way belief in a particular religion—typically the religion of one's parents—is acquired.

A second characteristic of political socialization is its cumulative nature. Earlier learning influences later learning. The beliefs that people hold will affect their response to new ideas and developments. Of course, people's beliefs are not completely fixed. Change in a person's views is possible, especially when previous and current experiences are at odds. However, individuals have psychological defense mechanisms that protect their ingrained beliefs. Faced with situations that might challenge their original views, people often come up with reasons for holding onto them. For example, many people throughout their lives hold onto their belief in the superiority of the Republican or Democratic party even when their policy opinions indicate that the opposing party's positions are closer to their own.

Widespread political change is rare, and when it has occurred, it has nearly always been preceded by a catastrophic event. Younger adults are usually more responsive to such events because their beliefs are less firmly rooted than those of older adults. The **age-cohort tendency** holds that a significant change in the pattern of political socialization is almost always concentrated among younger citizens. For example, President Franklin Roosevelt's New Deal, which sought to alleviate the economic hardship of the Great Depression, prompted many younger Republicans, but not many older ones, to shift their loyalty to the Democratic party.

age-cohort tendency The tendency for a significant break in the pattern of political socialization to occur among younger citizens, usually as the result of a major event or development that disrupts preexisting beliefs.

The Agents of Political Socialization

The socialization process takes place through a variety of agents, including family, schools, mass media, peers, and political leaders and events. It is helpful to consider briefly some of these **agents of socialization** and how they affect political learning.

agents of socialization Those agents, such as the family and the media, that have a significant impact on citizens' political socialization.

Families

The family is a powerful agent of socialization because it has a near-monopoly on the attention of the young child, who places great trust in what a parent says. By the time the child is a teenager and is not likely to listen to any advice a parent might offer, many of the beliefs and values that will stay with the child throughout life are already in place. Many adults are Republicans or Democrats today largely because their parents backed that party. They can give all sorts of reasons for preferring their party to the other, but the reasons come later in life. The loyalty comes first, during childhood. The family also contributes to basic orientations that, while not directly political, have political significance. For example, the American family tends to be more egalitarian than families in other nations, and American children often have a voice in family decisions. Basic American values such as equality, individualism, and personal freedom have their roots in patterns of family interaction.[12]

Students in a North Carolina school reciting the Pledge of Allegiance. Such childhood socialization experiences can have a profound impact on an individual's basic political beliefs.

Schools

The school, like the family, has its major impact on children's basic political beliefs rather than on their opinions about specific issues. Teachers at the elementary level extol the exploits of national heroes such as George Washington, Abraham Lincoln, and Martin Luther King Jr. and praise the country's economic and political systems.[13] Although students in the middle and high school grades receive a more nuanced version of American history, it tends to emphasize the nation's great moments—for example, its decisive role in the two world wars. U.S. schools are probably more instrumental in building support for the nation than are the schools in other democracies. The Pledge of Allegiance, which is recited daily in many U.S. schools, has no equivalent in European countries. Schools also contribute to Americans' sense of social equality. Most American children, regardless of family income, attend public schools and study a fairly standard curriculum. In many countries, even some countries in Europe, schoolchildren are separated at an early age, with some placed in courses that train them to become manual laborers while others take courses that will prepare them for college.

Mass Media

The mass media are another powerful socializing agent. The themes and images that prevail in the media affect people's perceptions of their world. For example, exposure to crime and lawlessness on television can lead people to believe that society itself is more violent than it actually is. Similarly, people's perceptions of political leaders are affected to some extent by how those leaders are reported in the media. When leaders are repeatedly portrayed as manipulative and self-interested, for example, people tend to see them as manipulative and self-interested.[14]

Peers

Peer groups—friends, neighbors, and coworkers—tend to reinforce what a person already believes. One reason is that most people trust the opinions of their friends and associates. Many individuals are also unwilling to deviate too far from what their peers think. In *The Spiral of Silence*, Elisabeth Noelle-Neumann contends that most individuals are conformists and are reluctant to speak out against prevailing opinions. One effect, she argues, is to make such opinions appear to be more widely held than they are, which can lead public officials to give them more attention than they may deserve.[15]

Political Institutions and Leaders

Citizens look to political leaders and institutions, particularly the president and political parties, as guides to opinion. In the period immediately after the terrorist attacks on the World Trade Center and the Pentagon on September 11, 2001, most Americans were confused about who the enemy was and how the attack should be dealt with. That state of mind changed dramatically ten days later after a televised speech by President Bush in which he identified the Al Qaeda and Taliban forces in Afghanistan as the immediate target of what would become a war on terrorism. In polls taken after the speech, nine of every ten Americans said they agreed with Bush's plan of action.

Churches

Since the Puritans in the seventeenth century, churches have played a substantial role in shaping Americans' social and political opinions. Most Americans say they believe in God, most attend church at least occasionally, and most belong to a religion that includes teachings on the proper nature of society. Moreover, most Americans say that religion has answers to many of the problems facing today's society. In these and other respects, churches and religion are a more powerful force in the United States than in most other Western countries (see "How the United States Compares").

Scholars have not studied the impact of churches on political socialization as closely as they have studied influences such as the schools and the media.[16] Nevertheless, churches are a source of political attitudes, including ones related to society's obligations to children, the poor, and the unborn. (The impact of religion is discussed further in a later section of this chapter.)

Religion is a powerful socializing force in American life. Churches, synagogues, mosques, and temples are places where Americans acquire values and beliefs that can affect their opinions about politics.

HOW THE UNITED STATES COMPARES

Americans as a Political People

Religion has long been a powerful force in American life. Several of the original colonies were established as havens for religious groups that had suffered persecution in the Old World. Not surprisingly, religious beliefs and imagery flowed into political discourse. America as the "Shining City upon a Hill" of which President Ronald Reagan spoke so eloquently and so often during the 1980s was derived from a sermon delivered by John Winthrop in 1630. He in turn had derived his sermon from a passage (5:14–16) in Matthew's version of the Gospel.

Religion was also the source of the country's "blue laws"—state and local regulations mandating certain activities and banning others. The first blue laws were enacted in the 1600s and made church attendance compulsory while prohibiting work on Sunday. Subsequent blue laws banned such things as the sale of liquor on Sunday.

In the nineteenth century and early twentieth century, religion was a source of deep political divisions, as Catholics and Protestants found themselves in opposite camps. Religion's political influence declined during and after World War II, but then reemerged in the 1960s as new issues rose to prominence. Today, many of the nation's political debates—over abortion, war, poverty, and same-sex marriage, for example—have a religious component.

Religion is a more salient part of American life than of European life. Of course, there are many countries in the less developed regions of the world—the Middle East, Africa, and Latin America, particularly—where religion is as important to people as it is to Americans. Compared with Europeans and Canadians, however, Americans are far more likely to say that religion is personally important. A 2002 cross-national survey by the Pew Research Center for the People and the Press illustrates the difference:

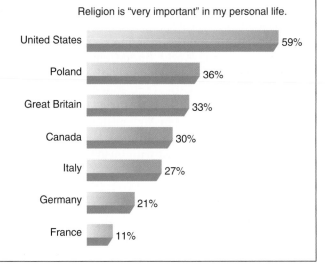

Religion is "very important" in my personal life.

United States	59%
Poland	36%
Great Britain	33%
Canada	30%
Italy	27%
Germany	21%
France	11%

FRAMES OF REFERENCE: HOW AMERICANS THINK POLITICALLY

What are the frames of reference that guide the political thinking of Americans? The question is important in at least two respects. First, the ways in which citizens think politically provide clues about the way in which public opinion is likely to affect government. The government in a democratic system is expected to act more often in accordance with public opinion than against it.

A second reason why it is important to understand how the people think politically is that a shared frame of reference can bring citizens together in the pursuit of a common goal. The opinions of millions of Americans would mean almost nothing if each opinion were different from all the others. If enough people think the same way, however, they may be able to exert political power.

The subject of how Americans think politically fills entire books. Outlined here are four major frames of reference through which Americans evaluate political alternatives. The first tends to unite Americans; the other three give rise to opposing opinions.

Cultural Thinking: Common Ideas

As was indicated in Chapter 1, Americans embrace a common set of ideals. Principles such as liberty, equality, and individualism have always meant somewhat different things to Americans but nonetheless are a source of agreement. For example, government programs aimed at redistributing wealth from the rich to the poor are popular among Europeans but are less appealing to Americans, who have a deeper commitment to individualism.

There are limits, of course, to the degree to which Americans' basic beliefs shape their policy opinions. For nearly two centuries, African Americans were inferior by law to white Americans, despite the American creed that "all men are created equal." Such inconsistencies speak to the all-too-human capacity to voice one idea and live another.

Nevertheless, Americans' political ideals have a powerful influence on their opinions. These ideals affect the way in which disputes are argued and also what Americans regard as reasonable and desirable. These shared ideals place boundaries on political action.

Ideological Thinking: The Outlook of Some

Analysts sometimes use words such as *liberal, conservative, populist,* and *libertarian* to describe how ordinary Americans think about politics (see "States in the Nation"). These are ideological terms, as are such terms as socialism and communism. An **ideology** is a consistent pattern of political attitudes that stems from a core belief. The core belief of socialism, for example, is that society should ensure that every person's basic economic needs are met. Accordingly, a socialist would support public policies that provide for economic security, such as a government-guaranteed annual income for all families.

Although ideological terms are useful analytically, they can be misleading. Many Americans who call themselves liberal or conservative have no real idea of what the term means. As well, people frequently hold inconsistent opinions.[17] They may take a liberal position on one issue and a conservative position on a related one. People's opinions are even contradictory at times.[18] As we saw earlier, many Americans want steep tax cuts while also wanting government to spend more heavily on health, education, and other programs. Studies indicate that no more than a third of Americans hold coherent opinions across a wide range of policy issues. Thus, by the strict definition of what constitutes a political ideology—"a *consistent* pattern of political attitudes"—most Americans do not have one.

Nevertheless, ideological terms are a meaningful shorthand way to describe broad tendencies in political attitudes. When millions of Americans during the

ideology A consistent pattern of opinion on particular issues that stems from a core belief or set of beliefs.

1930s Great Depression wanted the federal government to help them economically, they may not have thought of themselves as economic liberals, but their belief was strong enough to change how government operated in the economic realm.

America's major ideologies are rooted in beliefs about equality and liberty. The importance that people attach to one or the other of these ideals, and the degree to which they think government involvement promotes or impedes it, affect their ideological stance. Economic liberals, for example, look to government to create a more equal society than that which results from unregulated markets or untaxed incomes. In contrast, economic conservatives believe that too much government involvement in the economy undermines personal liberty and initiative.

Today, ideological conflict in the United States centers on the scope of government programs and the intrusiveness of government action. In order to measure public attitudes on these two dimensions, pollsters have developed a variety of methods. The Gallup Poll uses a two-question method that is widely used:

1.   Some people think the government is trying to do too many things that should be left to individuals and businesses. Others think that government should do more to solve our country's problems. Which view is closer to your own?

2.   Some people think the government should promote traditional values in our society. Others think that the government should not favor any particular set of values. Which view is closer to your own?

liberals Those who believe government should do more to solve the nation's problems but reject the notion that government should favor a particular set of social values.

conservatives Those who believe government tries to do too many things that should be left to firms and individuals but look to government to uphold traditional values.

libertarians Those who believe government tries to do too many things that should be left to firms and individuals and who oppose government as an instrument of traditional values.

populists Those who believe government should do more to solve the nation's problems and look to it to uphold traditional values.

The Gallup Poll's two questions are used to categorize Americans into four ideological types. **Liberals** are those who say that government should do more to solve the country's problems and who say that government ought not to support traditional values at the expense of less conventional ones. Thus, for example, a liberal would be inclined to favor an increase in government-provided health care and also to support civil unions for same-sex couples. **Conservatives** are those who think government should be sparing in its programs and who feel government should use its power to uphold traditional values. Thus, a conservative would be likely to oppose an increase in government-provided health care and to oppose civil unions. **Libertarians** are those who are reluctant to use government either as a means of economic redistribution or as a means of favoring particular social values. Thus, a libertarian would prefer that government not get more deeply involved in health-care provision and would be inclined to permit civil unions. **Populists** are those who would use government for both the purpose of economic redistribution and the purpose of guarding traditional values. Thus, a populist would be inclined to support increased health-care spending and to oppose civil unions. (To determine your ideology by this method, see "Liberty, Equality & Self-Government.)

During the 1990s, according to the Gallup method, both conservatives and libertarians easily outnumbered both liberals and populists. Since 2002, liberals and populists together have slightly outnumbered the combination of conservatives and libertarians, largely as a result of a rise in the number of Americans who feel that government should do more to solve society's problems.[19]

Again, ideology in its strictest sense is not an attribute that accurately describes how most Americans think politically. Nevertheless, ideological tenden-

STATES IN THE NATION

Conservatives and Liberals

In the United States, self-identified conservatives substantially outnumber those who call themselves liberals. Only in twelve states and the District of Columbia are liberals greater or nearly equal in number to conservatives.

Q. Why is the concentration of conservatives especially high in the southern, plains, and mountain states?

A. The southern, plains, and mountain states are less urbanized. Accordingly, their residents traditionally have been less dependent on and less trusting of government.

Most conservative

Next most conservative

Least conservative

Source: CNN exit polls, 2000. Classification based on the difference in the proportions of self-identified conservatives and liberals in each state.

cies do help to explain the political choices that Americans make and the conflicts that divide them. Until the 1970s, for example, liberal attitudes were ascendant. Gradually, however, Americans became less trusting of government and more worried about its financial cost. The rollback in federal taxes in the 1980s was fueled by a belief that government was trying to do too much. Recently, Americans have been more sharply divided over issues of the scope

Liberty, Equality & Self-Government

What's Your Opinion?

Americans' Ideologies

In the United States, the key dimensions of political conflict center on the extent of government intervention in the economic marketplace and in the maintenance of traditional values. Government intervention in either sphere has implications for liberty—the amount of freedom you should have in deciding on your lifestyle and in making economic choices. Government intervention in the economic sphere can also affect equality: government has been the principal means of providing economic security for those vulnerable to market forces.

You can test your own ideology—and thus in a way your own conception of liberty and equality—by asking yourself the two measurement questions used in Gallup surveys:

1. Some people think the government is trying to do too many things that should be left to individuals and businesses. Others think that government should do more to solve our country's problems. Which view is closer to your own?

   a. Government is doing too much
   b. Government should do more

2. Some people think that the government should promote traditional values in our society. Others think the government should not favor any particular set of values. Which view is closer to your own?

   a. Government should promote traditional values
   b. Government should not favor particular values

If you had been a respondent in a poll that asked these questions, you would have been classified as a *conservative* if you agreed with the first statement of each question (1a and 2a); a *liberal* if you agreed with the second statement of each question (1b and 2b); a *libertarian* if you agreed with the first statement of the first question (1a) and the second statement of the second question (2b); and a *populist* if you agreed with the second statement of the first question (1b) and the first statement of the second question (2a).

and intrusiveness of government. As a result, political conflict has intensified. Some observers believe that the United States is now more deeply divided ideologically than at any time since the 1930s.

Group Thinking: The Outlook of Many

For most citizens, groups are a more important reference than ideology.[20] Many Americans see politics through the lens of a group to which they belong or with which they identify. Farmers, for example, are more likely to follow agricultural issues than labor-management issues. A group outlook is a source of both consensus and conflict. Farmers generally approve of government price supports for commodities, an opinion that unites farmers but pits them against other groups, including consumers.

Because of the country's great size, its settlement by various immigrant groups, and its economic pluralism, Americans are a very diverse people. Later chapters examine group tendencies more fully, but it is useful here to mention a few major group orientations: religion, class, region, race and ethnicity, gender, and age.

Economic class is related to Americans' opinions on a range of social and economic issues. Shown here is a work crew constructing formed wooden beams.

Religion

Religious beliefs have always been a source of solidarity within a group and a source of conflict with outsiders. As Catholics and Jews came to America in large numbers in the nineteenth and early twentieth centuries, they encountered intense hostility from Protestant reactionaries. Today, Catholics, Protestants, and Jews have similar opinions on most policy issues.

Nevertheless, some important religious differences remain, although the opposing sides are not always the same. Fundamentalist Protestants and Roman Catholics oppose legalized abortion more strongly than do other Protestants and Jews. In contrast, on welfare issues such as food programs for the poor, Catholics and Jews are more supportive than Protestants. Such differences have at least a partial basis in religious beliefs. A belief in self-reliance, for example, is part of the so-called Protestant ethic. Attitudes on abortion are tied to religious beliefs about whether human life begins at conception or at a later stage in the development of the fetus.

The most powerful religious force in contemporary American politics is the so-called religious right, which consists primarily of individuals who see themselves as born-again Christians and who view the Bible as infallible truth. Their views on issues such as gay rights, abortion, and school prayer differ significantly from those of the population as a whole. A Time/CNN survey found, for example, that born-again Christians are 37 percent more likely than other Americans to agree that "the Supreme Court and the Congress have gone too far in keeping religious and moral values like prayer out of our laws, schools, and many areas of our lives."

Class

Economic class has less influence on political opinion in the United States than in Europe, but it is nevertheless related to opinions on certain economic issues. For example, lower-income Americans are more supportive of social welfare programs, business regulation, and progressive taxation than are those in higher-income categories.

An obstacle to class-based politics in the United States is that people with similar incomes but differing occupations do not share the same opinions. Support for collective bargaining, for example, is substantially higher among factory workers than among small farmers, service workers, and those in the skilled crafts, even though the average income of members of all these groups is similar. The interplay of class and opinion is examined more closely in Chapter 9, which discusses interest groups.

Region

Region has declined as a basis of political opinions. The increased mobility of the U.S. population has resulted in the relocation of millions of Americans from the Northeast and Midwest to the South and West. Their beliefs on issues such as social welfare tend to be more liberal than those of people native to these regions. Nevertheless, regional differences are still evident in the areas of social welfare, civil rights, and national defense. Conservative opinions on these issues are more prevalent in the southern and mountain states than elsewhere.

Race and Ethnicity

As Chapter 5 pointed out, race and ethnicity have a significant influence on opinions. Whites and African Americans, for example, differ on issues of integration: black people are more in favor of affirmative action, busing, and other measures designed to promote racial equality and integration. Racial and ethnic groups also differ on economic issues, largely as a result of differences in their economic situations. The crime issue is another area in which opinion differences are pronounced and predictable: minorities are less trusting of police and the judicial system. A 1999 American Bar Association survey found, for example, that only half as many nonwhites as whites believe that "law enforcement officials and police try to treat whites and minorities alike."

Gender

Although male-female differences of opinion are small on most issues, gender does affect opinion in some policy areas. For example, women are slightly more supportive than men of abortion rights and affirmative action. A Gallup poll found a 63 percent to 53 percent difference in support for affirmative action. The difference is even larger on some social welfare issues, such as poverty and education assistance.[21] A Washington Post/ABC News poll, for example, found that 72 percent of women, compared with 57 percent of men, favored increased spending for education. Some analysts suggest that such differences are accounted for in part by a tendency for women to think more in terms of the community as a whole and for men to think more in terms of self-reliance.

Women and men differ most significantly in their opinions on the use of military force. In nearly every case, women are less supportive of military action than men are. The terrorist attacks on the World Trade Center and the Pentagon on September 11, 2001, produced an exception to the normal pattern.

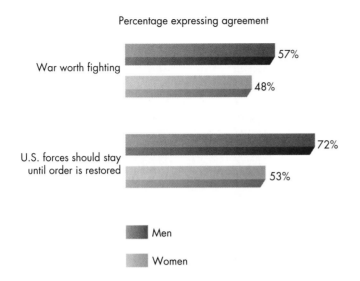

Percentage expressing agreement

War worth fighting — Men 57%, Women 48%

U.S. forces should stay until order is restored — Men 72%, Women 53%

Men

Women

Figure 6–2

Gender and the Iraq Conflict
Compared with men, women are somewhat less inclined to support military force as a means of resolving international conflicts. This difference was evident in a poll taken six months after the United States invaded Iraq. Women were less likely than men to think that the war was worth fighting and that U.S. troops should stay in Iraq until order was fully restored.
Source: ABC News/Washington Post poll, November 12–16, 2003.

Men and women were almost equally likely (90 percent and 88 percent, respectively) to favor a military response. But they differed in expected ways when questioned about other recent military actions. Women were less likely than men to think that military intervention in Iraq was worthwhile (see Figure 6–2).

Differences such as these are a factor in the gender gap discussed in Chapter 5. Women and men do not differ greatly in their political views, but persistent and predictable differences lead them to respond somewhat differently to issues, events, and candidates.

Age

Age has always affected opinions, but the gap between young and old is growing. In her book *Young v. Old*, political scientist Susan MacManus notes that the elderly tend to oppose increases in public school funding while supporting increases in social security and Medicare (government-assisted medical care for retirees). MacManus predicts that issues of age will increasingly dominate American politics and that the elderly have the political clout to prevail. They vote at a much higher rate than do young people, are better organized politically (through groups such as the powerful AARP), and are increasing in number as a result of lengthened life spans (the so-called graying of America).[22]

Crosscutting Cleavages

Although group loyalty can have a powerful impact on people's opinions, this influence is diminished when identification with one group is offset by identification with other groups. In a pluralistic society such as the United States, groups tend to be "crosscutting"—that is, each group includes individuals who also belong to many other groups. Crosscutting cleavages tend to produce moderate opinions. Faced with conflicting feelings arising out of identification with several groups, most people seek a balanced opinion. In America, for example,

Figure 6–3

Partisanship and Issue Opinions

Republicans and Democrats differ significantly in their opinions on many policy issues.

Source: In order of questions: Washington Post/ABC News, 2003; ICA, 2003; Washington Post/ABC News, 2004; Pew Research Center for the People and the Press, 2003.

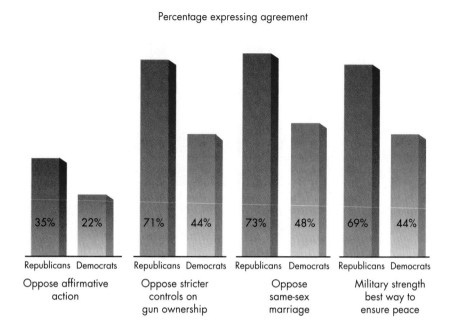

Percentage expressing agreement

Republicans	Democrats	Republicans	Democrats	Republicans	Democrats	Republicans	Democrats
35%	22%	71%	44%	73%	48%	69%	44%
Oppose affirmative action		Oppose stricter controls on gun ownership		Oppose same-sex marriage		Military strength best way to ensure peace	

Catholics and Protestants are not at each other's throats, largely because each group includes people of varying income, education, region, and so on. However, in societies such as Northern Ireland where group loyalties are reinforcing rather than crosscutting (Catholics tend to have much lower incomes, Protestants much higher ones), opinions are intensified by group identifications, and deep hatreds among the opposing camps result.

Partisan Thinking: The Line That Divides

In the everyday world of politics, no source of opinion more clearly divides Americans than that of their partisanship. Figure 6–3 provides examples, but these show only a few of the differences. On nearly every major political issue, Republicans and Democrats have views that are at least somewhat different. In many cases, such as spending programs for the poor, the differences are substantial.

party identification The personal sense of loyalty that an individual may feel toward a particular political party.

Party identification refers to a person's ingrained sense of loyalty to a political party. Party identification is not formal membership in a party but rather an emotional attachment to a party—the feeling that "I am a Democrat" or "I am a Republican." Scholars and pollsters typically have measured party identification with a question of the following type: "Generally speaking, do you think of yourself as a Republican, a Democrat, an Independent, or what?" About two-thirds of adults call themselves Democrats or Republicans. Of the one-third who prefer the label "Independent," most say they lean toward one party or the other and tend to vote primarily for that party's candidates.

Early studies concluded that party loyalties were highly stable and seldom changed over the course of adult life.[23] Subsequent studies have shown that party loyalties are more fluid than originally believed; they can be influenced by

John Kerry during his campaign as the 2004 Democratic presidential nominee. Partisanship is one of the strongest influences on the political opinions that people hold.

the issues and candidates of the moment.[24] Nevertheless, most adults do not switch their party loyalties easily, and a substantial proportion never waver from their initial commitment to a party, which can often be traced to childhood influences.

Once acquired, partisanship affects how people perceive and interpret events. For example, when the U.S. Supreme Court ruled against a manual recount of Florida votes, which decided the 2000 presidential election in favor of George W. Bush, 53 percent of Democrats and 25 percent of Independents but only 12 percent of Republicans said in a national poll that they had "less respect" for the Court because of its action.

For most people, partisanship is not simply blind faith in the party of their choice. Some Republicans and Democrats know very little about their party's policies and unthinkingly embrace its candidates. However, party loyalties are not randomly distributed across the population but follow a pattern that would be predicted from the parties' traditions. The Democratic party, for example, has been the driving force behind social welfare and workers' rights policies, while the Republican party has been the spearhead for probusiness and tax reduction policies. The fact that most union workers are Democrats and most business-people are Republicans is not a coincidence. Their partisanship is rooted in their different economic circumstances and the different policy traditions of the two parties.[25] This and other issues of partisanship are examined in more detail at various points later in this book, particularly in Chapters 7, 8, 11, and 12.

 # THE INFLUENCE OF PUBLIC OPINION ON POLICY

Yet unanswered in our discussion is the central question about public opinion: what impact does it have on government?

Figure 6–4

Americans' Opinion on Whether the U.S. Government Serves the People

Most Americans believe that the government operates on behalf of the public.

Source: The Pew Research Center for the People and the Press, Global Attitudes Survey, 2002.

Percentage agreeing that, "generally, the U.S. government is run for the benefit of all the people."

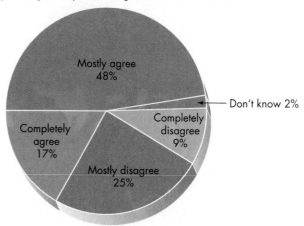

The fundamental principle of democracy is that the people's view ought to prevail on public issues, but this principle is difficult to put into practice. In any society of appreciable size, it is simply not possible for the people to directly formulate public policies and programs. However, democracy can be said to exist when elections are free and fair and when officials take the public's views into account when making policy decisions.[26] If Americans are the judge, the United States would be said to meet these criteria. A majority believe that government is responsive to their views and concerns. A 2002 survey found that two-thirds felt that "government is run on behalf of all the people" (see Figure 6–4).

Some analysts argue, however, that the public's views do not count for enough; the elites, it is claimed, are so entrenched and remote that they pay little attention to the preferences of ordinary citizens.[27] The most comprehensive study ever conducted of the relationship between public opinion and policy concluded otherwise. In a study spanning fifty years of trends, Benjamin Page and Robert Shapiro found a substantial relationship between changes in public opinion and subsequent changes in public policy, particularly on highly visible issues. More often than not, policy changed when opinion changed. Furthermore, the more important the issue, the more likely it was that policy changed in the direction of public opinion. Page and Shapiro concluded that U.S. officials are in fact reasonably responsive to public opinion.[28]

Not all scholars have interpreted the evidence on public opinion and policy so favorably.[29] Research points to a widening gap between public opinion and policy, apparently because elected leaders from both political parties have tilted toward the more extreme positions favored by powerful groups within their respective parties (such as the Christian Right within the Republican party and lifestyle liberals within the Democratic party).[30] Nevertheless, there are many actions that politicians willingly take in order to appeal to the public.[31] In late 1999, for example, the GOP-controlled Congress passed a budget than included funding to hire thousands of new public school teachers. Congressional Republicans had opposed the measure, but education ranked near the top in polls of Americans' policy priorities and the 2000 election was just around the corner. Republicans, reluctant to hand the Democrats a potent campaign issue, enacted the funding measure.

TABLE 6–1	Anatomy of the Iraq Conflict: Public Opinion and Policy	
APPROXIMATE TIME PERIOD	**POLICY SITUATION**	**U.S. PUBLIC OPINION**
Spring 2002	Indications surface that the Bush administration is preparing for a possible war with Iraq.	A slight majority support using U.S. troops to topple the Saddam Hussein regime, this opinion has existed since the end of the first Gulf War in 1991.
Fall 2002	U.S. troop buildup in the vicinity of Iraq is underway; Congress passes a resolution authorizing use of force if necessary against Iraq; efforts begin to get UN weapons inspectors into Iraq to check for Weapons of Mass Destruction (WMDs).	Majority support exists for using U.S. troops but majority also indicates a preference to resolve the problem with sanctions or, if through war, with the backing of the UN and America's allies.
Winter 2002	As troop buildup and UN debate continues, Bush administration makes clear its intention to go to war with or without broad international backing.	Majority support exists for military option but 40 percent say they oppose it without UN backing; about 25 percent fully opposed to war.
March 2003	Against the objections of France, Germany, Russia, and other countries, Bush orders an attack on Iraq. The attack is essentially carried out by U.S. and British troops only.	More than 70 percent express support for war with roughly 25 percent opposed. Bush's approval rating rises to the 70-percent level.
April 2003	Intense combat phase of the war ends with the defeat of the Iraqi army.	More than 70 percent say the war was successful and was worth fighting. Bush approval rating remains high.
Summer 2003	The WMDs that were used as justification for the war are not found and doubts surface that they will be found. U.S. troops take almost daily casualties as a result of ambushes and suicide bombings.	Those who believe war was worth fighting drops below 60 percent. Bush approval rating dropping.
Fall 2003	Turmoil in Iraq continues, as does the financial burden as a result of the troop deployment and reconstruction effort. In late fall, Bush announces a speeded-up timetable for returning sovereignty to Iraqis.	Those who believe war was worth fighting continues to slide, as does Bush's approval rating.
Spring 2004	Continued turmoil in Iraq. Revelations by arms inspectors and terrorist experts raise questions about the U.S. intelligence reports that were used to justify the war and raise questions about whether the Bush administration was determined to go to war with Iraq regardless of circumstances. Abuses of war prisoners by U.S. troops are revealed.	Americans are evenly split on whether war was worth fighting and whether the United States is safer or less safe as a result of the war.
June 2004	Handover of authority to Iraqi officials, although the United States continues to exercise control over military and some other operations.	A slight majority of Americans believe that the war was a mistake and that it was fought on a false pretext. Bush's approval rating falls below 50 percent.
Fall 2004	As it has been throughout the 2004 presidential campaign, the Iraq conflict is a source of heated debate between the Bush camp and its Democratic opponents.	Americans believe Iraq and the economy are the top issues in the presidential campaign. On balance, the Iraq issue hurts Bush's candidacy more than it helps.

After U.S. forces captured Baghdad and President Bush declared that the war had been "won," guerrilla forces and terrorists continued to attack American troops. The casualties from these attacks weakened public support for the intervention in Iraq, which was among the reasons the Bush administration accelerated the timetable for returning control of Iraq to the Iraqis.

There is also little question that the broad public's views place a boundary on what policymakers can reasonably do. There are many actions that officials dare not take for fear of public retribution. Leading politicians in recent decades, for example, have rarely risked proposing anything other than small changes in the social security program, which has broad public support.

The war in Iraq is also an instructive case study in the power of public opinion (see "Anatomy of the Iraq Conflict"). While Americans' opinions gave President Bush wide latitude in whether and when to invade Iraq, Bush's options narrowed when, after the combat phase ended, U.S. troops continued to die and the financial cost of rebuilding Iraq climbed. Bush was forced to speed up his timetable for placing Iraqis in charge of aspects of their government and to seek more support from the UN and from Europe, including European governments that had opposed the U.S. invasion. The American public's aversion to a costly transition in Iraq limited Bush's ability to decide on his own the policies that the United States would pursue.

Such examples, however, do not provide an answer to the question of whether government is *sufficiently* responsive to public opinion. This question is a normative one, the answer to which rests on assumptions about the proper relationship between people's everyday opinions and the actions of government. The question is also complicated by the fact that politics includes a battle over the control of public opinion. People's views are neither fixed nor simply a product of personal circumstances. Public opinion is dynamic and can be changed, activated, and crystallized through political action.

In fact, one of the best indicators of the power of public opinion is the effort made by political leaders to harness it in support of their goals. In American politics, popular demand for a policy is a powerful argument for that policy. For this reason and others, great effort is made to organize and represent public opinion through elections (Chapter 7), political parties (Chapter 8), interest groups (Chapter 9), the news media (Chapter 10), and political institutions (Chapters 11 through 14).

Summary

Self-Test
www.mhhe.com/pattersontad7

Public opinion can be defined as those opinions held by ordinary citizens that they openly express. Public officials have many ways of assessing public opinion, such as the outcomes of elections, but they have increasingly come to rely on public opinion polls. There are many possible sources of error in polls, and surveys sometimes present a misleading portrayal of the public's views. However, a properly conducted poll can be an accurate indication of what the public is thinking and can dissuade political leaders from thinking that the views of the most vocal citizens (such as demonstrators and letter writers) are also the views of the broader public.

The process by which individuals acquire their political opinions is called political socialization. During childhood, the family and schools are important sources of basic political attitudes, such as beliefs about the parties and the nature of the U.S. political and economic systems. Many of the basic orientations that Americans acquire during childhood remain with them in adulthood, but socialization is a continuing process. Major shifts in opinion during adulthood are usually the consequence of changing political conditions; for example, the Great Depression of the 1930s was the catalyst for wholesale changes in Americans' opinions on the government's economic role. Short-term fluctuations in opinion can result from new political issues, problems, and events. Individuals' opinions in these cases are affected by prior beliefs, peers, political leaders, and the news media. Events themselves are also a significant short-term influence on opinions.

The frames of reference that guide Americans' opinions include cultural beliefs, such as individualism, that result in a range of acceptable and unacceptable policy alternatives. Opinions can also stem from ideology, although most citizens do not have a strong and consistent ideological attachment. In addition, individuals develop opinions as a result of group orientations, notably religion, income level, occupation, region, race, ethnicity, gender, and age. Partisanship is perhaps the major source of political opinions; Republicans and Democrats differ in their voting behavior and views on many policy issues.

Public opinion has a significant influence on government but seldom determines exactly what government will do in a particular instance. Public opinion serves to constrain the policy choices of officials. Some policy actions are beyond the range of possibility because the public will not accept change in existing policy or will not seriously consider policy that seems clearly at odds with basic American values. Evidence indicates that officials are reasonably attentive to public opinion on highly visible and controversial issues of public policy.

STUDY CORNER

Key Terms

age-cohort tendency *(p. 193)*

agents of socialization *(p. 193)*

conservatives *(p. 198)*

ideology *(p. 197)*

liberals *(p. 197)*

libertarians *(p. 198)*

party identification *(p. 204)*

political socialization *(p. 191)*

population *(p. 189)*

populists *(p. 198)*

probability sample *(p. 190)*

public opinion *(p. 185)*

public opinion poll *(p. 189)*

sample *(p. 189)*

sampling error *(p. 189)*

Self-Test

1. The process by which individuals acquire political opinions is called:
   a. public opinion polling.
   b. efficacy.
   c. selective incorporation.
   d. political socialization.
   e. sampling error.

2. Most studies on the influence of ideology on public opinion agree that:
   a. most people think of themselves as liberals.
   b. most people think of themselves as libertarians.
   c. most people think of themselves as isolationists.
   d. only a minority of Americans truly understand and apply ideological frames of reference.

3. Public officials increasingly rely on what way to assess public opinion?
   a. talk show ratings
   b. election outcomes
   c. public opinion polls
   d. what editorial writers in newspapers are saying about the public
   e. mail received by elected representatives in Washington, D.C.

4. Partisan thinking is linked to:
   a. loyalty to a political party.
   b. preference for interest groups over political parties.
   c. voting for the individual rather than the party.

   d. considering oneself an independent.
   e. voting on the basis of issues rather than party.

5. According to your text, a person who favors economic individualism and traditional social values can be labeled as a:
   a. liberal.
   b. conservative.
   c. libertarian.
   d. populist.
   e. nationalist.

6. The political opinions of males and females differ most significantly on issues of:
   a. the environment.
   b. crime and the judicial system.
   c. the use of military force.
   d. global trade.

T 7. In general, the larger the size of the sample in a poll, the smaller the sampling error. (T/F)

F 8. Most American citizens apply a fully developed ideological frame of reference to political issues. (T/F)

F 9. When asked whether they are liberal, conservative, or moderate, most Americans describe themselves as liberal. (T/F)

F 10. Most Americans pay close attention to and are well informed about the workings of their government. (T/F)

Critical Thinking

What factors limit the influence of public opinion on the policy choices of public officials?

Suggested Readings

Alvarez, R. Michael, and John Brehm. *Hard Choices, Easy Answers: Values, Information, and American Public Opinion*. Princeton, N.J.: Princeton University Press, 2002. An analysis that argues that what citizens know about politics is assessed in the context of their values and beliefs.

Asher, Herbert. *Polling and the Public*, 6th ed. Washington, D.C.: Congressional Quarterly Press, 2004. A guide to public opinion poll methods and analysis.

Delli Carpini, Michael X., and Scott Keeter. *What Americans Know About Politics and Why It Matters*. New Haven, Conn.: Yale University Press, 1996. A synthesis of the American public's knowledge about politics.

Green, Donald, Bradley Palmquist, and Eric Schickler. *Partisan Hearts and Minds*. New Haven, Conn.: Yale University Press, 2002. An analysis that concludes partisanship powerfully affects how citizens respond to candidates and issues.

Jacobs, Lawrence, and Robert Shapiro. *Politicians Don't Pander*. Chicago: University of Chicago Press, 2000. An analysis that concludes politicians are not driven by polls.

MacManus, Susan A. *Young v. Old: Generational Combat in the Twenty-first Century*. Boulder, Colo.: Westview Press, 1996. A study of the emerging conflict in the political self-interest of younger and older Americans.

Sobel, Richard. *The Impact of Public Opinion on U.S. Foreign Policy Since Vietnam*. New York: Oxford University Press, 2001. A study of the relationship between public opinion and foreign policy.

Zaller, John R. *The Nature and Origins of Mass Opinion*. New York: Cambridge University Press, 1992. A superb analysis of the nature of public opinion.

List of Websites

http://www.policy.com/

A nonpartisan site that provides a wealth of information about current public issues.

http://www.people-press.org/

Website of the Pew Research Center for the People and the Press; it includes an abundance of recent polling results, including cross-national comparisons.

http://www.princeton.edu/~abelson/

The Princeton Survey Research Center's site; it offers results from surveys conducted by a variety of polling organizations.

http://www.publicagenda.org/

The nonpartisan Public Agenda's site; it provides opinions, analyses, and educational materials on current policy issues.

Participate!

At the website of a polling organization such as the Pew Research Center for the People and the Press (www.people-press.org), examine the poll results on a current policy issue. Study the extent to which opinions differ, if at all, between men and women and between Republicans and Democrats. Would an informal poll of the people you know result in a similar distribution of opinion? Why or why not?

Extra Credit

For up-to-the-minute *New York Times'* articles, interactive simulations, graphics, study tools, and more links and quizzes, visit the text's Online Learning Center at www.mhhe.com/pattersontad7.

(Self-Test Answers: 1. d   2. d   3. c   4. a   5. b   6. c   7. T   8. F   9. F   10. F)

Political Participation and Voting:

Expressing the Popular Will

"We are concerned in public affairs,
but immersed in our private ones."

—*Walter Lippmann*[1]

At stake in the 2004 election was control of the presidency and the Congress. Which party would have the leading voice on legislation affecting education, health, welfare, and the environment? Which party would have the greater say in how America responded to the challenges posed by the domestic and global economies? Which party would be entrusted with national security? With so much at stake, it might be thought that Americans would have been eager to cast their ballots for the party of their choice. But in fact tens of millions of American adults did not vote in the 2004 election. Despite a concerted get-out-the-vote campaign by the political parties, news media, and civic groups, the number of people who did not vote was far greater than the number of votes the winning side received.

Voting is a form of **political participation**—involvement in activities intended to influence public policy and leadership. Political participation involves other activities in addition to voting, such as joining political parties and interest groups, writing to elected officials, demonstrating for political causes, and giving money to political candidates.

Democratic societies are distinguished by their emphasis on citizen participation. The concept of self-government is based on the idea that ordinary people have a right to participate in the affairs of state. Related issues include whether people exercise that right and whether participation is evenly spread across society. As it happens, the United States is an unusual case relative to other democracies, as this chapter will show. The major points made in this chapter are the following:

- *Voter turnout in U.S. elections is low in comparison with that of other democratic nations.* The reasons for this difference include the nature of U.S. election laws, particularly those pertaining to registration requirements and the scheduling of elections.

- *Most citizens do not participate actively in politics in ways other than voting.* Only a small proportion of Americans can be classified as political activists.

- *Most Americans make a sharp distinction between their personal lives and national life.* This attitude reduces their incentive to participate and contributes to a pattern of participation dominated by citizens with higher levels of income and education.

political participation Involvement in activities intended to influence public policy and leadership, such as voting, joining political parties and interest groups, writing to elected officials, demonstrating for political causes, and giving money to political candidates.

suffrage The right to vote.

Historical Background

VOTER PARTICIPATION

At the nation's founding, **suffrage**—the right to vote—was restricted to property-owning males. Tom Paine ridiculed this policy in *Common Sense*. Observing that a man whose only item of property was a jackass would lose his right to vote if the jackass died, Paine asked, "Now tell me, which was the voter, the man or the jackass?" It was not until 1840 that all states extended suffrage to propertyless white males, a change made possible by their continued demand for the vote and by the realization on the part of the wealthy that the nation's abundance and openness were natural protections against an assault on property rights by the voting poor.

Women did not secure the vote until 1920, with the ratification of the Nineteenth Amendment. In the 1870s, Susan B. Anthony tried to vote in her hometown of Rochester, New York, asserting that she had a right to do so as a U.S. citizen. The men who placed her under arrest charged her with "illegal voting" and insisted that her proper place was in the home. By 1920, men had run out of excuses for keeping the vote from women. As Senator Wendell Phillips observed: "One of two things is true: either woman is like man—and if she is, then a ballot based on brains belongs to her as well as to him. Or she is different, and then man does not know how to vote for her as she herself does."[2]

African Americans had to wait nearly fifty years longer than women to be granted full suffrage. Blacks seemed to have won the right to vote with passage of the Fifteenth Amendment after the Civil War, but as explained in Chapter 5, they were effectively disenfranchised in the South by a number of electoral tricks, including poll taxes, literacy tests, and whites-only primary elections. The poll tax was a fee of several dollars that had to be paid before a person could register to vote. Because most blacks in the South were too poor to pay it, the poll tax barred them from voting. Not until the ratification of the Twenty-fourth Amendment in 1964 was the poll tax outlawed in federal elections. Supreme Court decisions and the Voting Rights Act of 1965 swept away other legal barriers to fuller participation by African Americans.

In 1971, the Twenty-sixth Amendment extended voting rights to include citizens eighteen years of age or older. Previously, nearly all states had restricted voting to those twenty-one years of age or older.

Today virtually any American—rich or poor, man or woman, black or white—who is determined to vote can legally and actually do so. Americans attach great importance to the power of their votes. They claim that voting is their greatest source of influence over political leadership and their strongest protection against an uncaring or corrupt government.[3] They also claim that voting is a basic act of citizenship (see Table 7–1). In view of this attitude and the historical struggle of various groups to gain voting rights, the surprising fact is that millions of Americans choose not to vote regularly, a tendency that sets them apart from citizens of most other Western democracies.

After a hard-fought, decades-long campaign, American women finally won the right to vote in 1920.

Factors in Voter Turnout: The United States in Comparative Perspective

Voter turnout is the proportion of persons of voting age who actually vote in a given election. Since the 1960s, the voter turnout in presidential elections has averaged only about 55 percent (see Figure 7–1). Turnout is even lower in the midterm congressional elections that take place between presidential elections. Midterm election turnout has not reached 50 percent since 1920, nor has it made it past the 40 percent mark since 1970. After one midterm election, cartoonist Rigby showed an election clerk eagerly asking a stray cat that had wandered into a polling place, "Are you registered?"[4]

Nonvoting is far more prevalent in the United States than in nearly all other democracies (see "How the United States Compares"). In recent decades, turnout in major national elections has averaged less than 60 percent in the United States, compared with more than 90 percent in Belgium, and more than 80 percent in France, Germany, and Denmark.[5] The disparity in turnout between the United States and other nations is not as great as these official voting rates indicate. Some nations calculate turnout solely on the basis of eligible adults, whereas the United States bases its figures on all adults, including noncitizens and other ineligible groups. Nevertheless, even when such statistical disparities are corrected, turnout in U.S. elections is relatively low.

Contributing to the relatively low turnout in U.S. elections are registration requirements, the frequency of elections, and the lack of clear-cut differences between the political parties.

voter turnout The proportion of persons of voting age who actually vote in a given election.

TABLE 7–1	Opinions on Obligations of Citizens Americans rank voting as one of the essential obligations of citizenship.			
	ESSENTIAL OBLIGATION	VERY IMPORTANT OBLIGATION	SOMEWHAT IMPORTANT	PERSONAL PREFERENCE
Treating all people equally regardless of race or ethnic background	57%	33%	6%	4%
Voting in elections	53	29	9	9
Working to reduce inequality and injustice	41	42	12	6
Being civil to others with whom we may disagree	35	45	14	6
Keeping fully informed about the news and other public issues	30	42	19	10
Donating blood or organs to help with medical needs	20	37	18	26
Volunteering time to community service	16	42	26	16

Source: Used by permission of the 1996 Survey of American Political Culture, James Davison Hunter and Carol Bowman, Directors, Institute for Advanced Studies in Culture, University of Virginia.

Figure 7–1

Voter Turnout in Presidential Elections, 1960–2004
Voter turnout has declined since the 1960s.
Source: U.S. Bureau of the Census.

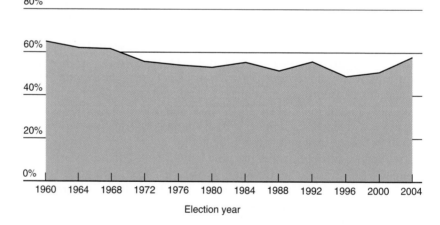

Percentage of adults who voted

Election year

Registration Requirements

registration The practice of placing citizens' names on an official list of voters before they are eligible to exercise their right to vote.

Before Americans are allowed to vote, they must be registered—that is, their names must appear on an official list of eligible voters. **Registration** began around 1900 as a way of preventing voters from casting more than one ballot during an election. Fraudulent voting had become a favorite tactic of political party machines in communities where the population was too large for residents to be personally known to poll watchers. However, the extra effort in-

HOW THE UNITED STATES COMPARES

Voter Turnout

The United States ranks near the bottom among the world's democracies in the percentage of eligible citizens who participate in national elections. One reason for the low voter turnout is that individual Americans are responsible for registering to vote, whereas in most other democracies, voters are automatically registered by government officials. In addition, unlike some other democracies, the United States does not encourage voting by holding elections on the weekend or by imposing penalties, such as fines, on those who do not participate.

Another factor affecting voter turnout rate in the United States is the absence of a major labor or socialist party, which would serve to bring lower-income citizens to the polls. America's individualist culture and its electoral system (see Chapter 8) have inhibited the establishment of a major labor or socialist party. In democracies where such parties exist, the turnout difference between upper- and lower-income groups is relatively small. In the United States, however, lower-income persons are much less likely to vote than are higher-income persons.

COUNTRY	APPROXIMATE VOTER TURNOUT	AUTOMATIC REGISTRATION?	SOCIAL DEMOCRAT, SOCIALIST, OR LABOR PARTY?	ELECTION DAY A HOLIDAY OR WEEKEND DAY?
Belgium	90%	Yes	Yes	Yes
Germany	85%	Yes	Yes	Yes
Denmark	85%	Yes	Yes	No
Italy	80%	Yes	Yes	Yes
Austria	80%	Yes	Yes	Yes
France	80%	No	Yes	Yes
Great Britain	60%	Yes	Yes	No
Canada	60%	Yes	No	No
Japan	60%	Yes	Yes	Yes
United States	55%	No	No	No

Source: Developed from multiple sources.

volved in registering placed an added burden on honest citizens. Because citizens could now vote only if they had registered beforehand, those people who forgot or otherwise failed to do so found themselves unable to participate on election day. Turnout in U.S. elections declined steadily after registration was instituted.

Although other democracies also require registration, they place this responsibility on government. In most European nations, public officials have the duty to enroll citizens on registration lists. The United States—in keeping with its individualistic culture—is one of the few democracies in which registration is the individual's responsibility. In addition, registration laws have traditionally been established by the state governments, and some states make it relatively difficult for citizens to qualify. Registration periods and locations usually

Although Americans have voted in relatively low numbers in recent U.S. elections, the turnout rate increased in 2004 in response to the issue and candidates of the moment.

are not highly publicized, and many citizens simply do not know when or where to register.[6] Eligibility can also be a problem. In most states, a citizen must establish legal residency by living in the same place for a minimum period, usually thirty days, before becoming eligible to register.

States with a tradition of lenient registration laws generally have a higher turnout than other states. Idaho, Maine, Minnesota, New Hampshire, Wisconsin, and Wyoming, which are states that allow people to register at their polling place on election day, have high turnout rates. Those states that have erected the most barriers are in the South, where restrictive registration was originally intended to prevent black people from voting. These historical differences continue to be reflected in state voter turnout (see "States in the Nation").

In 1993, in an effort to increase registration levels nationwide, Congress enacted a voting registration law known as "motor voter." It requires states to permit people to register to vote when applying for a driver's license and when applying for benefits at certain state welfare offices. Registration does not occur automatically in these situations; the citizen must fill out an application form. Congressional Republicans made their support of the legislation contingent on this nonmandatory provision. They had blocked the legislation for several years, believing that the bill as written would increase the proportion of lower-income Americans on the registration rolls and thereby help the Democratic party.

According to Federal Election Commission estimates, the motor-voter law has resulted in a net increase of more than ten million registrants. (A larger number of people have been registered through the law, but many of them would have registered anyway under the old system.) Nevertheless, the overall turnout rate has not increased since the law was passed. Other factors have combined to offset the gain in voters attributable to the legislation. Clearly, the registration requirement is only one of several factors underlying America's low turnout rate.

STATES IN THE NATION

Voter Turnout in Presidential Elections

The United States has a low voter turnout relative to most other Western democracies. However, the state-to-state variation is considerable. In a few states, including Minnesota and New Hampshire, nearly seven in ten adults vote in presidential elections. In contrast, there are a few states, including Hawaii and Texas, where barely more than four in ten adults vote.

Q. Why does the South have lower turnout than other regions? Why do states in the Southwest have relatively low turnout rates?

A. Southern states have more poverty and a tradition of more restrictive registration laws (dating to the Jim Crow era of racial segregation). Both factors are associated with lower voting rates. States with large populations of recent immigrants, including those states in the Southwest, also tend to have lower voting rates.

Source: Compiled by author from various sources; based on recent midterm and presidential elections.

Frequency of Elections

The United States holds more elections than any other nation. No other democracy has elections for the lower chamber of its national legislature (the equivalent of the U.S. House of Representatives) as often as every two years, and none

Ballots Cast but Not Counted

In the 2000 election, more than one hundred million votes were officially recorded as having been cast for president. However, more than two million other votes were cast but not counted. Some could not be read by a voting machine because the voter had not marked the ballot clearly or had placed a mark outside the designated space. Some were punch-card ballots that could not be read because the hole in the card was not punched through completely.

It has been estimated that 2 percent of all ballots cast in U.S. elections are spoiled for one reason or another. These votes rarely receive attention because they do not affect an election's outcome. In the 2000 presidential election, however, they may have been decisive. George W. Bush won the presidency on the basis of a 537-vote victory in Florida, where tens of thousands of ballots went uncounted.

His opponent, Al Gore, mounted a legal challenge to get the ballots counted, but it failed when the U.S. Supreme Court intervened to stop a hand recount on the grounds that the standards for determining a legal ballot were vague (see Chapter 14). The Florida vote highlighted a glaring weakness in the conduct of U.S. elections. Many communities in Florida and elsewhere were unable or unwilling to invest public funds in balloting systems that have a low error rate. Most of the inadequate machinery was found in minority areas. In Chicago, for example, the error rate was three times higher in African American neighborhoods, where older and less reliable ballot methods were used, than in white neighborhoods. After the 2000 election, Congress passed legislation that provided money and set standards intended to reduce the percentage of uncounted ballots.

schedules elections for chief executive as often as every four years.[7] In addition, elections of state and local officials in the United States are often scheduled separately from national races. Four-fifths of the states elect their governors in nonpresidential election years,[8] and 60 percent of U.S. cities hold elections of municipal officials in odd-numbered years.[9]

The frequency of U.S. elections reduces turnout by increasing the effort required to participate in all of them.[10] Most European nations have less frequent elections, and the responsibility of voting is thus less burdensome. Many European nations also schedule their elections on Sundays or declare election day a national holiday, thus making it more convenient for working people to vote. In the United States, elections are traditionally held on Tuesdays, and most people must vote before or after work.

Party Differences

A final explanation for low voter turnout in the United States has to do with people's perceptions of the two major parties (see Figure 7–2). At times, as in the 2004 presidential election, Americans have thought that a lot was at stake in the choice between the two parties. At other times, as in the 2000 election, they have been less convinced that it will make a big difference whether the Republicans or the Democrats win. And indeed, the two major parties do not ordinarily differ sharply on most policy issues. Each party depends on citizens of all economic and social backgrounds for support, and thus neither party can afford to adopt positions that will alienate sizable segments of the electorate. American parties do not completely avoid controversial issues, but they do not routinely take sharp stands on a wide range of them.

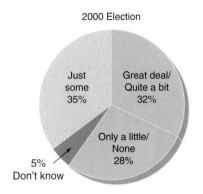
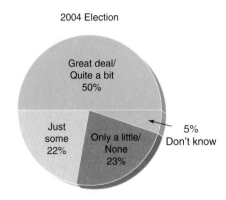

Figure 7–2

The Perceived Effect of Electing a Republican or a Democratic President

Many Americans believe that the country will not be greatly affected by whether the Republican or Democratic presidential candidate is elected. However, the proportion holding this belief shrinks when, as in the case of the 2004 campaign, Americans think important issues are at stake in the election.

Source: The Vanishing Voter Project, Shorenstein Center on the Press, Politics and Public Policy, Harvard University. Published by permission of project director.

European voters have more clearly defined options. Most European democracies have three or more significant political parties, which have formed along class divisions and sometimes along religious and social divisions as well. Labor parties abound in Europe, as do middle-class and right-wing parties. In order to hold onto their core constituencies and to distinguish themselves from multiple competitors, European parties take relatively sharp positions on most issues. This tendency has diminished somewhat in recent decades as old antagonisms, such as religion and class, have diminished in intensity. Nevertheless, European parties typically provide alternatives that are more clear-cut than those presented to America's voters.[11]

Why Some Americans Vote and Others Do Not

Even though turnout is lower in the United States than in other democracies, some Americans do vote regularly while other Americans seldom or never vote. Among the factors that explain this difference are civic attitudes, age, education, and income.

Civic Attitudes

Regular voters are characterized by a strong sense of **civic duty.** They believe that citizens are obliged to vote, regardless of the expected outcome of an election. In 1996, for example, it was clear from the polls that Bill Clinton would handily defeat Bob Dole, yet regular voters were undeterred. Although they knew their votes would not sway the election, they voted anyway in order to fulfill their duty as citizens. Civic duty is an attitude that is usually acquired as part of childhood socialization. When parents vote regularly and take an

civic duty The belief of an individual that civic and political participation is a responsibility of citizenship.

Volunteers at a community event attempt to interest citizens in registering so that they can vote in the next election. Nearly all democracies have automatic voter registration. The United States does not, which makes voter registration efforts an important factor in election turnout.

interest in politics, their children are likely to acquire the belief that voting is an obligation of citizenship.

Many citizens do not have a strong sense of civic duty, and some display almost no interest in politics. **Apathy** is the term that describes a general lack of interest in or concern with politics. Just as some people would not attend the Super Bowl even if it were free and being played across the street, some people would not bother to vote even if a ballot were delivered to their door. As with civic duty, a sense of apathy is often the consequence of childhood socialization. When parents disparage voting and other forms of political participation, their children are likely to hold a similar view when they reach voting age.

Alienation is the term that describes a sense of personal powerlessness that includes the notion that government does not care about the opinions of people like oneself. Alienation diminishes people's interest in political participation.[12] Citizens who do not trust government are less likely to vote than those who do. It might be thought foolish for alienated citizens to withdraw from politics as opposed to getting more deeply involved in an effort to shake up the system. However, citizens recognize that a single vote is unlikely to make a difference, and they may choose not to cast their vote if they believe government is unresponsive to their interests.

Even among citizens who are not politically apathetic or alienated, interest in voting can be diminished by disenchantment with election politics. Most Americans believe, for example, that money plays too large a role in determining who gets elected and that candidates will say almost anything to get elected (see Table 7–2). As long as Americans feel so negatively about campaigns, it might be difficult to consistently draw them to the polls in huge numbers.

apathy A feeling of personal disinterest in or unconcern with politics.

alienation A feeling of personal powerlessness that includes the notion that government does not care about the opinions of people like oneself.

TABLE 7–2	Opinions on Election Politics *Americans are generally dissatisfied with election politics.*		
	AGREE	DISAGREE	DON'T KNOW
Political candidates are more concerned with fighting each other than with solving the nation's problems.	70%	26%	4%
Most political candidates will say almost anything in order to get themselves elected.	78	18	4
Political campaigns today seem more like theater or entertainment than like something to be taken seriously.	65	30	5
Interest groups and donors who give large sums of money to political campaigns have way too much influence on what candidates do once they are elected.	80	16	4

Source: National poll by The Vanishing Voter Project, Joan Shorenstein Center on the Press, Politics, and Public Policy, John F. Kennedy School of Government, Harvard University, October 20–24, 2000. Used by permission of the Director, The Vanishing Voter Project.

Age

When viewers tuned in MTV at various times in the 2000 presidential campaign, they might have thought at first that they had selected the wrong channel. Rather than a video of their favorite rock star, they saw the presidential candidates urging young people to vote.

The candidates had targeted the right audience for their get-out-the-vote message. Young adults are much less likely to vote than are middle-aged citizens. Even senior citizens, despite the infirmities of old age, have a far higher turnout rate than do voters under the age of thirty. Young people are less likely to have the political concern that can accompany such lifestyle characteristics as homeownership, a permanent career, and a family.[13] In fact, citizens under the age of thirty have the lowest turnout rate of any major demographic group.

Young voters account for much of the decline in voter turnout in recent decades. Of the eligible eighteen- to twenty-four-year-olds, about half voted in 1972 compared with a third recently. During this same period, turnout among those forty-five years of age and older declined only a few percentage points.

Education

What does your college education mean? One thing it means is that you have a higher likelihood of becoming an active citizen. Persons with a college education are about 40 percent more likely to vote than are persons with a grade

Liberty, Equality & Self-Government

What's Your Opinion?

Voting: A Right?

On election day, officials unfailingly urge Americans "to get out and vote." Some of these officials are not to be taken seriously. On the whole, U.S. elections are conducted fairly and openly with the support of tens of thousands of public-minded officials and volunteer poll watchers. Lurking in the shadows, however, are policies that serve to depress the vote. The worst abuses, such as whites-only primaries and poll taxes, are in the past. But official obstacles to voting are still part of the electoral system. For example, registration in most states closes two or more weeks in advance of election day. Many officials in these states have no interest in adopting the election day registration policy that is currently in effect in six states. They prefer a smaller voter turnout because it is more manageable and predictable. Another obstacle is early poll closings. Half the states close the polls before 8 P.M. in the evening, which disadvantages people who are at work during daylight hours.

More so than in other Western democracies, voting in the United States has been subject to political manipulation. America's electoral history is replete with examples of public policies designed to deny or suppress the vote. Voting has been treated as a privilege rather than an inalienable right, as something to be earned (or, in some cases, arbitrarily withheld) rather than something so intrinsic to citizenship that government makes every reasonable effort to promote its exercise.

What, in your opinion, explains the historical tendency? Do you think Americans' claim to self-government has been diminished by the tendency?

Young adults have the lowest voter turnout rate of any major demographic group. Efforts to increase their participation include MTV's "Rock the Vote" campaign, which often features celebrity participants. Pictured here are (from left to right) humorist Bill Maher and singers Macy Gray and Moby.

school education. Education generates an interest in politics, confidence that one can make a difference politically, and peer pressure to participate—all of which are related to the tendency to vote.[14]

Education is the single best predictor of voter turnout. This fact led analysts in the 1950s to conclude that increasing the overall level of education was the best way to increase levels of turnout. Paradoxically, the overall education level of the American people has increased greatly since then, but voter turnout has dropped. The positive effect of increased education levels has been more than offset by people's declining interest in politics.

Economic Class

Turnout is also closely related to economic status (see Figure 7–3). Americans at the bottom of the income ladder are only half as likely to vote in presidential elections as are those at the top.[15]

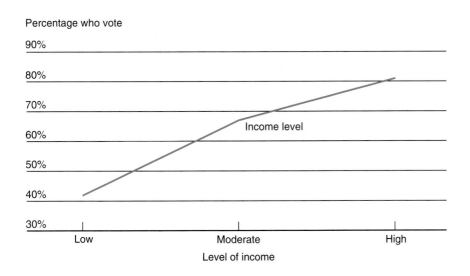

Percentage who vote

Figure 7–3

Voter Turnout and Level of Income
Americans with lower income are much less likely to vote.
Source: U.S. Bureau of the Census.

In European democracies, economic status does not affect turnout to such a high degree. Lower-income Europeans are encouraged to participate by class-based organizations and traditions—strong socialist or labor parties, politically oriented trade unions, and class-based political ideologies. The United States does not have, and never has had, a major socialist or labor party.[16] Although the Democratic party by and large represents the working class and the poor, it is more attentive to the middle class, which, because of its size and voting regularity, is the key to victory in U.S. elections. Americans in the bottom third by income are more likely than those in the top third to say that election outcomes have no appreciable effect on their lives.[17]

The Impact of the Vote

Through their votes, the people choose the representatives who will govern in their name. But what effect does the vote have on these representatives? Fuller answers to this question will be provided later (see Chapters 8, 11, and 12), but it is useful to consider at least a partial response at this point.

Elections do *not* ordinarily produce a policy mandate for the winning candidate. A mandate requires that voters consciously choose between candidates on the basis of the promises they make during the campaign. A problem with this interpretation of election results is that voters are not usually well informed about candidates' policy positions. In most campaigns, fewer than half the voters can identify the candidates' positions on major issues.[18]

Several influences combine to limit the voters' issue awareness. First, the candidates do not always make their positions clear, either because they fear that taking a firm stand will lose them votes or because they do not have specific policies in mind. Many candidates have dodged the abortion issue in recent years by expressing personal opposition to it while at the same time promising to uphold a woman's right to choose as long as the courts permit it. Additionally, the news media concentrate on election strategy and tactics rather than on the candidates' policy positions. Finally, voters can hardly be aware of

Voter Participation: Why It Matters

Some observers take comfort in low-turnout elections. They claim that the country is better off if less interested and less knowledgeable citizens stay home on election day. In a 1997 cover story in *Atlantic Monthly*, Robert Kaplan wrote: "The last thing America needs is more voters—particularly badly educated and alienated ones—with a passion for politics." The gist of this age-old argument is that low turnout protects society from erratic or even dangerous shifts in power. However, America's voters have not acted whimsically. Except for an interlude in the 1780s, when the Articles of Confederation governed the United States, erratic voting has not been a persistent source of political instability.

On the other hand, a low participation rate is a problem. As the electorate has shrunk, it has become increasingly less representative of the public as a whole in its opinions. Polls indicate that the outcomes of several recent elections would have changed if turnout had been substantially higher. And even if greater voter turnout would not have altered the outcomes, campaign platforms have always been tailored to those who vote. As the political scientists Steve Rosenstone and Mark Hanson note in *Mobilization, Participation, and Democracy in America* (1993): "The idle go unheard: They do not speak up, define the agenda, frame the issues, or affect the choices leaders make."

Voting can strengthen democracy in other ways, too. When people vote, they are more attentive to politics and are better informed about issues affecting them. As the philosopher John Stuart Mill theorized a century ago, voting also deepens community involvement. Studies indicate that voters participate more frequently in community affairs and are more likely to work with others on community projects. Of course, these associations say more about the type of person who votes than about the effect of voting. But recent evidence, as Harvard University's Robert Putnam notes in *Bowling Alone* (2000), "suggests that voting itself encourages volunteering and other forms of good citizenship."

Voting among young adults in particular has fallen off dramatically. When eighteen- to twenty-one-year-old citizens gained eligibility to vote in the 1972 election, nearly 50 percent of them voted. In 2000, only about 30 percent did so. The hotly contested 2004 election, waged against the backdrop of a soft economy and turmoil in Iraq, produced increased turnout among young adults, although the level was substantially below that in 1972. Unless increased turnout among young voters can be sustained, the overall voting rate will continue to stagnate, because the oldest generation, those who grew up during the Depression and World War II, participate at very high rates.

Changes in registration laws have made it easier for students to vote if they choose to do so. Voting is not a time-consuming task, and the benefits to the individual and society are considerable. Have you registered yet?

---

prospective voting A form of electoral judgment in which voters choose the candidate whose policy positions most closely match their own preferences.

retrospective voting A form of electoral judgment in which voters support the incumbent candidate or party when its policies are judged to have succeeded and oppose the incumbent party or candidate when its policies are judged to have failed.

issues if they are not paying attention. Most citizens do not follow campaigns closely and do not necessarily gain knowledge even of highly publicized issues.[19] In 2000, for example, only about half of adults could identify Bush's and Gore's positions even on the candidates' top issues—tax cuts and prescription drugs for the elderly, respectively.[20]

There are, to be sure, some voters who are highly informed on the issues and cast their ballots on this basis. **Prospective voting** is a term used to describe this forward-looking type of voting. Prospective voting occurs when voters know the issue stands of the candidates and choose the candidate whose positions best match their own.

A more prevalent form of voting is **retrospective voting,** a term that describes the situation in which voters support the incumbent candidate or party when they are pleased with its performance and oppose it when they are displeased. George W. Bush's 2004 reelection campaign illustrates the importance voters attach to past performance. Bush's popularity, which had reached a record high after the 2001 terrorist attacks on the World Trade Center and the Pentagon, fell in 2004 as a result of economic weakness at home and turmoil in Iraq. Bush, who earlier had seemed a virtual shoo-in for reelection, suddenly found himself in a tight race with Democratic nominee John Kerry.

Although foreign policy issues affect voters' assessments of candidates, economic issues ordinarily have a much larger impact. When voters' confidence in the in-party's handling of the economy has been high, its nominee usually has won the presidential election. Conversely, its nominee usually has lost when the voters are dissatisfied with the economy.[21]

Retrospective voting is a weaker form of public control than is prospective voting, because it occurs after the fact: government has already acted, and nothing can change what has taken place. Nevertheless, retrospective voting can be an effective form of popular control over policy. The fear that they might be voted out of office because of their policies encourages officials to take public opinion into account in their decisions.[22]

 ## CONVENTIONAL FORMS OF PARTICIPATION OTHER THAN VOTING

In one sense, voting is an unrivaled form of citizen participation. Free and open elections are the defining characteristic of democratic government, so voting is regarded as the most basic duty of citizens. Furthermore, most citizens in most democracies vote in elections. No other active form of political participation is so widespread.

In another sense, however, voting is a restricted form of participation. Citizens have the opportunity to vote only at a particular time and place, and only on those items listed on the ballot. Other activities, such as campaign work or community participation, offer citizens a fuller opportunity to express themselves.

Campaign Activities

A citizen may engage in campaign-related activities such as working for a candidate or a party, attending election rallies, contributing money, and wearing a campaign button. The more demanding of these activities, such as doing volunteer work for a candidate or a party, require a lot more time than voting does. These activities are also less imbued with notions of civic duty than is voting.[23] Not surprisingly, the proportion of citizens who engage in these activities is relatively small. Annually, fewer than one in twenty adult Americans say they worked for a party or a candidate.

Nevertheless, campaign participation is higher in the United States than in Europe. A five-country comparative study found that Americans were more likely to contribute money and time to election campaigns than citizens of Germany, Austria, the Netherlands, and Great Britain.[24] One reason why Americans are more active in campaigns, even though they vote at a lower rate, is that they have more opportunities to become active.[25] The United States is a

Youthful volunteers work to fix up a children's playground. Americans are more likely than citizens of other democracies to take part in voluntary community activities.

federal system with campaigns for national, state, and local offices. A citizen who wishes to participate is almost certain to find an opportunity at one level of office or another. Most of the governments in Europe are unitary in form (see Chapter 3), which means that there are fewer elective offices and thus fewer campaigns in which to participate.

Community Activities

Many Americans participate in public affairs not through campaigns and political parties but through local organizations such as parent-teacher associations, neighborhood groups, business clubs, church-affiliated groups, and hospital auxiliaries. The actual number of citizens who participate actively in a community group is difficult to estimate, but the number is surely in the tens of millions. The United States has a tradition of local participation that goes back to colonial days. Moreover, compared with cities and towns in Europe, those in the United States have more authority over policy issues, which is an added incentive to participation. Because of increased mobility and other factors, Americans may be less tied to their local communities than in the past and therefore less involved in community action. Nevertheless, half of Americans claim that they volunteer time to groups and community causes, compared with 20 percent or less in most European countries. Americans also surpass Europeans when it comes to donating money to a group.

social capital The sum of the face-to-face interactions among citizens in a society.

In a widely publicized book titled *Bowling Alone*, Harvard's Robert Putnam claims that America has been undergoing a long-term decline in its **social capital** (the sum of the face-to-face civic interactions among citizens in a society).[26] Putnam attributes the decline to television and other factors that draw people inward and away from participation in civic and political groups. Not all scholars accept Putnam's interpretation of trends in civic involvement (some indicators point toward a rise in certain types of participation),[27] but no one challenges his assumption about the importance of civic participation. It brings people together, gives them an understanding of other points of view, and builds skills that make them more effective as citizens.

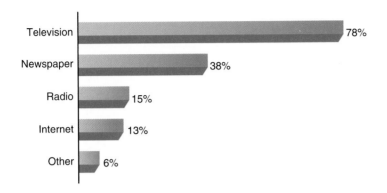

Figure 7–4

Americans' Major News Sources
When Americans are asked where they get most of their news, they mention television most often.
Source: Pew Research Center for the People and the Press, January 2004. Totals more than 100 percent because of multiple responses.

Lobbying Group Activities

Increasingly, Americans are also involved in public affairs through membership in lobbying groups. This form of participation seldom consists of more than the contribution of annual dues that enable a professionally managed national organization to pressure government officials or otherwise attempt to influence public policy.[28] Examples of these groups are the National Organization for Women, Common Cause, the Christian Moral Government Fund, the American Civil Liberties Union, and the National Conservative Political Action Committee. Chapter 9 discusses lobbying groups more fully.

Following Politics in the Media

Campaign work and community participation are active forms of political involvement. There is also a passive form: following politics in the news. It can safely be said that no act of political participation takes up more of people's time than does news consumption. The news is important to citizen participation: if people are to participate effectively and intelligently in politics, they must be aware of what is taking place in their communities, in their nation, and in the world.

News about politics is within easy reach of nearly all Americans. More than 95 percent of U.S. homes have a television set, and about 50 percent of Americans receive a daily newspaper. However, the regular audience for news is much smaller than these figures suggest. The mere fact of having a television or getting a daily paper does not mean that a person pays close attention to the news. About a third of Americans regularly read a newspaper's political sections or watch a television newscast. Another third follow the news intermittently, catching an occasional newscast or scanning a paper's news sections somewhat often. The final third pay no appreciable attention to the news either on television or in a newspaper.

Television is the medium of choice for most Americans (see Figure 7–4). Citizens who say television is their main source of news substantially outnumber those who rely mainly on a newspaper. Radio and magazines account for even smaller proportions. The figures are somewhat misleading in that people are asked where they get "most" of their news, not how much news they

Figure 7–5

Debate Audiences Have Steadily Declined

The audience for the October presidential debates has fallen by half since the 1970s.

Source: The Vanishing Voter Project, John F. Kennedy School of Government, Harvard University.

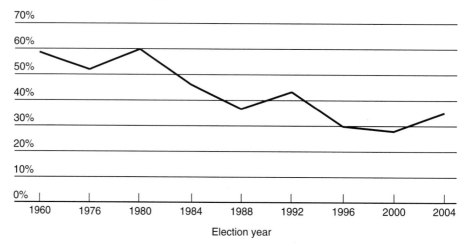

Percentage of TV households tuned in

Election year

actually get. Some of the people who say they get "most" of their news from television do not watch the news a lot. Because they do not read a newspaper at all, even a little exposure to television news makes it their leading news source.

The news audience has been shrinking. Newspapers have lost readers to television newscasts, which in turn have lost viewers to entertainment broadcasts. Before cable television was widely available, many television viewers had no alternative to a newscast during the dinner hour. With cable, viewers always have a variety of choices, and many viewers—as many as 40 percent by some estimates—choose to ignore the news unless a sensational event occurs.

The audience for major televised political events has also fallen off (see Figure 7–5). Although they are still a major attraction, even the October presidential debates receive less attention than before.[29] The four Kennedy-Nixon debates in 1960 each attracted roughly 60 percent of all households with television sets. When debates resumed with Carter and Ford in 1976, viewers again flocked to their TVs, as they did for the single Reagan-Carter face-off in 1980. Since then, however, debate audiences have declined. The 2004 debates had an audience rating exceeding that of the 2000 debates, but far below that of the 1960 debates.

Young Americans in particular are ignoring politics. Today's young adults are less politically interested and informed than any cohort of young people on record. Most of them do not regularly watch television news or read a daily newspaper.[30]

Virtual Participation

The prospect of an entire generation of politically inattentive citizens is disturbing to many observers. Yet there is a glimmer of hope—the Internet. It is used more heavily by younger people and is packed with political information and participation possibilities.

A student works at the computer in her room. The Internet has vast but as yet unrealized potential as an instrument of mass political participation.

It is unclear whether the Internet will actually serve as an entry into the world of politics for large numbers of citizens. Most people use it primarily for entertainment, school assignments, shopping, and personal and business communication. Nevertheless, there are thousands of chat rooms in which politics and public affairs are discussed. In addition, some organizations have successfully used the Internet to mobilize young adults. One example is MoveOn, which claims to have two million "online activists," many of whom are under the age of thirty. MoveOn raised more than $3.5 million in small contributions to support candidates in the 2002 midterm elections and has used e-mail appeals to exert grassroots pressure on Washington officials. Another example is Howard Dean's 2004 presidential campaign, which had great success in attracting youthful volunteers and raising campaign funds through the Internet. John Kerry's 2004 campaign also raised millions of dollars through the Internet.

However, the full impact of the Internet on citizen participation is not likely to be known until its technological capacity is fully developed and today's computer-literate children reach adulthood. Some analysts foresee a day when the Internet will be the prime medium of political information and involvement, but the evidence to date does not provide a basis for a firm prediction.[31]

 ## UNCONVENTIONAL ACTIVISM: SOCIAL MOVEMENTS AND PROTEST POLITICS

Before mass elections became prevalent, the public often resorted to protest as a way of expressing dissatisfaction with government. Tax and food riots were commonplace. The advent of elections allowed the masses to communicate their views in an institutionalized and less disruptive way. Elections are double-edged, however. Although they are commonly viewed as a means by which the people control the government, *elections are also a means by which the government controls the people.*[32] Because representatives are freely chosen by the people, they can claim that their policies reflect the popular will. It is difficult for people

Should Voting Through the Internet Be Allowed?

As nonvoting has increased and Internet use has spread, it was only a matter of time before voting through the Internet would be considered. In 2000, Arizona voters had the opportunity to vote online in the state's Democratic presidential primary. Several states are moving toward online voting for all elections, and the U.S. military has established a pilot online voting option for troops overseas. Advocates see online voting as the answer to the downward trend in voter turnout. Not everyone agrees that Internet voting is the solution, however. Opponents say that Internet voting would lead to a sharp increase in election fraud. They also note that Internet voting would disadvantage groups, primarily the poor and minorities, that have limited access to the Internet.

Yes: Few benefits of online interactivity are of such potential importance—or are so often overlooked—as the Internet's promise for improving democracy. . . . Voting is an important example of an information activity that could be improved with the help of the Internet. Where I live, we vote for judges, but I often don't know who deserves my ballot, since little information about their judicial records is readily available. I look forward to an Internet-based alternative. Instead of voting in person or mailing in an absentee ballot, I expect to be able to vote from my PC. While pondering the choices at my leisure, I'll be able to see what the candidates say about themselves, listen to speeches they've given, check their judicial records, read or watch news reports, survey their endorsements or the recommendations of nonpartisan groups, or even ask individuals I trust who they intend to vote for—all electronically. The result will be a better-informed vote, and probably greater participation. I'm an optimist about information technology because I've seen how it can improve the effectiveness of businesses and how it's beginning to positively influence education. It's no secret that many governments could be more efficient and responsive, and I'm confident that PCs and the Internet will play a welcome role in improving civic life and political dialogue around the world.

—*Bill Gates, chair, Microsoft Corporation*

No: Internet voting initially presents itself as a benevolent new platform for election administration, with the potential to reach voters not currently engaged in the process. But given the inequities of access to the Internet, "remote" Internet voting—voting via the Internet in a nonpolling-place environment such as a home, office or library—results in discrimination. . . . Whites are more likely to have Internet access from home than most racial and ethnic minorities have from *any* location. . . . Even if special pains were taken to create cybervillages in publicly accessible locations, remote Internet voting would be less likely among minority voters. By making voting more convenient for voters who have ready access—predominantly white—a bias is set up that boosts the potential turnout for connected voters while diluting the power of individual minority voters' ballots. . . . By confining Internet voting to polling places, you immediately bring parity to the process, while gaining time to address the complex issues of how to bridge the digital divide. Otherwise, the premature use of remote Internet voting will result in an America where all voters are created equal, but some are more equal than others.

—*Deborah Phillips, chair and president, Voting Integrity Project*

to argue that they are justified in rioting against government policy that has been enacted by representatives they themselves have elected to office.

Voting in elections is also limited to the options listed on the ballot. America's voters effectively have only two choices: the Democratic or Republican party. No other party has much chance of victory, and citizens who are dissatisfied with both parties have no realistic way to exercise power through the ballot.

The high point of the civil rights movement was Dr. Martin Luther King Jr.'s "I Have a Dream" address on the capitol mall in Washington, D.C., on August 28, 1963. A quarter of a million people, the largest gathering on the mall to that date, turned out for the rally.

Social movements are an alternative form of influence. **Social movements,** or **political movements** as they are sometimes called, refer to broad efforts to achieve change by citizens who feel that government is acting improperly.[33] These efforts are sometimes channeled through traditional forms of participation, such as political lobbying, but citizens can also take to the streets in protest against government. A dramatic example occurred in late 1999 when a host of activists—trade unionists, environmentalists, and others—engaged police in what became known as the "Battle in Seattle." The World Trade Organization

social (political) movements Active and sustained efforts to achieve social and political change by groups of people who feel that government has not been properly responsive to their concerns.

Figure 7–6

Americans' Opinions of Iraq War Protests

A majority supported the right of antiwar protesters to demonstrate, although some Americans felt they should not be allowed to do so.

Source: ABC News/Washington Post poll, March 23, 2003.

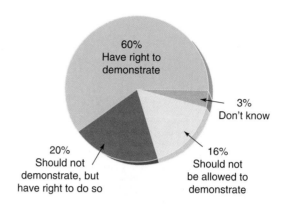

60%
Have right to demonstrate

3%
Don't know

20%
Should not demonstrate, but have right to do so

16%
Should not be allowed to demonstrate

(WTO) was meeting in Seattle to discuss global economic issues, and the activists were protesting the weak environmental and labor provisions that had marked earlier trade agreements. In 2003, as the Bush administration was preparing for war with Iraq, protest demonstrations were held in many U.S. cities, including Washington and San Francisco. Two percent of adult Americans said they participated in an antiwar demonstration.[34]

Social movements do not always succeed, but they sometimes enable otherwise politically weak persons to force government to respond to their desires. For example, the timing and scope of the landmark 1964 Civil Rights Act and 1965 Voting Rights Act can be explained only as a response by Congress to the pressure created by the civil rights movement. Another effective social movement in the 1960s was the farm workers' movement, whose protests led to improved working and living conditions for migrant workers.

Protest politics in America goes back to the Boston Tea Party and earlier, but it has taken on new forms in recent years. Protest was traditionally a desperate act that began, often spontaneously, when a group had lost hope that it could succeed through more conventional methods. Today, however, protest is usually a calculated act—a means of bringing added attention and impetus to a cause.[35] These tactical protests often involve a great deal of planning, including, in some instances, the busing of thousands of people to Washington for a rally staged for television. Civil rights, environmental, agricultural, and pro- and antiabortion groups are among those that have staged tactical protests in Washington within the past few years.

Citizens who participate in social movements tend to be younger than nonparticipants, a reversal of the situation with voting.[36] Participants in social movements also tend to emphasize nonmaterial values more than do nonparticipants. Social movements often develop in response to real or perceived injustices and thus attract idealists.[37]

The public's response to protest movements has at times been antagonistic. The duration and intensity of the Vietnam War protests, which in limited cases were accompanied by the burning of draft cards and of the American flag, turned many Americans against the demonstrators. When unarmed student protesters at Kent State University and Jackson State University were shot to death in May 1970 by members of the National Guard, a majority of Americans polled blamed the students, not the guardsmen, for the tragedy.

The public was much more accepting of protests against the 2003 war with Iraq (see Figure 7–6). Even after the fighting had begun, according to an ABC

News/Los Angeles Times poll, three in every five Americans said they saw the protests as "a sign of a healthy democracy." Still, almost two in five felt that "opponents of the war should not hold antiwar demonstrations"; about half of these said that antiwar demonstrations should be banned. In another poll, about a third of respondents said that protesters were "the kind of people who tend to blame America first."[38]

Yet there is a basic tolerance of protest activity. Rarely are protesters attacked by those who disagree with their actions, and most Americans display at least some understanding of protest as part of America's tradition of free expression. In that sense, protest is seen as something to be allowed if not embraced.

PARTICIPATION AND THE POTENTIAL FOR INFLUENCE

Although Americans claim that political participation is important, most of them do not practice what they preach. Most citizens show little interest in participation except to vote, and a significant minority cannot even be persuaded that voting is worth their while. However, Americans are not completely apathetic: many millions of them give their time, effort, and money to political causes, and roughly a hundred million vote in presidential elections.

Protesters demonstrate (in 2003) against the war in Iraq. Although protest movements are an American tradition, they do not routinely receive strong public support.

Yet sustained political activism does not engage a large proportion of the public. Moreover, many of those who do participate are drawn to politics by a habitual sense of civic duty rather than by an intense concern with current issues. The emphasis that American culture places on individualism tends to discourage a sense of urgency about political participation. "In the United States, the country of individualism *par excellence*," William Watts and Lloyd Free write, "there is a sharp distinction in people's minds between their own personal lives and national life."[39] Although wars and severe recessions can lead the American public to turn to government, most people under most conditions expect to solve their own problems. This is not to say that Americans have a disdain for collective action. In their communities particularly, citizens frequently take part in collective efforts to support a local hospital, improve the neighborhood, and the like. But most Americans tend not to see their material well-being as being greatly dependent on involvement in politics of the traditional kind.

This tendency contributes to a class bias in American politics. For one thing, it helps maintain a relatively sharp distinction between that which is properly public (political) and that which is properly private (economic). The private component, which includes most economic relationships, is largely beyond the realm of political debate and action. Americans, according to political scientist Robert Lane, prefer to see benefits distributed primarily through the economic marketplace rather than through the policies of government.[40] For example, access to medical care in the United States, unlike in Europe where government-provided health care is available to all, is to some degree based on a person's ability to pay for it. Roughly forty million Americans do not have access to adequate health care because they cannot afford health insurance.

Political Culture

One People out of Many

Exercise of the Vote

After decades of struggle, women gained the right to vote in 1920. Nevertheless, many women did not take advantage of this right. Voter turnout had been 62 percent in 1916. It dropped to 49 percent in 1920 as less than 40 percent of women voted. Even as late as 1960, women voted at a rate that was nearly 10 percentage points below that of men. Not until 1980 did the women's vote reach the same level as the men's vote.

The history of the exercise of women's right to vote is similar to that of other newly enfranchised groups. As groups and individuals have gained the right to vote through changes in suffrage laws or through citizenship, they have been slow to exercise that right. Hispanics who have become citizens in recent decades are about a third less likely than other citizens to vote on election day.

It might be thought that individuals who have just gained the right to vote would be the ones most eager to exercise it. However, like other aspects of social and cultural assimilation, a voting habit takes root slowly. Education and income are a reason; newly enfranchised groups usually rank below more established groups in these areas. The tendency also reflects the fact that the newly enfranchised are not accustomed to or necessarily comfortable with their newly granted right to vote. "It was not to be expected that the adult women who suddenly find themselves in possession of the franchise should be as conscientious in its exercise as men who from childhood had been encouraged to think politically," wrote Arthur M. Schlesinger and Erik McKinley Eriksson in a 1924 *New Republic* article.

Sixty years passed before the voting rate of women reached that of men. Only recently has the voting rate of black Americans reached a level that is close to the turnout rate among white Americans. The rate for Hispanics, though rising, is still far below the national average. The history of the franchise for immigrants from Ireland, Italy, and other countries is similar. Voting is not something that blossoms overnight. The merging of peoples and cultures—the creation of one out of many—is a slow and fitful process, even when it comes to voter turnout on election day.

Lower-income Americans are a relatively weak force in the nation's politics. Higher-income Americans are more likely to have the financial resources and communication skills that encourage participation in politics and make it personally rewarding. Among citizens who are most active in politics, three times as many have incomes in the top third as in the bottom third.[41] This difference is much greater than in other Western democracies, where poorer citizens are assisted through automatic voter registration and by the presence of class-based political organizations. By comparison, the poor in the United States must arrange their own registration and must choose between two political parties that are attuned primarily to middle-class interests.

The low participation rate of lower-income Americans reduces their influence on public policy. Studies indicate that representatives are more responsive to the demands of participants than to those of nonparticipants,[42] although it must be kept in mind that participants do not always promote only their own interests. It would be a mistake, however, to conclude that large numbers of people regularly support policies that would mainly benefit others. For example, a turning point in the defeat of President Bill Clinton's health care reform proposal came when middle-class Americans decided that it might increase the cost and reduce the quality of their own medical care. According to Time/CNN

Suggested Readings

Bimber, Bruce, and Richard Davis. *Campaigning Online: The Internet in U.S. Elections*. New York: Oxford University Press, 2003. A careful study of citizens' use of the Internet in elections.

Burns, Nancy, Kay Lehman Schlozman, and Sidney Verba. *The Private Roots of Public Action: Gender, Equality, and Public Action*. Cambridge, Mass.: Harvard University Press, 2001. An analysis of gender differences in political participation.

Leighley, Jan. *Strength in Numbers: The Political Mobilization of Racial and Ethnic Minorities*. Princeton, N.J.: Princeton University Press, 2001. A study of the factors that motivate blacks and Hispanics to participate.

Patterson, Thomas E. *The Vanishing Voter*. New York: Knopf, 2002. A study of the decline in electoral participation and what might be done to reverse the trend.

Putnam, Robert. *Bowling Alone*. New York: Simon and Schuster, 2000. A provocative analysis of the trend in civic participation.

Schudson, Michael. *The Good Citizen: A History of American Civic Life*. New York: Free Press, 1998. A thoughtful history of civic participation in America.

Skocpol, Theda. *Diminished Democracy: From Membership to Management in American Civic Life*. Norman: University of Oklahoma Press, 2003. An analysis of the trend away from active membership in civic and political organizations.

Verba, Sidney, Kay Schlozman, and Henry Brady. *Voice and Equality*. Cambridge, Mass.: Harvard University Press, 1995. A careful study of political attitudes and participation.

List of Websites

http://www.rockthevote.org/

Rock the Vote is an organization dedicated to helping young people realize and utilize their power to affect the civic and political life of their communities.

http://www.umich.edu/~nes/

The University of Michigan's National Election Studies (NES) site provides survey data on voting, public opinion, and political participation.

http://www.vanishingvoter.org/

Harvard University's election study site provides information on voter participation.

http://www.vote-smart.org/

Project Vote Smart includes information on Republican and Democratic candidates and officials; also has the latest in election news.

Participate!

If you are not currently registered to vote, consider registering. You can obtain a registration form from the election board or clerk in your community of residence. There are several websites that contain state-by-state registration information. One such site is www.vanishingvoter.org. If you are already registered, consider participating in a registration or voting drive on your campus. Although students typically register and vote at relatively low rates, they will often participate if encouraged by other students to do so.

Extra Credit

For up-to-the-minute *New York Times* articles, interactive simulations, graphics, study tools, and more links and quizzes, visit the text's Online Learning Center at www.mhhe.com/pattersontad7.

(Self-Test Answers: 1. b   2. d   3. c   4. b   5. c   6. d   7. T   8. T   9. F   10. T)

8

Political Parties, Candidates, and Campaigns:
Defining the Voter's Choice

> Political parties created democracy and . . . modern democracy is
> unthinkable save in terms of the parties.
>
> *E. E. Schattschneider*[1]

Two hundred miles and five weeks apart, the two parties faced off, each offering its own vision of a better America. The Democrats met first, in Boston. The Democrats' platform included tax benefits for low- and middle-income families, reproductive freedom for women, a commitment to multilateralism in international affairs, and pledges to strengthen the nation's environmental, educational, and health systems. The Democrats chose Massachusetts Senator John Kerry as their presidential nominee and North Carolina Senator John Edwards as his running mate.

The Republicans met in New York City. The Republicans renominated the same ticket—George W. Bush and Dick Cheney—that had carried them to victory in 2000. The 2004 GOP platform included proposals for stimulating business investment, increasing the level of defense spending, delegating policy authority to the states, and waging the war on terrorism.

A **political party** is an ongoing coalition of interests joined together in an effort to get its candidates for public office elected under a common label.[2] Political parties are an indispensable component of democratic government. By offering voters a choice between policies and leaders, parties give them a chance to influence the direction of government. "It is the competition of [parties] that provides the people with an opportunity to make a choice," political scientist E. E. Schattschneider once wrote. "Without this opportunity popular sovereignty amounts to nothing."[3]

This chapter examines political parties and the candidates who run under their banners. U.S. campaigns are **party-centered politics** in the sense that the Republican and Democratic parties compete across the country election after election. Yet campaigns are also **candidate-centered politics** in the sense that individual candidates devise their own strategies, choose their own issues, and form their own campaign organizations. The following points are emphasized in this chapter:

- *Political competition in the United States has centered on two parties, a pattern that is explained by the nature of America's electoral system, political institutions, and political culture.* Minor parties exist in the United States but have been unable to compete successfully for governing power.

- *To win an electoral majority, candidates of the two major parties must appeal to a diverse set of interests; this necessity normally leads them to advocate moderate and somewhat overlapping policies.* Only during periods of stress are America's parties likely to present the electorate with starkly different choices.

Democratic nominee John Kerry is surrounded by party faithful during the 2004 presidential campaign.

political party An ongoing coalition of interests joined together to try to get their candidates for public office elected under a common label.

party-centered politics Election campaigns and other political processes in which political parties, not individual candidates, hold most of the initiative and influence.

candidate-centered politics Election campaigns and other political processes in which candidates, not political parties, have most of the initiative and influence.

party competition A process in which conflict over society's goals is transformed by political parties into electoral competition in which the winner gains the power to govern.

- *U.S. party organizations are decentralized and fragmented.* The national organization is a loose collection of state organizations, which in turn are loose associations of autonomous local organizations. This feature of U.S. parties can be traced to federalism and the nation's diversity, which have made it difficult for the parties to act as instruments of national power.

- *The ability of America's party organizations to control nominations and election to office is weak, which in turn enhances the candidates' role.*

- *Candidate-centered campaigns are based on the media and utilize the skills of professional consultants.* Money, strategy, and televised advertising are key components of today's presidential and congressional campaigns.

PARTY COMPETITION AND MAJORITY RULE: THE HISTORY OF U.S. PARTIES

Through their numbers, citizens have the potential for great influence, but that potential cannot be realized unless citizens have the capacity to act together. Parties give them that capacity. When Americans go to the polls, they have a choice between the Republican and Democratic parties. This **party competition** narrows their options to two and in the process enables people with different backgrounds and opinions to unite behind a single alternative. In casting a majority of its votes for one party, the electorate chooses that party's candidates, philosophy, and policies over those of the opposing party.

The history of democratic government is virtually synonymous with the history of parties. When the countries of Eastern Europe gained their freedom more than a decade ago, one of their first steps toward democracy was the legalization of parties. When the United States was founded over two centuries ago, the formation of parties was also a first step toward the building of its democracy. The reason is simple: it is the competition among parties that gives popular majorities a chance to influence how they will be governed.[4]

The First Parties

America's early leaders mistrusted parties. George Washington in his farewell address warned the nation of the "baneful effects" of parties, and James Madison likened parties to special interests. However, Madison's initial misgivings about parties gradually gave way to a grudging admiration; he recognized that they provided a way for like-minded people to work together to achieve their mutual goals.

America's parties originated in the rivalry within George Washington's administration between Thomas Jefferson, a supporter of states' rights and small landholders, and Alexander Hamilton, who promoted a strong national government and commercial interests (see Figure 8–1). When Hamilton's ideas prevailed in Congress, Jefferson and his followers formed a political party, the Republicans. By adopting this label, which was associated with popular government, the Jeffersonians sought to portray themselves as the rightful heirs to the American Revolution's legacy of self-government and political equality.

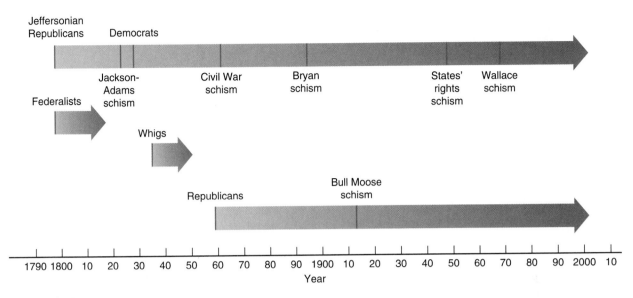

Figure 8–1

A Graphic History of America's Major Parties
The U.S. party system has been remarkable for its continuity. Competition between two major parties has been a persistent feature of the system.

Hamilton responded by organizing his supporters into a formal party—the Federalists—and in the process created America's first competitive party system. The Federalists took their name from the faction that had supported ratification of the Constitution, thereby implying that they represented America's political values and traditions. However, the Federalists' preoccupation with commercial and wealthy interests fueled Jefferson's claim that the Federalists were bent on establishing a government of the rich and wellborn. After Adams's defeat by Jefferson in the presidential election of 1800, the Federalists and their philosophy never again held sway.

During the so-called Era of Good Feeling, when James Monroe ran unopposed in 1820 for a second presidential term, it appeared as if the political system might operate without parties. Yet by the end of Monroe's second term, policy differences had split the Republicans. The dominant faction, led by Andrew Jackson, retained Jefferson's commitment to the interests of ordinary people. This faction called itself Democratic Republicans, later shortened to Democrats. Thus, the Republican party of Jefferson is the forerunner of today's Democratic party rather than of today's Republican party.

Historical Background

Andrew Jackson and Grassroots Parties

For all its shortcomings, competition between parties is the only system that can regularly mobilize collective influence on behalf of the many who are individually powerless against those few who have extraordinary wealth and prestige.

Andrew Jackson

(1767–1845)

Andrew Jackson rose to national fame when, as a major general, he defeated the British at the Battle of New Orleans during the War of 1812. A Tennessee native, he won the presidency in 1828 after having lost in 1824 despite receiving the most popular votes. He instituted political changes including grassroots parties that were designed to strengthen popular rule. The term "Jacksonian Democracy" became synonymous with his belief that ordinary people were capable of governing themselves.

grassroots party A political party organized at the level of the voters and dependent on their support for its strength.

This realization led Jackson during the 1820s to develop a **grassroots party.** Whereas Jefferson's party had been well organized only at the leadership level, Jackson sought a party that was built from the bottom up. Jackson's Democratic party consisted of committees and clubs at the local, state, and national levels, with membership open to all eligible voters. These organizational activities, along with more liberal suffrage laws, contributed to a nearly fourfold rise in voter turnout during the 1830s.[5] At the peak of Jacksonian democracy, Alexis de Tocqueville wrote, "The People reign in the American political world as the Deity does in the universe."[6] Although Tocqueville exaggerated the people's true power, he caught the spirit of popular government that was behind the development of grassroots parties under Andrew Jackson.

In this period, a new opposition party, the Whigs, emerged to challenge the Democrats. The Whigs were a catchall party. Its followers were united not by a coherent philosophy of their own but by their opposition for one reason or another to the policies of the Jacksonian Democrats.

Competition between the Whigs and the Democrats was relatively short-lived. During the 1850s the slavery issue began to tear both parties apart. The Whig party began to disappear, and a northern-based new party, calling itself Republican, arose as the main challenger to the Democrats. In 1860, the Democratic party's northern faction nominated for president Stephen A. Douglas, who held that the question of whether a new territory would permit slavery was for a majority of its voters to decide, while the southern faction nominated John C. Breckinridge, who called for the legalization of slavery in all territories. The Democratic vote in the fall election was split sharply along regional lines between these two candidates—with the result that the Republican nominee, Abraham Lincoln, was able to win the presidency with only 40 percent of the popular vote. Lincoln's election prompted the southern states to secede from the Union, which led to the Civil War. For the first and only time in the nation's history, the party system had failed to peaceably resolve Americans' conflicting goals.[7] The issue of slavery proved too explosive to be settled through electoral competition.

Republicans Versus Democrats: Realignments and the Enduring Party System

After the Civil War, the nation settled into the pattern of competition between the Republican and Democratic parties that has prevailed ever since. The durability of these two parties is due not to their ideological consistency but to their remarkable ability to adapt during periods of crisis. By abandoning at these crucial times their old ways of doing things, the Republican and Democratic parties have repeatedly remade themselves—with new bases of support, new policies, and new public philosophies.

These periods of great political change are known as *realignments*. A **party realignment** involves four basic elements:

1. The disruption of the existing political order because of the emergence of one or more unusually powerful and divisive issues
2. An election contest in which the voters shift their support strongly in favor of one party
3. A major change in policy through the action of the stronger party
4. An enduring change in the party coalitions, which works to the lasting advantage of the dominant party

Abraham Lincoln
(1809–1865)

Abraham Lincoln was a member of Congress from Illinois before his election to the presidency in 1860. Homely and gangly, Lincoln is regarded by many as America's greatest president for his principled leadership during the Civil War. His greatest legacy is the preservation of the American Union. The Emancipation Proclamation and the Gettysburg Address are two of his other legacies. He was assassinated at Ford's Theater in the nation's capital shortly after the start of his second term as president.

Realignments are rare. They do not occur simply because one party wrests control of government from the other. They involve deep and lasting changes in the party system that affect not just the most recent election but later ones as well. By this standard, there have been three clear-cut realignments since the 1850s.

The Civil War realignment, for example, brought about a thorough change in the party system. The Republicans replaced the Democrats as the nation's majority party. The Republicans were the dominant party in the larger and more populous North, while the Democratic party was left with a stronghold in what became known as "the Solid South." During the next three decades, the Republicans held the presidency except for Grover Cleveland's two terms of office and had a majority in Congress for all but four years.

The 1896 election resulted in a further realignment of the Republican-Democratic party system. Three years earlier, an economic panic following a bank collapse had resulted in a severe depression. The Democrat Cleveland was president when the crash happened, and people blamed him and his party. The Democrats then nominated William Jennings Bryan in 1896 on a cheap-credit platform (unlimited coinage of silver) that frightened many voters into believing that inflation would destroy their savings and the economy. As a result, the Republicans made additional gains in the Northeast and Midwest, solidifying their position as the nation's dominant party. During the four decades between the 1890s realignment and the next one in the 1930s, the Republicans held the presidency except for Woodrow Wilson's two terms and had a majority in Congress for all but six years.

The Great Depression of the 1930s triggered a thoroughgoing realignment of the American party system. The Republican Herbert Hoover was president when the stock market crashed in 1929, and many Americans blamed Hoover, his party, and its business allies for the economic catastrophe that followed. The Democrats became the country's majority party. Their political and policy agenda called for an expanded social and economic role for the national government. Franklin D. Roosevelt's presidency was characterized by unprecedented policy initiatives in the areas of business regulation and social welfare (see Chapter 3). His election in 1932 began a thirty-six-year period of Democratic presidencies that was interrupted only by Dwight D. Eisenhower's

party realignment An election or set of elections in which the electorate responds strongly to an extraordinarily powerful issue that has disrupted the established political order. A realignment has a lasting impact on public policy, popular support for the parties, and the composition of the party coalitions.

Realignments in History

The new order begins: Franklin D. Roosevelt rides to his inauguration with outgoing president Herbert Hoover after the realigning election of 1932.

1960 "de-alignment

two terms in the 1950s. In this period the Democrats also dominated Congress, losing control only in 1947–1948 and 1953–1954.

The reason realignments have such a substantial effect on future elections is that they affect voters' *party identification* (see Chapter 6). Young voters in particular are likely to identify with the newly ascendant party, and they tend to retain that identity, giving the party a solid base of support for years to come. In the 1930s, for example, the Democratic party's image as the party of the common people, jobs, and social security was vastly more appealing to young voters than the Republican party's image as the party of business and wealthy interests. First-time voters in the 1930s came to identify with the Democratic party by a two-to-one margin, establishing it as the nation's majority party and enabling it to dominate national politics for the next three decades.[8]

Today's Party Alignment and Its Origins

A party realignment inevitably loses strength over time, because the issues that gave rise to it eventually decline in importance. By the late 1960s, with the Democratic party divided over the Vietnam War and civil rights, it was apparent that the era of New Deal politics was ending.[9]

The change was most dramatic in the South. The region had been solidly Democratic at all levels since the Civil War, but the Democratic party's leadership on civil rights angered white conservatives.[10] In the 1964 presidential election, five southern states voted Republican, and the South is now a Republican bastion in presidential politics. The Republican party also made gains, though more gradually, in elections for other offices. Today most top officials in the southern states are Republicans.

More slowly and less completely, the northeastern states have become more Democratic. The shift is partly attributable to the growing size of minority populations in the Northeast. But it is also due to the declining influence of the Republican party's moderate wing, which was concentrated in these states. As southern conservatives became Republican in ever larger numbers, the party's stands on social issues such as abortion and affirmative action tilted toward the right, reducing the party's appeal among northeastern voters.

Party conflict also extended to federal spending on education, health, and economic security programs. The Democrats, who had started nearly all of these programs, defended them, while Republicans attacked them as being too expensive. Taxing and spending became perennial campaign issues, resulting in a further alignment of liberals against conservatives.

The GOP (short for "Grand Old Party" and another name for the Republican party) gained the most from these changes in party politics. Since 1968, Republicans have held the presidency for twice as many years as the Democrats have. Also, since 1994—except for a brief interlude—the GOP has controlled both houses of Congress. Republicans, after trailing for decades,

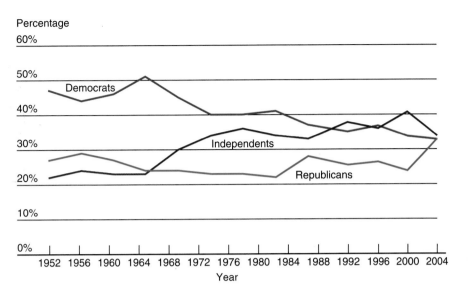

Figure 8–2

Partisan Identification
After trailing for decades, Republican identifiers reached parity with Democratic identifiers in 2004. Of the roughly one-third of voters who describe themselves as Independents, most also say they "lean" toward one of the two major parties. The leaners divide almost evenly between the two parties.
Source: National Election Studies, 1952–2000; various surveys, 2004.

have also drawn even with Democrats in terms of party identification (see Figure 8–2). In 2004, the Gallup Organization released a report, based on 40,000 interviews, that described America as a nation equally split between the two parties. Voters who identified with or leaned toward the Republican party comprised 45 percent of the nation's adults, exactly the same percentage that identified with or leaned toward the Democratic party.[11]

The shift toward the Republican party is not a party realignment in the traditional sense. Rather than occurring abruptly in response to a single overriding issue, as was the case in the 1860s and 1930s realignments, the change has taken place slowly and somewhat fitfully. For a period in the 1970s, for example, Republican strength stagnated. Further, the partisan intensity that marks a full-scale party realignment has at times been missing. The percentage of self-described Independent voters rose sharply during the 1960s and early 1970s. The level of voter turnout also fell after 1960, an indication that many party identifiers did not feel strongly enough about their party to go to the polls. Some analysts have described these developments as a *dealignment*—a partial but enduring weakening of partisanship.[12]

Nevertheless, partisanship is alive and well in America and has in fact intensified since the 1980s. Conflict between Republican and Democratic leaders in Washington has increased substantially (see Chapters 11 and 12), and the gap in the policy opinions of people identifying themselves as Republican and Democratic has widened (see Chapter 6). In addition, fewer voters now cast a **split ticket.** When offices at all levels are taken into account, ticket splitting is widespread: roughly half of voters select at least one candidate from each party when casting a ballot that includes a range of offices. In the past quarter century, however, ticket splitting among candidates for national office has declined, as can be seen from a comparison of presidential and congressional voting (see Figure 8–3). In 1980, 28 percent of voters backed one party's candidate for president and the other party's candidate for the House of Representatives. By 1996, the figure had fallen below 20 percent.

split ticket The pattern of voting in which the individual voter in a given election casts a ballot for one or more candidates of each major party.

Figure 8–3

Split-Ticket Voting in Presidential and Congressional Races

The level of split-ticket voting, as measured by the percentage who backed one party's candidate for president and the other party's candidate for the House of Representatives, has declined in recent elections. The change reflects an increased level of partisanship among America's voters.

Source: National Election Studies. The 2004 percentage is estimated from preelection polls.

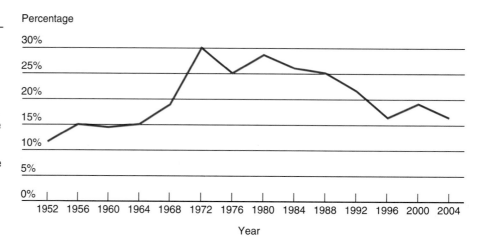

Analysts are divided in their opinions on where the party system is heading. Some project a period of Republican dominance as the GOP consolidates its recent gains and adds to them.[13] Others foresee a resurgent Democratic party fueled by the increasing voting power of minority groups, particularly blacks and Hispanics.[14] One thing is virtually certain: as they have for over 150 years, Americans will continue to look to the Republican and Democratic parties for political leadership. The enduring strength and appeal of the two major parties is a hallmark of American politics.

ELECTORAL AND PARTY SYSTEMS

two-party system A system in which only two political parties have a real chance of acquiring control of the government.

The United States traditionally has had a **two-party system:** Federalists versus Jeffersonian Republicans, Whigs versus Democrats, and Republicans versus Democrats. These have not been the only American parties, but they have been the only ones with a realistic chance of acquiring political control. A two-party system, however, is the exception rather than the rule (see "How the United States Compares"). Most democracies have a **multiparty system,** in which three or more parties have the capacity to gain control of government, separately or in coalition. Why the difference? Why are there three or more major parties in most democracies but only two in the United States?

multiparty system A system in which three or more political parties have the capacity to gain control of government separately or in coalition.

The Single-Member-District System of Election

single-member districts The form of representation in which only the candidate who gets the most votes in a district wins office.

A chief reason for the persistence of America's two-party system is the fact that the nation chooses its officials through plurality voting in **single-member districts.**[15] Each constituency elects a single candidate to a particular office, such as U.S. senator or representative; only the party that gets the most votes (a plurality) in a district wins the office. This system discourages minor parties. Assume, for example, that a minor party received exactly 20 percent of the vote in each of the nation's 435 congressional races. Even though one in five voters

HOW THE UNITED STATES COMPARES

Party Systems

For nearly 160 years, electoral competition in the United States has centered on the Republican and Democratic parties. By comparison, most democracies have a multiparty system, in which three or more parties receive substantial support from voters. The difference is significant. In a two-party system, the parties tend to have overlapping coalitions and programs, because each party must appeal to the middle-of-the-road voters who provide the margin of victory. In multiparty systems, particularly those with four or more strong parties, the parties tend to separate themselves as each tries to secure the enduring loyalty of voters who have a particular viewpoint.

Whether a country has a two-party or a multiparty system depends on several factors, but particularly the nature of its electoral system. The United States has a single-member, plurality district system in which only the top vote getter in a district gets elected. This system is biased against smaller parties; even if they have some support in a great many races, they win nothing unless one of their candidates places first in an electoral district. By comparison, proportional representation systems enable smaller parties to compete; each party acquires legislative seats in proportion to its share of the total vote. All the countries in the chart that have four or more parties also have a proportional representation system of election.

Number of Competitive Parties

TWO	THREE	FOUR OR MORE
United States	Canada (at times)	Belgium
	Great Britain	Denmark
		France
		Germany
		Italy
		Netherlands
		Sweden

nationwide backed the minor party, it would not win any seats in Congress because none of its candidates placed first in any of the 435 single-member-district races. The winning candidate in each case would be the major-party candidate who received the larger proportion of the remaining 80 percent of the vote.

By comparison, most European democracies use some form of **proportional representation,** in which seats in the legislature are allocated according to a party's share of the popular vote. This type of electoral system provides smaller parties an incentive to organize and compete for power. In the 2002 German elections, the Green party received nearly 9 percent of the national vote and thereby won 55 seats in the 603-seat Bundestag, the German parliament. If the Greens had been competing under American electoral rules, they would not have won any seats and would have had no chance of exercising a share of legislative power. In Germany, the Greens even gained a share of executive power. The Social Democratic party won the most legislative seats in the 2002 German election but failed to gain an outright majority. The Social Democrats then formed a coalition with the Green party, which received cabinet posts in return for its backing of a Social Democrat–led government.

proportional representation A form of representation in which seats in the legislature are allocated proportionally according to each political party's share of the popular vote. This system enables smaller parties to compete successfully for seats.

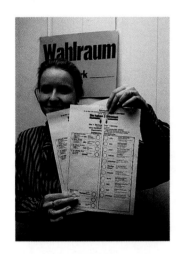

Germany's electoral system allocates legislative seats on the basis both of single-district voting and of the overall proportion of votes a party receives. This system requires that the German voter cast two ballots in legislative races: one to choose among the candidates in the particular district and one to choose among the parties. Shown here is a ballot from a German election. The left column lists the candidates for the legislative seat in a district, and the right column lists the parties. (Note the relatively large number of parties on the ballot.)

Politics and Coalitions in the Two-Party System

The overriding goal of a major American party is to gain power by getting its candidates elected to office. Because there are only two major parties, however, the Republicans or Democrats can win consistently only by attracting majority support. In Europe's multiparty systems, a party can hope for a share of power if it has the firm backing of a minority faction. Not so in the United States. If either party confines its support to a narrow segment of society, it forfeits its chance of gaining control of government.

Seeking the Center

American parties, Clinton Rossiter said, are "creatures of compromise."[16] The two parties usually take stands that have broad appeal, or at least will not alienate significant blocs of voters. Any time a party makes a pronounced shift toward either extreme, the political center is left open for the opposing party. Barry Goldwater, the Republican presidential nominee in 1964, proposed the elimination of mandatory social security and said he might consider the tactical use of small nuclear weapons in such wars as the Vietnam conflict—extreme positions that cost him many votes. Eight years later, the Democratic nominee, George McGovern, took positions on Vietnam and income security that alarmed many voters; like Goldwater, he got buried in one of the greatest landslides in presidential history.

It is impossible to understand the dynamics of the U.S. party system without recognizing that the true balance of power in American elections rests with the moderate voters in the center rather than with those who hold more extreme positions. When congressional Republicans mistook their 1994 election victory as a mandate to trim assistance programs for the elderly, the poor, and children, they alienated many of the moderate voters who had contributed to their 1994 victory. These voters wanted "less" government but not a government that neglected society's most vulnerable citizens. After weak showings in the 1996 and 1998 elections, congressional Republicans shifted course. They unseated Speaker Newt Gingrich, replacing him with a more pragmatic conservative, Dennis Hastert. "We still need to prove that we can be conservative without being mean," was how one Republican member of Congress described the change in strategy.[17] The change in Republican outlook was also apparent in GOP presidential candidate George W. Bush's 2000 campaign slogan: "compassionate conservatism." These adjustments reflect a basic truth about U.S. politics: party ideology is acceptable as long as it is tinged with moderation.

Nonetheless, the Republican and Democratic parties do offer somewhat different alternatives and, at times, a clear choice. When Roosevelt was elected president in 1932, Johnson in 1964, and Reagan in 1980, the parties were relatively far apart in their priorities and programs. Roosevelt's New Deal, for example, was an extreme alternative within the American political tradition and caused a decisive split along party lines. A lesson of these periods is that the center of the American political spectrum can be moved. Candidates risk a crushing defeat by straying too far from established ideas during normal times, but they may do so with some chance of victory during turbulent times.

Another lesson of such periods is that public opinion is the critical element in partisan change. Critics who say that the Democratic and Republican parties fail to offer the voters a real choice ignore the parties' tendency to tailor their appeals to majority opinion.[18] When the public's mood shifts, the parties usually also shift. The Republicans' Contract with America in 1994, for example, was a response to public discontent with the federal government's taxing and spending policies. After the Republicans won in 1994, many Democratic officeholders also embraced cutbacks in federal power, thus shifting the entire party system toward the right. Perhaps Republican leaders misjudged just how far right the public was willing to go, but they nonetheless redirected the nation's politics. President Clinton, a Democrat, summed up the change in his 1996 State of the Union address when he said "The era of big government is over."

Party Coalitions

The groups and interests that support a party are collectively referred to as the **party coalition.** In multiparty systems, each party is supported by a relatively narrow range of interests. European parties tend to divide along class lines, with the center and right parties drawing most of their votes from the middle and upper classes and the left parties drawing theirs from the working class. By comparison, America's two-party system requires each party to accommodate a wide range of interests in order to gain the voting plurality necessary to win elections. The Republican and Democratic coalitions are therefore very broad. Each includes a substantial proportion of voters of nearly every ethnic, religious, regional, and economic grouping. There are only a few sizable groups that are tightly aligned with a party. African Americans are the clearest example; they vote about 85 percent Democratic in national elections.

Although the Republican and Democratic coalitions overlap, they are hardly identical (see Figure 8–4). Each party likes to appear to be all things to all Americans, but in fact each builds its coalition through a process of both unification and division. If a party did not stand for something—if it never took sides—it would lose all support.

Since the 1930s, the major policy differences between the Republicans and the Democrats have involved the national government's role in solving social and economic problems. Each party has supported government action to promote economic security and social equality, but the Democrats have consistently favored a greater degree of government involvement. Virtually every

Ronald Reagan's successful runs for the presidency in 1980 and 1984 illustrate that candidates with less moderate positions can win elections when Americans are seeking a change in national policy.

party coalition The groups and interests that support a political party.

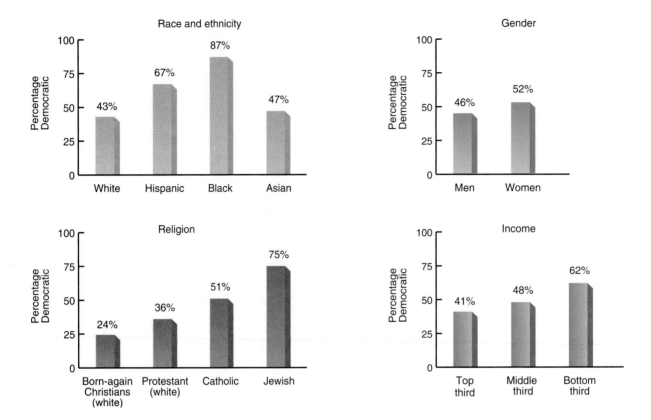

Figure 8–4

The Vote of Selected Demographic Groups in Recent Presidential Elections
Although the Democratic and Republican coalitions overlap substantially, there are important differences, as illustrated by the Democratic party's percentage of the two-party vote among some major demographic groups in recent elections.
Source: Compiled by author from NES and other surveys.

major assistance program for the poor, the elderly, and low-wage workers has been initiated by the Democrats. To some extent, the Democratic coalition draws support disproportionately from society's underdogs—blacks, union members, the poor, city dwellers, Hispanics, Jews, and other "minorities."[19] For a long period, the Democratic party was also the clear choice of the nation's elderly as a result of its support for old-age assistance programs and because the basic political loyalties of the elderly were acquired during the New Deal era, a period favorable to the Democrats. Recently, however, elderly voters have split their vote nearly evenly between the parties.

The Democratic party's biggest gains recently have been among women, who traditionally had a voting pattern very similar to that of men. Recent elections, however, have shown a gender gap (see Chapter 6). Women have voted disproportionately for the Democratic party, apparently as a result of its positions on issues such as abortion rights, education spending, employment policies, and gun control. The Democratic party, as a result of its leadership on civil

Parties and Your Vote

In civics classes, students are often told to "vote for the person, not the party" or "vote on the issues, not the party." Commentators sometimes make the same pitch. On the whole, it's pretty bad advice.

To vote for the person is to assume that the individual officeholder wields singular power. But that's not true even in the case of the president. In choosing one presidential candidate over another, Americans are choosing more than the person who will sit behind the desk in the Oval Office. They are also selecting several hundred other executive officers, including the secretary of state, the attorney general of the United States, and the director of the Central Intelligence Agency. The president also nominates all federal judges and justices. The great majority of these individuals, including the judicial officers, will be of the same party as the president.

The election of a senator or a representative is also more than a decision about which individual will occupy a seat in Congress. Rarely does a single member of Congress have a decisive voice in legislation. Congress works through collective action. Power resides with the majority party in each chamber.

By the same token, a vote based on an issue is usually shortsighted. Once in office, a successful candidate will vote on scores of policy issues, not just the one or two issues that were the cornerstone of the election campaign. And what is the best predictor of how the successful candidate will vote on these issues? In nearly every case, the best predictor is the political party to which the officeholder belongs.

An issue that dominates an election can be overtaken by events and be a secondary issue by the time the winning candidates are sworn into office. Partisanship, on the other hand, tends to endure. Today's Democratic and Republican candidates and officeholders are not all that different in their policy leanings from their partisan counterparts of a decade or two ago.

In recent decades, Americans have increasingly called themselves Independents rather than Democrats and Republicans. They pride themselves on "voting on the issue or the candidate rather than the party." Do you agree with that outlook? What argument would you make to support it?

rights issues, has also made gains among gays and lesbians, who are now the party's third most loyal voting bloc (after blacks and Jews).

The Republican coalition consists mainly of white middle-class Protestants. The GOP has historically been the party of tax cuts and business incentives. It has also been more supportive of traditional values, as reflected, for example, in its support of school prayer and its opposition to abortion. Not surprisingly, the GOP has generally been the stronger party in the suburbs and other areas, such as the West and Midwest, where traditional values and a desire for lower taxes and less government regulation of economic activity are more pronounced.

The Republican party has made big gains in recent decades among white fundamentalist Christians, who have been drawn to the GOP by its positions on abortion, school prayer, same-sex marriage, and other social issues. In recent presidential elections, the Republican nominee has garnered the votes of roughly three-fourths of fundamentalist Christians.

Minor Parties

Although the U.S. electoral system discourages the formation of third parties, the nation has always had minor parties—more than a thousand over the nation's history.[20] Most of them have been short-lived, and only a few have had a lasting impact. Only one minor party, the Republican party, has ever achieved majority status.

Minor parties in the United States have formed largely to promote policies that their followers believe are not being adequately represented by either of the two major parties. A major party is always somewhat captive to its past, which is the source of many of its ideas and most of its followers. When conditions change, major parties are often slow to respond, and a minor party can capitalize on neglected issues.

When a minor party gains a large following, as has happened a few times in history, the major parties are forced to pay attention to the problems that are driving people to look outside the two-party system for leadership. In such a situation, one or both major parties typically awaken to the new issues, at which time the minor party usually begins to lose support. Nevertheless, the minor party will have served the purpose of making the major parties more responsive to the public's concerns.

Single-Issue Parties

Some minor parties form around a single issue of overriding interest to their supporters, such as the present-day Right-to-Life party, which was formed to oppose the legalization of abortion. Some single-issue parties have seen their policy goals enacted into law. The Prohibition party contributed to the ratification in 1919 of the Eighteenth Amendment, which prohibited the manufacture, sale, and transportation of alcoholic beverages (but which was repealed in 1933). Single-issue parties usually disband when their issue is favorably resolved or fades in importance.[21]

Factional Parties

Although the Republican and Democratic parties are normally adept at managing internal divisions, there have been times when internal conflict has led a faction to break away and form its own party.

The most successful of these factional parties at the polls was Theodore Roosevelt's Bull Moose party. In 1908, Roosevelt, after having served eight years as president, declined to seek a third term and handpicked William Howard Taft for the Republican nomination. When Taft as president showed neither Roosevelt's enthusiasm for a strong presidency nor his commitment to the goals of the Progressive movement, Roosevelt challenged Taft for the 1912 Republican nomination but lost out. Backed by Progressive Republicans, Roosevelt proceeded to form the Bull Moose party (a reference to Roosevelt's claim that he was "as strong as a bull moose"). Roosevelt won 27 percent of the presidential vote to Taft's 25 percent, but the split within Republican ranks enabled the Democratic nominee, Woodrow Wilson, to win the 1912 presidential election.

The States' Rights party in 1948 and George Wallace's American Independent party in 1968 are other examples of strong factional parties. These parties were formed by white southern Democrats angered by northern Democrats' support of civil rights for black Americans.

Deep divisions within a party give rise to factionalism and can lead eventually to a change in its coalition. The conflict over civil rights that began within the Democratic party during the late 1940s continued for the next quarter-century, leading many southern whites to shift their party loyalty to the GOP.

Ideological Parties

Other minor parties are characterized by their ideological commitment to a broad and radical philosophical position, such as redistribution of economic resources. Modern-day ideological parties include the Citizens party, the Socialist Workers party, and the Libertarian party, each of which operates on the fringes of American politics.

One of the strongest ideological parties in the nation's history was the Populist party. Its candidate in the 1892 presidential election, James B. Weaver, gained 8.5 percent of the national vote and won twenty-two electoral votes in six western states. The party began as an agrarian protest movement in response to an economic depression and the anger of small farmers over low commodity prices, tight credit, and the high rates charged by railroad monopolies to transport farm goods. The Populists' ideological platform called for government ownership of the railroads, a graduated income tax, low tariffs on imports, and elimination of the gold standard.[22]

Third-party candidate Ralph Nader speaks during a campaign appearance. Nader's presidential candidacies illustrate that, although third-party candidates have no realistic chance of victory, they can siphon off votes from the major-party nominees.

The strongest minor party today is the Green party, an ideological party that holds liberal positions on the environment, labor, taxation, social welfare, and other issues. Its 2000 presidential nominee, consumer-rights advocate Ralph Nader, received 3 percent of the national vote. According to polls, Nader (who ran as an Independent in 2004) got most of his support from voters who otherwise would have backed Democrat Al Gore, thus tipping the election to the more conservative Republican nominee, George W. Bush. This outcome stirred a debate within Green party ranks over whether the party should concentrate on local and state races and forego the presidential contest. In 2004, the Green party did decide to compete in the presidential race, but in a way designed to reduce the chance of tipping the election to the Republicans. The Green party rejected Nader's bid for its 2004 nomination, choosing instead Green-party activist David Cobb, a little-known Texas lawyer.

Historical Background

Before the 2000 presidential election, America's strongest minor party was the Reform party. It originated in the 1992 independent candidacy of Ross Perot, who gained 19 percent of the presidential vote (second only to Roosevelt's 1912 percentage among candidates who were not major-party nominees). Perot's campaign was based on middle-class discontent with the major parties and was funded by more than $60 million of his own money. Perot ran again in 1996 but as the nominee of the Reform party, which he created after the 1992 campaign. In his 1996 run, Perot accepted public funds for his campaign, which limited his spending to roughly $30 million (see Chapter 12). He attracted 8 percent of the vote, which qualified the Reform party for public funding again in 2000. Perot chose not to run in 2000, setting off a bitter struggle for the Reform party's nomination and public funding. Pat Buchanan, a conservative who had twice failed to win the GOP nomination, won out. His nomination split the party, and he won only 1 percent of the national vote. In 2004, the party did not hold a nominating convention but its leaders endorsed independent candidate Ralph Nader.

PARTY ORGANIZATIONS

The Democratic and Republican parties have organizational units at the national, state, and local levels. The main purpose of these **party organizations** is the contesting of elections.

party organizations The party organizational units at national, state, and local levels; their influence has decreased over time because of many factors.

A century ago, party organizations enjoyed almost complete control of nominations and elections. The party organizations still perform all the activities they formerly engaged in. They recruit candidates, raise money, develop policy positions, and canvass for votes. But they do not control these activities as completely as they once did.[23] For the most part, these activities are now directed by the candidates themselves.[24]

The Weakening of Party Organizations

nomination The designation of a particular individual to run as a political party's candidate (its "nominee") in the general election.

Nomination refers to the selection of the individual who will run as the party's candidate in the general election. Until the early twentieth century, nominations were entirely the responsibility of party organizations. To be nominated, an individual had to be loyal to the party organization, a requirement that included a willingness to share with it the spoils of office—government jobs and contracts. The situation allowed party organizations to acquire campaign workers and funds, but it also enabled unscrupulous party leaders to extort money from those seeking political favors. Reform-minded Progressives argued that the power to nominate should rest with ordinary voters rather than with the party leaders (see Chapter 2).

primary election (direct primary) A form of election in which voters choose a party's nominees for public office. In most primaries, eligibility to vote is limited to voters who are registered members of the party.

The result was the introduction of the **primary election** (or **direct primary**) as a method of choosing nominees. The primary system places nomination in the hands of the voters (see Chapters 2 and 12).

Primary elections take several forms. Most states conduct closed primaries, in which participation is limited to voters registered or declared at the polls as members of the party whose primary is being held. Other states use open primaries, a form that allows independents and voters of either party to vote in a party's primary, although voters are prohibited by law from participating in both parties' primaries simultaneously. A few states have a third form of primary, known as the blanket primary. These states provide a single primary ballot listing both the Republican and Democratic candidates by office. Each voter can cast only one vote per office but can select a candidate of either party.

Louisiana has a variation on this form in which all candidates are listed on the ballot but are not identified by party.

In most states, the winner of a primary election is the candidate who receives the largest number of votes, even if this number is not a majority. Some border and southern states, however, have a provision for a runoff primary if no candidate receives a majority of the vote (or, in North Carolina, 40 percent of the vote) in the regular primary. Slightly more than half the states have a sore-loser law that prevents a candidate who loses a primary from running as an independent or third-party candidate in the general election.

Primaries are the severest impediment imaginable to the strength of the party organizations. If primaries did not exist, candidates would have to work through party organizations in order to gain nomination, and they could be denied renomination if they were disloyal to the party's goals. Because of primaries, however, candidates have the option of seeking office on their own, and once elected (with or without the party's help), they can build a personal following that effectively places them beyond the party's direct control.

Party organizations also lost influence over elections because of a decline in patronage. When a party won control of government a century ago, it also gained control of public jobs, which were doled out to loyal party workers. However, as government jobs in the early twentieth century shifted from patronage to the merit system (see Chapter 13), the party organizations lost control of many of these positions. Today, because of the expanded size of government, thousands of patronage jobs still exist. These government employees help staff the party organizations (along with volunteers), but most of them are more indebted to an individual politician than to a party organization. The people who work for members of Congress, for example, are all patronage employees, but they owe their jobs and their loyalty to their senator or representative, not to their party.

In the process of taking control of nominations, candidates have also acquired control of most campaign money. At the turn of the last century, when party machines were at their peak, most campaign funds passed through the hands of party leaders. Today, most of the money spent on congressional and presidential campaigns goes to the candidates directly, without first passing through the parties.

In Europe, where there are no primary elections, the situation is very different. Parties control their nominations, and because of this they also control campaign money and workers. A party's candidates are expected to campaign on the national platform and, if elected as a governing majority, to support its planks, which are formulated in conjunction with organizational leaders. A candidate who repudiates the party's platform is likely to be denied renomination in the next election.

The Structure and Role of Party Organizations

Although the influence of party organizations has declined, parties are not about to die out. Political leaders and activists need an ongoing organization through which they can work together, and the party serves that purpose.

Figure 8-5

Formal Organization of the Political Party

U.S. parties are loosely structured alliances of national, state, and local organizations; most local parties are not as well organized as the formal chart implies.

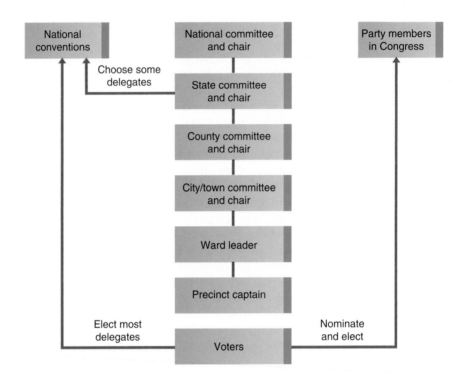

Moreover, certain activities, such as voter registration drives and get-out-the-vote efforts on election day, affect all of a party's candidates and therefore are more efficiently conducted through the party organization. Indeed, parties have staged a comeback of sorts.[25] National and state party organizations in particular have developed the capacity to assist candidates with fund-raising, polling, research, and media production, all essential ingredients of a successful modern campaign.

Structurally, U.S. parties are loose associations of national, state, and local organizations (see Figure 8–5). The national party organizations cannot dictate the decisions made by the state organizations, which in turn do not control the activities of local organizations. However, there is communication between the levels because they all share a common interest in strengthening the party's position.

Local Party Organizations

In a sense, U.S. parties are organized from the bottom up, not the top down. There are about five hundred thousand elective offices in the United States, of which fewer than five hundred are contested statewide and only two—the presidency and vice presidency—are contested nationally. All the rest are local offices; not surprisingly, at least 95 percent of party activists work within local organizations.

It is difficult to generalize about local parties because they vary greatly in their structure and activities. Today only a few local party organizations, including the Democratic organizations in Albany, Philadelphia, and Chicago, bear even a faint resemblance to the fabled old-time party machines that, in return for jobs and even welfare services, were able to control the vote on election day. Nevertheless, local parties tend to be strongest in urban areas and in the Northeast and Midwest, where parties traditionally have been more highly organized. In any case, local parties tend to specialize in elections that coincide with local electoral boundaries. Campaigns for mayor, city council, state legislature, county offices, and the like motivate most local parties to a greater degree than do congressional, statewide, and national contests.

In most urban areas, the party organizations do not have enough workers to staff even a majority of local precincts (voting districts) on an ongoing basis. However, they become more active during campaigns, when they open campaign headquarters, conduct registration drives, send mailings or deliver leaflets to voters, and help get out the vote. These activities are not trivial. Most local campaigns are not well funded, and the party's backing of a candidate can spell the difference between success and failure.

In most suburbs and towns, the party's role is less substantial. The parties exist organizationally but typically have little money and few workers; hence they cannot operate effectively as electoral organizations. The individual candidates must carry nearly the entire burden.

Chicago mayor Richard Daley speaks at a campaign event. He is the son of the legendary Chicago mayor of the same name, who headed the last of the big-city party machines. The earlier Mayor Daley "ruled" Chicago during a twenty-year, six-term reign that ended in the 1970s.

State Party Organizations

At the state level, each party is headed by a central committee made up of members of local party organizations and local and state officeholders. These state central committees do not meet regularly, and they provide only general policy guidance for the state organizations. Day-to-day operations and policy are directed by a chairperson, who is a full-time, paid employee of the state party. The central committee appoints the chairperson, but it often accepts the individual recommended by the party's leading politician, usually the governor or a U.S. senator.

The state chairperson is supported by a staff, the size of which varies widely from state to state depending on the amount of money the party has. Nevertheless, virtually all the state party organizations engage in activities, such as fund-raising and voter registration, that are designed to improve their candidates' chances of success. State party organizations concentrate on statewide races, including those for governor and U.S. senator,[26] and also focus on races for the state legislature. They play a smaller role in campaigns for national or local offices, and in most states they do not endorse candidates in statewide primary contests.

Source: Provided courtesy of the Democratic National Committee.

Source: Provided courtesy of the Republican National Committee.

The home pages of the websites of the Democratic National Committee (DNC) and the Republican National Committee (RNC).

National Party Organizations

The national party organizations are structured much like those at the state level: they have a national committee, a national party chairperson, and a support staff. The national headquarters for the Republican and Democratic parties are located in Washington, D.C. Although in theory the national parties are run by their committees, neither the Democratic National Committee (DNC) nor the Republican National Committee (RNC) has great power. The RNC (with more than 150 members) and the DNC (with more than 300 members) are too cumbersome to act as deliberative bodies. They meet only periodically, and their power is largely confined to setting organizational policy, such as determining the site of the party's presidential nominating convention and the rules governing the selection of convention delegates. They have no power to decide nominations or to determine candidates' policy positions.

The national party's day-to-day operations are directed by a national chairperson chosen by the national committee, although the committee defers to the president's choice when the party controls the White House. The national chairperson is supported by a permanent staff that concentrates on providing assistance in presidential and congressional campaigns.

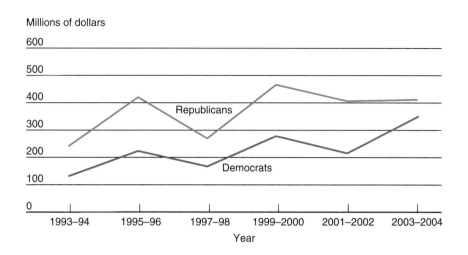

Millions of dollars

Figure 8–6

National Party Fund-raising, 1993–2004

Over the years, the Republican party has raised significantly more money than the Democratic party has. The figures include fund-raising by the DNC, RNC, DCCC, NRCC, DSCC, and NRSC. Soft-money (nonfederal) fund-raising is not included.

Source: Federal Elections Commission. The 2003–2004 data are based on projections from incomplete cycle.

This focus began in the 1970s when Republican leaders decided that a re-vamped national party organization could play a larger contributing role in campaigns. The RNC developed campaign-management "colleges" and "seminars" for candidates and their staffs, compiled massive amounts of computer-based electoral data, and sent field representatives to assist state and local party leaders in modernizing their operations. The range of services that the RNC provides is impressive. For example, the RNC tapes C-SPAN's televised coverage of congressional debate and can instantly retrieve the statement of any speaker on any issue. Republican challengers use this material to create attack ads directed at Democratic incumbents, while Republican incumbents use it to show themselves speaking out on issues of concern to their constituents. The Republican model has also filtered down to most of the state Republican party committees, which, to varying degrees, provide the types of media, data research, and educational services that the national committee offers.

The DNC in the early 1980s followed the Republicans' example, but its later start and less affluent followers have kept the Democrats behind. In every recent election, Republicans have raised and spent more money than the Democrats have (see Figure 8–6), reflecting the greater affluence of the GOP's constituents. Modern campaigns, as David Adamany notes, are based on "cash," and Democrats are relatively cash-poor.[27]

The Parties and Money

The parties' major role in campaigns is the raising and spending of money. The RNC and the DNC are major sources of campaign funds, as are the party campaign committees in the House and the Senate. These include the Democratic Congressional Campaign Committee (DCCC), the National Republican Congressional Committee (NRCC), the Democratic Senatorial Campaign Committee (DSCC), and the National Republican Senatorial Committee (NRSC).

These committees have more of a **service relationship** than a power relationship with their party's candidates. The party offers help to virtually any of

service relationship The situation where party organizations assist candidates for office but have no power to require them to support the party's main policy positions.

its candidates who have a chance of victory. Without the ability to control the nominating process, the party has little choice but to embrace a strong candidate who runs under its banner. If the candidate wins, the party at least has denied the office to the opposing party. Of course, the party will acquire some additional loyalty from officeholders as a result of the contributions it makes to their campaigns. But because the party is more or less willing to support any candidate whatever his or her policy positions, its money does not give it substantial control over how party members conduct themselves after they take office.

A party can legally give $10,000 directly to a House candidate and $37,500 to a Senate candidate. This funding, along with the money a candidate receives from individual contributors ($2,000 maximum per contributor) and interest groups ($5,000 maximum per group), is termed **hard money;** it goes directly to the candidate and can be spent as he or she chooses.

Limits on party contributions were established when the campaign finance laws were reformed in the 1970s in response to the Watergate scandal. However, a loophole in the laws was exposed when a court ruling gave the parties a nearly unlimited opportunity to raise and spend campaign funds provided the funds were not channeled directly to a party's candidates. Although the law limited how much an individual could give directly to a candidate for federal office, it did not restrict individual contributions to a political party. Thus, whereas a wealthy contributor could legally give a candidate only a limited amount, that same contributor could give an unlimited amount to the candidate's party. These contributions were termed **soft money** in that a party could not hand it over directly to a candidate. But the party could use these contributions to support party activities, such as voter registration efforts, get-out-the-vote drives, and party-centered televised ads, that could indirectly benefit its candidates. The party could also funnel soft money to state and local party organizations and, by concentrating it on organizations in areas with close races, could influence the outcome of those races. In some cases, the line between the use of hard and soft money was hard to distinguish. In 1996, for example, the Democratic party ran a $100 million ad campaign that did not directly urge voters to support Clinton but did include pictures of him and references to his accomplishments as president.

In his surprisingly strong bid for the 2000 Republican presidential nomination, John McCain proposed a ban on soft money, which contributed to heightened interest within Congress in closing the loophole. Revelations that the bankrupt Enron Corporation had made soft money contributions as part of its strategy to influence national energy policy strengthened the drive to end the practice. In the previous decade, Enron had contributed $4.4 million to Republican candidates and committees and $1.5 million to Democratic candidates and committees. Prodded by these revelations, Congress in 2002 enacted a law that prohibits the national parties from raising or spending soft money. The law also bans the state parties from spending soft money on federal election activities.

Although the Supreme Court upheld these restrictions in 2003,[28] few people thought the new law would fully solve the soft money problem and, indeed, a loophole has surfaced. The ban on soft money does not fully apply to so-called "527 groups." (Section 527 of the Internal Revenue Code defines the rules governing not-for-profit political groups.) Although such groups are prohibited

hard money Campaign funds given directly to candidates to spend as they choose.

soft money Campaign contributions that are not subject to legal limits and are given to parties rather than directly to candidates.

Should Soft Money Have Been Banned?

Few campaign finance issues have received more attention in recent years than has soft money—unrestricted contributions to political parties. More than a billion dollars in soft money was donated to campaigns during the 1990s alone, leading Congress in 2002 to enact a ban on soft money contributions in federal election campaigns. The congressional vote on the ban was close, as was the Supreme Court decision upholding it. Five justices concluded that the ban was legal, while four justices, including Antonin Scalia, held that it was not. Like many opponents of the ban, Scalia argued that campaign contributions are a form of free speech because they fund televised political advertising, among other things. Proponents of the ban argue that soft money corrupts the political process by giving wealthy donors and interest groups undue influence on public policy.

Debating the Issues

Yes: Special interests who give large amounts of soft money to political parties do in fact achieve their objectives. They do get special access. Sitting Senate and House members have limited amounts of time, but they make time available in their schedules to meet with representatives of business and unions and wealthy individuals who gave large sums of money to their parties. These are not idle chit-chats about the philosophy of democracy. In these meetings, these special interests, often accompanied by lobbyists, press elected officials ... to adopt their position on a matter of interest to them. [Members of Congress] are pressed by their benefactors to introduce legislation, to amend legislation, to block legislation, and to vote on legislation in a certain way. No one says: "We gave money so you should help us with this." No one needs to say it—it is perfectly understood by all participants in every such meeting. . . . Large soft money contributions in fact distort the legislative process. They affect what gets done and how it gets done. They affect whom Senators and House members see, whom they spend their time with, what input they get, and—make no mistake about it—this money affects outcomes as well.

—*Warren Rudman, former U.S. senator*

No: This is a sad day for the freedom of speech. Who could have imagined that the same court which, within the past four years, has sternly disapproved of restrictions upon such inconsequential forms of expression as virtual child pornography, tobacco advertising, dissemination of illegally intercepted communications, and sexually explicit cable programming would smile with favor upon a law that cuts to the heart of what the First Amendment is meant to protect: the right to criticize the government. . . . The premise of the First Amendment is that the American people are neither sheep nor fools, and hence fully capable of considering both the substance of the speech presented to them and its proximate and ultimate source. If that premise is wrong, our democracy has a much greater problem to overcome than merely the influence of amassed wealth. Given the premises of democracy, there is no such thing as too much speech. . . . The first instinct of power is the retention of power, and, under a Constitution that requires periodic elections, that is best achieved by the suppression of election-time speech. . . . It is not the proper role of those who govern us to judge which campaign speech has "substance" and "depth" (do you think it might be that which is least damaging to incumbents?) and to abridge the rest.

—*Antonin Scalia, associate justice of the Supreme Court*

from using soft money to attack a candidate directly, they can use it for issue advocacy. They have found it rather easy to craft televised issue-advocacy ads that are thinly disguised attacks on a candidate. Such groups spent more than $100 million to influence the 2004 presidential campaign. A major spender was America Coming Together, a 527 group that spent more than $15 million, including $5 million provided by the financier George Soros, to criticize Bush administration policies. Just as water seems to run downhill, money always seems to find its way into election politics.

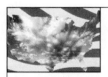

STATES IN THE NATION

Public Funding of State Elections

About half the states have public funding of election campaigns. Some of them give the money to political parties, which allocate it to candidates or spend it on party activities, such as get-out-the-vote efforts. Other states give funds directly to candidates, although this funding is typically limited to candidates for designated offices, such as governor.

Q. What might explain the fact that there is no clear-cut regional pattern to the public funding of state elections?

A: Public funding of elections is relatively new, so additional states may adopt it in the next decade or two, at which time a regional tendency could emerge. (If your state does not have public funding, do you think it is likely to adopt it anytime soon? Why?)

Source: From Thomas Patterson, *We the People*, 5th Edition. Copyright © 2004 The McGraw-Hill Companies. Reprinted by permission of The McGraw-Hill Companies.

 # THE CANDIDATE-CENTERED CAMPAIGN

Although competition between the Republican and Democratic parties provides the backdrop to today's campaigns, the campaigns themselves are largely controlled by the candidates, particularly in congressional, statewide, and presidential races. Each candidate has a personal organization, created especially for the campaign and disbanded once it is over.

Today's candidates tend to be self-starters. Some candidates still rise through the ranks of the party or are drafted because no other qualified persons are willing to run. But most candidates seek high office because they aspire to careers in politics. They are entrepreneurs who play what political consultant Joe Napolitan called "the election game."[29] The game begins with money—lots of it.

Seeking Funds: The Money Chase

Campaigns for high office are expensive, and the costs keep rising. In 1980, about $250 million was spent on all Senate and House campaigns combined. The figure had jumped to $425 million by 1990 and topped $1 billion ($1,000 million) in 2000.

As might be expected, incumbents have a distinct advantage in fund-raising. They have contributor lists from past campaigns and have acquired the public visibility and political clout that donors want. In recent House and Senate races, incumbents have outspent their challengers by more than two to one.[30]

Because of the high cost of campaigns, candidates are forced to spend much of their time raising funds, which come primarily from individual contributors, interest groups (through PACs, discussed in Chapter 9), and political parties. The **money chase** is relentless.[31] A U.S. senator must raise $20,000 a week on average throughout the entire six-year term in order to raise the minimum of $6 million that it takes to run a competitive Senate campaign in many states. A Senate campaign in a large state can cost several times that amount. In 2000, Representative Rick Lazio and First Lady Hillary Clinton spent nearly $70 million on the New York Senate race. House campaigns are less costly, but expenditures of $1 million or more are commonplace. As for presidential elections, even the nominating race is expensive. A candidate needs at least $20 million to have a reasonable chance of gaining nomination. In 2004, Senator John Kerry spent roughly $40 million during the contested phase of the Democratic race. (In presidential races, but not congressional ones, candidates are eligible to receive federal funds, a topic discussed in Chapter 12.)

money chase A term used to describe the fact that U.S. campaigns are very expensive and candidates must spend a great amount of time raising funds in order to compete successfully.

Creating Organization: Hired Guns

The key operatives in today's campaigns are campaign consultants, pollsters, media producers, and fund-raising and get-out-the-vote specialists. They are **hired guns** who charge hefty fees for their services. "The new king-makers" is the way writer David Chagall characterized these pros.[32]

Some of the hired guns are specialists in campaign management. Inexperienced candidates often think that campaigns are simple to run and entrust the job to an amateur, often a relative or friend. They soon discover that their campaign is headed nowhere. At this point, if they have the money, they hire a seasoned professional. Over the years, some of these operatives, like James Carville, Joe Napolitan, Ed Rollins, Dick Morris, and Roger Ailes, have developed almost legendary reputations.

hired guns A term that refers to the professional consultants who run campaigns for high office.

U.S. Senator Hillary Clinton is the only first lady to seek elective office. She moved to New York to compete in the state's 2000 Senate race, which she won. Clinton is shown here campaigning on the streets of New York City.

Fund-raising specialists are also part of the new politics. Direct-mail operators have developed contributor lists for every state and nearly every type of candidacy, and they flood the mail with computer-generated letters. There are also numerous specialty mailing lists, such as EMILY's List (*early money is like yeast*, "it makes the dough rise"). EMILY's List was started in the 1980s to provide seed money for liberal women candidates. Effective fund-raisers also know how to tap into the networks of large contributors and interest groups who give to election campaigns (see Chapter 9).

Polling is another ingredient of the modern campaign. Although candidates make use of the public polls conducted by Gallup, the news media, and other organizations, they also hire their own pollsters.[33] They also rely on focus groups—small groups of voters assembled to talk at length about the issues and candidates and, in some instances, to evaluate proposed themes and materials, such as televised political ads. Polls and focus groups enable candidates to identify messages that are likely to resonate with the voters. At one point in the 2004 presidential race, for example, John Kerry shifted from the issue of jobs to the issue of health care after polls indicated this issue was having a larger impact on undecided voters.

Media consultants are another staple of the modern campaign. These experts are adept at producing televised political advertising and creating the "photo-ops" and other staged events that attract news coverage. They also teach the candidates how to use the media properly. Inexperienced candidates soon discover that they cannot "just be themselves" when talking with journalists or participating in televised debates. They have to conform to the demands of the media, such as the preference of television journalists for sound bites, short pithy statements that add zest and zing to a news story.[34]

Devising Strategy: Packaging the Candidate

In the old days, candidates were nearly prepackaged. They were labeled as Democrats or Republicans, which was about all the guidance most voters wanted or needed. Party labels are still meaningful, but today's campaigns are also based on media images.

Often depicted as hollow deceptions, images are more typically rooted in factual arguments.[35] They are constructed by placing aspects of the candidate's partisanship, policy positions, record, and personality in the context of the voters' "ideal" candidate, a process known as the **packaging** of a candidate.[36] The voters want a representative who is honest, able, straightforward, resolute, and responsive to their interests, but there are limits on the claims a candidate can reasonably make. It would be difficult, for example, for Democratic incumbents who have been long-time advocates of domestic spending programs to convincingly portray themselves as fiscal conservatives. Instead, they would base their images as responsive legislators on other issues, such as health and education. In any case, officeseekers try to create a favorable portrayal of their candidacy that is also plausible. In a way, this type of packaging is as old as politics itself. Andrew Jackson's self-portrayal as "the champion of the people" is an image that any modern candidate could appreciate. What is new is the need to fit the image to the requirements of a media campaign. The image must conform to a world of sound bites, thirty-second ads, and televised debates.

Air Wars

The major battleground of the modern campaign is the mass media, particularly television. Television emerged in the 1960s as the major medium of presidential and congressional politics and has remained the dominant medium ever since.

Candidates spend heavily on televised political advertising, which enables them to communicate directly—and on their own terms—with voters.[37] The production and the airing of political ads account for half or more of the expenditures in presidential campaigns and in most congressional races. Indeed, televised ads are usually cited as the main reason for the high cost of U.S. campaigns. In most democracies, televised campaigning takes place through parties, which receive free air time to make their pitch. Many democracies even prohibit the purchase of televised advertising time by candidates (see Table 8–1).

Air wars is the term that political scientist Darrell West applies to candidates' use of televised ads. Candidates increasingly play off each other's ads, seeking to gain the strategic advantage.[38] Modern production techniques enable well-funded candidates to get new ads on the air within a few hours' time, which allows them to rebut attacks and exploit fast-breaking developments, a tactic known as *rapid response.*

Candidates also use the news media to get their message across, although the amount of coverage they can expect varies widely by location and office. Many House candidates are nearly ignored by their local news media. The New York City media market, for example, includes more than a score of House districts in New York, New Jersey, Pennsylvania, and Connecticut, and candidates in these districts get little or no coverage from the New York media. The presidential campaign, in contrast, gets daily coverage from both national and local media. Between these extremes are Senate races and House races in less populated areas, which always get some news coverage and, if hotly contested, may get heavy coverage.

Simulation
www.mhhe.com/pattersontad7

packaging A term of modern campaigning that refers to the process of recasting a candidate's record into an appealing image.

air wars A term that refers to the fact that modern campaigns are often a battle of opposing televised advertising campaigns.

TABLE 8–1	Television Campaign Practices in Selected Democracies
	In many democracies, free television time is provided to political parties, and candidates are not allowed to buy advertising time. The United States provides no free time to parties and allows candidates to purchase air time. Television debates are also a feature of many U.S. campaigns.

COUNTRY	PAID TV ADS ALLOWED?	UNRESTRICTED FREE TV TIME PROVIDED?	TV DEBATES HELD?
Canada	Yes	Yes	Yes
France	No	Yes	Yes
Germany	Yes	Yes	Yes
Great Britain	No	Yes	No
Italy	No	Yes	Yes
Netherlands	No	No	Yes
United States	Yes	No	Yes

Debates are also part of the media campaign. Debates often attract a large and attentive audience but can be risky encounters, because they give viewers a chance to compare the candidates directly. A weak or bumbling performance can hurt a candidate. Some analysts believe, for example, that Al Gore's performance in the first of the 2000 general election debates, when he grimaced and sighed loudly when George W. Bush was talking, cost him the election. Gore had been slightly ahead in the opinion polls but lost his lead immediately after the debate.

Ground Wars

Candidates' first priority in a close election is "swing voters"—those voters who conceivably could be persuaded to vote for either side. As election day nears, however, candidates concentrate on getting their supporters to the polls.

The get-out-the-vote effort traditionally has been borne by the parties and other organizations, such as labor unions. Although these groups remain the cornerstone of the effort, the candidates are also involved, and increasingly so. As partisanship has intensified in recent years, candidates have found it more difficult to persuade voters to switch sides. It has therefore become important for them to get as many of their supporters as possible to the polls on election day. Some campaign money that formerly would have been spent on televised advertising is now channeled into voter turnout efforts. In the final phase of the 2004 presidential election, millions of potential voters were contacted by phone or in person by the Republican and Democratic campaigns.

Web Wars

New communication technology usually makes its way into campaign politics, and the Internet is no exception. Each of the nine candidates for the 2004

Citizenship

Getting Involved, Making a Difference

Political Strategy

"Political strategy" is a practice synonymous with modern campaigning, and it is a practice that is often scorned. The term seems to imply some form of manipulation. Nevertheless, strategy is an essential part of political action. Ideas don't suddenly turn into policies and programs. Candidates don't miraculously get elected to office. Strategic action is required to make these things happen.

Political strategy has always existed. It might be difficult today to acknowledge, for example, that the Constitution became law through strategic action. The Framers were men of vision, but they were also masterful politicians. They acted strategically from the moment of their arrival in Philadelphia. They closed the deliberations to outsiders and proceeded to ignore Congress's instructions that they were only to amend the Articles of Confederation. Proponents of the Virginia Plan rushed to get their proposal on the table, knowing that the order of discussion could well determine the outcome. When they were finished, the delegates stacked the dice in favor of the Constitution by declaring that it would become law when approved by nine states as opposed to the full thirteen that Congress had mandated.

The Framers used many of the strategic tools that today's political activists employ. They ran a media campaign. In scores of newspaper articles, Madison and Hamilton made the case for ratification. They were masters at framing their message. Their arguments were cast in the most favorable terms possible, while a negative spin was placed on the Anti-Federalists' arguments. The Framers also shamelessly played on Americans' admiration of George Washington by saying he would become the nation's first president and would ensure the Constitution's success. And in the end, they used coercion to get North Carolina and Rhode Island to ratify; they said to these states that the others would not come to their defense if they were attacked by a foreign power.

The point is not that the Framers hoodwinked Americans. The Framers believed that the government of the Constitution was the best available option, and they made the strongest case possible for it. It was not, however, the only alternative available to Americans in 1787. The Anti-Federalists' idea of a state-centered union also had its backers. But the Anti-Federalists were not as well organized and were less effective in making their case, and the Framers' vision of a new government prevailed.

In sum, strategic thinking is a basic aspect of effective political action. Strategy is basically a plan for pursuing a particular goal. Strategy is not incompatible with the democratic process. Autocrats have no need for strategy; they rule by dictate. In a democracy, however, popular consent is the basis of government, and strategy is part of the process of acquiring consent. Whether taking action on your campus or in your community, you should not hesitate to think strategically in the pursuit of your civic goals.

Democratic presidential nomination, for example, had a website dedicated to providing information, generating public support, attracting volunteers, and raising money. Howard Dean's website was by far the most successful. Through it, Dean raised more than $20 million and developed a network of a half-million supporters.

Although television is still the principal medium of election politics, some analysts believe that the Internet may eventually overtake it. E-mail is much cheaper than television advertising (and both much cheaper and much faster than traditional mail). Because it is a targeted medium, the Internet could

A campaign volunteer works the phone on behalf of George W. Bush's presidential campaign. In the past few elections, as partisan attitudes have hardened, candidates have placed somewhat more emphasis on getting their supporters to the polls on election day.

become the channel through which candidates reach particular voting groups. But the Internet also has some weaknesses compared to television. The most obvious and most important is that the individual user has greater control over Internet messages. With television, when a political ad appears during a favorite program, most viewers will watch it. An unsolicited message on the Internet is more easily ignored or deleted. Future candidates may conclude that the Internet is the preferred medium for interacting with die-hard supporters and that television is the best medium for achieving public recognition and reaching less-interested voters.

 ## PARTIES, CANDIDATES, AND THE PUBLIC'S INFLUENCE

Candidate-centered campaigns have some distinct advantages. First, they can infuse new blood into electoral politics. Candidate recruitment is normally a slow process in party-centered systems. Would-be officeholders pay their dues by working in the party and, in the process, tend to adopt the outlook of those already there. By comparison, a candidate-centered system is more open and provides opportunities for total newcomers to gain office quickly. John Edwards is a case in point. Edwards had never run for public office when, in 1997, he called a Democratic political consultant to say that he was thinking about running for the senate. The consultant assumed that Edwards, a little-known trial lawyer, had the North Carolina state senate in mind. Edwards shocked him by saying that he was eyeing the upcoming 1998 U.S. Senate race. Edwards proceeded to gain the Democratic Senate nomination and then poured millions of his own money into a successful general-election campaign against incumbent Republican Senator

John Edwards campaigns during the 2004 election. Edwards epitomizes today's candidate-centered politics. On his own initiative, he ran for U.S. Senate in 1998 even though he had not previously held public office. Then, in 2003 and again on his own initiative, Edwards entered the race for the 2004 Democratic presidential nomination. Though Edwards lost that bid, he ran strongly enough to convince John Kerry to choose him as the 2004 Democratic vice-presidential nominee.

Lauch Faircloth. In 2003, Edwards decided against seeking a second term in the Senate and entered the race for the 2004 Democratic presidential nomination. Though Edwards lost that bid, he ran so strongly in the primaries that the winner, John Kerry, picked him as his vice presidential running mate.

Candidate-centered campaigns also lend flexibility to electoral politics. When political conditions and issues change, self-directed candidates quickly adjust, bringing new ideas into the political arena. Strong party organizations are rigid by comparison. Until recently, for example, the British Labour party was controlled by old-line activists who refused to concede that changes in the British economy called for changes in the party's trade unionist and economic policies. The result was a series of humiliating defeats at the hands of the Conservative party that ended only after Tony Blair and other proponents of "New Labour" successfully rebuilt the party's image.

Second, candidate-centered campaigns encourage national officeholders to be responsive to local interests. In building personal followings among their state and district constituents, members of Congress respond to local needs. Nearly every significant domestic program enacted by Congress is adjusted to accommodate the interests of states and localities that otherwise would be hurt by the policy. Members of Congress are not obliged to support the legislative position of their party's majority, and they often extract favors for their constituents as the price of their support. Where strong national parties exist, national interests take precedence over local concerns. In both France and Britain, for example, the pleas of representatives of underdeveloped regions have often gone unheeded by their party's majority.

In other respects, however, candidate-centered campaigns have some real disadvantages. Often they degenerate into mere personality contests, and they are fertile ground for powerful special interest groups, which contribute much of the money that underwrites candidates' campaigns. Many groups give

Liberty, Equality & Self-Government

What's Your Opinion?

Parties and Equality

Historically, parties have given weight to the voice of disadvantaged people. Their strength is in their numbers rather than in their wealth or status, and elections give them a chance to exercise that strength if they act together. It is no accident that the Jacksonian Democrats created the first American grassroots party in order to mobilize lower-class voters. The role of the political party in giving voice to the lower classes is even more evident in Europe, where labor and socialist parties emerged out of workers' movements.

As U.S. parties have changed in recent decades, so has the political influence of Americans of lower income

levels. The voting rate of citizens at the bottom of the income ladder is now about half that of citizens at the top. Party conflict in the first half of the twentieth century centered on the working class. It now inhabits the periphery of policy debates. The candidate-centered politics of today is mainly a politics of media and money and is primarily responsive to middle-class interests.

What do you make of this development? Is there a good alternative to the political party as an instrument for giving voice to the aspirations of lower-income Americans? What might be done to increase the parties' responsiveness to their interests?

large sums of money to incumbents of both parties, which enables them to insulate themselves from an election's outcome: whether the Republicans win or the Democrats win, these contributors are assured of having friends in high places.

Candidate-centered campaigns also weaken accountability by making it easier for officeholders to deny responsibility for government's actions. If national policy goes awry, an incumbent can always say that he or she is only one vote out of many and that the real problem resides with the president or with "others" in Congress. The problem of accountability in the U.S. system is illustrated by surveys that have asked Americans about their confidence in Congress. Although most citizens do not have a high opinion of Congress as a whole, most citizens also say that they have confidence in their own representative in Congress. This paradoxical attitude prevails in so many districts that the net result in most elections is a Congress whose membership is not greatly changed from the previous one (see Chapter 11). In contrast, party-centered campaigns are characterized by collective accountability. When problems occur, voters tend to hold the majority party responsible and invariably vote many of its members out of office.

In sum, candidate-centered campaigns strengthen the relationship between the voters and their individual representative while at the same time weakening the relationship between the full electorate and their representative institutions. Whether this arrangement serves the public's interest is debatable. Nevertheless, it is clear that Americans do not favor party-centered politics. Parties survived the shift to candidate-centered campaigns and will persist, but their organizational heyday has passed. (Congressional and presidential campaigns are discussed further in Chapters 11 and 12, respectively.)

Summary Self-Test

www.mhhe.com/pattersontad7

Political parties serve to link the public with its elected leaders. In the United States, this linkage is provided by the two-party system; only the Republican and Democratic parties have any chance of winning control of government. The fact that the United States has only two major parties is explained by several factors: an electoral system—characterized by single-member districts—that makes it difficult for third parties to compete for power; each party's willingness to accept differing political views; and a political culture that stresses compromise and negotiation rather than ideological rigidity.

Because the United States has only two major parties, each of which seeks to gain majority support, their candidates normally tend to avoid controversial or extreme political positions. Candidates typically pursue moderate and somewhat overlapping policies. Nonetheless, Democratic and Republican candidates sometimes do offer sharply contrasting policy alternatives, particularly in times of political change.

America's parties are decentralized, fragmented organizations. The national party organization does not control the policies and activities of the state organizations, and these in turn do not control the local organizations. Traditionally the local organizations have controlled most of the party's work force because most elections are contested at the local level. Local parties, however, vary markedly in their vitality. Whatever their level, America's party organizations are relatively weak. They lack control over nominations and elections. Candidates can bypass the party organization and win nomination through primary elections. Individual candidates also control most of the organizational structure and money necessary to win elections. The state and national party organizations have recently expanded their capacity to provide candidates with modern campaign services. Nevertheless, party organizations at all levels have few ways of controlling the candidates who run under their banners. They assist candidates with campaign technology, workers, and funds, but they cannot compel candidates' loyalty to organizational goals.

American political campaigns, particularly those for higher office, are candidate centered. Most candidates are self-starters who become adept at "the election game." They spend much of their time raising campaign funds, and they build their personal organizations around hired guns: pollsters, media producers, fund-raisers, and election consultants. Strategy and image making are key components of the modern campaign, as is televised political advertising, which accounts for half or more of all spending in presidential and congressional races.

The advantages of candidate-centered politics include a responsiveness to new leadership, new ideas, and local concerns. Yet, this form of politics can result in campaigns that are personality-driven, dependent on powerful interest groups, and blur responsibility for what government has done.

STUDY CORNER

Key Terms

air wars *(p. 267)*
candidate-centered politics *(p. 242)*
grassroots party *(p. 244)*
hard money *(p. 262)*
hired guns *(p. 265)*
money chase *(p. 265)*
multiparty system *(p. 248)*
nomination *(p. 256)*

packaging (of a candidate) *(p. 267)*
party-centered politics *(p. 242)*
party coalition *(p. 251)*
party competition *(p. 243)*
party organizations *(p. 256)*
party realignment *(p. 245)*
political party *(p. 242)*

primary election (direct primary)
   (p. 256)
proportional representation *(p. 249)*
service relationship *(p. 261)*
single-member districts *(p. 248)*
soft money *(p. 262)*
split ticket *(p. 247)*
two-party system *(p. 248)*

Self-Test

1. The formation of political parties:
   a. acts as a support for an elitist government.
   b. makes it difficult for the public to participate in politics.
   c. can mobilize citizens into collective action to compete for power with those who have wealth and prestige.
   d. can function as an alternative to a free and open media.

2. A major change in party activity in the South since the 1960s is:
   a. the emergence of a viable third party.
   b. a sharp decline in voter turnout.
   c. a decline in the level of two-party competition in state and local elections.
   d. a switch to support of Republican candidates in presidential elections.

3. The chief electoral factor supporting a two-party system in the United States is:
   a. proportional representation.
   b. multimember election districts.
   c. single-member districts with proportional voting.
   d. single-member districts with plurality voting.

4. The high cost of campaigns in the United States is largely related to:
   a. televised ads.
   b. developing a colorful website.
   c. organizing door-to-door canvassing efforts.
   d. the legal and accounting expenses related to filing information about campaign donors and expenditures with the Federal Elections Commission.

5. In recent decades state political party organizations in the United States have:
   a. become weaker and less effective.
   b. taken over control and direction of the national parties.
   c. been hurt by services provided by the national party organizations.
   d. become more professional in staffing and support of statewide races.

6. European and American political parties differ in which of the following ways?
   a. the degree to which they are party-centered as opposed to candidate-centered
   b. the nature of their party organizations: the extent to which they are organized at the local and national levels and the amount of power that exists at each of these levels
   c. the type of electoral system in which they elect their candidates to office
   d. all of the above

7. The coalitions of voters that make up the Republican and Democratic parties are virtually identical. (T/F)

8. Primary elections helped strengthen party organizations in the United States. (T/F)

9. U.S. political parties are organized from the bottom up, not the top down. (T/F)

10. Modern-day parties in the United States are described in the text as having more of a service than a power relationship with candidates. (T/F)

Critical Thinking

Why are elections conducted so differently in the United States than in European democracies? Why are the campaigns so much longer, more expensive, and more candidate-centered?

Suggested Readings

Aldrich, John H. *Why Parties? The Origin and Transformation of Political Parties in America*. Chicago: University of Chicago Press, 1995. An insightful analysis of what parties are and how they emerge and develop.

Flanigan, William H., and Nancy H. Zingale. *Political Behavior of the American Electorate*, 10th ed. Washington, D.C.: Congressional Quarterly Press, 2002. A study of Americans' electoral behavior.

Greenberg, Stanley B. *The Two Americas: Our Current Political Deadlock and How to Break It*. New York: Thomas Dunne Books, 2004. An assessment of party politics in today's America.

Lijphardt, Arend. *Electoral Systems and Party Systems: A Study of Twenty-Seven Democracies, 1945–1990*. New York: Oxford University Press, 1994. A comprehensive study of the relationship between electoral systems and party systems.

Patterson, Kelly D. Political *Parties and the Maintenance of Liberal Democracy*. New York: Columbia University Press, 1996. A systematic look at the effects of political parties on American government and politics.

Rosenstone, Steven J., Roy L. Behr, and Edward H. Lazarus. *Third Parties in America*, 2d ed. Princeton, N.J.: Princeton University Press, 1996. An analysis of America's third parties and their impact on the two-party system.

Stonecash, Jeffrey. *Class and Party in American Politics*. Boulder, Colo.: Westview Press, 2001. An insightful analysis that argues that class is still very much a part of America's party politics.

West, Darrell M. *Air Wars: Television Advertising in Election Campaigns, 1952–2000*, 3d ed. Washington, D.C.: Congressional Quarterly Press, 2001. A thorough study of the role of televised advertising in election campaigns.

List of Websites

http://www.democrats.org/

The Democratic National Committee's site; it provides information on the party's platform, candidates, officials, and organization.

http://www.greenparties.org/

The Green party's website; it contains information on the party's philosophy and policy goals.

http://www.rnc.org/

Home page of the Republican National Committee; it offers information on Republican leaders, policy positions, and organizations.

http://www.jamescarvillesoffice.com/

The website of James Carville, one of the nation's top campaign consultants.

Participate!

Consider becoming a campaign volunteer. The opportunities are numerous. Candidates at every level from the presidency on down seek volunteers to assist in organizing, canvassing, fund-raising, and other campaign activities. As a college student, you have communication and knowledge skills that would be valuable to a campaign. You might be pleasantly surprised by the tasks you are assigned.

Extra Credit

For up-to-the-minute *New York Times* articles, interactive simulations, graphics, study tools, and more links and quizzes, visit the text's Online Learning Center at www.mhhe.com/pattersontad7.

(Self-Test Answers: 1. c   2. d   3. d   4. a   5. d   6. d   7. F   8. F   9. T   10. T)

9

Interest Groups:
Organizing for Influence

The flaw in the pluralist heaven is that the heavenly chorus sings with
a strong upper-class bias.

—*E. E. Schattschneider*[1]

They launched their attack within hours of the announcement that congressional Republicans had included Medicare in their balanced-budget proposal. The GOP lawmakers planned a $1.1 trillion reduction in federal spending over seven years, including a $270 billion cut in health care for the elderly. Senior-citizen groups assailed the plan and quickly organized a mass demonstration outside the Capitol. The next step was an orchestrated campaign involving thousands of angry calls, letters, telegrams, and faxes from retirees to their congressional representatives.

President Clinton sided with the seniors' lobby and promised to veto the Republican bill, which led to a showdown between Congress and the White House that forced a temporary shutdown of some federal programs, including the national parks. In January 1996, after a six-week battle and with their poll ratings dropping almost daily, Republican lawmakers shelved their balanced-budget proposal.

The campaign against the Republicans' Medicare initiative suggests why interest groups are both admired and feared. On one hand, groups have a legitimate right to express their views on public policy issues. It is entirely appropriate for senior citizens or any other group—whether farmers, consumers, business firms, or college students—to actively promote their interests through collective action. In fact, the *pluralist* theory of American politics (see Chapter 1) holds that society's interests are most effectively represented through the efforts of groups.

On the other hand, groups can wield too much power. If a group gets its way at an unreasonable cost to the rest of society, the public interest is harmed. When the Republican budget package was prepared in Congress, polls indicated that most Americans wanted a balanced federal budget and were willing to bear a fair share of the costs. Did the senior-citizen lobby, in pursuit of its own interest, derail a sound budgetary proposal? Or did the Republican package, which also included tax cuts for upper-income Americans, place too much of the burden of a balanced budget on the elderly?

Opinions on these questions differ widely, but there is no doubt that the special interest in some cases wrongly prevails over the general interest. Indeed, most observers are of the opinion that groups have achieved too much influence over public policy in recent decades. Some analysts describe the situation as the triumph of **single-issue politics:** separate groups organized around nearly every conceivable policy issue, with each group pressing its demands and influence to the utmost, no matter the cost to the

The American Association of Retired Persons (AARP) has roughly thirty million members and is the largest citizens' group. It regularly encourages its members to contact Congress on issues facing retirees, as in this electronic message on prescription drugs. Source: www.aarp.org. Reprinted with permission.

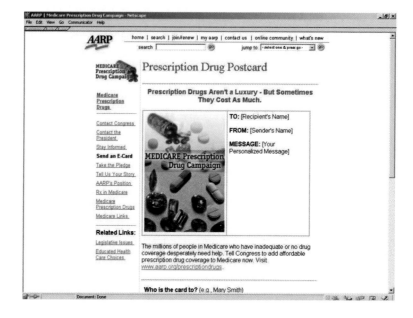

single-issue politics The situation in which separate groups are organized around nearly every conceivable policy issue and press their demands and influence to the utmost.

interest group A set of individuals who are organized to promote a shared political interest.

broader society. The structure of the American political system provides fertile ground for group influence. The system's elaborate checks and balances make it relatively easy for a group, if it has strong support even within a single corner of government, to pursue its goals effectively. (This "Madisonian dilemma" is explored more fully in the chapter's concluding section.)

An **interest group,** also called a "faction" or "pressure group" or "special interest," has two characteristics: an organized membership and the pursuit of policy goals that stem from its members' shared interest. Thus, a bridge club or an amateur softball team is not an interest group because it does not seek to influence the political process. Organizations such as the Association of Wheat Growers, Common Cause, the National Organization for Women, the World Wildlife Fund, the National Rifle Association, and the Anti-Defamation League of B'nai B'rith are interest groups because, despite their differences, each is an organized entity and each seeks to further its members' interests through political action.

Interest groups are similar to political parties in certain respects, but the two types of organizations differ in important ways. Major political parties address a broad range of issues so as to appeal to diverse blocs of voters. Parties exist to contest elections. They change their policy positions as the voters' preferences change; for the party, winning is almost everything. In contrast, interest groups focus on specific issues of immediate concern to their members; farm groups, for example, concentrate on agricultural policy. A group may involve itself in elections, but its purpose is to influence public policy.

This chapter examines the degree to which various interests in American society are represented by organized groups, the process by which interest groups exert influence, and the costs and benefits of group politics with respect to the public good. The main points made in the chapter are the following:

- *Although nearly all interests in American society are organized to some degree, those associated with economic activity, particularly business enterprises, are by far the most thoroughly organized.* Their advantage rests on their superior financial resources and on the fact that they offer potential members private goods (such as wages and jobs).

- *Groups that do not have economic activity as their primary function often have organizational problems.* They pursue public or collective goods (such as a safer environment) that are available even to individuals who are not group members, and so individuals may choose not to pay the costs of membership.

- *Lobbying and electioneering are the traditional means by which groups communicate with and influence political leaders.* Recent developments, including grassroots lobbying and PACs, have heightened interest groups' influence on policy.

- *The interest-group system overrepresents business interests and higher-income groups and fosters policies that serve a group's interest more than the public interest.* Thus, although groups are an essential part of the democratic process, they also distort that process.

THE INTEREST-GROUP SYSTEM

In the 1830s, the Frenchman Alexis de Tocqueville wrote that the "principle of association" was nowhere more evident than in America.[2] The country's tradition of free association has always made it easy for Americans to join together for political purposes, and their diverse interests have given them reason to seek influence through specialized groups (see "How the United States Compares").

However, the nation's various interests are not equally well organized. Organizations develop when people with shared interests have the opportunity and the incentive to join together. Some individuals have the skills, money, contacts, or time to participate effectively in group politics, but others do not. Moreover, some groups are inherently more attractive to potential members than others and thus find it easier to build large or devoted followings. Organizations also differ in their access to financial resources and thus differ in their capacity for political action.

Therefore, a first consideration in regard to group politics in America is the issue of how thoroughly various interests are organized. Interests that are highly organized stand a good chance of having their views heard by policymakers. Poorly organized interests run the risk of being ignored.

Economic Groups

No interests are more fully or effectively organized than those that have economic activity as their primary purpose. An indication of their advantage is the fact that Washington lobbyists who represent economic groups outnumber those of all other groups by more than two to one.

Corporations, labor unions, farm groups, and professional associations, among others, exist primarily for economic purposes: to make profits, provide jobs, improve pay, or protect an occupation. For the sake of discussion, we will

HOW THE UNITED STATES COMPARES

Groups: "A Nation of Joiners"

"A nation of joiners" is how the Frenchman Alexis de Tocqueville described the United States during his visit to this country in the 1830s.

Even today, Americans are more actively involved in groups and community causes than are Europeans. The American tradition of group activity is only one reason. Another is the structure of the U.S. political system. Because of federalism and the separation of powers, the American system offers numerous points at which groups can try to influence public policy. If unsuccessful with legislators, groups can turn to executives or to the courts. If thwarted at the national level, groups can turn to state and local governments. By comparison, the governments of most other democratic nations are not organized in ways that facilitate group access and influence. France's unitary government, for example, concentrates power at the national level.

Such differences are reflected in citizens' participation rates. Americans are more likely to belong to groups than are the French, Italians, British, or Germans, as the accompanying figures from the World Values Survey indicate.

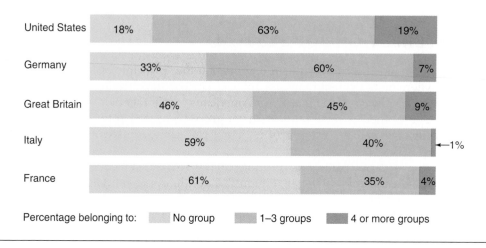

	No group	1–3 groups	4 or more groups
United States	18%	63%	19%
Germany	33%	60%	7%
Great Britain	46%	45%	9%
Italy	59%	40%	1%
France	61%	35%	4%

Percentage belonging to: ▢ No group ▢ 1–3 groups ▢ 4 or more groups

economic groups Interest groups that are organized primarily for economic reasons but that engage in political activity in order to seek favorable policies from government.

call such organizations **economic groups,** although it is important to recognize that their political goals can include policies that transcend the narrow economic interests of their members. Although the AFL-CIO, for example, concentrates on labor policies, it also takes positions on other foreign and domestic issues.

An Organizational Edge

One reason for the abundance of economic groups is their access to financial resources. Political activity does not come cheap. If a group is to make its views known, it normally must have a headquarters, an expert staff, and communication facilities. Economic groups can obtain the requisite money and expertise from their economic activities. Corporations have the greatest built-in advantage. They do not have to charge membership dues or conduct fund-raisers to support their lobbying. Their political money comes from their business activity.

Some economic groups do depend on dues for their support, but they can offer prospective members a powerful incentive to join: **private (individual) goods,** which are the benefits that a group can grant directly to the individual member. For example, workers in the state of Michigan cannot hold automobile assembly jobs unless they belong to the United Auto Workers (UAW). The UAW has a **material incentive**—the economic lure of a high-paying job—to attract potential members. Economic groups are highly organized in part because they serve the economic needs of potential members. The predominance of economic interests was predicted in *Federalist* No. 10, in which James Madison declared that property is "the most common and durable source of factions." Stated differently, nothing seems to matter quite so much to people as their pocketbooks and livelihoods.

Types of Economic Groups

Most economic groups are of four general types: business groups, labor groups, agricultural groups, and professional groups.

Business Groups   More than half of all groups formally registered to lobby Congress are business organizations. Nearly all large corporations and many smaller ones are politically active. They concentrate their activities on policies that touch directly on business interests, such as tax, tariff, and regulatory decisions.

Business firms are also represented through associations such as the U.S. Chamber of Commerce, which includes nearly three million businesses of all sizes. Other business associations, such as the American Petroleum Institute, are confined to a single trade or industry. Because each trade association represents a single industry, it can promote the interests of member corporations even when these interests conflict with those of business generally. Thus, while the Chamber of Commerce promotes a global free trade policy, some trade associations seek protective tariffs because their member firms want barriers against foreign competition.

Business interests have the advantage of what economist Mancur Olson calls "the size factor."[3] Although large groups can claim that government should pay more attention to them because they represent more people, small groups are usually more cohesive. Everyone is a consumer, but most consumers do not see any benefit in paying money to join a consumer advocacy group. On the other hand, because business firms in a particular industry are few in number, they are likely to recognize the significance of working together. When the "Big Three" U.S. automakers—General Motors, Ford, and Chrysler—fought recently against higher mileage-efficiency standards, the defection of any one of them would likely have meant defeat. But they stayed together and gained concessions from the government. In the process, each automaker saved hundreds of millions of dollars because they did not have to design and manufacture new engines. Their gain came at an unknown cost to consumers, whose newly purchased automobiles were less fuel efficient than they could have been.

Labor Groups   Since the 1930s, organized labor has been politically active on a large scale. Its goal has been to promote policies that benefit workers in general

private (individual) goods Benefits that a group (most often an economic group) can grant directly and exclusively to individual members of the group.

material incentive An economic or other tangible benefit that is used to attract group members.

America's "Big Three" automakers—Chrysler, Ford, and General Motors—actively lobby government, sometimes working together to achieve policy goals that will promote their industry.

and union members in particular. Although there are some major independent unions, such as the United Mine Workers, the dominant labor group is the AFL-CIO, which has its national headquarters in Washington, D.C. The AFL-CIO has more than thirteen million members in its ninety-seven affiliated unions, which include the International Brotherhood of Electrical Workers, the Sheet Metal Workers, the Communication Workers of America, and the International Brotherhood of Teamsters.

At one time, about a third of the U.S. work force was unionized, but today only about a seventh of all workers belong to unions. Skilled and unskilled laborers have historically been the core of organized labor, but their numbers are decreasing while the numbers of professionals, technicians, and service workers are increasing. Professionals have shown little interest in union organization, perhaps because they identify with management or see themselves as economically secure. Service workers and technicians are also difficult for unions to organize because they work closely with managers and, often, in small offices.

Nevertheless, in recent decades unions have made inroads in their efforts to organize service and public employees. Teachers, postal workers, police, firefighters, and social workers are among the public employee groups that have become increasingly unionized. Today, the nation's largest unions are those that represent service and public employees rather than skilled and unskilled laborers (see Table 9–1).

Agricultural Groups   Farm organizations represent another large economic lobby. The American Farm Bureau Federation is the largest of the farm groups, with more than four million members. The National Farmers Union, the National Grange, and the National Farmers Organization are smaller farm lobbies. Agricultural groups do not always agree on policy issues. For instance, the Farm Bureau sides with agribusiness and owners of large farms, while the Farmers Union promotes the interests of smaller "family" farms.

There are also numerous specialty farm associations, including the Association of Wheat Growers, the American Soybean Association, and Associated Milk Producers. Each association acts as a separate lobby to try to obtain policies beneficial to its members' specific interest.

TABLE 9-1	**The Largest Labor Unions, 1950 and 2000** The largest labor unions today represent service and public employees; fifty years ago, the largest unions represented skilled and unskilled workers.

1950	2000
1. United Auto Workers	1. National Education Association
2. United Steel Workers	2. International Brotherhood of Teamsters
3. International Brotherhood of Teamsters	3. United Food and Commercial Workers International
4. United Brotherhood of Carpenters & Joiners	4. American Federation of State, County, & Municipal Employees
5. International Association of Machinists	5. Service Employees International

Source: U.S. Department of Labor.

Professional Groups   Most professions have lobbying associations. Among the most powerful of these groups is the American Medical Association (AMA), which, with nearly three hundred thousand members, represents about half the nation's physicians. The AMA has consistently opposed any government policy that would limit physicians' autonomy. Other professional groups include the American Bar Association and the American Association of University Professors, each of which maintains a lobbying office in Washington.

Citizens' Groups

Although economic interests are the best-organized groups, they do not have a monopoly on group activity. There are a great number and variety of other organized interests, which are referred to collectively as **citizens' groups** (or **noneconomic groups**). The members of groups in this category are drawn together not by the promise of direct economic gain but by **purposive incentives**—opportunities to promote a cause in which they believe.[4] Whether a group's goal is to protect the environment, reduce the threat of nuclear war, return prayer to the public schools, or feed the poor at home or abroad, there are citizens who are willing to participate simply because they believe the cause is a worthy one.[5]

Compared to economic groups, citizens' groups have a harder time acquiring the resources necessary for organization. These groups do not generate profits or fees as a result of economic activity. Moreover, the incentives they offer prospective members are not exclusive. As opposed to the private or individual goods provided by many economic groups, most noneconomic groups offer **collective goods** (or **public goods**) as an incentive for membership. Collective goods are, by definition, benefits that must be shared; they cannot be granted or withheld on an individual basis. The air people breathe and the national forests people visit are examples of collective goods. They are available to one and all, those who pay dues to a clean-air group or a wilderness group as well as those who do not.

citizens' (noneconomic) groups Organized interests formed by individuals drawn together by opportunities to promote a cause in which they believe but that does not provide them significant individual economic benefits.

purposive incentive An incentive to group participation based on the cause (purpose) that the group seeks to promote.

collective (public) goods Benefits that are offered by groups (usually citizens' groups) as an incentive for membership but that are nondivisible (e.g., a clean environment) and therefore are available to nonmembers as well as members of the particular group.

This 1873 lithograph illustrates the benefits of membership in the National Grange, an agricultural interest group.

The Free-Rider Problem

The shared characteristic of collective goods creates what is called the **free-rider problem:** individuals can receive the good even when they do not contribute to the group's effort. Take the case of National Public Radio (NPR). Although NPR's programs are funded primarily through listeners' donations, those who do not contribute can hear the programs. The noncontributors are free riders: they receive the benefit without paying any of the costs of providing it. About 90 percent of regular listeners to NPR do not contribute to their local station.

As economist Mancur Olson noted, it is not rational, in a purely economic sense, for individuals to contribute to a group when they can obtain its benefit without paying for it.[6] Moreover, the dues paid by any single member are too small to affect the group's success one way or another. Why pay dues to an environmental group when any improvements in the air, water, or wildlife from its lobbying efforts are available to everyone and when one's individual contribution is too small to make a real difference? Although many people do join such groups anyway, there is no doubt that the free-rider problem is a reason why citizens' groups are less highly organized than economic groups.

Citizens' groups try to surmount the free-rider problem by creating individual benefits, akin to those offered by economic groups, to make membership more attractive. Organizational newsletters and social activities are among the individual benefits that some citizens' groups offer as an incentive to membership. Computer-assisted direct mail has also helped citizens' groups attract members. Group organizers buy mailing lists and flood the mails with computer-typed "personal" letters asking recipients to pay a small annual membership fee. For some individuals, a fee of $25 to $50 annually represents no great sacrifice and offers the momentary satisfaction of supporting a cause in which they believe. Until the computer era, citizens' groups had great difficulty identifying and contacting potential members, which is a reason why the number of such groups was so much smaller in the past than is true today.

The Internet has also been a boon to citizens' groups. Nearly every such group of any size has its own website and e-mail list. One of the most successful citizen lobbying efforts in history was conducted largely through the Internet: a global campaign that succeeded in getting one hundred countries to sign an international treaty banning the use of land mines. Its organizer, Jody Williams, linked activists and groups throughout the world and received the Nobel Peace Prize for her work. MoveOn is another example of the Internet's organizing capacity. MoveOn was started by a handful of liberal activists working out of a garage. By 2004, they had created an Internet network

free-rider problem The situation in which the benefits offered by a group to its members are also available to nonmembers. The incentive to join the group and to promote its cause is reduced because nonmembers (free riders) receive the benefits (e.g., a cleaner environment) without having to pay any of the group's costs.

Simulation
www.mhhe.com/pattersontad7

The Internet has made it easier for citizens' groups to organize and increase their membership. One of the most successful examples is MoveOn. It was founded by a small group of liberal activists, including Wes Boyd and Joan Blades, shown here standing outside their home in California.

that linked hundreds of thousands of citizens who could be mobilized in support of liberal causes.

On the whole, however, the organizational advantages rest with economic groups. In nearly every respect, they have the upper hand over citizens' groups (see Table 9–2).

Types of Citizens' Groups

Most citizens' groups are of three general types: public-interest groups, single-issue groups, and ideological groups.

Public-Interest Groups   Public-interest groups are those that claim to represent the broad interests of society as a whole. Despite their label, public-interest groups are not led by people elected by the public at large, and the issues they target are ones of their own choosing, not the public's. Moreover, people often disagree on what constitutes "the public interest," which raises the issue of whether any particular viewpoint can truly be said to represent that interest. Nevertheless, there is a basis for distinguishing the so-called public-interest groups from economic groups: the latter seek direct material benefits for their members, while the former seek benefits that are less tangible and more broadly shared. For example, the National Association of Manufacturers, an economic group, seeks policies favorable to large corporations, while the League of Women Voters, a public-interest group, seeks policies—such as simplified voter registration—that can benefit the public in general.

More than half of the currently active public-interest groups were established after 1960. One of these organizations is Common Cause, which has more than two hundred thousand members and describes itself as "a national citizens' lobby"; it concentrates on political reform in such areas as campaign finance.

TABLE 9–2	Advantages and Disadvantages Held by Economic and Citizens' Groups Compared with economic groups, citizens' groups have fewer advantages and more disadvantages.

ECONOMIC GROUPS	CITIZENS' GROUPS
Advantages	*Advantages*
Economic activity provides the organization with the resources necessary for political action.	Members are likely to support leaders' political efforts because they joined the group in order to influence policy.
Individuals are encouraged to join the group because of economic benefits they individually receive (e.g., wages).	*Disadvantages*
Disadvantages	The group has to raise funds, especially for its political activities.
Persons within the group may not support leaders' political efforts because they did not join the group for political reasons.	Potential members may choose not to join the group because they get collective benefits even if they do not join (the free-rider problem).

Environmental activists protest against automobile and truck emissions, which are a leading cause of air pollution. Although environmental groups have been quite successful in attracting public support, they still confront the so-called free-rider problem—the fact that people will gain the benefit of a group's effort even if they do not contribute to it.

Single-Issue Groups   A single-issue group is organized to influence policy in just one area. Notable current examples are the National Rifle Association and various right-to-life and pro-choice groups that have formed around the issue of abortion. The number of single-issue groups has risen sharply in the past three decades, and they now pressure government on almost every conceivable issue, from nuclear arms to day care centers to drug abuse.

Environmental groups are sometimes classified as public-interest groups, but they may also be considered single-issue organizations in that most of them seek to influence public policy in a specific area, such as pollution reduction, wilderness preservation, or wildlife protection. The Sierra Club is one of the oldest environmental groups. It was formed in the 1890s to promote the preservation of scenic areas. Also prominent are the National Audubon Society, the Wilderness Society, the Environmental Defense Fund, Greenpeace U.S.A., and the Izaak Walton League. Since 1960, membership in environmental groups has more than tripled as a result of the public's increased concern about the quality of the environment.[7]

Ideological Groups   Single-issue groups have a narrowly focused policy agenda. In contrast, ideological groups have a broad agenda that derives from a philosophical or moral position. An example is the Christian Coalition of America, which was organized to restore "Christian values" to American life and politics. The group has addressed a wide range of issues, including school prayer, law and order, abortion, and television programming. Ideological groups on both the left and the right have increased substantially in number since the 1960s.

The Rev. Pat Robertson (standing at the microphones) founded the Christian Coalition of America, an ideological group. The Christian Coalition's website contains the phrase "America's Leading Grassroots Organization Protecting Our Godly Heritage."

Groups such as the National Organization for Women (NOW) and the National Association for the Advancement of Colored People (NAACP) can also be generally classified as ideological groups. Although they represent particular demographic groups, they do so across a wide range of issues. For example, NOW addresses issues that range from jobs to reproduction to political representation.

A Special Category of Interest Group: Governments

While the vast majority of organized interests in the United States represent private concerns, a growing number of interest groups represent governments, both foreign and subnational.

The U.S. federal government makes policies that directly affect the economic development, political stability, and security of nations throughout the world. Arms sales, foreign aid, immigration, and import restrictions and other trade practices have a great impact on foreign nations. For this reason, most foreign nations supplement the political efforts made through their embassies with the services of paid lobbyists in Washington.[8] Foreign governments are prohibited from engaging in certain lobbying activities, including contributions to U.S. election campaigns.

States, cities, and other governmental units within the United States also lobby heavily. Most major cities and two-thirds of the states have at least one Washington lobbyist. Lobbying also occurs through groups such as the Council of State Governments, the National Governors Conference, the National Association of Counties, the National League of Cities, and the U.S. Conference of Mayors. These organizations sometimes play a large role in policy debates.[9] For example, as Congress was preparing in 2005 to renew and amend the USA Patriot Act that had gone into effect four years earlier, the National Governors Conference and the U.S. Conference of Mayors lobbied to ensure that the changes reflected state and local experiences with the legislation.

Citizenship

Getting Involved, Making a Difference

Groups and Social Capital

When the Frenchman Alexis de Tocqueville came to the United States in the 1830s, he marveled at the abundance of civic and political groups and concluded that they were the underlying strength of American democracy. Little has happened in the nearly two centuries since to change this conclusion. Recent research, in fact, confirms it. In his pioneering *Making Democracy Work* (1993), Harvard University's Robert Putnam found that the more abundant a society's voluntary associations are, the more likely it is that the society's institutions will act in the public interest. Putnam uses the term *civic community* to describe a society in which voluntary associations flourish.

Citizens *should* participate in voluntary groups. By doing so, they contribute to improvements in their community, whether it be a college campus, a town, a state, or the nation. Moreover, the relationships that develop among people as a result of civic participation enable individuals to better understand the opinions and values of others.

These benefits are substantial. Democratic theorists such as Rousseau, Jefferson, Mill, and Dewey argued that communities should be constructed in ways that encourage the individual to participate as fully as possible in civic affairs. The theorists' assumption was that citizens "invest" in a community when they are an integral part of it. The theorists also assumed that participation expands the individual's vision, giving him or her the capacity, in Rousseau's words, for "seeing things in general." Said differently, civic participation enables individuals to surmount a narrowly self-interested view of what is best for society.

Putnam argues that America has undergone a long-term decline in its *social capital* (the sum of its civic relationships). In *Bowling Alone* (2000), Putnam presents evidence that indicates Americans are now less involved in community groups and other forms of social interaction. He attributes the change to television and other factors that produce social isolation. Not all scholars agree with Putnam's view of the trend (some indicators point toward a rise in certain types of group membership), but no one has challenged his assumption about the importance of maintaining high levels of civic participation. The relationships fostered by this participation are a foundation of democratic life. And no democratic theorist has suggested that there can be "too much" civic participation. The higher the level of participation, the firmer the democratic base.

INSIDE LOBBYING: SEEKING INFLUENCE THROUGH OFFICIAL CONTACTS

Modern government provides a supportive environment for interest groups. First, modern government is involved in so many issues—business regulation, income maintenance, urban renewal, cancer research, and energy development, to name only a few—that hardly any interest in society could fail to benefit significantly from having influence over federal policies or programs.

Second, modern government is oriented toward action. Officials are inclined to respond to problems rather than let problems linger. For example, when forest fires raged out of control in California and other western states in 2004 and destroyed property worth millions, Washington granted immediate assistance to residents who had incurred losses and cleanup costs.

Groups seek support through **lobbying,** a term that refers broadly to efforts by groups to influence public policy through contact with public officials. The two main lobbying strategies have been labeled "inside lobbying" and "outside lobbying."[10] Each strategy involves communication between public officials and group lobbyists, but the strategies differ in what is communicated and who does the communicating. This section discusses **inside lobbying,** which is based on group efforts to develop and maintain close ("inside") contacts with policymakers. (Outside lobbying is described in the next section.)

Acquiring Access to Officials

Inside lobbying is designed to give a group direct access to officials in order to influence their decisions. Access is not the same as influence, which is the capacity to affect policy decisions. But access is a critical first step in the influence process.[11]

Lobbying once depended significantly on tangible inducements, sometimes including indirect or even outright bribes. This old form of lobbying survives, but modern lobbying generally involves subtler and more sophisticated methods than providing money or personal favors to officials. It focuses on supplying officials with information and indications of group strength that will persuade them to adopt the group's perspective.[12]

For the most part, inside lobbying is directed at policymakers who are inclined to support the group rather than at those who have opposed it in the past. This tendency reflects both the difficulty of persuading opponents to change long-held views and the advantage of having trusted allies who will work actively to promote the group's policy positions. Thus, union lobbyists work mainly with pro-labor officeholders, just as corporate lobbyists work mainly with policymakers who support business interests.

Money is the basic ingredient of inside lobbying efforts. The American Petroleum Institute, for example, with its abundant financial resources, can afford a downtown Washington office staffed by lobbyists, petroleum experts, and public relations specialists who help the oil companies maintain access to and influence with legislative and executive leaders.[13] Many groups spend $1 million or more annually on lobbying. Other groups survive on much less, but it is hard to run an effective lobbying effort on less than $100,000 a year. Given the costs of maintaining a Washington lobby, the domination by corporations and trade associations is understandable. They have the money to retain high-priced lobbyists, while many other interests do not.

The targets of inside lobbying are officials of all three government branches—legislative, executive, and judicial.

Inside lobbying offers groups a chance to make their policy views known. Access to public officials is critical to the inside-lobbying strategy.

lobbying The process by which interest-group members or lobbyists attempt to influence public policy through contacts with public officials.

inside lobbying Direct communication between organized interests and policymakers, which is based on the assumed value of close ("inside") contacts with policymakers.

Lobbying Congress

The benefits of a close relationship with members of Congress are substantial. With support in Congress, a group can obtain the legislative help it needs to achieve its policy goals. By the same token, members of Congress also gain from

The Revolving Door: Officials and Lobbyists

As government has grown increasingly complex, people in Washington who know how the system works have become increasingly important actors. Not surprisingly, a revolving door has developed between positions in government and positions in lobbying groups. For example, Representative Bob Livingston, chair of the House Appropriations Committee, resigned from Congress in 1999 and soon thereafter started the Livingston Group, which lobbies Congress on behalf of business firms.

High-level officials and top lobbyists are familiar with the policy process and the issues within their sphere of responsibility. These skills are easily transferable from one type of job to the other.

The revolving door has obvious benefits. Policymakers need to be knowledgeable about public policy problems and need to have access to groups affected by these problems. The complexity of many issues today is such that it is impossible to make good policy decisions without detailed information about them. Moreover, because the U.S. governing system itself is complex—a result of its size and the division of powers—it is difficult for individuals to accomplish much of anything unless they know how to work the system.

Nevertheless, the revolving door between government and interest groups can result in abuses of power. When former lobbyists take a government position, they can do special favors for the groups they once represented. When former government officials take a lobbying post, they can use their contacts within government to obtain favorable treatment for the groups they now represent. To guard against unwarranted influence, there are some restrictions on those individuals who pass through the revolving door. The 1978 Ethics in Government Act, for example, prohibits former executive branch employees from lobbying their former agency for a year after leaving it and for two years on any matter that came within the employee's area of responsibility. There is only a one-year limit on former members of Congress. Moreover, they have the unique right to go directly onto the floor of the House or Senate to speak with current members. Former members usually represent groups with which they had close ties while they were in office.

The news media and public interest groups such as Congress Watch have taken on responsibility for guarding the revolving door. When they see a lobbyist-official relationship that has become too cozy, they try to bring it into public view. However, much of what transpires between lobbyists and officials takes place in private. What do you think should be done to ensure that the revolving door works to the public's benefit?

working closely with lobbyists. The volume of legislation facing Congress is enormous, and members rely on trusted lobbyists to identify bills that deserve their attention and support. When Republican lawmakers took control of Congress in 1995, they invited corporate lobbyists to participate directly in drafting legislation affecting business. Congressional Democrats complained loudly, but Republicans said they were merely getting help from those who best understood business's needs and accused Democrats of having engaged in the same practice with organized labor when they were in power.

Lobbyists' effectiveness with members of Congress depends in part on their reputation for fair play. If a group is adamant about getting everything it wants—"my way or no way"—it is likely to end up with nothing. Lobbyists are also expected to play it straight. Said one congressman: "If any [lobbyist] gives me false or misleading information, that's it—I'll never see him again."[14] Arm-twisting is another unacceptable practice. During the debate over the North American Free Trade Agreement in 1993, the AFL-CIO threatened retaliation against congressional Democrats who supported the legislation. The backlash from these Democrats was so intense that the union backed down on its threat. The safe lobbying strategy is the aboveboard approach: provide information, rely on longtime allies among members of Congress, and push steadily but not too aggressively for legislative goals.

Lobbying Executive Agencies

As the scope of the federal government has expanded, lobbying of the executive branch has increased in importance. Bureaucrats make key administrative decisions and develop policy initiatives that the legislative branch later makes into law. By working closely with executive agencies, groups can influence policy decisions at the implementation and initiation stages. In return, groups assist agencies by providing information and support when their programs are reviewed by Congress and the president.

Nowhere is the link between groups and the bureaucracy more evident than in the regulatory agencies that oversee the nation's business sectors. For example, the Federal Communications Commission (FCC), which regulates the nation's broadcasters, uses information provided by broadcast organizations to decide many of the policies governing their activities. The FCC is sometimes cited as an example of agency capture. The capture theory suggests that regulatory agencies pass through a series of phases that constitute a life cycle. Early in an agency's existence, it regulates an industry on the public's behalf, but as the agency matures, its vigor declines until at best it protects the status quo and at worst it falls captive to the very industry it is supposed to regulate. In 2003, for example, media corporations successfully lobbied the FCC to issue a ruling that would increase the number of media outlets in a community that a single firm could own. Citizen groups and many members of Congress claimed the ruling would only enrich the media corporations. With less competition, news outlets would have less incentive to provide citizens with quality local news.

Research has shown that the capture theory describes only some agencies —and then only some of the time.[15] Agencies selectively cooperate with or oppose interest groups, depending on which strategy better suits agency purposes.[16] Agency officials are aware that they can lose support in Congress, which controls agency funding and program authorization, if they show too much favoritism toward an interest group.[17]

Lobbying the Courts

Court rulings in areas such as education and civil rights have made interest groups recognize that the judiciary too can help them reach their goals.[18] Interest groups have several judicial lobbying options, including efforts to influence the selection of federal judges. Right-to-life groups have pressured Republican administrations to make opposition to abortion a prerequisite for nomination to the federal bench. Democratic administrations have in turn faced pressure from pro-choice groups in their judicial nominations.

Groups rely on lawsuits in their efforts to influence the courts. For some organizations, such as the American Civil Liberties Union (ACLU), legal action is the primary means of lobbying government. The ACLU often takes on unpopular causes, such as the free speech rights of fringe groups. Such causes have no chance of success in legislative bodies but may prevail in a courtroom.

As interest groups increasingly resort to legal action, they often find themselves facing one another in court. Environmental litigation groups such as the Sierra Club Legal Defense Club, the Environmental Defense Fund, and the Natural Resources Defense Council have frequently sued oil, timber, and mining corporations.

Webs of Influence: Groups in the Policy Process

Lobbying efforts provide an incomplete picture of how groups obtain influence. To get a fuller picture, it is necessary to also consider two policy processes—iron triangles and issue networks—in which many groups are enmeshed.

Iron Triangles

iron triangle A small and informal but relatively stable group of well-positioned legislators, executives, and lobbyists who seek to promote policies beneficial to a particular interest.

An **iron triangle** consists of a small and informal but relatively stable set of bureaucrats, legislators, and lobbyists who seek to develop policies beneficial to a particular interest.[19] The three "corners" of one such triangle are the Department of Veterans Affairs (bureaucrats), the veterans' affairs committees of Congress (legislators), and veterans' groups such as the American Legion and the Veterans of Foreign Wars (lobbyists). Together they determine many of the policies affecting veterans. Of course, the support of other players, including the president and a majority in Congress, is needed to enact programs helpful to veterans. However, these players often defer to the policy views of the veterans' triangle. Its members know the problems and policy needs of veterans.

A group in an iron triangle has an inside track to those legislators and bureaucrats who are in the strongest position to help its cause. And because it has something of value to offer each of them, the relationships tend to be ironclad. The group provides lobbying support for the agency's funding and programs and makes campaign contributions to its congressional allies. Agricultural groups, for example, contribute millions of dollars to congressional candidates in each election. Most of this money is given to incumbents, and most of these contributions go to the campaigns of members of the House and Senate agriculture committees. Figure 9–1 summarizes the benefits that flow to each member of an iron triangle.

Issue Networks

issue network An informal and relatively open network of public officials and lobbyists who have a common interest in a given area and who are brought together by a proposed policy in that area. Unlike an iron triangle, an issue network disbands after the issue is resolved.

Iron triangles represent the pattern of influence in only certain policy areas and are less common now than in the past. A more frequent pattern of influence today is the **issue network,** which is an informal grouping of officials, lobbyists, and policy specialists (the "network") who are brought together temporarily by their shared interest in a particular policy problem (the "issue").

Issue networks are a result of the increasing complexity of policy problems. Participants must have specialized knowledge of the issue at hand in order to participate effectively. Thus, unlike iron triangles, where a participant's position

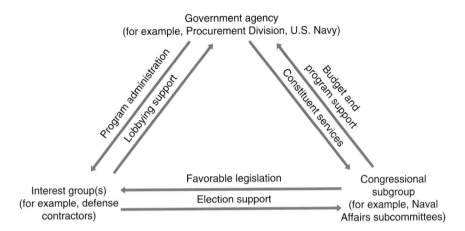

Figure 9–1

How an Iron Triangle Benefits its Participants

An iron triangle works to the advantage of each of its participants—an interest group, a congressional subgroup, and a government agency.

is everything, an issue network is built around specialized interests and information. On any given issue, the participants might come from a variety of executive agencies, congressional committees, interest groups, and institutions such as universities or think tanks. And, compared to iron triangles, issue networks are less stable. As the issue develops, new participants may join the debate and old ones drop out. Once the issue is resolved, the network disbands.[20]

An example of an issue network is the set of participants who would come together over the issue of whether a large tract of old forest should be opened to logging. A few decades ago, that issue would have been settled in an iron triangle consisting of the timber companies, the U.S. Forest Service, and relevant members of the House and Senate agriculture committees. But as forestlands have diminished and environmental concerns have grown, such issues can no longer be contained within the cozy confines of an iron triangle. Today, an issue network would form that included logging interests, the U.S. Forest Service, House and Senate agriculture committee members, research scientists, and representatives of environmental groups, the housing industry, and animal-rights groups. Unlike the old iron triangle, which was confined to like-minded interests, this issue network would include opposing interests (for example, the loggers and the environmentalists). And unlike an iron triangle, the issue network would dissolve once the issue was resolved, and the various parties would go their separate ways.

Issue networks, then, differ substantially from iron triangles. In an iron triangle, a common interest brings the participants together in a stable, long-lasting, and mutually beneficial relationship. In an issue network, an immediate issue brings the participants together in a temporary network that is based on their ability to address the issue in a sophisticated way and where they play out their separate interests before disbanding once the issue is settled.

Iron triangles and issue networks, however, do have one thing in common: they are arenas in which organized interests operate. The interests of the general public may be taken into account in these webs of influence, but the interests of the participating groups are paramount.

The policy issues surrounding the technological revolution are extraordinarily complex, and issue networks tend to form when policy issues of this type arise.

OUTSIDE LOBBYING: SEEKING INFLUENCE THROUGH PUBLIC PRESSURE

Although an interest group may rely solely on inside lobbying, this approach is not likely to be successful unless the group can demonstrate convincingly that its concerns reflect those of a vital constituency. Accordingly, groups make use of constituency connections when it is advantageous for them to do so. They engage in **outside lobbying,** which involves bringing public ("outside") pressure to bear on policymakers (see Table 9–3).[21]

outside lobbying A form of lobbying in which an interest group seeks to use public pressure as a means of influencing officials.

grassroots lobbying A form of lobbying designed to persuade officials that a group's policy position has strong constituent support.

Constituency Advocacy: Grassroots Lobbying

One form of outside pressure is **grassroots lobbying**—that is, pressure designed to convince government officials that a group's policy position has popular support.

No group illustrates grassroots lobbying better than AARP (American Association of Retired Persons). With more than thirty million members and a staff of sixteen hundred, AARP is a powerful lobby on retirement issues such as social security and Medicare. When major legislation affecting retirees is pending, AARP swings into action. Congress receives more mail from members of AARP than it does from members of any other group.[22] AARP's support was critical to passage in 2003 of a controversial prescription drug program for the elderly. Until AARP's last-minute endorsement, the program was headed for a narrow defeat in Congress.

As with other forms of lobbying, the precise impact of grassroots campaigns is often difficult to assess. Some members of Congress downplay its influence, but all congressional offices monitor letters and phone calls as a way of tracking constituents' opinions.

TABLE 9-3	Tactics Used in Inside and Outside Lobbying Strategies
	Inside and outside lobbying are based on different tactics.

INSIDE LOBBYING	OUTSIDE LOBBYING
Developing contacts with legislators and executives	Encouraging group members to write or phone their representatives in Congress
Providing information and policy proposals to key officials	Seeking favorable coverage by news media
Forming coalitions with other groups	Encouraging members to support particular candidates in elections
	Targeting group resources on key election races
	Making PAC contributions to candidates

Electoral Action: Votes and PAC Money

An "outside" strategy can also include election campaigns. "Reward your friends and punish your enemies" is a political adage that loosely describes how interest groups view elections. Organized groups work to elect their supporters and defeat their opponents. The possibility of electoral opposition from a powerful group can keep an officeholder from openly obstructing the group's goals. For example, opposition from the three-million-member National Rifle Association is a major reason why the United States has lagged behind other Western societies in its handgun control laws, despite polls that show most Americans favor such laws.

Grassroots lobbying is based on pressure from constituents. These farmers traveled to Washington to protest the low prices they were getting for agricultural goods.

The principal way interest groups try to gain influence through elections is by contributing money to candidates' campaigns. As one lobbyist said, "Talking to politicians is fine, but with a little money they hear you better."[23] Members of Congress sometimes get into hot water by listening too closely to the groups that fund their campaigns. When the Enron Corporation collapsed into bankruptcy in 2002, depleting the retirement accounts of its employees in the process, its deep connections in Washington quickly became known. In the previous decade, Enron and its top officials had contributed $6 million in campaign funds. Some members of Congress found themselves in the embarrassing position of holding investigative hearings on a company that they had consulted on policy issues and from which they had taken campaign money.

Have Interest Groups Hijacked the Initiative Process?

The initiative was pioneered by the Progressives of the early twentieth century, who saw it as a way to wrest power from the political bosses and corporate robber barons and place it in the hands of ordinary citizens. Twenty-four states allow the initiative, which requires the gathering of a sufficient number of citizens' signatures to place a legislative proposal (initiative) on the ballot. If a majority of voters approve it, the initiative becomes law, just as if it had been enacted by the legislature itself. In recent years, however, the initiative process has been used by interest groups to advance their policy agendas. These groups have the money to pay for the signature-gathering phase and to conduct a campaign for enactment of the initiative. To some observers, this tendency has corrupted the initiative process. Other observers claim that the initiative remains a bulwark of citizen-based politics.

Yes: The initiative process came to the United States about 100 years ago, imported from Switzerland by populists and progressives worried about the influence of money on legislatures. The purpose was twofold: one, break the power of interest groups, and two, empower people to write the laws themselves on the ballot. The system worked pretty well [for a time]; it produced a great deal of progressive legislation. . . . [Today, however, the initiative process is] being driven very much by money. With their own political agendas, interest groups of all kinds have latched onto this device as a way of writing the law the way they would like it written without having to go through all the hoops of the normal governmental process. . . . I think it's particularly ironic that a device that was introduced into this country as a way of fighting special interest influence and the power of money now has been largely taken over by those same interest groups and by very wealthy millionaires who have the resources that it now takes to get an initiative on the ballot and to fight these campaigns to get them passed or defeated in the states.

—*David S. Broder, author and* Washington Post *columnist*

No: Many of the concerns about initiatives seem unfounded, and so addressing them in turn seems unfounded as well. Political scientists have found that, whereas 40 percent of all initiatives on the California ballot from 1986 to 1996 passed, only 14 percent of initiatives promoted by special interests passed. Many people are predisposed to believe that money influences elections. But when it comes to initiative campaigns, the proof does not exist. In an era of growing government, the people need a mechanism to check government. Many claim that the people already have that check—elections. But that is a fallacy. Most people who support the initiative process and who use the process use it as a tool for addressing single issues. They want for the most part to keep a particular elected official, and so voting that official out of office for failing to deal with one specific issue is considered an extreme step, far more extreme than allowing the people to make laws occasionally. . . . Representative government and the initiative process are perfect complements to each other—two imperfect systems of government each designed to help the people and both carefully constructed to balance the weaknesses of one with the strengths of the other.

—*M. Dane Waters, president,* The Initiative & Referendum Institute

political action committee (PAC) The organization through which an interest group raises and distributes funds for election purposes. By law, the funds must be raised through voluntary contributions.

    A group's election contributions are given through its **political action committee (PAC).** A group cannot give organizational funds (such as corporate profits or union dues) to candidates, but through its PAC, a group can raise money for election campaigns by soliciting voluntary contributions from members or employees. A PAC is legally limited in the amount it can contribute to the campaign of a candidate for federal office. The ceiling is $10,000 per candidate—$5,000 in the primary campaign and $5,000 in the general election campaign; there is no legal limit on the number of candidates a PAC can sup-

The Houston headquarters of the now-bankrupt Enron Corporation. Until its collapse due to illegal business practices, Enron was one of the nation's largest corporations and one of the most active lobbying groups in Washington.

port. These financial limits do not apply to candidates for state and local office. Their campaigns are regulated by state laws, and many states allow PACs to make unlimited campaign contributions.

PACs increased eightfold after favorable changes were made in campaign finance laws in 1974 (see Figure 9–2). There are now more than four thousand PACs, and PAC contributions account for roughly a third of total contributions to congressional campaigns. Their role is less significant in presidential campaigns, which are larger in scale and publicly funded in part and therefore are less dependent on PAC contributions.

PACs contribute more than five times as much money to incumbents as to their challengers. PACs are well aware of the fact that incumbents are likely to win and thus to remain in a position to make policy. One PAC director, expressing a common view, said, "We always stick with the incumbent when we agree with them both."[24]

The tendency of PACs to back incumbents has to some extent blurred longstanding partisan divisions in campaign funding. Business interests are especially pragmatic. Although they tend to favor Republican candidates, they are reluctant to anger Democratic incumbents. The result is that Democratic incumbents, particularly in House races, have received substantial support over the years from business-related PACs.[25] Other PACs, of course, are less pragmatic. The Christian Moral Government Fund, for example, backs only candidates who take conservative stands on issues such as school prayer and abortion.

More than 40 percent of all PACs are associated with corporations (see Figure 9–3). Examples include the Ford Motor Company Civic Action Fund, the Sun Oil Company Political Action Committee (Sunpac), and the Coca-Cola

Figure 9–2

Growth in the Number of PACs

The number of PACs began to increase sharply after campaign finance reforms were enacted in the early 1970s.

Source: Federal Election Commission, 2004.

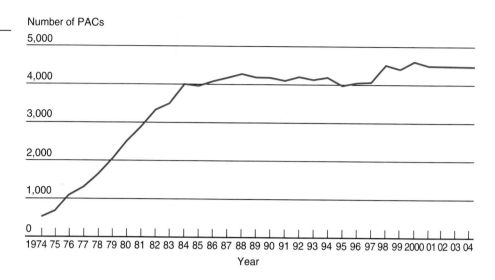

Figure 9–3

Percentage of PACs by Category

Most PACs represent business. Corporate and trade association PACs make up 65 percent of the total.

Source: Federal Election Commission, 2004.

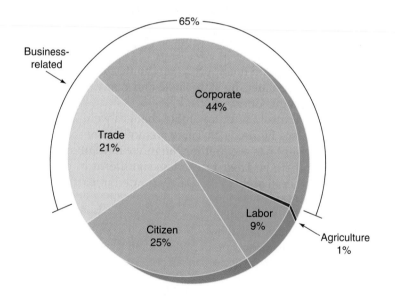

PAC. The next largest group of PACs consists of those linked to citizens' groups (that is, public-interest, single-issue, and ideological groups), such as the liberal People for the American Way and the conservative National Conservative Political Action Committee (NCPAC). Ranking third are PACs tied to trade and professional associations, such as AMPAC (American Medical Association) and R-PAC (National Association of Realtors). Labor unions, once the major source of group contributions, now rank fourth.

Advocates of PACs claim that groups have a right to be heard, which includes the right to express themselves with money. Advocates also say that a campaign finance system based on pooled contributions by individuals is superior to one in which candidates rely on a few wealthy donors.[26]

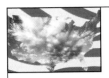

STATES IN THE NATION

Limits on PAC Contributions

Elections of state officials (such as governors and state legislators) are regulated by state law rather than by federal law. In some states, there is no law limiting how much money PACs can contribute to a candidate. Of the states that limit PAC contributions, only New York and Nevada allow contributions in excess of $10,000.

Q. Why might states located to the west of the Mississippi River (which runs down the eastern borders of Minnesota, Iowa, Missouri, Arkansas, and Louisiana) place fewer limits on PAC contributions than other states?

A. A possible explanation is that the political cultures of the westernmost states, as a result of their frontier heritage, are less accepting of government restraints on economic and political activity.

PAC contribution limits

$2,000 or less

More than $2,000 but not unlimited

Unlimited

Source: Federal Elections Commission.

Critics argue, however, that PACs give interest groups altogether too much influence with public officials.[27] Opposition to PACs has increased in recent years as citizens have come to believe that interest groups have gained too much power over public policy. Although members of Congress deny that they are unduly influenced, there has been a growing sentiment even within Congress to place some restrictions on PACs. Agreement on the changes, however, has been difficult to achieve because Democrats and Republicans have different ideas about how to reform the process and also because many incumbents are unwilling to support any change that would reduce the advantage they derive from the present system.

THE GROUP SYSTEM: INDISPENSABLE BUT BIASED

As noted in the chapter's introduction, pluralist theory holds that organized groups are a source of sound governance. On one level, this claim is beyond dispute. Without groups to carry their message, most of society's interests would find it difficult to get government's attention and support. Yet the issue of representation is also a question of whether all interests in society are fairly represented through the group system, and here the pluralist argument is less compelling.

The Contribution of Groups to Self-Government: Pluralism

Group activity is an essential part of self-government. A major obstacle to popular sovereignty is the difficulty that public officials encounter in trying to discover what the people want from government. To discern their wishes, lawmakers consult public opinion polls, meet with constituents, and assess election results. The activities of organized groups are also a clue to what people are seeking. On any given issue, the policy positions that are likely to be expressed most clearly and intensely are those held by organized interests.

Moreover, government does not exist simply to serve majority interests. The fact that most people are not retirees or labor union members or farmers or college students or Hispanics does not mean that the concerns of such "minorities" are unworthy of attention. And what better instrument exists for promoting their interests than organizations formed by them?

Some pluralists even question the usefulness of terms such as *the common good* and *the collective interest*. If people disagree on society's goals and priorities, as they always do, how can it be said that people have a "common" or "collective" interest? As an alternative, pluralists contend that, because society has so many interests, the common good ultimately is best served by a process that enables a great many interests to gain favorable policies. Thus, if manufacturing interests prevail on one issue, environmentalists on another, farmers on a third, minorities on a fourth, and so on until many interests are served, the collective interest of society will have been promoted.[28]

Finally, interest groups often take up issues that are neglected by the party system. Party leaders typically shy from issues, such as affirmative action and abortion, on which the party's voters disagree. Such issues would get less notice if not for the groups that promote them. And when groups succeed in drawing attention to these issues, the parties are nearly compelled to address them as well. In this sense, as political scientist Jack Walker noted, the party and group systems "are complementary and together constitute a more responsive and adaptive system than either would be if they somehow operated on their own."[29]

Sometimes the interests of a group clearly diverge from majority opinion, as when the National Association of Auto Dealers lobbied successfully against legislation that would have required automobile dealers to inform customers about any defects in used cars.

Flaws in Pluralism: Interest-Group Liberalism and Economic Bias

Although pluralist theory includes some compelling arguments, it also has questionable aspects. Political scientist Theodore Lowi argues that there is no concept of society's collective interest in a system that gives special interests the ability to determine the policies affecting them.[30] The basis of decision in such cases is not majority (collective) rule but minority (special-interest) rule.

It is seldom safe to assume that what most people would favor is what a special-interest group wants. Consider the case of the federal law that required auto dealers to list the known defects of used cars on window stickers. The law was repealed after an extensive lobbying campaign financed by contributions of more than $1 million by the National Association of Automobile Dealers to the reelection campaigns of members of Congress.

Lowi uses the term **interest-group liberalism** to describe the tendency of officials to support the policy demands of the interest group or groups that have a special stake in a policy. In practical terms, it is the group as much as the government that decides policy. The adverse effects include an inefficient use of society's resources: groups get what they want, whether or not their priorities match those of society as a whole.

Another flaw in the pluralist argument resides in its claim that the group system is representative. Pluralists recognize that better-organized interests have more influence but argue that the group process is relatively open and that few interests are at a serious disadvantage. These claims contain an element of truth, but they are far from the complete truth.

As this chapter has pointed out, organization is a political resource that is distributed unequally across society. Economic interests, particularly

interest-group liberalism The tendency of public officials to support the policy demands of self-interested groups (as opposed to judging policy demands according to whether they serve a larger conception of "the public interest").

Liberty, Equality & Self-Government

What's Your Opinion?

Interest Groups

Rarely is the tension between liberty and equality more evident than in the activities of interest groups. "Liberty is to faction what air is to fire," wrote James Madison in *Federalist* No. 10. Madison was lamenting the self-interested behavior of factions or, as they are called today, interest groups. Yet Madison recognized that the only way to suppress this behavior was to destroy the liberty that allows people to organize.

Interest groups tend to strengthen the already powerful and thus contribute to political inequality. As political scientist E. E. Schattschneider said, the group system "sings with a strong upper-class bias."

Numerous efforts have been made to harness the power of groups without infringing on Americans' rights of free expression, assembly, and petition. Laws have been enacted that require lobbyists to register, report their lobbying expenditures, and identify the issues on which they are working. Other laws restrict group contributions to candidates for public office. Yet nothing in the end seems to be all that effective in harnessing the self-interested actions of groups. Is there an answer to "Madison's dilemma"? Or are the excesses of group politics simply one of the costs of living in a free society?

corporations, are the most highly organized, and some analysts argue that group politics works chiefly to the advantage of business. Of course, economic groups do not dominate everything, nor do they act unchecked. Many of the public interest groups formed since the 1960s were deliberately created as a check against the influence of corporate lobbies.[31] Activist government has also brought the group system into closer balance; the government's poverty programs have spawned groups that act to protect these programs. Nevertheless, nearly two-thirds of all lobbying groups in Washington are business-related. The interest-group system is biased toward America's economically oriented groups, particularly its corporations.

The group system is also slanted toward the interests of upper-middle-class Americans. Studies indicate that individuals of higher socioeconomic status are disproportionately represented among group members and even more so among group leaders. Educated and affluent Americans have the money, communication skills, and savvy to participate effectively in special-interest politics. The poor, minorities, women, and the young are greatly underrepresented in the group politics system. A lack of organization does not ensure an interest's failure, just as the existence of organization does not guarantee success. However, organized interests are obviously in a better position to promote their views.

The business and class bias of the group system is especially significant because the most highly organized interests are, in a sense, those least in need of political clout. Corporations and affluent citizens already control the largest share of society's resources. The group system magnifies their power.

A Madisonian Dilemma

James Madison recognized the dilemma inherent in group activity. Although he worried that interest groups would have too much political control, he realized that a free society is obliged to permit the advocacy of self-interest. Unless people can promote the separate opinions that stem from differences in their talents, needs, values, and possessions, they do not have liberty.

Ironically, Madison's constitutional solution to the problem of factions has become part of the problem. The American system of checks and balances, with a separation of powers at its core, was designed primarily to prevent a majority faction from trampling on the interests of smaller groups. This same system, however, makes it relatively easy for minority factions—or, as they are called today, special-interest groups—to gain government support. If they can get the backing of even a small number of well-placed policymakers, as in the case of iron triangles, they are likely to get many of the benefits they seek. Because of the system's division of power, they have numerous points at which to exert influence. Often, they need only to find an ally in one place, whether that be a congressional committee or an executive agency or a federal court, to get at least some of what they seek. And once they obtain a government benefit, it is likely to persist. Benefits are hard to eliminate because concerted action by the executive branch and both houses of Congress is usually required. If a group has strong support in even a single institution, it can usually fend off attempts to terminate its benefits. Such support ordinarily is easy to acquire, because the group has resources—information, money, and votes—that officeholders want. (Chapters 11 and 13 discuss further the issue of interest-group power.)

Summary Self-Test
www.mhhe.com/pattersontad7

A political interest group is composed of a set of individuals organized to promote a shared political concern. Most interest groups owe their existence to factors other than politics. These groups form for economic reasons, such as the pursuit of profit, and maintain themselves by making profits (in the case of corporations) or by providing their members with private goods, such as jobs and wages. Economic groups include corporations, trade associations, labor unions, farm organizations, and professional associations. Collectively, economic groups are by far the largest set of organized interests. The group system tends to favor interests that are already economically and socially advantaged.

Citizens' groups do not have the same organizational advantages as economic groups. They depend on voluntary contributions from potential members, who may lack interest and resources or who recognize that they will get the collective good from a group's activity even if they do not participate (the free-rider problem). Citizens' groups include public-interest, single-issue, and ideological groups. Their numbers have increased dramatically since the 1960s despite their organizational problems.

Organized interests seek influence largely by lobbying public officials and contributing to election campaigns. Using an inside strategy, lobbyists develop direct contacts with legislators, government bureaucrats, and members of the judiciary in order to persuade them to accept the group's perspective on policy. Groups also use an outside strategy, seeking to mobilize public support for their goals. This strategy relies in part on grassroots lobbying—encouraging group members and the public to communicate their policy views to officials. Outside lobbying also includes efforts to elect officeholders who will support group aims. Through political action committees (PACs), organized groups now provide nearly a third of all contributions received by congressional candidates.

The policies that emerge from the group system bring benefits to many of society's interests, and in some instances these benefits also serve the general interest. But when groups can essentially dictate policies, the common good is not served. The majority's interest is subordinated to group (minority) interests. In most instances, the minority consists of individuals who already enjoy a substantial share of society's benefits.

STUDY CORNER

Key Terms

citizens' (noneconomic) groups
  (p. 283)
collective (public) goods (p. 283)
economic groups (p. 280)
free-rider problem (p. 284)
grassroots lobbying (p. 294)
inside lobbying (p. 289)

interest group (p. 278)
interest-group liberalism (p. 301)
iron triangle (p. 292)
issue network (p. 292)
lobbying (p. 289)
material incentive (p. 281)
outside lobbying (p. 294)

political action committee (PAC)
  (p. 296)
private (individual) goods (p. 281)
purposive incentive (p. 283)
single-issue politics (p. 278)

Self-Test

1. Interest groups tend to do all but which one of the
   following?
   a. try to influence the political process
   b. pursue members' shared policy goals
   c. contribute support to candidates and officials who
      favor their goals
   d. change policy positions in order to win elections

2. If an interest group wants to influence policy
   decisions at the implementation stage, efforts should
   be directed primarily toward the:
   a. judiciary.
   b. bureaucracy.
   c. White House.
   d. Congress.

3. Interest-group politics is aligned with the political
   theory of:
   a. elitism.
   b. inclusion.
   c. communitarianism.
   d. pluralism.

4. When lobbyists supply policymakers with
   information and indications of group strength to
   persuade them to adopt the group's perspective, the
   activity is called:
   a. arm twisting.
   b. wrangling.
   c. purposive persuasion.
   d. inside lobbying.

5. Economic interest groups have an advantage over
   other groups chiefly because of their:
   a. ability to muster large numbers of members.
   b. emphasis on training people to run for Congress.
   c. devotion to promoting the broad public interest.
   d. access to financial resources.

6. Political action committees:
   a. raise money for election campaigns by soliciting
      voluntary contributions from members or
      employees.
   b. have declined rapidly in number since the passage
      of the recent campaign finance reform legislation.
   c. are under no restrictions regarding the amount of
      money each PAC can give to the election campaign
      of a single candidate for federal office.
   d. are not an important source of funds in
      congressional campaigns.

7. The free-rider problem results when individuals can
   benefit from the activities of an interest group even if
   they do not contribute to the group's activities. (T/F)

8. The key tactic of outside lobbying activity is to seek
   influence through public pressure. (T/F)

9. Interest-group liberalism is a term used by Theodore
   Lowi to express the tendency of interest-group
   politics to favor narrow interests over majority
   interests. (T/F)

10. Affluent citizens and business groups dominate the
    interest-group system. (T/F)

Critical Thinking

Why are there so many more organized interests in
the United States than elsewhere? Why are so many of

these groups organized around economic interests—
particularly business interests?

Suggested Readings

Berry, Jeffrey M. *The New Liberalism: The Rising Power of Citizen Groups.* Washington, D.C.: Brookings Institution Press, 1999. An exploration of the influence that citizen groups exercise.

Browne, William P. *Cultivating Congress: Constituents, Issues, and Interests in Agriculture Policymaking.* Lawrence: University Press of Kansas, 1995. An analysis of the limits of "iron triangles" as a description of congressional policymaking.

Cigler, Allan J., and Burdett A. Loomis. *Interest Group Politics,* 6th ed. Washington, D.C.: Congressional Quarterly Press, 2002. A comprehensive analysis of interest-group politics.

Grossman, Gene M., and Elhanan Helpman. *Interest Groups and Trade Policy.* Princeton, N.J.: Princeton University Press, 2002. An examination of the impact of groups' campaign and lobbying activities on trade policy.

Herrnson, Paul S., Ronald G. Shaiko, and Clyde Wilcox, eds. *The Interest Group Connection: Electioneering, Lobbying, and Policymaking in Washington.* Chatham, N.J.: Chatham House Publishers, 1998. Essays and commentaries on groups and officials and the linkages between them.

Lowi, Theodore J. *The End of Liberalism,* 2d ed. New York: Norton, 1979. A thorough critique of interest groups' influence on American politics.

Olson, Mancur, Jr. *The Logic of Collective Action,* rev. ed. Cambridge, Mass.: Harvard University Press, 1971. A pioneering analysis of why some interests are more fully and easily organized than others.

Rozell, Mark J., and Clyde Wilcox. *Interest Groups in American Campaigns.* Washington, D.C.: Congressional Quarterly Press, 1999. An assessment of the election role of interest groups.

List of Websites

http://www.fec/gov/

The Federal Election Commission site; it offers information on elections, voting, campaign finance, parties, and PACs. It also includes a citizens' guide to campaign contributions.

http://www/pirg.org/

The Public Interest Research Group (PIRG) site; PIRG has chapters on many college campuses, and the site provides state-by-state policy and other information.

http://www.sierraclub.org/

The Sierra Club, one of the oldest environmental protection interest groups, promotes conservation; its website provides information on its activities.

http://www.townhall.com/

The website of the American Conservative Union (ACU); it includes policy and political information and has a lively chat room.

Participate!

Consider contributing to a citizens' interest group. Such groups depend on members' donations for operating funds. Citizens' groups cover the political spectrum from right to left and touch on nearly every conceivable public issue. You will not have difficulty locating a group through the Internet that has policy goals consistent with your beliefs and values.

Extra Credit

For up-to-the-minute *New York Times* articles, interactive simulations, graphics, study tools, and more links and quizzes, visit the text's Online Learning Center at www.mhhe.com/pattersontad7.

(Self-Test Answers: 1. d   2. b   3. d   4. d   5. d   6. a   7. T   8. T   9. T   10. T)

10

The News Media:
Communicating Political Images

Chapter Outline

"The press in America . . . determines what people will think and talk about—an authority that in other nations is reserved for tyrants, priests, parties, and mandarins."

—*Theodore H. White*[1]

Early on the morning of April 22, 2000, the television networks interrupted their coverage to report a breaking story from Miami. Federal agents had just forced their way into the home where six-year-old Elian Gonzalez was staying and rushed him to a waiting plane that would fly him to Washington to be reunited with his father. During the next few days, Elian's seizure and the reactions to it filled the airwaves and front pages. The seizure was the latest episode in a running news story that had begun months earlier when Elian was rescued at sea after his mother drowned while trying to escape Cuba by boat. The young boy became the object of a political tug-of-war between Florida's Cuban American community and Cuba's Fidel Castro. Every move and countermove provoked a torrent of news coverage.

Not all developments receive such intensive news coverage. More new immigrants have arrived in the United States in the past three decades than during any comparable period in the nation's history. Their sheer number has strained the capacity of schools and other public organizations. In some communities, mobile homes have been converted into makeshift schoolrooms simply to get a roof over all students' heads. This great wave of immigration will affect U.S. communities and public policies for years to come. Yet this development has only occasionally been mentioned in the news, let alone emblazoned in the headlines month after month.

Although the news has been compared to a mirror held up to society, it is actually a highly selective portrayal of reality. The **news** is mainly an account of obtruding events, particularly those that are *timely* (new or unfolding developments rather than old or static ones), *dramatic* (striking developments rather than commonplace ones), and *compelling* (developments that arouse people's emotions).[2] These tendencies have their origin in a number of factors, not the least of which is that the news organizations seek to make a profit, which leads them to prefer news stories that will attract and hold an audience. Thus, Elian Gonzalez became headline news the instant he was plucked from the sea, and he remained newsworthy while the political and legal process surrounding his status unfolded. The larger issue of the influx of immigrants into the United States during the past three decades is not considered particularly newsworthy because it is a slow and steady process that is dramatic only in its long-term implications. Columnist George Will noted that a development requires a defining event before it can become big news.[3] Without such an event, reporters have no peg on which to hang their stories.

Federal agents seize Elian Gonzalez from the home of his Miami relatives. The Gonzalez story was one of the most heavily covered news events of recent years.

news The news media's version of reality, usually with an emphasis on timely, dramatic, and compelling events and developments.

press (news media) Those print and broadcast organizations that are in the news-reporting business.

News organizations and journalists, of either the print media (newspapers and magazines) or the broadcast media (radio and television), are referred to collectively as the **press** or the **news media.** The press is an increasingly important political actor. Its heightened influence is attributable in part to changes within the media. New technology, from broadcast television to cable to satellites, has dramatically increased the reach and speed of communication. In addition, the press has filled some of the void created by the decline in political parties and other political institutions.

In some ways, the press is better positioned than parties or groups to serve the public. On a daily basis, Americans connect to politics more through the news than through the activities of parties or groups. This chapter argues, however, that the news media are a very different kind of intermediary than either parties or interest groups and that problems arise when the press is expected to perform the same functions as these organizations. The chapter begins with a review of the media's historical development and the current trends in news reporting. It concludes with an analysis of the roles the press can and cannot perform adequately in the American political system. The main ideas represented in this chapter are the following:

- *The American press initially was tied to the nation's political party system (the partisan press) but gradually developed an independent position (the objective press).* In the process, the news shifted from a political orientation, which emphasizes political values and ideas, to a journalistic orientation, which stresses newsworthy information and events.

- *Although the United States has thousands of separate news organizations, they present a common version of the news that reflects journalists' shared view of what the news is.* Freedom of the press in the United States does not result in a robust marketplace of ideas.

- *In fulfilling their responsibility to provide public information, the news media effectively perform three significant roles—those of signaler (the press brings relevant events and problems into public view), common carrier (the press serves as a channel through which political leaders can address the public), and watchdog (the press scrutinizes official behavior for evidence of deceitful, careless, or corrupt acts).* These roles are within the news media's capacity because they fit with the values, incentives, and accountability of the press.

- *The press cannot do the job of political institutions, even though it increasingly tries to do so.* The nature of journalism as it has evolved is incompatible with the characteristics required for the role of public representative.

THE DEVELOPMENT OF THE NEWS MEDIA: FROM PARTISANSHIP TO OBJECTIVE JOURNALISM

Democracy requires a free flow of information. Communication enables a free people to keep in touch with one another, with their leaders, and with important events.

America's early leaders were quick to recognize the importance of the press. At Alexander Hamilton's urging, the *Gazette of the United States* was founded by John Fenno to promote the policies of George Washington's administration. Hamilton, as secretary of the treasury, supported Fenno's paper by granting it the Treasury Department's printing contracts. Thomas Jefferson, who was secretary of state and Hamilton's political adversary, complained that the newspaper's content was "pure Toryism." Jefferson persuaded Philip Freneau to start the *National Gazette* as the opposition Republican party's publication and supported it by granting Freneau authority to print State Department documents.

Early newspapers were printed on flat presses, a process that limited production and kept the cost of each copy beyond the reach of ordinary citizens—most of whom were illiterate anyway. Leading papers such as the *Gazette of the United States* had fewer than fifteen hundred subscribers and could not have survived without party support. Not surprisingly, the "news" they printed was a form of party propaganda.[4] In this era of the **partisan press,** publishers openly took sides on partisan issues. Their employees were expected to follow the party line. President James K. Polk once persuaded a leading publisher to fire an editor who was critical of Polk's policies.[5]

partisan press Newspapers and other communication media that openly support a political party and whose news in significant part follows the party line.

From a Partisan Press to an "Objective" One

Technological changes helped bring about the gradual decline of America's partisan press. After the introduction of the telegraph in 1837, editors could receive timely information on developments in Washington and the state capital, and they had less reason to fill their pages with partisan arguments.[6] The invention in 1815 of the hand-cranked rotary press enabled publishers to print their

Yellow journalism was characterized by its sensationalism. William Randolph Hearst's *New York Journal* whipped up public support for a war in Cuba against Spain through inflammatory reporting on the sinking of the battleship *Maine* in Havana Harbor in 1898.

objective journalism A model of news reporting that is based on the communication of "facts" rather than opinions and that is "fair" in that it presents all sides of partisan debate.

newspapers more rapidly and cheaply. The *New York Sun* was the first paper to pass on the benefit of higher-speed printing to subscribers by reducing the price of a daily copy from six cents to a penny. The *Sun*'s circulation rose to five thousand in four months and to ten thousand in less than a year.[7] Increased circulation meant increased advertising revenue, which freed newspapers from their dependence on government printing contracts.

By the late nineteenth century, helped along by the invention of newsprint and power-driven presses, many American newspapers were printing fifty thousand or more copies a day, and their large circulations enabled them to charge high prices for advertising. The period marked the height of newspapers' power and the low point in their sense of public responsibility. A new style of reporting—"yellow journalism"—had emerged as a way of boosting circulation.[8] It was "a shrieking, gaudy, sensation-loving, devil-may-care kind of journalism which lured the reader by any possible means."[9] A circulation battle between William Randolph Hearst's *New York Journal* and Joseph Pulitzer's *New York World* is believed to have contributed to the outbreak of the Spanish-American War through sensational (and largely inaccurate) reports on the cruelty of Spanish rule in Cuba. A young Frederic Remington (who later became a noted painter and sculptor), working as a news artist for Hearst, planned to return home because Cuba appeared calm and safe, but Hearst cabled back: "Please remain. You furnish the pictures and I'll furnish the war."[10]

The excesses of yellow journalism led some publishers to consider ways of reporting the news more responsibly. One step was to separate the newspaper's advertising department from its news department, thus reducing the influence of advertisers on news content. A second development was a new model of reporting called **objective journalism,** which was based on the reporting of "facts" rather than opinions and was "fair" in that it presented both sides of partisan debate.[11]

A chief advocate of this new form of journalism was Adolph Ochs of the *New York Times.* Ochs bought the *Times* in 1896, when its circulation was 9,000; four years later, its readership had grown to 82,000. Ochs told his reporters that he "wanted as little partisanship as possible . . . as few judgments as possible."[12] The *Times*'s approach to reporting particularly appealed to educated readers, and by the early twentieth century it had acquired a reputation as the country's best newspaper. Objective reporting was also promoted through newly formed journalism schools. Among the first of these professional schools were those at Columbia University and the University of Missouri.

Objective journalism is still a component of news coverage. Although most newspapers have a partisan bias on their editorial pages, they tend to treat the Republican and Democratic parties equally on their news pages. Nevertheless, the influence of objective journalism is waning. Newspapers increasingly rely

Franklin D. Roosevelt was the first president to make effective use of the radio to communicate directly with the American people. He broadcast a series of fireside chats that reached millions of listeners across the country.

on **interpretive reporting,** a style of reporting in which the journalist's job is to analyze and explain developments rather than merely report them. The older form of objective journalism (called **descriptive reporting,** because of its straightforward description of events) required that reporters stick to the "facts." The newer interpretive style allows them to tell their audience what the facts mean. As explained later in the chapter, interpretive reporting has greatly increased journalists' ability to construct the news to fit their own beliefs, including their skeptical opinion of politicians' motives and accomplishments.

interpretive reporting The style of reporting that aims to explain *why* something is taking place or has occurred.

descriptive reporting The style of reporting that aims to describe *what* is taking place or has occurred.

The Development of the Broadcast Media

Radio and Television: The Truly National Media

Until the early twentieth century, the print media were the only form of mass communication. Within a few decades, however, hundreds of radio stations were broadcasting throughout the nation. Broadcasting was the first truly *national* mass medium. Newspapers had local readerships, whereas radio could reach millions of Americans across the country simultaneously.

Television followed radio, and by the late 1950s more than 90 percent of American homes had a television set. However, television newscasts of the 1950s were brief, lasting no more than fifteen minutes, and relied on news gathered by other organizations, particularly the Associated Press and other wire services. In the early 1960s, the three commercial networks—CBS, NBC, and ABC—expanded their evening newscasts to thirty minutes, and their audience ratings increased. Simultaneously, they increased the size and funding of their news divisions, and television soon became the principal news medium of national politics.

Today, television provides a twenty-four-hour forum of political news and information. The creation of the Cable News Network (CNN) and C-SPAN in the late 1970s brought Americans round-the-clock public-affairs coverage. Television talk shows, such as *Larry King Live*, have broadened the range of choices available to politically interested viewers. A parallel development is the emergence of radio talk shows. Nearly a sixth of the American public claim to listen regularly to politically oriented radio talk shows, most of which have a conservative slant.

Even more so than their newspaper counterparts, television journalists rely on an interpretive style of reporting. The reason is that television journalists use a narrative or storytelling mode in order to appeal to an audience accustomed to entertainment programming. "Facts" alone do not tell a story; they have to be interpreted in a way that makes them into a story. Reuven Frank, a network executive and pioneer in television journalism, once told his correspondents: "Every news story should, without any sacrifice of probity or responsibility, display the attributes of fiction, of drama. It should have structure and conflict, problem and denouement, rising action and falling action, a beginning, a middle and an end."[13]

Government Licensing and Regulation of Broadcasters

At first the government did not carefully regulate broadcasting. Chaos was the result. Nearby stations often used the same or adjacent radio frequencies, interfering with each other's transmissions. Finally, in 1934, Congress passed the Communications Act, which requires that broadcasters be licensed and meet certain performance standards. Congress established the Federal Communications Commission (FCC) to administer the act through regulations pertaining to such matters as signal strength, advertising rates, and political coverage.

The principle of scarcity justifies the licensing and regulation of broadcast media. Because the number of available broadcasting frequencies is limited, those few individuals who are granted a broadcasting license are expected to serve the public interest in addition to their own. In principle, licensing is a means of controlling broadcasting. If a station fails to comply with federal broadcast regulations, the FCC can withdraw its license. However, the FCC seldom even threatens to revoke a license, for fear of being accused of restricting freedom of the press. A broadcast station can apply for renewal of its license by postcard and is virtually guaranteed FCC approval, which covers seven years for radio and five for television.

Because broadcast frequencies are a scarce resource, licensees are required by law to be somewhat evenhanded during election campaigns. Section 315 of the Communications Act imposes on broadcasters an "equal-time" restriction, which means that they cannot sell or give air time to a political candidate without granting equal opportunities to the other candidates running for the same office. (Election debates are an exception; broadcasters can televise them even if participation is limited to the Republican and Democratic nominees only.)

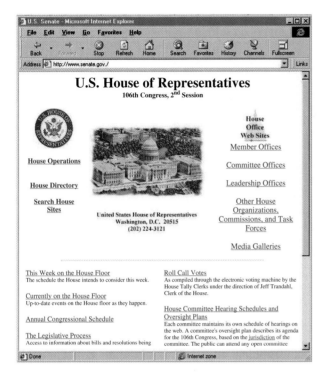

The Internet has weakened the traditional news media's control of the political information that Americans receive. Through the Internet, citizens and political leaders alike can communicate widely without having their messages filtered through the news media. Pictured here are the home pages of the U.S. House and Senate.

The Emergence of the Internet

Although the First Amendment protects each individual's right to press freedom, in practice the right has been reserved for a tiny few. Journalist A. J. Liebling wrote that freedom of the press belongs to those with the money to own a broadcast station or newspaper.[14] Even a smaller broadcast station or daily newspaper costs millions to buy; the larger are worth hundreds of millions.

Access to the Internet is no substitute for ownership of a major news outlet, but it does provide ordinary citizens with an opportunity to exercise their free-press rights. By creating a website, the ordinary citizen can post information about public affairs, harangue officials, argue for public policies, and attempt to mobilize the support of others. There is no assurance of a wide audience, and in fact most citizens have neither a personal website nor, if they do, a large following. But the Internet has reduced the barriers to citizen communication to a level not seen since colonial days, when citizen-produced pamphlets were the major form of political expression. The Internet has also provided political leaders and organizations with a direct channel to the public. At all political levels, office-holders, parties, and interest groups now have websites that they use to inform and mobilize their followers.

Figure 10–1

Opinions on Press Censorship in Time of War
When U.S. forces were attacking Afghanistan, more Americans said they would support government censorship than said they would give the press free rein in its reporting.
Source: Pew Research Center Survey, November 13–19, 2001.

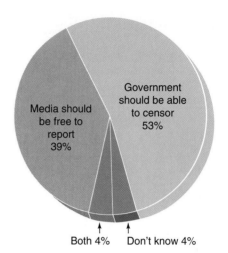

Government should be able to censor 53%

Media should be free to report 39%

Both 4%   Don't know 4%

FREEDOM AND CONFORMITY IN THE U.S. NEWS MEDIA

Some democracies impose significant legal restraints on the press. In Britain, for example, the news media are barred from reporting on subjects that have been designated "official secrets" by the government, and they are inhibited by tough libel laws from publishing unsubstantiated claims that will damage a person's reputation.

In the United States, as pointed out in Chapter 4, the First Amendment gives the press more leeway. The courts have consistently upheld the right of U.S. newspapers to report on politics pretty much as they choose. Broadcasters, as the equal-time restriction indicates, have less freedom under the law, but they are subject to much less government control than are broadcasters in Europe. In the case of both U.S. newspapers and broadcasters, the government cannot block publication of a news story unless it can convincingly demonstrate in court that the information would jeopardize national security. Although most Americans would permit censorship in time of war (see Figure 10–1), the courts have strictly limited the government's ability to impose it. U.S. libel laws also strongly favor the press. A public figure who is attacked in a news story cannot collect libel damages unless he or she can demonstrate convincingly that the news organization was false in its accusations and was knowingly or recklessly careless in its search for the truth. This imposing standard has come to mean in practice that the press is virtually immune from charges of libel.

Moreover, the U.S. government gives the news media a lot of economic support. Newspapers and magazines have a special postal rate that helps them keep their circulation costs low, and broadcasters pay only a few dollars annually in license fees for broadcasting rights worth hundreds of billions of dollars. Such policies have contributed to the development of a truly enormous news industry in the United States: 1,600 daily newspapers; 8,500 weeklies; 9,500 radio stations; 6 national television news networks; 850 local television stations; and 10,500 cable television systems.[15]

Liberty, Equality & Self-Government

What's Your Opinion?

Press Freedom

In the United States, government has little power to block the press from reporting information that could damage national security. The principle of "no prior restraint" holds that government cannot stop a publication or broadcast program unless it can convince a court that grave harm to the nation would result from release of the information. The U.S. press is also protected, as explained in Chapter 4, by an imposing legal standard for libel. It is nearly impossible for a U.S. official to win a libel suit against a newspaper, magazine, or broadcast organization even in situations where his or her reputation has been destroyed by false allegations.

By comparison, Britain's government has the power to prevent news organizations from reporting on national security issues. For example, there was a long period during which British journalists were prohibited from reporting stories on the Irish separatist issue that presented the conflict from the viewpoint of separatists who advocated violence. British libel law also differs from American law when it comes to libel. Although libel judgments in Britain typically result in relatively small monetary awards, the standard of proof in British courts is such that a person whose reputation has been unfairly tarnished by a news reporter or organization has a reasonable chance of winning a libel judgment.

Which model of press freedom—the American or the British—do you prefer? What arguments would you make for and against each model?

The audience reach of leading news organizations is substantial. Each weekday evening, more than twenty million Americans tune into a network newscast. The *New York Times*, the *Wall Street Journal*, *USA Today*, and the *Los Angeles Times* each have daily circulations exceeding one million readers. Three dozen other newspapers each have circulations in excess of 250,000 readers. The average daily circulation of America's newspapers is roughly forty million; on Sunday, newspaper circulation jumps to sixty million.[16]

In view of the great number and the freedom of news organizations in the United States, it might be expected that Americans would have a lot of diversity in the news they receive. However, the opposite is true. Newspapers and broadcast stations from coast to coast tend to highlight the same national news stories and to interpret them in similar ways. Any number of terms—*pack journalism, groupthink, media concentration*—have been used to describe this tendency.

A reason for the tendency is that U.S. reporters, aside from some journalists in a few outlets such as Fox News, do not deliberately put a partisan spin on the news. There is not a Republican version of the news and an opposing Democratic version of the news. U.S. journalists do differ somewhat in the issues they highlight, but this difference is a far cry from the partisan disputes that filled the pages of nineteenth-century American newspapers or that can be found, today, in many European newspapers.

Of course, today's news organizations differ in the way they tell a given story. Broadcast news tends to be, in effect, headline news with pictures. A

STATES IN THE NATION

In the News, or Out?

Most of the news that reaches Americans wherever they might live originates with a handful of news outlets, such as NBC News. This coverage, however, concentrates on events in a few places. The map shows the relative frequency with which each of the fifty states was mentioned on NBC News during a recent one-year period.

A. Why do some states get more coverage than other states do?

B. The heavily covered states are the more populous ones, which increases the likelihood that a newsworthy event will occur. In NBC's case, coverage is also heavier in states where one of its news bureaus is located. NBC has bureaus in New York, Washington, Los Angeles, Dallas, Atlanta, Chicago, and Boston.

Source: Data compiled by author from Nexis.

thirty-minute network news broadcast typically presents a dozen or so stories in the roughly twenty minutes allotted to news content (the other ten minutes are devoted to commercials). Newspapers have the space to present news developments in greater depth; some, like the *New York Times* (which labels itself "the newspaper of record"), provide substantial detail. The reporting styles of

The audience reach of the U.S. news media is truly substantial. More than twenty million Americans each evening watch a network newscast, and about half the adult population read a daily paper. However, the news audience is shrinking, which has caused alarm among those in the news industry and those who believe that attention to news is critical to an informed citizenry.

news organizations also vary. Although most of them present the news in an understated way, others tend toward sensationalism. For example, when Jeffrey Dahmer, a convicted murderer who had cannibalized his victims, was himself murdered in a Wisconsin prison, the *New York Post* gave its whole front page to the headline "Death of a Monster." The *New York Times*, in contrast, gave the story a standard-size front-page headline, "Jeffrey Dahmer, Multiple Killer, Is Bludgeoned to Death in Prison." Such differences in approach, however, do not disguise the fact that most news organizations tell their various audiences the same stories each day.

Domination of News Production

Another reason for the lack of diversity in national news reporting is that a few news organizations produce most of it. The Associated Press (AP) is the major contributor. It has three hundred full-time reporters stationed throughout the country and the world to gather news stories, which are relayed by satellite to subscribing newspapers and broadcast stations. More than 95 percent of the nation's dailies are serviced by AP, and some also subscribe to other wire services, such as Reuters and the New York Times.[17] Smaller dailies lack the resources to gather news outside their own localities and thus depend on wire-service reports for their national and international coverage.[18]

Television news production is similarly dominated by just a few organizations. The six major networks—ABC, CBS, NBC, PBS, Fox, and CNN—generate most of the television coverage of national and international politics. For news of the nation and the world, local stations depend on video transmissions fed to them by the networks.

News Values and Imperatives

Competitive pressures also lead the producers of news to report the same stories. No major news organization wants to miss an important story that others are reporting.

The networks, the wire services, and a few elite dailies, including the *New York Times*, the *Washington Post*, the *Wall Street Journal*, the *Los Angeles Times*, and the *Chicago Tribune*, establish a national standard of story selection. Whenever one of them highlights a story, the others jump on the bandwagon. The top trendsetter is the *New York Times*, which has been described as "the bulletin board" for other major newspapers, newsmagazines, and television networks.

The imperatives of the fast pace of daily journalism also tend to make the news homogeneous.[19] Journalists have the task each day of filling a newspaper or broadcast with stories. Thus, editors assign reporters to such beats as the White House and Congress, which can be relied on for a steady supply of news. On these beats the reporters of various news organizations see and hear the same things, exchange views on what is important, and, not surprisingly, produce similar news stories.

Finally, shared professional values guide journalists in their search for news.[20] Reporters are on the lookout for aspects of situations that lend themselves to interesting news stories—novel, colorful, and compelling developments. Long practice at reporting leads journalists to develop a common understanding of what comprises news. After the White House press corps has listened to a presidential speech, for example, nearly all the journalists in attendance are in agreement on what was most newsworthy about the speech—often only a single statement within it.

"Megamedia": Mergers, Profits, and the News

Over the past three decades, media ownership has become increasingly concentrated. The ABC network and its news division, for example, are part of the Disney corporation, while CNN is part of Time Warner. The trend reflects the high profitability of the media business and the economies of scale: the larger the media organization, the more it can leverage advertisers and achieve efficiencies in the production of news and entertainment. The net result is that U.S. news is largely in the hands of what political scientist Dean Alger calls the "megamedia."[21]

Should so few entities control so much of what Americans see and hear through the mass media? Some observers say that the change is not all that significant because there is still competition between news organizations and because news organizations enjoy a degree of independence within their corporate structures. Alger is not convinced:

> It is . . . vital for democracy to have a truly diverse set of media sources present in the public arena. . . . The continued advance of megamedia and their increasing domination of the prime mass media spell a profound constriction of that diversity and a severe diminution of the marketplace of ideas, and thus a danger to democracy.[22]

Do Media Mergers Serve the Public Interest?

Giant corporations now control most of the nation's communication capacity. Most daily newspapers and all three major broadcast networks are embedded in media conglomerates. For example, the American Broadcasting Company (ABC) is owned by the entertainment giant Disney. Are such concentrations of media power in the public interest? Advocates of these mergers claim that they foster the accumulation of capital necessary for the production and distribution of high-value information on a broad scale. Critics say that media concentration places corporate profits above a diversity of voices and the free flow of information. These differences are reflected in claims that were made when the Federal Communication Commission (FCC) decided in 2003 to relax the legal limits on media ownership, opening the door to a further concentration of media ownership.

Debating the Issues

Yes: Do we even need free television? From a public policy perspective, I believe the answer is yes—we absolutely need to maintain a viable free television service for the welfare of our citizens. Free broadcast television remains an important service for those citizens that cannot afford pay television. Additionally, free television continues to play a vital role in informing the public during national and local emergencies. . . . That's why the FCC passed a new set of broadcast ownership limits, modernizing a regulatory regime that was made for the bygone era of the big three [ABC, CBS, NBC] to reflect today's dynamic media marketplace. Those rule modifications were made, in part, to strengthen free television to give it a chance to remain viable for our citizens to enjoy for decades to come. . . . [The] rule changes, such as allowing cross-ownership or the ownership of more than one local television broadcast outlet in some markets, will [also] bring consumers more and better quality local news coverage and will help fund the transition to high definition digital television. . . . Free television has been an important service to the American public for over 50 years. If our efforts do not provide free television with the ability to better compete in today's vibrant media marketplace, we risk losing its services for the next 50 years.

—*Michael Powell, Chairperson, FCC*

No: When nationwide companies own local media outlets, they often shrink news departments, cut staff, and avoid controversial issues to please advertisers. These news cutbacks produce results like what happened in Minot, North Dakota, when a train derailed in the early hours of a cold January morning in 2002. After the accident, Minot was covered in a toxic cloud of anhydrous ammonia fertilizer that killed one person. But when local law enforcement officials tried to warn the community by calling radio station KCJB, they couldn't get through to anyone. . . . It happened because media giant Clear Channel owns all six of Minot's commercial radio stations, which were staffed by one full-time news employee. . . . Opposition to FCC rules changes spans the ideological spectrum. Some of the strongest opposition . . . comes from groups like the National Rifle Association which warned that, "gun-hating media giants like AOL Time Warner, Viacom/CBS and Disney/ABC . . . [could refuse] to sell us television, radio or newspaper advertising at any price." . . . Media consolidation also makes it difficult for women and minority groups, who only recently have gained the economic power sufficient to buy radio and TV stations, to become owners. Ownership limits have been a way for government to encourage diversity among broadcast owners.

—*Common Cause*

Another issue is the impact of media conglomerates on the quality of news content. As news organizations were absorbed by larger corporations, they were pressured to increase their profit margins. A result was a cutback in news-gathering capacity. ABC, CBS, and NBC News, for example, closed many of their overseas news bureaus.

News divisions have also been directed to compete more aggressively for audiences, because audience size determines advertising revenues.[23] As a

HOW THE UNITED STATES COMPARES

Partisan Neutrality as a News Value

In the nineteenth century, the United States had a partisan press. Journalists were partisan actors, and news was a blend of reporting and advocacy. Facts and opinions were freely intermixed in news stories. This type of reporting gradually gave way to a model of journalism that emphasizes the "facts" and covers the two major parties more or less equally. American journalists, through both print and television, seek impartiality in their daily news reporting. For example, a political scandal, whether it involves a Democrat or a Republican, is a big story for any major U.S. news organization.

European news organizations are less committed to poliltical neutrality. Many European newspapers are aligned with a party, and although they focus on events, their coverage has a partisan component. In Great Britain, for example, the *Daily Telegraph* often serves as a voice of the Conservative party, while the *Guardian* favors the liberals. Broadcasters in most European countries are politically neutral by law and practice, but there are exceptions, as in the case of French and Italian broadcasters.

The difference between the U.S. and European media is evident in a five-country survey that asked journalists whether they thought journalists should remain neutral in reporting on political parties. Compared with their counterparts in Great Britain, Germany, Sweden, and Italy, U.S. journalists were more likely to believe in partisan neutrality.

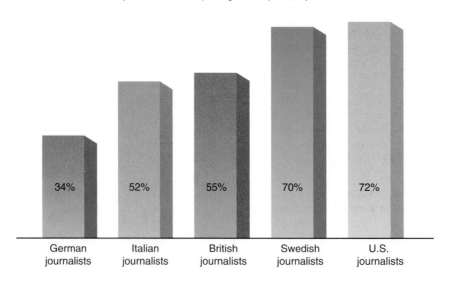

Percentage expressing strong agreement that journalists should stay neutral when reporting on the political parties

German journalists 34% | Italian journalists 52% | British journalists 55% | Swedish journalists 70% | U.S. journalists 72%

Source: Thomas E. Patterson, Media and Democracy Project, in progress. Reprinted by permission of the author.

consequence, the news has become increasingly entertainment oriented. Critics say it is "infotainment" rather than real news. A study of network evening newscasts found that, over the past decade, the amount of news time devoted to government, politics, and public affairs has declined significantly while the amount given to lifestyle issues, celebrities, and human-interest subjects has risen sharply.[24]

THE NEWS MEDIA AS LINK: ROLES THE PRESS CAN AND CANNOT PERFORM

When the objective model of reporting came to dominate American news coverage, the relationship between the press and the public was fundamentally altered. The nineteenth-century partisan press gave its readers clear-cut cues as to how to evaluate political issues and leaders. In the presidential election campaign of 1896, the *San Francisco Call* devoted 1,075 column-inches of photographs to the Republican ticket of McKinley-Hobart and only 11 inches to the Democrats, Bryan and Sewell.[25] Many European newspapers still function in this way, guiding their readers by applying partisan or ideological values to current events. The *Daily Telegraph,* for example, is an unofficial but fiercely loyal mouthpiece of Britain's Conservative party (see "How the United States Compares").

The modern American press operates by a different standard. Partisanship is accepted on talk shows and editorial pages but is discouraged in news reporting. Journalists are expected to concentrate on describing and explaining events and developments. The media thus are very different from political parties and interest groups, the other major links between the public and its leaders. Parties and groups exist to promote political positions. The media are driven by the search for interesting and important stories.

This distinction provides a basis for determining what roles the media can and cannot be expected to fulfill. The press is capable of fulfilling only those public responsibilities that are compatible with journalistic values: the signaler role, the common-carrier role, and the watchdog role. The media are less successful in their attempts to perform a fourth and more politically oriented role: public representative.

U.S. journalists covering the war in Iraq. The top correspondents were from the major networks, the wire services, and leading newspapers such as the *New York Times.* These news organizations supply most of the national and international news that Americans receive.

The Signaler Role

As journalists see it, their responsibilities include the **signaler role.** They seek to alert the public to important developments as soon as possible after they happen—a state visit to Washington by a foreign leader, a bill that has just been passed by Congress, a change in the nation's unemployment level, a terrorist bombing in a foreign capital.

signaler role The accepted responsibility of the media to alert the public to important developments as soon as possible after they happen or are discovered.

The U.S. media are well equipped to play the signaler role. They are poised to converge on any major news event anywhere in the nation and nearly anywhere in the world. For instance, as the United States prepared to attack Iraq in 2003, hundreds of U.S. journalists descended on that part of the world. Many of them were "embedded" in U.S. combat units. When the attack began, they traveled into battle with the troops. Their news stories kept Americans abreast of the war and the subsequent effort to create a stable government in Iraq.

The media are particularly well suited to signal developments from Washington. More than half of all national news coverage emanates from the nation's capital, most of it from the White House and Congress. Altogether, more than ten thousand people in Washington work in the news business. The key players are the leading correspondents of the television networks and the major newspapers, the heads of the Washington news bureaus, and a few top editors.[26]

The press, in its capacity as signaler, has the power to focus the public's attention. The term **agenda setting** has been used to describe the media's ability to influence what is on people's minds.[27] By covering the same events, problems, issues, and leaders—simply by giving them space or time in the news— the media place them on the public agenda. The press, as Bernard Cohen notes, "may not be successful much of the time in telling people what to think, but it is stunningly successful in telling them what to think about."[28] This influence is most obvious in situations such as the U.S. war in Iraq, a development that captivated Americans.

agenda setting The power of the media through news coverage to focus the public's attention and concern on particular events, problems, issues, personalities, and so on.

The Common-Carrier Role

common-carrier role The media's function as an open channel through which political leaders can communicate with the public.

The press also plays a **common-carrier role** in that it provides political leaders a channel through which to communicate with the public. The importance of this role to officials and citizens alike is obvious. Citizens cannot very well support or oppose a leader's plans and actions if they do not know about them, and leaders need news coverage if they are to get the public's attention. Indeed, national news is mainly about the actions of political leaders and institutions, as is reflected in the hundreds of reporters who station themselves regularly at the Capitol and the White House.

Officials try to get the most favorable news coverage they can. For example, the White House Press Office and the White House Office of Communications try to shape information in a way favorable to the president. Sometimes they succeed in placing their spin (that is, the president's interpretation) on the media's coverage of events.

Even though the president and Congress can expect coverage, the press increasingly places its own spin on stories out of Washington. Journalists, because of their increased celebrity status, their heightened skepticism of politicians since Vietnam and Watergate, and the greater latitude afforded them by the interpretive style of reporting, have become accustomed not only to covering what newsmakers say but also to having their own say. In 2004, as the Bush administration was trying to get out the message that the economy was gaining strength, the press was playing up the situation in Iraq, carrying almost daily reports of the risks and problems associated with the U.S. occupation of that country.

In fact, the news today is as much journalist centered as it is newsmaker centered. For every minute the presidential candidates spoke on the network newscasts during coverage of the 2004 campaign, for example, the journalists who were covering them talked for six minutes. In the 1960s, a candidate's sound bite (the length of time within a television story that the candidate speaks without interruption) was more than forty seconds in length on

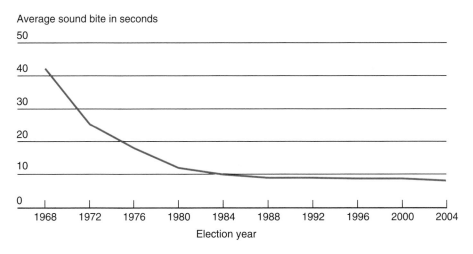

Average sound bite in seconds

Figure 10–2

The Shrinking Sound Bite of Television Election Coverage
The average length of time that presidential candidates are shown speaking without interruption on broadcast television newscasts has declined sharply in recent elections.
Source:Adapted from Daniel C. Hallin, "Sound Bite News: Television Coverage of Elections 1968–1988." *Journal of Communication* 42 (Spring 1992): 6. The 1992–2004 data are from the Center for Media and Public Affairs.

average.[29] In recent campaigns, the average sound bite has been less than ten seconds, barely enough time for the candidate to utter a long sentence (see Figure 10–2).

The Watchdog Role

Traditionally, the American press has accepted responsibility for protecting the public from deceitful, careless, incompetent, and corrupt officials. In this **watchdog role,** the press stands ready to expose any official who violates accepted legal, ethical, or performance standards.

The press was acting in its watchdog role in 2004 when it reported the abuse of prisoners by U.S. soldiers in Iraq. Graphic photos of naked Iraqi prisoners forced into humiliating sexual poses and acts shocked the nation and the world. Allegations of abuse in U.S. military prisons in Iraq had been circulating for months, but publication of the photos brought the issue into the open. High-ranking U.S. officials, including Secretary of Defense Donald Rumsfeld, had learned of the photos months earlier but had not shared their discovery with President Bush or Congress. After the photos were aired on television and published in newspapers, Congress launched hearings to discover why U.S. troops had violated laws governing the treatment of war prisoners and who should be held responsible.

Acting in its watchdog role, the press in recent decades has vigorously pursued allegations of official wrongdoing. The Watergate scandal is the most renowned example. Led by the *Washington Post,* the press uncovered evidence that high-ranking officials in the Nixon administration had lied about their role in the burglary of the Democratic National Committee's headquarters and the subsequent cover-up. President Richard Nixon was forced to resign, as was his attorney general, John Mitchell. The press also exposed illegal government activity (the Iran-Contra scandal) during the Reagan presidency and illicit personal behavior (the Monica Lewinsky scandal) during the Clinton presidency.

watchdog role The accepted responsibility of the media to protect the public from deceitful, careless, incompetent, and corrupt officials by standing ready to expose any official who violates accepted legal, ethical, or performance standards.

Simulation
www.mhhe.com/pattersontad7

GLOBAL Perspective

Americans in an Interdependent World

Global Television and Foreign Policy

As the casualties continued to mount after President George W. Bush declared that the war in Iraq was over, he came under increasing pressure to revise his timetable for handing sovereignty back to the Iraqis. Bush initially had wanted a lengthy transition in which the United States controlled policies. By 2004, however, he was committed to a drastically shortened timetable.

Was Bush's decision to change his policies wholly a response to unanticipated problems in Iraq? Or was it forced partly by television footage of the deaths of U.S. soldiers and other unfavorable developments in Iraq?

In just the past few decades, global television networks such as CNN have developed the capacity to provide live television coverage from almost anywhere in the world. The Iraq war was not the first time television viewers had been saturated with pictures of armed conflict. During the previous decade, Americans had been eyewitnesses to fighting in places such as the Persian Gulf, Somalia, Bosnia, Kosovo, and Afghanistan. The Iraq war illustrated yet again that global television had broken down the boundaries of space and time that once formed a buffer between Americans and warfare in distant areas of the globe.

Some analysts believe that television coverage has had a major influence on U.S. foreign policy. They point, for example, to U.S. intervention in Somalia in the early 1990s. Civil war and famine in that country had created widespread malnutrition and resulted in thousands of deaths. CNN's pictures of long lines of starving refugees touched a responsive chord in the United States and other countries, and the United Nations sent a humanitarian mission to Somalia that included American soldiers. This intervention turned sour when warring Somalia clans threatened the mission. An American military unit was ambushed, and several dozen U.S. soldiers died. Television captured the haunting image of one of the dead soldiers being dragged by a mob through the streets of the Somalia capital, and public opinion quickly shifted. Americans had supported the humanitarian mission, but they now wanted U.S. troops pulled out of Somalia as rapidly as possible. Within a short period, the troops were withdrawn.

Although the effect of global television on public policy can easily be exaggerated, it can sometimes force policymakers to act more hastily or in different ways than they might otherwise act. With its preference for action and drama, television in its war coverage tends to play up conflict and death rather than cooperation and progress. The compelling news story out of Iraq after the active combat phase was not the reopening of schools or the rebuilding of the oil industry. The coverage concentrated instead on the deaths of U.S. soldiers, the frustrating search for weapons of mass destruction, and the abuse of Iraqi prisoners, contributing to declining public support for a protracted stay in Iraq.

Some analysts see this type of coverage as a positive development because it mobilizes public opinion and makes leaders more responsive to it. They claim that it makes it harder for leaders to paint rosy scenarios that encourage Americans to support a policy simply because their leaders present it as the proper course of action. Other analysts are critical of the development. They argue that television's pictures tend to reflect only the most incendiary aspects of a situation and thus serve to distort both the situation and the public's response to it, possibly forcing policymakers to base policy choices on short-time political considerations rather than on long-term policy objectives.

These examples indicate that the press, as watchdog, is a vital part of the American system of checks on those who hold positions of power.

There is an inherent tension between the watchdog role and the common-carrier role. The watchdog role demands that the journalist maintain a skeptical view of government and keep it at a distance. The common-carrier role requires the journalist to maintain close ties with government officials. In the period before Watergate, the common-carrier role was clearly the dominant orientation. It perhaps still is, but journalists have become increasingly critical of political leaders and institutions.

Journalists are intent on publicizing the missteps of political leaders. Given the enormous size of the U.S. government, there is plenty to criticize if journalists want to focus on the negative. The media's preference for "bad news" can be seen, for example, in the fact that the negative coverage of presidential candidates has risen steadily in recent decades and now exceeds the positive coverage (see Figure 10–3).

"Bad news" characterizes the coverage of Democrats and Republicans alike. Although surveys indicate that most journalists lean toward the Democratic party in their personal beliefs, studies have found partisan bias to be a relatively small factor in political coverage.[30] Other influences, including the norm of objectivity, counterbalance the effect of partisanship on journalists' news decisions. On the other hand, there is no rule of journalism that limits negativity.[31] Coverage of the Democrat-controlled Congress of 1993–1994 by the national media was nearly 70 percent negative;

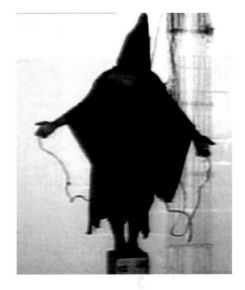

The publication of photos showing the abuse of Iraqi prisoners by U.S. soldiers undermined the U.S. government's claim that allegations about prisoner abuse were exaggerated. The press was acting in its watchdog role when it published the photos and reported on conditions in U.S. military prisons in Iraq. The news coverage led to a congressional investigation.

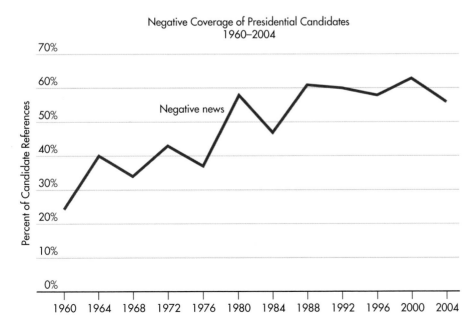

Negative Coverage of Presidential Candidates
1960–2004

Negative news

Percent of Candidate References

70%
60%
50%
40%
30%
20%
10%
0%

1960 1964 1968 1972 1976 1980 1984 1988 1992 1996 2000 2004

Figure 10–3

Negative Coverage of Major-Party Presidential Nominees, 1960–2004

In the 1960s, candidates received largely favorable news coverage. Today their coverage is mostly negative.

Source: Thomas E. Patterson, *Out of Order* (New York: Vintage, 1994), 20, for 1960–1992; Center for Media and Public Affairs, for 1996. The 2000–2004 estimates were derived from multiple sources. The 2004 percentage is based on preliminary data.

Presidential politics is a favorite topic of the press. Here, Democratic presidential nominee John Kerry is surrounded by reporters during a 2004 campaign stop. Like that of all other recent presidential nominees, Kerry's news coverage was substantially negative in tone.

when the Congress shifted to Republican hands in 1995–1996, coverage was also nearly 70 percent negative in tone.[32] The fact is that the real bias of the press is not a liberal as opposed to a conservative bent, but a pronounced tendency to report what is wrong with politics and politicians rather than what is right.

Critics argue that the press has gone too far in its search for bad news, claiming that it now faults nearly everything that politicians say and do, thereby undermining the public trust on which effective leadership is built. Journalists claim that they are merely doing their job—that the public is better served by a highly skeptical and intrusive press than by a compliant one. CNN correspondent Bob Franken said, "We historically are not supposed to be popular, and it's almost our role to be the bearer of bad news."[33]

The Public-Representative Role

public-representative role A role whereby the media attempt to act as the public's representatives.

Traditionally, the **public-representative role**—that of spokesperson for and advocate of the public—has belonged to political leaders, political institutions, and political organizations. Today, however, many reporters believe they also have a mandate to represent the public. "[Our] chief duty," newscaster Roger Mudd claims, "is to put before the nation its unfinished business."[34]

Although the press has to some degree always acted as a stand-in for the people, the desire of journalists to play the role of public advocate increased significantly after the 1960s. As journalists' status rose, they became more assertive, a tendency sharpened by the trend toward interpretive reporting. Vietnam and Watergate also contributed to the change; these events convinced many journalists that their judgments were superior to those of political leaders. James Reston of the *New York Times* said of Vietnam, "Maybe the historians will agree that the reporters and cameras were decisive in the end. They brought the issue of the war to the people, before the Congress and the courts, and forced the withdrawal of American power from Vietnam."[35]

Allegations in 1998 of a sexual relationship between intern Monica Lewinsky and President Bill Clinton unleashed a media feeding frenzy that disrupted the White House's policy agenda.

Nevertheless, there are at least two basic reasons for concluding that journalists are not nearly as well suited as political leaders to the role of public representative. First, the news media are not subject to the level of public accountability required of a public representative. Political institutions are made responsible to the public by a formal mechanism of accountability—elections. The vote gives officeholders a reason to act in the majority's interest, and it offers citizens an opportunity to boot from office anyone they feel has failed them. Thousands of elected officials have lost their jobs this way. The public has no comparable hold over the press. Journalists are neither chosen by nor removable by the people.

A second obstacle to journalists' attempts to play the role of public representative is that representation requires a point of view. Politics is essentially the mobilization of bias—that is, it involves the representation of particular values and interests. Political parties and interest groups, as explained in Chapters 8 and 9, exist to represent particular interests in society. But what political interests do the media represent? A few news outlets, such as Fox News, promote a point of view, but the large majority do not. As a television executive once said, journalists cover news "from nobody's point of view."[36] What he was saying, in effect, was that journalists do not consistently represent the political concerns of any segment of society. They respond to news opportunities, not to political interests. Above all, they prize good stories.[37]

The 2004 criminal trials of Michael Jackson, Kobe Bryant, Scott Peterson, and Martha Stewart are prime examples. These trials, and the hoopla surrounding them, received far more news coverage in 2004 than health care, unemployment, drug abuse, education, and every other domestic policy problem.

Underlying the press's obsession with the dramatic story is its quest for profits. The bottom line, rather than the public interest, increasingly drives news coverage. Audience competition has intensified with the spread of cable and satellite television, and the news has become increasingly sensational. During the 2004 campaign, as the public was expressing concern with Iraq and the economy, the press spent weeks on end covering the events of thirty years earlier: whether George W. Bush had fulfilled his National Guard duties and whether the heroic portrayal of John Kerry's Vietnam service was fully accurate.

Even when the media cover policy developments, the reporting can be distorted by the quest for higher ratings. The U.S. invasion of Iraq in 2003, for example, was dominated by audience-pleasing reports from the battlefield, while other important aspects were underplayed. This imbalance affected perceptions of the war. Many Americans wrongly believed, for example, that the U.S. invasion had the support of most countries in the world.[38]

The relentless search for attention-getting stories weakens the press's ability to provide citizens with a clear understanding of what is broadly at issue in politics. Journalist Walter Lippmann put it plainly when he said:

> The press is no substitute for [political] institutions. It is like the beam of a searchlight that moves restlessly about, bringing one episode and then another out of darkness into vision. Men cannot do the work of the world by this light alone. They cannot govern society by episodes, incidents, and interruptions.[39]

 ## ORGANIZING THE PUBLIC IN THE MEDIA AGE

Lippmann's point was not that news organizations are somehow inferior to political organizations but that each has a different role and responsibility in society. Democracy cannot operate effectively without a free press that fulfills its signaler, common-carrier, and watchdog roles. Citizens must have access to timely and uncensored news about public affairs. However, the media cannot also be expected to do the job of political institutions.

As previous chapters have emphasized, the challenge of citizen influence lies in organizing the public so that people can act together effectively. The news media merely appear to meet this challenge. The fact that millions of people each day receive the same news about their government does not mold them into an organized community. The news creates a pseudo-community: citizens who feel they are part of a functioning whole until they try to act on their news awareness. The futility of media-centered democracy was dramatized in the movie *Network* when its central character, a television anchorman, became enraged at the nation's political leadership and urged his viewers to go to their windows and yell "I'm mad as hell and I'm not going to take it anymore!" Citizens heeded his instructions, but the main effect was to raise the network's ratings. It was not clear what officials in Washington were expected to do about several million people leaning out their windows and shouting a vague slogan. The film vividly illustrated the fact that the news can raise public consciousness as a prelude to action but cannot itself organize the public in any meaningful way. When public opinion on an issue is already formed, the media can serve as a channel for the expression of that opinion. But when society's choices are in their formative stage, the media are not ordinarily an adequate guide to what action should be taken.[40]

Why Should I Care?

Informative News

For nearly four months in 2001, the Gary Condit story dominated America's news. It was not a distinction that was earned by Rep. Condit's stature (he was a backbench member of the House of Representatives) or by new developments (the known facts hardly changed at all during the story's run). The story's prominence owed to its ingredients—power, sex, and Condit's possible involvement in the disappearance of congressional intern Chandra Levy.

On September 11, 2001, the Condit story abruptly disappeared. The attacks on the World Trade Center and the Pentagon swept it out of the news.

Before September 11, however, international terrorism was not a leading news subject, even though there were public warnings of the danger it posed. Earlier that year, the U.S. Commission on National Security had predicted a "catastrophic attack" by international terrorists and had urged the creation of a homeland security agency. CIA director George Tenet had also sounded the alarm, saying in a Senate hearing that Osama bin Laden's "global network" was the "most immediate and serious" threat facing the nation. These warnings were almost completely ignored by the U.S. press. In the year preceding the World Trade Center and Pentagon attacks, for example, the Al Qaeda terrorist network was

mentioned by name only once on the network's evening newscasts.

The Condit and terrorism examples illustrate a frequent failing of U.S. news media in recent decades. In their pursuit of higher ratings, they have often been more interested in entertaining their audience than informing it. In the process, they have failed to fully meet their public service responsibility. The press has an obligation to provide its audience with a view of the world that does not lead people to think they are in the Land of Oz when in fact they are traveling through Kansas.

Of course, citizens themselves contribute to the problem by consuming titillating or trivial news. During the summer of 2001, the highest-rated television program was ABC correspondent Connie Chung's interview with Gary Condit. Unless citizens show a preference for serious news coverage, they are unlikely to get it on a regular basis.

Nevertheless, the press has an obligation to provide the public with informative news. As former NBC executive Reuven Frank said in a 1998 article in the *Columbia Journalism Review:* "This business of giving people what they want is a dope pusher's argument. News is something that people don't know they're interested in until they hear about it. The job of the journalist is to take what's important and make it interesting."

Summary Self-Test
www.mhhe.com/pattersontad7

In the nation's first century, the press was allied closely with the political parties and helped the parties mobilize public opinion. Gradually the press freed itself from this partisan relationship and developed a form of reporting, known as objective journalism, that emphasizes the fair and accurate reporting of newsworthy developments. The foundation of modern American news rests on the presentation and evaluation of significant events, not on the advocacy of partisan ideas. The nation's news organizations do not differ greatly in their reporting; broadcast stations and newspapers throughout the country emphasize many of the same events, issues, and personalities, following the lead of the major broadcast networks, a few elite newspapers, and the wire services.

The press performs four basic roles in a free society. First, in their signaler role, journalists communicate infor-

mation to the public about events and problems that they consider important, relevant, and therefore newsworthy. Second, the press serves as a common carrier in that it provides political leaders with a channel for addressing the public. Third, the press acts as a public protector, or watchdog, by exposing deceitful, careless, or corrupt officials. The American media can and, to a significant degree, do perform these roles adequately.

The press is less well suited, however, to the fourth role it plays, that of public representative. This role requires a consistent political viewpoint and public accountability, neither of which the press possesses. The media are not a substitute for effective political institutions. The press's strength lies ultimately in its capacity to inform the public, not in its attempts to serve as the public's representative.

STUDY CORNER

Key Terms

agenda setting *(p. 322)*

common-carrier role *(p. 322)*

descriptive reporting *(p. 311)*

interpretive reporting *(p. 311)*

news *(p. 308)*

objective journalism *(p. 310)*

partisan press *(p. 309)*

press (news media) *(p. 308)*

public-representative role *(p. 326)*

signaler role *(p. 321)*

watchdog role *(p. 324)*

Self-Test

1. Recent trends in news reporting include:
   a. presenting liberal rather than conservative columnists.
   b. combining the activities of the news and advertising departments.
   c. an interpretive style of reporting.
   d. a decentralization of media ownership and along with that greater diversity in coverage.

2. When the media are playing the role of watchdog, they are primarily:
   a. protecting the public from deceitful, careless, incompetent, or corrupt public officials.
   b. conveying objective information about an event and minimizing reporting bias.
   c. trying to get their audience more interested in issues of animal rights.
   d. trying to help their favorite political party at the expense of the other.

3. The news is said to provide a selective depiction of reality because it:
   a. emphasizes dramatic events rather than the slow and steady social, economic, and political developments that typically have a larger impact on the nation.
   b. is biased in favor of a Democratic point of view.
   c. emphasizes the daily lives of ordinary Americans rather than the actions of public officials.
   d. places more emphasis on international affairs than these developments deserve.

4. Broadcasting revolutionized the American media because it:

   a. was the first truly national mass medium.
   b. opened a direct, instantaneous channel between a leader and the people.
   c. reached millions of people simultaneously.
   d. all of the above.

5. The news media have grown more visible and powerful in recent decades and, in the process, have shown that they can do the job of:
   a. political parties.
   b. interest groups.
   c. elected representatives.
   d. none of the above.

6. Desire for profit making and an increased share of the audience market encourage the media to:
   a. prefer dramatic news stories.
   b. keep public policy issues at the top of the news coverage agenda.
   c. shun sensational stories.
   d. provide the public with a clear understanding of what is broadly at issue in politics.

7. Objective journalism is based on the reporting of opinions in preference to "facts." (T/F)

8. The United States' libel laws strongly favor the press. (T/F)

9. News organizations seek to make a profit, which leads them to prefer news stories that will attract and hold an audience. (T/F)

10. In the past few decades, media ownership has been broken up and decentralized. (T/F)

Critical Thinking

Why does almost every U.S. news outlet, despite having the freedom to say nearly anything it wants, cover virtu-

ally the same national stories in virtually the same way as other news organizations?

Suggested Readings

Bagdikian, Ben H. *The Media Monopoly*, 6th ed. Boston: Beacon Press, 2000. An examination of the growing power of the press, including tendencies toward monopolies of ownership and news production.

Baum, Matthew. *Soft News Goes to War*. Princeton, N.J.: Princeton University Press, 2003. A study of the impact of soft-news coverage of war.

Cook, Timothy E. *Governing with the News: The News Media as a Political Institution*. Chicago: University of Chicago Press, 1997. An analysis of the press in its role as a political institution.

Hamilton, James T. *All the News That's Fit to Sell*. Princeton, N.J.: Princeton University Press, 2004. A careful study of the economic influences on news content.

Jamieson, Kathleen Hall, and Paul Waldman. *The Press Effect*. New York: Oxford University Press, 2002. A penetrating analysis of U.S. journalism and news coverage.

Maltese, John Anthony. *Spin Control: The White House Office of Communications and the Management of Presidential News*. Chapel Hill: University of North Carolina Press, 1994. An assessment of how presidents attempt to manage news coverage.

Patterson, Thomas E. *Out of Order*. New York: Vintage Books, 1994. An analysis of how election news coverage has changed in recent decades.

Sparrow, Bartholomew H. *Uncertain Guardians*. Baltimore, Md.: Johns Hopkins University Press, 1999. A systematic assessment of the news media's political role and tendencies.

List of Websites

http://www.cmpa.com/

The website for the Center for Media and Public Affairs (CMPA), a nonpartisan organization that analyzes news coverage on a continuing basis; provides analyses of news content that are useful to anyone interested in the media's political coverage.

http://www.drudgereport.com/

The website through which Matt Drudge (The Drudge Report) has challenged the traditional media's control of the news.

http://www.fcc.gov/

The Federal Communications Commission (FCC) website, which provides information on broadcasting regulation and current issues.

http://www.newslink.org/

Provides access to more than a thousand news organizations, including most U.S. daily newspapers.

Participate!

If you are like most citizens, news consumption is the politically related activity that takes up most of your time. And if you are like most citizens, you will spend this time without thinking critically about what you are seeing and hearing. The next time you watch a television newscast or read a newspaper, pay attention to how a story is constructed. Is it framed in terms of conflict? Does it sensationalize the material? Is it framed critically—that is, does it present a negative view of a development, institution, or leader? How else might the same factual information have been presented? Do significant items of information or points of view seem to be missing from the story?

Extra Credit

For up-to-the-minute *New York Times* articles, interactive simulations, graphics, study tools, and more links and quizzes, visit the text's Online Learning Center at www.mhhe.com/pattersontad7.

(Self-Test Answers: 1.c   2.a   3.a   4.d   5.d   6.a   7.F   8.T   9.T   10.F)

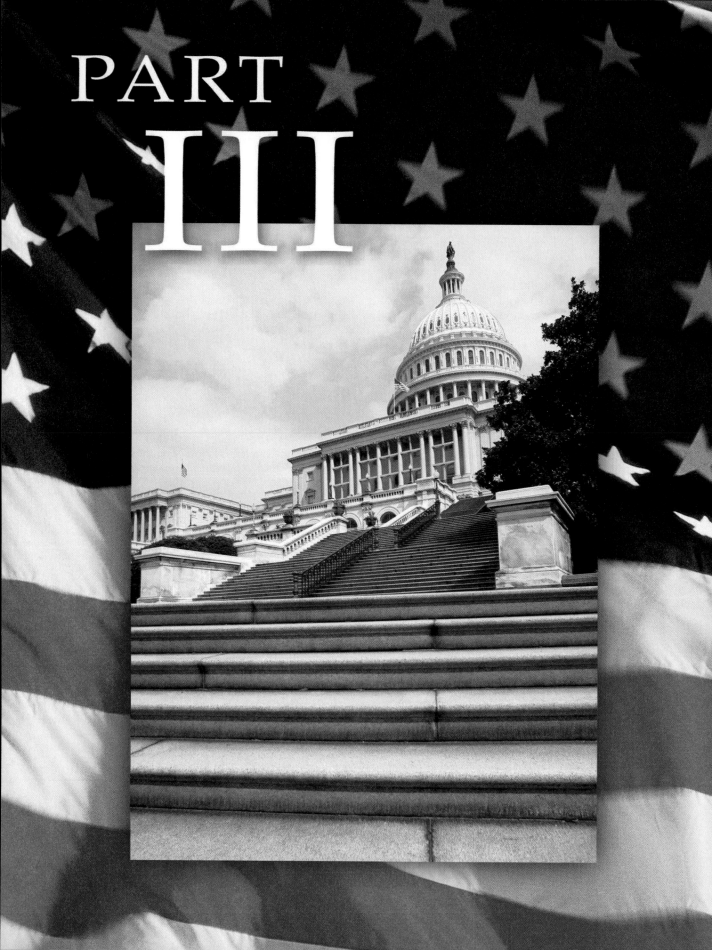

PART
III

Governing Institutions

American democracy is often described as government by the people. But direct democracy is a practical impossibility in a nation the size of the United States. Americans are governed largely through institutions.

A debate has long raged over the proper relationship between a people and their representatives. One view holds that representatives should follow the expressed opinions of the governed; if they do not, they will promote their own narrow interests. Another view, first elaborated by the English theorist Edmund Burke, holds that representatives should exercise their best judgment in deciding policy; if they listen too closely to those who elected them, they will serve parochial interests rather than the general interests of society.

The governing system of the United States embodies both conceptions of representation. The presidency is a truly national office that, as Chapter 12 will describe, encourages its incumbent to take a national view of issues. On the other hand, Congress, as Chapter 11 will show, is both a national institution and a body subject to powerful local influences.

Americans are also governed through unelected bureaucrats and appointed judges whose decisions, as Chapters 13 and 14 will describe, can in some instances be as far-reaching as those made by the people's elected representatives.

PART THREE OUTLINE

11

Congress:
Balancing National Goals and Local Interests

There are two Congresses. . . . The tight-knit complex world of
Capitol Hill is a long way from [the member's district], in perspective
and outlook as well as in miles.

Roger Davidson and Walter Oleszek[1]

In late 2003, Congress faced the reality of a ballooning federal deficit that was the product of a slow economy, steep tax cuts, increased spending on social services, and the rising cost of military operations abroad. A budget shortfall of $400–500 billion dollars was projected for 2004. How would Congress respond? How would it cut spending?

As it happened, the appropriations bill that was forged in Congress contained more than $20 billion in new spending on pork-barrel projects. Nearly every House and Senate member could point to one project or another that would benefit his or her home district or state. Fifty million dollars, for example, was designated for construction of a rain forest exhibit in the state of Iowa. The sponsor was Senator Charles Grassley, a Republican with a reputation for fiscal conservatism. Grassley, chair of the Senate Finance Committee, which oversees the appropriations process in the Senate, argued that the rain forest project would be good for the country as well as for Iowa. While it would boost tourism in Iowa, it would also serve as a national laboratory for testing clean energy ideas. What Grassley did not say was that it would also be good politics. The 2004 election was less than a year away, and although citizens routinely complain of government waste, they rarely consider a federally funded project for their own district or state a bad idea.

The story of the 2004 appropriations bill illustrates the dual nature of Congress: it is both a lawmaking institution for the country and a representative assembly for states and districts.[2] Members of Congress have both an individual duty to serve the interests of their separate constituencies and a collective duty to protect the interests of the nation as a whole. Attention to constituency interests is the common denominator of a national institution in which each member must please the voters back home in order to win reelection.[3]

This chapter examines Congress, beginning with congressional election and organization and concluding with congressional policymaking. The following points are emphasized in this chapter:

- *Congressional elections tend to have a strong local orientation and to favor incumbents.* Congressional office provides incumbents with substantial resources (free publicity, staff, and legislative influence) that give them (particularly House members) a major advantage in election campaigns. However, incumbency also has some liabilities that contribute to turnover in congressional membership.

The U.S. Capitol in Washington, D.C., with the House wing in the foreground. The Senate meets in the wing at the right of the central rotunda (under the dome). The offices of the House and Senate party leaders—Speaker, vice president, majority and minority leaders and whips—are located in the Capitol. Other members of Congress have their offices in nearby buildings.

- *Although party leaders in Congress provide collective leadership, the work of Congress is done mainly through its committees and subcommittees, each of which has its separate leadership and policy jurisdiction.* The committee system of Congress allows a broad sharing of power and leadership, which serves the power and reelection needs of Congress's members but fragments the institution.

- *Congress lacks the direction and organization required for the development of comprehensive national policies, but it is well organized to handle policies of relatively narrow scope.* At times, Congress takes the lead on broad national issues, but ordinarily it does not do so.

- *Congress's policymaking role is based on three major functions: lawmaking, representation, and oversight.*

CONGRESS AS A CAREER: ELECTION TO CONGRESS

In the nation's first century, service in the Congress was not a career for most of its members. Before 1900, at least a third and sometimes as many as half the seats in Congress changed hands at each election. Most members left voluntarily. Because travel was slow and arduous, serving in the nation's capital required members to spend months away from their families. And because the national government was not the center of power and politics that it is today, many politicians preferred to serve in state capitals.

The modern Congress is very different. Most of its members are professional politicians, and a seat in the U.S. Senate or House is as high as most of them can expect to rise in politics. The pay (about $155,000 a year) is reasonably good, and the prestige of their office is substantial, particularly if they serve in the Senate. A lengthy career in Congress is the goal of most of its members.[4]

Electoral Competition: Why It's Important to You

During the past half-century, congressional elections have increasingly resulted in the reelection of incumbents. Their advantages are enormous. At taxpayer expense, they have a large staff in Washington and a smaller one in their district or state, and most of these staff resources are used to promote their standing with constituents. When an election year arrives, they also have a substantial fund-raising advantage as a result of their constituency contacts and the support they receive from interest groups that have a stake in gaining favor with members of Congress.

In combination with incumbents' other advantages, the effect of this support is to dampen electoral competition. About 95 percent of House incumbents are reelected. Their margin of reelection typically is very high. In recent House races, about two-thirds of incumbents have won by more than 60 percent of the vote. In fact, more than 10 percent of House incumbents have been reelected unopposed—the other major party did not even bother to field a candidate.

This situation weakens the voters' ability to influence government through their votes. When incumbents win almost as a matter of routine and when elections are one-sided, the vote is not a very powerful instrument. People may still vote out of a sense of civic duty, but they have no real reason to think, in most races, that their vote is going to make all that much difference. And because turnover in Congress is limited in any given election, the likelihood that an election will serve as a basis for major policy change is slim.

Electoral competition is the lifeblood of democracy. It is through their votes that ordinary people have the greatest chance of influencing the course of policy. But if that vote is diminished because of the enormous advantages of incumbency, the public's influence is diminished accordingly.

What do you think might be done to strengthen the competitiveness of congressional elections? Would you favor limits on the number of terms a member of Congress could serve? Would you favor public funding of elections? Would you favor reductions in the size of congressional staffs so that incumbents would have only the staff required for their legislative activities? Would you favor restrictions on PAC contributions?

Incumbents have a high probability of being reelected (see Figure 11–1). In recent elections, 95 percent of House incumbents and nearly 90 percent of Senate incumbents seeking another term have been reelected. These figures overestimate slightly an incumbent's chances of reelection. A few incumbents retire from Congress when faced with a campaign they believe they will lose. On balance, however, incumbents have an edge on their opponents, as their margin of victory indicates. In recent elections, two-thirds of House incumbents and nearly half of Senate incumbents seeking reelection have received 60 percent or more of the vote. Even when voters are convinced that Congress as an institution is performing badly, they reelect a large majority of its members. One reason is that many congressional districts and a few states are so lopsidedly Democratic or Republican that the candidate of the weaker party has no realistic chance of victory. However, whether their district is lopsided or competitive, incumbents have several built-in advantages over their challengers.

Using Incumbency to Stay in Congress

An incumbent promotes his or her reelection prospects by catering to the **constituency**: the body of citizens eligible to vote in their state or district.

constituency The individuals who live within the geographical area represented by an elected official. More narrowly, the body of citizens eligible to vote for a particular representative.

Figure 11–1

Recent Reelection Rates of House and Senate Incumbents

Congressional incumbents have a very good chance of winning another term, as indicated by the reelection rates of U.S. representatives and senators who sought reelection during the past five congressional elections.

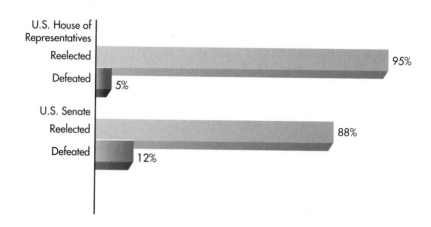

pork-barrel projects Laws whose tangible benefits are targeted at a particular legislator's constituency.

service strategy Use of personal staff by members of Congress to perform services for constituents in order to gain their support in future elections.

Members of Congress pay attention to constituency opinions when choosing positions on legislation, and they work hard to get their share of **pork-barrel projects** (a term referring to legislation that funds a special project for a particular locale, such as a new highway or hospital). They also respond to their constituents' individual needs, a practice known as the **service strategy.** Whether a constituent is seeking information about a government program, expressing an opinion about pending legislation, or looking for help in obtaining a federal benefit, the representative's staff is ready to assist.

Congressional staffers spend most of their time not on legislative matters but on constituency service and public relations—efforts that pay off on election day.[5] Each House member receives an office allowance of $750,000 a year, which supports a personal staff of fifteen to twenty full-time staff members.[6] Senators receive allowances that vary according to the population size of the state they represent. Senators' personal staffs average about forty employees.[7] Each member of Congress is also permitted several free mailings annually to constituent households, a privilege known as the frank.

Finally, incumbents have a decided advantage when it comes to raising campaign funds. Congressional elections have become increasingly expensive in recent decades because of the high cost of polling, televised advertising, and other modern techniques (see Figure 11–2). Today a successful House campaign in a competitive district will cost more than a million dollars. The price of victory in competitive Senate races is much higher, ranging from several million dollars in small states to $15 million or more in larger states. A study by the *Congressional Quarterly* found that only 10 percent of incumbents said they had trouble raising enough money to conduct an effective campaign, compared with 70 percent of challengers.[8] Many challengers are able to raise only enough money for a token campaign.

Incumbents obtain a fund-raising advantage from their past campaigns and constituent service, which enable them to develop mailing lists of potential contributors. Individual contributions, most of which are $100 or less, account for about 50 percent of all funds raised by candidates and are obtained mainly through fund-raising events and direct-mail solicitation. Incumbents also have an edge with political action committees, or PACs, which are the fund-raising

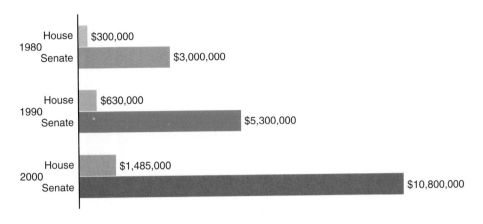

Figure 11–2

Congressional Campaign Expenditures
The cost of running for congressional office has risen sharply as campaign techniques—television advertising, opinion polling, and so on—have become more elaborate and sophisticated. The increase in spending can be seen from a comparison of the approximate average spending by both candidates per House or Senate seat at ten-year intervals, beginning in 1980.
Source: Federal Election Commission.

arm of interest groups (see Chapter 9). Most PACs are reluctant to oppose an incumbent unless it is clear that the candidate is vulnerable. More than 85 percent of PAC contributions in recent elections have been given to incumbents; their challengers received less than 15 percent (see Figure 11–3). "Anytime you go against an incumbent, you take a minute and think long and hard about what your rationale is," said Desiree Anderson, director of the Realtors PAC.[9] (A race without an incumbent—called an **open-seat election**—usually brings out a strong candidate from each party and involves heavy spending, especially when the parties are evenly matched in the state or district.)

open-seat election An election in which there is no incumbent in the race.

The Pitfalls of Incumbency

Incumbency is not without its liabilities. Potential pitfalls include troublesome issues, personal misconduct, variation in turnout, strong challengers, and, for some House members, redistricting.

Troublesome Issues

Disruptive issues are a potential threat to incumbents. Most elections are not waged in the context of such issues, but when they exist, incumbents are at greater risk. In the 1992 and 1994 elections, when the public was angry over economic and social conditions and believed Congress was mired in partisan bickering, the number of incumbents who were defeated exceeded 10 percent. After that, the economy improved and the number dropped to roughly 5 percent.

Figure 11–3

Allocation of PAC Contributions Between Incumbents and Challengers in Congressional Races That Included an Incumbent, 1978–2004.

In allocating campaign contributions, PACs favor incumbent members of Congress over their challengers by a wide margin.

Source: Federal Elections Commission. Figures for 2004 based on preliminary data.

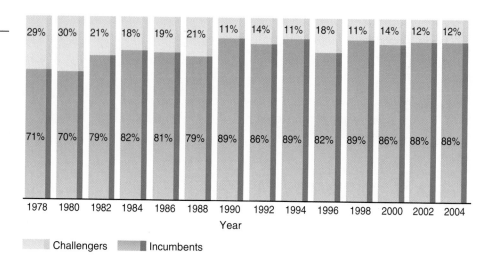

	Challengers	Incumbents
1978	29%	71%
1980	30%	70%
1982	21%	79%
1984	18%	82%
1986	19%	81%
1988	21%	79%
1990	11%	89%
1992	14%	86%
1994	11%	89%
1996	18%	82%
1998	11%	89%
2000	14%	86%
2002	12%	88%
2004	12%	88%

Year

Personal Misconduct

Members of Congress can also fall prey to scandal. Life in Washington can be fast paced, glamorous, and expensive, and some members of Congress get caught up in influence peddling, sex scandals, and other forms of misconduct. Roughly a fourth of House incumbents who lost their bid for reelection in the past two decades were shadowed by ethical questions. "The first thing to being reelected is to stay away from scandal, even minor scandal," says political scientist John Hibbing.[10] Representative Gary Condit found that out in 2002 when he was defeated in the Democratic primary. A married man, Condit had been romantically linked to Chandra Levy, an intern in his office who was missing and later found dead from foul play. Even top congressional leaders are not immune from the effects of scandal, as illustrated by the experience of former House Ways and Means Committee Chairman Dan Rostenkowski. Accused of gross misuse of congressional funds, he lost his House seat in 1994 despite having won by 20 percentage points two years earlier and outspending his 1994 opponent by more than ten to one.

Turnout Variation: The Midterm Election Problem

Historically, the party holding the presidency loses seats in the midterm congressional elections, particularly in the House of Representatives. The 2002 midterm elections, when the Republicans had George W. Bush in the White House and picked up a handful of House seats, was only the fourth time in more than a century that the president's party gained seats.

The pattern is largely attributable to a drop-off in turnout for midterm elections.[11] The voters who go to the polls only during presidential election years tend to have weaker party loyalties and therefore are more responsive to the issues of the moment. In any given election, these issues tend to favor one party, which contributes to the success of its congressional candidates as well as its presidential nominee. Most of the party's congressional candidates who win

U.S. Representative William (Bill) Clay represents a heavily Democratic district in St. Louis. The biggest reelection obstacles for House members from one-sided districts are redistricting, personal impropriety, scandal, and a well-funded primary election opponent. In the absence of any such factor, as in Clay's case, reelection is nearly a sure thing.

narrowly owe their margin of victory to these voters. However, these voters stay home during midterm elections. Thus, unless these incumbents can make inroads among midterm voters who backed their opponent two years earlier, they stand a good chance of losing. Since many of these voters are strong partisans, they are not easily swayed, and the result is the midterm defeat of some of these incumbents.

Strong Challengers: A Problem for Senators

Incumbents are also vulnerable to strong challengers. Senators are particularly likely to face formidable opponents: after the presidency, the Senate is the highest rung of the political ladder. Governors and House members are frequent challengers for Senate seats, and they have the electoral base, reputation, and experience to compete effectively. Moreover, the U.S. Senate lures wealthy challengers. Maria Cantwell spent $10 million of her own money to defeat Senator Slade Gorton in the state of Washington's Senate race in 2000. Cantwell made her fortune as an executive with RealNetworks, a high-tech company.

House incumbents have less reason to fear strong challengers. A House seat often is not attractive enough to induce prominent local politicians, such as mayors or state legislators, to risk their political careers in a challenge to an incumbent.[12] This situation leaves the field open to weak opponents with little or no governmental or political experience. Indeed, in recent elections, more than 10 percent of House incumbents have run unopposed for reelection.

Redistricting: A Problem for House Members

Every ten years, after each population census, the 435 seats in the House are reallocated among the states in proportion to their population. This process is called **reapportionment.** States that have gained population since the last

reapportionment The reallocation of House seats among states after each census as a result of population changes.

When Massachusetts was redistricted in 1812, Governor Elbridge Gerry had the lines of one district redrawn in order to ensure that a candidate of his party would be elected. Cartoonist Elkanah Tinsdale, noting that the strangely shaped district resembled a salamander, called it a "Gerry-mander."

redistricting The process of altering election districts in order to make them as nearly equal in population as possible. Redistricting takes place every ten years, after each population census.

gerrymandering The process by which the party in power draws election district boundaries in a way that is to the advantage of its candidates.

census may acquire additional House seats, while those that have lost population may lose seats. New York and Illinois were among the states that lost one or more House seats as a result of the 2000 census; Arizona and Washington were among the states that gained one or more seats. (The Senate is not affected by population change, because each state has two senators regardless of its size.)

The responsibility for redrawing House election districts after a reapportionment—a process called **redistricting**—rests with the state governments. States are required by law to make their districts as nearly equal in population as possible. There are many ways, however, to divide a state into districts of nearly equal size, and the party in power in the state legislature will do so in a way that favors candidates of its party. One method is to stack a few districts with overwhelming numbers of voters from the opposing party. This tactic ensures that the opposing party will win easily in these districts, but it also reduces the number of voters from that party in other districts, thus placing it at a disadvantage in most races. The process by which one party draws district boundaries to its advantage is called **gerrymandering.**

Reapportionment, redistricting, and gerrymandering are a potential threat to House incumbents. Turnover in House elections typically is higher after a new census than in previous elections. The newly redrawn districts include voters who are unfamiliar with the incumbent, thereby diminishing an advantage that incumbents typically have over their challengers. Moreover, when a state loses congressional seats, there are fewer districts than there are incumbents, and incumbents may end up running against each other. Finally, incumbents of the party that does not control the state legislature may find themselves having to compete in redrawn districts that are stacked with the opposition party's voters.

In 2003, congressional redistricting may have entered a new phase that could further threaten incumbents. Although congressional redistricting traditionally has taken place only once after each new census, the Republican-controlled Texas legislature decided that it did not like the results of the redistricting that had occurred after the 2000 census. In the 2002 elections, Democrats won seventeen of Texas's thirty-two House seats. In 2003, the Texas legislature redrew district boundaries in a way designed to allow Republican candidates to pick up an additional half dozen seats in the House. Republicans in Colorado tried the same tactic, but the Colorado Supreme Court disallowed it, noting that the state's constitution provided for a single redistricting after each census. The Texas constitution has no such provision, and the courts upheld Texas's new redistricting arrangement.

Safe Incumbency and Representation

Although incumbents can and do lose their reelection bids, they normally win easily. An effect is to reduce Congress's responsiveness to political change. Research indicates that incumbents tend to hold relatively stable policy posi-

Should Partisan Gerrymandering Be Abolished?

Elections to the U.S. House of Representatives are uncompetitive and have been made so deliberately through a process of partisan gerrymandering. In redrawing election-district boundaries after the census, the states tend to draw the lines in ways designed to create safe Democratic or Republican districts. Of the 435 House districts today, roughly 400 are safely in the hands of one party. An issue is whether partisan gerrymandering puts election of House members in the hands of the states rather than in the hands of the voters. In *Vieth v. Jubelirer* (2004), the Supreme Court by a 5-4 vote refused to overturn Pennsylvania's redistricting arrangement, saying that, although there might be constitutional limits on partisan redistricting, workable standards for determining fairness in redistricting do not exist. Following are excerpts from two amicus curiae briefs filed in the Pennsylvania case.

Debating the Issues

Yes: Challengers to incumbents and third party voters and candidates are disadvantaged when the two political parties create safe seats for themselves. '[Partisan]' gerrymandering violates the Constitution's Equal Protection Clause by intentionally discriminating against identifiable groups and diminishing those groups' political power. Congressional elections are becoming less competitive every year. . . . Over ninety percent of Americans live in congressional districts that are essentially one-party monopolies. The situation is even worse in some states. For example, in California, 50 out of 53 races were decided by margins of greater than 20 percent. In a related phenomenon, incumbents are now more than ever, nearly guaranteed reelection. . . . This situation is not mere happenstance, but rather the result of carefully orchestrated political gerrymandering—sometimes by one of the major political parties to the disadvantage of the other, and sometimes by the two parties colluding to protect their seats and their incumbents. . . . [E]ven though most states are close to evenly divided between the two major political parties, the vast majority of districts for the U.S. House of Representatives are drawn so as to prevent any real competition.

—*Center for Voting and Democracy*

No: Fairness in the redistricting process [has evaded] resolution for generations. Scholars cannot even agree on such foundational points as (1) whether there is a problem at all with respect to the ability of Republicans and Democrats to compete for control of the legislature; (2) if there is a problem, whether redistricting is to blame for it; (3) whether creation of safe seats is a bad thing, and, if so, whether it can be avoided; and (4) whether neutral, nonpartisan redistricting standards are either theoretically or practically possible. . . . Justice White [once] cited the work of the late Robert G. Dixon, Jr., "one of the foremost scholars of reapportionment," for the proposition "that there are no neutral lines for legislative districts . . . every line drawn aligns partisans and interest blocs in a particular way different from the alignment that would result from putting the line in some other place." Elsewhere, Professor Dixon rebuked those of his colleagues who aspire to discover universal principles of fair representation: "My own experience tells me that although I may find nonpartisanship in heaven, in the real world, and especially in academia, there are no nonpartisans, although there may be noncombatants."

—*Leadership of the Alabama Senate and House of Representatives*

tions during their time in office.[13] Thus, because few congressional seats normally change hands during an election, Congress does not normally change its direction all that much from election to election. Even when people are dissatisfied with national conditions, congressional elections sometimes produce only a small turnover in congressional membership.

Safe incumbency weakens the public's influence on Congress. Democracy depends on periodic shifts in power between the parties to bring public policy into closer alignment with public opinion. In European democracies, incumbents tend to win or lose depending on their political party's popularity, which

Constitutional Qualifications for Serving in Congress

Representatives: "No person shall be a Representative who shall not have attained to the age of twenty-five years, and been seven years a citizen of the United States, and who shall not, when elected, be an inhabitant of that State in which he shall be chosen." [Article I, Section 2]

Senators: "No person shall be a Senator who shall not have attained to the age of thirty years, and been nine years a citizen of the United States, and who shall not, when elected, be an inhabitant of the State for which he shall be chosen." [Article I, Section 3]

can change markedly from one election to the next. In the United States, incumbents are often able to overcome adverse political change through constituency service and other efforts on behalf of the residents of their particular state or district. It is worth noting that national legislators in other democracies do not have the large personal staffs and the substantial travel and publicity budgets that members of Congress have.

Who Are the Winners in Congressional Elections?

Although members of the House and Senate are elected to represent their constituents, the average representative is very different from the average American in virtually every respect.[14] Although only one in every three hundred fifty Americans is a lawyer, about one in three members of Congress has studied law. Attorneys are attracted to politics in part by Congress's role in lawmaking and by the public visibility that a campaign for office helps build, which in turn can make a private law practice more successful. Along with lawyers, professionals such as business executives, educators, bankers, and journalists account for more than 90 percent of congressional membership.[15] Blue-collar workers, clerical employees, and homemakers are seldom elected to Congress. Farmers and ranchers are not as rare; a fair number of House members from rural districts have agricultural backgrounds.

Finally, members of Congress are disproportionately white and male. Minority-group members and women each account for less than 15 percent of the Congress (see Chapter 5). This proportion, however, is twice that of a decade ago. Safe incumbency is a major obstacle to the election to Congress of more women and minorities.[16] In open-seat races in which they have run, they have won about half the time. However, they have been no more successful than other challengers in dislodging congressional incumbents. In elections to state and local office, where incumbency is less important, women and minority candidates have made greater inroads (see "States in the Nation").

 CONGRESSIONAL LEADERSHIP

The way Congress works is related to the way its members win election. Because of their independent power base in their state or district, members of Congress have substantial independence within the institution they serve. The Speaker of the House and the other top leaders in Congress are crucial to its

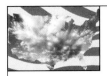

STATES IN THE NATION

Women in the State Legislatures

More than one in five state legislators is a woman, a four-fold increase since 1970. The state of Washington, with more than 35 percent, has the highest proportion of women legislators. Alabama, with fewer than 10 percent, has the lowest.

Q. Why do the northeastern and western regions have the most women legislators?

A. The northeastern and western regions have a higher proportion of college-educated women in the work force than do other regions. College-educated women are more likely to run for public office and to actively support those who do run.

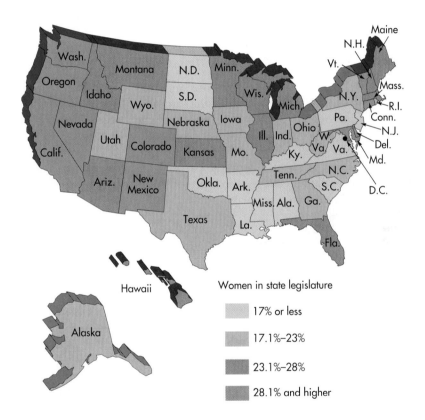

Women in state legislature

- 17% or less
- 17.1%–23%
- 23.1%–28%
- 28.1% and higher

Source: Created from data gathered by the Center for the American Woman and Politics (CAWP). National Information Bank on Women in Public Office. Eagleton Institute of Politics, Rutgers University, 2004.

operation, but unlike their counterparts in European legislatures, they cannot demand the loyalty of the members they lead. There is an inherent tension in Congress between the institution's need for strong leadership at the top and the individual members' need to exercise power on behalf of their constituents. The result is an institution in which the power of the top leaders rests on the willingness of other members to support them.

TABLE 11-1	Number of Democrats and Republicans in the House of Representatives and Senate, 1985–2006										
	85–86	87–88	89–90	91–92	93–94	95–96	97–98	99–00	01–02	03–04	05–06
House											
Democrats	253*	258*	262*	268*	259	205*	207*	212*	213	208	203
Republicans	182	177	173	167	176	230	228	223	222	227	232
Senate											
Democrats	47	54*	55*	56*	56	46*	45*	45*	51*	49	45
Republicans	53	46	45	44	44	54	55	55	49	51	55

*Chamber not controlled by the president's party. Independents are included in the total for the party with which they caucused.

Party Leadership in Congress

The House and Senate are organized along party lines. When members of Congress are sworn in at the start of a new two-year session, they automatically are members of either the Republican or the Democratic **party caucus** in their chamber. Through the caucuses, the Democrats and Republicans in each chamber meet periodically to plan strategy and discuss their differences in the process of settling on the party's legislative program. The caucuses also select the **party leaders** who represent the party's interests in the chamber and give direction to the party's goals.

party caucus A group that consists of a party's members in the House or Senate and that serves to elect the party's leadership, set policy goals, and determine party strategy.

party leaders Members of the House and Senate who are chosen by the Democratic or Republican caucus in each chamber to represent the party's interests in that chamber and who give some central direction to the chamber's deliberations.

The House Leadership

The main party leaders in the House are the Speaker, majority leader, majority whip, minority leader, and minority whip. The Constitution provides only for the post of Speaker. The Constitution further provides that the Speaker is to be elected by the members of the House. In practice, this means that the Speaker will be a member of the majority party, because it has enough votes to ensure that one of its own members is chosen. (Table 11–1 shows the party composition in Congress during the past two decades.)

The Speaker is often said to be the second most powerful official in Washington, after the president. The Speaker is active in developing the party's positions on issues and in persuading party members in the House to support these positions.[17] Although the Speaker cannot force party members to support the party's program, they look to the Speaker for leadership. The Speaker also has certain formal powers, including the right to speak first on legislation during House debate and the power to recognize members—that is, give them permission to speak from the floor. Because the House places a time limit on floor debate, not everyone has a chance to speak on a given bill, and the Speaker can sometimes influence legislation simply by exercising the power to decide who will speak and when. The Speaker also chooses the chairperson and the majority-party members of the powerful House Rules Committee, which controls the scheduling of bills for debate. Legislation that the Speaker wants passed is likely to reach the floor under conditions favorable to its enactment; for example, the Speaker may ask the Rules Committee to delay sending a bill to the floor until there is enough support for its passage. The Speaker has other ways of influencing the work of the House. The Speaker assigns bills to committees, places time limits on the reporting of bills out of committees, and assigns members to conference committees. (The importance of these powers over committee action will become apparent later in this chapter.)

The Speaker is assisted by the House majority leader and the House majority whip, who are elected by the majority party's members. The majority leader acts as the party's floor leader, organizing the debate on bills and working to line up legislative support. The whip has the important job of soliciting votes from party members and of informing them when critical votes are scheduled. As voting is getting under way on the House floor, the whip will sometimes stand at a location that is easily seen by party members and let them know where the leadership stands on the bill by giving them a thumbs-up or thumbs-down signal.

The minority party has its own leaders in the House. The House minority leader heads the party's caucus and its policy committee and plays the leading role in developing the party's legislative positions. The minority leader is assisted by a minority whip.

The power of House majority leader Tom DeLay (R-Texas), like that of other party leaders in Congress, rests on the trust placed in him by members of his party.

The Senate Leadership

In the Senate, the most important party leadership position is that of the majority leader, who heads the majority-party caucus. The majority leader's role is much like that of the Speaker of the House in that the Senate majority leader formulates the majority party's legislative agenda and encourages party members to support it. Like the Speaker, the Senate majority leader chairs the party's policy committee and acts as the party's voice in the chamber.[18] The majority leader is assisted by the majority whip, who sees to it that members know when important votes are scheduled and ensures that the party's strongest advocates on a legislative measure are present for the debate. The Senate also has a minority leader and a minority whip, whose roles are comparable to those performed by their counterparts in the House.

Unlike the Speaker of the House, the Senate majority leader is not the chamber's presiding officer. The Constitution assigns this responsibility to the vice president of the United States. However, because the vice president is allowed to vote in the Senate only to break a tie, the vice president normally is not in the Senate chamber unless support for a bill is so closely divided that a tie vote appears possible. The Senate has a president pro tempore, who, in the absence of the vice president, has the right to preside over the Senate. President pro tempore is largely an honorary position that by tradition is usually held by the majority party's senior member. The presiding official has limited power, because each senator has the right to speak at any length on bills under consideration.

The Senate's tradition of unlimited debate stems mainly from its relatively small size (only 100 members, compared with the House's 435 members). Moreover, senators like to view themselves as the equals of all others in their

HOW THE UNITED STATES COMPARES

Legislative Leadership and Authority

The U.S. House and Senate are separate and co-equal chambers, each with its own leadership and rules. This type of legislative structure is not found in most democracies. Many democracies, for example, have a single legislative chamber, which is apportioned by population. If the United States had an equivalent legislature, it would consist only of the House of Representatives.

Even most of the democracies that have a bicameral (two-chamber) legislature organize it differently from how the U.S. Congress is organized. The U.S. Senate is apportioned strictly by geography: there are two senators from each state. Germany is among the democracies that have a chamber organized along geographical lines, but Germany's upper house (the Bundesrat) differs from the U.S. Senate. Each of the German states (known as Länder) has at least three representatives in the Bundesrat, but the more populous states have more than three representatives.

Moreover, in most bicameral legislatures, one legislative chamber has substantially less power than the other. In the British Parliament, for example, the House of Lords is far weaker than the House of Commons; the House of Lords can delay legislation in some instances but cannot kill it. In the German Parliament, the Bundesrat has a voice on constitutional policy issues but not on most national policy issues, and its vote can in some cases be overridden by the population-based chamber (the Bundestag). In the United States, the Senate and House are equal in their legislative powers; without their joint agreement, a law cannot be enacted.

The U.S. Congress is fragmented in other ways as well: it has elected leaders with limited formal powers, a network of relatively independent and powerful committees, and members who are free to follow or ignore other members of their party. It is not uncommon for a fourth or more of a party's legislators to vote against their party's position on important legislative issues. In contrast, European legislatures have a centralized power structure: top leaders have substantial authority, the committees are weak, and the parties are unified. European legislators are expected to support their party unless granted permission to vote otherwise on a particular bill. Legislative leadership is much easier to exercise in Europe's hierarchical parliaments than in America's "stratarchical" Congress.

COUNTRY	FORM OF LEGISLATURE
Canada	One house dominant
France	One house dominant
Germany	One house dominant (except on certain issues)
Great Britain	One house dominant
Israel	One house only
Japan	One house dominant
Mexico	Two equal houses
Sweden	One house only
United States	Two equal houses

chamber and thus are reluctant to take orders from their leadership. For these reasons, the Senate majority leader's position is weaker than that of the Speaker of the House.

The Power of Party Leaders

The power of all party leaders, in the Senate and House alike, rests largely on the trust placed in them by the members of their party. They do not have the strong formal powers of parliamentary leaders (see "How the United States Compares"), but they are expected to lead. If they are adept at promoting ideas and building coalitions, they can exercise considerable power within their chamber. By the same token, their power is diminished if they make a mistake that hurts their party. In 2002, Republican Senate leader Trent Lott of Mississippi resigned his post after he placed his party at the center of an unwanted controversy by publicly praising the South's segregated past.

Party leaders are in a stronger position today than they were a few decades ago as a result of changes in the composition of the congressional parties. The GOP once had a substantial progressive faction within it, but this faction has been eclipsed by its conservative wing. At the same time, the Democratic party's conservative wing, represented by its southern lawmakers, has withered away almost entirely. As congressional Republicans have become more alike in their thinking and more different from congressional Democrats, each group has found it easier to band together and stand against the opposing party. Accordingly, the party leaders through the party caucus have found it easier to bring their party's lawmakers together on legislative issues.

In her book *Majority Leadership in the U.S. House*, Barbara Sinclair provided a perspective on legislative leadership that is now widely accepted.[19] Applying the *principal-agent model*, she saw party leaders as agents of party members, the principals. Members delegate power to their agents, the party leaders, which frees the members to pursue other activities. The task of the leader is to manage self-interested party members in ways that make them effective as a group. To do this well, party leaders must create harmony among the members and forge party positions that are agreeable enough to the members to enable them to act in concert. As agents of the members, party leaders must be attuned to their interests but, because the members will have somewhat different policy views, party leaders must also be creative in determining how to position the party on legislation. If they fail to do this well, the party's collective power will be diminished.

Party leaders have a challenging role because most party members are virtually guaranteed reelection and thus can decide for themselves whether to support the party's position on a bill. Until a few decades ago, congressional folkways dictated that newer members, particularly on the House side, would mostly listen and learn, awaiting the day when, through seniority, they were positioned to assume a larger role in the institution. There were always a few mavericks, but most new members willingly took a back seat. Of course, a back seat in the Senate was not the same as a back seat in the House. Because the Senate is a small body and operates on rules that are more egalitarian, a junior senator could rise to prominence more quickly than a junior House member could. Nevertheless, the Senate too had a tight inner circle dominated by its more senior members.[20]

Today, junior House and Senate members are less deferential. They are elected in a system that rewards self-starters, and they want the attention that comes with a more visible role in Washington policy debates. They also are likely to have close ties to the special interests that support their campaigns, and these groups expect them to vigorously pursue legislative goals. Finally, television has provided a path to prominence for junior members who are articulate and engaging. The visibility they obtain outside Congress through the media magnifies their voice within the institution. The old axiom that junior members "should be seen and not heard" is no longer an accurate description of life in Congress.

Simulation
www.mhhe.com/pattersontad7

U.S. senators Orrin Hatch (R-Utah) and Patrick Leahy (D-Vermont) confer at a Judiciary Committee hearing. Most of the legislative work of Congress is done in committees and their subcommittees.

Committee Chairs: The Seniority Principle

Party leaders are not the only important leaders in Congress. Most of the work of Congress takes place in the meetings of its thirty-five standing (permanent) committees and their numerous subcommittees, each of which is headed by a chairperson. A committee chair schedules committee meetings, determines the order in which committee bills are considered, presides over committee discussions, directs the committee's majority staff, and can choose to lead the debate when a committee bill reaches the floor of the chamber for a vote by the full membership.

seniority A member of Congress's consecutive years of service on a particular committee.

Committee chairs are always members of the majority party, and they usually have the most **seniority** (the most consecutive years of service on a particular committee). Seniority is based strictly on time served on a committee, not on time spent in Congress. If a member switches committees, the years spent on the first committee do not count toward seniority on the second one.

The seniority system has several important advantages: it reduces the number of bitter power struggles that would occur if the chairs were decided each time by open competition, it provides experienced and knowledgeable committee leadership, and it enables members to look forward to the reward of a position as chair after years of service on the same committee.

A drawback of the seniority system is that it places the committee chairs outside the immediate control of the House and Senate's elected leaders. In an effort to counter this problem, Republican leaders upon gaining a majority of the House in 1995 placed a limit of three terms on committee chairs. In 2001, a dozen committee chairs lost their positions due to this term-limit policy.

Congressional organization and leadership extend into subcommittees, smaller units within each committee formed to conduct specific aspects of the committee's business. Altogether there are about two hundred subcommittees in the House and Senate, each with a chairperson who decides its order of business, presides over its meetings, and coordinates its staff. In both chambers, a subcommittee chair is often the most senior member on the panel, but seniority is not as important in these appointments as it is in the designation of committee chairs.

Oligarchy or Democracy: Which Principle Should Govern?

In 1995, House Republicans gave committee chairs the power to select the chairs of their subcommittees and to appoint all majority-party staff members, including those who work for the subcommittees. Committee chairs were to use this power to promote within their committees the Republican party's overall policy goals. The changes reversed House reforms of the 1970s that gave subcommittees and their chairs greater autonomy in order to disperse power more widely among House members.[21]

The opposing forces embedded in the 1970s and 1995 reforms have played themselves out many times in the history of Congress. The institution is at once a place for conducting the nation's business and a venue for promoting constituency interests. At times, the position of top party leaders has been strengthened. At other times, the position of rank-and-file members has been enhanced. At all times, there has been an attempt to create a workable balance of the two. The result is an institution very different from European parliaments, where power is concentrated at the top (an arrangement reflected even in the name for rank-and-file members: "backbenchers"). The distinguishing feature of congressional power is its division among the membership, with provision for added power at the top.

THE COMMITTEE SYSTEM

As indicated earlier, most of the work in Congress is conducted through **standing committees,** permanent committees with responsibility for a particular area of public policy.[22] At present there are nineteen standing committees in the House and sixteen in the Senate (see Table 11–2). Both the House and the Senate, for example, have a standing committee that specializes in handling foreign policy issues. Other important standing committees are those that deal with agriculture, commerce, the national budget, the interior (natural resources and public lands), defense, government spending, labor, the judiciary, and taxation. House committees, which average about thirty-five to forty members each, are about twice the size of Senate committees. Each standing committee has legislative authority in that it can draft and rewrite proposed legislation and can recommend to the full chamber the passage or defeat of the legislation it considers.

Each standing committee in Congress has its own staff. Unlike the members' personal staffs, which concentrate on constituency relations, the committee staffs perform an almost entirely legislative function. They help draft legislation, organize hearings, and participate in altering bills within committee. In fact, experienced staffers sometimes play as large a role in the writing of legislation as do the members themselves.

In addition to its standing committees, Congress also has a number of *select committees,* which are created to perform specific tasks. An example is the Senate Select Committee on Intelligence, which oversees the work of intelligence agencies, such as the CIA. Congress also has *joint committees,* composed of members of both houses, which perform advisory or coordinating functions for the House and the Senate. The Joint Committee on the Library, for example, oversees

standing committees
Permanent congressional committees with responsibility for a particular area of public policy. An example is the Senate Foreign Relations Committee.

TABLE 11–2   The Standing Committees of Congress

HOUSE OF REPRESENTATIVES	SENATE
Agriculture	Agriculture, Nutrition, and Forestry
Appropriations	Appropriations
Armed Services	Armed Services
Budget	Banking, Housing, and Urban Affairs
Education and the Workforce	Budget
Energy and Commerce	Commerce, Science, and Transportation
Financial Services	Energy and Natural Resources
Government Reform	Environment and Public Works
House Administration	Finance
International Relations	Foreign Relations
Judiciary	Governmental Affairs
Resources	Health, Education, Labor, and Pensions
Rules	Judiciary
Science	Rules and Administration
Small Business	Small Business and Entrepreneurship
Standards of Official Conduct	Veterans' Affairs
Transportation and Infrastructure	
Veterans' Affairs	
Ways and Means	

conference committees
Temporary committees formed to bargain over the differences in the House and Senate versions of a bill. A committee's members are usually appointed from the House and Senate standing committees that originally worked on the bill.

the Library of Congress, which is the largest library in the world. Finally, Congress has **conference committees,** which are joint committees formed temporarily to work out differences in House and Senate versions of a particular bill. The role of conference committees is discussed more fully later in the chapter.

Congress could not possibly handle its workload without the help of its committee system. About ten thousand bills are introduced during each two-year session of Congress. The sheer volume of legislation would paralyze the institution if it did not have a division of labor. Yet the very existence of committees and subcommittees helps fragment Congress: each of these units is relatively secure in its power, jurisdiction, and membership.

Committee Membership

Each committee includes Republicans and Democrats, but the majority party holds the majority of seats on each committee and its subcommittees. The ratio of Democrats to Republicans on each committee is approximately the same as the ratio in the full House or Senate, but there is no fixed rule on this matter, and the majority party decides what the ratio will be (mindful that at the next

There are dozens of informal caucuses in Congress that aim to represent the concerns of particular constituencies. Pictured here is U.S. Representative Loretta Sanchez (D-Calif.), a member of the Hispanic caucus.

election it could become the chamber's minority party). Members of the House typically serve on only two committees. Senators often serve on four, although they can sit on only two major committees, such as Foreign Relations and Finance. There are also limits on subcommittee assignments; no House member, for example, can serve on more than five subcommittees.

Each standing committee has a fixed number of members, and a committee must have a vacancy before a new member can be appointed. Vacancies usually occur at the start of a new congressional session, when the committee positions of members who have retired or been defeated for reelection are reallocated. On nearly all committees, members retain their seats unless they decide to relinquish them or are forced to do so by changes in party ratios or committee size. The biggest change in committee membership comes when a party loses control of the House or Senate; several Democrats had to relinquish their committee assignments when the Republicans took control of the Senate after the 2002 midterm elections.

Each party has a special committee in each chamber with responsibility for deciding who will fill vacancies on standing committees. Several factors influence these decisions, including the preferences of the legislators themselves. Most newly elected members of Congress receive a committee assignment that they have requested. New members usually ask for assignment to a committee on which they can serve their constituents' interests and at the same time increase their reelection prospects. For example, when Hillary Clinton was elected to the Senate in 2000 from New York, a state that depends heavily on human services programs, she asked for and received an appointment on the Senate Health, Education, Labor, and Pensions Committee.

Members of Congress also prefer membership on one of the most important committees, such as Foreign Relations or Finance in the Senate and Appropriations or Ways and Means in the House. A seat on these committees is coveted because they deal with large and visible issues, such as taxes and international affairs. Such factors as members' intelligence, experience, party loyalty, ideology, region, length of congressional service, and work habits weigh heavily in the determination of appointments to these prestigious committees.[23]

Subcommittee assignments are handled differently. The members of each party on a committee decide who among them will serve on each of its subcommittees. The members' preferences, seniority, and personal backgrounds and the interests of their constituencies are key influences on subcommittee assignments.

Committee Jurisdiction

The 1946 Legislative Reorganization Act requires that each bill introduced in Congress be referred to the proper committee. An agricultural bill introduced in the Senate must be assigned to the Senate Agriculture Committee, a bill dealing with foreign affairs must be sent to the Senate Foreign Relations Committee, and so on. This requirement is a major source of each committee's power. Even if its members are known to oppose certain types of legislation, bills clearly within its **jurisdiction**—the policy area in which it is authorized to act—must be sent to it for deliberation.

However, policy problems are increasingly complex, and jurisdiction accordingly has become an increasingly contentious issue, particularly with regard to major bills. Which House committee, for example, should handle a major bill addressing the role of financial institutions in global trade? The Financial Services Committee? The Commerce Committee? The International Relations Committee? All committees seek legislative influence and each is jealous of its jurisdiction, so bills that overlap committee boundaries provoke conflict. Political scientist David King describes these conflicts as "turf wars." They also involve the party leaders, who are in charge of assigning bills to committee. The party leaders can take advantage of these situations by shuttling a bill to the committee that is most likely to handle it in the way they would like. But party leaders depend on the committee chairs for support, so they cannot regularly ignore a committee that has a strong claim to a bill. At times, party leaders have responded by dividing up a bill, handing over some of its provisions to one committee and other provisions to a second committee.

House and Senate subcommittees also have relatively secure jurisdictions. Thus, responsibility in Congress is thoroughly divided, with each subcommittee having authority over a small area of public policy. The House International Relations Committee, for instance, has six subcommittees: Europe, Middle East and Central Asia, Asia and the Pacific, Western Hemisphere, Africa, and International Terrorism, Nonproliferation, and Human Rights. Each subcommittee has about a dozen members, and these few individuals do most of the work and have the major voice in the disposition of most bills in their policy domain.

jurisdiction (of a congressional committee) The policy area in which a particular congressional committee is authorized to act.

 ## HOW A BILL BECOMES LAW

Parties, party leaders, and committees are critical actors in the legislative process. Their role and influence, however, vary with the nature of the legislation under consideration.

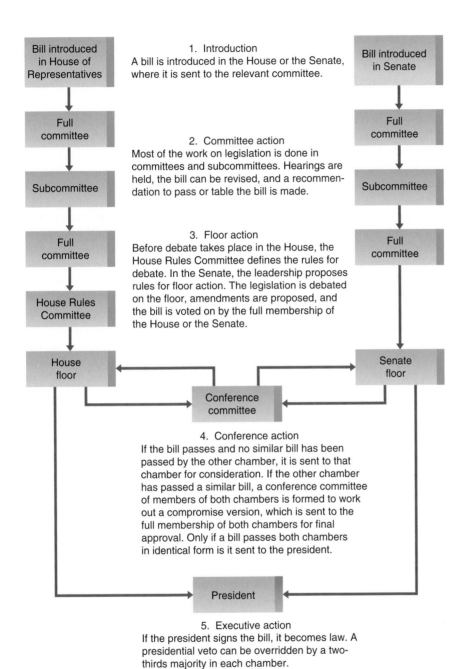

1. Introduction
A bill is introduced in the House or the Senate, where it is sent to the relevant committee.

2. Committee action
Most of the work on legislation is done in committees and subcommittees. Hearings are held, the bill can be revised, and a recommendation to pass or table the bill is made.

3. Floor action
Before debate takes place in the House, the House Rules Committee defines the rules for debate. In the Senate, the leadership proposes rules for floor action. The legislation is debated on the floor, amendments are proposed, and the bill is voted on by the full membership of the House or the Senate.

4. Conference action
If the bill passes and no similar bill has been passed by the other chamber, it is sent to that chamber for consideration. If the other chamber has passed a similar bill, a conference committee of members of both chambers is formed to work out a compromise version, which is sent to the full membership of both chambers for final approval. Only if a bill passes both chambers in identical form is it sent to the president.

5. Executive action
If the president signs the bill, it becomes law. A presidential veto can be overridden by a two-thirds majority in each chamber.

Figure 11–4

How a Bill Becomes Law
Although the legislative process can be short-circuited in many ways, this diagram describes the normal way a bill becomes law.

Committee Hearings and Decisions

The formal process by which bills become law is shown in Figure 11–4. A **bill** is a proposed legislative act. Many bills are prepared by executive agencies, interest groups, or other outside parties, but members of Congress also draft bills, and only they can formally submit a bill for consideration by their chamber. Once a bill is introduced by a member of the House or Senate, it is given a number and

bill A proposed law (legislative act) within Congress or another legislature.

a title and is then sent to the appropriate committee, which assigns it to one of its subcommittees. Most bills that reach a subcommittee are tabled on the grounds that they are not worthwhile. Less than 10 percent of the bills that committees consider reach the floor for a vote; the others are "killed" when committees decide that they do not warrant further consideration and table them. The full House or Senate can overrule committee decisions, but this rarely occurs.

The fact that committees kill more than 90 percent of the bills submitted in Congress does not mean that committees exercise 90 percent of the power in Congress. A committee rarely decides fully the fate of legislation that is important to the majority party or its leadership. Most bills die in committee because they are of little interest to anyone other than a few members of Congress or are so poorly conceived that they lack merit. Some bills are not even supported by the members who introduce them. A member may submit a bill to appease a powerful constituent group and then quietly inform the committee to ignore it.

If a bill seems to have merit, the subcommittee will schedule hearings on it. The subcommittee invites testimony on the proposed legislation from lobbyists, administrators, and experts, who inform members about the suggested policy, provide an indication of the support the bill has, and disclose possible weaknesses in the proposal. After the hearings, if the subcommittee still feels that the legislation is warranted, members recommend the bill to the full committee, which can hold additional hearings. In the House, both the full committee and a subcommittee can "mark up," or revise, a bill. In the Senate, markup is usually reserved for the full committee.

From Committee to the Floor

If a majority of the committee vote to recommend passage of the bill, it is referred to the full chamber for action. In the House, the Rules Committee has the power to determine when the bill will be voted on, how long the debate on the bill will last, and whether the bill will receive a "closed rule" (no amendments will be permitted), an "open rule" (members can propose amendments relevant to any of the bill's sections), or something in between (for example, only certain sections of the bill will be subject to amendment). The Rules Committee has this scheduling power because the House is too large to operate effectively without strict rules for the handling of legislation by the full chamber. The rules are also a means by which the majority party controls legislation. House Democrats employed closed rules to prevent Republicans from proposing amendments to major bills, a tactic House Republicans said they would forgo when they took control in 1995. Once in control, however, the Republicans applied closed rules to a number of major bills. The tactic was too effective to ignore.

On most House bills, only a small percentage of the legislators will have an opportunity to speak on the floor. In most cases, the decision as to who will speak is delegated to the bill's chief sponsor and one of the bill's leading opponents. Typically, both of these House members are members of the committee that handled the bill.

The Senate also has a rules committee, but it has much less power than in the House. In the Senate, the majority leader, usually in consultation with the minority leaders, schedules bills. All Senate bills are subject to unlimited debate unless a three-fifths majority of the full Senate votes for **cloture**, which limits

cloture A parliamentary maneuver that, if a three-fifths majority votes for it, limits Senate debate to thirty hours and has the effect of defeating a filibuster.

debate to thirty hours. Cloture is a way of thwarting a Senate **filibuster,** a procedural tactic whereby a minority of senators prevent a bill from coming to a vote by holding the floor and talking until other senators give in and the bill is withdrawn from consideration. For example, Senate Democrats used the filibuster to block several of President George W. Bush's judicial nominees. Democrats did not have the votes to defeat the nominees directly and used the filibuster to prevent the nominations from being voted upon.

The Senate also differs from the House in that its members can propose any amendment to any bill. Unlike House amendments, those in the Senate do not have to be germane to a bill's content. For example, a senator may propose an antiabortion amendment to a bill dealing with defense expenditures. Such an amendment is called a **rider,** and riders are frequently introduced.

Leadership and Floor Action

Committee action is usually decisive on bills that address small issues. If a majority of committee members favor such a bill, it normally is passed by the full chamber, often without amendment. In a sense, the full chamber merely votes to confirm or modify decisions made previously by committees and subcommittees. Of course, these units do not operate in a vacuum. In making its decisions, a committee takes into account the fact that its action can be reversed by the full chamber, just as a subcommittee recognizes that the full committee can overrule its decision.[24] Partisanship also serves as a check on committee action. When a committee's vote is sharply divided along party or regional lines, other members may conclude that they need to look more closely at the bill before deciding whether to support it.

On major bills, the party leaders are the critical actors. They will have worked closely with the committee during its deliberations and may assume leadership of the bill when it clears the committee. (In the case of "minor" bills, leadership during floor debate is normally provided by committee members.)

The majority party's leaders (particularly in the House) have increasingly set the legislative agenda and defined the debate on major bills.[25] They shape the bills' broad outlines and set the boundaries of the floor debate. In these efforts, they depend on the support of their party's members. To obtain this support, they consult their members informally and through the party caucus. **Party discipline**—the willingness of a party's House or Senate members to act together as a cohesive group—is increasingly important in congressional action and is the key to party leaders' ability to shape major legislation. (The role of parties in Congress is discussed further in the section on Congress's representation function.)

Senator John Edwards (D-North Carolina) speaks during confirmation hearings for Michael Powell to become chair of the Federal Communications Commission. Edwards served in the U.S. Senate from 1998 through 2004.

filibuster A procedural tactic in the U.S. Senate whereby a minority of legislators prevent a bill from coming to a vote by holding the floor and talking until the majority gives in and the bill is withdrawn from consideration.

rider An amendment to a bill that deals with an issue unrelated to the content of the bill. Riders are permitted in the Senate but not in the House.

party discipline The willingness of a party's House or Senate members to act together as a cohesive group and thus exert collective control over legislative action.

Conference Committees and the President

For a bill to pass, it must receive the support of a simple majority (50 percent plus one) of the House or Senate members voting on it. To become a law, however, a bill must be passed in identical form by both the House and the

Simulation
www.mhhe.com/pattersontad7

law (as enacted by Congress) A legislative proposal, or bill, that is passed by both the House and the Senate and is either signed or not vetoed by the president.

veto The president's rejection of a bill, thereby keeping it from becoming law unless Congress overrides the veto.

Senate. About 10 percent of all proposals that are approved by both chambers—the proportion is larger for major bills—differ in important respects in their House and Senate versions and are referred to conference committees to resolve the differences. Each conference committee is formed temporarily to handle a particular bill; its members are usually appointed from the House and Senate standing committees that worked on the bill originally. The conference committee's job is to bargain over the differences in the House and Senate versions and to develop a compromise version, which then goes to the House and Senate floors. There it can be passed, defeated, or returned to conference, but not amended.

Legislation that is passed by the House and the Senate is not assured of becoming law. The president also plays a role. If the president signs the bill, it becomes a **law.** If the president exercises the **veto,** a rejection of a bill, the bill is sent back to its originating chamber with the president's reasons for the veto. Congress can override a veto by a two-thirds vote of each chamber; the bill then becomes law. If the president fails to sign a bill within ten days (Sundays excepted) and Congress has remained in session, the bill automatically becomes law anyway. If the president fails to sign a bill within ten days and Congress has adjourned for the term, the bill does not become law. This last situation, called a pocket veto, forces Congress in its next session to start from the beginning: the bill again must pass both chambers and again is subject to presidential veto.

CONGRESS'S POLICYMAKING ROLE

The Framers of the Constitution expected Congress to be the leading branch of the national government. It was to the legislature—the embodiment of representative government—that the people were expected to look for policy leadership. During most of the nineteenth century, Congress, not the president, was clearly the dominant national institution. Aside from a few strong leaders such as Jackson and Lincoln, presidents did not play a major legislative role (see Chapter 12). However, as national and international forces combined to place greater leadership and policy demands on the federal government, the president became a vital part of the national legislative process. Today Congress and the president substantially share the legislative effort, although their roles differ greatly.[26]

Congress's policymaking role revolves around its three legislative functions: lawmaking, representation, and oversight. In practice, the three functions overlap, but they are conceptually distinct.

The Lawmaking Function of Congress

lawmaking function The authority (of a legislature) to make the laws necessary to carry out the government's powers.

Under the Constitution, Congress is granted the **lawmaking function:** the authority to make the laws necessary to carry out the powers granted to the national government. The constitutional powers of Congress are substantial; they include the power to tax, to spend, to regulate commerce, and to declare war. However, whether Congress takes the lead in the making of laws depends heavily on the type of policy at issue.

Kay Bailey Hutchison was elected to the U.S. Senate from Texas in 1993 to fill the seat vacated by Lloyd Bentsen, who had resigned to become Secretary of the Treasury. Hutchison is among the growing number of women who sit in the U.S. Congress.

Broad Issues: Fragmentation as a Limit on Congress's Role

Congress is structured in a way that makes agreement on large issues difficult to obtain. Congress is not one house but two, each with its own authority and constituency base. Neither the House nor the Senate can enact legislation without the other's approval, and the two chambers are hardly two versions of the same thing. California and North Dakota have exactly the same representation in the Senate, but in the House, which is apportioned by population, California has fifty-three seats compared to North Dakota's one.

Congress also includes a lot of people: 100 members of the Senate and 435 members of the House. They come from different constituencies and represent different and sometimes opposing interests. Because each member has a separate power base and depends on it for reelection, the members can be expected to take different positions on legislative issues even when they agree on the general goal. Nearly every member of Congress, for example, supports the principle of global free trade. When it comes to specific trade provisions, however, members often disagree. Foreign competition means different things to manufacturers who produce automobiles, computer chips, or underwear; it means different things to farmers who produce corn, sugar, or grapes; and it means different things to firms that deal in international finance, home insurance, or student loans. And because it means different things to different people in different parts of the country, members of Congress who represent these areas have conflicting views on what the nation's trade policy should be.

For such reasons, Congress often has difficulty taking the lead on broad issues of national policy. A legislative institution can easily lead on such issues only if it assigns this authority to its top leadership. Although the rise in party discipline in Congress has strengthened the role of its leaders, the fact remains that House and Senate members are relatively free to go their separate ways if they so choose. Thus, Congress often struggles when faced with the task of developing comprehensive policies that address broad national problems.

The presidency is better suited to the task of addressing broad issues. First, whereas Congress's authority is divided, the presidency's authority is not. Executive power is vested constitutionally in the hands of a single individual—the president. The president can adopt a policy position without having to negotiate with anyone, much less with scores or hundreds of legislators, each with a different opinion as to the best course of action. Second, whereas members of Congress tend to see issues mainly from the perspective of their state or district, the president tends to see them from a national perspective.

Presidential leadership means that Congress normally will pay attention to White House proposals, not that it will adopt them. Congress typically accepts a presidential initiative only as a starting point in its deliberations. It may reject the proposal outright—particularly when the president is from the opposing party—but any such proposal provides Congress with a tangible bill on which to focus. If the proposal is at all close to what a congressional majority would regard as acceptable, Congress will use it as a baseline from which to make changes that will bring it in line with the thinking of a congressional majority. (The legislative roles of Congress and the president are discussed further in Chapter 12.)

In its lawmaking activities, Congress has the support of three congressional agencies. One is the Congressional Budget Office (CBO), which was created as part of the Budget Impoundment and Control Act of 1974. Before this time, the president, through the Office of Management and Budget (OMB), had a significant advantage in budgetary matters. Congress had no independent way to systematically assess the president's budgetary proposals or their projected impact. The CBO gives Congress this capacity. Its two hundred fifty employees provide Congress with general economic projections, overall estimates of government expenditures and revenues, and specific estimates of the costs of proposed programs. Since the CBO's inception, its calculations have often been at odds with those of the OMB. For example, the OMB's estimates of the cost of presidential initiatives are usually optimistic, and the CBO's figures have been a basis by which Congress has trimmed or rejected these proposals. (The budgetary process is described more fully in later chapters.)

A second congressional agency is the General Accounting Office (GAO). With three thousand employees, the GAO is the largest congressional agency. Formed in 1921, it has primary responsibility for overseeing executive agencies' spending of money that has been appropriated by Congress. The programs that the executive agencies administer are authorized and funded by Congress. The GAO's responsibility is to ensure that executive agencies operate in the manner prescribed by Congress.

The third and oldest congressional agency is the Congressional Research Service (CRS). It has a staff of one thousand employees and operates as a non-partisan reference agency. It conducts research and provides information upon request from congressional committees and members.

Newt Gingrich and three hundred Republican congressional candidates stand in front of the Capitol to dramatize their Contract with America. After their stunning victory in the 1994 elections, they launched an aggressive attempt to reduce the scope of the federal government, illustrating that, in some instances, Congress can take the lead on broad national issues.

Congress in the Lead: Fragmentation as a Policymaking Strength

Congress occasionally does take the lead on large issues. Except during Roosevelt's New Deal, Congress has been a chief source of major labor legislation. Environmental legislation, federal aid to education, and urban development are other areas in which Congress has played an initiating role.[27] The Republicans' Contract with America that was introduced during the 1994 election is yet another example of congressional policy leadership. The contract included broad fiscal, regulatory, and social initiatives. In 1996, for example, the Republican-controlled Congress led the way on legislation that fundamentally changed the nation's welfare system. Nevertheless, Congress does not routinely develop broad policy programs and carry them through to passage. "Congress remains organized," James Sundquist notes, "to deal with narrow problems but not with broad ones."[28]

As it happens, the great majority of the hundreds of bills that Congress considers each session deal with narrow issues. The leading role in the disposition of these bills falls not on the president but on Congress and, in most cases, on a relatively small number of its members. The same fragmentation that makes it difficult for Congress to take the lead on a broad issue makes it easy for Congress to tackle scores of narrow issues simultaneously. Most of the legislation passed by Congress is "distributive"—that is, it distributes benefits to a particular group while spreading the costs among the general public. Veterans' benefits and business tax incentives are examples.[29]

Such legislation, because it directly benefits a constituent group, is the type of policy that members of Congress are most inclined to support. It is also the

Liberty, Equality & Self-Government

What's Your Opinion?

Minority Redistricting

Congressional representatives tend naturally to favor the opinions of the voters who supported them. This tendency can result in the underrepresentation of minority-group members because only rarely will they constitute an electoral majority in a congressional district. In 1982, Congress signaled that race could be taken into account in congressional redistricting, and after the 1990 census, the boundaries of some House districts were drawn so that black Americans were a voting majority. In a 1996 decision, the Supreme Court held that race cannot be the determining factor in redistricting decisions (because this action violates the Fourteenth Amendment's equal protection clause), although there might be circumstances in which it could be considered along with other factors. Then, in a 2001 decision, the Court held that racial redistricting is permissible if it is the consequence of a reapportionment plan motivated by partisan rather than racial considerations (for example, if the primary purpose was to create a district favorable to the Democratic candidate).

What's your view on racial redistricting? What's your view on partisan redistricting?

---

type of policy that Congress, through its committee system, is organizationally best suited to handle. Most committees parallel a major constituent interest, such as agriculture, commerce, or labor.

The Representation Function of Congress

In the process of making laws, the members of Congress represent various interests within American society, giving them voice and attention in the national legislature. The proper approach to the **representation function** has been debated since the nation's founding. A recurrent issue has been whether the primary concern of a representative should be the interests of the nation as a whole or those of his or her own constituency. These interests overlap to some degree but rarely coincide exactly. Policies that are of benefit to the full society are not always equally advantageous to particular localities and can even cause harm to some constituencies.

representation function The responsibility of a legislature to represent various interests in society.

Representation of States and Districts

The choice between national and local interests is not a simple one, even for a legislator who is inclined toward either orientation. To be fully effective, members of Congress must be reelected time and again, a necessity that compels them to pay attention to local demands. Yet, as part of the nation's legislative body, no member can easily put aside his or her judgment as to the nation's needs. In making the choice, most members of Congress, it appears, tend toward a local orientation. They are particularly reluctant to oppose local

Members of Congress are keenly sensitive to local opinion on issues of personal interest to their constituents. Representatives from urban areas are more supportive of gun control than are those from rural areas, where sport hunting is widespread.

sentiment on issues of intense concern. Support for gun control legislation, for example, has always been much lower among members of Congress representing rural areas where sporting guns are part of the fabric of everyday life.

Local representation also occurs through the committee system.[30] Although studies indicate that the views of committee members are not radically different from the views of the full House or Senate membership,[31] senators and representatives typically sit on committees and subcommittees with policy jurisdictions that coincide with state or district interests. For example, farm-state legislators dominate the membership of the House and Senate Agriculture committees, and westerners dominate the Interior committees (which deal with federal lands and natural resources, most of which are concentrated in the West). Committees are also the site of most of the congressional **logrolling,** the practice of trading one's vote with another member so that each gets what he or she most wants. It is not uncommon, for example, for agriculture committee members from livestock-producing states of the North to trade votes with committee members from the South, where crops such as cotton, tobacco, and peanuts are grown.

logrolling The trading of votes between legislators so that each gets what he or she most wants.

Nevertheless, representation of constituency interests has its limits. A representative's constituents have little interest in most issues that come before Congress and even less information about them. Whether the government should appropriate a few million dollars in foreign aid for Bolivia or should alter patent requirements for copying machines is not the sort of issue that local constituent groups are likely to know or care about. Moreover, members of Congress often have no choice but to go against the wishes of a significant portion of their constituency. The interests of small and large farmers in an agricultural state, for example, can differ considerably.

Of course, constituent groups are not the only groups that get legislators' support. The nation's capital is filled with powerful lobbies that contribute funds to congressional campaigns. These lobbying groups sometimes have as much influence with a member of Congress as do groups in the member's home district or state.

Representation of the Nation through Parties

When a clear-cut and vital national interest is at stake, members of Congress can be expected to respond to that interest. The difficulty of using the common good as a routine basis for thinking about representation, however, is that Americans often disagree on what constitutes the common good and what government should do to further it.

Most Americans believe, for example, that the nation's education system requires strengthening. The test scores of American school children on standardized reading, math, and science examinations are significantly below those of children in many other industrial democracies. This situation creates pressure for political action. But what action is necessary and desirable? Does more money have to be funneled into public schools, and, if so, which level of government—federal, state, or local—should provide it? Or does the problem rest with teachers? Should they be subject to higher certification and performance standards? Or is the problem a lack of competition for excellence? Should schools be required to compete for students and the tax dollars they represent? Should private schools be part of any such competition, or would their participation wreck the public school system? There is no general agreement on such issues. The quality of America's schools is of vital national interest, and quality schools would serve the common good. But the means to that end are the subject of endless dispute.

In Congress, debates over national goals occur primarily along party lines.[32] Republicans and Democrats have different perspectives on national issues because their parties differ philosophically and politically. In the end-of-the-year budget negotiations in 1998 and 1999, for example, Republicans and Democrats were deadlocked on the issue of new funding to hire thousands of public school teachers. The initiative had come from President Clinton and was supported by congressional Democrats. But it was opposed by congressional Republicans, who objected to spending federal (as opposed to state and local) funds for that purpose and who also objected to the proposed placement of the new teachers (most of whom would be placed in overcrowded schools, most of which are in Democratic constituencies). Democrats and Republicans alike agreed that more teachers were needed, but they disagreed on how that goal should be reached. In the end, through concessions in other areas, Clinton and the congressional Democrats obtained federal funding for new teachers, but it was obtained through an intensely partisan process.

Partisanship is the main source of division within Congress.[33] Real and substantial differences between members of the two parties often result in their voting on the opposite sides of legislative issues. In the past two decades, party-line voting has been relatively high on *roll-call votes* (those on which each member's vote is recorded), reflecting the rise of party discipline in Congress and the widening gap in the policy views of the Democrats and Republicans who serve there (see Figure 11–5). There are now in Congress fewer liberal Republicans and fewer conservative Democrats, as well as fewer moderates of both parties. Traditionally, the Senate, as the more deliberative body, was the chamber where the two parties tended to reach compromise positions. In the past few years, however, the party divide has been even greater in the Senate than in the House.

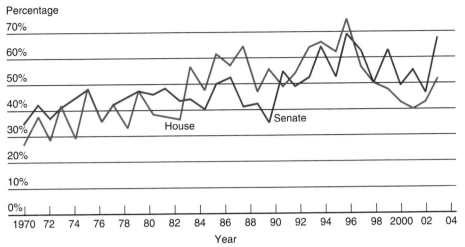

Figure 11–5

Percentage of Roll-Call Votes in House and Senate in Which a Majority of Democrats Voted Against a Majority of Republicans
Democrats and Republicans in Congress are often on opposite sides of issues; party-line voting has been relatively high since the 1980s.

Source: *Congressional Quarterly Weekly*, various dates.

Partisanship also affects the president's relationship with Congress. Presidents serve as legislative leaders not so much for the whole Congress as for members of their own party. More than half the time, opposition and support for presidential initiatives divide along party lines. Accordingly, the president's legislative success can depend on which party controls Congress. After Republicans in the 2002 midterm elections took full control of Congress, President Bush was in a stronger position to get his major programs enacted into law.

In short, any accounting of representation in Congress that minimizes the influence of party is faulty. If constituency interests drive the thinking of many members of Congress, so do partisan values. In fact, constituent and partisan influences are often difficult to separate in practice. In the case of conflicting interests within their constituencies, members of Congress naturally side with those that align with their party. When local business and labor groups take opposing sides on issues before Congress, for example, Republican members tend to back business's position, while Democratic members tend to line up with labor.

The Oversight Function of Congress

Although Congress enacts the nation's laws and appropriates the money to implement them, the administration of these laws is entrusted to the executive branch. Congress has the responsibility to see that the executive branch carries out the laws faithfully and spends the money properly, a supervisory activity referred to as the **oversight function** of Congress.[34]

Oversight is carried out largely through the committee system of Congress and is facilitated by the parallel structure of the committees and the executive bureaucracy: the House International Relations and Senate Foreign Relations committees oversee the work of the State Department, the House and Senate Agriculture committees look after the Department of Agriculture, and so on.

oversight function A supervisory activity of Congress that centers on its constitutional responsibility to see that the executive branch carries out the laws faithfully and spends appropriations properly.

The Legislative Reorganization Act of 1970 spells out each committee's responsibility for overseeing its parallel agency:

> Each standing committee shall review and study, on a continuing basis, the application, administration, and execution of those laws, or parts of laws, the subject matter of which is within the jurisdiction of that committee.

However, oversight is easier to mandate than to carry out. If congressional committees were to try to monitor all the federal bureaucracy's activities, they would have no time or energy to do anything else. Most members of Congress are more interested in working out new laws and looking after constituents than in laboriously keeping track of the bureaucracy. Although Congress is required by law to maintain "continuous watchfulness" over programs, committees have little incentive to take a hard look at programs on which their constituent groups depend. Oversight normally is not pursued aggressively unless members of Congress are annoyed with an agency, have discovered that a legislative authorization is being grossly abused, or are reviewing a program for possible major changes.

When an agency is suspected of serious abuses, a committee is likely to hold hearings. Except in cases involving *executive privilege* (the right to withhold confidential information affecting national security), executive-branch officials must testify at these hearings if asked to do so. If they refuse, they can be cited for contempt of Congress, which is a criminal offense. Congress's investigative power is not listed in the Constitution, but the judiciary has not challenged that power, and Congress has used it extensively.

Most federal programs must have their funding renewed every year, a requirement that gives Congress crucial leverage in its ongoing oversight function. If an agency has acted improperly, Congress may reduce the agency's appropriation or tighten the restrictions on the way its funds can be spent. A major difficulty is that the House and Senate Appropriations committees must review nearly the entire federal budget, a task that limits the amount of attention they can give any particular program.

Oversight conducted after the bureaucracy has acted has an obvious drawback: if a program has been administered improperly, some damage has already been done. For this reason, Congress in recent years has developed ways of limiting the bureaucracy's discretion in advance. One method is to include detailed instructions in appropriations bills. Such instructions serve to limit bureaucrats' flexibility when they spend funds on programs and provide a firmer basis for holding them accountable if they disregard the intent of Congress. Another oversight device is the **sunset law,** which fixes a date on which a program will end (or "fade into the sunset") unless it is renewed by Congress. Sunset provisions help prevent a program from outliving its usefulness, because once its expiration date is reached, Congress can reestablish it only by passing a new law. The "legislative veto" is a more intrusive and controversial oversight tool. It requires that an executive agency have the approval of Congress before it can take a specified action. Legislative vetoes are under challenge as an unconstitutional infringement on executive authority, and their future is unclear.

sunset law A law containing a provision that fixes a date on which a program will end unless the program's life is extended by Congress.

Citizenship

Getting Involved, Making a Difference

Becoming a Legislative Intern

Each year, thousands of college students serve as interns in Congress or state legislatures. Many internships are unpaid, but students can receive college credit for the experience.

Internships provide an opportunity to see the legislative process firsthand. They are not always a great adventure. Many legislative interns envision themselves contributing ideas and research that might influence public policy only to find that they are answering letters, developing mailing lists, or duplicating materials. Nevertheless, few interns conclude that their experience was a waste of time. Most find it rewarding and, ultimately, memorable.

Many executive agencies at the federal and state levels also accept interns, and some have well-organized internship programs. The Department of State has one of the best internship programs, but it is in heavy demand and has an early application deadline. The internships offered by executive agencies typically are more challenging than those provided by legislative offices.

Legislators dedicate a lot of their staff time to constituency service, whereas agencies concentrate on the administration of policies and programs. On the other hand, legislative offices are usually more spirited, and interns in these offices are more likely to strike up friendships with other interns in the same office or in nearby offices.

Information about internships can be obtained from the American Political Science Association (www.apsa.org). In addition, there are organizations in Washington that arrange internships in Congress and the executive agencies. These organizations frequently charge a fee for their services, so you might want to contact a legislative office or executive agency directly. It is important to make your request as early as possible in the college year, because some internship programs have deadlines and nearly all offices receive more requests than they can accommodate. You could also check with the student services office at your college or university. Some of these offices have information on internship programs and can be of assistance.

The biggest obstacle to effective oversight is the sheer magnitude of the task. With its hundreds of agencies and thousands of programs, the bureaucracy is beyond comprehensive scrutiny. Even some of Congress's most publicized oversight activities are relatively trivial when viewed against the extensive scope of the bureaucracy. For example, congressional investigations into the Defense Department's purchase of small hardware items, such as wrenches and hammers, at many times their market value do not begin to address the issue of whether the country is overspending on the military. Overpriced hand tools represent pocket change in a defense budget of billions of dollars. The real oversight question is whether the defense budget as a whole provides cost-effective national security. It is a question that Congress has neither the capacity nor the determination to investigate fully.

Congress's zeal for oversight changes dramatically when allegations of scandal or wrongdoing attract national media attention. Then members of Congress use the oversight process to hold high-profile hearings. The most noteworthy hearings of the past decade were those that investigated President

Clinton's relationship with a White House intern, Monica Lewinsky. (Chapter 12 describes the impeachment hearings in greater detail.) The collapse of Enron Corporation as a result of financial manipulation is another example. Several congressional committees held hearings in 2002 to grill Enron officials on the practices that led stockholders to lose billions of dollars and Enron employees to lose their retirement pensions. The hearings in the Democratic-controlled Senate were the more heated. Enron had close ties to President Bush and Vice President Cheney, and the Enron hearings gave Senate Democrats a chance to embarrass and pressure the White House.

CONGRESS: TOO MUCH PLURALISM?

Congress is an institution divided between service to the nation and service to the separate constituencies within it. Its members have responsibility for the nation's laws, yet for reelection they depend on the voters of their states and districts and are highly responsive to constituency interests. This latter focus is facilitated by the committee system, which is organized around particular interests. Agriculture, labor, education, banking, and commerce are among the interests represented through this system. It is hard to conceive of a national legislature structured to respond to special interests more closely than the Congress of the United States. It is even harder to conceive of a national legislature that gives as much real power to these interests through committees as Congress does.

Pluralists admire this feature of Congress. They argue that the United States has a majoritarian institution in the presidency and that Congress is a place where a *diversity* of interests is represented. Critics of this view say that Congress is sometimes so responsive to particular interests that it neglects the overall national interest. This criticism is blunted from time to time by a strong majoritarian impulse in Congress. The current period is one of those moments. The high level of party discipline in recent years, coupled with a widening ideological gap between the parties, has placed Congress at the center of many national policy debates, including the issue of the balance of power between Washington and the states.

The fact is that Congress cannot be an institution that is highly responsive both to diverse interests and to the national interest. These interests often conflict, as the rise and fall of former Speaker Newt Gingrich illustrate. He sought to make the Republican congressional majority into the driving force in American national politics, but he was ousted from his position when the conflicts generated by the uncompromising pursuit of conservative policy goals began to weaken the GOP's support in the states and districts, threatening the reelection chances of Republican incumbents. This inherent tension between Congress's national role and its local base has been replayed many times in U.S. history. In a real sense, the strengths of Congress are also its weaknesses. The features of congressional election and organization that make Congress responsive to separate constituencies are often the very ones that make it difficult for Congress to act as a strong instrument of a national majority. The perennial challenge for members of Congress is to find a workable balance between what Roger Davidson and Walter Oleszek call the "two Congresses": one embodied by the Capitol in Washington and the other embodied by the members' separate districts and states.[35]

Summary

Members of Congress, once elected, are likely to be reelected. Members of Congress can use their office to publicize themselves, pursue a service strategy of responding to the needs of individual constituents, and secure pork-barrel projects for their states or districts. House members gain a greater advantage from these activities than do senators, whose larger constituencies make it harder for them to build close personal relations with voters and whose office is more likely to attract strong challengers. Incumbency does have some disadvantages. Members of Congress must take positions on controversial issues, may blunder into political scandal or indiscretion, must deal with changes in the electorate, or may face strong challengers; any of these conditions can reduce members' reelection chances. By and large, however, the advantages of incumbency far outweigh the disadvantages. Incumbents' advantages extend into their reelection campaigns: their influential positions in Congress make it easier for them to raise campaign funds from PACs and individual contributors.

Congress is a fragmented institution. It has no single leader; rather, the House and Senate have separate leaders, neither of whom can presume to speak for the other chamber. The principal party leaders of Congress are the Speaker of the House and the Senate majority leader. They share leadership power with committee and subcommittee chairpersons, who have influence on the policy decisions of their committee or subcommittee.

It is in the committees that most of the day-to-day work of Congress is conducted. Each standing committee of the House or the Senate has jurisdiction over congressional policy in a particular area (such as agriculture or foreign relations), as does each of its subcommittees. In most cases, the full House and Senate accept committee recommendations about the passage of bills, although amendments to bills are quite common and committees are careful to take other members of Congress into account when making legislative decisions. Congress is a legislative system in which influence is widely dispersed, an arrangement that suits the power and reelection needs of its individual members. However, partisanship is a strong and binding force in Congress. It is the basis on which party leaders are able to build support for major legislative initiatives. On this type of legislation, party leaders and caucuses, rather than committees, are the central actors.

The major function of Congress is to enact legislation. Yet the role it plays in developing legislation depends on the type of policy involved. Because of its divided chambers and committee structure, as well as the concern of its members with state and district interests, Congress, through its party leaders and caucuses, only occasionally takes the lead on broad national issues; Congress instead typically looks to the president for this leadership. Nevertheless, presidential initiatives are passed by Congress only if they meet its members' expectations and usually only after a lengthy process of compromise and negotiation. Congress is more adept at handling legislation that deals with problems of narrow interest. Legislation of this sort is decided mainly in congressional committees, where interested legislators, bureaucrats, and groups concentrate their efforts on issues of mutual concern.

A second function of Congress is the representation of various interests. Members of Congress are highly sensitive to the state or district on which they depend for reelection. They do respond to overriding national interests, but for most of them, local concerns generally come first. National and local representation often work through party representation, particularly on issues that divide the Democratic and Republican parties and their constituent groups.

Congress's third function is oversight, the supervision and investigation of the way the bureaucracy is implementing legislatively mandated programs. Although oversight is a difficult process, it is an important means of legislative control over the actions of the executive branch.

STUDY CORNER

Key Terms

bill *(p. 355)*
cloture *(p. 356)*
conference committees *(p. 352)*
constituency *(p. 337)*
filibuster *(p. 357)*
gerrymandering *(p. 342)*
jurisdiction *(p. 354)*
law *(p. 358)*
lawmaking function *(p. 358)*

logrolling *(p. 363)*
open-seat election *(p. 339)*
oversight function *(p. 365)*
party caucus *(p. 346)*
party discipline *(p. 357)*
party leaders *(p. 346)*
pork-barrel projects *(p. 338)*
reapportionment *(p. 341)*
redistricting *(p. 342)*

representation function *(p. 362)*
rider *(p. 357)*
seniority *(p. 350)*
service strategy *(p. 338)*
standing committees *(p. 351)*
sunset law *(p. 366)*
veto *(p. 358)*

Self-Test

1. General characteristics of the U.S. Congress include all **except** which one of the following?
   a. Congress is a fragmented institution.
   b. Influence in Congress is widely dispersed.
   c. Congress rather than the president usually takes the lead in addressing broad national issues.
   d. Both the House and the Senate are directly elected by the voters.

2. In Congress, the role of representation of the nation through political parties is illustrated by all **except** which one of the following?
   a. conflicts over national goals primarily along party lines
   b. the emphasis that members of Congress place on pork-barrel legislation
   c. a common division of votes along party lines in committee voting
   d. Republicans aligned against Democrats on roll-call votes.

3. Which of the following give(s) the president a policymaking advantage over Congress on broad national issues?
   a. the public's expectation that the president will take the lead on such issues
   b. the fragmented leadership structure of Congress
   c. the president's position as the sole chief executive and thus the authoritative voice of the executive branch
   d. all of the above

4. Which of the following factors usually plays the largest role in the reelection of members of Congress?
   a. incumbency
   b. positions taken on issues
   c. popularity with the president
   d. gender

5. Most bills that are introduced in Congress:
   a. are defeated in committee.
   b. are passed in committee and defeated on the floor.
   c. are passed and become laws.
   d. are sent to executive agencies for review.

6. The most important party leadership position in the U.S. Senate is that of:
   a. Speaker.
   b. majority leader.
   c. president pro tempore.
   d. vice president of the United States.

7. Congressional incumbents receive fewer campaign contributions from PACs than their opponents do. (T/F)

8. The Speaker is the only officer of the House of Representatives provided for in the Constitution. (T/F)

9. Most of the work done in Congress is conducted through standing committees. (T/F)

10. A bill must be passed in identical form by both chambers of Congress before it can be sent to the president for approval or veto. (T/F)

Critical Thinking

How does the structure of Congress (for example, its two chambers and its committee system) affect its policymaking role?

Suggested Readings

Dwyre, Diana, and Victoria Farrar-Myers. *Legislative Labyrinth: Congress and Campaign Finance Reform.* Washington, D.C.: Congressional Quarterly Press, 2001. An inside look at the mix of Congress and campaign money.

Herrnson, Paul S. *Congressional Elections: Campaigning at Home and in Washington,* 4th ed. Washington, D.C.: Congressional Quarterly Press, 2003. A study that argues members of Congress run two campaigns, one at home and one in Washington.

Hibbing, John R., and Elizabeth Theiss-Morse. *Congress as Public Enemy: Public Attitudes Toward American Political Institutions.* New York: Cambridge University Press, 1995. An analysis through survey and focus group data of Americans' attitudes toward Congress.

Jacobson, Gary C. *The Politics of Congressional Elections,* 5th ed. New York: Longman, 2001. An overview of the congressional election process and its impact on policy and representation.

King, David C. Turf Wars: *How Congressional Committees Claim Jurisdiction.* Chicago: University of Chicago Press, 1997. An innovative study on how congressional committees claim jurisdiction.

Sidlow, Edward. *Challenging the Incumbent: An Underdog's Undertaking.* Washington, D.C.: Congressional Quarterly Press, 2003. A fascinating case study of the difficulties for those who dare to challenge an incumbent.

Sinclair, Barbara. *Unorthodox Lawmaking: New Legislative Processes in the U.S. Congress,* 2nd ed. Washington, D.C.: Congressional Quarterly Press, 2000. A detailed analysis of the American legislative process.

List of Websites

http://www.usafmc.org/default.asp?pagenumber=8

The website of the United States Association of Former Members of Congress, which has a "Congress to Campus" program that upon request brings former congressional members to campuses for talks.

http://thomas.loc.gov/

The Library of Congress site, named after Thomas Jefferson, that provides information about the congressional process, including the status of pending legislation.

http://www.house.gov/

The U.S. House of Representatives' website; it has information on party leaders, pending legislation, and committee hearings, as well as links to each House member's office and website.

http://www.senate.gov/

The U.S. Senate's website, which is similar to that of the House and provides links to each senator's website.

Participate!

Each year, thousands of college students serve as interns in Congress or in state legislatures. Many internships are unpaid, but students often can get college credit for the work experience. If a legislative internship is of interest to you, you can get information from the American Political Science Association (www.apsa.org). In addition, there are organizations in Washington that arrange congressional internships. Many of these organizations charge a fee, so you might want to contact a legislative office directly. Students normally get a better response when they contact their own legislator (representative or senator) rather than one from another district or state. You could also check with the student services office at your college or university. Some of these offices have information on internship programs, and some even offer application assistance.

Extra Credit

For up-to-the-minute *New York Times* articles, interactive simulations, graphics, study tools, and more links and quizzes, visit the text's Online Learning Center at www.mhhe.com/pattersontad7.

(Self-Test Answers: 1. c   2. b   3. d   4. a   5. a   6 b.   7. F   8. T   9. T   10. T)

12

The Presidency:
Leading the Nation

"[The president's] is the only voice in national affairs. Let him once win the admiration and confidence of the people, and no other single voice will easily overpower him."

Woodrow Wilson[1]

George W. Bush was sinking in the polls. His approval rating, which had been above 60 percent, was less than 55 percent. The economy was weakening, and the president was being criticized for not doing enough to reverse the downtrend. Bush was also getting heat for the defection of Senator James Jeffords of Vermont, which cost Republicans control of the Senate. The press was also starting to attack the president. Journalists had given him the honeymoon period traditionally accorded a new president, but they were now turning on him.

Everything changed on September 11, 2001. The terrorist attacks on the World Trade Center and the Pentagon led Americans to rally around their president. Bush vowed that America would not rest until the terrorists were brought to justice and the international network of which they were a part was destroyed. His presidential approval rating reached 96 percent, the highest level ever recorded. Not even Franklin Roosevelt and Harry Truman had received approval ratings that high during the Second World War. During the next two years, buoyed by public support, Bush led the nation into wars in Afghanistan and Iraq as part of his "war on terrorism." However, the U.S. invasion of Iraq was followed by problems the Bush administration had not anticipated. Continued attacks on U.S. forces, a failure to find weapons of mass destruction, abuses of Iraqi prisoners by U.S. soldiers, and the mounting cost of financing the reconstruction of Iraq combined to erode public support for Bush's policies. In 2004, for the first time in his presidency, Bush's approval rating fell below 50 percent.

The Bush story is but one in the saga of the ups and downs of the modern presidency. Lyndon Johnson's and Richard Nixon's dogged pursuit of the Vietnam War led to talk of "the imperial presidency," an office so powerful that constitutional checks and balances were no longer an effective constraint on it. Within a few years, because of the undermining effects of Watergate and of changing international conditions during the Ford and Carter presidencies, the watchword became "the imperiled presidency," an office too weak to meet the nation's demands for executive leadership. Ronald Reagan's policy successes before 1986 renewed talk heard in the Roosevelt and Kennedy years of "a heroic presidency," an office that is an inspirational center of American politics. After the Iran-Contra scandal in 1986, Reagan was more often called a lame duck. The first George Bush's handling of the Gulf crisis—leading the nation in 1991 into a major war and emerging from it with a stratospheric public approval rating—bolstered the heroic

President George W. Bush during a surprise visit to U.S. troops in Iraq on Thanksgiving Day 2003. The president's constitutional authority as commander in chief of the nation's armed forces is a major source of presidential power.

conception of the office. A year later, Bush was on his way to being removed from office by the voters. Bill Clinton overcame a fitful start to his presidency to become the first Democrat since Franklin D. Roosevelt in the 1930s to win re-election. As Clinton was launching an aggressive second-term policy agenda, however, he got entangled in an affair with a White House intern, Monica Lewinsky, that led to his impeachment by the House of Representatives and weakened his claim to national leadership.

No other political institution has been subject to such varying characterizations as the modern presidency. One reason is that the formal powers of the office are somewhat limited and thus presidential power changes with national conditions, political circumstances, and the personal capacity of the office's occupant.[2] The American presidency is always a central office in that its occupant is a focus of national attention. Yet the presidency is not an inherently powerful office in the sense that presidents routinely get what they want. Presidential power is conditional. It depends on the president's own abilities, but even more on the circumstances—on whether the situation demands strong leadership and whether the political support for that leadership exists. When conditions are favorable, the president will look powerful. When conditions are adverse, the president will appear vulnerable.

This chapter examines the roots of presidential power, the presidential selection process, the staffing of the presidency, and the factors associated with the success or failure of presidential leadership. The main ideas of this chapter are the following:

- *Public expectations, national crises, and changing national and world conditions have required the presidency to become a strong office.* Underlying this development is the public support the president acquires from being the only nationally elected official.

- *The modern presidential election campaign is a marathon affair in which self-selected candidates must plan for a strong start in the nominating contests and center their general-election strategies on media, issues, and a baseline of support.* The lengthy campaign process heightens the public's sense that the presidency is at the center of the U.S. political system.

- *The modern presidency could not operate without a large staff of assistants, experts, and high-level managers, but the sheer size of this staff makes it impossible for the president to exercise complete control over it.*

- *The president's election by national vote and position as sole chief executive ensure that others will listen to the president's ideas; but to lead effectively, the president must have the help of other officials and, to get their help, must respond to their interests as they respond to the president's.*

- *Presidential influence on national policy is highly variable.* Whether presidents succeed or fail in getting their policies enacted depends heavily on the force of circumstance, the stage of their presidency, partisan support in Congress, and the foreign or domestic nature of the policy issue.

FOUNDATIONS OF THE MODERN PRESIDENCY

The writers of the Constitution knew what they wanted from a president —national leadership, statesmanship in foreign affairs, command in time of war or insurgency, enforcement of the laws—but they could devise only general phrases to describe the president's constitutional authority. Compared with Article I, which enumerates Congress's specific powers, Article II of the Constitution contains relatively vague statements on the president's powers.[3]

Over the course of American history, each of the president's constitutional powers has been extended in practice beyond the Framers' intention. For example, the Constitution grants the president command of the nation's military, but only Congress can declare war. In *Federalist* No. 69, Alexander Hamilton wrote that a surprise attack on the United States was the only justification for war by presidential action. Nevertheless, the nation's presidents have sent troops into military action abroad more than two hundred times. Of the more than a dozen wars included in that figure, only five were declared by Congress.[4] All of America's most recent wars—the Korean, Vietnam, Persian Gulf, Balkans, Afghanistan, and Iraq conflicts— have been undeclared.

The Constitution also empowers the president to act as diplomatic leader with the authority to appoint ambassadors and to negotiate treaties with other countries, subject to approval by a two-thirds vote of the Senate. The Framers anticipated that Congress would define the nation's foreign policy objectives, while the president would oversee their implementation. However, the president has become the principal architect of U.S. foreign policy and has even acquired the power to make treaty-like arrangements with other nations, in the form of executive agreements. In 1937, the Supreme Court ruled that such agreements, signed and approved only by the president, have the same legal status as treaties, although Congress can cancel executive agreements with which it disagrees.[5] Since World War II, presidents have negotiated more than

---

The President's Constitutional Authority

Commander in chief: Article II, Section 2: "The President shall be commander in chief of the Army and Navy of the United States, and of the militia of the several states."

Chief executive: Article II, Section 2: "He may require the opinion, in writing, of the principal officer in each of the executive departments, upon any subject relating to the duties of their respective offices, and he shall have power to grant reprieves and pardons for offences against the United States, except in cases of impeachment."

Article II, Section 2: "He shall have power, by and with the advice and consent of the Senate, to make treaties, provided two thirds of the senators present concur; and he shall nominate, and by and with the advice and consent of the Senate, shall appoint ambassadors, other public ministers and consuls, judges of the Supreme Court, and all other officers of the United States, whose appointments are not herein otherwise provided for, and which shall be established by law."

Article II, Section 2: "The President shall have power to fill up all vacancies that may happen during the recess of the Senate, by granting commissions which shall expire at the end of their next session."

Article II, Section 3: "He shall take care that the laws be faithfully executed, and shall commission all the officers of the United States."

Chief diplomat: Article II, Section 2: "He shall have power, and with the advice and consent of the Senate, to make treaties, provided two thirds of the senators present concur."

Article II, Section 3: "He shall receive ambassadors and other public ministers."

Legislative leader: Article II, Section 3: "He shall from time to time give to the Congress information of the state of the Union, and recommend to their consideration such measures as he shall judge necessary and expedient; he may, on extraordinary occasions, convene both houses, or either of them, and in case of disagreement between them, with respect to the time of adjournment, he may adjourn them to such time as he shall think proper." (Article I, Section 7, which defines the president's veto power, is also part of his legislative authority.)

---

ten thousand executive agreements, compared to fewer than one thousand treaties ratified by the Senate.[6]

The Constitution also vests "executive power" in the president. This power includes the responsibility to execute the laws faithfully and to appoint major administrators, such as heads of the various departments of the executive branch. In *Federalist* No. 76, Hamilton indicated that the president's real authority as chief executive was to be found in this appointive capacity. Presidents have indeed exercised substantial power through their appointments, but they have found their administrative authority—the power to execute the laws—to be of even greater value, because it enables them to determine how laws will be interpreted and applied. President Ronald Reagan used his executive power to *prohibit* the use of federal funds by family-planning clinics that offered abortion counseling. President Bill Clinton exerted the same power to *permit* the use of federal funds for this purpose. The *same* act of Congress was the basis for each of these actions. The act authorizes the use of federal funds for family-planning services, but it neither requires nor prohibits their use for abortion counseling, enabling the president to decide this issue.

Finally, the Constitution provides the president with legislative authority, including use of the veto and the opportunity to recommend proposals to

Congress. The Framers expected this authority to be used in a limited and largely negative way. George Washington acted as the Framers anticipated: he proposed only three legislative measures and vetoed only two acts of Congress. Modern presidents have a different, more activist view of their legislative role. They routinely submit legislative proposals to Congress and often veto legislation they find disagreeable.

The presidency is a more powerful office than the Framers envisioned, for many reasons. But two features of the office in particular—*national election* and *singular authority*—have enabled presidents to make use of changing demands on government to claim the position of leader of the American people. It is a claim that no other elected official can routinely make, and it is a key to understanding the role and power of the president.

Asserting a Claim to National Leadership

The first president to forcefully assert a claim to popular leadership was Andrew Jackson, who had been swept into office in 1828 on a tide of public support that broke the hold of the upper classes on the presidency. Jackson used his popular backing to challenge Congress's claim to national policy leadership, contending that he was "the people's tribune."

Historical Background

However, Jackson's view was not shared by most of his successors during the nineteenth century, because national conditions did not routinely call for strong presidential leadership. The prevailing conception was the **Whig theory,** which held that the presidency was a limited or constrained office whose occupant was confined to the exercise of expressly granted constitutional authority. The president had no implicit powers for dealing with national problems but was primarily an administrator, charged with carrying out the will of Congress. "My duty," said President James Buchanan, a Whig adherent, "is to execute the laws . . . and not my individual opinions."[7]

Whig theory A theory that prevailed in the nineteenth century and held that the presidency was a limited or restrained office whose occupant was confined to expressly granted constitutional authority.

Theodore Roosevelt rejected the Whig tradition upon taking office in 1901. He attacked the business trusts, pursued an aggressive foreign policy, and pressured Congress to adopt progressive domestic policies. Roosevelt embraced the **stewardship theory,** which calls for an assertive presidency that is confined only at points specifically prohibited by law. As "steward of the people," Roosevelt said, he was permitted "to do anything that the needs of the Nation demanded unless such action was forbidden by the Constitution or by the laws."[8]

stewardship theory A theory that argues for a strong, assertive presidential role, with presidential authority limited only at points specifically prohibited by law.

Roosevelt's image of a strong presidency was shared by Woodrow Wilson, but his other immediate successors reverted to the Whig notion of the limited presidency.[9] Herbert Hoover's restrained conception of the presidency prevented him from taking decisive action even during the devastation of the Great Depression. Hoover said that he lacked the constitutional authority to establish public relief programs for jobless Americans. However, Hoover's successor, Franklin D. Roosevelt, shared the stewardship theory of his distant cousin Theodore Roosevelt, and FDR's New Deal signaled the end of the limited presidency. As FDR's successor, Harry Truman, wrote in his memoirs: "The power of the President should be used in the interest of the people and in order to do that the President must use whatever power the Constitution does not expressly deny him."[10]

Liberty, Equality & Self-Government

What's Your Opinion?

The Presidency

When the Constitution was drafted, fear of executive power was widespread. The Framers worried that a too-powerful executive would threaten Americans' hard-won liberty, equality, and self-government.

Presidents have at times pursued policies that have made Americans less free, but presidents more often have led efforts to enlarge the practice of America's core principles. Thomas Jefferson, Abraham Lincoln, Franklin Roosevelt, and Lyndon Johnson are among the presidents whose names are nearly synonymous with such efforts. Johnson's leadership, for example, was critical to passage of the 1964 Civil Rights Act and the 1965 Voting Rights Act.

Can this development be explained by the nature of executive power? Unlike legislative power, which is widely shared, executive power is vested in a single individual. Have presidents taken the lead on issues of liberty, equality, and self-government largely because of their greater capacity for assertive action?

Today the presidency is an inherently strong office.[11] The modern presidency becomes a more substantial office in the hands of a persuasive leader such as Ronald Reagan, but even a less forceful person such as Jimmy Carter is expected to act assertively. This expectation not only is the legacy of former strong presidents but also stems from changes that have occurred in the federal government's national and international policy responsibilities.

The Need for Presidential Leadership of an Activist Government

During most of the nineteenth century (the Civil War being the notable exception), the United States did not need a strong president. The federal government's policymaking role was small, as was its bureaucracy. Moreover, the nation's major issues were of a sectional nature (especially the North-South split over slavery) and thus were suited to action by Congress, which represented state and local interests. The U.S. government's role in world affairs was also small. As these conditions changed, however, the presidency also changed.

Foreign Policy Leadership

The president has always been the nation's foreign policy leader, but the role was initially a rather undemanding one. The United States avoided entanglement in the turbulent affairs of Europe, and though it was involved in foreign trade, it was preoccupied with internal development. By the end of the nineteenth century, however, the nation was seeking to expand the world market for its goods. President Theodore Roosevelt advocated an American economic

Harry S Truman's presidency was characterized by bold foreign policy initiatives. He authorized the use of nuclear weapons against Japan in 1945, created the Marshall Plan as the basis for the economic reconstruction of postwar Europe, and sent U.S. troops to fight in Korea in 1950. Truman is shown here greeting British Prime Minister Winston Churchill at a Washington airport in early 1952.

empire and looked south toward Latin America and west toward Hawaii, the Philippines, and China for new markets (the "Open Door" policy). However, the United States' tradition of isolationism remained a powerful influence on national policy. The United States fought in World War I but immediately thereafter demobilized its armed forces. Over President Woodrow Wilson's objections, Congress then voted against the entry of the United States into the League of Nations.

World War II fundamentally changed the nation's international role and the president's role in foreign policy. In 1945, the United States emerged as a global superpower, a giant in world trade, and the recognized leader of the noncommunist world. The United States today has a military presence in nearly every part of the globe and an unprecedented interest in trade balances, energy supplies, and other international issues affecting the nation.

The effect of these developments on America's political institutions has been one-sided. Because of the president's constitutional authority as chief diplomat and military commander and the special demands of foreign policy leadership, the president, not Congress, has taken the lead in addressing the nation's increased responsibilities in the world. Foreign policy requires singleness of purpose and, at times, fast action. Congress—a large, divided, and unwieldy institution—is poorly suited to such a response. In contrast, the president, as sole head of the executive branch, can act quickly and speak authoritatively for the nation as a whole in its relations with other nations.

This capacity has rarely been more evident than after the terrorist attacks of September 11, 2001. The initiative in the war on terrorism rested squarely with the White House. President Bush decided on the U.S. response to the attacks and took the lead in obtaining international support for U.S. military,

The White House contains, on the first floor, the president's Oval Office, other offices, and ceremonial rooms. The First Family's living quarters are on the second floor.

intelligence, and diplomatic initiatives. Congress backed these actions enthusiastically. The joint resolution that endorsed Bush's decision to attack the Taliban government in Afghanistan passed unanimously in the Senate and with only a single dissenting vote in the House. In reality, however, Congress had little choice but to support whatever policies Bush chose. Americans wanted decisive action and were looking to the president, not Congress, for leadership.

In other situations, of course, Congress is less compliant. In recent decades, it has contested presidential positions on issues such as global trade and international human rights. Nevertheless, the president is clearly the leading voice in U.S. foreign policy. (The changing shape of the world and its implications for presidential power and leadership are discussed more fully later in the chapter.)

Domestic Policy Leadership

Historical Background

The change in the president's domestic leadership role has also been substantial. Throughout most of the nineteenth century Congress jealously guarded its constitutional powers, making it clear that domestic policy was its business. James Bryce wrote in the 1880s that Congress paid no more attention to the president's views on legislation than it did to the editorial positions of prominent newspaper publishers.[12]

By the early twentieth century, however, the national government was taking on regulatory and policy responsibilities imposed by the nation's transition from an agrarian to an industrial society, and the executive branch was growing ever larger. In 1921, Congress conceded that it lacked the centralized authority to coordinate the growing national budget and enacted the Budget and Accounting Act, which provided for an executive budget. Federal departments and agencies would no longer submit their annual budget requests directly to Congress. Instead, the president would oversee the initiation of the budget by working the various agencies' requests into a comprehensive budgetary proposal, which then would be submitted to Congress as a starting point for its deliberations.

During the Great Depression of the 1930s, Franklin D. Roosevelt's New Deal responded to the public's demand for economic relief with a broad program that involved a level of policy planning and coordination beyond the capacity of Congress. In addition to initiating public works projects and social welfare programs aimed at providing immediate relief, the New Deal made the government a partner in nearly every aspect of the nation's economy. If economic regulation was to work, unified and continuous policy leadership was needed, and only the president could routinely provide such leadership.

Presidential authority has continued to grow since Roosevelt's time. In response to pressures from the public, the national government's role in such areas as education, health, welfare, safety, and protection of the environment has expanded greatly, which in turn has created additional demands for presidential leadership.[13] Big government, with its emphasis on comprehensive planning and program coordination, has favored executive authority at the expense of legislative authority. All democracies have seen a shift in power from their legislature to their executive. In Britain, for example, the prime minister has taken on responsibilities that once belonged to the cabinet or to Parliament.

CHOOSING THE PRESIDENT

As the president's policy and leadership responsibilities changed during the nation's history, so did the process of electing presidents. The changes do not parallel each other exactly, but they are related both politically and philosophically. As the presidency drew ever closer to the people, their role in selecting the president grew ever more important.[14] The United States in its history has had four systems of presidential selection, each more "democratic" than its predecessor (see Table 12-1). The justification for each new electoral system was **legitimacy,** the idea that the choice of a president should be based on the will of the people as expressed through their votes.

legitimacy (of election) The idea that the selection of officeholders should be based on the will of the people as expressed through their votes.

Toward a More "Democratic" System of Presidential Election

The delegates to the constitutional convention of 1787 feared that popular election would make the presidency too centralized and too powerful and thereby undermine the principles of federalism and separation of powers. The Framers devised a novel system, which came to be called the Electoral College. Under the Constitution, the president is chosen by a vote of electors who are appointed by the states; the candidate who receives the majority of electoral votes is elected president. Each state is entitled to an elector for each member it has in Congress (House and Senate combined).

Historical Background

TABLE 12-1	The Four Systems of Presidential Selection	
SELECTION SYSTEM	**PERIOD**	**FEATURES**
1. Original	1788–1828	Party nominees are chosen in congressional caucuses. Electoral College members act somewhat independently in their presidential voting.
2. Party convention	1832–1900	Party nominees are chosen in national party conventions by delegates selected by state and local party organizations. Electoral College members cast their ballots for the popular-vote winner in their respective states.
3. Party convention, primary	1904–1968	As in system 2, except that a *minority* of national convention delegates are chosen through primary elections (the majority still being chosen by party organizations).
4. Party primary, open caucus	1972–present	As in system 2, except that a *majority* of national convention delegates are chosen through primary elections.

In choosing the nation's first presidents, electors acted somewhat independently, exercising their own judgment in casting their votes. This pattern changed after the election in 1828 of Andrew Jackson, who believed the people's will had been denied four years earlier when he placed first in the popular voting but failed to gain an electoral majority. Jackson could not persuade Congress to support a constitutional amendment that would have eliminated the Electoral College, but he did obtain the next-best alternative: he persuaded the states to tie their electoral votes to the popular vote. Under Jackson's reform, which is still in effect today, each party in a state has a separate slate of electors who gain the right to cast a state's electoral votes if their party's candidate places first in the state's popular voting. Thus, the popular vote for the candidates directly affects their electoral vote, and one candidate is likely to win both forms of the presidential vote. Since Jackson's time, only Rutherford B. Hayes (in 1876), Benjamin Harrison (in 1888), and George W. Bush (in 2000) have won the presidency after having lost the popular vote.

Jackson also championed the national convention as a means of nominating the party's presidential candidate (before this time, nominations were made by party caucuses in Congress and in state legislatures). The parties' strength was at the grass roots, among the people, and Jackson saw the convention process as a means of bringing the citizenry and the presidency closer together. Since Jackson's time, presidential nominees have been formally chosen at national party conventions. Each state party sends delegates to the national convention, and these delegates select the party's nominee.

Jackson's system of presidential nomination remained fully intact until the early twentieth century, when the Progressives devised the primary election as

Should the Electoral College Be Abolished?

As the votes in the 2000 election were counted, the country was thrown into turmoil by the electoral vote system. The president is chosen by an indirect system of election. Voters cast ballots for candidates, but their votes choose only each state's electors, whose subsequent ballots result in the actual selection of the president. Electoral votes are apportioned by states based on their representation in Congress, which creates the possibility that the candidate who receives the most popular votes will not receive the most electoral votes and thus will not be elected president. The 2000 election was of this type, and it renewed the debate about retaining the electoral vote system.

Debating the Issues

Yes: It's time to abolish the Electoral College and to count the votes of all Americans in presidential elections. . . . Two centuries ago the Constitutional Convention considered many ways to select the president of the emerging republic, from popular election to assigning the decision to the Congress. The Electoral College was a compromise that reflected a basic mistrust of the electorate—the same mistrust that denied the vote to women, African-Americans, and people who did not own property. The Electoral College may or may not have made sense in 1787. But through 21st-century eyes it is as anachronistic as the limitations on suffrage itself. Whether or not you like the results of a particular election . . . your vote should count. . . . If the Electoral College merely echoes the election results, then it is superfluous. If it contradicts the voting majority, then why tolerate it? It is a remarkable and enduring virtue of our political system that our elections are credible and decisive—and that power changes hands in a coherent and dignified manner. . . . Every other public official is chosen by majority vote. That's the way it's supposed to work in a democracy. For reasons both philosophical and practical, that's also how we should elect the president.

—*William D. Delahunt, U.S. representative (D-Mass.)*

No: The pundits will argue that it is not fair to deny the presidency to the man who received the most total votes. After all, to do so would be "undemocratic." This argument ignores the fundamental nature of our constitutional system. The Founding Fathers sought to create a loose confederacy of states, joined together by a federal government with very little power. They created a constitutionally limited republic, not a direct democracy. They did so to protect fundamental liberties against the whims of the masses. The Electoral College likewise was created in the Constitution to guard against majority tyranny in federal elections. The President was to be elected by the states rather than the citizenry as a whole, with votes apportioned to states according to their representation in Congress. The will of the people was to be tempered by the wisdom of the Electoral College. By contrast, election of the President by pure popular vote totals would damage statehood. Populated areas on both coasts would have increasing influence on national elections, to the detriment of less populated southern and western states. A candidate receiving a large percentage of the popular vote in California and New York could win a national election with very little support in dozens of other states! A popular vote system simply would intensify the populist pandering which already dominates national campaigns.

—*Ron Paul, U.S. representative (R-Texas)*

a means of curbing the power of the party bosses (see Chapter 2). State party leaders had taken control of the nominating process by handpicking their states' delegates. The Progressives sought to shift control to the voters by allowing them to select the convention delegates. Such a process is called an *indirect primary*, because the voters are not choosing the nominees directly (as they do in House and Senate races) but rather are choosing delegates who in turn select the nominees.

Presidential nominating campaigns often attract a large number of contenders. The 2004 Democratic race had a huge field. Pictured here in one of their earliest televised debates are (left to right) John Kerry, Bob Graham, Joseph Lieberman, Wesley Clark, Dennis Kucinich, John Edwards, Howard Dean, Al Sharpton, Carol Mosley-Brown, and Richard Gephardt. Graham dropped out of the race shortly after this debate.

The Progressives were able to persuade only a minority of states to switch to the primary system. As a result, party leaders continued to control a majority of the delegates and therefore continued to have the larger voice in the nominating process.

In 1968, the Democratic nomination went to Vice President Hubert Humphrey, who had not entered a single primary and was closely identified with the Johnson administration's Vietnam policy. After Humphrey narrowly lost the 1968 general election to Richard Nixon, reform-minded Democrats forced changes in the nominating process. The new rules gave rank-and-file party voters more control by requiring that states choose their delegates through either primary elections or **open party caucuses** (meetings open to any registered party voter who wants to attend). Although the Democrats initiated the change, the Republicans were also affected by it. Most states that adopted a presidential primary in order to comply with the Democrats' new rules also required Republicans to select their convention delegates through a primary.

open party caucuses
Meetings at which a party's candidates for nomination are voted on and that are open to all the party's rank-and-file voters who want to attend.

Today it is the voters in state primaries and open caucuses who play the decisive role in the selection of the Democratic and Republican presidential nominees.[15] A state's delegates are awarded to candidates in accordance with how well they do in the state's primary or caucus. Thus, to win the majority of national convention delegates necessary for nomination, a candidate must place first in a lot of states and do at least reasonably well in most of the rest. (About forty states choose their delegates through a primary election; the others use a caucus system.)

In sum, the presidential election system has changed from an elite-dominated process to one based on voter support. This arrangement has strengthened the presidency by providing the office with the reserve of power that popular election confers on democratic leadership.

The Campaign for Nomination

The fact that voters pick the party nominees has opened the nominating races to any politician with the energy and resources to run a major national campaign. Nominating campaigns, except those in which an incumbent president is seeking reelection, typically attract a half-dozen contenders. The 2004 Democratic race drew an even larger number. Nine candidates were on the ballot: John

Kerry, John Edwards, Richard Gephardt, Carol Mosley-Brown, Wesley Clark, Dennis Kucinich, Joe Lieberman, Al Sharpton, and Howard Dean.

A key to success in the nominating campaign is **momentum**—a solid showing in the early contests that leads to a buildup of public support in subsequent ones. If candidates start off strongly, the press will cover them more heavily, contributors will provide them with more funding, and voters will give more thought to supporting them. For these reasons, presidential contenders now give extraordinary attention to the early contests, particularly the first caucuses in Iowa and the first primary in New Hampshire. Solid wins in these two states in 2004 propelled John Kerry to the Democratic nomination.

Money, always a critical factor in elections, has become increasingly important in the last three decades because states have moved their primaries and caucuses to the early weeks of the nominating period in order to increase their influence on the outcome. To compete effectively in so many contests over such a short period, candidates need money—lots of it. A candidate can be in only one place at a time, so the campaign must be carried to other voters through televised political advertising. Ads are expensive to produce and broadcast, and analysts claim that it takes at least $20 million to $30 million to run a competitive nominating campaign. George W. Bush raised more than $75 million in 2000 for his successful nominating campaign, far more than any of his Republican rivals. In every nominating race but one from 1984 to 2004, the winner was the candidate who had raised the most money before the start of the primaries. (The exception occurred in 2004, when Howard Dean was the top fund-raiser in advance of the Iowa caucuses.)

Candidates in primary elections receive federal funding if they meet the eligibility criteria. The Federal Election Campaign Act of 1974 (as amended in 1979) provides for federal matching funds. Under the program, the government matches the first $250 of each private donation received by a primary election candidate, provided the candidate raises at least $5,000 in individual contributions of up to $250 in at least twenty states. This provision is designed to restrict matching funds to candidates who can show they have a reasonable amount of public support. In addition, any candidate who receives matching funds must agree to limit expenditures for the nominating phase to a set amount overall ($45 million in 2004) and in particular states (the limits in 2004 in Iowa and New Hampshire, for example, were $1.3 million and $725,000, respectively). The limits are adjusted upward each election year to account for inflation. Taxpayers fund the matching program by checking a box on their income-tax return allocating $3 of their taxes to it.

In 2004, Kerry and Dean chose not to accept matching funds. This enabled them to outspend their Democratic opponents in Iowa, New Hampshire, and the other early contests. Kerry spent more than $10 million in Iowa and New Hampshire alone. President Bush also decided not to take matching funds in 2004. Although he had no opponent for the Republican nomination, Bush raised roughly $200 million for his nominating campaign—more than three times as much as the top Democratic fund-raiser. Once the Democratic race was decided in favor of Kerry, the Bush campaign unleashed the money, concentrating on states where the race against Kerry was tightest. The strategy was perfectly legal, as long as the money was spent in the period before the Republican convention in late August. Clinton pursued a similar strategy in his successful 1996 reelection campaign.

momentum A strong showing by a candidate in early presidential nominating contests, which leads to a buildup of public support for the candidate.

Simulation
www.mhhe.com/pattersontad7

The Front-Loading of Presidential Primaries

Fifteen states in 2000 held their presidential primaries on March 7. So many contests were held on this day that opponents did not stand a chance against George W. Bush's and Al Gore's superior name recognition, financing, and organization. Bill Bradley quit the Democratic race the next day. John McCain retreated to his Arizona home and, two days later, announced he was dropping out of the Republican contest. The 2004 nominations were also decided by early March, as were the 1996 nominations. Each time, the races ended before most states had held their primary or caucus. Voters in these states were effectively disenfranchised as a result.

The reason the races end abruptly is *front-loading*—the tendency of states to position their contests toward the front end of the nominating process. Front-loading exists because states gradually came to recognize that the power in the nominating process resides in the early contests. A state that holds back risks losing its opportunity to influence the outcome. Nevertheless, many states do hold back. Some small and medium-size states realize their contest will not get much attention from the candidates if it is scheduled at the same time as a dozen contests that include several large-state primaries, including those of California and New York. Other states hold back because they have decided that a March primary is too soon in the year to select nominees for other offices. A statewide primary is expensive to run, and most states therefore are unwilling to conduct an early primary for the presidential race and a later one for other races.

Nevertheless, enough states have moved to the front of the process to give a huge advantage to a candidate with lots of money and high name recognition. In fact, every presidential nominee since 1984 except one has been the candidate who raised the most money in advance of the first contest. A poorly funded candidate can sometimes win in a single-state contest such as New Hampshire's primary, as McCain did in 2000, but after that, face-to-face campaigning gives way to televised political ads, which cost huge sums.

In *The Vanishing Voter* (2002), Thomas Patterson shows how front-loading has produced two different nominating electorates, one formed by residents of early-contest states and one comprised of residents of late-contest states. The first electorate chooses the nominees and is exposed to an active campaign, that includes televised advertising, candidate visits, and media attention. The second electorate has no meaningful voice in the process and is more or less ignored by the candidates and the media.

Which category is your state in? Does it hold its presidential nominating contest early or late in the process? (The schedule can be found at www.vote-smart.org/election_president_state_primary_dates.php.)

The national party conventions mark the end of the nominating campaign. In an earlier era, the convention was where the nomination was actually decided. State party delegations would come together at their convention to bargain and choose among potential nominees. Since 1972, when the delegate-selection process was changed, the leading candidate in every case has acquired enough delegates in the primaries to lock up the nomination before the convention begins. Nevertheless, the convention is a major event. It brings together the delegates elected in the state caucuses and primaries, who then approve a party platform and formally nominate the party's presidential and vice presidential candidates.

By tradition, the choice of the vice presidential nominee rests with the presidential nominee. In 2004, Kerry alone decided upon John Edwards as his running mate. Critics say the vice presidential nomination should be decided in open competition, because the vice president could become president someday (see Table 12-2). The chief argument for the existing method is that the president needs a trusted and like-minded vice president.

TABLE 12–2	The Path to the White House		
PRESIDENT	**YEARS IN OFFICE**	**HIGHEST PREVIOUS OFFICE**	**SECOND-HIGHEST OFFICE**
Theodore Roosevelt	1901–1908	Vice president*	Governor
William Howard Taft	1909–1912	Secretary of war	Federal judge
Woodrow Wilson	1913–1920	Governor	None
Warren G. Harding	1921–1924	U.S. senator	Lieutenant governor
Calvin Coolidge	1925–1928	Vice president*	Governor
Herbert Hoover	1929–1932	Secretary of commerce	War relief administrator
Franklin D. Roosevelt	1933–1945	Governor	Assistant secretary of Navy
Harry S Truman	1945–1952	Vice president*	U.S. senator
Dwight D. Eisenhower	1953–1960	None (Army general)	None
John F. Kennedy	1961–1963	U.S. senator	U.S. representative
Lyndon Johnson	1963–1968	Vice president*	U.S. senator
Richard Nixon	1969–1974	Vice president	U.S. senator
Gerald Ford	1974–1976	Vice president*	U.S. representative
Jimmy Carter	1977–1980	Governor	State senator
Ronald Reagan	1981–1988	Governor	None
George Bush	1989–1992	Vice president	Director, CIA
Bill Clinton	1993–2000	Governor	State attorney general
George W. Bush	2000–	Governor	None

*Became president on death or resignation of incumbent.

The Campaign for Election

The winner in the November general election is certain to be either the Republican or the Democratic candidate. Two-thirds of the nation's voters identify with the Republican or Democratic party, and most Independents lean toward one or the other of them. As a result, the major-party presidential nominees have a built-in source of votes. Even Democrat George McGovern, who had the lowest level of party support in the past half-century, was backed in 1972 by 60 percent of his party's identifiers. The level of party support for a major-party nominee can be quite high. In 2004, Bush was backed by 93 percent of self-identified Republicans while Kerry was supported by 89 percent of Democrats.

A third-party candidate has no hope of overcoming this disadvantage. Even Ross Perot, who in 1992 ran the most successful third-party campaign in nearly a century, was able to garner only a fifth of the vote, far less than was needed for victory. On the other hand, third-party candidates have sometimes caused problems for a major party by siphoning votes away from its nominee. In 2000 and again in 2004, third-party candidate Ralph Nader drew the bulk of his support from voters who indicated they otherwise would have backed the Democratic nominee.

Election Strategy

The candidates' strategies in the general election are shaped by many considerations, including the constitutional provision that each state shall have electoral votes equal in number to its representation in Congress. Each state thus gets two electoral votes for its Senate representation and a varying number of electoral votes depending on its House representation. Altogether, there are 538 electoral votes (including 3 for the District of Columbia, even though it has no voting representatives in Congress). To win the presidency, a candidate must receive at least 270 votes, an electoral majority. (If no candidate receives a majority, the election is decided in the House of Representatives. No president since John Quincy Adams in 1824 has been elected in this way. The procedure is defined by the Constitution's Twelfth Amendment, which is reprinted in this book's appendix.)

The importance of the electoral votes is magnified by the existence of the **unit rule:** all the states except Maine and Nebraska grant all their electoral votes as a unit to the candidate who wins the state's popular vote. For this reason, candidates are concerned with winning the most populous states, such as California (with 55 electoral votes), Texas (34), New York (31), Florida (27), Pennsylvania (21), Illinois (21), Ohio (20), Michigan (17), and Georgia, New Jersey, and North Carolina (15 each).

Even more so than a state's size, however, the closeness of the vote in a state dictates how much attention it will get from the candidates. Because of the unit rule, a state that is lopsidedly Democratic or Republican will be ignored. Its electoral votes are already locked up. Thus, the fall campaign becomes a fight over the toss-up states or, as they have come to be called, the battleground states. In 2004, only one-third of the states—many of them in a band that stretched west from Pennsylvania through Iowa and Minnesota—were seen by the Bush and Kerry campaigns as states that realistically could be won by either candidate. The two candidates spent nearly all their money and time in the battleground states during the closing months of the campaign. Other states might just as well have been located in Canada for the attention they received from the candidates. A large number of states, including Kansas and Mississippi, had no impact on the candidates' strategies.

At campaign's end, electoral votes and not popular votes determine the winner (see "States in the Nation"). In 2000, Bush was elected with 271 electoral votes, two more than required, even though he received 550,000 fewer popular votes than Al Gore. Bush was the first president since Harrison in 1888 to win the presidency despite losing the popular vote. In 2004, Bush won with 286 electoral votes. His popular margin exceeded 3 million votes, but he would have lost if Kerry had attracted 150,000 more votes in Ohio, which would have earned him Ohio's 20 electoral votes, enough for an electoral college victory.

Media and Money

The modern presidential campaign is a media campaign. At one time, candidates relied heavily on party organization and rallies to carry their messages to the voters, but now they rely on the media, particularly television. Candidates strive to produce the pithy ten-second sound bites that the television networks

unit rule The rule that grants all of a state's electoral votes to the candidate who receives most of the popular votes in the state.

STATES IN THE NATION

Electoral Votes in the 2004 Election

There are a total of 538 electoral votes and a candidate must receive a majority to win the presidency. In 2004, George W. Bush was elected to a second term with 286 electoral votes—sixteen more than required. If John Kerry had gathered roughly 150,000 more popular votes in Ohio, he would have had an electoral vote majority and become president, even though he trailed Bush by 3.5 million popular votes nationwide. Because electoral votes are allocated on a state-by-state basis, the loser of the national popular vote can gain an electoral-vote victory. In 2000, Bush trailed Democratic nominee Al Gore by half a million popular votes nationwide, but became president by virtue of a 537-vote popular margin in Florida. Bush was the first president since Benjamin Harrison in 1898 to win the presidency while losing the national popular vote.

States can determine for themselves how their electors will be chosen. Today, all state except two (Maine and Nebraska, which give one electoral vote to the winner of each congressional district and two electoral votes to the statewide winner), give all of their electoral votes to the popular-vote winner in the state.

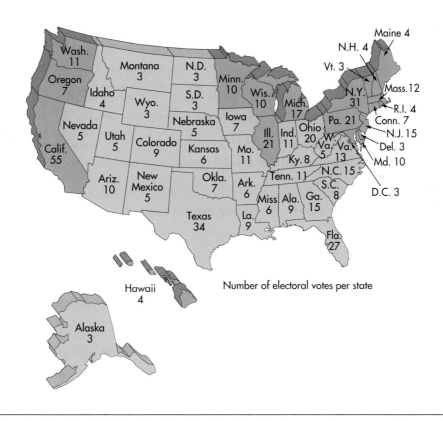

Number of electoral votes per state

Democratic nominee John Kerry addresses a crowd at City College of New York during the 2004 presidential election campaign.

prefer to highlight on the evening newscasts. They also rely on the power of the "new media," making frequent appearances on programs such as *Larry King Live* and creating their own Internet websites.

Television is the forum for the major confrontation of the fall campaign: the presidential debates. The first televised debate took place in 1960 between Kennedy and Nixon, and an estimated one hundred million people saw at least one of their four debates.[16] Televised debates resumed in 1976 and have become a fixture of presidential campaigns. Debates can influence voters' assessments of the candidates. In 2000, Gore drew a negative response from first-debate viewers when he huffed and grimaced while Bush was talking. Gore slipped in the polls after the debate and was unable in the second and third debates to fully overcome the harm to his image resulting from the first one. In 2004, George Bush's weak performance in the debates—polls indicate that viewers felt John Kerry won all three encounters—hurt his candidacy. Before the first debate, the polls showed Bush with a clear lead. By the last debate, the race was nearly a dead heat.

The television campaign includes political advertising. Televised commercials are by far the most expensive part of presidential campaigns, accounting for about half the candidates' general election expenditures.

The Republican and Democratic nominees are each eligible for federal funding of their general election campaigns even if, as in Kerry's and Bush's case in 2004, they did not accept it during the primaries. The amount for the general election was set at $20 million in 1975 and has been adjusted for inflation in succeeding elections. The major-party nominees in the 2004 presidential election each received about $75 million. The only string attached to this money is that candidates who accept it can spend no additional funds on their campaigns (although each party is allowed to spend some money—in 2004, roughly $4 million—on behalf of its nominee).

Candidates can choose not to accept public funds, in which case the amount they spend is limited only by their ability to raise money privately. However, all major-party nominees since 1976 have accepted public funding in the general election. Other candidates for the presidency qualify for federal funding if they

---

Formal and Informal Requirements for Becoming President

Formal requirements. Article II of the U.S. Constitution requires a president to be:

- At least thirty-five years old
- A natural-born U.S. citizen
- A resident in the United States for at least fourteen years

Informal requirements. In the nation's history, presidents have been:

- Male, without exception
- White, without exception

- Protestant, with the exception of John F. Kennedy
- Married, with the exceptions of James Buchanan and Grover Cleveland (who married in the White House)
- Career public servants—four were army generals, thirteen were vice presidents (seven succeeded upon a president's death, one upon a president's resignation), eight were federal administrators, and the remainder were U.S. senators, U.S. representatives (only one), or state governors.

---

receive at least 5 percent of the vote and do not spend more than $50,000 of their own money on the campaign. Such candidates receive an amount of funds equal to the proportion of their vote to the average of that of the two major-party nominees. In 1992, Perot spent over $60 million of his own money and thus was ineligible for federal funding. He accepted $29 million in federal funding in 1996, receiving about half as much as the major-party nominees because his 1992 vote total was roughly half that averaged by the two major-party candidates. In 2000, Perot's party, the Reform party, received more than $10 million in federal funding by virtue of Perot's 8 percent of the vote in 1996.

The Winners

The Constitution specifies only that the president must be at least thirty-five years old, a natural-born U.S. citizen, and a U.S. resident for at least fourteen years. Yet the holding of high public office is nearly a prerequisite for gaining the presidency. Except for four army generals, all presidents to date had served previously as vice presidents, members of Congress, state governors, or top federal executives.

All presidents have been white and male, but it is likely only a matter of time before the nation has its first minority-group president or its first woman president. Until the early 1950s, a majority of Americans polled said they would not vote for a woman for president. Today, fewer than 10 percent hold this view. A similar change of opinion preceded John Kennedy's election to the presidency in 1960. Kennedy was the nation's first Catholic president and only the second Catholic to have received a major party's nomination.

Graphics
www.mhhe.com/pattersontad7

STAFFING THE PRESIDENCY

When Americans go to the polls on election day, they have in mind the choice between two individuals, the Democratic and the Republican presidential nominees. In effect, however, they are choosing a lot more than a single executive

Presidents rely heavily on their top-ranking cabinet officers and personal assistants in making major policy decisions. During the Cuban missile crisis in 1962, this group of advisers to President John F. Kennedy helped him decide on a naval blockade as a means of forcing the Soviet Union to withdraw its missiles from Cuba.

leader. They are also picking a secretary of state, the director of the FBI, the chair of the Federal Reserve Board, and a host of other executives. Each of these is a presidential appointee.

Presidential Appointees

Newly elected presidents gain important advantages from their appointment powers. First, their appointees are a source of policy information. Modern policymaking requires a detailed understanding of policy issues, and this knowledge is a source of considerable power in Washington. Second, the appointees extend the president's reach into the huge federal bureaucracy by exerting influence on the day-to-day workings of the agencies they head. Not surprisingly, presidents have tended to appoint individuals who are members of their political party.

The Executive Office of the President

The key staff organization is the Executive Office of the President (EOP), created by Congress in 1939 to provide the president with the staff necessary to coordinate the activities of the executive branch.[17] The EOP has since become the command center of the presidency. Its configuration is determined by the president, and it currently consists of the Office of the Vice President and thirteen other organizations (see Figure 12-1). These include the White House Office (WHO), which consists of the president's closest personal advisers; the Office of Management and Budget (OMB), which consists of experts who formulate and then administer the federal budget; the National Security Council (NSC), which advises the president on foreign and military affairs; and the Council of Economic Advisers (CEA), which advises the president on the national economy.

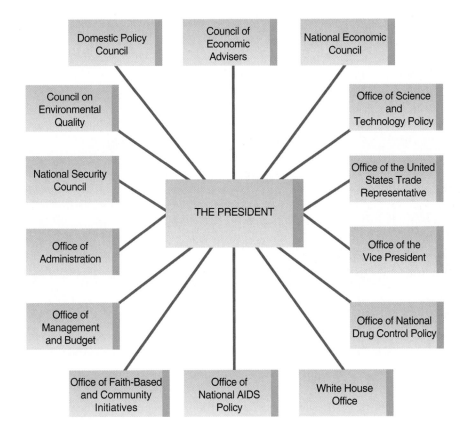

Figure 12–1

Executive Office of the President (EOP)
The EOP helps the president manage the rest of the executive branch and promotes the president's policy and political goals.
Source: White House, 2004.

The Vice President   Although the vice president works in the White House, no constitutional executive authority comes with this office. Accordingly, the president decides the role the vice president will play. Earlier presidents often refused to assign any significant duties to their vice presidents, which diminished the office's appeal. Nomination to the vice presidency was refused by many leading politicians, including Daniel Webster and Henry Clay. Said Webster, "I do not propose to be buried until I am really dead."[18] Recent presidents, however, have assigned important duties to their vice presidents. George W. Bush, for example, chose Dick Cheney as his running mate in part because of Cheney's experience as White House chief of staff and secretary of defense during previous Republican administrations. Cheney played such a large role in setting Bush administration policy that critics said he had too much power, a claim that would have astonished Daniel Webster. The vice president is supported by an administrative staff (the Office of the Vice President) of about a dozen people, including a domestic policy adviser and a national security policy adviser.

The White House Office   Of the EOP's thirteen other organizations, the White House Office serves the president most directly and personally. The units within the WHO include the Communications Office, the Office of the Press Secretary, the Office of the Counsel to the President, and the Office of

The Constitution assigns no policy authority to the vice president, whose role is determined by the president. Recent vice presidents, including Dick Cheney, pictured here with President Bush, have been assigned major policy responsibilities. Earlier vice presidents played smaller roles.

Legislative Affairs. As these names suggest, the WHO consists of the president's personal assistants, including close personal advisers, press agents, legislative and group liaison aides, and special assistants for domestic and international policy. They work in the White House, and the president can hire and fire them at will. The personal assistants do much of the legwork for the president and serve as a main source of advice. Most of them are skilled at developing political strategy, recognizing political opportunities, and communicating with the public, Congress, state and local governments, key groups, and the news media. Because of their closeness and loyalty to the president, they are among the most powerful individuals in Washington.

Policy Experts   The president is also served by the policy experts in the EOP's other organizations, who include economists, legal analysts, national security specialists, and others. The president is advised on economic issues, for example, by the National Economic Council (NEC). The NEC gathers information to develop indicators of the economy's strength and applies economic theories to various policy alternatives. Modern policymaking cannot be conducted in the absence of such expert advice and knowledge.

The President's Cabinet

cabinet A group consisting of the heads of the (cabinet) executive departments, who are appointed by the president, subject to confirmation by the Senate. The cabinet was once the main advisory body to the president but it no longer plays this role.

The heads of the fifteen executive departments, such as the Department of Defense and the Department of Agriculture, constitute the president's **cabinet.** They are appointed by the president, subject to confirmation by the Senate. Although the cabinet once served as the president's main advisory group, it has

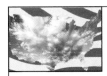

STATES IN THE NATION

Divided Power in the Executive

The president operates in a system of divided power in which joint action by Congress is often required for the president's programs to be adopted. The chief executives in the American states are the governors, nearly all of whom must contend with a further division: a separation of power within the executive itself. Maine and New Jersey are the only states in which executive power is vested solely in a governor. Five other states have separately elected and (unlike the vice president) constitutionally empowered lieutenant governors. In most of the other states, other major executive officials, such as the attorney general and the secretary of state, are also elected. Finally, there are twelve states in which even minor executive officials, such as commissioner of education, are chosen by the voters. In the case of the federal government, these other major and minor officials are appointed by the president.

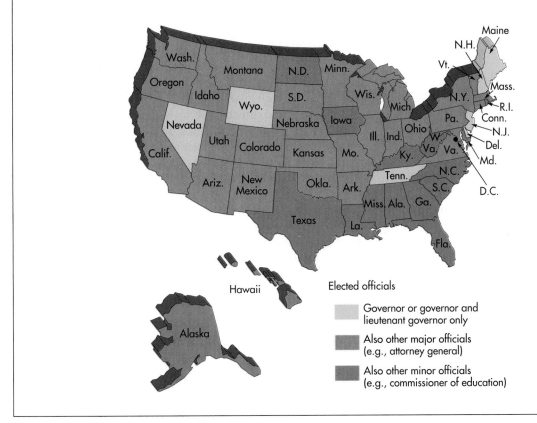

Elected officials

Governor or governor and lieutenant governor only

Also other major officials (e.g., attorney general)

Also other minor officials (e.g., commissioner of education)

not played this role since Herbert Hoover's administration. As national issues have become increasingly complex, the cabinet has become outmoded as a policymaking forum: department heads are likely to understand issues only in their respective policy areas.[19] Cabinet meetings have been largely reduced to gatherings at which only the most general matters are discussed.

Nevertheless, cabinet members, as individuals who head major departments, are important figures in any administration. The president chooses them for their prominence in politics, business, government, or the professions. Many of them bring to their office a high level of experience in public affairs.[20] The office of secretary of state is generally regarded as the most prestigious of the cabinet positions.

Other Presidential Appointees

In addition to cabinet secretaries, the president appoints the heads and top deputies of federal agencies and commissions. Altogether, the president appoints a few thousand executive officials. However, most of these appointees are selected at the agency level or are part-time workers. This still leaves nearly seven hundred full-time appointees who serve the president more or less directly, a much larger number than is appointed by the chief executive of any other democracy.[21]

The Problem of Control

Although the president's appointees are a valuable asset, they also pose a problem: because they are so numerous, the president has difficulty controlling them. President Truman had a wall chart in the Oval Office listing more than one hundred officials who reported directly to him; he often told visitors, "I cannot even see all of these men, let alone actually study what they are doing."[22] Since Truman's time, the number of bureaucratic agencies has more than doubled, compounding the problem of presidential control over subordinates.[23]

The nature of the control problem varies with the type of appointee. The advantages of having the advice of policy experts, for example, are offset somewhat by the fact that these experts often have little political experience and tend to exaggerate the importance of their particular policy interests. As a result, their proposals are sometimes impractical or politically unacceptable. On the other hand, top political appointees, while adept at politics, have a tendency to act too independently. WHO assistants, for example, tend naturally to skew information in a direction that supports the course of action they favor.[24]

The problem of presidential control is even more severe in the case of appointees who work outside the White House, in the departments and agencies. The loyalty of agency heads and cabinet secretaries often is split between a desire to promote the president's goals and an interest in boosting themselves or the agencies they lead. In late 2002, Harvey Pitt, appointed by President Bush to chair the Securities and Exchange Commission (SEC), resigned amid charges that he had not aggressively pursued corporate accounting irregularities. The Enron, WorldCom, and other corporate scandals had put regulatory action in the spotlight, and Pitt's apparent favoritism toward accounting firms, which he had represented as a lawyer before his appointment to the SEC, was an embarrassment to the Bush administration.

Lower-level appointees within the departments and agencies pose a different type of problem. The president rarely, if ever, sees them, and they are typically political novices (most have fewer than two years of government experience) and not very knowledgeable about policy. These appointees are often "captured" by the agency in which they work because they depend for

HOW THE UNITED STATES COMPARES

Systems of Executive Policy Leadership

The United States instituted a presidential system in 1789 as part of its constitutional checks and balances. This form of executive leadership was copied in Latin America but not in Europe. European democracies adopted parliamentary systems, in which executive leadership is provided by a prime minister, who is a member of the legislature. In recent years, some European prime ministers have campaigned and governed as if they were a singular authority rather than the head of a collective institution. France in the 1960s created a separate chief executive office but retained its parliamentary form of legislature.

The policy leadership of a president can differ substantially from that of a prime minister. As a singular head of an independent branch of government, a president does not have to share executive authority but nevertheless depends on the legislative branch for support. By comparison, a prime minister shares executive leadership with a cabinet, but once agreement within the cabinet is reached, he or she is almost assured of the legislative support necessary to carry out policy initiatives.

PRESIDENTIAL SYSTEM	PRESIDENTIAL/ PARLIAMENTARY SYSTEM	PARLIAMENTARY SYSTEM
Mexico	Finland	Australia
United States	France	Belgium
Venezuela		Canada
		Germany
		Great Britain
		Israel
		Italy
		Japan
		Netherlands
		Sweden

advice on the agency's career bureaucrats. (Chapter 13 examines further the relationship between presidential appointees and career bureaucrats.)

In sum, the modern presidency is a double-edged sword. Presidents today have greater responsibilities than their predecessors, and this increase in responsibilities expands their opportunities to exert power. At the same time, the range of these responsibilities is so broad that presidents must rely on staffers who may or may not act in the president's best interests. The modern president's recurring problem is to find some way of making sure that aides serve the interests of the presidency above all others. (The subject of presidential control of the executive branch is discussed further in Chapter 13.)

 ## FACTORS IN PRESIDENTIAL LEADERSHIP

The president operates within a system of separate institutions that share power (see "How the United States Compares"). Significant presidential action normally depends on the approval of Congress, the cooperation of the bureaucracy, and sometimes the acceptance of the judiciary. Because other officials have their own priorities, presidents do not always get their way. Congress in particular— more than the courts or the bureaucracy— holds the key to presidential success. Without congressional authorization and funding, most presidential proposals are nothing but ideas, empty of action.

President Lyndon Johnson addresses a joint session of Congress in 1965. Johnson had an extraordinary record of success with Congress, which adopted the great majority of his legislative proposals.

Whether a president's initiatives succeed or fail depends substantially on several factors, including the force of circumstance, the stage of the president's term, the nature of the particular issue, the president's support in Congress, and the level of public support for the president's leadership. The remainder of this chapter examines each of these factors.

The Force of Circumstance

During his first months in office and in the midst of the Great Depression, Franklin D. Roosevelt accomplished the most sweeping changes in domestic policy in the nation's history. Congress moved quickly to pass nearly every New Deal initiative he proposed. In 1964 and 1965, Lyndon Johnson pushed landmark civil rights and social welfare legislation through Congress on the strength of the civil rights movement, the legacy of the assassinated President Kennedy, and large Democratic majorities in the House and Senate. When Ronald Reagan assumed the presidency in 1981, high unemployment and inflation had greatly weakened the national economy and created a mood for significant change, enabling Reagan to persuade Congress to support some of the most notable taxing and spending changes in history.

From such presidencies has come the popular impression that presidents single-handedly decide national policy. However, each of these periods of presidential dominance was marked by a special set of circumstances: a decisive election victory that gave added force to the president's leadership, a compelling national problem that convinced Congress and the public that bold presidential action was needed, and a president who was mindful of what was expected and who vigorously advocated policies consistent with those expectations.

When conditions are favorable, the power of the presidency appears awesome. The problem for most presidents is that conditions normally are not conducive to strong leadership. Political scientist Erwin Hargrove suggests that presidential influence depends largely on circumstance.[25] Some presidents serve in periods when resources are scarce or when important problems are surfacing in American society but have not yet become critical. Such a situation, Hargrove contends, works against the president's efforts to accomplish significant policy change. In 1994, reflecting on the constraints of budget deficits and other factors beyond his control, President Clinton said he had no choice but "to play the hand that history had dealt" him.

The Stage of the President's Term

If conditions conducive to great accomplishments occur infrequently, it is nonetheless the case that nearly every president has favorable moments. Such moments often come during the first months in office. Most newly elected presidents enjoy a **honeymoon period** during which Congress, the press, and the public anticipate initiatives from the Oval Office and are more predisposed than usual to support these initiatives.

Not surprisingly, presidents have put forth more new programs in their first year in office than in any subsequent year. James Pfiffner uses the term *strategic presidency* to refer to a president's need to move quickly on priority items in order to take advantage of the policy momentum gained from the election.[26] Later in their terms, presidents tend to be less successful in presenting initiatives and getting them enacted. They may run out of good ideas, get caught up in scandal, or exhaust their political resources; the momentum of their election is gone and sources of opposition have emerged. Even highly successful presidents like Johnson and Reagan tended to have weak records in their final years. Franklin Roosevelt began his presidency with a remarkable period of achievement—the celebrated "Hundred Days"—but during his last six years in office, few of his major domestic proposals were enacted.

An irony of the presidency, then, is that presidents are usually most powerful when they are least knowledgeable—during their first months in office. These months can, as a result, be times of risk as well as times of opportunity. An example is the Bay of Pigs fiasco during the first year of John Kennedy's presidency, in which a U.S.-backed invasion force of anticommunist Cubans was easily defeated by Fidel Castro's army.

> **honeymoon period** The president's first months in office, a time when Congress, the press, and the public are more inclined than usual to support presidential initiatives.

The Nature of the Issue: Foreign or Domestic

In the 1960s, political scientist Aaron Wildavsky wrote that although the nation has only one president, it has two presidencies: one domestic and one foreign.[27] Wildavsky was referring to Congress's greater tendency to defer to presidential leadership on foreign policy issues than on domestic policy issues. He had in mind the broad leeway Congress had granted Truman, Eisenhower, Kennedy, and Johnson in their foreign policies. Wildavsky's thesis is now regarded as a somewhat time-bound conception of presidential influence. He wrote before the Vietnam War had weakened congressional support for presidential leadership in foreign affairs. Today, many of the same factors that affect a president's domestic policy success, such as the partisan composition of Congress, also affect foreign policy success.

Nevertheless, presidents are still somewhat more likely to get what they want when the issue is foreign policy, because they have more authority to act on their own and are more likely to receive support from the opposite party in Congress.[28] The clash between powerful interest groups that occurs on many domestic issues is less prevalent in the foreign policy area. Additionally, the president is recognized by other nations as America's voice in world affairs, and members of Congress sometimes will back the president in order to maintain America's credibility abroad. In some cases, Congress effectively has no choice but to accept presidential leadership. When President Bush in 2002 pursued a congressional resolution to use force against Iraq, even some members of Congress who questioned such a broad grant of war-making authority to the president supported the resolution, realizing that its defeat might lead Iraq's

America's Greatest Presidents?

Historian Arthur Schlesinger, Sr., began the game of ranking U.S. presidents when he sought the opinions of other historians in a 1948 article for *Life* magazine. Since then, a great many scholars and analysts, including historian Arthur Schlesinger, Jr., have tried their hand at it. Here is the list from a survey in 2000 of seventy-eight history, political science, and law professors that was conducted by the Federalist Society and the Wall Street Journal. Unlike most such lists, this list ranks Abraham Lincoln second rather than first.

Great

1   George Washington
2   Abraham Lincoln
3   Franklin Roosevelt

Near Great

4   Thomas Jefferson
5   Theodore Roosevelt
6   Andrew Jackson
7   Harry Truman
8   Ronald Reagan
9   Dwight Eisenhower
10   James Polk
11   Woodrow Wilson

Above Average

12   Grover Cleveland
13   John Adams
14   William McKinley
15   James Madison
16   James Monroe
17   Lyndon Johnson
18   John Kennedy

Average

19   William Taft
20   John Quincy Adams
21   George H. W. Bush
22   Rutherford Hayes
23   Martin Van Buren
24   William Clinton
25   Calvin Coolidge
26   Chester Arthur

Below Average

27   Benjamin Harrison
28   Gerald Ford
29   Herbert Hoover
30   Jimmy Carter
31   Zachary Taylor
32   Ulysses Grant
33   Richard Nixon
34   John Tyler
35   Millard Filmore

Failure

36   Andrew Johnson
37T Franklin Pierce
37T Warren Harding
39   James Buchanan

Saddam Hussein to conclude that America lacked the unity and determination to pursue the disarmament of his regime. Some members of Congress did vote against the resolution. Nevertheless, it gained the backing of 77 percent of senators and 70 percent of House members. Five months later, Bush ordered U.S. forces to attack Iraq.

Presidents also gain some leverage in foreign and defense policy because of their commanding position with respect to the defense, diplomatic, and intelligence agencies, sometimes labeled "presidential agencies." As chief executive, the president is in charge of all federal agencies, but in practice the president's influence is strongest in those agencies that connect with his constitutional authority as chief diplomat and commander in chief, such as the Departments of State and Defense and the CIA. These agencies have a tradition of deference to presidential authority not found in agencies that deal primarily with domestic policy. The Department of Agriculture, for example, responds to presidential direction but is also responsive (perhaps even more responsive) to farm-state senators and representatives.

Americans in an Interdependent World

Fast-Track Authority on Trade

The president has always been the nation's foreign policy leader. Negotiations with other countries require that the nation speak with one voice so that these countries know where the United States stands on the issue under discussion.

Nevertheless, Congress ordinarily is unwilling to grant presidents a free hand in the area of foreign policy negotiations. In particular, it is not surprising that Congress has taken a keen interest in issues of international trade, because such trade has direct implications for U.S. firms and workers. An example is congressional ambivalence to granting the president fast-track authority on global trade. With this authority, the president can negotiate a trade agreement, which Congress then must accept or reject in its entirety. In the absence of this authority, Congress retains the power to reject or accept specific provisions of an agreement.

Presidents naturally prefer fast-track authority. It allows a president to guarantee another nation that any trade agreement negotiated with the United States will, if accepted, be accepted in its entirety. Because trade negotiations involve concessions on both sides, other nations at least know that the concessions they gained in the negotiations will not be selectively deleted from the agreement.

Presidents at times have had fast-track authority. At other times, Congress has withheld it. Support in Congress for fast-track authority is strongest among advocates of unrestricted free trade. It is weakest among members who believe that, too often, labor and environmental issues are not given enough weight in trade negotiations and members who believe that important industries in their state or district are disadvantaged by global free trade.

Where do you stand on this issue? Should the president have fast-track authority, or does this grant of power unreasonably restrict Congress's ability to oversee presidential action in the area of international trade?

GLOBAL
Perspective

Relations with Congress

Although the presidency is not nearly as powerful as most Americans assume, the capacity of presidents to influence the agenda of national debate is unrivaled, reflecting presidents' unique claim to represent the whole country. Whenever the president directs attention to a particular issue or program, members of Congress take notice. But will they take action? The answer is sometimes yes and sometimes no, depending in part on whether the president takes their concerns into account.

Seeking Cooperation from Congress

As the center of national attention, presidents can easily start to believe that their ideas should prevail over those of Congress. This line of reasoning invariably gets any president into trouble. Jimmy Carter had not held national office before he was elected president in 1976 and thus had no clear understanding of how Washington operates.[29] Soon after taking office, Carter deleted from his budget nineteen public works projects that he believed were a waste of

Secretary of State Colin Powell shakes hands with Israeli Prime Minister Ariel Sharon. The secretary of state is always a prominent member of the Administration, a reflection of the president's constitutional authority in the realm of foreign affairs.

taxpayers' money, ignoring the determination of members of Congress to obtain federally funded projects for their constituents. Carter's action set the tone for a conflict-ridden relationship with Congress.

In order to get the help of members of Congress, the president must respond to their interests as they respond to those of the president. Political scientist Fred Greenstein concludes that "whatever else his qualities, the president needs to be a working politician who can work with or otherwise win over the Washington community."[30]

The use of the presidential veto illustrates the point. Presidents can sometimes force Congress to accommodate their views through the use or threatened use of the veto. When a major civil rights bill was being debated in Congress in 1991, George Bush said flatly that he would veto any bill that imposed hiring "quotas" on employers; his ultimatum forced Congress to alter provisions of the bill. Yet the veto is more effective as a presidential restraint on Congress than as a device by which Congress can be forced to take positive action on the president's proposals.

The most basic fact about presidential leadership is that it takes place in the context of a system of divided powers. Although the president gets most of the attention, Congress has most of the constitutional authority in the American system. The powers of the presidential office are by themselves insufficient to keep the president in a strong position. Even the president's most direct legislative tool, the veto, has clear limits.[31] Congress can seldom muster the two-thirds majority in each chamber required to override a presidential veto, and so the threat of a veto can make Congress bend to the president's demands. Yet, as presidential scholar Richard Neustadt argues, the veto is as much a sign of presidential weakness as it is of strength, because it comes into play when Congress refuses to go along with the president's ideas.[32]

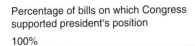

Percentage of bills on which Congress
supported president's position

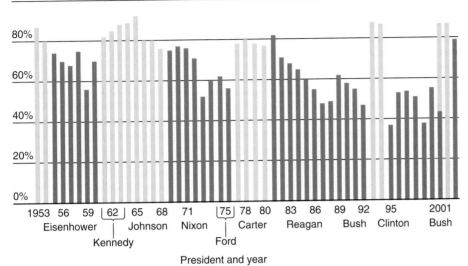

Control of Congress

President's party

Other party (one or both houses)

Figure 12–2

Percentage of Bills Passed by Congress on Which the President Announced a Position, 1953–2003
In most years, presidents have been supported by Congress on a majority of policy issues on which they have taken a stand. Presidents fare better when their party controls Congress.

Source: *Congressional Quarterly Weekly Report.* Copyright © 1999 by Congressional Quarterly Inc. Reproduced with permission of Congressional Quarterly Inc. in the format textbook via Copyright Clearance Center.

Congress is a constituency that all presidents must serve if they expect to have its support. Neustadt concludes that presidential power, at base, is "the power to persuade."[33] Like any singular notion of presidential power, Neustadt's has limitations. Presidents at times have the power to command and to threaten. They can also appeal directly to the American people as a means of pressuring Congress. But Congress can never be taken for granted. Theodore Roosevelt expressed the wish that he could "be the president and Congress, too," if only for a day, so that he would have the power to enact as well as to propose laws.

Benefiting from Partisan Support in Congress

For most presidents, the next best thing to being "Congress, too" is to have a Congress filled with members of their own party. The sources of division within Congress are many. Legislators from urban and rural areas, wealthier and poorer constituencies, and different regions of the country often have very different views of the national interest. To obtain majority support in Congress, the president must find ways to overcome these differences.

No source of unity is more important to presidential success than partisanship. Presidents are more likely to succeed when their own party controls Congress (see Figure 12-2). Between 1954 and 1992, each Republican president—Eisenhower, Nixon, Ford, Reagan, and Bush—had to contend with a Democratic majority in one or both houses of Congress. Congress passed a smaller percentage of the initiatives supported by each of these presidents than those supported by any Democratic president of the period: Kennedy, Johnson, or Carter. In his first two years in office, backed by Democratic majorities in the House and Senate, more than 85 percent of the bills Clinton supported were enacted into law. After Republicans took control of Congress in 1995, Clinton's legislative success rate sank below 40 percent, a dramatic illustration of the way presidential power is affected by whether the president's party controls Congress.

In 2001, George W. Bush had an 87 percent success rate, the highest since Lyndon Johnson's 93 percent in 1965. Bush's extraordinary success in winning congressional support was achieved in a way never before seen. When he took office, his Republican party controlled both the House and the Senate, which virtually ensured a responsive Congress. In mid-summer, however, Senator James Jeffords of Vermont bolted the GOP, leaving the Democrats in control of the Senate. This shift occurred shortly before Congress's summer recess, which meant that few bills were considered in the first weeks after Jeffords's defection. Then, shortly after Congress resumed its work, terrorist attacks on the World Trade Center and the Pentagon led congressional members of both parties to rally behind the president. After September 11, Bush's positions prevailed on eleven of twelve House votes and thirty of thirty-one Senate votes, contributing to the highest presidential success rate in more than three decades.

Colliding with Congress

On rare occasions, presidents have pursued their goals so zealously that Congress has been compelled to take steps to curb their use of power.

The ultimate sanction of Congress is its constitutional power to impeach and remove the president from office. The House of Representatives decides whether the president should be impeached (placed on trial), and the Senate conducts the trial and then votes on the president's case, with a two-thirds vote required for removal from office. In 1868, Andrew Johnson was impeached and came within one Senate vote of being removed from office for his opposition to Congress's harsh Reconstruction policies after the Civil War. In 1974, Richard Nixon's resignation halted congressional proceedings on the Watergate affair that almost certainly would have ended in his impeachment and removal from office.

The specter of impeachment arose again in 1998 when the House of Representatives by a vote of 258 to 176 authorized an investigation of President Clinton's conduct. He was accused of lying under oath about his relationship with Monica Lewinsky and of obstructing justice by trying to conceal the affair. The gravity of the allegations was leavened by the circumstances. The charges had grown out of an extramarital affair rather than a gross abuse of executive power and were tied to a controversial five-year, $40 million investigation by independent counsel Kenneth Starr. For their part, the American people were ambivalent about the whole issue. Most people approved of Clinton's handling of the presidency and did not believe his actions warranted removal from office but were also critical of his relationship with Lewinsky. Not surprisingly, congressional Republicans and Democrats differed sharply on the impeachment issue. At all formal stages of the process—the House vote to authorize an inquiry, the House vote on the articles of impeachment, and the Senate vote on whether to remove the president—the vote was divided largely along party lines. In the end, Clinton was acquitted by the Senate, but his legacy will forever be tarnished by his impeachment by the House.

Simulation
www.mhhe.com/pattersontad7

Impeaching, Convicting, and Removing the President

In October 1998, for only the third time in American history, Congress authorized an official impeachment investigation of the president of the United States. Bill Clinton joined Andrew Johnson and Richard Nixon as presidents whose legacy will be forever linked with the word *impeachment.*

Although *impeachment* technically applies only to the indictment stage of congressional action, it is commonly used to refer also to the removal stage. But these are separate stages, and the Constitution divides the responsibility for them. The House is granted under Article I, Section 2 of the Constitution the power to impeach (indict) the president. The Senate under Article I, Section 3 is given the power to remove the president.

The Constitution is not overly specific on the presidential acts that would justify removal from office. Article II, Section 4 states that impeachable acts are "Treason, Bribery, or Other High Crimes and Misdemeanors" but does not spell out what these other high crimes and misdemeanors shall include. Any such definition in the context of the presidential office would necessarily be somewhat subjective. As a result, the impeachment process is inevitably a political as well as a constitutional one. Nevertheless, it can be assumed that the contemporary use of the term *misdemeanors* includes lesser crimes (such as a speeding ticket) than the writers of the Constitution had in mind. It is also clear from the historical record that the Framers deliberately created a process that would make it difficult to remove the president from office in order to discourage Congress from seeking to get rid of a president for purely political reasons.

The steps that Congress would take in removing the president from office are the following:

1. The House of Representatives by simple majority vote would authorize an investigation of the president.

2. The House Judiciary Committee would conduct the inquiry and submit its findings to the full House.

3. The House through simple majority vote would indict the president on one or more charges (thus "impeaching" the president).

4. The Senate would hold a trial on the charges. The chief justice of the Supreme Court would preside over the trial, and the senators would be under oath to express themselves truthfully.

5. The Senate through a two-thirds majority would cause the president's removal from office. The Senate would be prohibited from imposing any additional penalty (although subsequent action against the president in a court of law would not be precluded).

The Clinton impeachment process ended with step 4; the Senate did not vote to remove. The course of Andrew Johnson's impeachment was the same, although the Senate, in his case, came within one vote of removal. Nixon resigned shortly before the House vote on impeachment (step 3).

The gravity of impeachment action makes it an unsuitable basis for curbing presidential power except in rare instances. More often, Congress has responded legislatively to executive abuses. An example is the Budget Impoundment and Control Act of 1974, which prohibits a president from indefinitely withholding funds that have been appropriated by Congress. The legislation was enacted in response to the Nixon administration's practice of withholding funds from programs it disliked.

Congress's most significant historical effort to curb presidential power is the War Powers Act. During the Vietnam War, presidents Johnson and Nixon repeatedly misled Congress, supplying it with intelligence estimates that painted a falsely optimistic picture of the military situation. This information contributed to Congress's willingness to appropriate the funds necessary for continuation of the war. However, congressional support changed abruptly in 1971

Richard M. Nixon

(1913–1994)

Richard Nixon is one of the most controversial presidents in the nation's history. His presidency saw major triumphs, including the reestablishment of relations with China and the reduction of tensions with the Soviet Union. However, his presidency also included major reversals. He was forced to resign his office because of the Watergate scandal, and his high-handed actions led Congress to enact the War Powers Act and the Budget Impoundment Act, which restricted presidential authority. Before gaining the presidency, Nixon served as a U.S. representative, U.S. senator, and vice president. He narrowly lost to John F. Kennedy in the 1960 presidential election. He gained the presidency by narrowly defeating Hubert Humphrey in 1968.

with publication in the *New York Times* of classified documents (the so-called Pentagon Papers) that revealed the Vietnam situation to be much worse than portrayed by Johnson and Nixon.

To prevent future presidential wars, Congress in 1973 passed the War Powers Act. Nixon vetoed the measure, but Congress overrode his veto. The act does not prohibit the president from sending troops into combat. However, the act requires the president to notify Congress of the reason for committing combat troops within forty-eight hours of their deployment; specifies that hostilities must end within sixty days unless Congress extends the period; gives the president an additional thirty days to withdraw the troops from hostile territory, although Congress can shorten this period; and requires the president to consult with Congress whenever feasible before dispatching troops into a hostile situation.

Every president since Nixon has claimed that the act infringes on his constitutional power as commander in chief, and each has refused to accept it fully. Nevertheless, the War Powers Act is a potentially significant constraint on the president's war-making powers.

Thus, the effect of executive efforts to circumvent congressional authority is heightened congressional opposition. Even if presidents gain in the short run by acting on their own, they undermine their capacity to lead in the long run if they fail to keep in mind that Congress is a coequal branch of the American governing system.

Public Support

Public support affects a president's ability to achieve policy goals.[34] Presidential power rests in part on a claim to national leadership, and the legitimacy of that claim is roughly proportional to the president's public support. With public backing, the president's leadership cannot easily be dismissed by other Washington officials. If the president's public support sinks, officials are less inclined to accept presidential leadership.[35]

Every recent president has had the public's confidence at the very start of his term of office. When asked in polls whether they "approve or disapprove of how the president is doing his job," a majority of Americans have expressed approval during the first months of the president's term. Sooner or later, however, all **presidential approval ratings** have slipped below this high point, and several recent presidents have left office with a rating below 50 percent (see Table 12–3).

presidential approval ratings
A measure of the degree to which the public approves or disapproves of the president's performance in office.

Events and Issues

The public's support for the president is affected by national and international conditions. Threats from abroad tend to produce a patriotic "rally 'round the flag" reaction that initially creates widespread support for the president. Every

TABLE 12-3	Percentage of Public Expressing Approval of President's Performance			
	Presidential approval ratings generally are higher at the beginning of the term than at the end.			
PRESIDENT	YEAR IN OFFICE	AVERAGE DURING PRESIDENCY	FIRST-YEAR AVERAGE	FINAL-YEAR AVERAGE
Harry Truman	1945–1952	41%	63%	35%
Dwight Eisenhower	1953–1960	64	74	62
John Kennedy	1961–1963	70	76	62
Lyndon Johnson	1963–1968	55	78	40
Richard Nixon	1969–1974	49	63	24
Gerald Ford	1974–1976	46	75	48
Jimmy Carter	1977–1980	47	68	46
Ronald Reagan	1981–1989	53	58	57
George Bush	1989–1992	61	65	40
Bill Clinton	1993–2000	57	50	60
George W. Bush	2001–	—	68	—

Source: Averages compiled from Gallup polls.

foreign policy crisis in the past four decades has followed this pattern. Americans were deeply divided in 2003 over the wisdom of war with Iraq, but, when the fighting began, President Bush's approval rating immediately increased.

Ongoing crises, however, can eventually erode a president's support if they are not resolved or pursued successfully. George W. Bush's approval rating rose above 70 percent with the attack on Iraq but then fell steadily as months passed and U.S. casualties mounted.

Economic downswings also tend to reduce the public's confidence in the president.[36] Ford, Carter, and the first President Bush lost their reelection bids when their popularity plummeted after the economy swooned. In contrast, Clinton's popularity rose in 1995 and 1996 as the economy strengthened, contributing to his reelection in 1996. In 2004, an improving economy contributed to George W. Bush's reelection. Of course, the irony is that presidents do not actually have that much control over the economy. If they did, it would always be strong.

The Televised Presidency

A major advantage that presidents enjoy in their efforts to nurture public support is their access to the media, particularly television.[37] Only the president can expect the television networks to provide free air time on occasion, and in terms of the amount of news coverage, the president and top presidential advisors receive half again as much coverage as all members of Congress combined.

Political scientist Samuel Kernell calls it "going public" when the president bypasses inside bargaining with Congress and promotes "himself and his policies by appealing to the American public for support."[38] Such appeals are at least as old as Theodore Roosevelt's use of the presidency as a "bully pulpit," but they have increased substantially in recent years.[39] As the president's role

Bush press secretary Ari Fleischer briefs reporters in the cramped space of the White House briefing room. Effective communication is an essential part of the modern presidency.

has moved from administrative leader to policy advocate and agenda setter, public support has become increasingly important to presidential success. Television has made it easier for presidents to go public with their programs. Ronald Reagan was called "the Great Communicator" in part because of his ability to use television to generate public support for his initiatives.

On the other hand, the press is adept at putting its own spin on events and tends to play up adverse developments. For example, although presidents get some credit in the press when the economy is doing well, they get mounds of negative coverage when the economy is doing poorly. Scandal is the biggest threat to a president's ability to influence news coverage. When the whiff of a possible scandal is detected, a media "feeding frenzy" ensues, and power shifts from the White House to the press and the president's political opponents. In 2004, for example, informed sources claimed that the Bush administration had targeted Iraq long before it ordered an invasion of that country. Secretary of Defense Donald Rumsfeld reportedly wanted to bomb Iraq immediately after the terrorist attacks of September 11, 2001, even though there was no evidence linking Iraq to the attacks. Rumsfeld was quoted by a White House insider as saying "There aren't any good targets in Afghanistan and there are lots of good targets in Iraq." The allegations were front-page news for days on end and placed the Bush administration on the defensive.

The Illusion of Presidential Government

Presidents have no choice but to try to counter this type of press coverage with their own version of their accomplishments. President George W. Bush did exactly that by scheduling blocks of interviews with journalists from local and regional news outlets to say that the real story of the Iraq effort—the success story of reopened schools, restored oil production, and renewed hope for the Iraqi people—was not being told by the Washington press corps. Such efforts can carry a president only so far, however. No president can fully control his communicated image, and national conditions ultimately have the largest impact on a president's public support. No amount of public relations can disguise adverse developments at home or abroad. Indeed, presidents run a risk by building up their images through public relations. If they are as powerful as they project themselves to be, they will be held responsible for policy failures as well as policy successes. By thrusting themselves into the limelight, presidents contribute to the public's belief that the president is in charge of the national government, a perception that political scientist Hugh Heclo calls "the illusion of presidential government."[40]

Because the public expects so much from its presidents, they get too much credit when things go well and too much blame when things go badly. Therein lies an irony of the presidential office. More than from any constitutional grant, more than from any statute, and more than from any crisis, presidential power derives from the president's position as the sole official who can claim to represent the entire American public. Yet because presidential power rests on a popular base, it erodes when public support declines. The irony is that the presidential office typically grows weaker as problems mount. Just when the country could most use effective leadership, strong leadership often is hardest to achieve.[41]

Self-Test
www.mhhe.com/pattersontad7

Summary

The presidency has become a much stronger office than the Framers envisioned. The Constitution grants the president substantial military, diplomatic, legislative, and executive powers, and in each case the president's authority has increased measurably over the nation's history. Underlying this change is the president's position as the one leader chosen by the whole nation and as the sole head of the executive branch. These features of the office have enabled presidents to claim broad authority in response to the increased demands placed on the federal government by changing world and national conditions.

During the course of American history, the presidential selection process has been altered in ways intended to make it more responsive to the preferences of ordinary people. Today, the electorate has a vote not only in the general election, but also in the selection of party nominees. To gain nomination, a presidential hopeful must gain the support of the electorate in state primaries and open caucuses. Once nominated, the candidates receive federal funds for their general election campaigns, which today are based on televised appeals.

Although the campaign tends to personalize the presidency, the responsibilities of the modern presidency far exceed any president's personal capacities. To meet their obligations, presidents have surrounded themselves with large staffs of advisers, policy experts, and managers. These staff members enable the president to extend control over the executive branch while at the same time providing the information necessary for policymaking. All recent presidents have discovered, however, that their control of staff resources is incomplete and that some things that others do on their behalf can work against what they are trying to accomplish.

As sole chief executive and the nation's top elected leader, presidents can always expect that their policy and leadership efforts will receive attention. However, other institutions, particularly Congress, have the authority to make presidential leadership effective. No president has come close to winning approval of all the programs he has placed before Congress, and the presidents' records of success have varied considerably. The factors in a president's success include whether national conditions that require strong leadership from the White House are present and whether the president's party has a majority in Congress.

To hold onto an effective leadership position, the president depends on the backing of the American people. Recent presidents have made extensive use of the media to build support for their programs; yet they have had difficulty maintaining that support throughout their terms of office. A major reason is that the public expects far more from its presidents than they can deliver.

STUDY CORNER

Key Terms

cabinet *(p. 394)*

honeymoon period *(p. 399)*

legitimacy (of election) *(p. 381)*

momentum *(p. 385)*

open party caucuses *(p. 384)*

presidential approval ratings *(p. 406)*

stewardship theory *(p. 377)*

unit rule *(p. 388)*

Whig theory *(p. 377)*

Self-Test

1. Which two features of the presidency have enabled it to become more powerful than the Framers envisioned?

   a. power to disregard Supreme Court and also Congress during national emergencies

   b. power to use presidential resources to defeat members of Congress and power to veto acts of Congress

   c. election by national vote and president's position as sole chief executive

   d. power to appoint federal judges and to appoint high-ranking executives

2. Key presidential appointees who are responsible for coordinating the activities of the executive branch are located in the:

   a. Office of the General Counsel.

   b. Attorney General's Office.

   c. General Accounting Office.

   d. Executive Office of the President.

3. A president is most successful passing legislative initiatives when Congress is:

   a. in recess.

   b. acting in an election year as opposed to a year when no federal election is scheduled to be held.

   c. controlled by the president's own party.

   d. concentrating on domestic policy issues as opposed to foreign policy issues.

4. Which of the following is **not** an important factor in the success that presidents have had in getting their policy proposals enacted into law?

   a. a force of circumstance, such as war or economic stability

   b. stage of the president's term

   c. level of public support for the president's leadership

   d. ability to raise campaign funds

5. Systems that have been used in the United States for presidential selection include all **except** which one of the following?

   a. congressional caucus

   b. national party convention

   c. direct election by popular vote

   d. combination of national convention and primary elections

   e. party primary and open party caucus

6. Advantages that newly elected presidents gain from their appointment powers include all **except** which one of the following?

   a. gain a source of information for policymaking

   b. can force Congress to confirm the appointment even of nominees Congress judges as unfit to hold executive office

   c. can extend the president's authority into the federal bureaucracy

   d. can make sure that some people in key positions share the president's political and policy goals

7. A candidate running for president has to accept federal campaign funding. (T/F)

8. Under the War Powers Act, the president must have the formal consent of Congress to send U.S. troops into combat. (T/F)

9. National conditions, such as the state of the economy, rarely affect the level of public confidence in the president. (T/F)

10. Big government after the Roosevelt era has favored the growth of legislative authority at the expense of executive authority. (T/F)

Critical Thinking

Why is presidential power "conditional"—that is, why is it affected so substantially by circumstance, the makeup of Congress, and popular support? (The separation of powers should be part of your answer.)

Suggested Readings

Cohen, Jeffrey E. *Presidential Responsiveness and Public Policymaking: The Publics and the Policies That Presidents Choose.* Ann Arbor: University of Michigan Press, 1997. An accounting of presidential responsiveness and public policymaking.

Eisinger, Robert M. *The Evolution of Presidential Polling.* New York: Cambridge University Press, 2003. A close look at the use of opinion polls by the White House and how their use has changed since Franklin Roosevelt.

Entman, Robert M. *Projections of Power: Framing News, Public Opinion, and U.S. Foreign Policy.* Chicago: University of Chicago Press, 2003. An assessment of the president's power to set the news agenda.

Jackson, John S., and William J. Crotty. *The Politics of Presidential Selection.* New York: Longman, 2001. A careful look at the presidential election process by two of its best analysts.

Milkis, Sidney, and Michael Nelson. *The American Presidency: Origins and Development, 1776–2002,* 4th ed. Washington, D.C.: Congressional Quarterly Press, 2003. A thoughtful assessment of the factors and conditions that have molded the presidential office.

Neustadt, Richard E. *Presidential Power and the Modern Presidents: The Politics of Leadership from Roosevelt to Reagan.* New York: Free Press, 1990. The classic analysis of the limitations on presidential power.

Pika, Joseph A., and John Anthony Maltese. *The Politics of the Presidency,* 6th ed. Washington, D.C.: Congressional Quarterly Press, 2004. An insightful look at the leadership skills demanded of presidents.

Walcott, Charles E., and Karen M. Hult. *Governing the White House: From Hoover through LBJ.* Lawrence: University Press of Kansas, 1995. An innovative study of how the organization of the White House affects presidential performance.

List of Websites

http://sunsite.unc.edu:80/lia/president
A site with general information on specific presidents and links to the presidential libraries.

http://www.ipl.org/ref/POTUS
Profiles of the nation's presidents, their cabinet officers, and key events during their time in office.

http://www.vote-smart.org/executive
Information on the presidency and the Executive Office of the President as well as links to key executive agencies and organizations.

http://www.whitehouse.gov/
The White House's home page; it has an e-mail guest book and includes information on the president, the vice president, and current White House activities.

Participate!

Consider writing a letter or sending an e-mail to the president or a top presidential appointee that expresses your opinion on an issue that is currently the object of executive action. You can inform yourself about the administration's policy or stance on the issue through the website of the White House (www.whitehouse.gov) or of the agency in question (for example, the State Department's site is www.state.gov).

Extra Credit

For up-to-the-minute *New York Times* articles, interactive simulations, graphics, study tools, and more links and quizzes, visit the text's Online Learning Center at www.mhhe.com/pattersontad7.

(Self-Test Answers: 1. c   2. d   3. c   4. d   5. c   6 b.   7. F   8. F   9. F   10. F)

13

The Federal Bureaucracy:
Administering the Government

[No] industrial society could manage the daily operations of its public affairs
without bureaucratic organizations in which officials play a major
policymaking role.

—*Norman Thomas*[1]

Early on the morning of September 7, 1993, a truck pulled up to the south lawn of the White House and unloaded pallets stacked with federal rules and regulations. The display was the backdrop for a presidential speech announcing the completion of the National Performance Review or, as it is commonly called, NPR. The federal regulations piled atop the pallets symbolized bureaucratic red tape, and NPR was a statement of the Clinton administration's effort to make government more responsive.

The origins of the National Performance Review were plain enough. For years, the federal bureaucracy had been derided as being too big, too expensive, and too intrusive. These charges gained weight as federal budget deficits increased and the public became increasingly dissatisfied with the performance of the government in Washington. Reform attempts in the 1970s and 1980s had had some success but had not stemmed the tide of federal deficits or markedly improved the bureaucracy's performance. Clinton campaigned on the issue of "reinventing government" and acted swiftly on the promise. During the transition phase, Vice President–elect Al Gore was placed in charge of the National Performance Review. Once in office, Gore assembled more than two hundred career bureaucrats, who knew firsthand how the bureaucracy operated, and organized them into "reinventing teams" that would recommend ways of improving government administration. NPR's report included 384 specific recommendations grouped into four broad imperatives: reducing red tape, putting customers first, empowering administrators, and cutting government back to basic services.[2]

NPR was the last in a lengthy list of major twentieth-century efforts to remake the federal bureaucracy. NPR was different in its particulars, but its claim to improve administration while saving money was consistent with the claims of earlier reform panels, including the Brownlow, Hoover, and Volcker commissions.[3] Like those efforts, NPR addressed an enduring issue of American politics: the bureaucracy's efficiency, responsiveness, and accountability.

Modern government would be impossible without a large bureaucracy. It is the government's enormous administrative capacity that makes it possible for the United States to have such ambitious programs as space exploration, social security, environmental protection, interstate highways, and universal postal service. Yet the bureaucracy also poses special problems and challenges. Even those who work in federal agencies agree that the bureaucracy does not always function well. It can be unresponsive, wasteful, and self-serving.

PART THREE · Governing Institutions

As one of thousands of services provided by the federal bureaucracy, the National Hurricane Service monitors hurricane activity and provides early warning to affected coastal areas.

This chapter examines both the need for bureaucracy and the problems associated with it. The chapter will describe the bureaucracy's responsibilities, organizational structure, and management practices and will explain the "politics" of the bureaucracy. The three constitutional branches of government impose a degree of accountability on the bureaucracy, but its sheer size and fragmented nature confound efforts to control it completely. The main points discussed in this chapter are the following:

- *Bureaucracy is an inevitable consequence of complexity and scale.* Modern government could not function without a large bureaucracy. Through authority, specialization, and rules, bureaucracy provides a means of managing thousands of tasks and employees.

- *The bureaucracy is expected simultaneously to respond to the direction of partisan officials and to administer programs fairly and competently.* These conflicting demands are addressed through a combination of personnel management systems—the patronage, merit, and executive leadership systems.

- *Bureaucrats naturally take an "agency point of view." They seek to promote and preserve their agency's programs and power.* They do this through their expert knowledge, support from clientele groups, and backing by Congress or the president.

- *Although agencies are subject to scrutiny by the president, Congress, and the judiciary, bureaucrats are able to achieve power in their own right.* The issue of bureaucratic power and responsiveness is a basis of efforts at "reinventing" government.

FEDERAL ADMINISTRATION: FORM, PERSONNEL, AND ACTIVITIES

For many Americans, the word *bureaucracy* brings to mind waste, mindless rules, and rigidity. This image is not unfounded, but it is one-sided. Bureaucracy is also an efficient and effective method of organization. Although

Americans tend to equate bureaucracy with the federal government, bureaucracy is found wherever there is a need to manage large numbers of people and tasks. All large-scale, task-oriented organizations—public and private—are bureaucratic in form.[4] General Motors is a bureaucracy, as is every university. The state governments are also every bit as "bureaucratic" as the federal government (see "States in the Nation").

In formal terms, **bureaucracy** is a system of organization and control that is based on three principles: hierarchical authority, job specialization, and formalized rules. **Hierarchical authority** refers to a chain of command whereby the officials and units at the top of a bureaucracy have authority over those in the middle, who in turn control those at the bottom. In a system of **job specialization,** the responsibilities of each job position are explicitly defined, and there is a precise division of labor within the organization. **Formalized rules** are the standardized procedures and established regulations by which a bureaucracy conducts its operations.

These features are the reason why bureaucracy, as a form of organization, is the most efficient means of getting people to work together on tasks of great magnitude and complexity. Hierarchy speeds action by reducing conflict over the power to make decisions: the higher an individual's position in the organization, the more decision-making power he or she has. Specialization yields efficiency because each individual is required to concentrate on a particular job: workers acquire specialized skills and knowledge. Formalized rules enable workers to make quick and consistent judgments because decisions are made on the basis of preestablished guidelines rather than by deliberation or personal inclination.

These organizational characteristics are also the cause of bureaucracy's pathologies. Administrators perform not as whole persons but as parts of an organizational entity. Their behavior is governed by position, specialty, and rule. At its worst, bureaucracy grinds on, heedless of the feelings and needs of its members or their clients. Fixed procedures become an end unto themselves, as anyone who has applied for a driver's license or a student loan knows all too well.

If bureaucracy is an indispensable condition of large-scale organization, gross bureaucratic inefficiency and unresponsiveness are not. At least that is the assumption underlying efforts to reform the administration of government, a topic examined later in this chapter.

bureaucracy A system of organization and control based on the principles of hierarchical authority, job specialization, and formalized rules.

hierarchical authority A basic principle of bureaucracy that refers to the chain of command within an organization whereby officials and units have control over those below them.

job specialization A basic principle of bureaucracy that holds that the responsibilities of each job position should be explicitly defined and that a precise division of labor within the organization should be maintained.

formalized rules A basic principle of bureaucracy that refers to the standardized procedures and established regulations by which a bureaucracy conducts its operations.

The Federal Bureaucracy in Americans' Daily Lives

The U.S. federal bureaucracy has roughly 2.5 million employees, who have the responsibility for administering thousands of programs. The president and Congress may get far more attention in the news, but it is the bureaucracy that has the more immediate impact on the daily lives of Americans. The federal bureaucracy performs a wide range of functions; for example, it delivers the daily mail, maintains the national forests and parks, administers social security, builds dams and generates hydroelectric power, enforces environmental protection laws, develops the country's defense systems, provides foodstuffs for school lunch programs, and regulates the stock markets.

STATES IN THE NATION

The Size of State Bureaucracies

Although the federal bureaucracy is often criticized as being "too big," it is actually smaller on a per capita basis than even the smallest state bureaucracy. There is 0.91 federal employee for every 100 Americans. Illinois, with 1.04 state employees for every 100 residents, has the smallest state bureaucracy on a per capita basis. Hawaii has the largest—4.48 state employees per 100 residents.

Q. What do the states with larger per capita bureaucracies have in common?

A. In general, the least populous states, especially those that are larger geographically, have larger bureaucracies on a per capita basis. This pattern reflects the fact that a state, whatever its population, has basic functions (such as highway maintenance and policing) that it must perform.

Number of state employees (full-time equivalents)

1.60 or fewer employees/100 residents

1.61–1.90 employees/100 residents

1.91 or more employees/100 residents

Source: U.S. Bureau of the Census, 2004.

Types of Administrative Organizations

The U.S. federal bureaucracy is organized along policy lines. One agency handles veterans' affairs, another specializes in education, a third is responsible for agriculture, and so on. No two units are exactly alike. Nevertheless, most of them take one of five general forms: cabinet department, independent agency, regulatory agency, government corporation, or presidential commission.

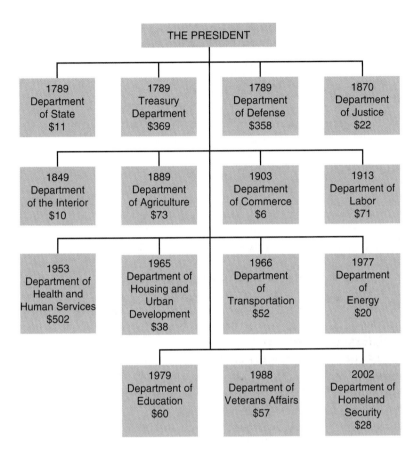

THE PRESIDENT

| 1789 Department of State $11 | 1789 Treasury Department $369 | 1789 Department of Defense $358 | 1870 Department of Justice $22 |

| 1849 Department of the Interior $10 | 1889 Department of Agriculture $73 | 1903 Department of Commerce $6 | 1913 Department of Labor $71 |

| 1953 Department of Health and Human Services $502 | 1965 Department of Housing and Urban Development $38 | 1966 Department of Transportation $52 | 1977 Department of Energy $20 |

| 1979 Department of Education $60 | 1988 Department of Veterans Affairs $57 | 2002 Department of Homeland Security $28 |

Figure 13–1

Cabinet (Executive) Departments

Each executive department is responsible for a general policy area and is headed by a secretary or, in the case of Justice, the attorney general, who serves as a member of the president's cabinet. Shown are each department's year of origin (above the title) and annual budget in billions of dollars (below the title). (The Attorney General's office was created in 1789 and became the Justice Department in 1870.)

Source: White House Office of Management and Budget, FY2004.

Cabinet Departments

The major administrative units are the fifteen **cabinet** (or **executive**) **departments** (see Figure 13–1). Except for the Department of Justice, which is led by the attorney general, the head of each department is its secretary (for example, the secretary of defense), who serves as a member of the president's cabinet.

Cabinet departments vary greatly in their visibility, size, and importance. The Department of State, one of the oldest and most prestigious departments, is also one of the smallest, with approximately twenty-five thousand employees. The Department of Defense has the largest work force, with more than six hundred thousand civilian employees (apart from the more than 1.4 million uniformed active service members). The Department of Health and Human Services has the largest budget; its activities account for more than a fourth of all federal spending, much of it in the form of social security benefits. The Department of Homeland Security is the newest department, dating from 2002.

Each cabinet department has responsibility for a general policy area. But executive departments are not monoliths: each department has a number of semiautonomous operating units that typically carry the label of "bureau," "agency," "division," or "service." The Department of Justice, for example, has thirteen such operating units, including the Federal Bureau of Investigation

cabinet (executive) departments The major administrative organizations within the federal executive bureaucracy, each of which is headed by a secretary or, in the case of Justice, the attorney general. Each department has responsibility for a major function of the federal government, such as defense, agriculture, or justice.

Graphic
www.mhhe.com/pattersontad7

(FBI), the Civil Rights Division, the Tax Division, and the Drug Enforcement Administration (DEA). In short, the Department of Justice is itself a large bureaucracy.

Independent Agencies

Independent agencies resemble the cabinet departments, but most of them have a narrower area of responsibility. They include organizations such as the Central Intelligence Agency (CIA) and the National Aeronautics and Space Administration (NASA). The heads of these agencies are appointed by and report to the president but are not members of the cabinet. Like the executive departments, each of the independent agencies is divided into smaller operating units. In general, the independent agencies exist apart from cabinet departments because their placement within a department would pose symbolic or practical policy problems. NASA, for example, could conceivably be located in the Department of Defense, but such positioning would suggest that the space program is intended solely for military purposes and not also for civilian purposes such as space exploration and satellite communication.

Regulatory Agencies

Regulatory agencies are created when Congress recognizes the importance of close and continuous regulation of an economic activity. Because such regulation requires more time and expertise than Congress can provide, the responsibility is delegated to a regulatory agency. The Securities and Exchange Commission (SEC), which oversees the stock and bond markets, is a regulatory agency. So is the Environmental Protection Agency (EPA), which monitors and prevents industrial pollution. Table 13–1 lists some of the regulatory agencies and other noncabinet units of the federal bureaucracy.

Beyond their executive functions, regulatory agencies have legislative and judicial functions. They issue regulations and judge whether individuals or organizations have complied with them. The SEC, for example, can impose fines and other penalties on business firms that violate regulations pertaining to the trading of stocks and bonds.

Some regulatory agencies, particularly the older ones (such as the SEC), are "independent" by virtue of their relative freedom from ongoing political control. They are headed by a commission of several members who are appointed by the president and confirmed by Congress but who are not subject to removal by the president. Commissioners serve for a fixed number of years, a legal stipulation intended to free them and thereby their agencies from political interference. The newer regulatory agencies (such as the EPA) lack such autonomy. They are headed by a presidential appointee who can be removed at the president's discretion.

Government Corporations

Government corporations are similar to private corporations in that they charge clients for their services and are governed by a board of directors. However, government corporations receive federal funding to help defray

TABLE 13–1	Selected U.S. Regulatory Agencies, Independent Agencies, Government Corporations, and Presidential Commissions

Central Intelligence Agency	National Labor Relations Board
Commission on Civil Rights	National Railroad Passenger Corporation (Amtrak)
Consumer Product Safety Commission	National Science Foundation
Environmental Protection Agency	National Transportation Safety Board
Equal Employment Opportunity Commission	Nuclear Regulatory Commission
Export-Import Bank of the United States	Occupational Safety and Health Review Commission
Farm Credit Administration	Office of Personnel Management
Federal Communications Commission	Peace Corps
Federal Deposit Insurance Corporation	Securities and Exchange Commission
Federal Election Commission	Selective Service System
Federal Emergency Management Agency	Small Business Administration
Federal Maritime Commission	U.S. Arms Control and Disarmament Agency
Federal Reserve System, Board of Governors	U.S. Information Agency
Federal Trade Commission	U.S. International Development Cooperation Agency
General Services Administration	U.S. International Trade Commission
National Aeronautics and Space Administration	U.S. Postal Service
National Archives and Records Administration	
National Foundation on the Arts and the Humanities	

Source: *The U.S. Government Manual.*

operating expenses, and their directors are appointed by the president with Senate approval. The largest government corporation is the U.S. Postal Service, with roughly seven hundred thousand employees. Other government corporations include the Federal Deposit Insurance Corporation (FDIC), which insures savings accounts against bank failures, and the National Railroad Passenger Corporation (Amtrak), which provides passenger rail service.

Presidential Commissions

Some **presidential commissions** are permanent bodies that provide ongoing recommendations to the president in particular areas of responsibility. Two such commissions are the Commission on Civil Rights and the Commission on Fine Arts. Other presidential commissions are temporary and disband after making recommendations on specific issues. An example is the President's Commission to Strengthen Social Security, which was established by President Bush in 2001 to study ways of reforming social security.

presidential commissions
Organizations within the bureaucracy that are headed by commissioners appointed by the president. An example of such a commission is the Commission on Civil Rights.

Federal Employment

The roughly 2.5 million civilian employees of the federal government include professionals who bring their expertise to the problems involved in governing a large and complex society, service workers who perform such tasks as the typing of correspondence and the delivery of mail, and middle and top managers who supervise the work of the various federal agencies.

More than 90 percent of federal employees are hired by merit criteria, which include educational attainment (in the case, for example, of lawyers and engineers), employment experience, and performance on competitive tests (such as the civil service and foreign service examinations). The merit system is intended to protect the public from the inept or discriminatory administrative practices that can result if partisanship is the employment criterion.

Federal employees are underpaid in comparison with their counterparts in the private sector. The large majority of federal employees have a GS (Graded Service) job ranking. The rankings range from GS-1 (the lowest rank) to GS-18 (the highest). College graduates who enter the federal service usually start at the GS-5 level, which provides a salary of about $22,000 for a beginning employee. With a master's degree, employees begin at level GS-9 with a salary of $33,000. Federal employees' salaries increase with rank and length of service. Public employees receive substantial fringe benefits, including full health insurance, secure retirement plans, and generous vacation time and sick leave.

Public service has its drawbacks. Federal employees can form labor unions, but their unions by law have limited authority: the government maintains full control of job assignments, compensation, and promotion. Moreover, the Taft-Hartley Act of 1947 prohibits strikes by federal employees and permits the firing of workers who do go on strike. When federal air traffic controllers went on strike anyway in 1981, they were fired by President Reagan. There are also some limits on the partisan activities of civil servants. The Hatch Act of 1939 prohibited them from holding key positions in election campaigns. In 1993, Congress relaxed this prohibition but retained it for certain high-ranking career bureaucrats.

The Federal Bureaucracy's Policy Responsibilities

policy implementation The primary function of the bureaucracy; it refers to the process of carrying out the authoritative decisions of Congress, the president, and the courts.

The Constitution mentions executive departments but does not grant them any powers. Their authority derives from grants of power to the three constitutional branches: Congress, the president, and the courts. Nevertheless, the bureaucracy is far more than an administrative extension of the three branches. It never merely follows orders. The primary function of administrative agencies is **policy implementation,** that is, carrying out decisions made by Congress, the president, and the courts.

Although implementation is sometimes described as "mere administration," it is a highly significant and creative function. In the course of their work, administrators come up with policy ideas that are then brought to the attention of the president or members of Congress. Administrative agencies also develop public policy in the process of implementing it. Most legislative acts identify general goals, which bureaucrats translate into specific programs. The Telecommunications Act of 1996, for example, had as its stated goal "to promote competition and reduce regulation in order to secure lower prices and higher quality services for American telecommunication consumers and encourage the rapid deployment of new telecommunications technologies." Although the act included specific provisions, its implementation was left in large part for the Federal Communications Commission (FCC) to decide. The FCC decided, for example, that regional telephone companies (the Bell companies) had to open their networks to AT&T and other competitors at wholesale rates far below what they were charging their retail customers. The purpose was to enable AT&T and other carriers to compete with the Bell companies for local phone customers; in other words, the FCC was responding to its legislative mandate "to promote competition." But it was the FCC, not Congress, that determined the wholesale rates and many of the interconnection rules. This development of policy—through *rulemaking* that determines how laws will work in practice—is perhaps the chief way that administrative agencies exercise real power.[5]

Agencies are also charged with the delivery of services—carrying the mail, processing welfare applications, approving government loans, and the like. Such activities are governed by rules, and in most instances the rules determine what gets done. But some services allow agency employees enough discretion that laws end up being applied arbitrarily, a situation that Michael Lipsky describes as "street-level bureaucracy."[6] For example, FBI agents are more diligent in their pursuit of organized crime than of white-collar crime, even though the laws do not say that white-collar crime should somehow be pursued less aggressively.

In sum, administrators necessarily exercise discretion in carrying out their policy responsibilities. They initiate policy, develop it, evaluate it, apply it, and determine whether others are complying with it. The bureaucracy does not simply administer policy, it also *makes policy.*

The U.S. Postal Service is one of the most efficient in the world, delivering hundreds of millions of pieces of mail each day, inexpensively and without undue delay. Yet, like many other government agencies, it is often criticized for its inefficiency and ineptness.

 ## DEVELOPMENT OF THE FEDERAL BUREAUCRACY: POLITICS AND ADMINISTRATION

Agencies are responsible for carrying out programs that serve society, yet each agency was created and is maintained in response to partisan interests. Each agency thus confronts two simultaneous but incompatible demands: that it administer programs fairly and competently and that it respond to partisan claims.

Historically, this conflict has worked itself out in ways that have made the organization of the modern bureaucracy a blend of the political and the

The Central Intelligence Agency (CIA) is located in Langley, Virginia, which is roughly ten miles from the nation's capital. The CIA is an independent federal agency that gathers intelligence used in deciding national security policy. The internal workings of the normally secretive agency came into public view in 2004 as a result of its faulty assessments of Iraqi weapon systems.

administrative. This dual line of development is reflected clearly in the mix of management systems that characterizes the bureaucracy today—the *patronage, merit,* and *executive leadership* systems.

Small Government and the Patronage System

The federal bureaucracy originally was small (three thousand employees in 1800, for instance). The federal government's role was confined mainly to defense and foreign affairs, currency and interstate commerce, and the delivery of the mail. The nation's first six presidents, from George Washington through John Quincy Adams, believed that only distinguished men should be entrusted with the management of the national government. Nearly all top presidential appointees were men of education and political experience, and many of them were members of socially prominent families. They often remained in their jobs year after year.

The nation's seventh president, Andrew Jackson, did not share his predecessors' admiration for the social elite. In Jackson's view, government would be more responsive to the public if it were administered by common people of good sense.[7] Jackson also believed that top administrators should remain in office for only short periods to ensure a steady influx of fresh ideas.

Jackson's version of the **patronage system** was popular with the public, but critics labeled it a **spoils system**—a device for placing political cronies in government office as a reward for partisan service. Although Jackson was motivated as much by a concern for responsive government as by his desire to reward partisan supporters, later presidents were often more interested in distributing the spoils of victory. Jackson's successors extended patronage to all levels of administration.

patronage system An approach to managing the bureaucracy whereby people are appointed to important government positions as a reward for political services they have rendered and because of their partisan loyalty.

spoils system The practice of granting public office to individuals in return for political favors they have rendered.

Growth in Government and the Merit System

Because the government of the early nineteenth century was relatively small and limited in scope, it could be managed by employees who had little or no administrative training or experience. As the century advanced, however, the nature of the country changed rapidly, and the bureaucracy changed along with it. The Industrial Revolution brought with it massive economic shifts, which prompted groups to look to government for assistance. Farmers were among these groups, and in 1889 Congress created the Department of Agriculture. Business and labor interests also pressed their claims, and in 1903 Congress established the Department of Commerce and Labor to "promote the mutual

Historical Background

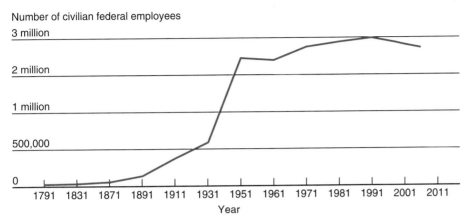

Number of civilian federal employees

Figure 13–2

Number of Persons Employed by the Federal Government
The federal bureaucracy grew slowly until the 1930s, when an explosive growth began in the number of programs that required ongoing administration by the federal government.

Source: Historical Statistics of the United States and Statistical Abstract of the United States, 1986, 322; recent figures from U.S. Office of Personnel Management.

interest" of the nation's firms and workers. (The separate interests of business and labor proved stronger than their shared concerns, and thus in 1913 Labor became a separate department.)

By 1930, federal employment had reached six hundred thousand, a sixfold increase over the level of the 1880s (see Figure 13–2). During the 1930s, as a result of President Franklin Roosevelt's New Deal, the federal work force again expanded, climbing to 1.2 million. Public demand for relief from the economic hardship and uncertainty of the Great Depression led to the formation of economic and social welfare agencies such as the Securities and Exchange Commission and the Social Security Board. An effect was to give the federal government an ongoing role in promoting Americans' economic well-being.

A large and active government requires skilled and experienced personnel. In 1883, Congress passed the Pendleton Act, which established a **merit** (or **civil service**) **system** whereby certain federal employees were hired through competitive examinations or by virtue of having special qualifications, such as an advanced degree in a particular field. The transition to a career civil service was gradual. Only 10 percent of federal positions in 1885 were filled on the basis of merit. But the pace accelerated when the Progressives (see Chapter 2) promoted the merit system as a way of eliminating partisan graft and corruption in the administration of government. By 1920, as the Progressive era was concluding, more than 70 percent of federal employees were merit appointees. Since 1950, the proportion of merit employees has never dipped below 80 percent.[8]

merit (civil service) system An approach to managing the bureaucracy whereby people are appointed to government positions on the basis of either competitive examinations or special qualifications, such as professional training.

The Pendleton Act created the Civil Service Commission to establish job classifications, administer competitive examinations, and oversee merit employees. The commission was replaced by two independent agencies in 1978. The Merit Service Protection Board handles appeals of merit employees who have been fired or who face other disciplinary action, and the Office of Personnel Management (OPM) supervises the hiring and classification of federal employees.

The administrative objective of the merit system is **neutral competence.**[9] A merit-based bureaucracy is "competent" in the sense that employees are hired and retained on the basis of their skills, and it is "neutral" in the sense that employees are not partisan appointees and thus are expected to do their work on behalf of everyone, not just those who support the incumbent president.

neutral competence The administrative objective of merit-based bureaucracy. Such a bureaucracy should be "competent" in the sense that its employees are hired and retained on the basis of their expertise and "neutral" in the sense that it operates by objective standards rather than partisan ones.

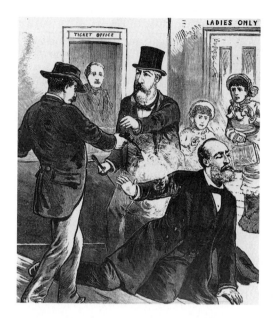

The assassination of President James A. Garfield in 1881 by Charles Guiteau, a disappointed officeseeker, did much to end the spoils system of distributing government jobs.

executive leadership system
An approach to managing the bureaucracy that is based on presidential leadership and presidential management tools, such as the president's annual budget proposal.

Although the merit system contributes to the impartial and proficient administration of government programs, it has its own sources of bias and inefficiency. Career bureaucrats tend to place their agency's interests ahead of those of other agencies and typically oppose substantial efforts to trim their agency's activities. They are not partisans in the sense of Democratic or Republican politics, but they are partisans when it comes to protecting their own positions and agencies, as explained more fully later in the chapter.

Big Government and the Executive Leadership System

As problems with the merit system surfaced after the early years of the twentieth century, reformers looked to a strengthened presidency—an **executive leadership system**—as a means of coordinating the bureaucracy's activities to increase its efficiency and responsiveness.[10] The president was to provide the general leadership that would overcome agency fragmentation and provide a common direction. As Chapter 12 describes, Congress in 1939 provided the president with some of the tools needed for improved coordination of the bureaucracy. The Office of Management and Budget (OMB) was created to give the president the authority to coordinate the annual budgetary process. Agencies would be required to prepare their budget proposals under the direction of the president, who would then submit the overall budget to Congress for its approval and modification. The president was also authorized to develop the Executive Office of the President, which oversees the agencies' activities on the president's behalf by assisting in the development and implementation of policy programs.

Like the merit and patronage systems, the executive leadership system has brought problems as well as improvements to the administration of government. In practice, the executive leadership concept can give the president too much leverage over the bureaucracy and thereby weaken Congress's ability to act as a check on presidential power. A case in point is the intelligence estimates the Bush administration gave Congress while seeking a congressional resolution authorizing a military attack on Iraq. The Bush administration claimed that the CIA had evidence that Iraq's Saddam Hussein was accumulating weapons of mass destruction (WMDs) that threatened the security of the United States. Bush also used this argument in the effort to generate public and international support for the war. In his 2003 State of the Union address, President Bush said, "The dictator of Iraq is not disarming. To the contrary, he is deceiving." In a speech to the United Nations, Secretary of State Colin Powell claimed, "The facts on Iraq's behavior demonstrate . . . that Saddam Hussein and his regime are concealing their efforts to produce more weapons of mass destruction."

Yet the facts proved quite different. In testimony before Congress in 2004, the chief U.S. weapons inspector in Iraq, David Kay, said that his team had failed to uncover any evidence of an Iraq weapons program on the scale

Debating the Issues

The Case of Iraq's Weapons of Mass Destruction: Did the CIA Play Politics?

The federal bureaucracy is a storehouse of knowledge that informs national policy. Though major policy decisions are made primarily by elected officials, these officials rely on agencies for policy-related information. Seldom has this relationship created more controversy than in the case of Iraq's weapons programs. The Bush administration justified its attack on Iraq in 2003 by saying that intelligence agencies had confirmed Iraq's possession of large stockpiles of weapons of mass destruction and its willingness to use them. After U.S. military forces took over Iraq, investigators could not find evidence of an Iraqi weapons program anywhere near the scale portrayed by the Administration. Suddenly the intelligence agencies themselves were on the spot. Had they misread their intelligence or slanted it to fit the Bush administration's agenda? Or had they offered their best judgment based on the intelligence they had? There were countless views on this issue, including those of Senator Carl Levin, a member of the Senate Select Committee on Intelligence, and George Tenet, the director of Central Intelligence.

Yes: There is now confirmation from the administration's own leading weapons inspector that the intelligence community produced greatly flawed assessments about Iraq's weapons of mass destruction in the months leading up to the invasion of Iraq. It is my opinion that flawed intelligence and the administration's exaggerations concerning Iraq's weapons of mass destruction resulted from an effort to make the threat appear more imminent and the case for military action against Iraq appear more urgent than they were. . . . Director Tenet, after 12 months of indefensible stonewalling, recently relented and declassified the material that I requested, which makes clear that his public testimony before the Congress on the extent to which the United States shared intelligence with the United Nations on Iraq's weapons of mass destruction programs was false. . . . In other words, honest answers by Director Tenet might have undermined the false sense of urgency for proceeding to war and could have contributed to delay, neither of which fit the administration's policy goals. . . . We rely on our intelligence agencies to give us the facts, not to give us the spin on the facts. The accuracy and objectivity of intelligence should never be tainted or slanted to support a particular policy.

—*Carl Levin, U.S. senator (D-Mich.)*

No: Much of the current controversy centers on our prewar intelligence on Iraq, summarized in the National Intelligence Estimate of October 2002. . . . This Estimate asked if Iraq had chemical, biological, and nuclear weapons and the means to deliver them. We concluded that in some of these categories, Iraq had weapons. And that in others—where it did not have them—it was trying to develop them. Let me be clear: analysts differed on several important aspects of these programs and those debates were spelled out in the Estimate. They never said there was an "imminent" threat. Rather, they painted an objective assessment for our policymakers of a brutal dictator who was continuing his efforts to deceive and build programs that might constantly surprise us and threaten our interests. No one told us what to say or how to say it. . . . Did these strands of information weave into a perfect picture—could they answer every question? No—far from it. But, taken together, this information provided a solid basis on which to <u>estimate</u> whether Iraq did or did not have weapons of mass destruction and the means to deliver them. It is important to underline the word <u>estimate.</u> Because not everything we analyze can be known to a standard of absolute proof.

—*George J. Tenet, director of Central Intelligence*

claimed by the Bush Administration. This and other revelations produced heated debate over who was to blame for the faulty claim. Did the blame rest largely with the White House, which had pressured the intelligence agencies to make the strongest case possible for war with Iraq, or did the blame rest largely with the intelligence agencies themselves? Many observers thought both sides deserved blame, concluding that the White House had overstated its case and that the intelligence agencies had been too eager to tell the White House what it wanted to hear.

TABLE 13-2	Strengths and Weaknesses of Major Systems for Managing the Bureaucracy	
SYSTEM	**STRENGTHS**	**WEAKNESSES**
Patronage	Makes the bureaucracy more responsive to election outcomes by allowing the president to appoint some executive officials.	Gives executive authority to individuals chosen for their partisan loyalty rather than for their administrative or policy expertise; can favor interests that supported the president's election.
Merit	Provides for *competent* administration in that employees are hired on the basis of ability and allowed to remain on the job and thereby become proficient, and provides for *neutral* administration in that civil servants are not partisan appointees and are expected to work in an evenhanded way.	Can result in fragmented, unresponsive administration because career bureaucrats are secure in their jobs and tend to place the interests of their particular agency ahead of those of other agencies or the nation's interests as a whole.
Executive leadership	Provides for presidential leadership of the bureaucracy in order to make it more responsive and to coordinate and direct it (left alone, the bureaucracy tends toward fragmentation).	Can upset the balance between executive and legislative power and can make the president's priorities, not fairness or effective management, the basis for administrative action.

Thus, the executive leadership system, like the patronage and merit systems, is not foolproof. It can make bureaucratic agencies overly dependent on the presidency, thereby distorting their activities and reducing congressional checks on executive power. Nevertheless, the executive leadership system is a necessary part of an overall strategy for the effective handling of the bureaucracy. At its best, the system imposes principles of effective management—such as eliminating wasteful duplication—on the work of government agencies.

The federal bureaucracy today embodies aspects of all three systems—patronage, merit, and executive leadership—a situation that reflects the tensions inherent in governmental administration. The bureaucracy is expected to carry out programs fairly and competently (the merit system), but it is also expected to respond to political forces (the patronage system) and to operate efficiently (the executive management system). Table 13–2 summarizes the major strengths and weaknesses of each of these three systems of administration.

 THE BUREAUCRACY'S POWER IMPERATIVE

A common misperception is that the president, as the chief executive, has the sole claim on the bureaucracy's loyalty. In fact, each of the elected institutions has reason to claim proprietorship: the president as chief executive and Congress as the source of the authorization and funding of the bureaucracy's programs. One presidential appointee asked a congressional committee whether it had any problem with his plans to reduce one of his agency's programs. The committee chairman replied, "No, you have the problem, because if you touch that bureau I'll cut your job out of the budget."[11]

The U.S. system of separate institutions sharing power results in a natural tendency for each institution to guard its turf. In addition, the president and members of Congress differ in their constituencies and thus in the interests to which they are most responsive. For example, although the agricultural sector is just one of many concerns of the president, it is of vital interest to senators and representatives from farm states. Finally, because the president and Congress are elected separately, the White House and one or both houses of Congress may be in the hands of opposing parties. Since 1968, this source of executive-legislative conflict has more often been the rule than the exception.

If agencies are to operate successfully in this system, they must seek support where they can find it—if not from the president, then from Congress. In other words, agencies must play politics.[12] Any agency that is content to sit idly by while new priorities with regard to money and policy are determined is virtually certain to lose out to other agencies that are willing to fight for power.

The Agency Point of View

Administrators have little choice but to look out for their agency's interests, a perspective that is called the **agency point of view.** This perspective comes naturally to most high-ranking civil servants. More than 80 percent of all top careerists reach their high-level positions by rising through the ranks of the same agency.[13] As one top administrator said when testifying before the House Appropriations Committee, "Mr. Chairman, you would not think it proper for me to be in charge of this work and not be enthusiastic about it . . . would you? I have been in it for thirty years, and I believe in it."[14]

agency point of view The tendency of bureaucrats to place the interests of their agency ahead of other interests and ahead of the priorities sought by the president or Congress.

Professionalism also cements agency loyalties. High-level administrative positions have increasingly been filled by scientists, engineers, lawyers, educators, physicians, and other professionals. Most of them take jobs in an agency whose mission they support, as in the case of the aeronautical engineers who work for NASA.

Studies confirm that bureaucrats believe in the importance of their agency's work. One study found that social welfare administrators are three times as likely as other civil servants to believe that social welfare programs should be a high policy priority.[15]

Sources of Bureaucratic Power

In promoting their agency's interests, bureaucrats rely on their specialized knowledge, the support of interests that benefit from the programs they run, and the backing of the president and Congress.

The Power of Expertise

Most of the policy problems that the federal government confronts do not lend themselves to simple solutions. Whether the issue is space travel or hunger in America, expert knowledge is essential to the development of effective public policy. Much of this expertise is held by bureaucrats. They spend their careers working in a particular policy area, and many of them have had scientific, technical, or other specialized training.[16]

HOW THE UNITED STATES COMPARES

Educational Backgrounds of Bureaucrats

To staff its bureaucracy, the U.S. government tends to hire persons with specialized educations to hold specialized jobs. This approach heightens the tendency of bureaucrats to take the agency point of view. By comparison, Great Britain tends to recruit its bureaucrats from the arts and humanities, on the assumption that general aptitude is the best qualification for detached professionalism. The conti-nental European democracies also emphasize detached professionalism, but in the context of the supposedly impartial application of rules. As a consequence, high-ranking civil servants in Europe tend to have legal educations. The college majors of senior civil servants in the United States and other democracies reflect these tendencies.

COLLEGE MAJOR OF SENIOR CIVIL SERVANTS	NORWAY	GERMANY	GREAT BRITAIN	ITALY	BELGIUM	UNITED STATES
Natural science/ engineering	8%	8%	26%	10%	20%	32%
Social science/ humanities/ business	38	18	52	37	40	50
Law	38	63	3	53	35	18
Other	16	11	19	—	5	—
	100%	100%	100%	100%	100%	100%

Adapted from *The Politics of Bureaucracy*, 5th ed. By B. Guy Peters. Copyright © 2001 by Routledge. Printed by permission of Thomsen Publishing Services.

By comparison, elected officials are generalists. To some degree, members of Congress do specialize through their committee work, but they rarely have the time or the inclination to acquire a commanding knowledge of a particular issue. The president's understanding of policy issues is even more general. Not surprisingly, the president and members of Congress regularly depend on the bureaucracy for policy advice and guidance.

All agencies acquire some power through their careerists' expertise. No matter how simple a policy issue may appear at first, it invariably involves more complexity than meets the eye. A recognition that the United States has a trade deficit with China, for example, can be the premise for policy change, but this recognition does not begin to address basic issues such as the form that the new policy might take, its probable cost and effectiveness, and its links to other issues, such as America's standing in Asia. Among the officials most likely to understand these issues are the career bureaucrats in the Commerce Department and the Federal Trade Commission.

The Power of Clientele Groups

Most agencies have **clientele groups,** special interests that benefit directly from an agency's programs. Clientele groups assist agencies by placing pressure on Congress and the president to support those programs from which they benefit.[17] For example, when House Speaker Newt Gingrich threatened in 1995 to "zero out" funding for the Corporation for Public Broadcasting, audience members and groups such as the Children's Television Workshop wrote, called, faxed, and cajoled members of Congress, saying that programs like *Sesame Street* and *All Things Considered* were irreplaceable. Within a few weeks, Gingrich had retreated from his position, saying that a complete cessation of funding was not what he had in mind.

In general, agencies both assist and are assisted by the clientele groups that depend on the programs they administer.[18] Many agencies were created for the purpose of promoting particular interests in society. For example, the Department of Agriculture's career bureaucrats are dependable allies of farm interests year after year. The same cannot be said of the president, Congress as a whole, or either political party, all of whom must balance farmers' demands against those of other interests.

The popular children's program *Sesame Street* is produced through the Corporation for Public Broadcasting, a government agency that gains leverage in budgetary deliberations from its public support. Singer Garth Brooks is shown here with two muppets during his appearance on *Sesame Street.*

clientele groups Special interest groups that benefit directly from the activities of a particular bureaucratic agency and therefore are strong advocates of the agency.

The Power of Friends in High Places

Although members of Congress and the president sometimes appear to be at war with the bureaucracy, they need it as much as it needs them. An agency's resources—its programs, expertise, and group support—can assist elected officials in their efforts to achieve their goals. When President George W. Bush in 2001 announced plans for a war on terrorism, he needed the help of careerists in the Central Intelligence Agency, the Department of Defense, and the Justice Department to make his efforts successful. At a time when other agencies were feeling the pinch of a tight federal budget, these agencies received substantial new funding.

Bureaucrats also seek favorable relations with members of Congress. Congressional support is vital because agencies' funding and programs are established through legislation. Agencies that offer benefits to major constituency interests are particularly likely to have close ties to Congress. In some policy areas, more or less permanent alliances—iron triangles—form among agencies, clientele groups, and congressional subcommittees. In other policy areas, temporary issue networks form among bureaucrats, lobbyists, and members of Congress. As explained in Chapters 9 and 11, these alliances are a means by which an agency can gain support from legislators and groups positioned to support its goals.

Figure 13-3

Opinions on Bureaucratic Inefficiency and Waste

Although Americans believe that government programs are inefficient and wasteful, they are not alone in their belief. Public opinion on this issue is remarkably consistent across democratic nations.

Source: Global Attitudes Survey, Pew Research Center on the People and the Press, 2002.

Percentage agreeing that "when something is run by the government, it is usually inefficient and wasteful."

Country	Percentage
Canada	61%
France	70%
Germany	65%
Great Britain	66%
Italy	82%
Japan	74%
Mexico	66%
United States	63%

 BUREAUCRATIC ACCOUNTABILITY

Even though most Americans say that they have a favorable impression of their most recent personal experience with the bureaucracy (as, say, when a senior citizen applies for social security), they have an unfavorable impression of the bureaucracy as a whole (see Figure 13–3). Along with citizens of other democracies, they see the programs of government bureaucracies as wasteful and inefficient. This view is somewhat unfair. In areas such as health care and retirement insurance, government bureaucracies are actually more efficient than private organizations. In other areas, efficiency is an inappropriate standard for government programs. The most efficient way to administer government loans to college students, for example, would be to give money to the first students who apply and then close down the program when the money runs out. However, college loan programs, like many other government programs, operate on the principles of fairness and need, which require that each application be judged on its merits.

This view is also somewhat unfair when applied to the American case in particular. Studies indicate that the U.S. bureaucracy compares favorably to government bureaucracies elsewhere.[19] Of course, not all U.S. agencies have strong performance records (see Figure 13–4). The Immigration and Naturalization Service (INS) is one agency that has been chronically mismanaged. Yet the performance of many U.S. agencies is superior to that of their counterparts in other industrialized democracies. The U.S. postal service, for example, has an on-time and low-cost record that few postal services can match.

Nevertheless, it is easy to see why most Americans hold a relatively unfavorable opinion of the federal bureaucracy. Americans have traditionally mistrusted political power, and the bureaucracy is the symbol of "big government." It is also a convenient target for politicians who claim that "Washington bureaucrats" are wasting taxpayer money. (The irony is that the bureaucracy has no power to create programs or authorize spending; these decisions are made by Congress and the president.) It is no surprise that Americans have qualms about the federal bureaucracy and want it to be more closely controlled.

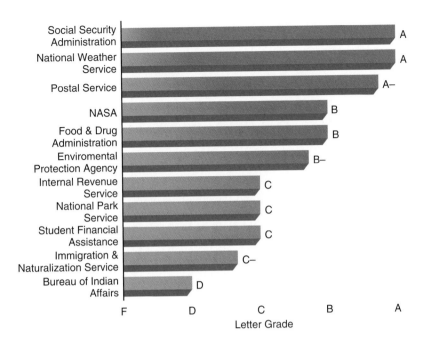

Figure 13–4

Rating Federal Agencies, Selected Examples

The Federal Performance Project evaluates federal agencies and gives them a "report card" based on the quality of their management of finances, human resources, programs, information, and physical assets. The Social Security Administration is one of the top-rated agencies. The Bureau of Indian Affairs is one of the lowest-rated agencies.

Source: Created from data in Anne Laurent, "Managing for Results," *Government Executive*, April 2001, 8–12.

Adapting the requirements of the bureaucracy to those of democracy has been a persistent challenge for public administration (see "Liberty, Equality, & Self-Government"). Bureaucracy is the antithesis of democracy. Bureaucrats are unelected and hold office indefinitely, and they make decisions based on fixed rules rather than on debate and deliberation. This situation raises the question of **bureaucratic accountability**—the degree to which bureaucrats are held accountable for the power they exercise. Bureaucratic accountability occurs primarily through oversight by the president, Congress, and the courts.[20]

bureaucratic accountability
The degree to which bureaucrats are held accountable for the power they exercise.

Accountability through the Presidency

The president can only broadly influence, not directly control, the bureaucracy. "We can outlast any president" is a maxim of bureaucratic politics. Each agency has its clientele and its congressional supporters as well as statutory authority for its existence and activities. No president can unilaterally eliminate an agency or its funding and programs. Nor can the president be indifferent to the opinions of career civil servants—not without losing their support and expertise in developing and implementing presidential policy objectives.

To encourage the bureaucracy to act responsibly, the president can apply management tools that have developed out of the "executive leadership" concept discussed earlier in this chapter. These tools include reorganization, presidential appointees, and the executive budget.

Reorganization

The bureaucracy's extreme fragmentation—its hundreds of separate agencies—makes presidential coordination of its activities difficult. Agencies pursue independent and even contradictory paths, resulting in an undetermined amount of

Liberty, Equality & Self-Government

What's Your Opinion?

Bureaucracy and Self-Government

The power of the bureaucracy is both undeniable and difficult to reconcile with the concept of self-government. Bureaucracy entails hierarchy, command, permanence of office, appointment to office, and fixed rules, whereas self-government involves equality, consent, rotation of office, election to office, and open decision making. At base, the conflict between bureaucracy and self-government centers on the degree of power held by unelected officials.

Eliminating the bureaucracy is not an answer to the problem. American society would collapse without the defense establishment, the education and welfare programs, the regulation of business, the transportation systems, and the hundreds of other activities of the federal bureaucracy.

Oversight by Congress, the president, and the judiciary has been America's answer to the problem. Can you think of ways this oversight might be made more effective? Can you also think of ways of reorganizing the bureaucracy that would enhance accountability? For example, do you think the bureaucracy would be more accountable if civil servants rotated from one agency to another every few years, much as military personnel rotate in their assignments? What would be the disadvantages of such a personnel system?

waste and duplication of effort. For example, more than one hundred governmental units are responsible for different pieces of federal education policy.

All recent presidents have tried to streamline the bureaucracy and make it more accountable.[21] Such changes seldom greatly improve things, but they can produce marginal gains.[22] For George W. Bush, the challenge came after the terrorist attacks on the World Trade Center and the Pentagon. Breakdowns in the FBI and CIA had undermined whatever chance there might have been to prevent the attacks. These agencies had neither shared nor vigorously pursued the intelligence information they had gathered. Bush concluded, and Congress agreed, that a reorganization of the FBI and CIA, as well as the creation of the Department of Homeland Security, was necessary. Nevertheless, neither the White House nor Congress was under the illusion that this reorganization would fully correct the coordination problems plaguing the agencies charged with stopping terrorist attacks on American soil.

Presidential Appointments

Although there is almost no direct confrontation with a bureaucrat that a president cannot win, the president does not have time to deal personally with every troublesome careerist or to make sure that the bureaucracy has complied with every presidential order. The president relies on political appointees in the agencies to ensure that directives are followed.

The power of presidential appointees is greater in those agencies where wide latitude exists in the making of decisions. Although the Social Security

Quality of the Federal Bureaucracy

Most Americans do not think highly of the federal bureaucracy. When questioned in polls, people say that the bureaucracy is wasteful of taxpayers' money and is staffed by people who are not particularly talented and who do not work all that hard.

These stereotypes have some basis. There is waste in federal programs, and some civil servants do take advantage of the job security provided by a civil service appointment. However, these problems are not as large as many people think. As former New York governor Mario Cuomo pointed out, fairness rather than efficiency is the goal of many federal programs. Loans to college students, for example, are awarded on the basis of need, which means they cannot simply be handed out in equal amounts to anyone who applies. That approach would be much less expensive to administer, but a need-based program requires a detailed application process and a case-by-case assessment of the applicants.

Some deadbeats work in the federal bureaucracy, which is not surprising in view of the fact that it has more than two million employees. Interestingly, when people are asked about their direct experiences with federal employees, they usually express satisfaction with the service they personally have received from postal workers, social security administrators, National Park Service rangers, and other civil servants.

However, the federal bureaucracy has had difficulty attracting top-notch employees. As the gap has widened between the pay and benefits in the public sector relative to the private sector, college graduates have shown less interest in careers in government. A 2001 survey found that only one in ten graduates was considering such a career path.

A government career is not without its frustrations. A 2002 study by Harvard's Kennedy School of Government found that management-level public-sector employees have less opportunity than comparable private-sector employees to pursue initiatives. Their work is more constrained because the operating rules and budget allocations are less flexible than in the private sector. However, the Kennedy School's study also found that public-sector managers get more intrinsic satisfaction from their work, which focuses on improving public life, than do private-sector managers.

The quality of the nation's public servants affects the quality of governance. Ultimately, an organization is no better than the people who staff it. What would it take for you to consider a career in government? What agency could you envision working in? For people who want to pursue a government career, a first step is often a master's degree program in public administration or public policy. Many of these programs require only a year of study after the bachelor's degree. For an entry-level employee with a master's degree rather than a bachelor's degree, the initial salary is 50 percent higher. Appointees with master's degrees enter the civil service at a higher rank (GS-9 rather than GS-5) and are placed in positions that entail greater responsibility than those assigned to newly hired appointees with bachelor's degrees.

Administration (SSA) has a huge budget and makes monthly payments to more than forty million Americans, the eligibility of recipients is determined by relatively fixed rules. The head of the SSA does not have the option, say, of granting a retiree an extra $100 a month because the retiree is facing financial hardship. In contrast, most regulatory agencies have broad discretion over regulatory policy, and the heads of these agencies have wide latitude in their decisions. For example, President Reagan's appointee to chair the Federal Trade Commission (FTC), James Miller III, was a strong-willed economist who shared Reagan's belief that consumer protection policy had gone too far and was adversely affecting business interests. In Miller's first year as head of the FTC, the commission

The Old Executive Office Building is adjacent to the west wing of the White House. Its occupants are part of the Executive Office of the President (EOP) and serve as contacts between the president and agency bureaucrats.

dropped one-fourth of its pending cases against business firms.[23] Overall, enforcement actions declined by about 50 percent during Miller's tenure compared with the previous period.

However, as noted in Chapter 12, there are limits to what a president can accomplish through appointments. High-level presidential appointees number in the hundreds, and their turnover rate is high: the average appointee remains in the Administration for less than two years before moving on to other employment.[24] No president can keep track of all appointees, much less instruct them in detail on all intended policies.

The Executive Budget

Faced with the difficulty of controlling the bureaucracy, presidents have come to rely heavily on their personal bureaucracy, the Executive Office of the President (EOP).

In terms of presidential management, the key unit within the EOP is the Office of Management and Budget (OMB). Funding, programs, and regulations are the mainstays of every agency, and the OMB has substantial influence on each of these areas. No agency can issue a major regulation without the OMB's verification that the regulation's benefits outweigh its costs, and no agency can propose legislation to Congress without the OMB's approval. However, the OMB's greatest influence over agencies derives from its budgetary role. At the start of the annual budget cycle, the OMB assigns each agency a budget limit in accord with the president's directives. The agency's tentative allocation requests are sent back to the OMB, which then conducts a final review of all requests before sending the full budget to Congress in the president's name.

In most cases, an agency's overall budget does not change much from year to year, indicating that a significant portion of the bureaucracy's activities persist regardless of who sits in the White House or Congress. It must be noted, however, that the bulk of federal spending is for programs such as social security that, although enacted in the past, enjoy the continuing support of the president, Congress, and the public.

Accountability through Congress

Congress has powerful means of influencing the bureaucracy. All agencies depend on Congress for their existence, authority, programs, and funding.

The most substantial control that Congress exerts on the bureaucracy is through its power to authorize and fund programs. Without authorization or funding, a program simply does not exist, regardless of the priority an agency claims it deserves. Congress can also void an administrative decision through legislation that instructs the agency to follow a different course of action. However, Congress lacks the time and expertise to work out complex policies down to the last detail.[25] The government would grind to a halt if Congress tried to define fully how programs will be designed and run.

The Budgetary Process: Funding the Agencies

The annual federal budget allocates the hundreds of billions of dollars that support federal agencies and programs. As Chapters 11 through 13 have indicated, Congress, the president, and the bureaucracy all play substantial roles in shaping the budget. The following is a simplified step-by-step summary of the process:

1. In the calendar year preceding enactment of the budget, the Office of Management and Budget (OMB) instructs each agency to prepare its budget request within guidelines established by the White House.

2. Agencies work out their budget proposals in line with White House guidelines and their own goals. Once completed, agency proposals are sent to the OMB for review and adjustment to fit the president's goals.

3. In January, the president submits the adjusted budget to Congress.

4. The president's budget is reviewed by the Congressional Budget Office (CBO) and is referred to the House and Senate budget and appropriations committees. The budget committees in each chamber then set expenditure ceilings in particular areas, which are voted upon by the members of Congress. Once set (usually in April), the budget ceilings establish temporary limits within which the appropriations committees must act.

5. Through subcommittee hearings, the House and Senate appropriations committees meet with agency heads and adjust the president's budgetary recommendations to fit congressional goals. Once the appropriations committees have completed their work, the proposals are submitted to the full House and Senate for a vote. Differences in the House and Senate versions are reconciled in conference committee.

6. The legislation is sent to the president for approval or veto. Before this point, the White House and Congress will have engaged in intense negotiations to resolve differences in their priorities. If the White House is satisfied with the outcome of the bargaining, the president can be expected to sign the legislation.

7. The new budget takes effect October 1, unless Congress has not completed its work by then or the president vetoes the legislation. If agreement has not been reached by this date, temporary funding (authorized by Congress and approved by the president) is required to keep the government in operation until a permanent budget can be enacted. If temporary funding is not provided, a shutdown of nonessential government services occurs.

Congress also exerts some control through its oversight function, which involves monitoring the bureaucracy's work to ensure compliance with legislative intent.[26] As noted in Chapter 11, however, oversight is a difficult and relatively unrewarding task, and members of Congress ordinarily place less emphasis on oversight than on their other major duties. Only when an agency has clearly stepped out of line is Congress likely to take decisive corrective action by holding hearings to ask tough questions and to warn of legislative punishment.

Because oversight is so burdensome, Congress has shifted much of the responsibility to the General Accounting Office (GAO). The GAO's primary function once was to keep track of the funds spent within the bureaucracy; now it also monitors whether policies are being implemented as Congress intended. The Congressional Budget Office (CBO) also carries out oversight studies. When the GAO or CBO uncovers a major problem with an agency's handling of a program, it notifies Congress, which can then take remedial action.

Of course, bureaucrats are kept in check by an awareness that misbehavior can trigger a response from Congress. Nevertheless, oversight cannot correct mistakes or abuses that have already occurred. Recognizing this limit on oversight, Congress has devised ways to constrain the bureaucracy *before* it acts. The simplest method is to draft laws that contain very specific provisions that limit bureaucrats' options when they implement policy. Another restrictive device is the sunset law, which establishes a specific date when a law will expire unless it is reenacted by Congress. Advocates of sunset laws see them as a means to counter the bureaucracy's reluctance to give up programs that have outlived their usefulness. Because members of Congress usually want the programs they create to last far into the future, however, most legislation does not include a sunset provision.

Accountability through the Courts

The judiciary's influence on agencies is less direct than that of the elected branches, but the courts too can and do act to ensure the bureaucracy's compliance with Congress's directives. Legally, the bureaucracy derives its authority from acts of Congress, and an injured party can bring suit against an agency on the grounds that it has failed to carry out the law properly. Judges can then order an agency to change its application of the law.[27]

However, the courts have tended to support administrators if their actions seem at all consistent with the laws they are administering. The Supreme Court has held that agencies can choose rule-making procedures that meet the minimal threshold set down by Congress, that agencies can apply any reasonable interpretation of statutes unless Congress has specifically stated something to the contrary, and that agencies in many instances have wide discretion in deciding whether to enforce statutes.[28] These positions reflect the need for flexibility in administration. The bureaucracy and the courts would both grind to a halt if judges routinely chose to substitute their interpretations of the law for those of administrators. The judiciary cannot conduct a decision-by-decision oversight of the bureaucracy. Judges recognize that constraints on the bureaucracy must work mainly through the Congress and the president. The judiciary has promoted bureaucratic accountability primarily by encouraging administrators to act responsibly in their dealings with the public and by protecting individuals and groups from the bureaucracy's worst abuses. In 1999, for example, a federal court approved a settlement in favor of African American farmers who alleged that the Department of Agriculture systematically favored white farmers in granting federal farm loans.[29]

Accountability within the Bureaucracy Itself

A recognition of the difficulty of ensuring adequate accountability of the bureaucracy through the presidency, Congress, and the courts has led to the development of mechanisms of accountability within the bureaucracy itself. Two measures, whistle-blowing and demographic representativeness, are particularly noteworthy.

Whistle-Blowing

Although the bureaucratic corruption that is rampant in some countries is relatively uncommon in the United States, a certain amount of waste, fraud, and abuse is inevitable in a bureaucracy as big as that of the federal government. **Whistle-blowing,** the act of reporting instances of official mismanagement, is a potentially effective internal check. To encourage whistle-blowers to come forward with their information, Congress enacted the Whistle Blower Protection Act to protect them against retaliation. Federal law also provides whistle-blowers with financial rewards in some cases.

Whistle-blower Richard Clarke testifies about Bush administration terrorist policies in the months before the September 11, 2001, attacks on the World Trade Center and the Pentagon. In high-profile appearances before Congress and the 9/11 Commission, Clarke accused the Bush administration, in which he had served as the top terrorist adviser, of ignoring warnings of a possible large-scale terrorist attack on the United States.

Nevertheless, whistle-blowing is not for the faint-hearted. Many federal employees are reluctant to report instances of mismanagement because they fear it could harm their careers or reputations. Their superiors might claim that they are malcontents or find subtle ways to punish them for revealing information that reflects badly on their agency or its leadership. Even their fellow employees are unlikely to think highly of "tattletales."

Accordingly, whistle-blowing sometimes does not occur until an employee has left an agency or quit government service entirely. A case in point is Richard Clarke, the former chief terrorist adviser in the Bush administration. In 2004, Clarke accused President Bush and other top White House officials of downplaying the terrorist threat and being preoccupied with Iraq in the period leading up to the September 11, 2001, terrorist attacks. "I believe the Bush administration in the first eight months considered terrorism an important issue, but not an urgent issue," Clarke told the 9/11 Commission, a bipartisan commission formed by Congress to investigate the attacks. The White House countered with accusations that Clarke was exaggerating his claims in order to boost sales of his recently published book. Vice President Dick Cheney claimed that Clarke "wasn't in the loop" and could not possibly have known what was going on in the Bush administration's inner circle. The White House slowed its attack on Clarke only after documents surfaced supporting some of his allegations. In a pre-9/11 memo prepared for Bush's national security advisor Condoleezza Rice, Clarke had expressed alarm at the slow pace of the administration's antiterrorism planning, saying "Imagine a day after hundreds of Americans lay dead at home or abroad after a terrorist attack."[30]

whistle-blowing An internal check on the bureaucracy whereby employees report instances of mismanagement that they observe.

Demographic Representativeness

Although the bureaucracy is an unrepresentative institution in the sense that its officials are not elected by the people, it can be representative in the demographic sense. If bureaucrats were a demographic microcosm of the general public, they presumably would treat the various groups and interests in society more fairly.[31]

TABLE 13-3	Federal Job Rankings (GS) of Various Demographic Groups Women and minority-group members are underrepresented in the top jobs of the federal bureaucracy, but their representation has been increasing.					
	WOMEN'S SHARE		BLACKS' SHARE		HISPANICS' SHARE	
GRADE LEVEL*	1976	2000	1982	2000	1982	2000
GS 1–4 (lowest ranks)	78%	68%	23%	27%	5%	9%
GS 5–8	60	68	19	25	4	8
GS 9–12	20	45	10	15	4	7
GS 13–15 (highest ranks)	5	31	5	10	2	4

*In general, the higher-numbered grades are managerial and professional positions, and the lower-numbered grades are clerical and manual labor positions.
Source: Office of Workforce Information, 2004.

At present, the bureaucracy is not demographically representative at its top levels (see Table 13–3). Roughly 60 percent of managerial and professional positions are held by white males. However, the employment status of women and, to a lesser extent, minorities has improved in recent decades, and top officials in the bureaucracy include a greater proportion of women and minorities than is found in Congress or the judiciary. Moreover, if all employees are considered, the federal bureaucracy comes reasonably close to being representative of the nation's population.[32]

demographic representativeness The idea that the bureaucracy will be more responsive to the public if its employees at all levels are demographically representative of the population as a whole.

Demographic representativeness is only a partial answer to the problem of bureaucratic accountability. A fully representative civil service would still be required to play agency politics. The careerists in, say, defense agencies and welfare agencies are similar in their demographic backgrounds, but they differ markedly in their opinions about policy. Each group believes that the goals of its agency should take priority. The inevitability of an agency point of view is the most significant of all political facts about the U.S. federal bureaucracy.

 # REINVENTING GOVERNMENT

There have been numerous attempts during the twentieth century to enhance the bureaucracy's efficiency, responsiveness, and accountability. Another wave of this reform effort, begun in the 1990s, sought to improve the administration of government by the reduction of its size, cost, and lines of authority.

In *Reinventing Government*, David Osborne and Ted Gaebler argue that the bureaucracy of today was created in response to earlier problems, particularly those spawned by the Industrial Revolution and a rampant spoils system. They claim that the information age requires a different kind of administrative structure, one that is leaner and more responsive. Osborne and Gaebler argued that government should set program standards but should not necessarily take on

Americans in an Interdependent World

Bureaucracy around the World

In polls, only about one in four Americans expresses confidence in the performance of the federal bureaucracy. Comparisons with other national bureaucracies, however, suggest that the U.S. bureaucracy is relatively effective. In fact, Charles Goodsell, a public administration expert, concludes that America's bureaucracy is among the best in the world. "Some national bureaucracies," he writes in *The Case for Bureaucracy*, "may be roughly the same [as the U.S. bureaucracy] in quality of overall performance, but they are few in number."

GLOBAL
Perspective

In many countries, the bureaucracy is thoroughly inefficient and corrupt. Tasks are completed slowly and sometimes not at all unless a bribe has been paid. In other countries, the bureaucracy is overly rigid, centralized, and remote. The rules are more important than the policy goals these rules are designed to achieve.

Neither of these extreme tendencies is characteristic of the U.S. federal bureaucracy. Comparisons of national postal services, for example, confirm that the U.S. postal bureaucracy is one of the best worldwide. The U.S. mail usually arrives on time, at the right destination, and with the proper postage. In many countries, the mail is chronically late, often misrouted, frequently lost, and sometimes posted at the wrong rate.

Such comparisons suggest that Americans' complaints are grounded less in how their particular bureaucracy performs than in how bureaucracies generally perform. An encounter with a bureaucracy may require the completion of a lengthy form and then a considerable wait before action is taken. If such steps are necessary to ensure that people in the same situation receive the same treatment, the process is a source of frustration. Americans at least have the satisfaction of knowing that their applications are likely to be acted upon and that the action will be fair. In many parts of the world, applicants have no such guarantee.

all program responsibilities. If, for example, a private firm can provide meals to soldiers at U.S. army posts at a lower cost than the military can provide them, it should be contracted to provide the meals. Osborne and Gaebler also argued that administrative judgments should be made at the lowest bureaucratic level feasible. If, for example, Department of Agriculture field agents have the required knowledge to make a certain type of decision, they should be empowered to make it, rather than being required to get permission from superiors. Finally, Osborne and Gaebler argued that the bureaucracy should focus on outputs (results) rather than inputs (dollars spent). Federal loans to college students, for example, should be judged by how many students stay in college as a result of these loans rather than by how much money they receive.[33]

These ideas informed the Clinton administration's National Performance Review (described in this chapter's introduction). Even though the Bush administration decided not to continue the initiative, NPR's impact is felt through laws and administrative practices established during its tenure. An example is a law that requires agencies to systematically monitor their performance by standards such as efficiency, responsiveness, and outcomes. These standards have long been considered gauges of administrative effectiveness but were often overlooked as bureaucrats went about their customary ways of doing business.

Some analysts question the logic and presumed consequences of the new philosophy of administration. They have asked, for example, whether the principles of decentralized management and market-oriented programs are as sound as their advocates claim. The delegation of control to lower-level administrators weakens the hierarchical connection between elected and administrative officials. A reason for hierarchy is to ensure that decisions made at the bottom of the bureaucracy are faithful to the laws enacted by Congress. Free to act on their own, lower-level administrators, as they did under the spoils system, might favor certain people and interests over others.[34] There is also the issue of the identity of the "customers" in a market-oriented administration.[35] Who are the Security and Exchange Commission's customers—firms, brokerage houses, or shareholders? Won't some agencies inevitably favor their more powerful customers at the expense of their less powerful ones?

Furthermore, there are practical limits on how much the federal bureaucracy can be trimmed. While some activities can be delegated to states and localities and others can be privatized, most of Washington's programs cannot be reassigned. National defense, social security, and Medicare are but three examples, and they alone account for more than half of all federal spending. National problems require national solutions, which is why national crises inevitably bring about an expansion of federal activity and authority. The war on terrorism that began in 2001, for example, has resulted in large increases in federal spending on military defense, intelligence gathering, law enforcement, and homeland security. Nor does the delegation of programs necessarily result in better performance. When the space shuttle Columbia exploded upon reentry in 2003, some analysts suggested that the tragedy was rooted in NASA's decision to assign many of the shuttle program's safety checks to private contractors in order to cut costs.

Thus, although the current wave of administrative reform is unique in its specific elements, it involves long-standing issues about the bureaucracy and about America's national needs. How can the federal government be made more efficient and yet accomplish all that Americans expect of it? How can it be made more responsive and yet act fairly? How can it be made more creative and yet be held accountable? As history makes clear, there are no easy or final answers to these questions.

Self-Test
www.mhhe.com/pattersontad7

Summary

Bureaucracy is a method of organizing people and work, based on the principles of hierarchical authority, job specialization, and formalized rules. As a form of organization, bureaucracy is the most efficient means of getting people to work together on tasks of great magnitude and complexity. It is also a form of organization that is prone to waste and rigidity, which is why efforts are being made to "reinvent" it.

The United States could not be governed without a large federal bureaucracy. The day-to-day work of the federal government, from mail delivery to provision of social security to international diplomacy, is done by the bureaucracy. Federal employees work in roughly four hundred major agencies, including cabinet departments, independent agencies, regulatory agencies, government corporations, and presidential commissions. Yet the bureaucracy is more than simply an administrative giant. Administrators exercise considerable discretion in their policy decisions. In the process of implementing policy, they make important policy and political choices.

Each agency of the federal government was created in response to political demands on national officials. Because of its origins in political demands, the administration of government is necessarily political. An inherent conflict results from two simultaneous but incompatible demands on the bureaucracy: that it respond to the preferences of partisan officials and that it also administer programs fairly and competently. This tension is evident in the three concurrent personnel management systems under which the bureaucracy operates: patronage, merit, and executive leadership.

Administrators are actively engaged in politics and policymaking. The fragmentation of power and the pluralism of the American political system result in a policy process that is continually subject to conflict and contention. There is no clear policy or leadership mandate in the American system, and hence government agencies must compete for the power required to administer their programs effectively. Accordingly, civil servants tend to have an agency point of view: they seek to advance their agency's programs and to repel attempts by others to weaken their position. In promoting their agency, civil servants rely on their policy expertise, the backing of their clientele groups, and the support of the president and Congress.

Administrators are not elected by the people they serve, yet they wield substantial independent power.

Because of this, the bureaucracy's accountability is a central issue. The major checks on the bureaucracy are provided by the president, Congress, and the courts. The president has some power to reorganize the bureaucracy and the authority to appoint the political head of each agency. The president also has management tools (such as the executive budget) that can be used to limit administrators' discretion. Congress has influence on bureaucratic agencies through its authorization and funding powers and through various devices (including sunset laws and oversight hearings) that hold administrators accountable for their actions. The judiciary's role in ensuring the bureaucracy's accountability is smaller than that of the elected branches, but the courts do have the authority to force agencies to act in accordance with legislative intent, established procedures, and constitutionally guaranteed rights. Nevertheless, administrators are not fully accountable. They exercise substantial independent power, a situation not easily reconciled with democratic values.

The National Performance Review is among recent efforts to scale down the federal bureaucracy. The reduction has included cuts in budgets, staff, and organizational units and also has involved changes in the way the bureaucracy does its work. This process is a response to political forces and also to new management theories.

STUDY CORNER

Key Terms

agency point of view (p. 427)
bureaucracy (p. 415)
bureaucratic accountability (p. 431)
cabinet (executive)
    departments (p. 417)
clientele groups (p. 429)
demographic
    representativeness (p. 438)

executive leadership system (p. 424)
formalized rules (p. 415)
government corporations (p. 418)
hierarchical authority (p. 415)
independent agencies (p. 418)
job specialization (p. 415)
merit (civil service) system (p. 423)
neutral competence (p. 423)

patronage system (p. 422)
policy implementation (p. 420)
presidential commissions (p. 419)
regulatory agencies (p. 418)
spoils system (p. 422)
whistle-blowing (p. 437)

Self-Test

1. America's governmental bureaucracy operates under which three personnel management systems?
    a. merit, patronage, civil service
    b. executive leadership, exchange theory, streamlined management
    c. patronage, merit, executive leadership
    d. executive agreements, civil service, merit

2. The strength of bureaucracy as a form of organization is that it:
    a. leads to flexibility in the completion of tasks.
    b. can only be used in the public sector.
    c. is the most efficient means of getting people to work together on tasks of great magnitude.
    d. allows individuals great latitude in making decisions.

3. Bureaucratic accountability through the president includes all of the following **except:**
    a. appointment of agency heads.
    b. budgetary oversight through the Office of Management Budget.
    c. the power to fire at will any civil servant that the president chooses to fire.
    d. the president's authority to recommend the reorganization of federal agencies.

4. Merit hiring has provided all **except** which one of the following advantages?
    a. a more competent work force through use of competitive exams
    b. ability to hire people with special qualifications
    c. greater responsiveness to presidential leadership

d. employees who are likely to treat clients and customers the same whether they are Republicans or Democrats.

5. Sources of bureaucratic power in the federal bureaucracy include all of the following **except:**
    a. power of the meritocracy.
    b. power of expertise.
    c. power of clientele groups.
    d. power of friends in Congress and the White House.

6. The primary function of America's federal bureaucracy is:
    a. oversight of the executive branch.
    b. developing laws for review by Congress.
    c. bringing cases for trial before the Supreme Court.
    d. policy implementation.

7. Bureaucracies are found only in the governmental sector of society and not in the private or corporate sectors. (T/F)

8. Regulatory agencies such as the Securities and Exchange Commission are permitted only to issue advisory opinions to the firms they regulate. Only the judiciary and Congress are allowed to take more decisive action if a firm disregards the law. (T/F)

9. Congress holds the bureaucracy accountable in part through its power to authorize and fund agency programs. (T/F)

10. Once they are in place, federal programs are often terminated at the request of their clientele groups. (T/F)

Critical Thinking

What are the major sources of bureaucrats' power? What mechanisms for controlling that power are available to the president and Congress?

Suggested Readings

Aberbach, Joel D., and Bert A. Rockman. *In the Web of Politics: Two Decades of the U.S. Federal Executive.* Washington, D.C.: Brookings Institution, 2000. An evaluation of the federal bureaucracy and its evolving nature.

Brehm, John, and Scott Gates. *Working, Shirking, and Sabotage: Bureaucratic Response to a Democratic Public.* Ann Arbor: University of Michigan Press, 1996. A generally favorable assessment of the bureaucracy's responsiveness to the public it serves.

Gormley, William T. Jr., and Steven J. Balla. *Bureaucracy and Democracy: Accountability and Performance.* Washington, D.C.: Congressional Quarterly Press, 2003. A close look at the effort to hold agencies accountable.

Kerwin, Cornelius M. *Rulemaking: How Government Agencies Write Law and Make Policy*, 3rd ed. Washington, D.C.: Congressional Quarterly Press, 2003. An analysis of rulemaking in the federal bureaucracy.

Osborne, David, and Ted Gaebler. *Reinventing Government: How the Entrepreneurial Spirit Is Transforming the Public Sector.* New York: Addison-Wesley, 1992. The book that Washington policymakers in the 1990s regarded as the guide to transforming the bureaucracy.

Sagini, Meshack M. *Organizational Behavior: The Challenges of the New Millennium.* Lanham, Md.: University Press of America, 2001. A comprehensive assessment of bureaucratic structures and behaviors.

Wood, B. Dan, and Richard W. Waterman. *Bureaucratic Dynamics: The Role of Bureaucracy in a Democracy.* Boulder, Colo.: Westview Press, 1994. A penetrating analysis of bureaucratic agencies and their power relationships with the president, Congress, and constituent groups.

List Of Websites

http://www.census.gov/

Website of the Census Bureau; the bureau is the best source of statistical information on Americans and the government agencies that administer programs affecting them.

http://www.whistleblower.org/

The Government Accountability Project's website; this project is designed to protect and encourage whistle-blowers by providing information and support to federal employees.

http://www.whitehouse.gov/government/cabinet.html

Lists the cabinet secretaries and provides links to each cabinet-level department.

Participate!

If you are considering a semester or summer internship, you might want to look into working for a federal, state, or local agency. Compared with legislative interns, executive interns are more likely to get paid and to be given significant duties. (Many legislative interns spend the bulk of their time answering phones or responding to mail.) Internship information can often be obtained through an agency's website. You should apply as early as possible; some agencies have application deadlines.

Extra Credit

For up-to-the-minute *New York Times* articles, interactive simulations, graphics, study tools, and more links and quizzes, visit the text's Online Learning Center at www.mhhe.com/pattersontad7.

(Self-Test Answers: 1. c   2. c   3. c   4. c   5. a   6. d   7. F   8. F   9. T   10. F)

14

The Federal Judicial System:
Applying the Law

It is emphatically the province and duty of the judicial department to say what the law is. Those who apply the rule to particular cases, must of necessity expound and interpret that rule. If two laws conflict with each other, the courts must decide on the operation of each.

—*John Marshall*[1]

Through its ruling in *Bush v. Gore*, the U.S. Supreme Court effectively ended the 2000 presidential election.[2] At issue was whether the "undervotes" in Florida—ballots on which counting machines had detected no vote for president—would be tabulated by hand. Florida's top court had ordered a statewide manual recount, but the U.S. Supreme Court by a narrow 5–4 margin had issued a rare emergency order halting the action. Three days later, the Supreme Court's majority delivered its ruling, saying that the manual recount violated the constitution's equal-protection clause. Florida's high court had said that officials should base the hand count on the "intent of the voter." The Supreme Court held that this standard gave county officials in Florida too much leeway and violated the right of citizens to have their votes counted fairly and equally.

The ruling brought charges that the Supreme Court had acted politically rather than on any strict interpretation of the law. In issuing a halt to the recount, the Court had divided sharply along ideological lines. The majority consisted of its most conservative members, all of whom were Republican appointees: Chief Justice William Rehnquist and associate justices Sandra Day O'Connor, Anthony Kennedy, Antonin Scalia, and Clarence Thomas. In a dissenting opinion, Justice John Paul Stevens said, "Preventing the recount from being completed will inevitably cast a doubt upon the legitimacy of the election." Stevens argued that the Florida high court's decision had properly reflected "the basic principle, inherent in our Constitution and our democracy, that every legal vote should be counted."

Bush v. Gore illustrates three key points about court decisions. First, the judiciary is an extremely important policymaking body. Some of its rulings are as consequential as a law passed by Congress or an executive action taken by the president. Second, the judiciary has considerable discretion in its rulings. The *Bush v. Gore* ruling was not based on any literal reading of the law: the justices invoked *their* individual interpretations of the law. Third, the judiciary is a political as well as legal institution. The *Bush v. Gore* case was a product of contending political forces, was developed through a political process, had political content, and was decided by political appointees.

This chapter describes the federal judiciary and the work of its judges and justices. Like the executive and legislative branches, the judiciary is an independent branch of the U.S. government, but unlike the two other branches, its top officials are not elected by the people. The judiciary is not a democratic institution, and its role is different from

Demonstrators rally outside the U.S. Supreme Court building during hearings on the *Bush v. Gore* case that effectively brought the 2000 presidential election to an end. At times, the policy rulings of the judiciary are as significant as the decisions of the president or Congress.

and, in some areas, more controversial than the roles of the executive and legislative branches. This chapter explores this issue in the process of discussing the following main points:

- *The federal judiciary includes the Supreme Court of the United States, which functions mainly as an appellate court; courts of appeals, which hear appeals; and district courts, which hold trials.* Each state has a court system of its own, which for the most part is independent of supervision by the federal courts.

- *Judicial decisions are constrained by applicable constitutional law, statutory and administrative law, and precedent.* Nevertheless, political factors have a major influence on judicial appointments and decisions; judges are political officials as well as legal ones.

- *The judiciary has become an increasingly powerful policymaking body in recent decades, raising the question of the judiciary's proper role in a democracy.* The philosophies of judicial restraint and judicial activism provide different answers to this question.

THE FEDERAL JUDICIAL SYSTEM

The writers of the Constitution were determined that the judiciary would be a separate and independent branch of the federal government but, for practical reasons, did not fully define the federal court system. The Framers established the Supreme Court of the United States but granted to Congress the power to decide the size and structure of the lower federal courts.

Federal judges are nominated by the president and, if confirmed by the U.S. Senate, are appointed by the president to the office. The Constitution states that judges "shall hold their offices during good behavior." However, the Constitution does not contain a precise definition of "good behavior," and no Supreme Court justice and only a tiny number of lower-court judges have been

Should All the Florida Ballots Have Been Counted?

In *Colegrove v. Green* (1946), Justice Felix Frankfurter warned the Supreme Court about getting involved in election politics, saying that it "ought not to enter this political thicket." In 2000, the Court thrust itself into the thorniest political thicket of all—a presidential campaign. In *Bush v. Gore*, the Court by a narrow majority blocked a statewide manual recount of uncounted ballots in Florida, thereby settling the election in favor of Republican George W. Bush. His Democratic opponent, Al Gore, had argued that all the Florida votes—not just those that could be read by machine—should count. Bush supporters retorted that a manual recount would be inherently subjective and open to mischief. These opposing views also existed within the Supreme Court, as the following opinions show.

Debating the Issues

Yes: Florida law holds that all ballots that reveal the intent of the voter constitute valid votes. . . . [The Florida Supreme Court] decided the case before it in light of the legislature's intent to leave no legally cast vote uncounted. In so doing, it relied on the sufficiency of the general "intent of the voter" standard articulated by the state legislature, coupled with a procedure for ultimate review by an impartial judge, to resolve the concern about disparate evaluations of contested ballots. If we assume—as I do—that the members of that court and the judges who would have carried out its mandate are impartial, its decision does not even raise a colorable federal question. . . . What must underlie petitioners' entire federal assault on the Florida election procedures is an unstated lack of confidence in the impartiality and capacity of the state judges who would make the critical decisions if the vote count were to proceed. Otherwise, their position is wholly without merit. . . . Although we may never know with complete certainty the identity of the winner of this year's Presidential election, the identity of the loser is perfectly clear. It is the Nation's confidence in the judge as an impartial guardian of the rule of law.

—John Paul Stevens, associate justice of the Supreme Court

No: The standards for accepting or rejecting contested ballots might vary not only from county to county but indeed within a single county from one recount team to another. . . . The question before the Court is not whether local entities, in the exercise of their expertise, may develop different systems for implementing elections. Instead, we are presented with a situation where a state court with the power to assure uniformity has ordered a statewide recount with minimal procedural safeguards. . . . It is obvious that the recount cannot be conducted in compliance with the requirements of equal protection and due process without substantial additional work. It would require not only the adoption (after opportunity for argument) of adequate statewide standards for determining what is a legal vote, and practicable procedures to implement them, but also orderly judicial review of any disputed matters that might arise. . . . The Supreme Court of Florida has said that the legislature intended the State's electors to "participat[e] fully in the federal electoral process." That statute, in turn, requires that any controversy or contest that is designed to lead to a conclusive selection of electors be completed by December 12. That date is upon us, and there is no recount procedure in place under the State Supreme Court's order that comports with minimal constitutional standards.

—Supreme Court's majority opinion

removed from office through impeachment and conviction by Congress. In practice, federal judges and justices serve until they retire or die.

Unlike the situation for the offices of president, senator, and representative, the Constitution places no age, residency, or citizenship qualifications on federal judicial office. Nor does the Constitution require a judge to have legal training. Tradition alone dictates that federal judges have an educational or professional background in the law.

The Supreme Court of the United States

The Supreme Court of the United States is the nation's highest court. The chief justice of the United States presides over the Supreme Court and, like the eight associate justices, is nominated by the president and is subject to Senate confirmation. The chief justice has the same voting power as the other justices but usually has exercised additional influence because of the position's leadership role.

The Constitution grants the Supreme Court both original and appellate jurisdiction. A court's **jurisdiction** is its authority to hear cases of a particular type. **Original jurisdiction** is the authority to be the first court to hear a case. The Supreme Court's original jurisdiction embraces legal disputes involving foreign diplomats and those in which the opposing parties are state governments. The Court in its entire history has convened as a court of original jurisdiction only a few hundred times and has rarely done so in recent years.

The Supreme Court does its most significant work as an appellate court. **Appellate jurisdiction** is the authority to review cases that have already been heard in lower courts and are appealed to a higher court by the losing party; these higher courts are called appeals courts or appellate courts. The Supreme Court's appellate jurisdiction extends to cases arising under the Constitution, federal law and regulations, and treaties. The Court also hears appeals involving admiralty or maritime issues and legal controversies that cross state or national boundaries. Appellate courts, including the Supreme Court, do not retry cases; rather, they determine whether a trial court acted in accord with applicable law.

Selecting and Deciding Cases

The primary function of the judiciary is to interpret the law in such a way that rules made in the past (for example, the Constitution or legislation) can be applied reasonably in the present. This function gives the courts—all courts—a role in policymaking. Antitrust legislation, for example, is designed to prevent uncompetitive business practices, but like all such legislation, it is not self-enforcing. It is up to the courts to decide whether and how these laws apply to the case at hand.

As the nation's highest court, the Supreme Court is particularly important in establishing legal precedents that guide lower courts. A **precedent** is a judicial decision that serves as a rule for settling subsequent cases of a similar nature. Lower courts are expected to follow precedent—that is, to resolve cases of a like nature in ways consistent with upper-court rulings. However, for reasons that will be explained later in this chapter, they do not always do so.

The Supreme Court's ability to set legal precedent is strengthened by its nearly complete discretion in choosing the cases it will hear. The large majority of cases that reach the Supreme Court do so through a **writ of certiorari** in which the losing party in a lower-court case explains in writing why its case should be ruled on by the Court. Four of the nine justices must agree to accept a particular case before it is granted a writ. Each year roughly seven thousand parties apply for certiorari, but the Court accepts only about a hundred cases for

---

jurisdiction (of a court) A given court's authority to hear cases of a particular kind. Jurisdiction may be original or appellate.

original jurisdiction The authority of a given court to be the first court to hear a case.

appellate jurisdiction The authority of a given court to review cases that have already been tried in lower courts and are appealed to it by the losing party; such a court is called an appeals court or appellate court.

precedent A judicial decision that serves as a rule for settling subsequent cases of a similar nature.

writ of certiorari Permission granted by a higher court to allow a losing party in a legal case to bring the case before it for a ruling; when such a writ is requested of the U.S. Supreme Court, four of the Court's nine justices must agree to accept the case before it is granted certiorari.

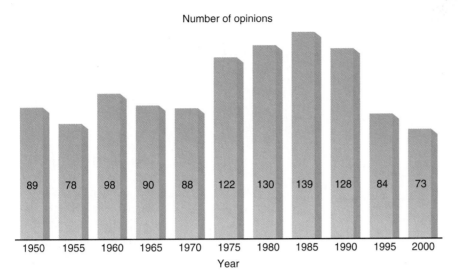

Number of opinions

| 89 | 78 | 98 | 90 | 88 | 122 | 130 | 139 | 128 | 84 | 73 |
| 1950 | 1955 | 1960 | 1965 | 1970 | 1975 | 1980 | 1985 | 1990 | 1995 | 2000 |

Year

Figure 14–1

Supreme Court Opinions, 1950–2000

The number of signed Supreme Court opinions each term is relatively small. The Court has considerable control over the cases it selects. The cases that are heard by the Supreme Court tend to be ones that have legal significance beyond the particular case itself. The Court's term runs from October 1 to June 30; the year indicated is the closing year of the term.

Source: Supreme Court of the United States.

a full hearing and signed ruling (see Figure 14–1). The Court issues another one hundred to two hundred per curiam ("by the court") decisions each year. Typically, these decisions are very brief, are issued without a hearing, and are a response to relatively noncontroversial issues. They are issued in the name of the full Court rather than signed by the particular justices who wrote the opinion.

The Court is most likely to grant certiorari when the U.S. government through the **solicitor general** (the high-ranking Justice Department official who serves as the government's lawyer in Supreme Court cases) requests it.[3] The solicitor general tracks cases in which the federal government is a party. When the government loses a case in lower court, the solicitor general decides whether to appeal it to the Supreme Court. Such cases often make up half or more of the cases the Court hears in a term.

The Court seldom accepts a routine case, even if the justices believe that a lower court has erred. The Supreme Court's job is not to correct every mistake of other courts but to resolve broad legal questions. As a result, the justices usually choose cases that involve substantial legal issues. This vague criterion essentially means that a case must center on an issue of significance not merely to the parties involved but to the nation. As a result, most cases heard by the Court raise major constitutional issues, affect the lives of many Americans, address issues that are being decided inconsistently by the lower courts, or involve rulings that conflict with a previous Supreme Court ruling.[4] When the Court does accept a case, chances are that most of the justices disagree with the lower court's ruling. In recent years, about three-fourths of the Supreme Court's decisions have reversed the judgments of lower courts.[5]

Once the Supreme Court accepts a case, it sets a date on which the attorneys for the two sides will present their oral arguments. Strict time limits, usually thirty minutes per side, are placed on these arguments. However, the oral arguments are less important than the lengthy written **brief** submitted earlier by each side, which contains the side's complete argument.

solicitor general The high-ranking Justice Department official who serves as the government's lawyer in Supreme Court cases.

brief A written statement by a party in a court case that details its argument.

The Supreme Court building is located across from the Capitol in Washington, D.C. The courtroom, the justices' offices, and the conference room are on the first floor. Administrative staff offices and the Court's records and reference materials occupy the other floors.

judicial conference A closed meeting of the justices of the U.S. Supreme Court to discuss and vote on the cases before them; the justices are not supposed to discuss conference proceedings with outsiders.

decision A vote of the Supreme Court in a particular case that indicates which party the justices side with and by how large a margin.

opinion (of a court) A court's written explanation of its decision, which serves to inform others of the legal basis for the decision. Supreme Court opinions are expected to guide the decisions of other courts.

majority opinion A court opinion that results when a majority of the justices are in agreement on the legal basis of the decision.

plurality opinion A court opinion that results when a majority of justices agree on a decision in a case but do not agree on the legal basis for the decision. In this instance, the legal position held by most of the justices on the winning side is called a plurality opinion.

concurring opinion A separate opinion written by a Supreme Court justice who votes with the majority in the decision on a case but who disagrees with their reasoning.

The oral session is also far less important than the **judicial conference** that follows, which is attended only by the nine justices. The conference's proceedings are kept strictly confidential. This secrecy allows the justices to speak freely about a case and to change their minds as the discussion unfolds.[6] After the discussion, the justices vote on the case.

Issuing Decisions and Opinions

After a case has been decided on in conference, the Court prepares and issues its ruling, which consists of a decision and one or more opinions. The **decision** indicates which party the Court supports and by how large a margin. The **opinion** explains the reasons behind the decision. The opinion is the most important part of a Supreme Court ruling because it informs others of the justices' interpretations of laws. For example, in the landmark *Brown v. Board of Education of Topeka* (1954) opinion, the Court held that government-sponsored school segregation was unconstitutional because it violated the Fourteenth Amendment provision that guarantees equal protection under the laws to all citizens. This opinion became the legal basis by which communities throughout the southern states were ordered by lower courts to end their policy of segregating public school students by race.

When a majority of the justices agree on the legal basis of a decision, the result is a **majority opinion.** In some cases there is no majority opinion because a majority of the justices agree on the decision but cannot agree on the legal basis for it. The result in such cases is a **plurality opinion,** which presents the view held by most of the justices who side with the winning party. Another type of opinion is a **concurring opinion,** which is a separate view written by a justice who votes with the majority but disagrees with its reasoning.

Types of Supreme Court Opinions

Per curiam: Unsigned decision of the Court that states the facts of the case and the Court's ruling.

Majority opinion: A written opinion of the majority of the Court's justices stating the reasoning underlying their decision on a case.

Plurality opinion: A written opinion that in the absence of a majority opinion presents the reasoning of most of the justices who side with the winning party.

Concurring opinion: A written opinion of one or more justices who support the majority position but disagree with the majority's reasoning on a case. This opinion expresses the reasoning of the concurring justices.

Dissenting opinion: A written opinion of one or more justices who disagree with the majority's decision and opinion. This opinion provides the reasoning underlying the dissent.

Justices on the losing side can write a **dissenting opinion** to explain their reasons for disagreeing with the majority position. Sometimes these dissenting arguments become the foundation of subsequent decisions. In a 1942 dissenting opinion, Justice Hugo Black wrote that defendants in state felony trials should have legal counsel even if they could not afford to pay for it. Two decades later, in *Gideon v. Wainwright* (1963), the Court adopted Justice Black's position.[7]

When part of the majority, the chief justice decides which justice will write the majority opinion. Otherwise, the senior justice in the majority determines the author. Chief justices have often given themselves the influential task of writing the majority opinion in important cases. John Marshall did so often: *Marbury v. Madison* (1802) and *McCulloch v. Maryland* (1819) were among the opinions he wrote. The justice who writes the Court's majority opinion has the responsibility to express accurately the majority's reasoning. The vote on a case is not considered final until the opinion is written and agreed upon, so plenty of give-and-take can occur during the writing stage.

> **dissenting opinion** The opinion of a justice in a Supreme Court case that explains his or her reasons for disagreeing with the majority's decision.

Other Federal Courts

There are more than one hundred federal courts but only one Supreme Court, and its position at the top of the country's judicial system gives the Supreme Court unparalleled importance. It is a mistake, however, to conclude that the Supreme Court is the only court of consequence. Judge Jerome Frank once wrote of the "upper-court myth," which is the view that appellate courts, and in particular the Supreme Court, make up the only truly significant judicial arena and that lower courts just dutifully follow the rulings handed down by courts at the appellate level.[8] The reality is very different, as the following discussion explains.

U.S. District Courts

The lowest federal courts are the district courts (see Figure 14–2). There are more than ninety federal district courts altogether—at least one in every state and as many as four in some states. District court judges, who number about

Figure 14–2

The Federal Judicial System
The simplified diagram shows the relationships among the various levels of federal courts and between state and federal courts. The losing party in a case can appeal a lower-court decision to the court at the next-highest level, as the arrows indicate. Decisions normally can be moved from state courts to federal courts only if they raise a constitutional question.

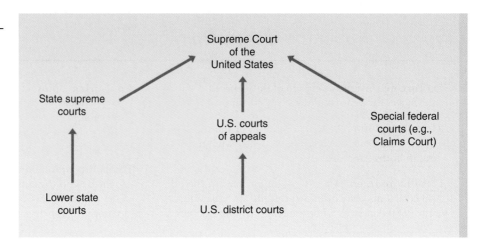

eight hundred in all, are appointed by the president with the consent of the Senate. Federal cases usually originate in district courts, which are trial courts where the parties argue their sides. District courts are the only courts in the federal system in which juries hear testimony. Most cases at this level are presented before a single judge.

Lower federal courts unquestionably rely on and follow Supreme Court decisions in their own rulings. The Supreme Court reiterated this requirement in a 1982 case, *Hutto v. Davis:* "Unless we wish anarchy to prevail within the federal judicial system, a precedent of this Court must be followed by the lower federal courts no matter how misguided the judges of those courts may think it to be."[9]

However, the idea that lower courts are guided strictly by Supreme Court rulings is part of the upper-court myth. District court judges may misunderstand the Supreme Court's position and deviate from it for that reason. In addition, the facts of a case before a district court are seldom identical to those of a case settled by the Supreme Court. The lower-court judge must decide whether a different legal judgment is appropriate. Finally, it is not unusual for the Supreme Court to issue a general ruling that is ambiguous enough to give lower courts some flexibility in deciding similar cases that come before them. Trial court judges then have a creative role in judicial decision making that rivals that of appellate court judges.

Most federal cases end with the district court's decision; the losing party does not appeal the decision to a higher court. This fact is another indication of the highly significant role of district court judges.

U.S. Courts of Appeals

When cases are appealed from district courts, they go to a federal court of appeals. These appellate courts make up the second level of the federal court system. Courts of appeals do not use juries. No new evidence is ordinarily submitted in an appealed case; rather, appellate courts base their decisions on a review of lower-court records. Appellate judges act as supervisors in the legal system, reviewing trial court decisions and correcting what they consider to be legal errors. Facts (i.e., the circumstances of a case) found by district courts are ordinarily presumed to be correct.

The Supreme Court is not the only federal court that "matters" in the American judicial system. Most federal cases originate in U.S. district courts, and most appealed cases are settled in U.S. courts of appeals, never reaching the Supreme Court. Shown here is testimony being given at a trial in district court, the only level in the federal system at which juries decide the outcome of cases.

The United States has twelve general appeals courts, each of which serves a "circuit" comprised of between three and nine states, except for the circuit that serves the District of Columbia only. In addition, the U.S. Court of Appeals for the Federal Circuit specializes in appeals of cases involving patents and international trade. Between four and twenty-six judges sit on each court of appeals, but each case is usually heard by a panel of three judges. On rare occasions, all the judges of a court of appeals sit as a body (*en banc*) in order to resolve difficult controversies, typically ones that have resulted in conflicting decisions within the same circuit. Each circuit is monitored by a Supreme Court justice, who normally takes the lead in reviewing appeals originating in that circuit.

Courts of appeals offer the only real hope of reversal for many appellants, because the Supreme Court hears so few cases. The Supreme Court reviews less than 1 percent of the cases heard by federal appeals courts.

Special U.S. Courts

In addition to the Supreme Court, the courts of appeals, and the district courts, the federal judiciary includes a few specialty courts. Among them are the U.S. Claims Court, which hears cases in which the U.S. government is being sued for damages; the U.S. Court of International Trade, which handles cases involving appeals of U.S. Customs Office rulings; and the U.S. Court of Military Appeals, which hears appeals of military courts-martial. Some federal agencies and commissions also have judicial powers (for example, the issuing of fines), and their decisions can be appealed to a federal court of appeals.

The State Courts

The American states are separate governments within the United State's federal system. The Tenth Amendment protects each state in its sovereignty, and each state has its own court system. Like the federal courts, state court systems have trial courts at the bottom level and appellate courts at the top.

GLOBAL Perspective

Americans in an Interdependent World

The International Criminal Court

After World War II, the United States led the way in establishing the temporary Nuremberg and Tokyo tribunals to try German and Japanese leaders accused of war crimes. The third such temporary tribunal in modern history is now under way at The Hague, Netherlands. The International Criminal Tribunal was established several years ago to assess the guilt and innocence of the people accused of war crimes in the Balkan wars of the 1990s. Slobodan Milosevic, the president of the former Yugoslavia, is the most prominent defendant.

In 1998, 120 member countries of the United Nations endorsed a plan to create, for the first time in world history, a permanent international court to handle atrocities committed under the guise of war. Although such atrocities in an earlier time might not have attracted worldwide attention, the globalization of the media and the widening role of international bodies such as the United Nations now ensure that they will be noticed. The permanent court—which is called the International Criminal Court (ICC)—will handle such cases. At the 1998 conference, it was decided that the ICC would begin its work after sixty nations had ratified the treaty authorizing it. This threshold was reached in 2002.

Not every nation supports the ICC. The United States is among the holdouts. The Bush administration refused to endorse the treaty, and a majority in Congress oppose its ratification. Many U.S. policymakers fear that an American might someday be brought before the ICC, which provides fewer legal protections than Americans enjoy under the Constitution. For example, the ICC offers no right to a trial by jury, and a majority vote of the judges is sufficient for conviction.

A larger concern of U.S. policymakers is that the ICC will become a means by which other countries would put American soldiers on trial. During the Iraq conflict, for example, U.S. forces killed several thousand noncombatants and abused dozens of Iraqi prisoners. Were such actions the unfortunate consequences of a deadly war, or were they, in some instances, crimes of war? Many U.S. leaders would prefer to leave that judgment to U.S. courts rather than entrusting it to the international court.

Some analysts believe that the United States has more to lose than to gain by refusing to support the International Criminal Court. They argue that the United States has enough clout in international circles to prevent the court from becoming a weapon in the hands of the nation's enemies. They say the only countries that need to fear the international court are autocratic regimes that use wanton murder and terrorism as instruments of national policy. They also point out that, under the ICC's rules, a nation has the option of trying in its own court system any of its citizens who are accused of war crimes.

Where do you stand on the question of whether the world needs the International Criminal Court and whether the United States should participate in it?

Each state decides for itself the structure of its courts and the method of judicial appointment. In some states judges are appointed by the governor, but in most states judgeships are *elective offices*. The common form involves competitive elections of either a partisan or a nonpartisan nature, although some states use a system called the *merit plan* (also called the "Missouri Plan" because Missouri was the first state to use it) under which the governor selects a judge

STATES IN THE NATION

Principal Methods of Selecting State Judges

The states use a variety of methods for selecting the judges on their highest court, including the merit plan, election, and political appointment. The states that appoint judges grant this power to the governor, except in Virginia, Connecticut, and South Carolina, where the legislature makes the choice.

Q. What might explain why a bloc of states in the middle of the nation use the merit plan for selecting judges?

A. The merit plan originated in the state of Missouri. Innovations in one state sometimes spread to adjacent states that have similar political cultures.

Source: Council of State Governments.

from a short list of acceptable candidates provided by a judicial selection commission. To stay on the bench, the judge selected must periodically receive the voters' support in a "yes" or "no" election (see "States in the Nation").

Besides the upper-court myth, there exists a "federal court myth," which holds that the federal judiciary is the most significant part of the judicial system and that state courts play a subordinate role. This view also is inaccurate. More than 95 percent of the nation's legal cases are decided in state courts. Most

The Florida Supreme Court hears the arguments that led it to order a statewide canvass of uncounted ballots in the Bush-Gore presidential contest. Less than a day after it was rendered, the court's order was blocked by the U.S. Supreme Court. It was a rare intervention. Upward of 95 percent of the nation's legal cases are decided entirely within the state court system, a refutation of the federal court myth.

crimes (from shoplifting to murder) and most civil controversies (such as divorces and business disputes) are defined by state or local law. Moreover, nearly all cases that originate in state courts also end there. The federal courts don't come into the picture because the case does not involve a federal issue.

In state criminal cases, after a person has been convicted and after all avenues of appeal in the state court system have been exhausted, the defendant can seek a writ of habeas corpus from a federal district court on grounds that constitutional rights were violated—as, for example, in a claim that local police failed to inform the suspect of the right to remain silent (see Chapter 4). If it accepts such an appeal, the federal court ordinarily confines itself to the federal aspects of the matter, such as whether the defendant's constitutional rights were in fact violated. In addition, the federal court accepts the facts determined by the state court unless such findings are clearly in error. In short, legal and factual determinations of state courts can bind the federal courts—a clear contradiction of the federal court myth.

However, issues traditionally within the jurisdiction of the states can become federal issues through the rulings of federal courts. In its *Lawrence v. Texas* decision in 2003, for example, the Supreme Court invalidated state laws that made it illegal for consenting adults of the same sex to engage in private sexual relations.[10] Earlier, the Court had held that states had the authority to decide for themselves whether to prohibit such acts.[11]

FEDERAL COURT APPOINTEES

The quiet dignity of the courtroom and the lack of fanfare with which a court delivers its decisions give the impression that the judiciary is as far removed from the world of politics as a governmental institution can possibly be. In reality, federal judges and justices are political officials who exercise the authority of a separate and powerful branch of government. All federal jurists bring their political views with them to the courtroom and have regular opportunities to

The justices of the U.S. Supreme Court pose for a photo. From left, they are: Clarence Thomas, Antonin Scalia, Sandra Day O'Connor, Anthony Kennedy, David Souter, Stephen Breyer, John Paul Stevens, Chief Justice William Rehnquist, and Ruth Bader Ginsburg.

promote their political beliefs through the cases they decide. Not surprisingly, the process by which federal judges are appointed is a partisan one.

The Selection of Supreme Court Justices and Federal Judges

The formal mechanism for appointments to the Supreme Court and the lower federal courts is the same: the president nominates, and the Senate confirms or rejects. Beyond that basic similarity, however, there are significant differences.

Supreme Court Nominees

A Supreme Court appointment is a critical choice for a president.[12] The cases that come before the Court tend to be controversial and to have far-reaching implications. And because the Court is a small body, each justice's vote can be crucial to the decisions it makes. Because most justices retain their positions for many years, presidents can influence judicial policy through their appointments long after they have left office. The careers of some Supreme Court justices provide dramatic testimony to the enduring effects of judicial appointments. Franklin D. Roosevelt appointed William O. Douglas to the Supreme Court in 1939, and for thirty years after Roosevelt's death in 1945, Douglas remained a strong liberal influence on the Court.

Presidents invariably seek nominees who share their political philosophy, but they also must take into account a nominee's acceptability to others. Every nominee is closely scrutinized by the legal community, interested groups, and the media; must undergo an extensive background check by the FBI; and then must gain the approval of a Senate majority. Within the Senate, the key body is the Judiciary Committee, whose members have responsibility for conducting hearings on judicial nominees and recommending their confirmation or rejection by the full Senate.

President Dwight D. Eisenhower shakes hands with William Brennan in the Oval Office after selecting Brennan to be an associate justice of the Supreme Court. Eisenhower would later say that he made a mistake in appointing Brennan to the Court. Brennan's decisions were more liberal than Eisenhower had expected.

Nearly 20 percent of presidential nominees to the Supreme Court have been rejected by the Senate on grounds of judicial qualification, political views, personal ethics, or partisanship. Most of these rejections occurred before 1900, and partisan politics was the main reason. Today a nominee with strong professional and ethical credentials is less likely to be blocked for partisan reasons alone. An exception was Robert Bork, whose 1987 nomination by President Reagan was rejected primarily because of strong opposition from Senate Democrats who disagreed with his judicial philosophy. On the other hand, nominees can expect easy confirmation if they have an unblemished personal background, hold relatively moderate views, and are selected through a process that makes some allowance for the views of senators of the opposing party. One such nominee, Ruth Bader Ginsburg, who was nominated by President Clinton in 1993, was confirmed by a 96–3 Senate vote.

Lower-Court Nominees

The president normally delegates to the deputy attorney general the task of screening potential nominees for lower-court judgeships. **Senatorial courtesy** is also a consideration in these appointments; this tradition, which dates back to the 1840s, holds that a senator from the state in which a vacancy has arisen should be given a say in the nomination if the senator is of the same party as the president.[13] If not consulted, the senator involved can request that confirmation be denied, and other senators will normally grant the request as a "courtesy" to their colleague. Not surprisingly, presidents have preferred to give senators a voice in judicial appointments.

senatorial courtesy The tradition that a U.S. senator from the state in which a federal judicial vacancy has arisen should have a say in the president's nomination of the new judge if the senator is of the same party as the president.

Although the president does not become as personally involved in selecting lower-court nominees as in naming potential Supreme Court justices, lower-court appointments are collectively a significant factor in the impact of a president's Administration. Recent presidents have appointed about two hundred judges during a four-year term of office.

Justices and Judges as Political Officials

Presidents generally manage to appoint jurists who have a similar political philosophy. Although Supreme Court justices are free to make their own decisions, their legal positions usually can be inferred from their prior work. A study by judicial scholar Robert Scigliano found that about three of every four appointees have behaved on the Supreme Court approximately as presidents could have expected.[14] Of course, a president has no guarantee that a nominee will fulfill

Why Should I Care?

Judicial Appointments

As a presidential campaign draws to a close, supporters of both candidates urge people to consider that, in choosing a president, they are also deciding who will be appointed to positions on the federal courts. Judging from opinion polls, not many voters are swayed one way or the other by this argument.

Nevertheless, the argument has some basis. For one thing, judicial appointments are essentially lifetime appointments, which means that a judicial nominee is likely to hold office long after the president leaves the White House. The most renowned jurist in American history, John Marshall, was appointed chief justice in 1801 by the second president, John Adams, and served until 1835, when the seventh president, Andrew Jackson, was nearing the end of his second term.

Second, the judiciary is a powerful and independent branch of the federal government. Because the United States has a federal system and a separation of powers, the judiciary is thrust into the middle of many controversies. The French theorist Alexis de Tocqueville observed that there is barely a political controversy in America that sooner or later does not become also a judicial controversy. Abortion, age-related discrimination, and Internet content are but a few recent examples. Moreover, unlike some national courts, U.S. federal courts have the power of judicial review. They are not simply empowered to hear cases arising under statutory and administrative law. They can invalidate state and national law if they conclude it violates the U.S. Constitution.

Third, partisanship affects the decisions that judges and justices make. Although the law is supposedly neutral, the partisan leanings of a judicial officer can affect the outcome of a case, particularly when the facts are murky or the applicable laws are vague. On civil rights cases, for example, there is a small but measurable tendency for Democratic appointees to side more often with the party alleging discrimination and for Republican appointees to side more often with the party alleged to have engaged in discrimination.

In sum, a president's judicial appointments are consequential. Whether you should weigh this fact heavily when you choose a presidential candidate is debatable, but you should not doubt that a president's nominees will leave their imprint on the law for years to come.

---

his hopes. Justices Earl Warren and William Brennan proved to be more liberal than President Dwight D. Eisenhower had anticipated. Asked whether he had made any mistakes as president, Eisenhower replied, "Yes, two, and they are both sitting on the Supreme Court."[15]

The Role of Partisanship

In nearly every instance, presidents have chosen members of their own party as Supreme Court nominees. Partisanship is also decisive in nominations to lower-court judgeships. More than 90 percent of recent district and appeals court nominees have been members of the president's own party.[16]

The fact that judges and justices are chosen through a partisan political process should not be interpreted to mean that they engage in blatant partisanship while on the bench. Judges and justices are officers of a separate branch and prize their judicial independence. All Republican appointees do not vote the same way on cases, nor do all Democratic appointees. Nevertheless, partisanship influences judicial decisions. A study of the voting records of appellate court judges, for example, found that Republican appointees are less likely than

TABLE 14-1	Justices of the Supreme Court, 2004 Most recent appointees held an appellate court position before being nominated to the Supreme Court.		
JUSTICE	YEAR OF APPOINTMENT	NOMINATING PRESIDENT	POSITION BEFORE APPOINTMENT
William Rehnquist*	1971	Nixon	Assistant attorney general
John Paul Stevens	1975	Ford	Judge, U.S. Court of Appeals
Sandra Day O'Connor	1981	Reagan	Judge, Arizona Court of Appeals
Antonin Scalia	1986	Reagan	Judge, U.S. Court of Appeals
Anthony Kennedy	1988	Reagan	Judge, U.S. Court of Appeals
David Souter	1990	Bush	Judge, U.S. Court of Appeals
Clarence Thomas	1991	Bush	Judge, U.S. Court of Appeals
Ruth Bader Ginsburg	1993	Clinton	Judge, U.S. Court of Appeals
Stephen Breyer	1994	Clinton	Judge, U.S. Court of Appeals

*Appointed chief justice in 1986.

Democratic appointees to side with parties that claim their civil rights or civil liberties have been violated.[17]

Other Characteristics of Judicial Appointees

In recent years, increasing numbers of federal justices and judges have had prior judicial experience; the assumption is that such individuals are best qualified for appointment to the federal bench. Most recent appellate court appointees have been district or state judges or have worked in the office of the attorney general.[18] Elective office (particularly a seat in the U.S. Senate) was once a common route to the Supreme Court,[19] but recent justices have typically held an appellate court judgeship before their appointment (see Table 14–1).

White males are greatly overrepresented on the federal bench, just as they dominate in Congress and at the top levels of the executive branch. However, the number of women and minority-group judges increased substantially as a result of the judicial appointments of President Clinton, a Democrat. Women and minority-group members are key constituencies of the Democratic party, and, not surprisingly, Democratic presidents have been more likely than Republican presidents to appoint them to the federal bench (see Figure 14–3).

The Supreme Court itself is demographically unrepresentative. Until 1916, when Louis D. Brandeis was appointed to the Court, no Jewish justice had ever served. At least one Catholic, but at most times only one, has been on the Court almost continuously for nearly a century. Thurgood Marshall in 1967 became the first black justice, and Sandra Day O'Connor in 1981 became the first woman justice. Antonin Scalia in 1986 became the Court's first justice of Italian descent. No person of Hispanic or Asian descent has ever been a member of the Court.

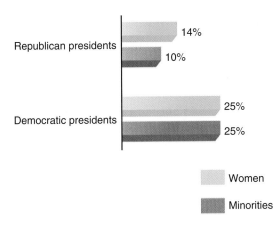

Figure 14–3

Political Parties, Presidents, and Women and Minority Judicial Appointees
Reflecting differences in their parties' coalitions, recent Republican and Democratic presidents have quite different records in terms of the percentage of their judicial appointees who have been women or minority-group members.
Source: Federal Judicial Center, 2004. Data based on appointees of Presidents Carter, Reagan, Bush (the elder), Clinton, and Bush (the younger).

THE NATURE OF JUDICIAL DECISION MAKING

Federal judges and justices are political officials: they constitute one of three co-equal branches of the national government. Yet, unlike members of Congress or the president, judges serve in a legal institution and make their decisions in a legal context. As a consequence, their discretionary power is less than that of elected officials. Article III of the Constitution bars a federal court from issuing a decision except in response to an actual case presented to it. As federal judge David Bazelon noted, a judge "can't wake up one morning and simply decide to give a helpful little push to a school system, a mental hospital, or the local housing agency."[20]

Judicial decisions are also restricted in scope. Technically, a court ruling is binding only on the parties involved. Its broader impact depends on the willingness of others to follow its lead. For example, if a court should decide that a school is bound by law to spend more on programs for the learning-disabled, the ruling would extend to other schools in the same situation only if those schools voluntarily responded or were forced by subsequent court action to do so. By comparison, if Congress were to pass legislation granting funds for programs for the learning-disabled, all eligible schools would receive the funding.

Another major restriction on the courts is the law itself. Although a president or Congress can make almost any decision that is politically acceptable, the judiciary must justify its decisions in terms of existing provisions of the law. When asked by a friend to "do justice," Oliver Wendell Holmes Jr. replied, "That is not my job. My job is to play the game according to the rules."[21] In playing according to the rules, judges engage in a creative legal process that requires them to identify the facts of the case, determine and sometimes formulate the relevant legal principles or rules, and then apply these to the case at hand.

The Constraints of the Facts

facts (of a court case) The relevant circumstances of a legal dispute or offense as determined by a trial court. The facts of a case are crucial because they help determine which law or laws are applicable in the case.

A basic distinction in any legal case is between "the facts" and "the laws." The **facts** of a case, as determined by trial courts, are the relevant circumstances of a legal dispute or offense. In the case of a person accused of murder, for example, key facts would include evidence about the murder and whether the rights of the accused were respected by police in the course of their investigation. The facts of a case are crucial because they determine which law or laws are applicable to the case. The courts must respond to the facts of a dispute. This restriction is a very substantial one. A murder case cannot be used as an occasion to pronounce judgment on freedom of religion, for example.

The Constraints of the Law

laws (of a court case) The constitutional provisions, legislative statutes, or judicial precedents that apply to a court case.

In deciding cases, the judiciary is also constrained by existing **laws.** To use an obvious comparison, the laws that apply to a case of alleged murder differ from those that apply to a case of alleged shoplifting. A judge must treat a murder case as a murder case, applying to it the laws that define murder and the penalties that can be imposed when someone is found guilty of that crime.

There are three sources of law that constrain the courts: the Constitution, statutes (and the administrative regulations derived from them), and precedents established by previous court rulings.

The Constitution and Its Interpretation

The Constitution of the United States is the nation's highest law, and judges and justices are sworn to uphold it. When a case raises a constitutional issue, a court has the duty to apply the Constitution to the case. For example, the Constitution prohibits the states from printing their own currency. If a state decided that it would do so anyway, a federal judge would be obligated to rule against the practice.

Nevertheless, constitutional provisions are open to interpretation in some cases. For example, the Fourth Amendment of the Constitution protects individuals against "unreasonable searches and seizures," but the meaning of "unreasonable" is not specified. Judges must decide upon its meaning in particular situations. Take, for example, the question of whether wiretapping, which was not invented until 150 years after ratification of the Fourth Amendment, is included in the prohibition on unreasonable searches and seizures. Reasoning that the Fourth Amendment was intended to protect individuals from government intrusion in their private lives, judges have ruled that indiscriminate wiretapping is unconstitutional.

criminal law cases Disputes in which an individual is charged by government with engaging in an act that is prohibited by law.

Statutes, Administrative Laws, and Their Interpretation

civil law cases Disputes between parties where no criminal act is alleged and where the parties are making conflicting claims, as in a property dispute.

The vast majority of cases that arise in courts involve issues of statutory and administrative law rather than constitutional law. Most **criminal law cases** (where an individual is charged with engaging in an illegal act, such as theft or murder) and **civil law cases** (where the parties are engaged in a noncriminal dispute, such as divorce proceedings or conflicting property claims) are covered either

Sources of Law That Constrain the Decisions of the Federal Judiciary

U.S. Constitution: The federal courts are bound by the provisions of the U.S. Constitution. The sparseness of its wording, however, requires the Constitution to be applied in the light of present circumstances. Thus, judges are accorded some degree of discretion in their constitutional judgments.

Statutory law: The federal courts are constrained by statutes and by administrative regulations derived from the provisions of statutes. Most laws, however, are somewhat vague in their provisions and often have unanticipated applications. As a result, judges have some freedom in deciding cases based on statutes.

Precedent: Federal courts tend to follow precedent (or stare decisis), which is a legal principle developed through earlier court decisions. Because times change and not all cases have a clear precedent, judges have some discretion in their evaluation of the way earlier cases apply to a current case.

by laws (statutes) created by legislative action or by administrative regulations that have been developed by government agencies on the basis of statutory law.

All federal courts are bound by federal statutes (laws passed by Congress) and by federal administrative regulations, as well as by treaties. When hearing a case involving statutory law or administrative regulation, judges must work within the limits of the applicable law or regulation. A company that is charged with violating federal environmental law will be judged within the context of that law—what it permits and what it prohibits, and the penalties that apply if the company is found to have broken the law.

When hearing such a case, judges will often try to determine whether the meaning of the statute or regulation can be determined by common sense (the "plain meaning rule"). The question for the judge is what the law or regulation was intended to safeguard (such as a particular issue of environmental protection). The law or regulation in most cases is clear enough that when the facts of the case are considered, the decision is fairly predictable. Not all cases, however, are clear-cut in their facts or in the applicable law or laws. Where, for example, do college admissions programs that take race into account cross the line from legal to illegal by placing too much weight on race? In such instances, courts have no choice but to exercise their judgment.

Legal Precedents (Previous Rulings) and Their Interpretation

The U.S. legal system developed from the English common-law tradition, which includes the principle that a court's decision on a case should be consistent with previous judicial rulings. This principle, known as precedent, reflects the philosophy of stare decisis (Latin for "to stand by things that have been settled"). Precedent holds that principles of law, once established, should be accepted as authoritative in subsequent similar cases. Judges and justices often cite past rulings as justification for their decisions in the cases before them.

Precedent is important because it gives predictability to the application of law. Government has an obligation to make clear what its laws are and how they are being applied. Precedent is one of the means by which greater consistency in the application of the law can be achieved. If courts routinely ignored how similar cases had been decided in the past, they would create confusion and uncertainty among those who must make choices on the basis of their understanding of how the law has been applied in previous situations. A business firm that is seeking to comply with environmental protection laws, for example, can develop company policies that will keep the company safely within the law if court decisions in this area are predictable. But if courts routinely ignore precedent, a firm might unintentionally engage in an activity that a court could arbitrarily conclude was unlawful.

POLITICAL INFLUENCES ON JUDICIAL DECISIONS

Although judicial rulings are constrained by existing laws, judges nearly always have some degree of discretion in their decisions.[22] The Constitution is a sparsely worded document and must be adapted to new and changing situations. The judiciary also has no choice at times but to apply its own judgment to statutory law. Congress often cannot anticipate or reach agreement on all the specific applications of a legislative act and therefore uses general language to state the act's purpose. It is left to the judiciary to decide what this language means in the context of a specific case arising under the act. Precedent is even less precise as a guide to decisions. Precedent is more a rule of thumb than a strict command; its significance must be weighed against the changes that have occurred since it was established. In the words of Justice Oliver Wendell Holmes Jr., precedent must be judged against the "felt necessities of the time."

The Supreme Court's ruling in a 1998 case (*Faragher v. City of Boca Raton*) involving sexual harassment in the workplace illustrates the ambiguity that can exist in the written law. The Court developed its ruling in the context of the antidiscrimination provisions of the Civil Rights Act of 1964. The act itself contains no description of, or even reference to, job-related sexual harassment. Nevertheless, the act does prohibit workplace discrimination, and the Court was unwilling to dismiss sexual harassment as an irrelevant form of job-related discrimination. In judging the case, however, the Court had no choice but to determine for itself which actions in the workplace are instances of harassment and which are not. In this sense, the Court was "making" law; it was deciding how legislation enacted by Congress applied to behavior that Congress had not addressed when it wrote the legislation.[23]

In sum, judges have leeway in their decisions. As a consequence, their rulings reflect not only legal influences but political ones, which can come from both outside and inside the judicial system.

Outside Influences on Court Decisions

The courts can and do make unpopular choices, but in the long run judicial decisions must be seen as fair if they are to be obeyed. In other words, the judi-

The judicial branch is increasingly an arena in which interest groups contend for influence. Many of these disputes have pitted environmental groups against economic interests. Shown here are demonstrators expressing their views on the issue of whether the Maine Atlantic Salmon should be declared an endangered species and placed off-limits to commercial fishing.

ciary cannot ignore the expectations of the general public, interest groups, and elected representatives.

Public Opinion and Interest Groups

Judges are responsive to public opinion, although much less so than elected officials are. In some cases, for example, the Supreme Court has tailored its rulings in an effort to gain public support or dampen public resistance. In the *Brown* case, the justices, recognizing that school desegregation would be an explosive issue in the South, required only that desegregation take place "with all deliberate speed" rather than immediately or on a fixed timetable. The Supreme Court typically has stayed close enough to public opinion to avoid seriously eroding public support for its decisions.[24]

Organized groups make their opinions known to the judiciary through the lawsuits they file. The range of interests that use lawsuits as a policy tactic includes traditional advocacy groups such as the American Civil Liberties Union (ACLU) as well as newer ones such as the Christian Legal Society's Center for Law and Religious Freedom. Groups also participate in cases brought by others through amicus curiae ("friend of the court") briefs, which they file in support of one of the parties to a case (see Chapter 9). Groups' influence on the courts has increased in recent decades as a result of both a sharp rise in group activity and the use of sophisticated judicial strategies. Groups carefully select the cases they pursue, choosing ones with the greatest chance of success. They also carefully pick the courts in which they file, because some judges are more sympathetic than others to their particular issue.

Congress and the President

Groups and the general public also make an impact on the judiciary indirectly, through their elected representatives. Both Congress and the president have powerful means of influencing the federal judiciary. Congress is constitutionally empowered to establish the Supreme Court's size and appellate jurisdiction, and Congress can rewrite legislation that it feels the judiciary has misinterpreted. Although Congress seldom undermines the judiciary directly, its members often express displeasure with judicial action. In a 1998 Senate speech, the chair of the Judiciary Committee, Orrin Hatch (R-Utah), lashed out at judges who he claimed were "making laws instead of interpreting the law."[25] Hatch argued that judges should be "strict constructionists." (*Strict constructionism* holds that a judicial officer should apply a narrow interpretation of the laws, whereas *loose constructionism* holds that a judicial officer can apply an expansive interpretation.)

The president also has ways of influencing the judiciary. The president is responsible for enforcing court decisions and has some control over the types of cases that come before the courts. Under President Ronald Reagan, for instance, the Justice Department pushed lawsuits that challenged the constitutionality of affirmative action programs.

Judicial appointments also provide the president with opportunities to influence the judiciary's direction. When Democrat Bill Clinton took office in 1993, more than a hundred federal judgeships were vacant. The first President Bush had expected to win reelection and had not moved quickly to fill vacancies as they arose. As it became apparent that he might lose the election, the Democrat-controlled Congress delayed action on the appointments. This enabled Clinton to fill many of the positions with loyal Democrats. The tables were turned in 2001. Senate Republicans had slowed action on Clinton nominees, enabling George W. Bush to appoint Republicans to existing vacancies when he took office.

In recent decades, the judicial appointment process has been unusually contentious, reflecting both the growing partisanship in Congress (see Chapter 11) and the widening range of issues (everything from abortion to the environment) being fought out in the courts. Nevertheless, the influence of elected officials on the judiciary is never total. Judges prize their independence. The fact that they are not popularly elected and hold their appointments indefinitely allows them to resist undue pressure from the elected branches of government. In 2004, for example, the Supreme Court rejected the Bush administration's claim that U.S. citizens charged with terrorism can be jailed indefinitely without a judicial hearing (see Chapter 4).

Inside Influences: The Justices' Own Political Beliefs

Although the judiciary symbolizes John Adams's characterization of the U.S. political system as "a government of laws, and not of men," judicial rulings are affected by the political beliefs of the men and women who sit on the courts.[26] Decisions of the Supreme Court, for example, often divide along political lines. During the 2003 Supreme Court term, for instance, forty-one cases were decided by nonunanimous vote. In more than two-thirds of these cases, justices Antonin Scalia and Clarence Thomas, each of whom was a Republican appointee, were opposed by justices Stephen Breyer and Ruth Bader Ginsburg, the two Democratic appointees on the Court.[27]

Arguably, partisanship was never more evident than in the Supreme Court's *Bush v. Gore* (2000) decision.[28] The five justices in the majority were the same justices who in previous decisions had upheld states' rights and had opposed expansive applications of the Fourteenth Amendment's equal protection clause. Yet they invoked the equal-protection clause to block the statewide manual recount that had been ordered by Florida's high court because no uniform standard for counting the ballots existed. When the Court issued a rare stay order to stop the recount, Justice Antonin Scalia claimed that it was justified because the recount could cast doubt on the legitimacy of Bush's election even though Bush had not yet been officially elected. Some observers suggested that if Bush had been trailing in the Florida vote, the Court's majority would have allowed the recount to continue. Justice John Paul Stevens, who thought the Florida high court had acted properly in ordering a manual count, accused the Court's majority of devising a ruling based on their partisan desires rather than on the law. Stevens noted that different standards for casting and counting ballots were found throughout the United States.[29]

Most Supreme Court justices do not change their views greatly during their tenure. As a result, major shifts in the Supreme Court's positions usually occur when its membership changes. Such shifts are related to political changes. When the Court in the 1980s moved away from the criminal justice rulings of the 1960s, for instance, it was largely because the more recently appointed justices, like the presidents who had nominated them, believed that government should have more leeway in its efforts to fight crime.

JUDICIAL POWER AND DEMOCRATIC GOVERNMENT

The issue of judicial power is heightened by the fact that federal judges are not elected. The principle of self-government asserts that lawmaking majorities have the power to decide society's policies. Because the United States has a constitutional system that places checks on the will of the majority, there is obviously an important role in the system for an institution such as the judiciary to play (see Table 14–2). Yet court decisions often reflect the political philosophy of the judges, who constitute a tiny political elite that wields significant power.[30] A critical question is how far unelected judges ought to go in substituting their policy judgments for those of legislative and executive officials who are elected by the people.

The judiciary's power is most evident when it declares executive or legislative action to be unconstitutional. The power of the courts to make such determinations, called **judicial review,** was first asserted in the landmark *Marbury v. Madison* case of 1803, when the Supreme Court rebuked both the president and Congress (see Chapter 2). Without judicial review, the federal courts would be unable to restrain an elected official or institution that has gone out of control.

Yet judicial review places the judgment of the courts above that of elected officials when interpretation of the Constitution is at issue, creating the possibility of conflict between the courts and the elected branches. The imposing

judicial review The power of courts to decide whether a governmental institution has acted within its constitutional powers and, if not, to declare its action null and void.

TABLE 14–2	**Significant Supreme Court Cases** Included are a few of the most significant cases decided by the U.S. Supreme Court.
CASE	**RULING**
Marbury v. Madison (1803)	Established principle of judicial review (Chapter 2)
McCulloch v. Maryland (1819)	Strengthened national power over states (Chapter 3)
Dred Scott v. Sanford (1857)	Decided that slaves were property and not citizens (Chapter 3)
Plessy v. Ferguson (1896)	Established the "separate but equal" doctrine (Chapter 5)
Gitlow v. New York (1925)	Protected free expression from state action by Fourteenth Amendment (Chapter 4)
Brown v. Board of Education of Topeka (1954)	Abolished the "separate but equal" doctrine and banned segregation in public schools (Chapter 5)
Gideon v. Wainwright (1963)	Decided that states must provide an attorney for poor defendants accused of committing felonies (Chapter 4)
Miranda v. Arizona (1966)	Decided that the police must inform suspects of their rights when they are arrested (Chapter 4)
Roe v. Wade (1973)	Decided that women have full freedom to choose abortion during the first three months of pregnancy under the right of privacy (Chapter 4)

nature of judicial review has led the judiciary to apply judicial review somewhat sparingly, although the Supreme Court alone has invoked it in more than a thousand cases. It should be noted that the large majority of these cases have involved action by state and local officials. Example cases include *Brown* (school desegregation), *Miranda* (right to remain silent), *Roe* (abortion), and *Lawrence* (relations between same-sex couples). Less than 10 percent of judicial review rulings have involved action by the president or Congress. An example is the 2002 Supreme Court decision that struck down part of the Americans with Disabilities Act, which Congress passed in 1990. (Chapters 2–5 discuss these and other judicial review cases.)

The Debate over the Proper Role of the Judiciary

legitimacy (of judicial power)
The issue of the proper limits of judicial authority in a political system based in part on the principle of majority rule.

The question of judicial power centers on the basic issue of **legitimacy:** the proper authority of the judiciary in a political system based in part on the principle of majority rule. The judiciary's policymaking significance and discretion have been sources of controversy throughout the country's history, but the controversies have seldom been livelier than during recent decades.

The judiciary at times has acted almost legislatively by defining broad social policies, such as abortion, busing, affirmative action, church-state relations,

Liberty, Equality & Self-Government

What's Your Opinion?

Judicial Review

Judicial review is the process by which a court invalidates legislative or executive action because it violates the Constitution. Judicial review is most dramatic in cases where the Supreme Court strikes down action taken by Congress or the president. However, most applications of judicial review take place in the context of action taken by state or local governments. The Supreme Court has struck down well over a thousand state laws and local ordinances, most of which involved issues of liberty and equality. Examples include *Near v. Minnesota*

(freedom of the press), *Brown v. Board of Education* (racial segregation in the schools), and *Gideon v. Wainwright* (legal counsel for the poor).

Why have encroachments on people's liberties occurred more frequently at the hands of state and local governments? Is it simply because there are so many of them that, by chance alone, most constitutional cases will arise at these levels? Or do you accept James Madison's claim (*Federalist* No. 10) that the smaller the sphere of government, the more likely it is that a dominant faction will disregard the interests of a weaker one?

Source: From Thomas Patterson, *We the People*, 5th Edition. Copyright © 2004 The McGraw-Hill Companies. Reprinted by permission of The McGraw-Hill Companies.

and prison reform. During the 1990s, for example, the prison systems in forty-two states were operating under court orders that mandated improvements in health care or overcrowding. School prayer is an older example. Until the Supreme Court in 1962 prohibited the reciting of prayer in public schools, the practice was governed by state legislatures and, in some cases, by local school districts. Through such actions the judiciary has restricted the policymaking authority of the states, has narrowed legislative discretion, and has made judicial action an effective alternative to election victory for certain interests.[31]

The judiciary has become more extensively involved in policymaking for many of the same reasons that Congress and the president have been thrust into new policy areas and become more deeply involved in old ones. Social and economic changes have required government to play a larger role in society, and this development has generated a seemingly endless series of new legal controversies. Environmental pollution, for example, was not a major issue until the 1960s; since then, it has been the subject of numerous court cases.

Judicial action raises an important question: How far should the judiciary go in asserting its authority when that authority collides with or goes beyond the action of elected institutions? There are two general schools of thought on this question. One advocates judicial restraint, and the other supports judicial activism. Although these terms are somewhat imprecise and often misused, they are helpful in efforts to clarify opposing philosophical positions on the Court's proper role.[32]

The Doctrine of Judicial Restraint

The doctrine of **judicial restraint** holds that the judiciary should be highly respectful of precedent and should defer to the judgment of legislatures. The

judicial restraint The doctrine that the judiciary should be highly respectful of precedent and should defer to the judgment of legislatures. The doctrine claims that the job of judges is to work within the confines of laws set down by tradition and lawmaking majorities.

The Supreme Court resists pressure from the public and from elected officials on some issues, such as school prayer, that it considers to be questions of individual rights rather than of majority opinion.

restraint doctrine holds that public issues should be decided in nearly all cases by elected officials rather than by judges. The judges' role is to determine how legislation and precedent apply in specific cases rather than to search for new principles that essentially create new laws or substantially redefine old ones.

Advocates of judicial restraint support their position with two major arguments. First, they contend that when the judiciary assumes policy functions that traditionally belong to elected institutions, it undermines the fundamental premise of self-government: the right of the majority to choose society's policies.[33] Second, judicial self-restraint is admired because it preserves the public support essential to the long-term legitimacy of the courts.[34] The judiciary must be concerned with **compliance**—with whether its decisions will be respected and obeyed. If judges impose their own views on the law, public confidence in the judiciary will be undermined.

compliance The issue of whether judicial decisions will be respected and obeyed.

Advocates of judicial restraint acknowledge that established law is never so precise as to provide exact answers to every question raised by every case and thus requires some degree of judicial discretion. In rare circumstances, decisive judicial action may be both appropriate and necessary, as in the historic *Brown v. Board of Education* decision (1954). The contradiction between the Fourteenth Amendment's equal-protection clause and government-created segregated schools is so blatant that even though the Constitution does not expressly prohibit racially segregated public schools, there is today no respectable jurist or legal scholar who would argue that such schools are constitutionally permissable.[35]

Yet advocates of judicial restraint see no constitutional justification for many of the Supreme Court's civil rights decisions. In *Romer v. Evans* (1996), for example, the Court's majority struck down an amendment to the Colorado constitution that was adopted by majority vote in a statewide referendum. The amendment had banned existing and future laws granting civil rights protections to gays and lesbians (see Chapter 5). Justice Antonin Scalia, who was in the Court's minority on the issue, said that the ruling was "an act not of judicial judgment but of political will." Scalia said that the statewide referendum was

HOW THE UNITED STATES COMPARES

Judicial Power

U.S. courts are highly political by comparison with the courts of most other democracies. First, U.S. courts operate within a common-law tradition, in which judge-made law becomes (through precedent) a part of the legal code. Many democracies have a civil-law tradition, in which nearly all law is defined by legislative statutes. Second, because U.S. courts operate in a constitutional system of divided power, they are required to rule on conflicts between state and nation or between the executive and the legislative branches, which thrusts the judiciary into the middle of political conflicts. It should not be surprising, then, that federal judges and justices are appointed through an overtly political process in which partisan views and activities are major considerations. Many federal judges, particularly at the district level, have no significant prior judicial experience. In fact, the United States is one of the few countries that does not mandate formal training for judges.

The pattern is different in most European democracies, where judgeships tend to be career positions. Individuals are appointed to the judiciary at an early age and then work their way up the judicial ladder largely on the basis of seniority. Partisan politics does not play a large role in appointment and promotion. By tradition, European judges see their

job as the strict interpretation of statutes, not the creative application of them.

The power of U.S. courts is nowhere more evident than in the exercise of judicial review—the voiding of a legislative or executive action on the grounds that it violates the Constitution. Judicial review had its origins in European experience and thought, but it was first formally applied in the United States when, in *Marbury v. Madison* (1803), the Supreme Court declared an act of Congress unconstitutional. Some democracies, including Great Britain, still do not allow broad-scale judicial review, but most democracies now provide for it.

In the so-called American system of judicial review, all judges can evaluate the applicability of constitutional law to particular cases and can declare ordinary law invalid when it conflicts with constitutional law. By comparison, the so-called Austrian system restricts judicial review to a special constitutional court. Judges in other courts cannot declare a law void on the grounds that it is unconstitutional: they must apply ordinary law as it is written. In the Austrian system, moreover, constitutional decisions are often made in response to requests for judicial review by political officials (such as the chief executive).

"the most democratic of procedures" and that the decision of Colorado voters should have been upheld.[36]

The Doctrine of Judicial Activism

Contrasting the judicial restraint position is the idea that the courts should take a generous view of judicial power and involve themselves extensively in interpreting and enlarging upon the law. Although advocates of this doctrine, known as **judicial activism,** acknowledge the principles of precedent and majority rule, they claim that the courts should not be overly deferential to existing legal principles or to the judgments of elected officials.

The doctrine of judicial activism is espoused by liberal activists who contend that courts should resort to general principles of fairness when existing law is inadequate. In areas in which social justice depends substantially on activist policies on behalf of the disadvantaged, liberal judicial activists argue that the courts have a responsibility to act positively and decisively. They believe, for example, that same-sex couples should have many of the same rights and

judicial activism The doctrine that the courts should develop new legal principles when judges see a compelling need, even if this action places them in conflict with the policy decisions of elected officials.

The handwritten letter that Clarence Gideon (insert) sent to the Supreme Court in 1962. The letter led eventually to the *Gideon* decision, in which the Court held that states must provide poor defendants with legal counsel (see Chapter 4). Seen by many people at the time as judicial activism, the ruling is now fully accepted.

I was sentenced to the State Penitentiary by the Circuit Court of Bay County, State of Florida. The present proceeding was commenced on a petition for a Writ of Habeus Corpus to the Supreme Court of the State of Florida to vacate the sentence, on the grounds that I was made to stand Trial without the aid of counsel, and, at all times of my incarseretion. The said Court refused to appoint counsel and therefore deprived me of Due process of law. and violate my rights in the Bill of Rights and the constitution of the United States.

Clarence Earl Gideon
5th day of Jan 1962 Petitioner.

Lawrence C Suyya
NOTARY PUBLIC

Notary Public
My Commis... Jan. 19, 1962
Bonded by American Surety Co. of N. Y.

Gideon's Letter to the Supreme Court
John F. Davis, Clerk, Supreme Court of the United States

privileges of opposite-sex couples, and thus they applauded the Supreme Court's decision in *Lawrence v. Texas* (2003), which struck down laws making it a crime for adults of the same sex to engage in consensual sexual relations.[37] These activists find justification for their philosophy in the U.S. Constitution's strong moral language and several of its provisions.[38] They view the Constitution as designed chiefly to protect individuals from unresponsive or repressive government, a goal that can be accomplished only by a judiciary that is willing to act when lawmaking majorities perpetrate or fail to correct injustice.

Judicial activism is not, however, confined to liberals. In the period from the 1860s to the 1930s, conservative activists on the Supreme Court struck down most legislative efforts to regulate economic activity (see Chapter 3). Judicial activism from the right recently loomed again when the Court overturned several precedents in the area of the rights of the accused. In 1990, Chief Justice William Rehnquist, in a rare action, asked Congress to restrict the right of those convicted in state courts to file habeas corpus appeals in federal courts. Congress rejected the proposal, and in 1991 a majority on the Rehnquist Court took action on its own to achieve the goal. In one ruling, the Court held that an inmate could not obtain a federal appeal simply because his or her lawyer had made a procedural mistake during the trial in a state court.[39]

Conservative activism is also evident in recent Supreme Court cases involving the issue of federalism. Since the late 1930s, the Court had deferred almost completely to Congress in this area, but it has recently struck down parts of several laws (see Chapter 3). The Court's four most conservative justices (Rehnquist, Scalia, Thomas, and Kennedy), joined by Justice O'Connor, supported the major decisions, each of which was decided by a 5–4 margin. In one of these cases, *Kimel v. Florida Board of Regents* (2000), the Court ruled that

Is the Supreme Court Suited to the Making of Broad Social Policy?

As the Supreme Court has extended its reach into areas that were once dominated by Congress and the president, some analysts have questioned whether the Court has the capacity (as distinct from the right) to devise workable policies in all these areas. The structure and procedures of the judiciary obviously differ greatly from those of elected institutions. The way in which the Supreme Court gathers information and formulates decisions bears little resemblance to the way in which Congress or the White House carries out its tasks. These differences, Donald Horowitz argues in *The Courts and Social Policy* (1977), prevent the Supreme Court from being a fully effective policymaking body when it comes to issues such as school integration.

Horowitz notes that, unlike members of Congress or executive officials, who usually start their policy deliberations from a general perspective, justices of the Supreme Court start with a particular case, which often involves unusual or extreme circumstances. The Court's initial busing decision in the 1971 *Swann* case, for example, involved Mecklenburg County, North Carolina, which had a long history of government-sponsored racial segregation. Yet the *Swann* decision became binding on a great number of communities, many of which had nothing approaching the level of institutionalized racism that existed in Mecklenburg County.

Horowitz also notes that the Court acts on the basis of less complete information than Congress, which often holds hearings, conducts research, and by other means considers a wide range of facts before deciding on policy. The basic function of courts is to resolve specific disputes, and admissible evidence is generally limited to material directly relevant to the case at hand. Research studies on social conditions, for example, cannot ordinarily be introduced in a court of law, because pieces of paper cannot be cross-examined on the witness stand. To be sure, the Supreme Court is more likely than lower courts to look for information beyond an immediate case. The justices can, for example, invite interested groups to submit amicus curiae ("friend of the

court") briefs in the hope that the advice thus obtained will broaden their understanding of a case's implications. The Court has a heavy schedule, however, and time and procedural tradition usually permit only a cursory assessment of information beyond what is contained in the trial record of a lower court.

Finally, the Court has no oversight mechanism of its own, which makes compliance a somewhat different issue than it is in the context of legislative or executive action. Although the Court has, for example, banned school prayer, prayer continues to be said daily in some public schools. There is not much the Court can do to compel teachers to stop the practice. On the other hand, Congress through its spending power and the executive through its administrative power are more readily able to get others to comply with their authoritative orders. The judiciary at times has resorted to direct action to achieve compliance. In some communities, for example, judges took on the role of overseeing busing plans for the purpose of achieving racial integration in public schools. However, courts are normally wary of getting directly involved in the implementation of their decisions, leaving this task to elected and administrative officers who, for their own reasons, may be less than zealous in forcing people and organizations to comply with Court rulings in sensitive areas of social policy.

Nevertheless, limits on the Court's policymaking capacity need to be kept in perspective. If the criterion for deciding whether an institution should establish broad policies was the likelihood of complete success, no institution would qualify. Every problem associated with judicial policymaking is also a problem confronted by legislative and executive institutions. Congress and the president also must act on the basis of imperfect information. In view of their resources, organization, and incentives, the elected institutions are better at fact-finding and are more representative than the Court, but they are not without flaws of their own. The difference is one of degree, not of kind.

Congress did not have the power to require states to comply with the federal age-discrimination law because age is not among the forms of discrimination expressly prohibited by the Fourteenth Amendment's equal-protection clause. The various rulings reflected Chief Justice William Rehnquist's long-held goal of limiting Congress's authority over the states.[40] "[The Rehnquist Court] doesn't defer to government at any level," said Walter Dellinger, a former solicitor general. "The Court is confident it can come up with the right decisions, and it believes it is constitutionally charged with doing so."[41]

Whether from the right or the left, judicial activism is characterized by a willingness to pit the judgment and power of the courts against the judgment and power of elected representatives or their administrative agents. To a degree, all judges are activists in the sense that their decisions are necessarily creative. The law as expressed through the Constitution, statutes, and precedent is not precise enough to provide an automatic answer to every court case. Judges and justices have no choice but to exercise judgment when the text of the law is inexact. And, to a degree, all judges are restrained in the sense that their decisions must have roots in the law. Judges cannot simply make any decision they might choose but are confined by the facts of a case and the laws that might reasonably be applied to it. Judges and justices vary in the degree to which they are willing to contest the judgment of elected officials and the degree to which they are willing to depart from the wording of the law. These differences are what separate the judicial activists from the practitioners of judicial restraint.

The Judiciary's Proper Role: A Question of Competing Values

The dispute between advocates of judicial activism and advocates of judicial restraint is a philosophical one that involves opposing values. The debate is important because it addresses the normative question of what role the judiciary ought to play in American democracy. Should unelected judges involve themselves deeply in policy by adopting a broad conception of their power, or should they grant wide discretion to elective institutions? Should judges defer to precedent, or should they be willing to change course, even at the risk of sending the law down uncharted paths? These questions cannot be answered simply on the basis of whether one personally agrees or disagrees with a particular judicial decision. The answer necessarily depends on a value judgment about the role the judiciary should play in a governing system based on the often-conflicting concepts of majority rule and individual rights.

The United States is a constitutional democracy that recognizes both the power of the majority to rule and the claim of the minority to protection of its rights. The judiciary was not established as the nation's moral conscience and does not have a monopoly on the issue of minority interests and rights. Yet the judiciary was established as a coequal branch of government and was charged with the responsibility of protecting individual rights and minority interests. In short, the constitutional question of how far the courts should be allowed to go in substituting their judgment for that of elected institutions and established law is open to interpretation. The trade-off is significant on all issues: minority rights versus majority rule, states' rights versus federal power, legislative authority versus judicial authority.

Summary

Self-Test
www.mhhe.com/pattersontad7

At the lowest level of the federal judicial system are the district courts, where most federal cases begin. Above them are the federal courts of appeals, which review cases appealed from the lower courts. The U.S. Supreme Court is the nation's highest court. Each state has its own court system, consisting of trial courts at the bottom and one or two appellate levels at the top. Cases originating in state courts ordinarily cannot be appealed to the federal courts unless a federal issue is involved, and then the federal courts can choose to rule only on the federal aspects of the case. Federal judges at all levels are nominated by the president, and if confirmed by the Senate they are appointed by the president to the office. Once on the federal bench, they serve until they die, retire, or are removed by impeachment and conviction.

The Supreme Court is unquestionably the most important court in the country. The legal principles it establishes are binding on lower courts, and its capacity to define the law is enhanced by the control it exercises over the cases it hears. However, it is inaccurate to assume that lower courts are inconsequential (the upper-court myth). Lower courts have considerable discretion, and the great majority of their decisions are not reviewed by a higher court. It is also inaccurate to assume that federal courts are far more significant than state courts (the federal court myth).

The courts have less discretionary authority than elected institutions do. The judiciary's positions are constrained by the facts of a case and by the laws as defined through the Constitution, statutes and government regulations, and legal precedent. Yet existing legal guidelines are seldom so precise that judges have no choice in their decisions. As a result, political influences have a strong impact on the judiciary. It responds to national conditions, public opinion, interest groups, and elected officials, particularly the president and members of Congress. Another political influence on the judiciary is the personal beliefs of judges, who have individual preferences that are evident in the way they decide on issues that come before the courts. Not surprisingly, partisan politics plays a significant role in judicial appointments.

In recent decades, the Supreme Court has issued broad rulings on individual rights, some of which have required governments to take positive action on behalf of minority interests. As the Court has crossed into areas traditionally left to lawmaking majorities, the legitimacy of its policies has been questioned. Advocates of judicial restraint claim that the justices' personal values are inadequate justification for exceeding the proper judicial role; they argue that the Constitution entrusts broad issues of the public good to elective institutions and that judicial activism ultimately undermines public respect for the judiciary. Judicial activists counter that the courts were established as an independent branch and should not hesitate to promote new principles when they see a need, even if this action brings them into conflict with elected officials.

STUDY CORNER

Key Terms

appellate jurisdiction (p. 448)

brief (p. 449)

civil law cases (p. 462)

compliance (p. 470)

concurring opinion (p. 450)

criminal law cases (p. 462)

decision (p. 450)

dissenting opinion (p. 451)

facts (of a court case) (p. 462)

judicial activism (p. 471)

judicial conference (p. 450)

judicial restraint (p. 469)

judicial review (p. 467)

jurisdiction (of a court) (p. 448)

laws (of a court case) (p. 462)

legitimacy (of judicial power) (p. 468)

majority opinion (p. 450)

opinion (of a court) (p. 450)

original jurisdiction (p. 448)

plurality opinion (p. 450)

precedent (p. 448)

senatorial courtesy (p. 458)

solicitor general (p. 449)

writ of certiorari (p. 448)

Self-Test

1. When nominating a justice to the U.S. Supreme Court, presidents:
   a. are required by law to consult with the American Bar Association.
   b. in accordance with senatorial courtesy have usually decided the choice by finding out who a majority of the senators in their party would like the nominee to be.
   c. tend to select a nominee who shares their political philosophy.
   d. get their nominee confirmed by the Senate only about half the time.

2. Judges in the U.S. judiciary:
   a. after issuing a ruling are personally responsible for seeing that the ruling is carried out by other officials.
   b. by law must attend public meetings from time to time and, while at these meetings, advise the public on judicial matters.
   c. are prohibited from issuing decisions except on actual cases that come to their court.
   d. have greater freedom than legislators or executives to choose the issues they will address.

3. The federal district courts are:
   a. courts of original jurisdiction.
   b. the only federal courts that regularly use juries to determine the outcome of cases.
   c. the courts that, in practice, make the final decision in most federal cases.
   d. the lowest level of federal courts.
   e. all of the above.

4. Most cases reach the U.S. Supreme Court through:
   a. appeal of cases that the court is bound by the Constitution or by act of Congress to hear even if it would prefer not to hear them.

   b. grant of a writ of certiorari.
   c. plea bargaining.
   d. its power of original jurisdiction.

5. Which constitutional power does the Congress have in relation to the Supreme Court?
   a. Congress can change the number of justices on the Supreme Court.
   b. Congress can change the Supreme Court's original jurisdiction.
   c. By two-thirds vote of both chambers, Congress determines which justice will become Chief Justice when that office becomes vacant.
   d. Congress can refuse to implement Supreme Court decisions when it disagrees with those decisions.

6. A court exercising judicial activism would likely:
   a. totally disregard judicial precedent.
   b. totally disregard legislative and executive action.
   c. not hesitate to act when it thought an important constitutional principle was at issue, even if such action would bring the court into conflict with public opinion or the elected branches.
   d. none of the above.

7. State court systems in the United States are lower-level administrative units of the federal court system, and not independent judicial units. (T/F)

8. The U.S. judiciary is not influenced by either public opinion or the actions of interest groups. (T/F)

9. The "federal court myth" implies that the federal courts are far more important than state courts. (T/F)

10. According to the text, social and economic changes have required the government, including the judiciary, to play a larger role in settling societal problems and conflicts. (T/F)

Critical Thinking

Which philosophy—that of judicial restraint or judicial activism—comes closer to your own thinking about the proper role of the courts? Does your support for restraint or activism depend on whether a judicial decision conforms to your own preference on the issue in question?

Suggested Readings

Baum, Lawrence. *The Supreme Court,* 8th ed. Washington, D.C.: Congressional Quarterly Press, 2003. A thorough book on the Supreme Court.

Carp, Robert A. *The Federal Courts,* 3d ed. Washington, D.C.: Congressional Quarterly Press, 1998. An overview of the federal judiciary system.

Gillman, Howard. *Votes That Counted: How the Court Decided the 2000 Presidential Election.* Chicago: University of Chicago Press, 2001. An accounting of the *Bush v. Gore* ruling.

McGuire, Kevin T. *Understanding the Supreme Court: Cases and Controversies.* New York: McGraw-Hill, 2002. An overview of Supreme Court decisions and approaches to legal disputes.

Salokar, Rebecca Mae. *The Solicitor General: The Politics of Law.* Philadelphia, Pa.: Temple University Press, 1992.

A study of the important and increasingly political role of the nation's top trial lawyer.

Sandler, Ross and David Schoenbrod. *Democracy by Decree: What Happens When Courts Run Government.* New Haven, Conn.: Yale University Press, 2003. A critical evaluation of the courts' growing policy role.

Seidman, Louis Michael. *Our Unsettled Constitution.* New Haven, Conn.: Yale University Press, 2002. A defense of constitutionalism and judicial review.

Watson, George L., and John Alan Stookey. *Shaping America: The Politics of Supreme Court Appointments.* New York: Longman, 1995. An examination of the process by which Supreme Court justices are nominated and confirmed.

List of Websites

http://www.courttv.com/cases

A website that allows you to take the facts of actual court cases, examine the law and the arguments, and then decide each case for yourself.

http://www.fjc.gov/

The home page of the Federal Judicial Center, an agency created by Congress to conduct research and provide education on the federal judicial system.

http://www.lib.umich.edu/libhome/Documents.center/fedjudi.html

A University of Michigan web page that provides detailed information on the federal judicial system.

http://www.rominger.com/supreme.htm

A vast site that provides links to the Supreme Court, pending cases, the state court systems, and other subjects.

Participate!

The right to a fair and open trial decided by a jury is one of the oldest hallmarks of the American justice system. If you have never done so, you might want to attend a trial at your local courthouse to see how the process works. If you live in or near Washington, D.C., or a state capital, you might choose instead to observe a session of a supreme court. Such courts are appellate courts, so there is no jury, but you are more likely to hear arguments on cases of broad significance. Finally, if you have the opportunity to serve on a jury, you should welcome the chance to participate in a decision that is important to society as well as to the parties directly involved. Too many Americans today see jury duty as a responsibility to be shirked.

Extra Credit

For up-to-the-minute *New York Times* articles, interactive simulations, graphics, study tools, and more links and quizzes, visit the text's Online Learning Center at www.mhhe.com/pattersontad7.

(Self-Test Answers: 1. c   2. c   3. e   4. b   5. a   6. c   7. F   8. F   9. T   10. T)

PART

IV

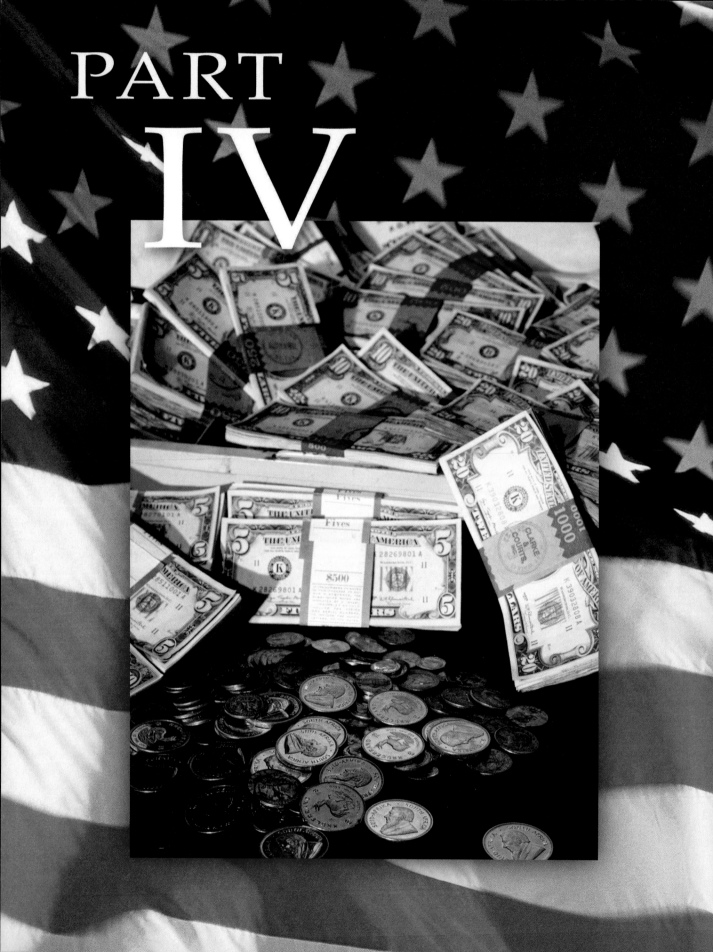

Public Policy

Politics, said Harold Lasswell, is the struggle over "who gets what, when, and how." Americans differ in many of their interests, and they also disagree over policy. Yet they are often able to find common ground. The typical response when a policy question arises is not only to fight over it but also to resolve it. This philosophy speaks volumes about the nature of American governance.

The four chapters in this section are designed mainly to address broad policy issue areas: the economy and environment (Chapter 15); welfare, education, and health (Chapter 16); foreign and defense policy (Chapter 17); and state and local politics and policy (Chapter 18).

There is a common pattern to policy action in these areas—it tends to be piecemeal and reactive. The nation's diversity and fragmented governing structure make it difficult for policymakers to deal with issues except in small parts and until they have reached the problem stage. This tendency increases the likelihood that major errors of policy will be avoided, but it also increases the chance that problems will be left to grow to the point where solutions are harder to find and more costly to implement.

Regardless, a democratic nation's policies reflect the nature of its political system and its people. They indicate the way a society has chosen to govern itself.

PART FOUR OUTLINE

15

Economic and Environmental Policy:
Contributing to Prosperity

Chapter Outline

Government as Regulator of the Economy
   Efficiency through Government Intervention
   Equity through Government Intervention
   The Politics of Regulatory Policy

Government as Protector of the Environment
   Conservationism: The Older Wave
   Environmentalism: The Newer Wave

Government as Promoter of Economic Interests
   Promoting Business
   Promoting Labor
   Promoting Agriculture

Fiscal Policy: Government as Manager of Economy, I
   Taxing and Spending Policy
   The Process and Politics of Fiscal Policy

Monetary Policy: Government as Manager of Economy, II
   The Fed
   The Politics of the Fed

We the people of the United States, in order to . . .
insure domestic tranquility . . .

—Preamble, U.S. Constitution

The stock market was downright scary. The Dow Jones and Nasdaq indexes had dropped steadily for two years, knocking trillions of dollars off the value of stocks. Stocks that sold on the technology-heavy Nasdaq index were particularly hard hit. By 2003, it had fallen 75 percent—a steeper decline over the same length of time than had occurred at the onset of the Great Depression. Was history about to repeat itself? Was the U.S. economy in danger of collapse?

In fact, Wall Street and the rest of America reacted rather calmly to the market downturn. Institutional and individual investors were unhappy with the drop in the value of their stocks, but they did not panic. Among the reasons was the existence of substantial government programs designed to stabilize and stimulate the U.S. economy. When the Great Depression struck, no such programs existed. Moreover, the response to the 1929–31 drop in stock prices made matters worse: businesses cut back on production, investors fled the stock market, depositors withdrew their bank savings, and consumers slowed their spending. All these actions accelerated the downward spiral. This time, however, government programs were in place to protect depositors' savings, slow the drop in stock prices, and steady the economy through adjustments in interest rates and spending programs.

This chapter examines the economic role of the government, focusing on its promotion and regulation of economic interests and its fiscal and monetary policies. Directly or indirectly, the federal government is a party to almost every economic transaction in which Americans engage. Although the private decisions of firms and individuals are the main force in the American economic system, these decisions are influenced by government policy. Washington seeks to maintain high productivity, employment, and purchasing power; regulates business practices that would otherwise harm the environment or result in economic inefficiencies and inequities; and promotes economic interests.

These activities are part of the **policy process**—the interplay of actors and institutions that leads to the adoption, modification, or rejection of public policy proposals. As previous chapters have suggested, the policy process takes different forms depending on who and what are involved. An issue that involves Congress, for example, involves different rules and actors than one that works itself out in the White House, a bureaucratic agency, or a federal court. (Nevertheless, the U.S. policy process has certain inherent tendencies; see "The U.S. Policy Process.") As will be seen in this chapter, the policy process for economic issues brings together a broad range of institutions and interests. The main ideas presented in this chapter are the following:

The collapse in 2002 of the Enron Corporation, which had been American's seventh largest firm, cost investors and Enron employees (through the loss of retirement accounts) billions of dollars. The debacle brought calls for closer government regulation of corporations, accounting firms, and pension plans. Shown here is a scene from Senate Commerce Committee hearings into the role that Enron's top executive, Ken Lay, played in the collapse. Lay is in the center of the group seated just behind the empty chairs on the left side of the photo.

policy process The interplay of actors and institutions that leads to the adoption, modification, or rejection of public policy proposals.

- *Through regulation, the U.S. government imposes restraints on business activity that are designed to promote economic efficiency and equity.* This regulation is often the cause of political conflict, which is both ideological and group-centered.

- *Through regulatory and conservation policies, the U.S. government seeks to protect and preserve the environment from the effects of business firms and consumers.*

- *Through promotion, the U.S. government helps private interests achieve their economic goals.* Business in particular benefits from the government's promotional efforts, which take place largely in the context of group politics.

- *Through its taxing and spending decisions (fiscal policy), the U.S. government seeks to maintain a level of economic supply and demand that will keep the economy prosperous.* The condition of the economy is generally the leading issue in American electoral politics and has a major influence on each party's success.

- *Through its money-supply decisions (monetary policy), the U.S. government— through the Fed—seeks to maintain a level of inflation consistent with sustained, controllable economic growth.*

economy A system of production and consumption of goods and services that are allocated through exchange among producers and consumers.

GOVERNMENT AS REGULATOR OF THE ECONOMY

laissez-faire doctrine A classic economic philosophy that holds that owners of business should be allowed to make their own production and distribution decisions without government regulation or control.

An **economy** is a system of production and consumption of goods and services that are allocated through exchange. When a shopper chooses groceries at a store and pays money for them, that transaction is one of the millions of economic exchanges that make up the economy. In *The Wealth of Nations* (1776), Adam Smith presented the case for the **laissez-faire doctrine,** which holds that private individuals and firms should be left alone to make their own production

The U.S. Policy Process

The American political system includes an imposing division of powers that can make it difficult to enact major initiatives. Legislation must be passed by both the House and the Senate and be signed by the president before it becomes law, and there are numerous obstacles at each step in this process. For example, a minority of senators can sometimes kill a bill through the filibuster.

This system contrasts with European parliamentary systems where a simple majority in one legislative chamber is sufficient for the enactment of legislation. Such systems are designed to empower majorities. The American system is designed to thwart majorities—a reflection of the determination of the writers of the Constitution to control governmental power.

One consequence is that U.S. policymakers are often slow in responding to a perceived need for policy change. Welfare reform is an example. The Welfare Reform Act of 1996, which changed the decades-old guarantee of federal assistance for low-income families with children, was not the first congressional attempt to alter the welfare system. A major change was nearly achieved as far back as the early 1970s, when policymakers first became aware that the welfare system needed fixing. Why did congressional action take so long?

In *Agendas, Alternatives, and Public Policy* (1995), John Kingdon tells why major policy changes are often slow to occur. As Kingdon describes it, the governing process is comprised of three largely separate "streams." One is the *policy stream*. It includes policy analysts, scholars, and other individuals who study policy situations closely. They are the main source of new policy ideas.

A second stream is the *problem stream*. It derives from the condition of society—the employment rate, the quality of the schools, the security of the nation, the safety of the streets, and so on. Conditions in any area are rarely optimal, but only certain conditions at an given time will be seen as "problems." Although there are always people without jobs, for example, it is only when the unemployment rate spirals upward that joblessness is seen as a policy problem.

The *political stream* is the third stream. It includes politicians, political parties, interest groups, and public opinion. It is the stream where problems are turned into political issues and where the power to change a policy resides.

Kingdon argues that significant policy action is likely to occur only when the three streams converge. The existence of a policy proposal is not sufficient by itself. In fact, most of the new programs devised and put forth by policy analysts are never acted upon. Nor is the acknowledgment of a policy problem sufficient by itself. People knew about the health risks of cigarettes long before policies to discourage smoking were implemented. Nor is a political actor's interest in a policy problem sufficient by itself. Unless many others in the political stream also agree that something is a problem, the broad support necessary to change existing policy will not be forthcoming.

However, when the streams flow together, the prospect for successful action is high. The problem is widely recognized, policy solutions exist, and politicians have an incentive to act. The 1996 Welfare Reform Act is a case in point. The policy stream had developed alternative approaches to welfare that had been tested in several states and appeared to be successful in moving people off welfare and into jobs; the problem stream had shifted as a result of a growing recognition of the financial and human costs of the existing welfare system; and the political stream had been altered by the Republican takeover of Congress after the 1994 elections. For the first time in decades, the three streams had converged on the issue of welfare, and the result was a sweeping change in policy.

Few policy efforts are as major as the revamping of the nation's welfare system. Nevertheless, timing is often a critical factor in policy change. "Timing is everything" is an old political adage. It is not "everything," but, as Kingdon's analysis suggests, it plays an important and sometimes decisive role in political action.

Timing is more important to action on legislation in the United States than in Europe. In both cases, windows of opportunity affect whether policy change is likely to occur. In the European case, however, the window does not have to be as large or stay open as long because political power in parliamentary democracies is more easily exercised, Thus, European democracies tend to act more quickly and decisively in response to policy problems, while policy action in the American case tends to be more reactive and tentative. The American approach increases the likelihood that problems will grow and, in the end, become more difficult and costly to solve. On the other hand, this approach decreases the likelihood that overt policy mistakes will be made. Because policy changes tend to be small and piecemeal, they are less likely to have harmful unanticipated effects.

Adam Smith
(1723–1790)

Born in Scotland and educated at Oxford, Adam Smith was a philosopher and economist best known for *The Wealth of Nations*, which provided a moral justification for a free-market economy. Smith claimed that government policies and personal efforts to promote the public good were of small consequence compared with the effects of an unrestricted marketplace. Before he wrote his economic classic, Smith was famed for a treatise on moral reasoning.

and distribution decisions. Smith reasoned that when there is a demand for a good (that is, when people are willing and able to buy a good), private entrepreneurs will respond by producing the good and distributing it to those places where demand exists. Smith argued that the desire for profit is the "invisible hand" that guides the system of demand and supply toward the greatest benefit for all.

Smith acknowledged that the doctrine of laissez-faire capitalism had limits. Certain areas of the economy, such as roadways and postal services, were natural monopolies and were better run by government than by private firms. In addition, by regulating banking, currency, and contracts, government could give stability to private transactions. Otherwise, Smith argued, the economy was best left in private hands.

In contrast, Karl Marx proposed a worker-controlled economy. In *Das Kapital* (*Capital*, 1867), Marx argued that a free market system is exploitative because producers, through their control of markets, can compel workers to labor at a wage below the value they add to production and can force consumers to pay higher prices for goods than are justified by the cost of production. To end the exploitation of labor, Marx proposed a collective economy. When the workers owned the means of production, the economy would operate in the interest of all people.

Marx and Smith represent the extremes of economic theory. No country in the world has an economy that conforms fully to either the laissez-faire or the collectivist model. All national economies today are of "mixed" form in that they contain elements of both private and public control. However, the world's economies vary in their mix. Compared with European countries and much more so compared with China, the United States relies more heavily on private ownership and initiative.

Nevertheless, the U.S. government plays a substantial economic role through the **regulation** of privately owned businesses. U.S. firms are not free to act as they please but rather must operate within production and distribution rules set by federal regulations. Regulatory policy is generally intended to promote either economic *efficiency* or *equity* (see Table 15–1).

regulation A term that refers to government restrictions on the economic practices of private firms.

Efficiency through Government Intervention

Economic efficiency results when firms fulfill as many of society's needs as possible while using as few of its resources as possible.[1] **Efficiency** refers to the relationship of inputs (the labor and material that go into making a product or service) to outputs (the product or service itself). The greater the output for a given input, the more efficient the production process.

Adam Smith and other classical economists believed that the free market was the optimal means of achieving efficiency. Producers would try to use as few resources as possible in order to keep their prices low so that they could compete successfully for customers. Efficient producers would be able to underprice inefficient ones, who would thereby be driven out of business.

efficiency An economic principle that holds that firms should fulfill as many of society's needs as possible while using as few of its resources as possible. The greater the output (production) for a given input (for example, an hour of labor), the more efficient the process.

TABLE 15–1	The Main Objectives of Regulatory Policy The government intervenes in the economy to promote efficiency and equity.	
OBJECTIVE	**DEFINITION**	**REPRESENTATIVE ACTIONS BY GOVERNMENT**
Efficiency	Fulfillment of as many of society's needs as possible at the cost of as few of its resources as possible. The greater the output for a given input, the more efficient the process.	Preventing restraint of trade; requiring producers to pay the costs of damage to the environment; reducing restrictions on business that cannot be justified on a cost-benefit basis.
Equity	When the outcome of an economic transaction is fair to each party.	Requiring firms to bargain in good faith with labor; protecting consumers in their purchases; protecting workers' safety and health.

Preventing Restraint of Trade

The assumption that the market always determines price is flawed. The same incentive—the profit motive—that drives producers to respond to demand can drive them to corner the market on a good. If a producer gains a monopoly on a good or colludes with other producers to fix its price, consumers are forced to pay an artificially high price. Rather than selling at a low price in order to attract customers, the producer will charge as high a price as the market will bear.

Restraint of trade was prevalent in the United States in the late nineteenth century when large trusts came to dominate many areas of the economy, including the oil, steel, railroad, and sugar markets. Railroad companies, for example, had no competition on short routes and charged such high rates that many farmers went broke because they could not afford to ship their crops to markets. In 1887, Congress took its first step toward regulating the trusts by enacting the Interstate Commerce Act. The legislation created the Interstate Commerce Commission (ICC), which was charged with regulating railroad practices and fares.

Business competition today is regulated by a wide range of federal agencies, including, for example, the Federal Trade Commission (FTC), the Food and Drug Administration (FDA), and the Antitrust Division of the Justice Department. The goal of regulatory activity is to protect consumers while preserving the market incentives that create a dynamic economy. In some cases, the government has prohibited mergers or required divestments in order to increase competition. In 1999, for example, the Federal Communications Commission (FCC) voided a proposed merger of Bell Atlantic and GTE, ruling that the companies had failed to show that the merger would not hurt consumers. In other cases, the government has pressured companies whose marketing practices threaten competition. An example is the Justice Department's suit against Microsoft for using its Windows operating system to promote its Internet Explorer at the expense of other web browsers such as Netscape Navigator.

In most cases, however, the government tolerates business concentration, even permitting the merger of competing firms, such as Time Warner's merger with America Online (AOL) in 2001. Although such mergers reduce

Microsoft's Bill Gates speaks to an audience about his firm's international scope. Microsoft's large market share and aggressive practices have made it a target of antitrust action.

competition, the government tolerates concentrated ownership in the oil, automobile, and other industries in which high capital costs make it difficult for smaller firms to compete successfully.[2] Government acceptance of corporate giants also reflects a realization that market competition no longer involves just domestic firms. For example, the "Big Three" U.S. automakers (General Motors, Ford, and Chrysler) face stiff competition from imports, particularly those from Japan and Germany. The merger of Chrysler and Germany's Daimler-Benz is testimony to the increased globalization of market competition.

The U.S. government's general policy toward corporate giants that act in restraint of trade has been to penalize them financially. In 1993, for example, a number of air carriers (including American, Delta, United, Northwest, and US Air) were found to have engaged in price fixing and were ordered to award hundreds of millions of dollars in certificates to travelers who could prove they had flown on these carriers during the period in question. More than four million individuals, organizations, and businesses filed claims.

Making Business Pay for Indirect Costs

Economic inefficiencies can result not only from restraint of trade but from the failure of businesses or consumers to pay the full costs of resources used in production. Classical economics assumed that market prices reflect all the costs of production, but this assumption is rarely warranted. Consider companies whose industrial wastes seep into nearby lakes and rivers. The price of these companies' products does not reflect the water pollution, and hence customers do not pay all the costs that society has incurred in the making of the products. Economists label such unpaid costs **externalities.**

externalities Burdens that society incurs when firms fail to pay the full costs of production. An example of an externality is the pollution that results when corporations dump industrial wastes into lakes and rivers.

Until the 1960s, the federal government did not require firms to pay such costs. The impetus to begin doing so came not only from lawmakers but also from the scientific community and environmental groups. The Clean Air Act of

1963 and the Water Quality Act of 1965 required industry to install antipollution devices to keep the discharge of air and water pollutants within specified limits. In 1970, Congress created the Environmental Protection Agency (EPA) to monitor firms and ensure their compliance with federal regulations governing air and water quality and the disposal of toxic wastes. (Environmental policy is discussed more fully later in the chapter.)

Overregulation

Although government intervention is intended to increase economic efficiency, it can have the opposite effect. Government regulation raises the cost of doing business. Firms have to expend work hours to monitor and implement government regulations, which in some instances (for example, pollution control) also require companies to buy and install expensive equipment. These costs are efficient to the degree that they produce commensurate benefits. Yet if government places needless or excessive regulatory burdens on firms, they waste resources in the process of complying. The result is higher-priced goods that are more expensive for consumers and less competitive in the domestic and global markets (see "How the United States Compares").

Overregulation can also be costly to governments. An example is a provision of the Safe Drinking Water Act that required communities to reduce contaminants in their water supply from the current level, whatever that level happened to be. In most communities, the effect was to improve the quality of the water supply. But in Anchorage, Alaska, the result was an absurd remedy. The city's water supply was already so clean that officials had to ask local fish-processing plants to dump their wastes into the sewer system so that Anchorage would have impurities to remove from its water.[3]

Situations of this kind have led to regulatory reform.[4] In 1995, Congress enacted legislation to tighten the regulatory process by requiring cost-benefit analysis and risk assessment (determining the severity of the problem) to be taken into account in certain regulatory decisions.

Deregulation

Another response to regulatory excess is the policy of **deregulation**—the rescinding of regulations already in force for the purpose of improving efficiency. This process began in 1977 with passage of the Airlines Deregulation Act, which eliminated government-set airfares and, in some instances, government-mandated air routes. The change had the intended effect: airfares declined, and competition between airlines increased on most routes. Congress followed airline deregulation with partial deregulation of the trucking, banking, energy, and communications industries, among others.

Reductions in regulation, however, can be carried too far.[5] Underregulation can result in harmful business practices. The profit motive can lead firms and their executives to manipulate the market illegally. Companies are more likely to try unlawful schemes when weak regulation leads them to believe they can escape detection. Such was the case with top executives of the Enron Corporation. They employed illegal maneuvers that falsely inflated the firm's

deregulation The rescinding of excessive government regulations for the purpose of improving economic efficiency.

HOW THE UNITED STATES COMPARES

Global Economic Competitiveness

The United States ranked second only to Finland in the World Economic Forum's 2003–2004 economic growth competitiveness survey. The World Economic Forum (WEF) is a private economic research organization in Switzerland.

To determine its rankings, the WEF takes into account factors such as a nation's corporate management, finance, institutional openness, government regulation, public infrastructure, science and technology, and labor. The United States ranks particularly high on its technology, management, and finance. A weakness is its labor practices. U.S. workers enjoy fewer protections and benefits (such as health care coverage) than their counterparts in many other industrialized societies.

The United States has been at or near the top of the WEF's rankings for a number of years. It has ranked substantially higher than some of its major economic rivals, such as Germany and Japan. These countries rank lower because their management, regulation, and finance systems are relatively rigid, reducing their ability to respond flexibly to the global marketplace.

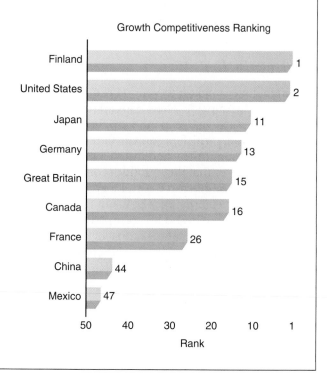

Growth Competitiveness Ranking

Country	Rank
Finland	1
United States	2
Japan	11
Germany	13
Great Britain	15
Canada	16
France	26
China	44
Mexico	47

earnings, which drove up the price of its stock. Only after the schemes failed and the firm went bankrupt in 2001 were their deceptions exposed. It was too late to help the stockholders who lost billions of dollars and the low-level Enron employees who lost their jobs as well as their company-based retirement savings.

The Enron scandal demonstrates that the issue of business regulation is not a simple question of whether or not to regulate. On one hand, too much regulation can burden firms with bureaucratic red tape, costly implementation procedures, and limited options. On the other hand, too little regulation can give firms the leeway to exploit the public unfairly or recklessly. Either too little or too much regulation can result in economic inefficiency. The challenge for policymakers is to strike the proper balance between regulatory measures and free-market mechanisms.

Equity through Government Intervention

The government intervenes in the economy to bring equity as well as efficiency to the marketplace. **Equity** occurs when an economic transaction is fair to each party.[6] Equity is judged by *outcomes*—whether they are reasonable and mutu-

equity (in relation to economic policy) The situation in which the outcome of an economic transaction is fair to each party. An outcome can usually be considered fair if each party enters into a transaction freely and is not unknowingly at a disadvantage.

Shown here are demonstrators protesting the practices of health maintenance organizations (HMOs). The central issue of business regulation is the proper balance of regulatory and free-market mechanisms. Critics of HMOs say the organizations are more interested in profits than in patients' health and that more regulation of their activities is warranted.

ally acceptable to the parties involved. A transaction can be considered fair if each party enters into it freely and is not unknowingly at a disadvantage (for example, if the seller knows a product is defective, equity requires that the buyer also know of the defect).

An early equity measure was the creation of the Food and Drug Administration (FDA) in 1907. Because consumers often are unable to tell whether foods and drugs are safe to use, the FDA works to keep adulterated foods and dangerous or ineffective drugs off the market. In the 1930s, financial reforms were among the equity measures enacted under the New Deal. The Securities and Exchange Act of 1934 and the Banking Act of 1934 were designed in part to protect investors and savers from dishonest or imprudent brokers and bankers. The New Deal also provided greater equity for organized labor, which previously had been in a weak position in its dealings with management. The Fair Labor Standards Act of 1938, for example, established minimum wages, maximum working hours, and constraints on the use of child labor.

Historical Background

The 1960s and 1970s produced the greatest number of equity reforms. From 1965 to 1977, ten federal agencies, including the Consumer Product Safety Commission, were established to protect consumers, workers, and the public from harmful effects of business activity. Among the products declared to be unsafe in the 1960s and 1970s were the insecticide DDT, cigarettes, and leaded gasoline. The rule eliminating lead in gasoline has given society a major benefit. Lead can cause severe brain damage in children; the average level of lead in children's blood has decreased by 75 percent since the regulation took effect.[7]

The Politics of Regulatory Policy

Economic regulation has come in waves, as changes in national conditions have produced intermittent bursts of social consciousness.

Deregulation: The Case of Your Phone Bill

Have you or your parents ever been sent an outlandish telephone bill for hundreds or even thousands of dollars? Lots of Americans have, and their experiences reveal the pitfalls of deregulation.

In 1984, the U.S. government deregulated long-distance telephone service. AT&T was forced to compete with other carriers in a market in which carriers could set their own rates rather than first having rates approved by the Federal Communications Commission (FCC). The theory was that competition would drive rates downward, which would benefit consumers.

Rates have come down, but deregulation has also created a buyer-beware marketplace. The unscrupulous practices of MCI-Worldcom alone are enough to fill a book. One of MCI's schemes was an illegal practice called "slamming." Through deceptive telemarketing and direct-mail advertising, MCI would trick people into changing to MCI as their carrier when they thought they were agreeing to something else, or in some cases not agreeing to anything at all. They found out the truth when a bill from MCI arrived in the mail. In 2000, the FCC fined MCI $3.5 million, the largest federal penalty ever for slamming.

MCI-Worldcom was also a leader in "cramming," which is the assessment of new rates and charges without informing customers of the change. MCI would attract customers with low advertised rates and later raise the rates. The first awareness that customers would have of the change would be when their bills arrived in the mail—too late for them to avoid paying the higher rate. In 2001, the FCC banned the practice. Telephone companies must now file a public notice when changing their rates and some states require that companies inform all their customers in writing before any such change can occur.

For customers who called MCI-Worldcom to say they were switching to another carrier, MCI had a final surprise in store. In the interval during which the switch was taking place (which could be a week or more), MCI moved the customer to a higher rate category, charging as much as twenty to thirty times the original rate.

To protect consumers against such practices, *Consumer Reports* and other publications have suggested guidelines for people who are ordering new phone service or changing their existing one. The guidelines include the following:

1. Read the fine print on any contract.
2. Ask a lot of questions. For example, some carriers charge only a few pennies more for calls to Canada, whereas others charge as much as $1.50 a minute for such calls. If you call Canada or any other country regularly, you will want to make sure that international calls are included in your plan. You will pay extra for this provision, but it can save you hundreds of dollars.
3. If you are switching from one long-distance carrier to another, inform only the new carrier and the local service provider. Do *not* inform your current long-distance carrier, or the company might increase your rate while the switch is being made.

Overall, deregulation has served consumers' interests. Telephone, airline, shipping, and other rates have come down. But consumers should recognize that deregulation means that they have fewer protections against unscrupulous business practices.

The Reforms of the Progressive and New Deal Eras

The first wave of regulation came during the Progressive era, when reformers sought to break the power of the trusts by placing constraints on unfair business practices. The second wave came in the New Deal era, when reformers sought to stimulate economic recovery through regulatory policies that were designed as much to save business as to restrain it.

Liberty, Equality & Self-Government

What's Your Opinion?

Economic Freedom, Equality and Equity

The U.S. economy is based on free-market principles. Producers and consumers are more or less free to act as they please, subject of course to their financial resources.

Few Americans would trade their free-enterprise system for a socialist system that would put more constraints on their economic activity in return for greater economic security (see Chapter 1). In fact, Americans' notions of liberty and economic freedom are closely connected. Americans want the liberty that attends economic freedom, even if it means that in the end only some of them will do well economically.

Paradoxically, a minimum of economic security ordinarily is required for people to exercise their liberty. If people have to scrape to make a living, they will have neither the energy nor the financial means to enjoy fully the fruits of liberty. This speaks to the issue of whether wealth in the United States is adequately spread across the society, without too much wealth at the top or too little at the bottom. In your opinion, is wealth distributed widely enough to allow nearly all Americans to enjoy the type of liberty that the economic marketplace can supply? Or do you believe that too many Americans lack the economic means to attain the full measure of their liberty?

Economic equity (as opposed to economic equality) is also tied to liberty. The issue of equity involves whether economic transactions are free and fair to each party or whether, instead, one party in the relationship is exploited because he or she lacks any real choice in the transaction. U.S. history is replete with examples of people who lacked the freedom to reject their own exploitation. Many of the millions of Irish, Italians, and Chinese who came to America in the nineteenth and early twentieth centuries, for example, had no power to bargain with their employers and virtually no choice—short of returning home or turning to a life of crime—but to work for long hours under adverse conditions for low pay. From your own experience and observations, do you think the large majority of today's Americans have the marketplace freedom that will assure them of economic equity?

Although business fought Progressive and New Deal reforms, long-term opposition was lessened by the fact that most of the resulting regulation applied to a particular industry rather than to firms of all types. This pattern makes it possible for an affected industry to gain influence with those officials responsible for regulating its activities. By cultivating close ties to the FCC, for example, the broadcast networks have managed to obtain policies that protect their near monopoly on broadcasting and give them high and sustained profits.[8] Although not all industries have as much leverage with their regulators as broadcasting has, it is generally true that industries have not been greatly hampered by the older form of regulation and in many cases have substantially benefited from it.

The Era of New Social Regulation

The third wave of regulatory reform, in the 1960s and 1970s, differed from the Progressive and New Deal phases in both its policies and its politics. This third wave has been called the era of "new social regulation" because of the social goals it addressed in its three major policy areas: environmental protection, consumer protection, and worker safety.

Most of the regulatory agencies established during the third wave have broader mandates than those created earlier. They have responsibility not for a single industry but for firms of all types, and their policy scope covers a wide range of activities. The EPA, for example, is charged with regulating environmental pollution of almost any kind by almost any firm. Unlike the older agencies that are run by a commission whose members serve for fixed terms, some of the newer agencies, including the EPA, are headed by a single director who is appointed by the president with Senate approval and is subject to immediate removal by the president.

Because newer agencies such as the EPA have a wide-ranging clientele, no one firm or industry can easily influence agency policy to a great extent. There is also strong group competition within some of the newer regulatory spheres. For example, business lobbies must compete with environmental groups such as the Sierra Club and Greenpeace for influence with the EPA.[9] The firms regulated by the older agencies, in contrast, face no powerful competition in their lobbying activities. Broadcasters, for example, are largely unopposed in their efforts to influence the FCC. Although television viewers and radio listeners have a stake in FCC decisions, they are not well enough organized to petition it effectively.

GOVERNMENT AS PROTECTOR OF THE ENVIRONMENT

Graphic
www.mhhe.com/pattersontad7

Few changes in public opinion and policy during recent decades have been as dramatic as those relating to the environment. Most Americans today recycle some of their garbage, and roughly two-thirds say they are either an active environmentalist or sympathetic to environmental concerns. In the 1960s, few Americans bothered to sort their trash, and few could have answered a polling question that asked them whether they were an "environmentalist." The term was not commonly used, and most people would not have understood its meaning.

The environmental movement gained impetus with the publication in 1962 of Rachel Carson's *The Silent Spring*.[10] Written at a time when the author was dying of breast cancer, *Silent Spring* revealed the threat of harmful pesticides such as DDT and challenged the notion that scientific progress was an unqualified benefit to society. Carson's appearance at a Senate hearing contributed to legislative action that produced the 1963 Clean Air Act and the 1965 Water Quality Act. It was the first time in the nation's history that the federal government had taken major steps to protect the nation's air, water, and ground from pollution. Today, environmental protection extends to nearly two hundred harmful forms of emission.

Conservationism: The Older Wave

Although government policy aimed at protecting the air, water, and soil is relatively new, the government has been involved in land conservation for more than a century.[11] The first national park was created at Yellowstone in 1872 and, like the later ones, was established to preserve the nation's natural heritage for

The federal government's environmental efforts include programs designed to conserve nature through the protection of forests and other natural assets. Shown here is a scene from Yellowstone National Park.

generations to come. The national park system serves more than one hundred million visitors each year and includes a total of eighty million acres, an area larger than every state except Alaska, Texas, California, and Montana.

The national parks are run by the National Park Service, an agency within the Department of Interior. Another agency, the U.S. Forest Service, located within the Department of Agriculture, manages the national forests, which cover an area more than twice the size of the national parks. They too have been preserved in part to protect America's natural heritage.

However, the nation's parks and forests are subject to a "dual use" policy. They are nature preserves and recreation areas, but they are also rich in natural resources—minerals, trees, and grazing lands. The federal government sells permits to ranchers, timber companies, and mining firms that give them the right to take some of these resources, a policy that can place their interests in conflict with those of conservationists. A case in point is Alaska's Arctic National Wildlife Refuge. The refuge is home to numerous species, including caribou and moose, but it also contains oil and natural gas. Oil companies have long wanted to drill in this wilderness area, while environmental groups have sought to prohibit drilling. Over the past few decades, the Arctic National Wildlife Refuge has periodically been the focus of intense political debate and lobbying. President Clinton threatened to veto any bill that would open the area to drilling. President Bush, in contrast, proposed to open the area to drilling as part of his program to increase the nation's energy supplies.

Environmentalism: The Newer Wave

The pivotal decade in the federal government's realization that Americans needed protection from the harmful effects of air, water, and ground pollutants was the 1960s. The period was capped by the first Earth Day. Held in the spring

Environmental regulations restricting the level of automobile pollution have greatly improved air quality in America's cities. However, motor vehicles are the major source of emissions that contribute to global warming.

of 1970, it was the brainchild of Senator Gaylord Nelson (D-Wis.), who had devoted nearly ten years to finding ways to draw the public's attention to environmental issues. With Earth Day, Nelson succeeded to a degree not even he could have imagined: ten thousand grade schools and high schools, two thousand colleges, and one thousand communities participated in the event, which included public rallies and environmental cleanup efforts. Earth Day has been held every year since 1970 and is now a worldwide event.

The year 1970 also marked the creation of the Environmental Protection Agency. Within a few months, the EPA was issuing new regulations at such a rapid pace that business firms had difficulty keeping track of all the mandates, much less complying fully with them. Corporations eventually found an ally in President Gerald Ford, who, in a 1975 speech to the National Federation of Industrial Business, claimed that business regulation was costing $150 billion annually, or $2,000 for every American family.[12] Although Ford's estimate exceeded that of economic analysts, his point was not lost on policymakers or the people. The economy was in a slump, and the costs of complying with the new regulations were impeding an economic recovery. Polls indicated a decline in public support for regulatory action.

Since then, environmental protection policy has not been greatly expanded, but neither has it greatly contracted. The emphasis has been on administering and amending the laws put into effect in the 1960s and 1970s. Nevertheless, the EPA has a broad mandate to protect America's air and water. In a 2001 decision, for example, the Supreme Court ruled unanimously that the EPA is to consider only public health and not industry costs in setting air quality standards.[13]

Environmental regulation has had a dramatic effect on air and water quality. Pollution levels today are far below their levels of the 1960s, when yellowish-gray fog ("smog") hung over cities like Los Angeles and New York and when bodies of water like the Potomac River and Lake Erie were open sewers. In the past four decades, toxic waste emissions have been cut by half, hundreds of polluted lakes and rivers have been revitalized, energy efficiency has increased, food supplies have been made safer, and urban air pollution has decreased by more than 60 percent.

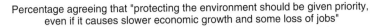

Percentage agreeing that "protecting the environment should be given priority, even if it causes slower economic growth and some loss of jobs"

Country	Percentage
Canada	82%
Italy	82%
Great Britain	81%
Germany	78%
Japan	72%
United States	69%
France	66%

Figure 15–1

Opinions on the Environment and Economic Growth

Majorities in industrialized democracies support environmental protection, even if it means somewhat slower economic growth. However, Americans are somewhat less likely than citizens elsewhere to accept this trade-off.

Source: The Pew Research Center for the People and the Press, Global Attitudes Survey, 2002.

Although environmental regulation has had positive effects, it remains an ongoing source of controversy.[14] The debate over global warming is an example. The scientific community has concluded that carbon emissions are creating a "greenhouse effect" (the trapping of heat in the atmosphere) that is producing a gradual rise in the earth's temperature. Global warming can be retarded only by controls on emissions but that solution would entail costly technological innovations and cutbacks in economic growth. So far, the pro-growth side has had the upper hand. The United States is the single largest source of worldwide carbon emissions, and U.S. policymakers have resisted demands at home and from abroad to enact substantial new restrictions on air pollution, fearing that any such policy would harm the U.S. economy. In 2002, for example, President George W. Bush declared that the United States would not participate in the Kyoto agreement, a multinational effort to reduce the emission of greenhouse gases (see "Debating the Issues").

Opinion polls indicate that a majority of Americans support environmental protection even when it would result in somewhat slower economic growth and some job loss. However, they are less willing to make this trade-off than are Canadians, the Japanese, or Western Europeans (see Figure 15–1).

GOVERNMENT AS PROMOTER OF ECONOMIC INTERESTS

The U.S. government has always made important contributions to the nation's economy. Congress in 1789 gave a boost to the nation's shipping industry by placing a tariff on imported goods carried by foreign ships. Since that first favor, the U.S. government has provided thousands of direct benefits to economic interests. The following sections provide brief examples of a few of these benefits.

Promoting Business

American business is not opposed to government regulation as such. Corporations object only to regulatory policies that hurt their interests. At various times and in different ways, as in the case of the FCC and broadcasters,

Debating the Issues

Should the United States Have Supported the Kyoto Agreement?

At a conference in Kyoto, Japan, representatives of the United States and other nations came together to address the problem of climate change as a result of the emission of greenhouse gases. The resulting accord, called the Kyoto Agreement, established targets that countries would meet to help reduce the carbon emissions contributing to global warming. In 2002, President George W. Bush announced that the United States would not sign the agreement, citing objections to it from U.S. firms and a majority in Congress. His decision provoked criticism from European countries, environmental groups, and some members of Congress, including Senator John McCain. Bush's rejection effectively doomed the Kyoto Agreement. The United States is the largest single producer of greenhouse emissions, and any comprehensive global agreement would virtually require its participation.

Yes: Given the fact that the United States produces approximately 25 percent of the total greenhouse gases emissions, the United States has a responsibility to cut its emissions of greenhouse gases. The United States must realize that when it comes to the climate, there are no boundaries. Therefore, climate change is a global problem and must be resolved globally. The current situation demands leadership from the United States. . . . There is going to be a world marketplace for carbon reductions, a marketplace that rewards improvements in energy efficiency, advances in energy technologies, and improvements in land-use practices—and we are running the risk that America is not going to be part of it. The risks that climate change poses for businesses have now increased. . . . While U.S. businesses are gaining experience with voluntary programs and are recognized as the world's experts in this area, they are increasingly recognizing that purely voluntary approaches will not be enough to meet the goal of preventing dangerous effects on the climate system. . . . As usual, industry is ahead of government in this area. . . . Deploying the power of a marketplace to pursue the least expensive answers is a unique and powerful American approach to the threat of climate change.

—*John McCain, U.S. senator (R-Ariz.)*

No: We do not know how much effect natural fluctuations in climate may have had on warming. We do not know how much our climate could, or will, change in the future. We do not know how fast change will occur, or even how some of our actions could impact it. Our country, the United States, is the world's largest emitter of man-made greenhouse gases. We account for almost 20 percent of the world's man-made greenhouse emissions. We also account for about one-quarter of the world's economic output. We recognize the responsibility to reduce our emissions. We also recognize the other part of the story—that the rest of the world emits 80 percent of all greenhouse gases. . . . Kyoto is, in many ways, unrealistic. Many countries cannot meet their Kyoto targets. The targets themselves were arbitrary and not based upon science. For America, complying with those mandates would have a negative economic impact, with layoffs of workers and price increases for consumers. And when you evaluate all these flaws, most reasonable people will understand that it's not sound public policy. . . . Yet, America's unwillingness to embrace a flawed treaty should not be read by our friends and allies as any abdication of responsibility. To the contrary, my administration is committed to a leadership role on the issue of climate change.

—*George W. Bush, president of the United States*

some regulatory agencies have promoted the interests of the very industries they are supposed to regulate in the public interest.

Providing loans and tax breaks is another way that government promotes business. Firms receive loan guarantees, direct loans, tax credits for capital investments, and tax deductions for capital depreciation. Over the past forty years, the burden of federal taxation has shifted dramatically from corporations to individuals. A few decades ago, the revenues raised from taxes on corporate income were roughly the same as the revenues raised from taxes on individual income. Today, individual taxpayers carry the heavier burden by a five-to-one ratio. Some analysts do not regard the change as particularly significant, arguing that higher corporate taxes would be passed along to the public anyway in the form of higher prices for goods and services.

The most significant contribution that government makes to business is the traditional services it provides, such as education, transportation, and defense. Colleges and universities, which are funded primarily by governments, furnish business with most of its professional and technical work force and with much of the basic research that goes into product development. The nation's roadways, waterways, and airports are other public-sector contributions without which business could not operate. In short, America's business has no bigger booster than government.

Striking janitors parade in Beverly Hills, California. Although government provides support for labor through a variety of policies, U.S. workers have less power and fewer rights than their European counterparts, a reflection of America's individualistic culture.

Promoting Labor

Laissez-faire thinking dominated government's approach to labor well into the twentieth century. The governing principle, developed by the courts in the early nineteenth century, held that workers had limited rights of collective action. Union activity was regarded as interference with the natural supply of labor and the free setting of wages. Government's hostility toward labor was evident, for example, in the use of U.S. Army troops during the late 1800s to break up strikes.

The 1930s brought significant changes. The key legislation was the National Labor Relations Act of 1935, which guaranteed workers the right to bargain collectively and prohibited business from discriminating against union employees and from unreasonably interfering with union activities. Government has also aided labor over the years by legislating minimum wages and maximum work hours, unemployment benefits, safer and more healthful working conditions, and nondiscriminatory hiring practices.

Although government support for labor extends beyond these examples, it is not nearly as extensive as its assistance to business. America's culture of individualism has resulted in public policies that are less favorable to labor than policies in European countries.

Promoting Agriculture

Until well into the twentieth century, most Americans still lived on farms and in small rural communities. Agriculture was America's dominant business and was assisted by government's land policies. The Homestead Act of 1862, for example, opened government-owned lands to settlement, creating spectacular "land rushes" by offering 160 acres of government land free to each family that staked a claim, built a house, and farmed the land for five years.

Farm programs today provide assistance to both small farmers and large commercial enterprises (agribusinesses) and cost the federal government billions of dollars annually. A major goal of this spending is to eliminate some of the risks associated with farming. Weather, world markets, and other factors can radically affect crop and livestock prices, and federal programs are designed to protect farmers from adverse developments.

Experience has shown that farmers need government's help. In 1996, Congress passed legislation that trimmed longstanding crop subsidy and crop allocation programs. The goal was to let the free trade market largely determine the prices farmers would get for their crops and to let farmers themselves decide on the crops they would plant. The result was a depressed farm economy—prices fell sharply because of the surplus production of particular crops. In 2002, Congress abandoned the free-market approach. Crop subsidies were increased and expanded to include more crops, and quotas were established for the planting of particular crops. The 2002 Farm Bill put farmers in line for hundreds of billions of dollars in government assistance in future years. At present, federal subsidies account for more than a third of net farm income.

FISCAL POLICY: GOVERNMENT AS MANAGER OF ECONOMY, I

Until the 1930s, the U.S. government adhered to the prevailing free-market theory and made no attempt to maintain the stability of the economy as a whole. The economy, which was regarded as largely self-regulating, was fairly prosperous, but it collapsed periodically, resulting in widespread joblessness and financial loss.

The greatest economic catastrophe in the nation's history—the Great Depression of the 1930s—finally brought an end to traditional economics. Franklin D. Roosevelt's government spending and job programs, designed to stimulate the economy and put Americans back to work, heralded the change. Although Roosevelt's use of government policy as an economic stimulus was highly controversial, today it is an accepted practice. Government is expected to pursue policies that will contribute to economic growth and stability.

TABLE 15–2	**Fiscal Policy: A Summary** Taxing and spending levels can be adjusted in order to affect economic conditions.	
PROBLEM	**FISCAL POLICY ACTIONS**
Low productivity and high unemployment	Demand side: increase spending
	Supply side: cut business taxes
Excess production and high inflation	Decrease spending
	Increase taxes

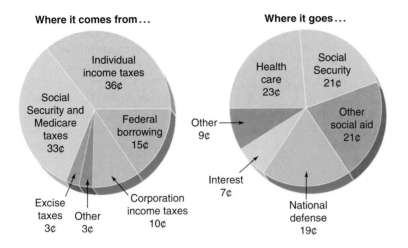

Where it comes from...

Where it goes...

Figure 15–2

The Federal Budget Dollar, Fiscal Year 2005
Source: Office of Management and Budget.

Taxing and Spending Policy

The government's efforts to maintain a thriving economy are made mainly through its taxing and spending decisions, which together are referred to as its **fiscal policy** (see Table 15–2).

The annual federal budget is the foundation of fiscal policy. Thousands of pages in length, the budget allocates federal expenditures among government programs and identifies the revenues—taxes, social insurance receipts, and borrowed funds—that will be used to pay for these programs (see Figure 15–2). From one perspective, the budget is the national government's allocation of costs and benefits. Every federal program benefits some interest, whether it be farmers who get price supports, defense firms that obtain military contracts, or retirees who receive monthly social security checks. Not surprisingly, the process of enacting the annual federal budget is highly political as agencies and interests compete for federal dollars.

From another standpoint, that of fiscal policy, the budget is a device for stimulating or dampening economic growth. Through changes in overall levels of spending and taxing, government can help keep the economy running smoothly.

Fiscal policy has its origins in the economic theories of John Maynard Keynes. In *The General Theory of Employment, Interest, and Money* (1936), Keynes noted that employers become overly cautious during a depression and will not expand production, even as wages drop. Challenging the traditional idea that government should draw back during depressions, Keynes claimed that severe economic downturns can be shortened only by increased government spending. Keynes said that government should engage in **deficit spending**—spending more than it gets from taxes, which can be accomplished through the borrowing and printing of money. By placing additional money in the hands of consumers and investors, government can stimulate production, employment, and spending and thereby promote recovery.[15]

fiscal policy A tool of economic management by which government attempts to maintain a stable economy through its taxing and spending policies.

deficit spending When the government spends more than it collects in taxes and other revenues.

John Maynard Keynes

(1883–1946)

Trained in mathematics and economics, John Maynard Keynes developed a theory of government spending and taxation that became the basis for government efforts to manage the economy through fiscal policy. His theory developed in part from his belief that there would be dire economic and hence dire political consequences from the heavy reparations levied on Germany after World War I. When the world economy went into a slump in 1929, Keynes set about developing a theory of economic cycles. The result was *The General Theory of Employment, Interest, and Money*, published in 1936.

economic depression A very severe and sustained economic downturn. Depressions are rare in the United States; the last one was in the 1930s.

economic recession A moderate but sustained downturn in the economy. Recessions are part of the economy's normal cycle of ups and downs.

demand-side economics A form of fiscal policy that emphasizes "demand" (consumer spending). Government can use increased spending or tax cuts to place more money in consumers' hands and thereby increase demand.

budget deficit Situation when the government's expenditures exceed its tax and other revenues.

national debt The total cumulative amount that the U.S. government owes to creditors.

According to Keynesian theory, the government's response should be commensurate with the severity of the problem. During an **economic depression**—an exceptionally steep and sustained downturn in the economy—the government should engage in massive new spending programs to hasten the recovery. During a less severe **economic recession,** new government spending should be less substantial.

Demand-Side Stimulation

Keynes's theory focused on government's efforts to stimulate consumer spending. This **demand-side economics** emphasizes the consumer "demand" component of the supply-demand equation. When the economy is sluggish, the government can increase its spending, thus placing more money in consumers' hands. With additional money to spend, consumers buy more goods and services. This increased demand, in turn, stimulates businesses to produce more goods and hire more workers. In this way, government spending contributes to economic recovery.

Although heightened spending is a tool that government can employ during a severe economic crisis, it is not a sensible response to every economic dip. Its application is affected by government's overall financial situation. In the early 1990s, for example, the U.S. economy was in its longest downturn since World War II, but policymakers chose not to boost federal spending temporarily as a means of blunting the recession. The reason was simple enough. During the previous two decades, there had been a **budget deficit**—each year, the federal government had spent more than it had received in tax and other revenues. The result was a huge **national debt,** which is the total cumulative amount that the U.S. government owes to creditors. By the early 1990s, the debt had reached $4 trillion, and an enormous amount of money was required each year merely to pay the interest on the national debt. Interest payments were roughly the total of all federal income taxes paid by Americans living west of the Mississippi River. This drain on the government's resources made it politically difficult for policymakers to increase the level of government spending in order to boost the economy.

The situation changed dramatically in the late 1990s. In 1998, for the first time since 1969, the U.S. government had a **balanced budget**—revenues were equal to government expenditures. Thereafter, there was a **budget surplus**—the federal government received more in tax and other revenues than it spent. The surplus was attributable to a surging U.S. economy that was in the midst of its longest period of sustained growth in the country's history. With more people working and with the stock market climbing ever higher, tax revenues had increased and government welfare expenditures had declined. The rosy budget picture also reflected the fiscal discipline of the Clinton administration and the Republican Congress, which had slowed the growth in federal expenditures.

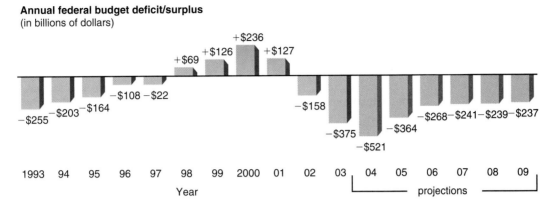

Figure 15–3

The Federal Budget Deficit/Surplus
The federal government ran a budget deficit until 1998, at which time a surplus that was expected to last for years emerged. In 2001, however, the surplus quickly disappeared as a result of an economic downturn, costs associated with the war on terrorism, and a cut in federal taxes.
Source: Office of Management and Budget, 2004.

The turnaround was relatively short-lived. The economy began to slow in 2000, and as income declined so did government tax revenues. The economic slowdown was accelerated by the terrorist attacks of September 11, 2001, which also led to sharp increases in defense spending in conjunction with military action in Afghanistan and Iraq. The effect of these and other developments was a huge budget deficit that is projected to last for years to come (see Figure 15–3). The severity of the deficit is a constraint on policymakers' ability to apply demand-side measures as a means of boosting the economy. Even though a large tax cut or major spending increase would contribute to economic growth, it would also increase the deficit.

The impact of demand-side fiscal policy, however, cannot be measured only by its effect during economic downturns. Although the United States has had recessionary periods since the 1930s, none of these downturns has come anywhere near the severity of the Great Depression. One reason is that government spending is now at permanently high levels. Each month, for example, roughly forty million Americans receive a social security check from the government. In turn, they spend it on food, clothing, housing, entertainment, and other goods and services. They pump billions of dollars each month into the U.S. economy, which creates jobs and income for millions of other Americans. And social security is only one—albeit the largest—of numerous federal spending programs. Every day, the federal government spends about $4 billion, more than the typical large corporation pumps into the economy during an entire year. The U.S. economy thus has a constant demand-side stimulus: government spending on an ongoing and massive scale.

balanced budget Situation when the government's tax and other revenues for the year are roughly equal to its expenditures.

budget surplus Situation when the government's tax and other revenues exceed its expenditures.

Supply-Side Stimulation

A fiscal policy alternative to demand-side stimulation is **supply-side economics,** which emphasizes the business (supply) component of the supply-demand

supply-side economics A form of fiscal policy that emphasizes "supply" (production). An example of supply-side economics is a tax cut for business.

equation. Supply-side theory was a cornerstone of President Reagan's economic program. He believed that economic growth could occur as easily from stimulation of the business sector as from stimulation of consumer demand. "Reaganomics" included substantial tax breaks for businesses and upper-income individuals.[16]

The Reagan administration overestimated the stimulus effect of its taxcuts policy. It had estimated that the increased tax revenues from increased business activity would soon offset the loss of revenue from reduced tax rates. However, the loss in tax revenues was much greater than the gain in revenues from the economic growth that followed. As a result, the tax cuts contributed to a growing budget deficit.

Despite this discouraging result, Reagan's supply-side measures contributed to the economic growth that began in the United States during the 1980s. The Reagan tax cuts allowed business firms to spend more on capital investments and enabled higher-income Americans to place more money into the stock markets, providing additional funds for business investment.

Supply-side theory was also the basis of President George W. Bush's economic program. Although his Economic Growth and Tax Reconciliation Act of 2001 included a demand-side component (an immediate cash rebate to taxpayers), supply-side measures were its signature: sharp cuts in the tax rate on individuals, with most of the gains going to high-income taxpayers, and a reduction in the **capital-gains tax,** the tax that individuals pay on gains in capital investments such as property and stocks. A reduction in the capital-gains tax increases the incentive for individuals to invest their money in capital markets. In turn, firms use this money to expand their operations and markets. The subsequent job creation and increased supply of goods can stimulate consumer demand and contribute to economic growth.

capital-gains tax Tax that individuals pay on money gained from the sale of a capital asset, such as property or stocks.

When Bush's tax bill was enacted in 2001, he had agreed—in order to get the congressional support necessary for its passage—to a phase-in of the individual and capital-gains tax cuts. In 2003, he went back to Congress and asked for a speeded-up timetable as a means of giving the economy a boost. Bush got what he requested. The capital-gains tax rate, which had been 28 percent in 2001, dropped to 15 percent, as did the tax rate for dividend income. Meanwhile, the highest marginal rate assessed on individual income fell to 35 percent, down from 39 percent in 2001. The great bulk of the tax savings resulting from Bush's policies went to high-income taxpayers—precisely those people who, according to supply-side economics, are the key to economic growth. (Bush's tax cuts are discussed further in Chapter 16.)

Controlling Inflation

inflation A general increase in the average level of prices of goods and services.

High unemployment and low production are only two of the economic problems that government is called on to solve. Another is **inflation,** an increase in the average level of prices of goods and services. Before the late 1960s, inflation was a minor problem: prices rose by less than 4 percent annually. But inflation rose sharply during the last years of the Vietnam War and remained high throughout the 1970s, reaching a postwar record rate of 13 percent in 1979 (see Figure 15–4). Since then, the annual inflation rate has averaged about 4 percent, and concern about inflation has lessened significantly.

Inflation rate since 1979 (Consumer Price Index)

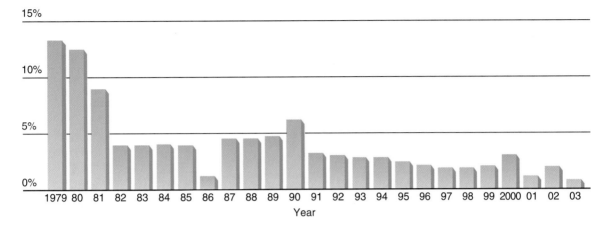

Figure 15–4

The Annual Rate of Inflation, 1979–2003
Price increases have declined in the last decade in comparison with the late 1970s.
Source: U.S. Department of Labor, 2004.

To fight inflation, government can apply remedies opposite to those used to fight unemployment and low productivity. Inflation normally occurs when jobs are plentiful and people have extra money to spend. Demand is high in such periods, and prices go up. By cutting spending or raising personal income taxes, government takes money from consumers, thus reducing demand and dampening prices. (The main policy tool for addressing inflation is monetary policy, which is discussed later in the chapter.)

The Process and Politics of Fiscal Policy

The president and Congress jointly determine fiscal policy, mainly through the annual budgetary process. The Constitution grants Congress the power to tax and spend, but the president, as chief executive, plays a major role in shaping the budget. The president's veto power also provides a strong tool in budget negotiations with Congress. In reality, the budgetary process involves give-and-take between Congress and the president as each tries to exert influence over the final budget.[17]

The Budgetary Process

The budgetary process is a very elaborate one, as could be expected when billions of dollars in federal spending are at issue. From beginning to end, the process lasts a year and a half (see Figure 15–5).

The budgetary process begins in the executive branch when the president, in consultation with the Office of Management and Budget (OMB), establishes general budget guidelines. The OMB is part of the Executive Office of the

Figure 15–5

Federal Budgetary Process
The budget begins with the president's instructions to the agencies and ends when Congress enacts the budget. The entire process spans about eighteen months.

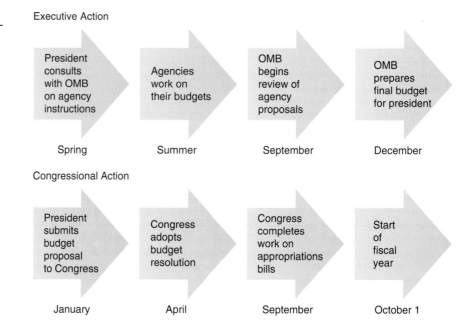

Executive Action

President consults with OMB on agency instructions — Spring

Agencies work on their budgets — Summer

OMB begins review of agency proposals — September

OMB prepares final budget for president — December

Congressional Action

President submits budget proposal to Congress — January

Congress adopts budget resolution — April

Congress completes work on appropriations bills — September

Start of fiscal year — October 1

President (see Chapter 12) and takes its directives from the president. Hundreds of agencies and thousands of programs are covered by the budget, and the OMB uses the president's decisions to determine the instructions that will guide each agency's budget preparations. For example, each agency is assigned a budget ceiling within which it must work.

The agencies receive these instructions in the spring and then work through the summer to develop a detailed agency budget, taking into account their existing programs and any new or proposed ones. These agency budgets then go to the OMB in September for a full review that invariably includes further consultation with each agency. The agency budgets are then finalized and combined into the full budget. Throughout, the OMB remains in close touch with the White House to ensure that the budget items conform to the president's objectives.

The agencies naturally tend to want more money, whereas the OMB has the job of matching the budget to the president's priorities. In fact, however, the president does not have any real say over most of the budget, about two-thirds of which involves mandatory spending. This spending is authorized by current law, and the government must allocate and spend the money unless the law itself is rescinded, an unlikely occurrence. Examples are social security and Medicare, which provide benefits to the elderly. The president does not have the authority to suspend or reduce these programs. Interest on the national debt is also part of the budget, and here too the president has no real option. The federal government is obligated to pay interest on the money it has borrowed.

The OMB focuses on the third of the budget that involves discretionary spending, which includes such areas as defense, foreign aid, education, national parks, space exploration, public broadcasting, and highways. In reality, even a large part of this spending is not truly discretionary. No president would even consider slashing defense spending to almost nothing or closing the national parks, and even modest cuts in a discretionary program may encounter resistance in Congress.

The president, then, works on the margins of the budget, trying to push it in directions that are consistent with administration goals. The effort in many policy areas consists of a modest increase or decrease in spending compared with the previous year. There are always a few areas, however, where the president will attempt a more dramatic adjustment. In 2003 and 2004, for example, President Bush asked for large increases in defense spending to assist in the war on terrorism and to pay for the Iraq war and reconstruction.

In January, the president transmits the full budget to Congress. This budget is only a proposal, because Congress has the constitutional power to appropriate funds. In reviewing the president's proposed budget, Congress relies heavily on the Congressional Budget Office (CBO), which, as discussed in Chapter 11, is the congressional equivalent of the OMB. The CBO reviews the items in the budget and develops estimates of their costs. If the CBO believes that an agency has misjudged the amount of money needed to meet its legislatively required programs, it will bring this information to the attention of the appropriate committees of Congress. Similarly, if the CBO concludes that the OMB has miscalculated how much the government can be expected to receive in taxes and other revenues, committees will be notified of the discrepancy.

The key congressional committees in the budgetary process are the budget and the appropriations committees. The House and Senate Budget Committees are responsible for drafting a "budget resolution," which includes projections of total spending, total revenues, and allocations between the mandatory and discretionary spending categories. These guidelines are then submitted to the full House and Senate for approval. The budget ceilings that are part of the resolution place a tentative limit on how much money will be allocated for each spending area.

The House Appropriations Committee through its subcommittees then takes on the primary task of reviewing the budget items, which includes hearings with each federal agency. There are thirteen such subcommittees, each of which has responsibility for a substantive area, such as defense or agriculture. Agency budgets are invariably changed at this stage. A subcommittee may cut an agency's budget because it believes that the agency's work is not very important or that the agency has asked for more funds than it needs for its programs. Or the subcommittee may decide to increase an agency's budget beyond what the president has requested. In any case, each subcommittee leaves its own mark on each agency's budget. The subcommittees' recommendations are then submitted to the House Appropriations Committee for final review and submission to the full House for a vote. The Senate Appropriations Committee and its subcommittees conduct a similar process, but the Senate is a smaller body and its review of agency requests is normally less thorough. To some degree, the Senate committee and its subcommittees serve as a "court of appeals" for agencies that have had their budget requests reduced by the House.

During Congress's work on the budget, the president's recommendations undergo varying degrees of change. The priorities of a majority in Congress are never exactly those of the president, even when they are of the same party. When they are of opposite parties, their priorities may differ greatly.

After the work of the appropriations committees has been completed and is approved by the full House and Senate, differences in the Senate and House versions of the appropriations bill are reconciled in conference committee (see Chapter 11). The legislation is then sent to the president for approval or veto. The threat of a presidential veto often is enough to persuade Congress to accept many of the president's recommendations. In the end, the budget inevitably reflects both presidential and congressional priorities. Neither branch ever gets everything it wants, but each branch always gets some of what it wants.

Once the budget has been passed by both the House and the Senate and is signed by the president, it takes effect on October 1, the starting date of the federal government's fiscal year. If agreement on the budget has not been reached by October 1, temporary funding is required in order to maintain government operations. In late 1995, President Clinton and the Republican Congress deadlocked on budgetary issues to such an extent that they could not even agree on temporary funding. Their standoff twice forced a brief shutdown of nonessential government activities.

Graphic
www.mhhe.com/pattersontad7

Partisan Differences

Partisan politics is a significant part of fiscal policy. The Democratic coalition has traditionally included the majority of lower-income and working-class Americans. Accordingly, the party's leaders are sensitive to rising unemployment because blue-collar workers are often the first and most deeply affected. Democrats in Washington have usually responded to a sluggish economy with increased government spending (demand-side fiscal policy), which offers direct help to the unemployed and stimulates consumption. Virtually every increase in federal unemployment benefits during the past fifty years, for example, has been initiated by Democratic officeholders.

Republican leaders are more likely to see an economic downturn through the eyes of business firms. Republicans in Washington typically have sought ways to protect or stimulate business activity as a means of economic recovery. Thus, in most cases, Republicans have resisted large increases in government spending (with the exception of defense spending) as a response to a sluggish economy. Such spending requires government to borrow money, which leads to upward pressure on interest rates. This pressure in turn raises the cost of doing business, because firms must pay higher interest rates for the money they borrow.

graduated personal income tax A tax on personal income in which the tax rate increases as income increases; in other words, the tax rate is higher for higher income levels.

Tax policy also has partisan dimensions. Democratic policymakers have typically sought tax policies that help working-class and lower-middle-class Americans. Democrats have favored a **graduated** (or progressive) **personal income tax,** in which the tax rate goes up substantially as income rises. Republicans have preferred to keep taxes on upper incomes at a relatively low level, contending that this policy encourages the savings and investment that foster economic growth (supply-side fiscal policy). These differences were evident, for example, in the battle over the Economic Growth and Tax Relief Reconciliation Act of 2001. Proposed by President Bush, the legislation contained the largest tax cut since 1981. The chief beneficiaries were upper-income taxpayers. In both the Senate and the House of Representatives, the bill had the overwhelming support of Republicans and very little support from Democrats.

STATES IN THE NATION

Federal Taxing and Spending: Winners and Losers

Fiscal policy (the federal government's taxing and spending policies) varies in its effect on the states. The residents of some states pay a lot more in federal taxes than they receive in benefits. The biggest loser is New Jersey, whose taxpayers get back in federal spending in their state only $0.62 for every dollar they pay in federal taxes. Connecticut taxpayers ($0.65 for every dollar) are the next-biggest losers. In contrast, the residents of some states get back more from federal spending programs than they contribute in taxes. The biggest winners are New Mexico and North Dakota, whose taxpayers get back $2.37 and $2.07, respectively, in federal spending in their states for every dollar they pay in federal taxes.

Q. Why are most of the "losers" in the northeastern section of the country?

A. The federal taxes that originate in a state reflect its wealth, and the northeastern states are generally the wealthier ones. Because they are wealthier, they also get less federal assistance for programs designed to help lower-income people and areas. Finally, most federal lands and military installations—sources of federal money—lie outside the northeastern region.

Taxes to spend ratio

$0.79 or lower
$0.80 – 1.09
$1.10 – 1.49
$1.50 or higher

In the Senate, for example, only two Republicans voted against it, whereas thirty-nine Democrats did so.[18] (Tax policy is discussed further in Chapter 15).

MONETARY POLICY: GOVERNMENT AS MANAGER OF ECONOMY, II

monetary policy A tool of economic management, available to government, based on manipulation of the amount of money in circulation.

Fiscal policy is not the only instrument of economic management available to government; another is **monetary policy,** which is based on manipulation of the amount of money in circulation (see Table 15–3). Monetarists such as economist Milton Friedman hold that control of the money supply is the key to sustaining a healthy economy. Too much money in circulation contributes to inflation because too many dollars are chasing too few goods, which drives up prices. Too little money in circulation results in a slowing economy and rising unemployment, because consumers lack the ready cash and easy credit required to push up spending levels. Monetarists believe in tightening or loosening the money supply as a way of slowing or invigorating the economy.

TABLE 15–3	**Monetary Policy: A Summary of the Fed's Role** The money supply can be adjusted in order to affect economic conditions.
PROBLEM	**MONETARY POLICY ACTIONS BY FEDERAL RESERVE**
Low productivity and high unemployment (require an increase in the money supply)	Lowers interest rate on loans to member banks Lowers cash reserve that member banks must deposit in Federal Reserve System
Excess productivity and high inflation (require a decrease in the money supply)	Raises interest rate on loans to member banks Raises cash reserve that member banks must deposit in Federal Reserve System

The Fed

Control over the money supply rests not with the president or Congress but with the Federal Reserve System (known as "the Fed"), which was created by the Federal Reserve Act of 1913. The Fed has a board of governors whose seven members serve for fourteen years, except for the chair and vice chair, who serve for four years. All members are appointed by the president with the approval of the Senate. The Fed regulates the activities of all national banks and those state banks that meet certain standards and choose to become members of the Federal Reserve System.

The Fed decides how much money to add to or subtract from the economy, seeking a balance that will permit steady growth without causing an unacceptable level of inflation. One way the Fed affects the money supply is by raising or lowering the cash reserve that member banks are required to deposit with the Federal Reserve. This reserve is a proportion of each member's total deposits. By increasing the reserve rate, the Fed takes money from member banks and thus takes it out of circulation. When the Fed lowers the reserve rate, banks have more money available and can make more loans to consumers and investors.

A second and more visible way the Fed affects the money supply is by lowering or raising the interest rate that member banks are charged when they borrow from the Federal Reserve. When the Fed raises the interest rate, banks also tend to raise the rate they charge for new loans, which discourages borrowing and thus reduces the amount of money entering the economy. Conversely, by lowering the interest rate, the Fed encourages firms and individuals to borrow from banks, which increases the money supply.

The Fed's interest-rate adjustments are often front-page news because they are a signal of the strength of the economy and thus affect the decisions of consumers and firms. As the economy weakened in 2001, for example, the Fed began a series of adjustments that by 2004 had reduced the interest rate to its lowest level in four decades. As the rate declined, home buying and refinancing soared, creating jobs in the construction industry, among other things. Some analysts credit the Fed's interest-rate policy with keeping the U.S. economy afloat as it struggled to regain strength.

Economists debate the relative effectiveness of monetary policy and fiscal policy, but monetary policy has one obvious advantage: it can be implemented more quickly than fiscal policy. The Fed can adjust interest and reserve rates on short notice, thus providing the economy with a psychological boost to go along with the financial effect of a change in the money supply. In contrast, changes in fiscal policy usually take much longer to implement. Congress is normally a slow-acting institution, and new taxing and spending programs ordinarily require a substantial preparation period before they can be put into effect. Moreover, Republicans and Democrats are often divided over which fiscal policy tool to use—taxing or spending—and may not be able to reach agreement on how to respond to a faltering economy. In 2003, for example, economic-stimulus legislation was delayed because Republicans wanted it to be rooted in tax cuts while Democrats pushed for spending on jobs-related programs.

The Politics of the Fed

The greater flexibility of monetary policy has positioned the Fed as the institution with primary policy responsibility for keeping the U.S. economy on a steady course. The Fed's power can easily be exaggerated. The U.S. economy is subject to a lot of influences, and the Fed's impact is relatively modest. Nevertheless, the Fed is a vital component of U.S. economic policy and has become increasingly important.[19]

The power of the Fed raises important questions. One is the issue of representation: whose interests does the Fed serve, those of the public as a whole or those of the banking sector? The Fed is not a wholly impartial body. Although it makes decisions in the context of economic theories and projections, it is "the bankers' bank" and as such is protective of monied interests. The Fed typically is more concerned with rising inflation, which erodes the value of money, than with rising unemployment, which has its greatest impact on people at the bottom of the economic ladder. The Fed tends to hike interest rates when signs of

University of Chicago economist Milton Friedman became the leading proponent of monetary policy as a tool for managing the economy. Friedman was named "Economist of the Century" by *Time* magazine.

GLOBAL Perspective

Americans in an Interdependent World

Economic Globalization

Economic globalization is a term that describes the increased interdependence of nations' economies. This development is both an opportunity for and a threat to U.S. economic interests. The opportunity rests with the possibility of increased demand abroad for U.S. goods and services as a result of open trade with other countries and of economic growth within these countries. The threat lies in the fact that foreign firms also compete in the global marketplace and may use their competitive advantages, such as low-wage labor, to produce goods more cheaply than U.S. firms can. In addition, as nations' economies become more interdependent, instability in one market can spread quickly to others, causing a broad decline in the global economy.

The effect of interdependency was evident in the summer of 1998 when the U.S. stock market dropped sharply in response to adverse economic developments in Asia and South America. The economic downturn in these regions also affected the U.S. balance of trade. As their economies slowed, their demand for goods declined, and U.S. exports declined accordingly. The reverse happened in 2001, when a slowdown in the U.S. economy contributed to slow growth in Europe, Asia, and South America.

Not surprisingly, global economic stability has been a high priority for U.S. officials. Working through international organizations, the U.S. government has provided financial and other assistance when economic instability occurs elsewhere in the world.

To what degree is your local area affected by the global economy? To what extent is your personal well-being affected? Think not only in terms of a job or jobs you might have had but also in terms of various products (for example, electronic items such as computer games) you might own.

---

rising inflation appear. Higher rates have the effect of slowing inflation, but they also slow job and income growth.

A related issue is one of accountability: should the Fed, an unelected body, have so much power? Though appointed by the president, members of the Federal Reserve Board are not subject to removal. They serve for fixed terms and are relatively insulated from political pressures, including the changes that take place through elections. Moreover, the Fed announces its decisions after closed-door meetings, although it has implemented a policy of signaling beforehand the policies it is likely to announce. Of course, the Fed, as a banking institution, has a vested interest in a healthy economy (too much inflation erodes banks' returns on loans, too much unemployment decreases demand for loans) and thus operates within its own system of checks and balances. Nevertheless, the restraints on the Fed are much weaker than those on popularly elected institutions.

At the time the Fed was created in 1913, economists had not yet "invented" the theory of monetary policy, and the Fed had no role in the management of the nation's economy. If the Fed were being created today, it would likely have a different structure, although there is general agreement among policymakers that some degree of independence is desirable.

The Fed is a preeminent example of *elitist* politics at work. Congress at some future point may decide that an overly independent Fed can no longer be tolerated and may bring monetary policy more closely under the control of elected institutions. Whether this move happens may hinge on the Fed's willingness to exercise power sparingly and in the broad interests of society. (The economic policies of the federal government in the areas of social welfare and national security are discussed in the next two chapters.)

Summary

Self-Test
www.mhhe.com/pattersontad7

Although private enterprise is the main force in the American economic system, the federal government plays a significant role through its policies to regulate, promote, and stimulate the economy.

Regulatory policy is designed to achieve efficiency and equity, which require government to intervene, for example, to maintain competitive trade practices (an efficiency goal) and to protect vulnerable parties in economic transactions (an equity goal). Many of the regulatory decisions of the federal government, particularly those of older agencies (such as the Federal Communication Commission), are made largely in the context of group politics. Business lobbies have an especially strong influence on the regulatory policies that affect them. In general, newer regulatory agencies (such as the Environmental Protection Agency) have policy responsibilities that are broader in scope and apply to a larger number of firms than those of the older agencies. As a result, the policy decisions of newer agencies are more often made in the context of party politics. Republican administrations are less vigorous in their regulation of business than are Democratic administrations.

Business is the major beneficiary of the federal government's efforts to promote economic interests. A large number of programs, including those that provide loans and research grants, are designed to assist businesses, which are also protected from failure through such measures as tariffs and favorable tax laws. Labor, for its part, obtains government assistance through laws concerning such matters as worker safety, the minimum wage, and collective bargaining. Yet America's individualistic cul-

ture tends to put labor at a disadvantage, keeping it less powerful than business in its dealings with the government. Agriculture is another economic sector that depends substantially on government's help, particularly in the form of income stabilization programs such as those that provide crop subsidies and price supports.

The U.S. government pursues policies that are designed to protect and conserve the environment. A few decades ago, the environment was not a policy priority. Today, there are many programs in this area, and the public has become an active participant in efforts to conserve resources and prevent exploitation of the environment.

Through its fiscal and monetary policies, Washington attempts to maintain a strong and stable economy—one characterized by high productivity, high employment, and low inflation. Fiscal policy is based on government decisions in regard to spending and taxing, which are aimed at either stimulating a weak economy or dampening an overheated (inflationary) economy. Fiscal policy is worked out through Congress and the president and consequently is responsive to political pressures. However, because it is difficult to raise taxes or cut programs, the government's ability to apply fiscal policy as an economic remedy is limited. Monetary policy is based on the money supply and works through the Federal Reserve System, which is headed by a board whose members hold office for fixed terms. The Fed is a relatively independent body, a fact that has given rise to questions as to whether it should have such a large role in influencing national economic policy.

STUDY CORNER

Key Terms

balanced budget *(p. 501)*
budget deficit *(p. 500)*
budget surplus *(p. 501)*
capital-gains tax *(p. 502)*
deficit spending *(p. 499)*
demand-side economics *(p. 500)*
deregulation *(p. 487)*
economic depression *(p. 500)*

economic recession *(p. 500)*
economy *(p. 482)*
efficiency *(p. 484)*
equity (in relation to economic policy) *(p. 488)*
externalities *(p. 486)*
fiscal policy *(p. 499)*
graduated personal income tax *(p. 508)*

inflation *(p. 502)*
laissez-faire doctrine *(p. 482)*
monetary policy *(p. 508)*
national debt *(p. 500)*
policy process *(p. 482)*
regulation *(p. 484)*
supply-side economics *(p. 501)*

Self-Test

1. Which of the following steps in the U.S. budget process is not in its proper sequential order?
   a. Office of Management and Budget compiles budget.
   b. Proposed budget is studied in the House and Senate Budget and Appropriations Committees.
   c. President sends budget proposal to Congress.
   d. Budget is approved by Congress and presented to the president to be signed.

2. The challenge for policymakers in devising and implementing regulatory and deregulatory policies is to:
   a. simply remove all regulations.
   b. not be concerned about economic inefficiency in protecting the public interest.
   c. favor equity at the expense of efficiency.
   d. strike a proper balance between regulatory measures and free-market mechanisms.

3. The institutions of the U.S. government involved in determining fiscal policy are:
   a. the executive and legislative branches.
   b. the Fed and the regulatory agencies.
   c. the judicial branch and the states.
   d. the legislative branch and the Fed.

4. The era of new social regulation in the 1960s and 1970s differed from that of previous eras in:
   a. narrowing the scope and range of activities regulated.
   b. concentrating on reforms of labor practices.
   c. expanding social goals to the areas of environment and consumer protection as well as worker safety.

   d. reducing the amount of lobbying by regulated firms.

5. Examples of services provided by government that aid business include:
   a. loan guarantees and direct loans to business.
   b. funding of public colleges and universities.
   c. subsidizing the building of roads, waterways, and airports.
   d. all of the above.

6. The Federal Reserve Board affects the economy by taking all **except** which one of the following actions?
   a. buying and selling securities on the open market
   b. lowering or raising interest charged on money borrowed by banks
   c. raising or lowering the cash reserve that member banks are required to deposit with regional Federal Reserve banks
   d. submitting monetary strategies to Congress for a vote

7. Early in the development of America's economy, there was hostility toward labor union activity. (T/F)

8. In times when the economy needs a quick fix, one would be better off to use fiscal policy than monetary policy because fiscal policy can be implemented within a faster time frame. (T/F)

9. Rachel Carson's *Silent Spring* encouraged the growth of the modern environmental protection movement. (T/F)

10. Fiscal policy has its origins in the economic theories of John Maynard Keynes. (T/F)

Critical Thinking

What are the tools of fiscal policy and monetary policy? What are the advantages and disadvantages of each of these two approaches to managing the economy?

Suggested Readings

Lindbloom, Charles E. *The Market System: What It Is, How It Works, and What to Make of It.* New Haven, Conn.: Yale University Press, 2001. A clear analysis of the advantages and disadvantages of the market system.

Mayer, Martin. *FED: The Inside Story of How the World's Most Powerful Financial Institution Drives the Markets.* New York: Free Press, 2001. A look at the Fed's impact on the economy and politics.

McChesney, Robert. *The Problem of the Media.* New York: Monthly Review Press, 2004. A scathing critique of media regulation.

Rosenbaum, Walter A. *Environmental Politics and Policy,* 5th ed. Washington, D.C.: Congressional Quarterly Press, 2001. A comprehensive examination of the politics of environmental policy.

Schick, Allen, with Felix Lostracco. *The Federal Budget: Politics, Policy, Process,* rev. ed. Washington, D.C.: Brookings Institution Press, 2000. An explanation of the federal budgetary process.

Shaiko, Ronald G. *Voices and Echoes for the Environment.* New York: Columbia University Press, 1999. The representation and communication of environmental groups.

Sheingate, Adam D. *The Rise of the Agricultural Welfare State.* Princeton, N.J.: Princeton University Press, 2003. A penetrating analysis of farm policy in the United States, France, and Japan.

Young, H. Peyton. *Equity: In Theory and Practice.* Princeton, N.J.: Princeton University Press, 1995. A systematic assessment of what economic equity entails in theory and actual situations.

List of Websites

http://www.federalreserve.gov/default.htm

The Federal Reserve System website; it describes the Fed, provides information about its current activities, and has links to some of the Fed's national and international information sources.

http://www.epa.gov/

The Environmental Protection Agency (EPA) website; it has information on environmental policy and regulations, EPA projects, and related subjects.

http://www.ftc.gov/

The website of the Federal Trade Commission, one of the older regulatory agencies; it describes the range of the FTC's activities.

http://www.whitehouse.gov/OMB

The home page of the Office of Management and Budget; it contains a summary of the annual federal budget and describes the OMB's operations and responsibilities.

Participate!

In recent decades, Americans have become increasingly aware of how their actions can harm the environment and what they might do to lessen the effect. Consider taking a personal inventory of your impact on the environment. Think about such things as your driving, eating, and living habits. For example, do you habitually turn off the lights when you leave a room? This simple practice conserves energy and reduces the pollution associated with energy production. A number of websites contain suggestions on what individuals can do to reduce harmful environmental effects. One of them is http://www.crd.bc.ca/rte/report/suggest.htm.

Extra Credit

For up-to-the-minute *New York Times* articles, interactive simulations, graphics, study tools, and more links and quizzes, visit the text's Online Learning Center at www.mhhe.com/pattersontad7.

16

Welfare and Education Policy:
Providing for Personal Security and Need

Chapter Outline

We the people of the United States, in order to . . .

promote the general welfare . . .

—*Preamble, U.S. Constitution*

As the Welfare Reform Act came up for renewal in 2002, there was cause for both hope and fear. The original legislation had been a stunning success. In the latter part of the 1990s, the number of people on the welfare rolls had been cut almost in half. In only three states—Hawaii, Rhode Island, and New Mexico—was the drop less than 20 percent (see "States in the Nation"). The trend defied what had been called welfare policy's "reverse gravity" law: welfare rolls that went up but never came down. Two factors accounted for the change. One was the booming national economy, with a steady decline in unemployment. As more Americans entered the work force, the demand for welfare decreased. The second factor was the 1996 Welfare Reform Act, which shortened the length of eligibility and required that able-bodied recipients find work or risk loss of benefits.

The situation in 2002 was starkly different. Those welfare recipients who had found work were the ones easiest to place in jobs. Many of those still unemployed lacked the education, skill, or temperament to find and hold a job. Moreover, the economy had weakened dramatically, and welfare rolls were starting to rise while tax revenues were declining. "At the beginning of welfare reform, we had the happy circumstance of a booming economy, low unemployment, falling welfare caseloads, and the states having the money to give more help to the poor, especially the working poor," said Sharon Parrott of the Center on Budget and Policy Priorities. "Now, everything is going the other way. Caseloads are rising, the value of the federal block grant is down, and state budgets are in catastrophic shape."[1]

The 2002 debate in Congress reflected these new realities. Yet it also brought out old differences of philosophy on how best to handle the welfare issue. Congressional Republicans wanted to increase pressure on the states to move more people off welfare and into work; they also argued for strict adherence to the eligibility rules, tight controls on federal spending, and increased work hours for welfare recipients. Congressional Democrats sought more funding for day care, education, and job-training programs; they also wanted to give the states more latitude in their administration of the welfare program. The differences were substantial enough to create a months-long deadlock between the Republican-controlled House and the Democratic-controlled Senate. "By stalling on . . . welfare reform," said Bill Thomas (R-Calif.) of the House Committee on

Ways and Means, "the Senate is shaping their legacy—inaction." Senate majority leader Tom Daschle (D-S. Dak.) was unbending, vowing to hold out until the Republicans agreed to "strong child care provisions."[2]

These opposing views typify opinions about social welfare policy. It's an area in which opposing philosophies of government collide. Many people, like Senator Daschle, believe the government must provide substantial and sustained assistance to those Americans who are less equipped to compete effectively in the marketplace. Others, like Representative Thomas, believe that welfare payments, except to those who are unmistakably unfit to work, discourage personal effort and create welfare dependency.

Another source of conflict over welfare policy is the country's federal system of government. Welfare was traditionally a responsibility of state and local governments. Only since the 1930s has the federal government also played a significant role. Some welfare programs are jointly run by the federal and state governments. They are funded at different levels from one state to the next but operate within guidelines set down by the national government and are partly funded by Washington. The strictness of federal guidelines and the amount that the federal government should contribute to these programs are sources of debate.

This chapter examines the social problems that federal welfare programs are designed to alleviate and describes how these programs operate. It also addresses public education policies. A goal of this chapter is to provide an informed basis for understanding issues of social welfare and education and to show why disagreements in these areas are so substantial. These issues involve hard choices that almost inevitably require trade-offs between federal and state power and between the values of individual self-reliance and egalitarian compassion. The main points of the chapter are the following:

- *Poverty is a large and persistent problem in America, deeply affecting about one in seven Americans, including many of the country's most vulnerable—children, female-headed families, and minority-group members.* Social welfare programs have been a major factor in reducing the extent of poverty in the United States.

- *Welfare policy has been a partisan issue, with Democrats taking the lead on government programs to alleviate economic insecurity and Republicans acting to slow down or reverse these initiatives.*

- *Social welfare programs are designed to reward and foster self-reliance or, when this is not possible, to provide benefits only to those individuals who are truly in need.* U.S. welfare policy is not based on the assumption that every citizen has a right to material security.

- *Americans favor social insurance programs (such as social security) over public assistance programs (such as food stamps).* As a result, most social welfare expenditures are not targeted toward the nation's neediest citizens.

- *A prevailing principle in the United States is equality of opportunity, which in terms of policy is most evident in the area of public education.* America invests heavily in its public schools and colleges.

STATES IN THE NATION

The Declining Number of Families on Welfare

The welfare rolls in the United States peaked in March 1994. After that, the number of American families on welfare dropped precipitously, which analysts attributed to both the surge in the U.S. economy and the 1996 welfare reform bill that instituted new work rules. The biggest drop (89 percent) was in Wisconsin. The smallest (7 percent) was in Hawaii.

Q: What might explain the state-to-state variation in the decline in the welfare rolls?

A: States that had weaker economies in the early 1990s had bigger drops in their welfare rolls in the latter part of the 1990s. These states had more laid-off workers on welfare and, as the economy strengthened, many of these unemployed workers found jobs.

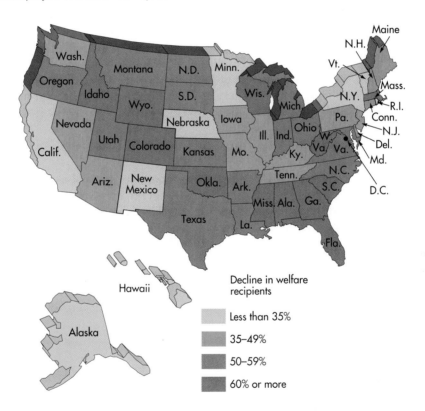

Decline in welfare recipients

- Less than 35%
- 35–49%
- 50–59%
- 60% or more

Figure 16–1

Percentage of Families Living in Poverty, By Family Composition and Race/Ethnicity

Poverty is far more prevalent among female-headed households and African American and Hispanic households.

Source: U.S. Bureau of the Census, 2004.

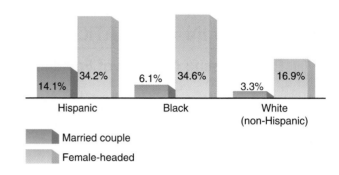

14.1%	34.2%	6.1% 34.6%	3.3% 16.9%
Hispanic		Black	White (non-Hispanic)

■ Married couple
■ Female-headed

POVERTY IN AMERICA: THE NATURE OF THE PROBLEM

In the broadest sense, social welfare policy includes any effort by government to improve social conditions. In a narrower sense, which is the way the term will be used in most of this chapter, social welfare policy refers to those efforts by government to help individuals meet basic human needs, including food, clothing, and shelter.

The Poor: Who and How Many?

Americans' social welfare needs are substantial. Although Americans are far better off economically than most of the world's peoples, poverty is a significant and persistent problem in the United States. The government defines the **poverty line** as the annual cost of a thrifty food budget for an urban family of four, multiplied by three to include the cost of housing, clothes, and other necessities. Families whose incomes fall below that line are officially considered poor. In 2005, the poverty line was set at an annual income of roughly $19,000 for a family of four. One in nine Americans—roughly thirty million people, including more than ten million children—lives below the poverty line. If they could all join hands, they would form a line stretching from New York to Los Angeles and back again.

America's poor include individuals of all ages, races, religions, and regions, but poverty is concentrated among certain groups. Children are one of the largest groups of poor Americans. One in every five children lives in poverty. Most poor children live in single-parent families, usually with the mother. In fact, as can be seen from Figure 16–1, a high proportion of Americans residing in families headed by divorced, separated, or unmarried women live below the poverty line. These families are at a disadvantage because most women earn less than men for comparable work, especially in nonprofessional fields. Women without higher education or special skills often cannot find jobs that pay significantly more than the child care expenses they incur if they work outside the home. Single-parent, female-headed families are roughly five times as likely as two-income families to fall below the poverty line, a situation referred to as "the feminization of poverty."

poverty line As defined by the federal government, the annual cost of a thrifty food budget for an urban family of four, multiplied by three to allow also for the cost of housing, clothes, and other expenses. Families below the poverty line are considered poor and are eligible for certain forms of public assistance.

HOW THE UNITED STATES COMPARES

Children Living in Poverty

The United States has the highest child poverty rate among industrialized nations. One in five American children live in poverty; in most other industrialized nations, the number is fewer than one in ten.

One reason for the difference is that income in the United States is less evenly distributed. As a consequence, the United States has the highest percentage of both rich and poor children in the industrialized world. In addition, the United States spends less on government assistance for the poor. Without government help, for example, the child poverty rates in the United States and France would be about equal—25 percent. Through its governmental programs, France has reduced the rate to less than 7 percent. Through its welfare programs, the United States has cut the rate only slightly.

Child poverty in the United States is made worse by the relatively large number of single-parent families, although Sweden, which has a similarly large number of such families, has one of the world's lowest rates of child poverty.

Source: United Nation's Children's Fund, 2001

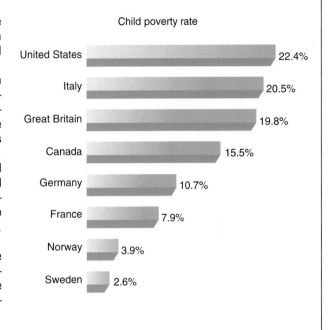

Child poverty rate

United States	22.4%
Italy	20.5%
Great Britain	19.8%
Canada	15.5%
Germany	10.7%
France	7.9%
Norway	3.9%
Sweden	2.6%

Poverty is also widespread among minority-group members. More than 20 percent of African Americans and Hispanics live below the poverty line, compared with 10 percent of whites.

Poverty is also geographically concentrated. Although it is often portrayed as an urban problem, it is somewhat more prevalent in rural areas. About one in seven rural residents—compared with one in nine urban residents— lives in a family with income below the poverty line. The urban figure is misleading, however, in that the poverty rate is very high in some inner-city areas. Suburbs are the safe haven from poverty. Because suburbanites are far removed from it, many of them have no sense of the impoverished condition of what Michael Harrington called "the other America."[3]

The "invisibility" of poverty in America is evident in polls that show that most Americans greatly underestimate the number of poor in their country. Certainly nothing in the daily lives of many Americans or in what they see on television would lead them to think that poverty rates are uncommonly high. Yet the United States has the highest level of poverty among the advanced industrialized nations, and its rate of child poverty is more than twice the average of the others (see "How the United States Compares").

Most people who are poor in America are victims of a temporary setback, such as job layoffs during an economic recession. Conversely, the number of Americans living below the poverty line shrinks substantially when the economy is prosperous and jobs are plentiful.

Living in Poverty: By Choice or Chance?

Many Americans hold to the idea that poverty is largely a matter of choice—that most low-income Americans are unwilling to make the effort to hold a responsible job and get ahead in life. In his book *Losing Ground*, Charles Murray argues that America has a permanent underclass of unproductive citizens who prefer to live on welfare and whose children receive little educational encouragement at home and grow up to be copies of their parents.[4] There are, indeed, many such people in America. They number in the millions. They are the toughest challenge for policymakers because almost nothing about their lives equips them to escape from poverty and its attendant ills.

Yet most poor Americans are in their situation as a result of circumstance rather than choice. A ten-year study of American families by a University of Michigan research team found that most of the poor are poor only for a while and that they are poor for temporary reasons such as the loss of a job or desertion by the father.[5] When the U.S. economy goes into a tailspin, the impact devastates many families. The U.S. Department of Labor reported that three million jobs were lost in the manufacturing sector alone during the recessionary period that began in 2001.

It is also true that a full-time job does not guarantee that a family will rise above the poverty line. A family of four with one employed adult who works forty hours a week at six dollars an hour (which is roughly the minimum wage level) has an annual income of about $12,000, which is well below the poverty line. Millions of Americans—mostly household workers, service workers, unskilled laborers, and farm workers—are in this position. The U.S. Bureau of Labor Statistics estimates that roughly 7 percent of full-time workers do not earn enough to lift their family above the poverty line.[6]

THE POLITICS AND POLICIES OF SOCIAL WELFARE

Welfare policy has generally been debated along partisan lines, a reflection of differences in the coalitions and philosophies of the Republican and Democratic parties. With its ties to labor, the poor, and minorities, the Democratic party has initiated nearly all major federal welfare programs. The key House of Representatives vote on the Social Security Act of 1935, for example, found 85 percent of Democrats voting for it and 99 percent of Republicans voting against it.[7]

Republicans gradually came to accept the idea that the federal government has a role in social welfare but argued that the role should be kept as small as practicable. Thus, in the 1960s, Republican opposition to President Lyndon Johnson's Great Society was substantial. His programs included federal initiatives in health care, education, public housing, nutrition, and other areas traditionally dominated by state and local governments. More than 70 percent of congressional Republicans voted against the 1965 Medicare and Medicaid programs, which provide government-paid medical assistance for the elderly and the poor. In contrast, the 1996 Welfare Reform Act, which was designed to cut

Graphics
www.mhhe.com/pattersontad7

President Clinton signs into law the 1996 welfare reform bill that ended the sixty-one-year-old federal guarantee of aid to the poor. The new legislation limits federal welfare assistance to a period of five years.

A New Beginning
Welfare to Work

welfare rolls and costs, had the overwhelming support of congressional Republicans, while a majority of congressional Democrats voted against it.

Although the Republican and Democratic parties have been at odds on social welfare issues, they have also had reason to work together. Millions of Americans need help from government if they are to meet their basic subsistence needs. This help includes job training efforts, special education programs, and income redistribution measures.

Job Training

The government's social welfare effort has included attempts to provide jobs and job training. Employment policy and welfare policy have been loosely linked since the Great Depression, when Franklin D. Roosevelt combined public jobs programs with social security legislation. At one point during the depression, a fifth of the nation's entire work force was employed in public jobs.

Work-related programs are Americans' preferred answer to the problem of poverty. Work is believed to foster initiative and responsibility, whereas welfare payments are thought to create dependency and irresponsibility. In a Los Angeles Times poll, respondents were asked what action government should take to help the poor. Only 6 percent responded that the government should provide money or services, whereas 20 percent preferred public works jobs and 72 percent favored job training.

The history of work and job training programs, however, is an uneven one. For example, an ambitious program that began in the early 1970s under Republican president Richard Nixon, and which at its peak provided employment for four million people, was terminated a decade later amid charges that it was too costly and had failed to place people in permanent jobs as opposed to subsidized temporary positions. Subsequent job training programs were less ambitious and, if anything, even less successful in moving the unemployed into permanent jobs.

The picture changed with passage of the 1996 Welfare Reform Act. The historic bill ended a six-decade federal guarantee of cash assistance to needy families and replaced it with a system of cash grants to the states, which were given the responsibility for caring for welfare recipients and getting them into jobs. The legislation's goal was to reduce long-term welfare dependency by limiting the time that recipients can receive welfare and by providing the states with incentives to prepare recipients for work. States may not let recipients receive federal welfare assistance for more than five years (although a fifth of recipients can be exempted from this requirement), and within two years of first receiving welfare a recipient must find work or face the loss of benefits. States receive federal funds with which to provide benefits, community service jobs, and job training, but unless they meet the program's goals, their federal assistance is reduced.

The long-term effectiveness of the new program is yet to be determined. The trend so far is cause for optimism. The number of Americans on welfare has declined sharply since the 1996 Welfare Reform Act was passed. Nevertheless, there is the lingering question of whether the states can train welfare recipients who are severely lacking in job skills. Most of the welfare recipients who have found employment since 1996 already had enough skills that they required little or, in most cases, no job training. Most of those who have been unable to find employment, in contrast, have limited education and few job-related skills.

Welfare recipients are not the only targets of federal jobs programs. In 1998, Congress passed the Workforce Investment Act, which is designed to help local communities place the unemployed in jobs. The legislation includes a significant role for local businesses; if they make job positions available, workers will be trained specifically for these positions. The program includes Youth Opportunities grants, for which localities compete. These grants are designed to train difficult-to-employ fourteen- to twenty-one-year-old youths. The program has been so popular with local leaders that the U.S. Conference of Mayors protested loudly when the Bush administration in 2002 proposed to cut the program's funding from $225 million to $45 million. Local leaders recognized that some federal programs would have to be cut because of the economic downturn and the cost of funding the war on terrorism, but they argued that a large reduction in the Youth Opportunities program was shortsighted.

Education Initiatives: Head Start

The social welfare effort also includes formal education programs, most notably Head Start. This program provides preschool education for poor children in order to give them a better chance to succeed when they enter school. Head Start was established in the 1960s as part of President Lyndon Johnson's war on poverty.

The Head Start education program is designed to give preschool children from poorer homes a better chance to succeed when they enter school. Shown here is a teacher reading to a Head Start class in Austin, Texas.

In the 1980s, Head Start's budget was dropped to a level that allowed only 10 percent of eligible children to participate. As evidence mounted of poverty's devastating impact on children's development, Congress concluded that Head Start was the kind of social investment that the country could hardly afford not to make, and its funding was increased substantially. Nevertheless, less than half of eligible children are enrolled in Head Start, and many who complete the program do not benefit in the long run because they get no educational support at home.

Income and Tax Measures

The United States has substantial income inequality (see Figure 16–2). The top fifth of Americans receive half of the total income, while the bottom fifth get less than a twentieth. This imbalance is greater than that found in any other industrialized democracy. The gap between rich and poor in the United States has widened recently, partly as a result of the tax policies of President George W. Bush. Arguing that high tax rates on the wealthy cripple economic growth, Bush persuaded Congress to enact a phased-in tax cut on upper incomes. Although his tax cuts also affected moderate and low incomes, the annual savings to Americans in the top 1 percent of income will eventually be $54,493, compared with an average of $67 for those in the bottom 20 percent and $611 for those in the middle 20 percent. In terms of total dollars, less than 1 percent of the cuts went to those in the bottom fifth by income, while those in the middle fifth got 8 percent of the cuts and those in the top fifth received 75 percent of the cuts.[8]

Figure 16–2

Income Inequality

The United States has the highest degree of income inequality of any industrialized democracy. Citizens in the top fifth get half of all income; those in the bottom fifth get less than a twentieth of all income.

Source: U.S. Bureau of the Census, 2004.

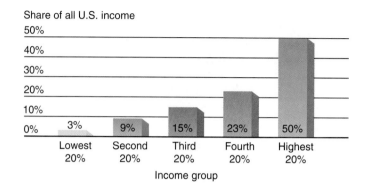

Share of all U.S. income

Income group

effective tax rate The actual percentage of a person's income that is spent to pay taxes.

Income taxes in the United States are not the instrument of economic redistribution that they are in other democracies. In 2004, the top tax rate in the United States was 35 percent, which applied only to income above $320,000. The tax code also includes numerous tax breaks for upper-income taxpayers, such as the deduction of mortgage interest on a second home. Moreover, the well-to-do escape social security taxes on most of their income. The social security tax is a flat rate of about 6 percent that begins with the first dollar earned each year and stops completely after roughly $90,000 in earnings is reached. Thus, individuals earning $90,000 or less pay social security taxes on every dollar they make, while those earning more than $90,000 pay no social security taxes on the dollars they make above this amount.

The net result is that the **effective tax rate** (the actual percentage of a person's income that is spent to pay taxes) of high- and middle-income Americans is not greatly different. When all taxes (including social security taxes, state sales taxes, and local property taxes) are combined, the average American family's effective tax rate is about three-fourths that of a family with an income over a million dollars.

In Europe, the effective tax rate on upper-income taxpayers is substantially higher than that on lower-income taxpayers. A top tax rate of around 50 percent is common in Europe, and there are fewer tax breaks for the well-to-do. Moreover, retirement programs typically are funded from general tax revenues rather than through a special tax that weighs more heavily on lower-income taxpayers.

These differences between Europe and the United States are to some extent a result of differences in their political cultures. As explained in Chapter 1, the American political culture places more emphasis on individualism and less emphasis on economic equality than does the European political culture. Thus, Americans are more accepting of widespread differences in wealth that result from the free-market economic system (see Figure 16–3).

Although well-to-do Americans pay relatively low taxes, the fact that they earn a lot of money means, in absolute terms, that they contribute the large share of tax revenues. The top 10 percent of earners pay about half the personal income taxes received by the federal government. Some of this tax revenue is redistributed downward to lower-income groups through social welfare programs.

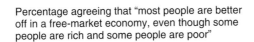

Percentage agreeing that "most people are better off in a free-market economy, even though some people are rich and some people are poor"

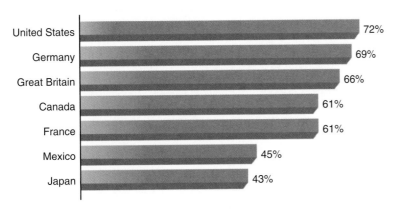

United States	72%
Germany	69%
Great Britain	66%
Canada	61%
France	61%
Mexico	45%
Japan	43%

Figure 16–3

Opinions on the Free Market
Americans are somewhat more supportive of a free-market economy and its effects than are citizens of other democracies.
Source: The Pew Research Center for the People and the Press, Global Attitudes Survey, 2002.

The United States also has a policy designed to reallocate income directly to lower-income families. This policy is the Earned Income Tax Credit (EITC). About ten million American families receive EITC payments; the maximum yearly payment to any one family is about $4,000. Eligibility for payment is determined when persons file their personal income taxes. Those with family incomes below a specified level receive the payment, which is phased out as income rises.

The EITC is widely regarded as one of the country's most successful welfare programs. According to the U.S. Census Bureau, 6 percent of Americans are living above the poverty line because of the extra income from their EITC payments. Without EITC, the poverty rate in America would exceed 15 percent. Moreover, because EITC payments are based on income tax returns, the program does not require a large and costly administrative structure. EITC payments are processed in the same way as refunds for overpayment of withholding taxes.

INDIVIDUAL-BENEFIT PROGRAMS

EITC involves what is called a **transfer payment,** or a government benefit that is given directly to an individual. All spending to promote the general welfare is designed to help individuals, but much of it—such as federal funds for public school construction or hospital equipment—is not in the form of transfer payments. Many federal programs, however, do transfer benefits directly to individuals, such as the monthly social security checks that retired people receive.

Individual-benefit programs are designed to alleviate the personal hardships associated with conditions such as joblessness, poverty, and old age. For most of these programs, any individual who meets the established criteria of eligibility is entitled to the benefits. For this reason, such programs are termed

transfer payment A government benefit that is given directly to an individual, as in the case of social security payments to a retiree.

Are Tax Cuts for High-Income Taxpayers Good for America?

Few issues spark more controversy than taxes. When a tax cut is at issue, the debate is usually over how the cut is to be divided. Supply-side economists have a unique answer to the question: those taxpayers who are personally least in need of tax relief are the ones who should get the largest share of the cut. Supply-side theory holds that high-income taxpayers will invest their extra income, thus boosting the economy and, along with the economy, the fortunes of everyone else. It is this argument that the Heritage Foundation's Daniel Mitchell makes below in support of President George W. Bush's supply-side tax initiatives, which substantially increase the after-tax income of America's wealthier individuals. Among the critics of the Bush tax program was Warren Buffett, one of America's richest people. Buffett called Bush's tax program "voodoo economics"—a term he borrowed from debates over the same issue in the 1980s. In his argument below, Buffett rejects both the logic and the symbolism of supply-side economics.

Yes: Pro-growth tax cuts are an important part of fiscal discipline. They take money out of Washington, thereby removing the temptation to spend tax dollars on programs that are wasteful, duplicative, or counterproductive. . . . Any money the government gives to one person must first be taken from someone else. This Keynesian approach—attempting to boost the economy by giving people more money to spend—makes sense only if one assumes that the money distributed by the government for tax relief or new spending materializes out of thin air. The essential insight of supply-side economics is that the right kind of tax cuts will help an economy by increasing incentives to work, save, and invest. This relationship is the reason why President Reagan's across-the-board reductions in marginal tax rates resulted in nearly 20 years of above-average economic performance. President Bush's . . . tax cut package seeks to reduce the tax penalty on productive behavior, so there is every reason to think it would yield significant benefits as well. . . . People invest in the expectation of earning after-tax income. . . . The argument for supply-side tax policy is simple: Lowering tax rates on productive behavior will improve the incentives to work, save, and invest.

—*Daniel J. Mitchell, senior fellow, the Heritage Foundation*

No: [These tax cuts] supply major aid to the rich in their pursuit of even greater wealth. . . . Administration officials say that the $310 million suddenly added to my wallet would stimulate the economy because I would invest it and thereby create jobs. But they conveniently forget that if Berkshire [Buffett's investment company] kept the money, it would invest that same amount, creating jobs as well. . . . Instead, give reductions to those who both need and will spend the money gained. Enact a Social Security tax "holiday" or give a flat-sum rebate to people with low incomes. Putting $1,000 in the pockets of 310,000 families with urgent needs is going to provide far more stimulus to the economy than putting the same $310 million in my pockets. When you listen to tax-cut rhetoric, remember that giving one class of taxpayer a "break" requires—now or down the line—that an equivalent burden be imposed on other parties. In other words, if I get a break, someone else pays. Government can't deliver a free lunch to the country as a whole. It can, however, determine who pays for lunch. And last week the [government] handed the bill to the wrong party.

—*Warren Buffett, chief executive officer, Berkshire Hathaway, Inc.*

entitlement program Any of a number of individual benefit programs, such as social security, that require government to provide a designated benefit to any person who meets the legally defined criteria for eligibility.

entitlement programs. In this sense, they have the same force in law as taxes. Just as individuals are required by law to pay taxes to government on the income they earn, individuals are entitled by law to receive government benefits for which they qualify.

All told, individual-benefit programs are the major component of U.S. social welfare policy. Federal spending on such programs is more than $1 trillion annually, more money than is spent on any other government activity, including national defense.

At an earlier time in the nation's history, the federal government spent almost nothing on social welfare. Welfare policy was deemed to fall within the powers reserved to the states by the Tenth Amendment and to be adequately addressed by them, even though they did not offer substantial welfare services. Individuals were expected to fend for themselves, and those unable to do so were usually supported by relatives and friends. This approach reflected the idea of **negative government,** which holds that government governs best by staying out of people's lives, thus giving them as much freedom as possible to determine their own pursuits and encouraging them to become self-reliant.

The situation changed dramatically with the Great Depression. The unemployment level reached 25 percent, prompting demands for help from the federal government. Franklin D. Roosevelt's New Deal brought economic relief in the form of public jobs and assistance programs and helped change opinions about the federal government's welfare role.[9] Americans came to look favorably on Washington's help. This new attitude reflected a faith in **positive government:** the idea that government intervention is necessary in order to enhance personal liberty and security when individuals are buffeted by economic and social forces beyond their control.

Since the 1930s, the federal government's welfare role has increased substantially, and individuals now expect the federal government to provide benefits to ease the loss of income caused by retirement, disability, unemployment, and the like. However, individual-benefit programs differ in their philosophy and level of public support. Individual-benefit programs fall into two general categories: *social insurance* and *public assistance*. Programs in the first category enjoy widespread public support and receive a higher level of funding; programs in the second category encounter substantial public opposition and receive less funding.

Franklin D. Roosevelt

(1882–1945)

Franklin D. Roosevelt won the presidency in 1932 during the depths of the Great Depression. FDR's job programs put Americans back to work, and his social programs met their immediate and long-term economic needs. His greatest domestic policy legacy is the Social Security Act of 1935, which for nearly eight decades has been the foundation of elderly Americans' financial security. Having been elected to an unprecedented third term in 1940, Roosevelt was in office when the Japanese attacked Pearl Harbor. His leadership during World War II was critical in the Allies' defeat of the Axis powers. FDR won a fourth term in 1944 but died in office of a cerebral hemorrhage as the war was coming to a close.

negative government The philosophical belief that government governs best by staying out of people's lives, thus giving individuals as much freedom as possible to determine their own pursuits.

positive government The philosophical belief that government intervention is necessary in order to enhance personal liberty and security when individuals are buffeted by economic and social forces beyond their control.

Social Insurance Programs

More than forty million Americans receive monthly benefits from social insurance programs—including social security, Medicare, unemployment insurance, and workers' compensation. The two major programs, social security and Medicare, cost the federal government more than $750 billion per year. Such programs are labeled **social insurance** because only those individuals who paid special payroll taxes when they were employed are eligible for these benefits. This self-financing feature of social insurance programs accounts for their strong public support.[10]

social insurance Social welfare programs based on the "insurance" concept, requiring that individuals pay into the program in order to be eligible to receive funds from it. An example is social security for retired people.

Social security benefits make it possible for many elderly Americans to maintain a secure, independent retirement.

Social Security

The leading social insurance program is social security for retirees. The program began with passage of the Social Security Act of 1935 and is funded through payroll taxes on employees and employers (currently set at 6.2 percent). Franklin D. Roosevelt emphasized that retiring workers would receive an insurance benefit that they had earned through their payroll taxes, not a handout from the government. Today, social security has Americans' full support. Public opinion polls indicate that upward of 90 percent of Americans favor current or higher levels of social security benefits for the elderly. Social security is one of the few welfare programs run entirely by the federal government. Washington collects the payroll taxes that fund the program and sends monthly checks directly to the nearly forty million social security recipients, who receive on average about $900 a month.

Although people qualify for social security by paying payroll taxes during their working years, the money they receive upon retirement is funded by payroll taxes on current workers' salaries. This arrangement poses a long-term threat to the viability of the social security program because people live longer than they once did. Roughly one in five Americans will be over age sixty-five in the year 2030, and there will not be enough workers then to pay for retirees' social security benefits. Some kind of adjustment in the current program will be required.

There are a number of ways of ensuring the solvency of social security, and there are proponents for nearly every possibility, from investing social security taxes in stocks, to raising the income level on which social security taxes are levied, to extending the retirement age. Many analysts believe that the plan most likely to be enacted is one that will preserve social security as a safety net for the elderly poor while creating limited opportunities for taxpayers to get a greater return on a portion of their social security payments through the stock market.

Social Security

For most college students, social security benefits are so far in the future that they seem barely worth a second thought. Indeed, recent polls indicate that many college-age Americans are not even counting on social security as part of their retirement income. Some young people say the social security system will not be around when they retire. A larger number say they will not have a financial need for social security benefits when they reach retirement age.

The social security system should not be so quickly dismissed. For one thing, it has relieved many young adults of the financial burden of supporting aging parents. There was a time in America when responsibility for the economic well-being of the elderly fell largely on their children. Now the federal government, through its social security and Medicare systems, bears most of this responsibility. And it has exercised that responsibility far more effectively than families ever did. At one time, nearly half of America's elderly lived in poverty. Now only about 10 percent do so. For many of the nation's elderly, monthly social security checks are the primary reason they live above the poverty line.

Social security is also available to young people who have the misfortune of losing one or both parents while they are still economically dependent. Many Americans are not aware that surviving family members receive social security benefits in some situations. Among those who are aware of it are the several million Americans who have had a portion of their college education funded with money received through social security.

Another reason young adults should care about social security is that it helps fuel the U.S. economy and, with that, helps create jobs. About forty million people each month receive a social security check. Most of them over the course of the month spend all or nearly all of it, thus contributing to the demand for goods and services that stimulates production and employment.

Finally, even the most promising retirement plans can go awry, leaving people thankful when they do finally reach retirement age that they have social security to back them up. Until 2002, employees of the Enron Corporation—America's seventh-largest firm—were anticipating comfortable retirements. The Enron stock in their individual pension plans was in many cases worth $1 million or more. When Enron collapsed under the weight of illegal financial schemes, the employees found out, almost overnight, that the value of their stock portfolios had fallen to almost nothing. Social security was the only retirement plan of value that remained for them.

Many scholars and commentators consider the social security system the most successful federal domestic program in the nation's history. It is a program worth caring about.

Unemployment Insurance

The 1935 Social Security Act provides for unemployment benefits for workers who have lost their jobs involuntarily. Unemployment insurance is a joint federal-state program. The federal government collects the payroll taxes that fund unemployment benefits, but states have the option of deciding whether the taxes will be paid by both employees and employers or by employers only (most states use the latter option). Individual states also set the tax rate, conditions of eligibility, and benefit level, subject to minimum standards established by the federal government. Although unemployment benefits vary widely among states, they average about a third ($275 a week) of what an average worker makes while employed, and in most cases the benefits are terminated after twenty-six to thirty-nine weeks.

The unemployment program does not have the same high level of public support that social security does. This situation reflects in part a common belief that the loss of a job, or the failure to find a new one right away, is somehow a personal failing. Unemployment statistics suggest otherwise. For example, U.S. Bureau of Labor statistics indicate that of those workers who lost their jobs in 2001, only 13 percent had made the decision to quit working or were fired. The rest became unemployed because of either a temporary layoff or the permanent elimination of a job position.

Medicare

After World War II, most European democracies created government-paid health care systems, and President Harry Truman, a Democrat, proposed a similar program for Americans. The American Medical Association (AMA) called Truman's plan "un-American" and threatened to mobilize local physicians to campaign against members of Congress who supported "socialized medicine." Truman's proposal never came to a vote in Congress. In 1961, President John F. Kennedy, also a Democrat, proposed a health care program restricted to social security recipients, but the AMA, the insurance industry, and conservative members of Congress succeeded in blocking the plan.[11]

The 1964 elections swept a tide of liberal Democrats into Congress, and the result was Medicare. Enacted in 1965, the program provides medical assistance to retirees and is funded primarily through payroll taxes. Medicare is based on the insurance principle and therefore has gained nearly the same high level of public support as social security.

Medicare provides for care in a hospital or nursing home, but the recipient pays part of the initial cost and pays most of the expenses after one hundred days. Medicare does not cover all physicians' fees, but enrollees in the program have the option of paying an insurance premium for fuller coverage of these fees. Enrollees who cannot afford the additional premium can apply to have the government pay it.

In 2003, Congress added a prescription drug benefit to the Medicare program that goes into effect in 2006. The program includes a recipient contribution and will primarily affect retirees who either are too poor to afford prescription drugs or have very high prescription drug costs. Retirees not in these categories receive a small benefit from the program but are required to pay most of the costs of their prescription drugs.

A major reform of the Medicare program may occur in the near future. The rising cost of medical care and the growing number of elderly have combined to threaten the solvency of the Medicare program; it is projected to run out of money within a decade unless new revenues and cost-cutting measures are devised. Among the options under consideration are increased payroll taxes, more cost-sharing by recipients, more use of managed care options, and more substantial controls on government payments to doctors and hospitals.

Public Assistance Programs

Unlike social insurance programs, **public assistance** programs are funded through general tax revenues and are available only to the financially needy. Eligibility for such entitlement programs is established by a **means test;** appli-

public assistance A term that refers to social welfare programs funded through general tax revenues and available only to the financially needy. Eligibility for such a program is established by a means test.

means test The requirement that applicants for public assistance must demonstrate that they are poor in order to be eligible for the assistance.

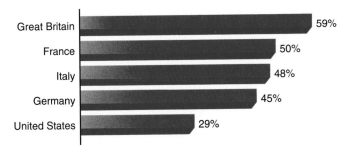

Percentage saying they "completely agree" that it is "the responsibility of the government to take care of very poor people who can't take care of themselves"

Great Britain	59%
France	50%
Italy	48%
Germany	45%
United States	29%

Figure 16–4

Opinions on Government's Responsibility for the Poor
Compared to Europeans and Canadians, Americans are much less likely to believe that government has a responsibility for the poor.
Source: The Pew Research Center for the People and the Press, Global Attitudes Survey, 2002.

cants must prove that they are poor enough to qualify for the benefit. These programs are often referred to as "welfare" and the recipients as "welfare cases."

Americans are much less supportive of public assistance programs than they are of social insurance programs. Americans tend to look upon social insurance benefits as having been "earned" by the recipient, while they see public assistance benefits as "handouts." Because of their individualistic culture, Americans are less inclined than Europeans to support the idea that government should provide substantial help to the poor (see Figure 16–4).

About twenty-five million Americans receive public assistance, typically through programs established by the federal government, administered mainly by the states, and funded jointly by the state and federal governments. Most Americans have the mistaken impression that public assistance programs account for the lion's share of welfare spending. A poll found that Americans believe welfare programs are the second-costliest federal program (foreign aid ranked first).[12] In fact, the federal government spends billions of dollars more on its two major social insurance programs, social security and Medicare, than it does on all public assistance programs combined.

Supplemental Security Income

A major public assistance program is Supplemental Security Income (SSI), which originated as federal assistance to the blind and elderly poor as part of the Social Security Act of 1935. By the 1930s, most states had begun or were considering such programs. Although the federal legislation was designed to replace their efforts, the states have retained a measure of control over benefits and eligibility and are required to provide some of the funding. Because SSI recipients (who now include the disabled in addition to the blind and elderly poor) have obvious reasons for their inability to provide for themselves, this public assistance program is not widely criticized.

Supplemental Security Income (SSI) is a combined federal-state program that provides public assistance to blind and disabled people.

Aid to Needy Families

Perhaps the most controversial of the major public assistance programs was Aid for Families with Dependent Children (AFDC). Partly funded by the federal government but administered by the states, the AFDC program was created in the 1930s as survivors' insurance to assist children whose fathers had died prematurely. Relatively small and noncontroversial at its inception, AFDC was the target of severe criticism by the 1970s. Although some attacks on it were based on false claims (for example, that most of the recipients were unwed teenage mothers when in fact less than 10 percent were in this category),[13] AFDC was widely unpopular because it was linked in people's minds to welfare dependency and irresponsibility. It was an entitlement program, which meant that any single parent (and in some states two parents) living in poverty could claim the benefit and keep it for as long as a dependent child was in the household. Some AFDC recipients were content to live on this assistance, and in some cases their children also grew to become AFDC recipients, creating what was called "a vicious cycle of poverty." By 1995, AFDC was supporting fourteen million Americans at an annual cost of more than $15 billion.

In 1996, AFDC was terminated as part of the Welfare Reform Act. Funding for AFDC was replaced by the Temporary Assistance for Needy Families (TANF) bloc grant, which gives each state an annual cash grant that it uses to design its own program for assisting needy families and moving welfare recipients into jobs. These programs operate within tight federal guidelines, including the following:

- Americans' eligibility for federal cash assistance is limited to no more than five years in their lifetime.
- Within two years, the head of most families on welfare will have to find work or risk the loss of benefits.
- Unmarried teenage mothers are qualified for welfare benefits only if they remain in school and live with a parent or legal guardian.
- Single mothers will lose a portion of their benefits if they refuse to cooperate in identifying for child support purposes the father of their children.

Although states are allowed to make exceptions to some of the rules (for example, an unmarried teenage mother who faces sexual abuse at home is permitted to live elsewhere), the exceptions are limited. States can even choose to impose more restrictive rules in some areas. For example, a state can deny increased benefits to an unwed mother on assistance who gives birth to another child.

The biggest challenge facing the states, in addition to ensuring that the poor do not wind up in the streets, is the development of welfare-to-work programs that actually do free families from welfare dependency. Republicans and Democrats alike agree that the success of the program will ultimately be determined by whether the able-bodied unemployed are able to find meaningful, long-term work.

Food Stamps

The food stamp program, which took its present form in 1961, is fully funded by the federal government. The program provides an **in-kind benefit**—not cash, but food stamps that can be spent only on grocery items.

Food stamps are available only to people who qualify on the basis of low income. The program is intended to improve the nutrition of poor families by enabling them to purchase qualified items—mainly foodstuffs—with food stamps. Some critics say that food stamps stigmatize their users by making it obvious to onlookers in the checkout line that they are "welfare cases." More prevalent criticisms are that the program is too costly and that too many undeserving people receive food stamps. The 1996 welfare reform bill allows states to restrict to three months in any three-year period the food-stamp eligibility of able-bodied adults with no children.

Shown here is a supermarket customer paying for groceries with food stamps. They are available to qualified low-income individuals and can be used only to purchase certain items, mainly foodstuffs. Critics say food stamps at the checkout counter stigmatize the user as a "welfare case." Several states are experimenting with Benefit Security Cards, debit cards that can be used in place of food stamps. These cards look like any other credit or debit card and thus are less obvious to onlookers than food stamps are.

in-kind benefit A government benefit that is a cash equivalent, such as food stamps or rent vouchers. This form of benefit ensures that recipients will use public assistance in a specified way.

Subsidized Housing

Low-income persons are also eligible for subsidized housing. Most of the federal spending in this area is on rent vouchers, an in-kind benefit. Under the voucher system, the individual receives a monthly rent-payment voucher, which is given in lieu of cash to the landlord, who then hands the voucher over to the government in exchange for cash. About five million households annually receive a federal housing subsidy.

The U.S. government spends much less on public housing than on tax breaks for homeowners, most of whom are middle- and upper-income Americans. Homeowners are allowed tax deductions for their mortgage interest payments and their local property tax payments. The total of these tax concessions is three times as much as is spent by the federal government on housing for low-income families.

Medicaid

When Medicare was enacted in 1965, Congress also established Medicaid, which provides health care for poor people who are already on welfare. It is considered a public assistance program, rather than a social insurance program like Medicare, because it is based on need and funded by general tax revenues. Roughly 60 percent of Medicaid funding is provided by the federal government, and about 40 percent by the states. More than twenty million Americans receive Medicaid assistance.

Medicaid is controversial because of its costs. As health care costs have spiraled far ahead of the inflation rate, so have the costs of Medicaid. It absorbs roughly half of all public assistance dollars spent by the U.S. government and has forced state and local governments to cut other services to meet their share of the costs. "It's killing us," was how one local official described the impact of Medicaid on his community's budget.[14] As is true of other public assistance programs, Medicaid has been criticized for supposedly serving too many people who could take care of themselves if they tried harder. This perception is contradicted, ironically, by the situation faced by many working Americans. There are roughly forty million Americans who make too much money to qualify for Medicaid but cannot afford health insurance.

EDUCATION AS EQUALITY OF OPPORTUNITY: THE AMERICAN WAY

All democratic societies promote economic security, but they do so to different degrees. Economic security has a higher priority in European democracies than in the United States. European democracies have instituted programs such as government-paid health care for all citizens, compensation for all unemployed workers, and retirement benefits for all elderly citizens. As this chapter shows, the United States provides these benefits only to some citizens in each category. For example, not all elderly Americans are entitled to social security benefits. If they paid social security taxes for a long enough period when they were employed, they (including their spouses) receive benefits. Otherwise, they do not, even if they are in dire economic need.

Such policy differences between Europe and the United States stem from cultural and historical differences. Democracy developed in Europe in reaction to centuries of aristocratic rule, which brought the issue of economic privilege to the forefront. When strong labor and socialist parties then emerged as a consequence of industrialization, European democracies initiated sweeping social welfare programs that brought about greater economic equality. In contrast, American democracy emerged out of a tradition of limited government that emphasized personal freedom. Equality was a lesser issue, and class consciousness was weak. No major labor or socialist party emerged in America during industrialization to represent the working class, and there was no persistent and strong demand for welfare policies that would bring about a widespread sharing of wealth.

Americans look upon jobs and the personal income that comes from work as the proper basis of economic security. Rather than giving welfare payments to the poor, Americans prefer that the poor be given training and education so that they can learn to help themselves. This attitude is consistent with Americans' preference for **equality of opportunity,** the idea that individuals

equality of opportunity The idea that all individuals should be given an equal chance to succeed on their own.

Political Culture

One People out of Many

Public Education

Public education has never been a uniform experience for American children. Cities in the late nineteenth century neglected the education of many immigrant children, who were thereby placed at a permanent disadvantage. During the first half of the twentieth century, southern public schools for black children were designed to keep them down, not lift them up. Today, many children in poorer neighborhoods attend overcrowded and understaffed public schools.

Nevertheless, the nation's public schools have been the primary means by which Americans of all nationalities, colors, creeds, and income levels have been brought together. At no time in most Americans' lives are they as thoroughly immersed in a socially diverse environment when, as children and adolescents, they attend public schools.

America's broad-based system of public education stems from a melding of its egalitarian and individualistic traditions. Leon Sampson, a nineteenth-century socialist, noted the stark difference between the philosophy of public education in the United States and that in Europe. "The European ruling classes," he wrote, "were open in their contempt for the proletariat. But in the United States equality, and even classlessness, the creation of wealth for all and political liberty were extolled in the public schools." Sampson concluded that American schools embodied a unique conception of equality. Everyone was being trained in much the same way so that each person would have the opportunity to succeed. "It is," he said, "a socialist conception of capitalism."

The making of one people out of many is fostered by the general philosophy of public education in America, which holds that students should share a common curriculum. A system that would seek instead to enhance the education of top students would work to the disadvantage of poor students and others who, for reasons of language or life circumstances, are less prepared to do well when they enter school. An elite-centered school system of the type found in some European societies would serve to widen the gap between the country's richer and poorer groups and to slow the assimilation into American society of its newer arrivals.

Of course, other institutions also contribute to the integration of American society; but no institution does it as well or as thoroughly as the public schools. This is not to say that the schools are mirrors of America's diversity. A great deal of ethnic, racial, and class segregation still exists in the schools. For example, in some suburban schools few of the children come from families that earn less than $75,000 a year. And in some urban schools few of the children come from families that earn more than $25,000 a year. Yet, were it not for public schools, America would be a substantially more stratified society, both in terms of one's classmates while in school and in terms of one's prospects for success after leaving school.

Public education in America was called "the great leveler" when it began in the early nineteenth century. Since then it has earned that label. Rarely has a public institution served so many so well for such a long period.

should have an equal chance to succeed on their own. The concept embodies *equality* in its emphasis on giving everyone a fair chance to get ahead. Yet equality of opportunity also embodies *liberty* because it allows people to succeed or fail on their own as a result of what they do with their opportunities. The expectation is that people will end up differently—some will be rich, some poor. It is sometimes said that equality of opportunity offers individuals an equal chance to become unequal.

In practice, equality of opportunity works itself out primarily in the private sector, where Americans compete for jobs, promotions, and other advantages. However, a few public policies have the purpose of enhancing equality of opportunity. The most significant of these policies is public education.

Public Education: Leveling through the Schools

During the nation's first century, the question of a free education for all children was a divisive issue. Wealthy interests feared that an educated public would challenge their power. The proponents of a more equal society wanted to use education as a means of enabling ordinary people to get ahead. The latter view won out. Public schools sprang up in nearly every community and were open free of charge to children who could attend.

Today, as discussed in Chapter 1, the United States invests more heavily in public education at all levels than does any other country. The curriculum in American schools is also relatively standardized. Unlike those countries that divide children even at the grade school level into different tracks that lead ultimately to different occupations, the United States aims to educate all children in essentially the same way. Of course, public education is not a uniform experience for American children. The quality of education depends significantly on the wealth of the community in which a child resides.

Nevertheless, the United States through its public schools educates a broad segment of the population. Arguably, no country in the world has made an equivalent effort to give children, whatever their parents' background, an equal opportunity in life through education. Per pupil spending on public elementary and secondary schools is roughly twice as high in the United States as it is in Western Europe. America's commitment to broad-based education extends to college. The United States is far and away the world leader in terms of the proportion of adults receiving a college education.[15]

The nation's education system preserves both the myth and the reality of the American dream. The belief that success can be had by anyone who works for it could not be sustained if the education system were tailored for a privileged elite. And educational attainment is related to personal success, at least as measured by annual incomes. In fact, the gap in income between those with and those without a college education is greater now than at any time in the country's history.

In part because the public schools play such a large role in creating an equal-opportunity society, they have been heavily criticized in recent years. Violence in the schools is a major parental concern. So too is student performance on standardized tests. American students are not even in the top ten internationally in terms of their test scores in science or math.[16]

Disgruntled parents have demanded changes, and these demands have led some communities to allow parents to choose the public school their children will attend. Under this policy, the schools compete for students, and those that attract the most students are rewarded with the largest budgets. Americans by a wide margin say they favor such a policy. Advocates of the policy contend that it compels school administrators and teachers to do a better job and gives students the option of rejecting a school that is performing poorly.[17] Opponents of the policy say that it creates a few well-funded schools and a lot of poorly funded ones, yielding no net gain in educational quality. Critics also claim that the policy discriminates against poor and minority-group children, whose parents are less likely to be in a position to steer them toward the better schools.[18]

A more contentious issue is a voucher system that allows parents to use tax dollars to send their children to private or parochial schools (see Figure 16–5).[19] The recipient school receives a voucher redeemable from the government, and the student receives a corresponding reduction in his or her tuition. Advocates claim that vouchers force failing schools to improve their instructional programs. Opponents argue that vouchers weaken the public schools by siphoning off revenue and students. They also note that vouchers are of little value to students from poor families because they cover only part of the cost of attending a private or parochial school. In *Zelman v. Simmons-Harris* (2002), the Supreme Court declared that vouchers are constitutionally permissible.[20]

The issue of school choice reflects the tensions inherent in the concept of equal opportunity. On one hand, competition between schools expands the number of alternatives available to students. On the other hand, not all students have the opportunity to choose from the alternatives.

The Federal Role in Education: Political Differences

Education has traditionally been a state and local responsibility. Most school policies—from length of the school year to teachers' qualifications—are set by state legislatures and local school boards. Over 90 percent of the funds spent on schools are provided through state and local tax revenues.

Federal intervention in school policy has often been resisted by states and localities, as exemplified by their response to desegregation and busing directives (see Chapter 5). State and local governments have been less hesitant when it comes to federal education grants, but it is difficult to get congressional support for grant programs targeted only at the schools that are most in need. Few members of Congress are willing to support large appropriations for education that do not benefit their constituents, which has reduced Washington's contribution to a goal—quality education for every American child—that nearly every official endorses, at least in principle.

Indeed, it was not until 1965 that Congress enacted the first general federal aid to education legislation: the Higher Education Act and the Elementary and Secondary Education Act. The former became the foundation for Pell Grants, federal loans to college students, and federally subsidized college work-study programs. The latter provided funding for items such as school construction, textbooks, special education, and teacher training.

These acts were not the first federal programs in the education area. A century earlier, for example, Congress had passed the Morrill Act, which provided states with free tracts of land if the land was used to establish colleges. America's great "land grant" universities are the consequence. Another program was the G.I. bill enacted after World War II that enabled millions of service veterans to attend college. A third program was the National Defense Education Act of 1958, which provided loans and special institutes for students in science and related fields. But not until the 1965 legislation did the federal government assume a broader, ongoing role in public education.

"Last year's Supreme Court decision says that the U.S. Constitution does not prevent a state from offering vouchers that parents can use to send their students to private schools at public expense. Do you favor or oppose your state making such vouchers available?"

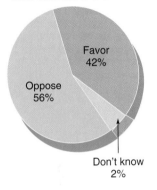

Favor 42%

Oppose 56%

Don't know 2%

Figure 16–5

Opinions on School Vouchers
Americans are divided in their opinions on school vouchers.
Source: 35th Annual Phi Delta Kappa/Gallup Poll of the Public's Attitudes Toward the Public Schools, 2003.

The Supreme Court has held that American children are entitled to an "adequate" education but do not have a right to an "equal" education. America's public schools differ greatly in quality primarily as a result of differences in the wealth of the communities they serve. Some public schools are overcrowded and have few facilities and little equipment. Others are very well equipped, have spacious facilities, and offer small class sizes.

Since then, federal assistance to public schools and colleges has been an important part of their financing, albeit a small part relative to the overall amount that the nation spends on public education. Federal funds during the past two decades have been split almost equally between support for college and support for public school elementary and secondary education.

As education has become increasingly an issue of national debate, Washington officials have been drawn into it. President Clinton rejected the idea of unrestricted school choice, arguing that it would weaken the nation's public schools and make them a repository of America's poorest and most difficult-to-educate children. Then, in 1998, Clinton persuaded Congress to pass a multibillion-dollar grant that enabled the nation's overcrowded schools to hire tens of thousands of new teachers.

In his 2000 presidential campaign, George W. Bush proposed a new direction in federal education policy. Once in office, he persuaded Congress to enact the No Child Left Behind Act of 2001. The legislation requires national testing in reading, math, and science and ties federal funding to test performance. Schools that show no improvement in students' test scores in the first two years of funding become eligible for additional funds. If these schools show no improvement by the end of the third year, however, their students will be eligible to transfer elsewhere and their federal assistance will be reduced.

Few federal education policies have provoked as much controversy as the No Child Left Behind Act. The National Education Association (NEA) claims that the law has forced teachers to teach to the national tests and thus interfered with real learning in the classroom. Congressional Democrats say that the program has failed to provide struggling schools with enough funds to improve the quality of classroom education. They see the legislation as punitive and as encouraging the flight of students from public to private schools. For their part, congressional Republicans have applauded the law, saying that it holds teachers and schools accountable for their students' performance. Congressman John Boehner (R-Ohio), chair of the House Committee on Education and the Workforce, said in 2003, "Money alone is not the answer to

One of the many ironies of U.S. social welfare policy is that tax deductions on home mortgages for the middle and upper classes are government subsidies, just as are rent vouchers for the poor, but only the latter are stigmatized as a government "handout."

the problems facing our children's schools. High standards and accountability for results—not just spending–are the key to erasing the achievement gap in education."[21]

Thus, many of the partisan and philosophical differences that affect federal welfare policy also affect federal education policy. Democratic lawmakers are more inclined to find the answer to how to improve schools in increased federal spending on education, particularly in less affluent communities. Republican lawmakers are more inclined to look toward marketlike mechanisms such as school choice and achievement tests.

CULTURE, POLITICS, AND SOCIAL WELFARE

Surveys have repeatedly indicated that a majority of Americans are convinced that most people on welfare could get along without it if they tried. Because public assistance programs have limited public support, there is constant political pressure to reduce welfare expenditures and to weed out undeserving recipients. The unwritten principle of social welfare in America, reflecting the country's individualistic culture, is that the individual must somehow earn any social welfare benefit, or, barring that, demonstrate a convincing need for the benefit. The result is a welfare system that is both *inefficient*, in that much of the money spent on welfare never reaches the intended recipients, and *inequitable*, in that most of the money spent on social welfare never gets to the people who are most in need of help.

Figure 16–6

The Cumbersome
Administrative Process by
Which Welfare Recipients
Receive Their Benefits

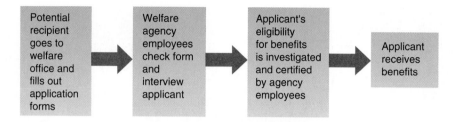

Inefficiency: The Welfare Web

The United States has the most complex system of social welfare in the world. Scores of separate programs have been established to address different, often overlapping needs. A single individual in need of public assistance may qualify for many, none, or one of these programs, and the eligibility criteria are sometimes bizarre. Consider the case of Gary Myers of Springfield, Missouri, who declared bankruptcy because he could not afford to pay $1,400 in hospital bills that his family had incurred. Had Myers made exactly $4 less than his $509 monthly wage as a security guard, he would have qualified for government payment of his medical expenses. Because he earned more than $505 a month, Myers was ineligible for assistance.

Beyond the question of the fairness of such rules is the question of their efficiency. The unwritten principle that the individual must somehow earn or deserve a particular benefit makes the U.S. welfare system heavily bureaucratic. For example, the 1996 welfare reform bill—which limits eligibility to families with incomes below a certain level and, in most instances, to families with a single parent living in the home—requires that the eligibility of each applicant be checked periodically by a caseworker. This procedure makes such programs doubly expensive; in addition to payments to the recipients, the programs must pay caseworkers, supervisors, and support staffs and must pay to process the extensive paperwork (see Figure 16–6).

The bureaucratic costs of welfare are substantially lower in Europe because eligibility is either universal, as in the case of health care, or less stringently defined. Proposals have been made to adopt a European-like system in the United States; President Nixon's attempt to establish a guaranteed annual income for every American family is an example. All these proposals have failed to win broad support, mainly because they run counter to Americans' belief in individualism.

Inequity: The Middle-Class Advantage

Most Americans hold to the traditional belief in individualism and self-reliance, which they generalize to other people. Although they recognize a need for programs for the poor and disadvantaged, they tend to minimize both the number of such individuals and the extent of their need. The result is that less advantaged Americans cannot count on a great deal of political support from other sectors of society. Even the much-heralded war on poverty of the 1960s was less a war than a skirmish. Weak middle-class support for the effort, reports that the programs were poorly administered and were not reaching the target audience,

Liberty, Equality & Self-Government

What's Your Opinion?

Gays, Lesbians, and Benefit Programs

In a 2003 survey, gays and lesbians ranked government and job-related benefits as one of the top issues facing their community. Their view reflected the fact that same-sex partners are ineligible for many benefits available to opposite-sex married couples.

The government's entitlement programs, such as social security and Medicare, are not universal in their application. Recipients must attain eligibility before they can receive benefits. In the case of social security and Medicare, for example, eligibility is achieved by working for a designated period of time at a job or series of jobs in which social security taxes are paid. Then, upon reaching a designated age, the individual becomes entitled to receive social security and Medicare benefits. However, eligibility is also granted to the married spouse of the recipient. The spouse receives Medicare benefits and, if the retired wage earner dies first, gets social security benefits.

Employee health care programs in both the public and the private sectors operate by similar rules. These programs offer health benefits to employees and also to their spouses and dependents.

Partners in gay and lesbian relationships see such arrangements as discriminatory. In general, partners in such relationships are not eligible for benefits to which spouses in opposite-sex relationships are entitled. For example, an elderly partner in a gay relationship cannot claim social security benefits upon the death of the partner who was receiving these benefits.

Do you think this form of inequality is justified? If not, what do you think is the proper way to address it? Some private firms and state and local governments have taken steps to make same-sex partners eligible for specific benefits, such as employee-based health care coverage. A more controversial approach is to permit civil unions or same-sex marriages, which would give same-sex couples the same legal status and thus the same claim on benefits as opposite-sex couples.

and the fiscal pressures of the Vietnam conflict combined to undermine the antipoverty effort. Annual congressional appropriations for the war on poverty programs never totaled as much as $500 per recipient.

Social security and Medicare are another story entirely. These two social insurance programs have broad public support, even though together they cost the federal government much more than is spent on all major public assistance programs. A reason for the higher public funding and approval for social security is that it benefits the majority. Most Americans are either actual or potential social security recipients. It is good politics for elected officials to appeal to the forty million retired Americans who get a monthly social security check.

Social security recipients feel entitled to their benefits by virtue of their payroll tax contributions. However, most recipients receive more in benefits than they have "earned" through their payroll taxes. These recipients are, in a sense, getting public assistance.

It is important to note, however, that the existence of social security substantially lessens the demand for other forms of public assistance. Monthly social security checks keep millions of Americans, mostly widows, out of poverty. About a fourth of social security recipients have no other significant source of income.

Nevertheless, many social security recipients, while legally entitled to the benefits they receive, have no actual financial need for them. Families in the top fifth of the income population receive more in federal social insurance benefits than is spent on TANF, food stamps, and housing subsidies combined. More than a fourth of America's high-income families receive a federal benefit of one type or another, usually social security and Medicare. That's a smaller proportion than for families in lower-income groups but a sizeable fraction nonetheless. Nor is there any reason to think that the situation will change. Because of lengthening life spans, social security payments will account for an increasingly larger share of federal social welfare expenditures in the years ahead. And social security is the one program where benefits go disproportionately to those who are comfortable financially—the more money that a person makes while working, the larger the social security benefit upon retirement.

The contradictions and difficulties of social welfare in America come together in the contrasting cases of social insurance and public assistance. Although the latter is targeted at the truly needy, it is less acceptable politically and culturally and receives much less funding. The situation testifies to the strength of traditional American values of individualism and self-reliance and to the power of money and votes. Social welfare is the arena in which many of the conflicts of the American political system come together: individualism versus equality, national authority versus local authority, public sector versus private sector, Republicans versus Democrats, poorer versus richer, social insurance versus public assistance. The politics of welfare is a politics of contradictory values and competing interests, which ensures that it will be a contentious issue well into the future.

Summary Self-Test
www.mhhe.com/pattersontad7

The United States has a complex social welfare system of multiple programs addressing specific welfare needs. Each program applies only to those individuals who qualify for benefits by meeting the specific eligibility criteria. In general, these criteria are designed to encourage self-reliance or, when help is necessary, to ensure that laziness is not rewarded or fostered. This approach to social welfare reflects Americans' traditional belief in individualism.

Poverty is a large and persistent problem in the United States. About one in nine Americans falls below the government-defined poverty line, including a disproportionate number of children, female-headed families, minority-group members, and rural and inner-city dwellers. The ranks of the poor are increased by economic recessions and are reduced through government assistance programs.

Welfare policy has been a partisan issue, with Democrats taking the lead on government programs to alleviate economic insecurity and Republicans acting to slow down or decentralize these initiatives. Changes in

social welfare have usually occurred through presidential leadership in the context of majority support for the change. Welfare policy has been worked out through programs to provide jobs and job training, education programs, income measures, and especially transfer payments through individual-benefit programs.

Individual-benefit programs fall into two broad categories: social insurance and public assistance. The former includes programs such as social security for retired workers and Medicare for the elderly. Social insurance programs are funded by payroll taxes paid by potential recipients, who thus, in a sense, earn the benefits they later receive. Because of this arrangement, social insurance programs have broad public support. Public assistance programs, in contrast, are funded by general tax revenues and are targeted toward needy individuals and families. These programs are not controversial in principle; most Americans believe that government should assist the truly needy. However, because of a widespread belief that most welfare recipients could get along without assistance if they tried, these programs do not have universal public support, are only modestly funded, and are politically vulnerable.

The balance between economic equality and individualism tilts more heavily toward individualism in the United States than in other advanced industrialized democracies. Entitlement to social security, for example, is not a universal right of the elderly in the United States, whereas it is elsewhere. Compared to other democracies, however, the United States attempts to more equally educate its children, a policy consistent with its cultural emphasis on equality of opportunity.

Social welfare is a contentious issue. A major reason is that opposing sides disagree fundamentally on the nature of the problem. In one view, social welfare is too costly and assists too many people who could help themselves; another view holds that social welfare is not broad enough and that too many disadvantaged Americans live in poverty. Because of these irreconcilable differences and because of federalism and the widely shared view that welfare programs should target specific problems, the existing system of multiple programs, despite its administrative complexity and inefficiency, has been the only politically feasible solution.

STUDY CORNER

Key Terms

effective tax rate *(p. 524)*
entitlement program *(p. 526)*
equality of opportunity *(p. 534)*
in-kind benefit *(p. 533)*

means test *(p. 530)*
negative government *(p. 527)*
positive government *(p. 527)*
poverty line *(p. 518)*

public assistance *(p. 530)*
social insurance *(p. 527)*
transfer payment *(p. 525)*

Self-Test

1. The shape of the U.S. welfare policy system has been strongly influenced by:
   a. the cultural emphasis placed on economic equality.
   b. the fact that the United States has a federal system of government.
   c. the fact that the United States is the wealthiest nation on earth and thus can afford the most generous benefit system.
   d. a and b only.

2. The 1996 Welfare Reform Act that Congress passed provides:
   a. an end to the federal guarantee of cash assistance to needy families.
   b. a limitation of five years in most cases for a person to receive assistance.
   c. that states must train and help welfare recipients find employment.
   d. all of the above.

3. Public assistance programs include all of the following **except:**
   a. subsidized housing.
   b. unemployment insurance.
   c. Medicaid.
   d. food stamps.

4. Regarding American education, all **except** which one of the following statements are true?
   a. The U.S. invests more heavily in public education than any other nation.
   b. U.S. law requires states to spend roughly equal amounts on each public school student, regardless of whether that student is going to school in a city, suburb, or rural area.
   c. Free public education provides a way that more people can gain the foundation for economic advantage.
   d. The curriculum in U.S. schools is relatively standardized on the assumption that children should be given an equal opportunity to get ahead in life.

5. Administrative costs of welfare are substantially lower in Europe than in the United States because:
   a. European eligibility is universal for certain programs, such as health care, and thus money does not have to be spent on the paperwork necessary to determine eligibility, which is the case in the United States.
   b. European eligibility for most programs is restricted to providing services to only the poorest 5 percent of the population.
   c. Europe has primarily unitary governments, which means they have to administer only one set of rules, rather than 50 different sets, as is the case in the United States because of state involvement in social welfare programs.
   d. a and c.

6. Regarding unemployment:
   a. according to research, the loss of a job or failure to immediately find a new job is in most cases the fault of the individual.
   b. U.S. Bureau of Labor statistics indicate that of those who have lost jobs, the large majority made the decision on their own to stop working rather than being terminated as part of a larger job layoff.
   c. government unemployment programs enjoy high levels of public support.
   d. none of the above.

7. The United States has almost the lowest poverty rate of any Western democracy. (T/F)

8. The Republican party has initiated nearly all major federal welfare programs. (T/F)

9. Social security and Medicare have widespread public support because they cost less than other welfare programs. (T/F)

10. There is a considerable gap in income levels between the top and bottom fifth of the American population. (T/F)

Critical Thinking

How has welfare and education policy been influenced by Americans' belief in individualism? By America's federal system of government?

Suggested Readings

Day, Phyllis J. *A New History of Social Welfare*. Boston: Allyn and Bacon, 1999. A comprehensive look at social welfare policy and traditions.

Diamond, Peter A. *Social Security Reform*. New York: Oxford University Press, 2002. A comprehensive look at the issue of social security reform.

Melnick, R. Shep. *Between the Lines: Interpreting Welfare Rights*. Washington, D.C.: Brookings Institution Press, 1994. An analysis of the intricate relationship between social welfare legislation and its interpretation in the courts.

Newman, Katherine S. *No Shame in My Game*. New York: Alfred A. Knopf and Russell Sage Foundation, 1999. A careful study of America's working poor.

Patterson, James T. *America's Struggle Against Poverty in the Twentieth Century*. Cambridge, Mass.: Harvard University Press, 2000. A careful study of poverty and its history.

Reed, Douglas S. *On Equal Terms: The Constitutional Politics of Educational Opportunity*. Princeton, N.J.: Princeton University Press, 2003. An insightful analysis of school reform issues.

Van Dunk, Emily, and Anneliese M. Dickman, *School Choice and the Question of Accountability*. New Haven, Conn.: Yale University Press, 2003. A careful look at the voucher system as applied in the Milwaukee school system.

Wilson, William Julius. *When Work Disappears: The World of the New Urban Poor*. New York: Knopf, 1996. An important analysis of jobs and poverty in the inner city.

List of Websites

http://www.doleta.gov/

The U.S. Department of Labor's website on the status of the welfare-to-work program, including state-by-state assessments.

http://www.nea.org/

The home page of the National Education Association; it provides information on the organization's membership and policy goals.

http://www.os.dhhs.gov/

The website of the Department of Health and Human Services—the agency responsible for most federal social welfare programs.

http://www.ssw.umich.edu/poverty/mission.html

The website of the University of Michigan's Program on Poverty and Social Welfare Policy; the program seeks to stimulate interest in policy issues and to transmit research findings to policymakers.

Participate!

Although conservatives and liberals disagree on the question of how far government should go in helping the poor, virtually all Americans—on the right and left—support private efforts to help the poor. Numerous local religious, civic, social, and economic groups have programs for the poor, such as food kitchens or clothing drives. Consider volunteering some of your time to such a group.

Extra Credit

For up-to-the-minute *New York Times* articles, interactive simulations, graphics, study tools, and more links and quizzes, visit the text's Online Learning Center at www.mhhe.com/pattersontad7.

(Self-Test Answers: 1. b   2. d   3. b   4. b   5. d   6. d   7. F   8. F   9. F   10. T)

17

Foreign and Defense Policy:
Protecting the American Way

"We the people of the United States, in order to . . .

provide for the common defense . . .

—Preamble, U.S. Constitution

Just after dark on March 19, 2003, the first bombs fell on Baghdad, signaling the start of the U.S. attack on Iraq. But if the progress of the fighting was necessarily foremost in the minds of U.S. policymakers, they also had their eye on a second set of issues: they were concerned about the economic consequences of the conflict with Iraq. There were fears that the war could destabilize the world economy, particularly if the flow of Middle Eastern oil was disrupted. There were also concerns about the effect of the war on the U.S. economy. The war would cost tens of billions of dollars—this at a time when the U.S. budget was already deeply in the red. Then there was the issue of the reconstruction of Iraq, which also would cost tens of billions of dollars yet was necessary if that nation was to become something other than a breeding ground for terrorists and an impediment to economic globalization. Securing an economically stable peace would be a more daunting task than waging a militarily successful war.

As America's war with Iraq illustrates, national security is an issue that ranges from military strength to economic vitality. The primary goal of U.S. foreign policy is protection of the American state. This objective requires military readiness in order to protect the territorial integrity of the United States, and it rises to the fore with every occurrence of an immediate threat, such as the terrorist attacks of September 11, 2001. But the American state also represents a society of nearly 300 million people whose livelihood depends in significant part on the nation's position in the international economy.[1] Through participation in economic policies that foster economic growth and international stability, the United States can secure the jobs and trade that are essential to the maintenance of a high standard of living.

The national security policies of the United States include an extraordinary array of activities—so many, in fact, that they could not possibly be addressed adequately in an entire book, much less a single chapter. There are some 190 countries in the world, and the United States has relations of one kind or another—military, diplomatic, economic—with all of them. This chapter narrows the subject by focusing on a few main ideas:

- *Since World War II, the United States has acted in the role of world leader, which has substantially affected its military, diplomatic, and economic policies.*

- *The policy machinery for foreign and defense affairs is dominated by the president and includes military, intelligence, diplomatic, and economic agencies and organizations.*

President George W. Bush talks with firefighters and police on the site of the collapsed World Trade Center buildings. The terrorist attacks of September 11, 2001, produced a fundamental change in U.S. foreign policy and public opinion.

- *The United States maintains a high degree of defense preparedness, which mandates a substantial level of defense spending and a worldwide deployment of U.S. conventional and strategic forces.*

- *Changes in the international marketplace have led to increased economic interdependence among nations, which has had a marked influence on the U.S. economy and on its security planning.*

THE ROOTS OF U.S. FOREIGN AND DEFENSE POLICY

For nearly half a century, U.S. defense policy was defined by conflict with the Soviet Union. From the Berlin airlift in 1948 to the Vietnam escalation in 1965 to the Star Wars initiative in 1983, the United States seemed willing to pay any price to halt the spread of communism. Then, in the late 1980s, the Soviet empire suddenly and dramatically began to fall apart. In December 1991, the Soviet Union itself ceased to exist. For decades, there had been two superpowers, the Soviet Union and the United States. Now there is only one.

Since the fall of the Soviet Union, the United States has redefined its foreign and defense policies. The country is still at the center of world politics, but its challenges have changed. The attacks on the World Trade Center and the Pentagon revealed to all what some analysts had been warning: the biggest threat to the physical security of the American people is not other nations but international terrorists who fight on behalf of causes. Developments in the previous decade had made another fact abundantly clear: a strong domestic base is the key to success in the increasingly important global economy.[2]

Although the age of superpower conflict is over, America's role in world affairs was shaped by that era. Accordingly, an understanding of the nation's foreign and defense policies and capabilities necessarily begins with an awareness of key developments during that period.

Historical Background

isolationism The view that the country should deliberately avoid a large role in world affairs and, instead, concentrate on domestic concerns.

internationalist Describing the view that the country should involve itself deeply in world affairs.

The United States as Global Superpower

Before World War II, the United States was an **isolationist** country, deliberately avoiding a large role in world affairs. A different America emerged from the war. It had more land, sea, and air power than any other country in the world, a huge military-industrial base, and several hundred overseas military bases. The United States had become an **internationalist** country, deeply involved in the affairs of other nations.

U.S. national security policy after World War II was built on concern with the power and intentions of the Soviet Union.[3] After the war, Soviet occupation forces assisted the communist parties in Eastern Europe in capturing state power, usually by coercive means. In the words of Britain's wartime minister, Winston Churchill, an "iron curtain" had fallen across Europe.

The Soviet Union's aggressive action led U.S. policymakers to assess Soviet aims. President Harry Truman saw the Soviet Union as an aggressive ideological foe that was bent on global domination and that could be stopped only by the forceful use of U.S. power. Truman's view was based on assumptions derived from territorial concessions made to Germany's Adolf Hitler by Britain and France at a conference in Munich in 1938; rather than appeasing Hitler, these concessions convinced him that Germany could bully its way to further gains. The idea that appeasement only encourages further aggression was the *lesson of Munich,* and it became the dominant view of U.S. policymakers in the postwar period. It contributed to the formulation of the doctrine of **containment,** which was based on the idea that the Soviet Union was an aggressor nation that had to be stopped from achieving its territorial ambitions.

Cold war propaganda, like this poster warning of the danger of communism, contributed to a climate of opinion in the United States that led to public support for efforts to contain Soviet power.

containment A doctrine, developed after World War II, based on assumptions that the Soviet Union was an aggressor nation and that only a determined United States could block Soviet territorial ambitions.

cold war The lengthy period after World War II when the United States and the USSR were not engaged in actual combat (a "hot war") but were nonetheless locked in a state of deep-seated hostility.

bipolar (power structure) A power structure dominated by two powers only, as in the case of the United States and the Soviet Union during the cold war.

The Cold War and Vietnam

Developments in the late 1940s embroiled the United States in a **cold war** with the Soviet Union. The term refers to the fact that the two countries were not directly engaged in actual combat (a "hot war") but were locked in a deep-seated hostility that lasted forty-five years. The structure of international power was **bipolar:** the United States stood firmly against the Soviet Union. Each side was supreme in its sphere and was blocked from expanding its influence by the power of the other.

The cold war included U.S. support for governments threatened by communist takeovers. In China, the Nationalist government had the backing of the United States, but it was defeated in 1949 by the Soviet-supplied communist forces of Mao Zedong. In June 1950, when the Soviet-backed North Koreans invaded South Korea, President Truman immediately committed U.S. troops to the conflict, which ended in stalemate and the loss of thirty-five thousand American lives.

In the jungle warfare of Vietnam, American soldiers had difficulty finding the enemy and adapting to guerrilla tactics.

For the United States, a major turning point in foreign policy was the Vietnam War. Responding to the threat of a communist takeover, the United States became ever more deeply involved in the civil war in Vietnam. By the late 1960s, 550,000 Americans were on station in South Vietnam. U.S. forces were technically superior in combat to the communist fighters, but they were fighting an enemy they could not easily identify in a society they did not fully understand.[4] Vietnam was a guerrilla war, with no front lines and few set battles. As the conflict dragged on, American public opinion, most visibly among the young, turned against the war, contributing to President Lyndon Johnson's decision not to run for reelection in 1968. Public opinion forced Richard Nixon, who became president in 1969, to aim not for victory but for a gradual disengagement. U.S. combat troops left Vietnam in 1973, and two years later North Vietnamese forces concluded their takeover of the country. Vietnam was the most painful and costly application of the containment doctrine: fifty-eight thousand American soldiers lost their lives in the fighting.

Détente and Disintegration of the "Evil Empire"

America's defeat in Vietnam forced U.S. policymakers to reconsider the country's international role. The *lesson of Vietnam* was that there were limits to the country's ability to assert its will in the world. Nixon claimed that the United States could no longer act as the "Lone Ranger" for the free world, and he sought to reduce tensions with communist countries. In 1972, for example, Nixon took a historic journey to the People's Republic of China, the first official contact with that country since the communists took power in 1949. Another indication of a change in policy was the Strategic Arms Limitation Talks (SALT), which presumed that the United States and the Soviet Union each had an interest in retaining enough nuclear weapons to deter the other from an attack but that neither side had an interest in an arms race that could lead to their mutual destruction. These efforts marked the start of a new era of communication and cooperation, or **détente** (a French word meaning "a relaxing"), between the United States and the Soviet Union.[5]

The period of détente did not last. The Soviet invasion of Afghanistan in 1979 convinced U.S. leaders that the USSR was still bent on expansion and threatened Western interests in the oil-rich Middle East. Ronald Reagan, elected president in 1980, called for a renewed hard line toward the Soviet Union, which he described as the "evil empire."

U.S. policymakers did not fully realize it at the time, but the Soviet Union was collapsing under its heavy defense expenditures, isolation from Western technology and markets, and inefficient centralized command economy. In March 1985, Mikhail Gorbachev became the Soviet leader and proclaimed a need to restructure Soviet society, an initiative known as *perestroika*. He also ordered the withdrawal of Soviet troops from Afghanistan (which had become his country's Vietnam) and sought to reduce tensions with the United States.

Gorbachev's efforts came too late to save the Soviet Union. In 1989, the withdrawal of Soviet troops from Eastern Europe accelerated a pro-democracy movement that was already under way in the region. Poland initiated major reforms. Hungary dismantled the "iron curtain" that had blocked free travel to Austria. Then, in November, the Berlin Wall between East and West Germany—the most visible symbol of the separation of East and West—came down. The Soviet Union itself was also disintegrating. On December 8, 1991, the leaders of the Russian, Belarus, and Ukrainian republics declared that the Soviet Union no longer existed. The bipolar power structure that had dominated world politics since the end of World War II had collapsed. The new structure was **unipolar**—the United States was now the unrivaled world power.

détente A French word meaning "a relaxing" and used to refer to an era of improved relations between the United States and the Soviet Union that began in the early 1970s.

unipolar (power structure) A power structure dominated by a single powerful actor, as in the case of the United States after the collapse of the Soviet Union.

A New World Order

The end of the cold war prompted the first President Bush in 1990 to call for a "new world order." His formulation abandoned the assumption that world affairs are a zero-sum game, in which for one nation to gain something, another nation has to lose. Bush contended that nations can move forward together. The concept emphasized **multilateralism**—the idea that major nations should act together in response to problems and crises.[6]

Multilateralism characterized the U.S. response to Iraq's invasion of Kuwait in August 1990. President Bush worked through the United Nations, which demanded the unconditional withdrawal of Iraqi forces and imposed a trade embargo on Iraqi oil. The military force arrayed against Iraq was also nominally a UN force, although it was led by a U.S. commander and consisted mostly of U.S. troops. Several countries, including Germany and Japan, supported the effort with money instead of troops.

The Gulf operation was successful from a strictly military perspective. Despite the size and combat readiness of Iraq's army, the shooting war ended quickly, prompting President Bush to claim that the United States had "kicked the Vietnam syndrome [the legacy of America's defeat in Vietnam] once and for all." But the outcome of the Gulf War was much less successful from another perspective. Bush's decision to stop the war short of a march on Baghdad left

multilateralism The situation in which nations act together in response to problems and crises.

Shown here is Slobodan Milosevic, president of the former Yugoslavia, during his trial at the United Nations war crimes tribunal in The Hague, Netherlands. Milosevic is accused of ordering and condoning atrocities in Bosnia and Kosovo during conflicts there in the 1990s. The war crimes tribunal is only one of the many ways that the United Nations works to promote peace and humanitarian goals.

Saddam Hussein in power, and he responded by refusing to cooperate with UN inspectors charged with dismantling Iraq's weapons programs.

Multilateralism was also applied in the Balkans. Beginning in 1992, the Bosnian Serbs, supported by the Serb-dominated Yugoslav government, attacked Muslims and Croats in Bosnia. Finally, in 1995, after UN economic sanctions and limited air strikes had failed to deter Serb aggression, planes of the United States and its Western allies undertook a bombing campaign that led to U.S.-negotiated peace talks (the Dayton Accords). The talks brought an end to hostilities and resulted in the deployment to Bosnia of sixty thousand peacekeeping troops (including twenty thousand from the United States). War in the Balkans flared again in 1999, after the Yugoslav Serbs began a campaign of "ethnic cleansing" in the Serbian province of Kosovo, which had a population that was 90 percent ethnic Albanian. After failed attempts at a negotiated settlement, planes from the NATO countries (North Atlantic Treaty Organization, discussed later in this chapter) attacked Serbia. (Yugoslavia is a federation that includes Serbia and Montenegro.) After weeks of intensive bombing, Yugoslav president Slobodan Milosevic (who was subsequently arrested and put on trial for war crimes) pulled his troops out of Kosovo. Ethnic Albanians moved back in and, despite the presence of UN peacekeeping troops, commenced revenge attacks on some of the Serbs who remained.

As these examples indicate, multilateralism has been only partly successful as a strategy for resolving international conflicts. With the deployment of enough resources, the world's major powers can intervene with some success in many parts of the developing world. However, these interventions offer no guarantee of long-term success. Regional and internal conflicts typically stem from enduring ethnic, religious, factional, or national hatreds or from chronic problems such as famine, overcrowding, or government corruption. Even if these hatreds or problems can be momentarily eased, they are often too deep-seated to be permanently resolved.

The War on Terrorism

When he took office in 2001, George W. Bush declared that the United States would play a less active role in international affairs. Bush announced that the United States would not participate in the Kyoto Accord (global climate change treaty) or the International Criminal Court (a permanent tribunal with jurisdiction over war crimes). Although Bush remained opposed to these arrangements, his position on America's role in the world abruptly changed when terrorists attacked the World Trade Center and the Pentagon, killing nearly three thousand people. The horror of the September 11 attacks prompted a massive international response that Bush called "the war on terrorism."

This war is unlike past wars because most of its targets are not nations but groups engaged in terrorism that is aimed at U.S. interests at home and abroad. A war without sharply defined battlefronts, it is being waged through a wide variety of instruments, including military force, intelligence gathering, law enforcement, foreign aid, international cooperation, and immigration control. The tactics are also unusual. The rooting out of terrorist cells in the United States and Europe, for example, is entrusted to law enforcement agencies rather than to military units.

The first U.S. military operation was an attack on Afghanistan. That country's Taliban-led government had provided training sites and protection to the Al Qaeda terrorist network, which had carried out the September 11 attacks. Backed by a UN resolution authorizing the use of force and supported by other NATO member countries, the United States toppled the Taliban government in early 2002; however, Al Qaeda leader Osama bin Laden and most of his top lieutenants evaded capture.

In March 2003, by order of President George W. Bush, U.S. troops attacked Iraq. The intense combat phase was relatively short, ending in the defeat of Iraqi forces. However, the reconstruction phase that followed was marked by continuing U.S. casualties and questions about the validity of the intelligence estimates that had been used to justify the attack.

In 2002, President Bush labeled Iraq, Iran, and North Korea an "axis of evil," thereby signaling a widening of the war on terrorism.[7] Shortly thereafter, he announced a new national security doctrine: the **preemptive war doctrine.** Speaking at West Point, President Bush said that the threat of international terrorism meant that the United States could not afford to wait until it was attacked by hostile nations. Bush declared that America was prepared to take "preemptive action."[8] This concept was not entirely new—U.S. officials had long maintained a right to strike first if faced with a serious and immediate threat. What was new about the Bush doctrine was that it extended the option to include military action against countries that might pose such a threat at an unspecified future time.

preemptive war doctrine The idea, espoused by President George W. Bush, that the United States could attack a potentially threatening nation even if the threat had not yet reached a serious and immediate level.

The Iraq War

In the summer of 2002, Bush targeted the regime of Iraq's Saddam Hussein claiming that it had accumulated weapons of mass destruction (WMDs)—chemical and biological weapons, and possibly even nuclear weapons. Bush asked Congress for a resolution authorizing the use of military force against Iraq if it did not fully and peaceably disarm. In October, Congress passed the resolution.

Facing the possibility of a Middle Eastern war, America's European allies urged the disarmament of Iraq through UN weapons inspectors. In late 2002,

Was the Iraq Intervention a Success?

The United States has unrivaled military power, and President George W. Bush used that power in 2003 to invade Iraq and topple the regime of Saddam Hussein. Bush acted without the broad international support that had underpinned the U.S. invasion of Afghanistan in the months following the terrorist attacks on the World Trade Center and the Pentagon. Americans were highly supportive of the decision to invade Iraq. Some of them began to have second thoughts, however, as the postwar reconstruction in Iraq bogged down in the wake of continuing attacks on U.S. troops and rising hostility of Iraqis toward the U.S. occupation. As a result, the Iraq war became a top issue of the 2004 presidential campaign. Bush and his opponent, John Kerry, spoke out frequently on the wisdom of the war, often (as in these excerpts) in sessions with journalists.

Yes: A secure and free Iraq is an historic opportunity to change the world and make America more secure. A free Iraq in the midst of the Middle East will have incredible change. It's hard—freedom is not easy to achieve. . . . We're changing the world. And the world will be better off and America will be more secure as a result of the actions we're taking. . . . Saddam Hussein was a threat. He was a threat because he had used weapons of mass destruction on his own people. He was a threat because he coddled terrorists. He was a threat because he funded suiciders. He was a threat to the region. He was a threat to the United States. . . . The Iraqis are really pleased we got rid of Saddam Hussein. And you can understand why. This is a guy who. . . . [made them] fearful of making decisions toward liberty. That's what we've seen recently. Some citizens are fearful of stepping up. . . . They're not happy they're occupied. I wouldn't be happy if I were occupied either. They do want us there to help with security, and that's why this transfer of sovereignty is an important signal to send, and it's why it's also important for them to hear we will stand with them until they become a free country.

—George W. Bush, president of the United States and 2004 Republican party presidential nominee

No: Nothing is more important than how a president takes a nation to war, how a president decides to put young men and women at risk for our nation. I believe this president broke faith with the rules of how a president does that. . . . Number one, you cannot bring other nations to the table through the back door. You cannot have America run the occupation, make all the reconstruction decisions, make the decisions of the kind of government that will emerge, and pretend to bring other nations to the table. . . . And the tragedy is that there were . . . opportunities for this administration to make it otherwise. Opportunity number one was when . . . the president broke his promise to build a legitimate coalition by being patient with the U.N. inspection process. . . . I will be a president who understands, as every president of the last century did, that multilateralism is not weakness, it is strength, and we need a president who understands how to reach out to other countries, build alliances. . . . [Moreover,] Iraq had nothing to do with al-Qaeda. . . . We had Osama bin Laden cornered. . . . [W]hat did we do? [We turned to Iraq and] let him escape.

—John Kerry, U.S. senator and 2004 Democratic party presidential nominee

the United Nations passed a resolution that required Iraq to accept weapons inspections. A two-track policy ensued. UN weapons inspectors entered Iraq in search of WMDs while at the same time the United States deployed combat units to the Middle East.

Over the strenuous objections of the French, German, and Russian governments and despite a failure to get UN authorization for military action,

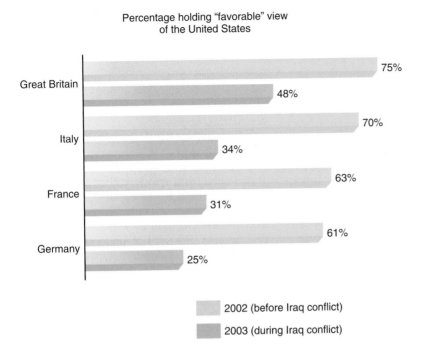

Percentage holding "favorable" view
of the United States

Great Britain — 75% / 48%
Italy — 70% / 34%
France — 63% / 31%
Germany — 61% / 25%

2002 (before Iraq conflict)
2003 (during Iraq conflict)

Figure 17–1

Impact of Iraq Conflict on Europeans' Opinion of the United States

The Iraq conflict in 2003 led to a sharp decline in Europeans' opinion of the United States.

Source: The Pew Research Center for the People and the Press surveys, July 2002 and March 2003. The 2003 survey was completed shortly before combat in Iraq began but after it became apparent that war was likely to occur.

President Bush in March 2003 ordered U.S. forces to attack Iraq, declaring that Hussein had sabotaged the weapons inspections. U.S. combat units, backed by their British allies, easily defeated the Iraqi army. However, the post-combat phase proved more deadly and costly than the Bush administration had anticipated. Roadside mines and suicide bombers took a heavy toll on U.S. soldiers, and the cost of rebuilding Iraq soon rose above $100 billion. Moreover, the WMDs that Bush had stated were the reason for the war could not be found. In early 2004, the chief U.S. weapons inspector, David Kay, testified before Congress that U.S. intelligence agencies had greatly overestimated the extent of Iraq's weapons program.

The American public, which initially had strongly backed the war on Iraq, came to question the war and its costs. They also expressed doubts about Bush's preemptive war doctrine. In polls, a majority said the United States henceforth should work more closely with other countries and should refrain from unprovoked attacks on other nations. Only 34 percent agreed that the "United States has the right and even the responsibility to overthrow dictatorships and help their people build a democracy."[9] Opinion elsewhere was more severe. For the first time since World War II, Western Europeans held that the United States should not be entrusted with world leadership. A year before the war, roughly 70 percent of Western Europeans had expressed a favorable opinion of the United States; fewer than 40 percent held that view in 2003 (see Figure 17–1).

Why World Opinion Is Important

As news of the terrorist attacks on the World Trade Center and the Pentagon spread throughout the world, an enormous outpouring of support for the United States occurred. Almost every nation offered help in combating global terrorism.

In a few Islamic countries, however, there were street celebrations of the attacks as well as demonstrations against America. Bush's subsequent "axis of evil" statement also produced street demonstrations in some Islamic countries. In Iran, one of the countries included in Bush's axis, the phrase "America, the Great Satan" was heard widely, just as it had been two decades before, at the time of Iran's Islamic Revolution.

There is no simple explanation for these adverse reactions to the United States, even though some commentary suggests otherwise. According to the simpleminded on the left, the attacks on the World Trade Center and the Pentagon occurred because the United States has arrogantly aligned itself against the Islamic world. But this perspective requires overlooking America's support for Muslims in the Bosnian and Kosovo conflicts and its role in developing the Oslo Accords, which could someday result in the creation of a sovereign Palestinian state. According to the simpleminded on the right, the terrorist attacks had no foundation whatsoever other than envy toward America as a bastion of freedom. This view requires overlooking the fact that America's cultural values and foreign policies are not universally admired and in some places are actively opposed.

Thoughtful appraisals are needed, perhaps more so than at nearly any time in the country's history. The war on terrorism is a battle for people's hearts and minds rather than a fight for territory or cultural hegemony. The world is becoming increasingly interdependent, and even single individuals can strike lethal blows at innocent people. Barriers to understanding need to be broken down, and policies need to be crafted that take into account the aspirations of those they affect. When, as in the fights against fascism and communism, the enemy was clearly identifiable, America could at least risk ignorance of the enemy's grievances. But when hostile forces have the same look as friendly ones, disarmament and victory are likely to be gained only by confronting squarely the sources of discontent that breed hostility. Not all such discontent is reasonable or rooted in fact, which means that irrational acts will occur. What may be achievable is a lowering of that discontent that is at least partly attributable to U.S. policies. John Dower, a historian at MIT and the author of *War Without Mercy*, says that America's tendency to see "itself as nothing but good and innocent" makes it difficult for the country to understand and respond effectively to those who object to U.S. policies.

During the 2004 presidential campaign, President Bush defended his preemptive war doctrine. "America will never seek a permission slip to defend the security of our country," he said.[10] Bush also said, however, that he had no plans in place for a second preemptive war. For his part, Democratic nominee John Kerry criticized Bush's policy: "We have a president who developed and exalted a strategy of war—unilateral, preemptive—and in my view, profoundly threatening to America's place in the world and the safety and prosperity of our own society." Kerry promised a foreign policy rooted in multilateralism. "As President," Kerry said, "I will not cede our security to any nation or institution—and adversaries will have no doubt of my resolve to use force if necessary—but I will always understand that even the only superpower on earth cannot succeed without cooperation and compromise with our friends and allies."[11]

Both candidates recognized, however, that the demise of Hussein's regime in Iraq hardly marked the end of the terrorist threat. Each pledged to fight terrorism with all the means at America's disposal. This reality was reflected in the federal budget for the 2005 fiscal year, which included substantial increases in spending on military defense, intelligence gathering, foreign assistance, and homeland security. The total amount was several hundred billion dollars more than had been spent in these areas in the fiscal year preceding the terrorist attacks of September 11, 2001.

THE PROCESS OF FOREIGN AND MILITARY POLICYMAKING

National security is unlike other areas of government policy because it rests on relations with actors outside rather than inside a country. As a result, the chief instruments of national security policy—diplomacy, military force, economic exchange, and intelligence gathering—differ from those of domestic policy.

The Policymaking Instruments

Diplomacy, one instrument of foreign policy, is the process of negotiation between countries. In most cases, nations prefer to settle their differences by talking rather than by fighting. Through negotiation, countries can usually reach agreement on common (mutual) problems. By definition, acts of diplomacy involve negotiations between two (bilateral) or more (multilateral) nations.

Military power, a second instrument of foreign policy, can be used unilaterally—that is, by a single nation acting alone. Most countries use military power as a defensive measure; they maintain forces, or enter into military alliances with other countries, in order to protect themselves from potential aggressors. Throughout the history of nations, however, there have always been a few countries that use military force more actively. The United States is such a nation. In the nineteenth century, it used force to take territory from Native Americans and from Mexico and Spain. Although the United States has not pursued territorial goals since then, it has made frequent use of its military power for other ends. Recent examples include the unilateral invasions of Grenada in 1983, Panama in 1989, and Haiti in 1994; the multilateral war against Iraq in 1991 and the bombing of Serbs in 1995 and 1999; the multilateral war against the Afghan regime in 2002; and the nominally multilateral but basically unilateral war against Iraq in 2003.

Economic exchange is a third instrument of world politics. This tool of international relations usually takes one of two forms: trade or assistance. Trade among nations is the more important form. Nearly all countries aspire to a strong trading position so as to have access to outside products and to markets for their products. Some countries, however, are so weak economically that they

Pictured here is a U.S. attack helicopter. America's military power rests substantially on the advanced state of its weaponry, as the wars in Afghanistan and Iraq showed. U.S. forces were able to inflict heavy casualties without incurring heavy casualties themselves.

require assistance from more prosperous countries. This assistance typically is also designed to help the stronger partner by providing a market for its goods.

A fourth instrument of world politics is intelligence gathering, or the process of monitoring other countries' activities. For many reasons, but primarily because all nations pursue their individual self-interest, each nation keeps a watchful eye on other nations.

The Policymaking Machinery

In the United States, the lead actor in the application of these four instruments of foreign policy is the president. The president shares power and responsibility for foreign and military policy with Congress, but the president has the stronger claim to leadership because of the constitutional roles of commander in chief, chief diplomat, and chief executive (see Chapter 12). For example, although President Bush briefed congressional leaders on his plans for the wars in Afghanistan and Iraq, they were not involved in formulating the plans or overseeing their execution.

The National Security Council (NSC), which is part of the Executive Office of the President (see Chapter 12), coordinates advice on foreign and military issues. Chaired by the president, the NSC includes the vice president and the secretaries of state and defense as full members and the director of the Central Intelligence Agency (CIA) and the chair of the Joint Chiefs of Staff as advisory members. Because the State Department, the Defense Department, and the CIA often have conflicting and self-centered views of national security, the NSC acts to keep the president in charge by providing a more comprehensive perspective. The NSC's staff of experts is directed by the president's national security advisor, who, with an office in the White House and access to defense, diplomatic, and intelligence sources, has become influential in the formulation of foreign policy.

The complexity of international politics makes it impossible for the president or any government agency to fully control U.S. policy. Moreover, as a world power, the United States relies on outside institutions, such as the United Nations, to pursue some of its policy objectives. The key organizational units in the foreign policy area can be categorized according to their primary functions—defense, intelligence, diplomacy, and trade.

Defense Organizations

The Department of Defense (DOD), which has more than one million uniformed personnel and seven hundred thousand civilian employees, is responsible for the military security of the United States. DOD was created in 1947 when the three military services—the Army, Navy, and Air Force—were placed under the secretary of defense. Each service has its own secretary, but they report to the defense secretary, who represents all the services in relations with Congress and the president. Each service naturally regards its mission and budget as more important than those of the other services. The defense secretary is expected to reduce the adverse effects of these interservice rivalries.

The president also receives military advice from the Joint Chiefs of Staff (JCS). The JCS includes a chair, a vice chair, and a member from each of the uniformed services—the Army, Navy, Air Force, and Marine Corps. The JCS helps shape military strategy and evaluates the military's personnel and weapons needs.

In 2002, the Department of Homeland Security was created to coordinate domestic efforts to protect the United States against terrorist attacks and threats. The responsibilities of the homeland security agency include securing the nation's borders, enhancing defense against biological attacks, preparing emergency personnel (police, firefighters, and rescue workers) for their roles in responding to terrorist attacks, and coordinating efforts to stop domestic terrorism.

Of the country's military alliances, the North Atlantic Treaty Organization (NATO) is the most important. NATO was created after World War II as a "forward defense" against the possible Soviet invasion of Western Europe. After the demise of the Soviet Union, NATO was restructured as a smaller, more flexible force that could deal with new risks, such as international terrorism and ethnic rivalries. The NATO forces, which now include troops from the United States, Canada, and most Western and Eastern European countries, conduct joint military exercises and engage in joint strategic and tactical military planning. NATO's attack on Serbia in 1999 was the first ever military campaign for the alliance. In 2003, NATO's status was thrown into doubt when several key members, including France, Germany, and Belgium, opposed America's war on Iraq, claiming that UN arms inspections were the better alternative. Since then, however, the countries in the NATO alliance have sought to repair the split caused by the Iraq war.

Intelligence Organizations

Foreign and military policy requires a high state of knowledge about what is happening in the world. Responsibility for the gathering of such information

GLOBAL Perspective

Americans in an Interdependent World

The Weapons of Global Terrorism

The September 11, 2001, attacks on the World Trade Center and the Pentagon awakened Americans to the threat of global terrorism. For many, it was their first real awareness that there was a deadly force loose in the world that aimed to do grave harm to America and Americans. Terrorists' weapons are not tanks, warplanes, and other conventional tools of war. Nevertheless, their weapons are frightening, in large part because they target civilian populations.

The September 11 attacks employed a weapon—transportation vehicles packed with explosive materials—that had been used in earlier attacks on Americans: the 1983 bombings of U.S. Marine barracks and the U.S. embassy in Lebanon, the 1993 bombing of the World Trade Center, the 1998 simultaneous bombings of U.S. embassies in Kenya and Tanzania, and the 2000 bombing of the U.S.S. Cole in Yemen. Such attacks were commonplace in Iraq after the U.S. invasion in 2003.

Assassination is a second terrorist weapon. The target is often an innocent civilian rather than a top government or military official, as in the case of *Wall Street Journal* reporter Daniel Pearl, who was murdered by Pakistani militants in 2002. Assassination is an old weapon of war, but it has taken on a new dimension with suicide bombers who blow themselves up in the process of killing and injuring those around them. Such attacks are designed to create fear and to inhibit people from traveling freely.

Weapons of mass destruction are also in the terrorist arsenal, but to date they have not been used to great effect. Biological and chemical weapons have the potential to kill thousands, even millions, of people. Shortly after the September 11 attacks, anthrax spores were mailed to several locations in the United States, including the Capitol building. Although several people died, the outbreak was contained by the fact that anthrax is not a communicable disease. Smallpox, however, is communicable, and U.S. officials fear that terrorist groups might obtain the smallpox virus. Smallpox vaccination in the United States was terminated three decades ago on the belief that the disease had been eradicated. Smallpox is easily transmitted from one person to another and is fatal in 30 percent of cases.

U.S. officials also worry that terrorists have or are developing the capacity to deploy nuclear weapons. If such a weapon were unleashed on the U.S. population, it would likely be delivered by land or ship rather than by a nuclear missile. If detonated in a congested area, thousands of people would be killed and the area of impact would be rendered uninhabitable.

A final terrorist weapon is propaganda. Terrorists realize they cannot win a conventional military showdown with the United States. Instead, they seek to weaken American resolve and to gain the support of peoples around the world who are resentful of regimes supported by the United States. In the end, the war on terrorism is a fight for people's hearts and minds. If the United States and other countries take actions that convince people around the world that grievances can be settled without resorting to terrorism, support for it will begin to diminish.

falls to specialized federal agencies, including the Central Intelligence Agency (CIA); the National Security Agency, which specializes in electronic communications analysis; and separate intelligence agencies within the Departments of State and Defense.[12] The federal government spends a vast amount annually on intelligence activities. The figure for fiscal year 2005 has been estimated at roughly $40 billion. However, the exact amount is secret information known only to select members of the executive and legislative branches (thus, it is called the "Black Budget").

With the decline of the Soviet threat, intelligence agencies have made increased efforts to stop international drug trafficking and terrorism. These efforts are a deterrent but cannot prevent all such activities. The U.S. embassies in Kenya and Tanzania, for example, had received no advance warning when terrorist bombs blew them apart in 1998, killing several hundred people, including a dozen Americans. Intelligence agencies also failed to uncover the terrorist planning that culminated in the September 11, 2001 attacks on the World Trade Center and the Pentagon, and they badly misjudged Iraq's weapons program in the run-up to the U.S. invasion of Iraq. Observers claimed that U.S. intelligence agencies were relying too heavily on spy satellites and other new technologies at the expense of field agents. In 2004, the bipartisan commission formed by Congress to investigate the September 11 attacks recommended a thorough restructuring of U.S. intelligence agencies.

President George W. Bush's national security advisor Condoleezza Rice is shown speaking at a White House gathering. The president's national security advisor is responsible for coordinating information provided by military, diplomatic, and intelligence agencies into advice on broad issues of foreign and defense policy.

Diplomatic Organizations

The Department of State conducts most of the country's day-to-day business with foreign countries through its embassies, headed by U.S. ambassadors. The secretary of state is one of the most visible and important members of the administration. The department's traditional duties include negotiating political agreements with other nations, protecting U.S. citizens and interests abroad, promoting U.S. economic interests, gathering foreign intelligence, and representing the United States abroad. For all its activities and prominence, the State Department is relatively small. Only about twenty-five thousand people—foreign service officers, policy analysts, administrators, and others—work in the State Department.

America's diplomatic efforts also take place through international organizations such as the Organization of American States (OAS) and the United Nations. The United Nations was established after the Second World War by the victorious allies. Its security council, which included the United States, France, Britain, the Soviet Union, and the Republic of China, was to be an instrument of multilateral policymaking. The world's strongest powers would work together for global harmony and prosperity. When the United States and Soviet Union entered into the cold war, all hope of such cooperation vanished.

The breakdown of the Soviet bloc in 1989 renewed the possibility that the world's great powers could work together to achieve common goals. The first major opportunity came in the Persian Gulf conflict of 1990–91, when the United States led a UN force that first blocked Iraqi forces and then attacked them. Yet, in 2003, the United States basically rejected attempts to use the United Nations as the means of resolving the issue of Iraq's weapons programs.

Some analysts believe that the UN might someday be able to play the large role in international affairs that was envisioned for it when it was chartered. International terrorism, ethnic conflict, territorial disputes, human rights abuses, and drug trafficking are among the areas in which the UN might take on a larger role. Other analysts are skeptical about the UN's capacity to solve difficult international problems. UN operations normally are effective only to the degree that member nations agree on a course of action and are determined to pursue it. Often, that collective will is lacking.

Economic Organizations

The increased importance of the global economy has brought to the fore a new set of government agencies, those representing economic sectors. The Agriculture, Commerce, Labor, and Treasury Departments are playing increasingly important roles in foreign affairs. In addition, some specialty agencies, such as the Federal Trade Commission and the Export-Import Bank of the United States, are involved in international trade and finance.

The United States also works through major international organizations that promote goals—such as economic development and free trade—that are consistent with U.S. policy objectives. The newest of these international organizations is the World Trade Organization (WTO), which was created in 1995 and is the formal institution through which most nations negotiate general rules of international trade. The WTO also adjudicates disagreements over the meaning of these rules. In 2003, for example, the WTO held that U.S. tariffs on imported steel, which were intended to protect U.S. steel makers, were illegal under international trade rules and had to be rescinded.

The World Bank and the International Monetary Fund (IMF) are older institutions. Created at the 1944 Bretton Woods Conference by the United States and Great Britain, these organizations provide financial assistance to developing countries. The World Bank makes long-term loans to poor countries for capital investment projects—such as the construction of dams, power plants, highways, and factories—that will promote economic growth. In contrast, the IMF makes short-term loans so that countries experiencing temporary problems will not collapse economically or resort to ruinous practices, such as the imposition of high tariffs. In 1997 and 1998, for example, the IMF made multibillion-dollar loans to Korea, Thailand, and other Asian countries whose economies had gone into a tailspin from poor investment practices and currency devaluation.

HOW THE UNITED STATES COMPARES

The Burden of Military Spending

The United States bears a disproportionate share of the defense costs of the NATO alliance. The U.S. military establishment is huge and is deployed all over the world, and taxpayers spend more than $400 billion per year to maintain it. These expenditures directly account for roughly 5 percent of the U.S. gross national product (GNP). By comparison, defense spending by Germany, Italy, and Canada accounts for 3 percent or less of their GNPs. The percentages for Britain and France are higher but not as high as for the United States. Japan, which is not part of NATO, spends only 1 percent of its GNP on defense. Japan's small military force is confined by World War II peace agreements to the country's islands and the adjoining waters.

The United States has pressured its allies to carry a larger share of the defense burden, but these countries have resisted, contending that the cost would be too high and that their security would not be substantially improved. A partial exception to this situation was the Persian Gulf War. U.S. troops and equipment accounted for the bulk of the military strength arrayed against Iraq, but the financial cost of the war effort was borne by other countries. Germany, Japan, Saudi Arabia, and Kuwait were among the countries that helped fund the war. In fact, other countries gave the United States $20 billion more than it spent on the war.

The war on terrorism has forced an increase in U.S. military spending that, to date, has not been matched by increased spending by America's allies. However, some U.S. officials prefer the imbalance because it gives the United States more freedom to act on its own when it prefers to do so.

The United States accounts for nearly half of the total defense spending worldwide.

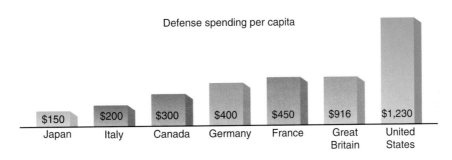

Defense spending per capita

Japan	Italy	Canada	Germany	France	Great Britain	United States
$150	$200	$300	$400	$450	$916	$1,230

Source: OECD and U.S. and British government statistics.

THE MILITARY DIMENSION OF NATIONAL SECURITY POLICY

The launching of the war on terrorism brought about the first major increase — tens of billions of dollars—in U.S. defense spending since the 1980s. The United States spends far more on defense, in both relative and absolute terms, than its allies do. On a per capita basis, U.S. military spending is more than twice that of other nations in the NATO alliance (see "How the United States Compares"). The U.S. defense budget is second to none in the world, but so is the military power it buys. In 2003, the Iraqi army, despite its numerical superiority, was no match for the United States' superior military equipment and technology. The combat phase of the war lasted less than a month.

Defense Capability

The United States owes its status as the world's only superpower in part to the strength of its conventional forces. The U.S. Navy has a dozen aircraft carriers, nearly one hundred attack submarines, and hundreds of other fighting and supply ships. The U.S. Air Force has thousands of high-performance aircraft. The U.S. Army has roughly five hundred thousand troops on active duty, and they are amply supported by tanks, artillery pieces, armored personnel carriers, and attack helicopters.

Assessments of military power have traditionally been based on the number of planes, tanks, and other weapons that a nation has. But these assessments increasingly must also account for the ability of a nation to connect these weapons to information. Surveillance devices (such as satellites), high-speed computers, and sophisticated software give military commanders the ability to gather, process, and disseminate information about tactical and strategic situations and thus to direct the use of their weaponry. In the war in Afghanistan, the United States was able to avoid the risk of committing large troop units to the fighting. Special forces soldiers, operating individually and in small groups, were deployed. Using their night-vision equipment and computer-assisted locators, they directed air strikes on Taliban and Al Qaeda positions. No other nation has anywhere near the advanced weapons systems that the United States possesses.

Despite this "revolution in military power," older weapons systems are still a part of the American arsenal. The nuclear weapons that starkly defined the nation's cold war with the Soviet Union are an example. During the cold war, the United States followed a policy of **deterrence,** which included a nuclear arsenal capable of destroying the Soviet Union many times over. Deterrence was based on the notion that the Soviet Union would be deterred from launching a nuclear attack by the knowledge that even if it destroyed the United States, it would be obliterated as well.

deterrence The idea that nuclear war can be discouraged if each side in a conflict has the capacity to destroy the other with nuclear weapons.

The Uses of Military Power

U.S. military forces have been trained for or called on for six types of military action, descriptions of which follow.

Unlimited Nuclear Warfare

The idea of an all-out nuclear war was always too horrible to imagine, but the fear of nuclear holocaust has diminished since the cold war ended. The United States and Russia have reduced their nuclear arsenals and have created monitoring systems designed to reduce the possibility that either side could launch a surprise attack. Nevertheless, both sides retain their capacity for a full-scale nuclear war. America's nuclear weapons are deployed in what is called the "nuclear triad." This term refers to the three ways these weapons can be launched—by land-based missiles, submarine-based missiles, and bombers. The triad provides a "second-strike capability"—the ability to absorb a first-strike nuclear attack and survive with enough nuclear power for massive retaliation (second strike).

Limited Nuclear Warfare

Some experts believe that although the risk of an all-out nuclear attack on the United States has diminished, the possibility that a single nuclear weapon might be used against the United States has increased. A major concern arising from the breakup of the Soviet Union has been control of its nuclear weapons, both strategic and tactical. In addition, terrorist groups and "outlaw" regimes, such as North Korea, are a threat because the technology and materials required to build nuclear weapons are more widely accessible than ever before. Accordingly, the United States, Russia, and other nuclear powers are cooperating to reduce the spread of nuclear weapons. One goal of the war on terrorism is the elimination of nuclear programs in countries such as North Korea.

U.S. Army troops in Afghanistan emerge from a small meeting room on the edge of the Kandahar Airport. The strategy session took place during the U.S. attack on Taliban and Al Qaeda forces, which was dubbed Operation Enduring Freedom.

Unlimited Conventional Warfare

The end of the cold war has also reduced the prospect of an unlimited conventional war. A great part of U.S. military preparedness and strategy in the past half-century was based on the scenario of an invasion of Western Europe by the Soviet Union and its allies. Even if the cold war should begin anew, Russia or any other part of the former Soviet Union would require years to build its military capacity to the point where it could pose a credible threat to the West. Since the end of the cold war, U.S. policy has aimed to prevent a resurgence of aggressive Russian nationalism. Through economic and other forms of encouragement, the United States and other industrialized nations have sought to assist Russia in making a transition to a more open and democratic political system.

Limited Conventional Warfare

Recent conflicts in Iraq, the Balkans, and Afghanistan have demonstrated that the United States has the military capacity to punish a well-armed foe. These conflicts have not demonstrated, however, that limited conventional wars routinely produce satisfactory results over the longer term. The reason is simple enough. If a political problem can be easily resolved, there is almost never a reason to apply military force; diplomatic, economic, and other forms of intervention are normally sufficient to achieve a resolution. Limited conventional warfare comes into play when other methods fail—that is, when the division between the contending parties is too deep to be resolved peacefully or when an aggressor is unrelenting. However, military force cannot always correct the problem that triggered the military response. Thus, in Iraq and Kosovo, intervention by the United States succeeded militarily but did not completely resolve the underlying problems.

Counterinsurgency

The Vietnam conflict was an **insurgency,** an uprising by irregular forces against an established government. In most Third World countries, insurgencies originate in the grievances of people who are struggling against the monopoly of economic and political power held by a ruling elite. In the past, the insurgents often received support in the form of military equipment from the Soviet Union. Most insurgencies therefore were seen by the United States as a threat to its political and economic interests.

U.S. involvement in Third World insurgencies dropped sharply after Vietnam and diminished even further with the end of the cold war. Neither the American public nor U.S. officials have wanted to involve the nation deeply in such wars, although more limited activities, such as the training and equipping of foreign troops, are a part of U.S. defense policy. Nearly a thousand U.S. troops were placed in an advisory role in the Philippines in 2002 as part of an effort to defeat a Muslim insurgent group with loose ties to the Al Qaeda terrorist network.

Police-Type Action

With the end of the cold war, U.S. policymakers began to pay closer attention to other global problems, including drug trafficking, political instability, population movement, and terrorism. The U.S. military has become increasingly involved with these problems. U.S. peacekeeping missions in Somalia, the Balkans, and Haiti are examples. U.S. military personnel have also been used to stop boat people fleeing Cuba, Haiti, and other Caribbean islands from entering the United States illegally.

U.S. military commanders have been reluctant to expand their mission to include police-type actions, such as immigration control and airport security, that traditionally have been a civilian responsibility. Nevertheless, it is likely that the pressure to use U.S. troops in unconventional ways will continue to grow.

The Politics of National Defense

All Americans would agree that the physical security of the United States is of paramount concern. The consensus sometimes breaks down, however, on specific issues. The 2003 Iraq war and its aftermath created deep divisions of opinion over the proper uses of America's military capacity. In contrast, U.S. policy in the Afghanistan war had majority support from start to end.

Public Opinion and Elite Conflict

Defense policy is a mix of *majoritarian* and *elite* politics. On issues of broad national concern, majority opinion is a vital component.[13] It was public opinion, for example, that ultimately forced U.S. policymakers to withdraw American troops from Vietnam in 1973 and compelled President Bush in 2004 to accelerate his timetable for returning control of Iraq to the Iraqi people.

Debates over foreign and defense policy, however, typically take place among political elites. Most citizens are not informed or interested enough to contribute significantly to such debates. Few Americans, for example, can name even half the countries in Africa, much less speak knowledgeably about their politics. This situation gives officials and policy specialists wide latitude in determining most issues of foreign policy.

The Military-Industrial Complex

Political disputes over defense policy are more than honest differences of opinion among people. They also involve billions of dollars in jobs and contracts.[14] In fiscal year 2005, the U.S. defense budget was roughly $400 billion, or about 5 percent of the gross national product. A high level of defense spending has been justified by reference to the nation's security needs. However, an alternative explanation for high defense spending points to the demands of the U.S. armed services and defense firms. In his 1961 farewell address, President Dwight D. Eisenhower warned against the "unwarranted influence" and "misplaced power" of what he termed "the military-industrial complex."

The **military-industrial complex** has three components: the military establishment, the arms industry, and the members of Congress from states and districts that depend heavily on the arms industry. All three benefit from a high level of defense spending, regardless of whether these expenditures can be justified from the standpoint of national security. The economic impact of even a single weapon system can be substantial. The B-1 bomber, for example, was built with the help of 5,200 subcontractors located in forty-eight states and in all but a handful of congressional districts. "This geographic spread gives all sections of the country an important stake in the airplane," concluded one assessment of the B-1.[15] Without doubt, some proportion of U.S. defense spending reflects the workings of the military-industrial complex rather than the requirements of national security. The problem is that no one knows exactly what this proportion is, and estimates vary widely.

military-industrial complex The three components (the military establishment, the industries that manufacture weapons, and the members of Congress from states and districts that depend heavily on the arms industry) that mutually benefit from a high level of defense spending.

THE ECONOMIC DIMENSION OF NATIONAL SECURITY POLICY

Economic considerations are a vital component of national security policy. In the simplest sense, economic strength is a prerequisite of military strength: a powerful defense establishment can be maintained only by a country that is economically well off. In a broader and more important sense, economic prosperity enables a people to "secure" their way of life. As President Eisenhower said, it is folly to weaken at home what one is trying to strengthen abroad.

Graphic
www.mhhe.com/pattersontad7

A Changing World Economy

Some aspects of U.S. superpower policy have economic benefits. The clearest example is the European Recovery Plan, better known as the Marshall Plan. Proposed in 1947 and named after one of its chief architects, the widely

Liberty, Equality & Self-Government

What's Your Opinion?

American Values

During the 1950s, President Dwight Eisenhower warned against neglecting at home the values that the United States is trying to promote abroad. He worried that measures designed to protect freedom elsewhere in the world could shrink freedom in the United States. He thought that excessive governmental secrecy and limits on civil liberties—justified in the name of national security—were a threat to American liberty and self-government.

This argument has resurfaced in the context of the war on terrorism. Nearly all Americans agree that the terrorist threat cannot be met without some changes in how government operates. However, disagreement has arisen over specific policies, such as the prolonged detention of noncitizens and the secrecy surrounding U.S. security activities.

How much latitude do you think policymakers should have in their pursuit of the war on terrorism? If you had to take a risk one way or the other, would you err on the side of a lot of latitude or a little?

Historical Background

respected General George Marshall, it is perhaps the boldest and most successful U.S. foreign policy initiative of the twentieth century. It called for $3 billion in immediate aid for the postwar rebuilding of Europe, with an additional $10 billion or so to follow. The Marshall Plan was unprecedented both in its scope (today, the equivalent cost would exceed $100 billion) and in its implications—for the first time, the United States had committed itself to an ongoing role in European affairs. The Marshall Plan enabled Western Europe to regain economic and political stability in a relatively short time.

Apart from enabling the countries of Western Europe to better confront the perceived Soviet threat, the Marshall Plan was also designed to meet the economic needs of the United States. Wartime production had lifted the country out of the Great Depression, but the end of the war in 1945 brought a recession and renewed fears of hard times. A rejuvenated Western Europe furnished a market for U.S. goods. In effect, Western Europe became a junior partner within a system of global trade that worked to the advantage of the United States.

Since then, major changes have taken place in the world economy. Germany has become an economic rival of the United States. Trade with Germany now results in a deficit for the United States. In addition, Western Europe, including Germany, has become a less receptive market for U.S. goods. European countries are now each other's best customers, trading among themselves through the European Union (EU).

In economic terms, the world is tripolar—power is concentrated in three centers. One center is the United States, which produces roughly 20 percent of the world's goods and services. Another center is Japan and China, which account for more than 15 percent of the world's economy. The third and largest

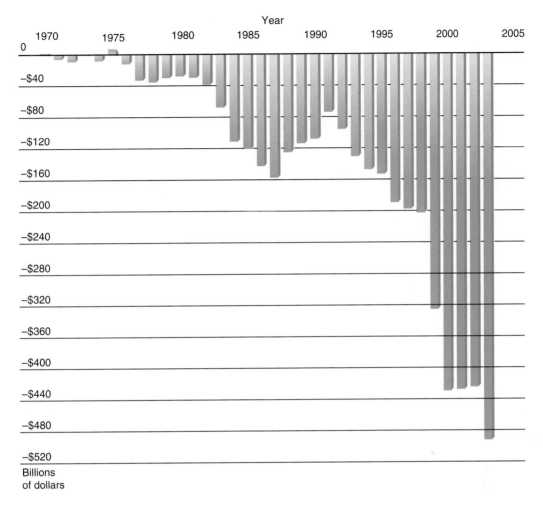

Figure 17-2

The U.S. Trade Deficit
Not since 1975 has the United States had a trade surplus; the deficit reached a record level in 2003.
Source: U.S. Bureau of the Census, Trade Data Services, 2004.

center, responsible for more than 25 percent of the world's economy, is the twenty-five-country EU. The EU is dominated by Germany, Britain, and France, which together account for more than half its economy.

By a few indicators, the United States is the weakest of the three economic centers. For example, it has the worst trade imbalance. Although the United States exports roughly $1 trillion annually in goods and services, the country imports an even larger amount. The result is a huge trade deficit that is easily the world's largest. The United States has not had a trade surplus since 1975 and in recent years has run deficits of more than $400 billion (see Figure 17-2).

In other ways, however, the United States is the strongest of the three economic powers. The American economy is the best balanced. Like the other economic powers, the United States has a strong industrial base, but it has a stronger agricultural sector and more abundant natural resources. Its vast fertile

Some U.S. firms are now as recognizable in other countries as they are in the United States. A Pepsi sign adorns the front of this small shop in Vietnam's Ho Chi Minh City (formerly Saigon).

Graphic
www.mhhe.com/pattersontad7

multinational corporations Business firms with major operations in more than one country.

economic globalization The increased interdependence of nations' economies. The change is a result of technological, transportation, and communication advances that have enabled firms to deploy their resources around the globe.

plains have made it the world's leading agricultural producer. The United States ranks among the top three countries worldwide in production of wheat, corn, potatoes, peanuts, cotton, eggs, cattle, and pigs. As for natural resources, the United States ranks among the top five nations in deposits of copper, uranium, lead, sulfur, zinc, coal, gold, iron ore, natural gas, silver, and magnesium.[16]

According to the Switzerland-based World Economic Forum, the United States also is more economically competitive than are its major trading rivals (see Chapter 15). The United States owes this position to factors such as the strength of its domestic economy and its technical know-how.[17]

This competitive advantage has been evident since the early 1990s. As Japan and parts of Europe have struggled with slow growth rates, the United States has enjoyed economic growth without the accelerated inflation that normally accompanies such a period. The slowdown in the U.S. economy that began in 2000 tempered the belief that technical know-how had unleashed unstoppable growth. Nevertheless, other countries have looked to the United States, particularly its technology sector, for policy and market innovations that might spark their own economic expansion.

America's Global Economic Goals

The United States depends on other countries for raw materials, finished goods, and capital to meet Americans' production and consumption demands. Meeting this objective requires the United States to exert influence on world markets. The broad goals of the United States in the world economy include the following:[18]

- Sustaining a stable and open system of trade that will promote prosperity at home
- Maintaining access to energy and other resources vital to the strength of the U.S. economy
- Keeping the widening gap between the rich and poor countries from destabilizing the world economy

Global Trade

International commerce is more competitive and important than in the past. Nations' economies are increasingly interconnected as a result of the transportation and communication revolution. Because of it, **multinational corporations** (firms with major operations in more than one country) now find it easy to manage worldwide operations. From a headquarters in New York, a firm has no difficulty directing a production facility in Thailand that is filling orders for markets in Europe and South America. Money, goods, and services today flow freely and quickly across national borders, and large firms increasingly think about markets in global rather than national terms.

Economic globalization is a term that describes the increased interdependence of nations' economies. This development is both an opportunity and a threat to U.S. economic interests. The opportunity rests with the possibility of increased demand abroad for U.S. products and lower prices to U.S. consumers as a result of inexpensive imports. The threat lies in the fact that foreign firms also compete in the global marketplace and may use their competitive advantages, such as cheaper labor, to outposition U.S. firms.

In general terms, the opposing sides on trade issues can be described as the protectionist and the free-trade positions. The **free-trade position** assumes that the long-term economic interests of all countries are advanced when tariffs and other trade barriers are kept to a minimum. Most free-trade advocates couple their advocacy with fair-trade demands, but they are committed philosophically and in practice to the idea that free trade fuels economic growth, results in a net gain for U.S. business, and provides American consumers with lower-priced goods.

In contrast, **protectionism** emphasizes the immediate interests of domestic producers and includes measures designed to enable them to compete successfully with foreign competitors in the domestic market. For some protectionists, the issue is simply a matter of defending domestic firms against the actions of their foreign competitors. For others, the issue is one of fair trade; they are protectionists in those instances where foreign firms have an unfair competitive advantage, as, for example, when government subsidies allow them to market their goods at an artificially low price.

The political leadership on free trade typically has come from the White House. From a presidential perspective—that is, from a national perspective—free trade is usually good politics. Although some firms and workers are invariably hurt by it, free trade generally helps the economy in the long term. Further, free trade is a means of building strong relationships with other countries, which presidents in their role as national leader seek to forge.

From a congressional perspective, free trade often looks better in theory than in practice. Some members of Congress are unabashed advocates of free trade. Many of them, however, take a protectionist stance when business firms in their state or district are threatened by foreign competition.

Opposing views on global trade clashed in 1993 over the issue of the North American Free Trade Agreement (NAFTA), which aims to create an EU-type market among the United States, Canada, and Mexico. Opponents of the agreement—who included organized labor, most environmental groups, and a majority of the Democrats in Congress—argued that it would result in the loss of countless jobs to Mexico. Its proponents—who included President Clinton, most large U.S. corporations, and most congressional Republicans—contended that the agreement would boost the economies of all three countries and was necessary if the United States was to maintain its leading position in global trade. The measure received majority support in Congress, but only after side agreements were worked out to protect some American producers from the adverse effects of open trade within North America.

In general, the free-trade position has prevailed during the past decade or so. A prime example is U.S. support for the WTO, which seeks to promote a global free market through reductions in tariffs, protections for intellectual property (copyrights and patents), and similar policies. WTO member nations (roughly 130 in number) have committed themselves to an open trade policy buttressed by regulations that are designed to ensure fair play among the participants. Trade disputes among WTO members are settled by arbitration panels consisting of representatives from the member nations.

free-trade position The view that the long-term economic interests of all countries are advanced when tariffs and other trade barriers are kept to a minimum.

protectionism The view that the immediate interests of domestic producers should have a higher priority (through, for example, protective tariffs) than should free trade between nations.

STATES IN THE NATION

Exports and State Economies

All states are affected by the global economy, but some states are more dependent on it. Exports are a larger fraction of the economies of these states. The state of Washington, with its aerospace, fishing, and logging industries, depends most heavily on trade with other countries. Exports account for nearly 20 percent of Washington State's economy.

Q. What do most of the states that rely heavily on exports have in common?

A. Most of the top exporting states are located on the nation's borders, which gives them easier access to other countries. For example, the state of Washington abuts Canada, and its seaports are a departure point for goods destined for Asia.

Highest exporters (more than 5%)

Intermediate exporters (3–5%)

Lowest exporters (less than 3%)

Numbers are exports as a percentage of state's total economy.

Although free trade has been the dominant philosophy,[19] protectionist sentiment has recently gained strength. The WTO, for example, has been criticized for placing trade ahead of environmental and human rights concerns. Some countries have gained a trade advantage through production processes that degrade the environment and exploit child labor. These issues have sparked mass demonstrations at WTO conferences, including a demonstration in Seattle in 1999 during which police used tear gas to drive back the protesters.

John Kerry speaking at the Council on Foreign Relations, an organization that for years has provided a sounding board for foreign policy ideas. Kerry's foreign policy views include close cooperation with America's traditional allies, multilateral approaches to international problems, and bolstering international organizations, such as the United Nations.

Loss of jobs has also become a major issue. The textile industry is one example. A half-century ago, textile firms began moving their plants from higher-wage northeastern states to lower-wage southeastern states. In the past decade, they have been moving their operations again, but this time to overseas locations. Even some high-tech and service sector jobs have been shipped abroad. Telephone-based financial and technical services, for example, often can be provided at lower operating cost by hiring educated English-speaking workers in Ireland or India rather than hiring educated American workers.

The jobs issue did not receive much attention during the late 1990s, when the overall U.S. economy was growing at a rapid pace. However, in the economic downturn that began in 2000, nearly three million U.S. manufacturing jobs were lost, thrusting the issue into prominence and dramatically changing opinions on global trade. In polls taken during the late 1990s, a majority of respondents favored global trade, believing that it was good both for them and for the country as a whole.[20] By 2004, Americans believed by almost an eight-to-one margin that more jobs had been lost than gained as a result of economic globalization (see Figure 17–3). They also felt that American businesses and consumers had benefited from international trade but that American workers had suffered.[21]

U.S. officials have struggled to find an effective response to this development. Economists argue that the job losses are simply part of the "creative destruction" that occurs naturally in free markets. Firms have no choice but to adapt if they are to survive. Public officials, however, cannot so easily take such a long-range view, because they face immediate pressures from constituents who have lost jobs and from communities that have lost firms. In the 2004 presidential campaign, both George W. Bush and John Kerry embraced the principle of free trade while promising to take steps to halt the overseas flight of jobs and firms. Kerry promised to change tax laws that give firms an incentive to move operations overseas, while Bush vowed to pursue strict enforcement of laws prohibiting other countries from gaining an unfair advantage by subsidizing

Figure 17–3

Americans' Opinion of the Effect of Global Trade on Jobs

By a wide margin, Americans believe that international trade has resulted in fewer jobs for U.S. workers.

Source: PIPA-Knowledge Networks survey, January 2004.

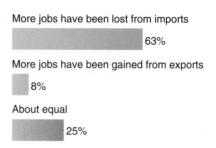

More jobs have been lost from imports
63%

More jobs have been gained from exports
8%

About equal
25%

their companies in ways that allow them to sell goods in the United States at artificially low prices.

Access to Natural Resources

Although the United States is rich in natural resources, it is not self-sufficient. The major deficiency is oil, with domestic production providing for only about half the nation's use.

Outside the United States, most of the world's oil is found in the Middle East, Latin America, and Russia. Access to this oil has occurred mainly through the marketplace, but U.S. military force has also been a factor. The 1990–91 war in the Persian Gulf is an example. Iraq's invasion of oil-rich Kuwait threatened Western supplies; Iraq's defeat quelled the threat.

Relations with the Developing World

Political instability in the less developed countries, as in the case of Iraq's invasion of Kuwait in 1990, is disruptive to world markets. Less developed countries also offer marketplace opportunities. In order to develop further, they need to acquire the goods and services that more industrialized countries can provide. To foster this demand, the United States and the other industrialized countries provide developmental assistance to poorer countries. Contributions include direct foreign aid and also indirect assistance through international organizations such as the International Monetary Fund and the World Bank. Since World War II, the United States has been far and away the leading source of aid to the developing countries of the world. The United States still contributes the most in terms of total dollars but not in terms of the percentage of its wealth (see Figure 17–4).

Foreign aid is a prime target of politicians. Upon being named chair of the Senate Foreign Relations Committee in 1995, Jesse Helms (R-N.C.) said he would trim millions in aid "going down foreign ratholes."[22] Many Americans share the view that the United States should not be funding discretionary programs abroad when there are pressing needs at home. The unpopularity of foreign aid is also a consequence of the public's exaggerated notion of how much the United States spends in this area. In a poll that asked respondents to name the largest federal programs, foreign aid was at the top of the list (27 percent said it was the most expensive federal program). In fact, foreign aid is far from the top, accounting for less than 1 percent of the total federal budget. The Iraq

Foreign aid, as percentage of GNI

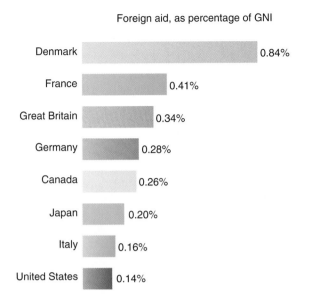

Denmark	0.84%
France	0.41%
Great Britain	0.34%
Germany	0.28%
Canada	0.26%
Japan	0.20%
Italy	0.16%
United States	0.14%

Figure 17-4

Assistance to Developing Countries, Percentage of Gross National Income
The United States ranks highest in terms of total amount spent on foreign aid to developing countries but ranks lower in terms of percentage of gross national income (GNI).
Source: OECD (Organization for Economic Cooperation and Development), 2004. Data are for assistance in 2003.

conflict, however, disrupted this pattern. U.S. reconstruction spending in Iraq alone in 2004 exceeded total foreign-assistance spending in any recent year.

Foreign aid, along with trade, has increasingly been tied to human rights issues. During the cold war, the United States backed virtually any regime—no matter how repressive—that opposed the Soviet Union. Since the end of the cold war, the United States has made a greater effort through its trade and assistance programs to promote human rights and democratic institutions. The Bush administration, for example, tied certain types of foreign assistance to a country's progress in achieving democratic reforms. Nevertheless, critics have argued that a desire for trade rather than a determination to promote democracy has been the driving force behind U.S. policy toward developing nations. China is a case in point. Although the United States has pressured China on human rights issues (for example, President Bush criticized China's restrictions on religious freedom during a 2002 trip to China), this pressure ordinarily has stopped at the point where it would interfere with trade relations. In 2000, despite objections from human rights groups, Congress voted to normalize trade with China on a continuing basis. Many supporters of this legislation claimed that it would actually speed up political reform in China. According to this view, improved trade results in higher living standards, which gradually create a demand for individual rights and democratic institutions. President Bush described free trade as "a forward strategy for freedom."

 A NEW WORLD

Although economic interests are a driving force in U.S. foreign policy, global terrorism has become America's top priority. "The world will never again be the same" was a common conclusion voiced about the effects of the events of September 11, 2001. Subsequent developments have shown that observation to

After Saddam Hussein's regime in Iraq was toppled, the United States began the task of reconstructing Iraqi oil operations, schools, hospitals, roads, and other facilities. The reconstruction costs were far higher than policymakers had anticipated and pushed total U.S. foreign assistance spending to new heights.

be true. Stopping terrorism has become the nation's most urgent policy goal, leading to huge increases in federal spending to combat the terrorist threat at home and abroad. The nation's intelligence and law-enforcement agencies have been reorganized to increase their capacity to blunt the threat. Shifts in policy toward the Middle East and South Asia have occurred. The U.S. attack on Iraq in 2003 was premised on the assumption that Iraq had chemical and biological weapons that could be funneled into the hands of anti-American terrorists. These are only a few examples of the changes brought about by the events of September 11. Almost no area of U.S. foreign and defense policy has been unaffected.

One of the largest changes has been in a direction the terrorists had not predicted. Through the September 11 attack as well as earlier attacks on American installations overseas, they sought to force the United States to reduce its presence in the Middle East and in the Arab world generally. The effect has been just the opposite. Just as Pearl Harbor ended Americans' isolationism, September 11 blunted a belief among some Washington policymakers that the United States had become too involved in regional conflicts and in the internal affairs of other nations. As security analyst Philip Gordon noted, "The result of the September 11 attacks will not be an American return to isolationism, but a reinvigoration of engagement."[24]

Summary

Self-Test
www.mhhe.com/pattersontad7

From 1945 to 1990, U.S. foreign and defense policies were dominated by a concern with the Soviet Union. During most of this period, the United States pursued a policy of containment based on the premise that the Soviet Union was an aggressor nation bent on global conquest. Containment policy led the United States to enter into wars in Korea and Vietnam and to maintain a large defense establishment. U.S. military forces are deployed around the globe, and the nation maintains a large nuclear arsenal. The end of the cold war, however, made some of this weaponry and much traditional military strategy less relevant to protecting America's security. A redefinition of the military's role in meeting the nation's security needs is taking place.

The first response of the United States after the end of the cold war was multilateralism: the idea that nations should work together toward achieving common goals, including efforts to address global problems such as drug trafficking and regional conflicts. The interventions in the Persian Gulf and the Balkans during the 1990s are examples of this multilateral approach to foreign affairs.

The terrorist attacks on the World Trade Center and the Pentagon resulted in a further adjustment in national security policy. The scope of the terrorist threat has led to large increases in spending on defense and homeland security. This expenditure has been coupled with a partial reorganization of intelligence, law-enforcement, immigration, and other agencies as well as new laws affecting the scope of their activities. The terrorist threat also forced the Bush administration to abandon its intention to reduce U.S. involvement abroad. The recent wars in Afghanistan and Iraq testify to that change. The September 11 attacks have deepened and broadened America's presence overseas while also producing changes at home, such as heightened airport security and intelligence gathering.

Economic considerations have also played a large role in defining national security policy. After World War II, the United States helped establish a global trading system within which it was the leading partner. The nation's international economic position gradually changed, however, owing to the emergence of strong economic competitors, particularly Europe and Japan, and then to economic globalization. Changes in communication, transportation, and computing have altered the way large corporations operate, and as they have changed their practices, nations have changed their foreign policies. The United States increasingly has defined its national security in economic terms, which means, for example, that trade considerations now play a larger role in defining its relationships with other countries.

The chief instruments of national security policy are diplomacy, military force, economic exchange, and intelligence gathering. These are exercised through specialized agencies of the U.S. government, such as the Departments of State and Defense, that are largely responsive to presidential leadership. National security policy has also relied on international organizations, such as the UN and the World Trade Organization, that are responsive to the global concerns of major nations.

STUDY CORNER

Key Terms

bipolar (power structure) *(p. 549)*

cold war *(p. 549)*

containment *(p. 549)*

détente *(p. 551)*

deterrence *(p. 564)*

economic globalization *(p. 570)*

free-trade position *(p. 571)*

insurgency *(p. 566)*

internationalist *(p. 548)*

isolationism *(p. 548)*

military-industrial complex *(p. 567)*

multilateralism *(p. 551)*

multinational corporations *(p. 570)*

preemptive war doctrine *(p. 553)*

protectionism *(p. 571)*

unipolar (power structure) *(p. 551)*

Self-Test

1. Diplomacy is distinct from military power as a foreign policymaking instrument in that diplomacy:
   a. is effective only when used in conjunction with other instruments.
   b. requires a bilateral relationship; it cannot be employed unilaterally.
   c. is subject to direction by the president.
   d. is sometimes applied through an international intermediary, such as the United Nations.

2. Economic exchange primarily takes place through:
   a. entering into military alliances that then turn into trading alliances.
   b. monitoring other countries' economic activities and enacting tariffs if necessary.
   c. developing trade relations with nations that are premised on the assumption that these relations will benefit both sides.
   d. military takeovers of countries that have raw materials of value.

3. Drawbacks to the pursuit of a policy of multilateralism include which of the following?
   a. Multilateral interventions are almost always less successful than when the United States acts unilaterally.
   b. Multilateral intervention does not guarantee long-term success in solving situations.
   c. Multilateral interventions abroad almost always reduce the president's popularity at home.
   d. All of the above.

4. The formal organization through which nations administer and negotiate the general rules governing international trade is called:

   a. UN.
   b. NATO.
   c. World Bank.
   d. WTO.

5. The *lesson of Vietnam* for the United States was that:
   a. there are limits to America's ability to assert its will in the world alone.
   b. America's military arsenal was obsolete and needed updating.
   c. appeasement only encourages further aggression.
   d. an isolationist foreign policy is the only safe direction for U.S. policy.

6. After World War II, the United States emerged as:
   a. an economically impoverished country.
   b. the major country with the least amount of domestic oil reserves.
   c. an internationalist country.
   d. the world's only superpower.

7. The main threat to the physical security of the United States after the attacks on the World Trade Center and the Pentagon is international terrorists who fight on behalf of causes. (T/F)

8. High levels of congressional support for an expensive weapons program are sometimes linked more to the jobs it creates than to its overall usefulness to the U.S. arsenal. (T/F)

9. The United States spends more on foreign aid as a percentage of its total national budget than do most Western democracies. (T/F)

10. U.S. military intervention both in the Persian Gulf and in Kosovo not only punished the aggressor party in each case but also settled the underlying dispute once and for all. (T/F)

Critical Thinking

What are the major objectives of U.S. foreign and defense policy? What are the mechanisms for pursuing those objectives?

Suggested Readings

Clarke, Richard A. *Against All Enemies: Inside America's War on Terror.* New York: Free Press, 2004. A best-selling book by the nation's former top-ranking presidential advisor on terrorism.

Fasulo, Linda. *An Insider's Guide to the UN.* New Haven, Conn.: Yale University Press, 2003. A correspondent's account of the United Nations.

Odom, William E. *Fixing Intelligence.* New Haven, Conn.: Yale University Press, 2003. A detailed critique of U.S. intelligence efforts by a former military intelligence officer.

Pillar, Paul R., and Michael A. Armacost. *Terrorism and U.S. Foreign Policy.* Washington, D.C.: Brookings Institution, 2001. A look at U.S. foreign policy from the perspective of the global terrorist threat.

Rothgeb, John M. *U.S. Trade Policy: Balancing Economic Dreams and Political Realities.* Washington, D.C.: Congressional Quarterly Press, 2001. A look at the politics and policies of global trade.

Sobel, Richard. *The Impact of Public Opinion on U.S. Foreign Policy Since Vietnam.* New York: Oxford University Press, 2001. A careful account of how public opinion has affected foreign policy.

Steger, Manfred B. *Globalism: The New Market Philosophy.* New York: Rowman & Littlefield, 2002. An award-winning critique of economic globalization.

Woodward, Bob. *Plan of Attack.* New York: Simon & Schuster, 2004. An inside look at the Bush administration's decision to go to war in Iraq.

List of Websites

http://www.defenselink.mil/
The U.S. Department of Defense's website; it provides information on each of the armed services, daily news from the American Forces Information Service, and other material.

http://www.foreignrelations.org/
A website that includes reports and assessments of the Council of Foreign Relations and transcripts of speeches by U.S. and world political leaders on topics of international interest.

http://www.igc.org/igc
Website of the Institute for Global Communications (IGC); it provides information and services to organizations and activists on a broad range of international issues, including human rights.

http://www.wto.org/
The World Trade Organization (WTO) website; it contains information on the organization's activities and has links to related sites.

Participate!

International conflicts stem from real causes but also have roots in cultural misunderstandings. American are thought to be more prone than most peoples to such misunderstandings because they have not been forced by geography to take different cultures, languages, and national identities fully into account. British social scientist Harold Lasswell remarked that Americans tend to view the world through the lens of their own experiences. This perspective has become a greater handicap as trade and communication have made the countries of the world ever more interdependent. Even the war on terrorism will depend for its success on a greater sensitivity to the beliefs and aspirations of other peoples. Individual Americans can do their part by educating themselves about the world. Consider taking a college course in history, political science, language and culture, geography, religion, or any other subject that will introduce you to a part of the world you have not previously studied. Close attention to the foreign affairs coverage in a quality newspaper or periodical can also deepen your understanding of other peoples and cultures.

Extra Credit

For up-to-the-minute *New York Times* articles, interactive simulations, graphics, study tools, and more links and quizzes, visit the text's Online Learning Center at www.mhhe.com/pattersontad7.

(Self-Test Answers: 1. b   2. c   3. b   4. d   5. a   6. c   7. T   8. T   9. F   10. F)

18

State and Local Politics:
Maintaining Our Differences

The powers not delegated to the United States by the Constitution, nor prohibited by it to the States, are reserved for the States . . .

—Tenth Amendment

The Supreme Court in *Reno v. Condon* (2000) upheld a federal law that prohibited states from selling their computer files of information acquired from drivers' license applicants. Some states had been making millions of dollars from the sale of the databases to mass-marketing and other firms. When citizens objected to the practice, Congress responded with the 1994 Drivers Privacy Protection Act. The state of South Carolina brought suit, claiming that Congress lacked the authority to tell the states what they could do with their databases. The Supreme Court ruled against South Carolina, saying that the law simply "regulates the states as owners of databases," an action permissible under Congress's constitutional power to regulate commerce. "[The] sale or release [of databases] into the interstate stream of business is sufficient to support Congressional regulation."[1]

One day earlier, however, the Supreme Court in *Kimel v. Florida Board of Regents* (2000) ruled that the states were not bound by the Federal Age Discrimination Act. The legislation was passed in 1967 and later amended to include state government employees, who were granted the power to sue in federal courts in cases of alleged age discrimination in the workplace. In 1995, a group of faculty members and librarians at Florida State University brought suit, charging that the state's wage policy violated the federal act. The State of Florida, in turn, claimed that the law infringed on its authority as a sovereign government. The Supreme Court ruled in Florida's favor, saying that the law "is not 'appropriate legislation' under1)…the Fourteenth Amendment." The Court said that age discrimination is not inherently unconstitutional and thus Congress lacked the authority to require state governments to apply a federal age-discrimination law.[2]

These cases reflect both the dynamic and the contentious nature of American federalism. The U.S. political system, as described in detail in Chapter 3 and discussed elsewhere in this text, divides power between a national government and the separate states.

During the more than two centuries that the United States has existed, there has been a gradual expansion of national power and a corresponding reduction in state-to-state differences. Yet the states and their creations, the local governments, continue to be vitally important centers of politics and policies. In terms of their day-to-day impact on Americans' lives, they are far more significant than the government in Washington. The roads Americans drive on, the schools they attend, the laws they obey, and much more are defined principally by state and local action rather than by federal action. In fact, contrary to what many Americans might believe, states and localities have nearly six times as many employees as the federal government (see Figure 18–1).

Figure 18–1

Employees of the Federal, State, and Local Governments

Levels of employment in state and local governments have increased in recent decades, whereas the number of federal government employees has remained fairly constant.

Source: U.S. Department of Labor, 2004.

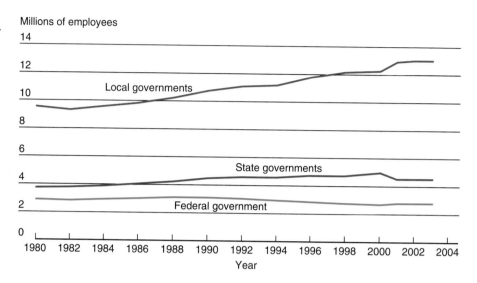

The purpose of this chapter is to describe more fully the American states and the localities within them. The great number of state and local governments and the variety they exhibit hinder any easy summary of what they are all about. Yet there are some general patterns, and it is these patterns on which this chapter concentrates. The chapter includes a comparison of the states that will explain some of the differences in their politics and policies. The main points of discussion in this chapter are the following:

- *All states apply the constitutional principle of separation of powers, but the states otherwise differ from one another—and from the federal government—in the way in which they structure their governments.* The use of elections as a means of choosing officials of all types, including judges and lesser executives (for example, state treasurer), is widespread.

- *Local governments are not sovereign; they are chartered by their state government, which sets the limits of their power.* Of the units of local government (county, municipality, township, school district, and special district), the basic unit is the municipality. A municipality may be governed in one of four ways—the strong mayor–council, weak mayor–council, commission, or city manager system.

- *States and localities have primary responsibility for most of the policies, such as public education, that directly touch Americans' daily lives.* The nature of these policies is affected by the wealth of the state or locality and also by its political culture, party system, and group system.

 ## THE STRUCTURE OF STATE GOVERNMENT

The Constitution of the United States contains provisions that forbid the states from interfering with the lawful exercise of national authority, and the states are required by the Constitution to provide their residents with a "republican" (that is, representative) form of government. In addition, the "supremacy clause" of the Constitution requires the states to comply with legitimate national laws, while the "full faith and credit" provision requires them to respect the laws of other states (for example, a contract issued by one state is ordinarily legally binding in other states).

Nevertheless, the Constitution was intended primarily to define national power and national institutions and does not say very much about the states or their powers. In fact, the Framers of the Constitution did not believe it was necessary to define the powers of the states. They held that the Constitution implied that the states held all legitimate governing powers not granted to the national government. This situation was unsettling to states'-rights advocates, who insisted on a constitutional amendment—the Tenth Amendment—which reserves for the states those powers not delegated to the national government (see Chapter 3).

The U.S. Constitution, in its emphasis on a separation of executive, legislative, and judicial power, has been a model for state constitutions. The U.S. Capitol Building has also served as a model for the states. Shown here is the capitol building of the state of Texas. It is located in Austin.

The Tenth Amendment is part of the Bill of Rights, whose provisions for individual rights initially applied only to action by the federal government. Not until the twentieth century was the Bill of Rights extended to include action by state and local governments (see Chapters 4 and 5). The Fourteenth Amendment was the basis for the change. It prohibits a state from depriving any person of "life, liberty, or property, without due process of law," or from denying any person within its jurisdiction the "equal protection of the laws."

The State Constitutions

Each state's constitution is its supreme law, except where valid national law applies. In each state, the constitution establishes executive, legislative, and judicial branches and defines the lawful powers of each branch. The concept of checks and balances—the notion that each branch will act as a curb on the power of the others—is embedded in all state constitutions. All of them also include a bill of rights.

Although the state constitutions in these respects resemble the Constitution of the United States, they have distinctive features. On average they are roughly four times the length of the U.S. Constitution. Vermont is the only state whose constitution is shorter than the nation's. Louisiana's constitution, until it was replaced in 1974, was by far the longest and most detailed. At 250,000 words, it was nearly thirty times the length of the U.S. Constitution. The longest state constitution still in effect today is Alabama's, which has approximately 175,000 words and has been amended more than five hundred times (compared with twenty-seven times for the U.S. Constitution).

The length of the state constitutions reflects the significant issues they address, such as the lawful powers and forms of local governments, the tax authority of both the state and local governments, and the executive agencies of the state government. However, the state constitutions also contain many

HOW THE UNITED STATES COMPARES

State Power in a Federal System

Federalism involves the division of sovereign authority between a national government and area (state) governments. As discussed in Chapter 3, the first federal system of government in world history was established in the United States in 1787. The American states already existed, and the only realistic alternative for the Framers of the Constitution was a form of government that protected the states' integrity and authority.

Other nations of the period had unitary systems (sovereignty invested solely in the national government), and most nations today still follow that system. However, the federal system has been adopted in some countries, including Canada and Germany.

Federal systems, however, are not the same everywhere. They differ primarily in the degree of autonomy granted to the subnational (state) governments. The United States allocates an extraordinary level of authority to the state governments. They have more discretionary authority and more far-reaching power than is typically the case in a federal system, a reflection of the American tradition of local control and of Americans' long-standing suspicion of centralized power.

The American states and their local units, for example, have a degree of control over education policy that is nearly unmatched. The federal government provides some of the funding for public schools and has imposed antidiscrimination requirements on these institutions. It has also established a national testing program that affects the amount of federal assistance a school is entitled to receive. However, the states and localities decide nearly all aspects of education policy. They set the school calendar, course requirements, achievement standards, teacher qualifications, and so on.

provisions that more properly belong in statutes than in a constitution. Enterprising state legislators have often preferred to embed their favorite policies in constitutional amendments, because they are harder to change than ordinary laws. For example, many of the state constitutions include benefits for special-interest groups, such as veterans, farmers, and businesses. Minnesota's constitution was amended in the early 1970s to permit the state to give each Vietnam veteran from the state a $600 bonus. California's constitution is filled with all sorts of tax provisions, which, among other things, limit the types and amount of taxation.

Most constitutional scholars would agree that the length of state constitutions is a drawback. The U.S. Constitution is a sparsely worded document, which, as indicated in Chapter 2, has enabled succeeding generations to adapt it to their changing needs. Not so with many of the state constitutions, which often are so loaded down with narrow and detailed provisions that they deny policymakers the flexibility to respond effectively to change.

The length of state constitutions reflects in part the relative ease with which they can be amended. Unlike the U.S. Constitution, for which amendments require a two-thirds majority in the House and Senate and then ratification by three-fourths of the state legislatures, a state constitution can be amended by legislative action combined with voter ratification. The typical process is a two-thirds vote of approval in each chamber of the state legislature and ratification by a simple majority of voters in the next election. Delaware is the only state where voter ratification is not required; however, two consecutive sessions of the Delaware legislature must approve an amendment for it to be ratified. More than forty states also provide for amendment by a **state constitutional convention,** and more than two hundred such conventions have been held. Finally, a third of the states permit amendment through a **constitutional initiative.** By obtaining the signatures of a certain number of registered voters, a citizen or group can petition to place a proposed amendment on the ballot at the next election. If it gets majority support, it becomes part of the constitution. In 1996, for example, California voters approved Proposition 209, which bans in the state any public employment, education, or contracting program that is based on race, ethnicity, or sex. California leads the nation in terms of the number of constitutional initiatives proposed and enacted; its constitution has roughly five hundred amendments, many of which were added through the initiative process.

state constitutional convention A state convention convened to amend the state constitution or draft a new one.

constitutional initiative The process by which a citizen or group can petition to place a proposed amendment on the ballot at the next election by obtaining the signatures of a certain number of registered voters; if the amendment gets majority support, it becomes part of the constitution.

Branches of Government

All states make use of the principle of checks and balances that underpins the national government (see Chapter 2). There is nothing in the Constitution of the United States that would prohibit a state from adopting a parliamentary form of government, but no state has tried it. The executive, legislature, and judiciary in each state are separate branches that share power. Each branch thus serves as a check on the power of the others.

The Executive Branch

Most states wrote their first constitutions during periods when mistrust of executive authority was high. Consequently, they provided for relatively weak governors. The model still applies in some states, especially in the South and in New England. Texas's governor, for example, has only modest formal powers. The governor can propose legislation, but by tradition the Texas House and Senate leaders set the legislative agenda without including the governor in their deliberations.[3]

Roughly half the states impose a two-term limit on their governors. Virginia, Mississippi, and Kentucky restrict the governor to a single term. In nearly all states, the governor's term of office is four years, but New Hampshire and Vermont limit it to two years.

Although the governorship in most states is not a highly powerful office, governors have gained power in recent decades as a result of an increase in the size and complexity of government. The initiation of the state budget now resides with the governor rather than with the legislature in nearly every state, and every state now grants the governor the power to veto legislative acts. There was a time when a number of states denied their governors this power. North Carolina was the last to change, amending its constitution in 1996 to give the governor veto power. In forty-three states, the governor also has a line-item veto, which enables the governor to reject a part of an appropriations bill without voiding the whole act.

Governors have the power to appoint the heads of agencies and commissions. This power has become increasingly important as state agencies have assumed broader policy responsibilities. In most states, governors also have the power to reorganize the executive branch (for example, the merging of two

In 2003, Hollywood actor Arnold Schwarzenegger was elected governor of California in a recall election that attracted scores of candidates.

agencies), subject to the legislature's veto. The extent of such powers, however, varies from state to state. Political scientist Thad Boyle has systematically evaluated the institutional powers of the states' governors and has concluded that the office is "very strong" in nine states (including Ohio, Pennsylvania, and Tennessee), "strong" in twenty-one states (including Arizona, Kentucky, and Michigan), "moderate" in seventeen states (including California, Florida, and Texas), and "weak" in three states (Vermont, North Carolina, and South Carolina).[4]

Regardless of formal powers, however, the governor is often the most visible and widely known politician in the state. The position provides a bully pulpit that allows the governor to assume a leadership role on policy issues.

In 2003, Arnold Schwarzenegger, a Hollywood actor who had not previously held a prominent public office, was elected California's governor in a recall election. He was an exception. Most governors have previously held other public office, such as state lieutenant governor, state attorney general, big-city mayor, or state legislator. Campaigns for governor, like those for the U.S. Senate, have become increasingly expensive. In a large state like New York or Texas, spending in the governor's campaign can easily top $20 million.

The governor is the state's chief executive but, in nearly every state, is not the sole elected executive official. In all but three states—Maine, New Hampshire, and New Jersey—the voters also directly choose one or more of the following executives: lieutenant governor, attorney general, secretary of state, state treasurer, education commissioner, agriculture commissioner, and public utilities commissioner. The governor shares executive power with these other officials, who are elected separately and who may belong to the opposite party.

The direct election of multiple executive officials has roots in early Americans' distrust of executive power and also in the Jacksonian and Progressive eras, when accountability to the people through the vote was a prevailing philosophy. The multiple executive system weakens the governor's control of the executive branch. At times, even the governor's control of his own office can be at risk. In California, for example, the lieutenant governor is elected separately from the governor and becomes acting governor when the governor travels outside the state's borders. When Jerry Brown was California's governor, the state's lieutenant governor, Mike Curb, was from the opposite party, and Brown would sometimes cancel, delay, or shorten a trip outside the state in order to prevent the lieutenant governor from taking action while he was away. On one of Brown's trips, Curb lifted the state's pollution control regulations. Upon his return, Brown issued an executive order reinstating them.[5]

Of the executive officials other than governor, the most powerful is the attorney general, who is elected to the post in forty-three states. The attorney general is the state's chief legal officer and sets priorities for legal action. An attorney general might decide, for example, to concentrate the state's legal resources on environmental protection or investigations of alleged political corruption. The office of attorney general has often been a stepping-stone to a governorship or a seat in the U.S. Senate.

The Legislature

Like Congress, state legislatures have within their authority the most impressive array of constitutional powers a democracy can bestow. The legislatures make the laws, appropriate the money, define the structure of the executive and the judiciary, oversee the operations of the other branches, and represent the people.

With one exception, the state legislatures are **bicameral legislatures**—that is, they have two chambers. The upper house in every state is called the senate. State senates average about forty members, who serve four-year terms in most states. The lower house is always the larger one. Lower houses average about 100 members, who are elected to two-year terms in most states. In nearly all states, the lower chamber is called either the house of representatives or the general assembly. Nebraska is the only state with a unicameral (one-house) legislature. It is called, simply enough, the Nebraska Unicameral Legislature.

bicameral legislatures
Legislatures having two chambers.

The state legislatures' organization and operation are similar to those of Congress (see Chapter 11). Their leadership is provided by party leaders chosen by each chamber's members, but most of the legislative work and executive oversight is carried out in committees. Unlike Congress, however, legislatures in some states can have legislative bills submitted for consideration directly by executive officials. In Congress, only the members themselves have the power to submit bills, although the bills are sometimes drafted in the executive branch.

Like Congress, the state legislatures could not manage their workload if they lacked committees to which tasks could be delegated. More than fifty thousand bills are enacted into law each year by state legislatures—an average of more than one thousand bills per state.

The distribution of power within state legislatures varies widely. Some legislatures are extraordinarily democratic in the sense that power is widely disbursed and the job of the leaders is primarily to organize the members' work. In other states, power is concentrated in the top leadership, and other members—especially relative newcomers—are expected to follow their lead. In New York State, the annual budget is determined through bargaining among three top officials: the senate majority leader, the speaker of the assembly, and the governor. They negotiate until a final "deal" is reached, which the legislature as a whole is then expected to enact in its entirety.

For a long period, state legislatures were synonymous with malapportionment. Cities were grossly underrepresented because rural legislators, who had controlled the state legislatures since the days when the United States was a farming nation, refused to reapportion the legislatures. Vermont was the extreme case. From 1793 to the 1960s, its legislative distribution did not change. In the state's lower house, each village, town, or city had one representative,

Shown here is the senate chamber of the New York legislature. Except for Nebraska, all the states have a two-chamber legislature.

regardless of population. Thus, the city of Burlington had exactly the same voting power in the legislature as the smallest village in the state. Not surprisingly, the policy needs of America's cities were neglected by state legislatures, while the interests of farmers and rural communities were quite well served.

Malapportionment ended in the early 1960s when the U.S. Supreme Court declared that state legislatures must represent people rather than communities or areas. The "one person, one vote" method of apportioning state legislatures immediately gave a larger share of legislative seats to populated urban areas—although, ironically, the cities never got their full due. By the time the Supreme Court outlawed malapportionment in the 1960s, so many people had moved out of the central cities that the suburbs gained the most advantage from reapportionment. The suburbs, like the rural areas, tend to be more conservative and more Republican than the cities; thus, there has never been a time when the concerns of cities have dominated the actions of state legislatures.

Until the past few decades, most of the state legislatures were relatively unimposing institutions. They were in session only for short periods each year, were deficient in staff and information resources, and were vulnerable to powerful lobbying groups. Beginning in the 1960s, however, they began to meet for longer periods and to expand their staffs. Legislators' pay also increased significantly at this time. The increase was substantial enough in a few states, such as New York and California, to create professional legislators—individuals whose chief occupation is an elective position within a state legislature. New York's legislators are paid more than $75,000 a year in salary.

Most analysts have welcomed the move toward more professional state legislatures. The Advisory Commission on Intergovernmental Relations, an agency established by Congress, noted in one of its reports: "Today's state legislatures are more functional, accountable, independent, and representative, and are equipped with greater information handling capacity than their predecessors."[6]

Some states have resisted the tendency toward longer sessions, larger staffs, and higher salaries. New Hampshire, Alabama, Texas, and Wyoming are among the states that pay their legislators $10,000 a year or less. A recent development that could partly restore the "citizen legislature" is *term limitations,* or legal restrictions on the number of years that elected officials can remain in office. The term-limitation movement has been based on the public's dissatisfaction with government, a belief that "professional" politicians are part of the problem, and a sense that an answer to the problem is to replace them with "amateurs" who are more closely connected to the people they serve. Voters in Oklahoma were the first to act on this belief, deciding by a two-to-one margin in 1990 to limit state legislators to twelve years of service. California and Colorado voters followed suit in the same year, and nearly half the states now have term limits for at least some offices.

The Courts

As a consequence of America's federal system, each state has its separate court system. Like the federal system, the state systems have trial courts at the bottom level and appellate courts at the top. About two-thirds of the states have two appellate levels, and the other third have only a single appellate court (the state's supreme court). Most of the less populated states have determined that they do not need a second appellate level. Those with a second appellate level have created it primarily to relieve the heavy caseload that would otherwise fall on the top court.

The states vary in the way they organize and label their courts. Most of the states have district courts and a supreme court, but the states also tend to give some lower courts specialized titles and jurisdictions. Family courts, for example, settle issues such as divorce and child custody disputes, and probate courts handle the disposition of the estates of people who have died. Below such specialized trial courts are less formal trial courts, such as magistrate courts and justice of the peace courts. These handle a variety of minor cases, such as traffic infractions, and usually do not use a jury. Jury trial is not a constitutional requirement of the states, nor do they have to follow the federal tradition of a twelve-member jury or of a unanimous verdict when a jury is used.

States also vary in their methods of selecting judges. In about a fourth of the states, judges are appointed by the governor, but in most states judgeships are elective offices. Several states use the Missouri Plan (so called because Missouri was the first state to use it), under which a judicial selection commission provides a short list of acceptable candidates from which the governor selects one. After a trial period of a year or more, the judge selected must be approved by the electorate in a yes-no vote in order to serve a longer term.

State courts are undeniably important. As indicated in Chapter 14, there is a federal court myth that holds that the federal courts are the more significant component of the American judicial system. In fact, the state judiciary is the locus of most court action. Upward of 95 percent of the nation's legal cases are decided in state courts (or local courts, which are agents of the states). Moreover, nearly all cases that originate in state courts also end there; the federal courts never enter the picture. Of course, one federal court—the U.S. Supreme Court— is a silent partner of the state and local courts, requiring them to act within the

Your State Government

Most Americans know less about their state government than about their national or local government. The main reason is simple enough: the news media cover Washington and city hall more closely than they cover the state capital.

The news media are in the audience delivery business. That is, they must attract and hold an audience in order to get advertisers to buy ads, which are their principal source of revenue. As a result, they concentrate on the concerns of people within their "media market." For network television and newspapers such as *USA Today*, the *Wall Street Journal*, and the *New York Times*, the media market is the nation as a whole. As a result, their news coverage concentrates on national government—the one government in which Americans have a common interest. All major news organizations have bureaus in Washington, D.C., and have reporters stationed at the White House and on Capitol Hill. For local newspapers and local television affiliates, the media market is the local community.

State governments are the odd entity. In most cases, state boundaries do not coincide with media markets. Media markets may even cut across state lines, as in the case of the St. Louis and Kansas City markets. Accordingly, state governments tend to get substantial coverage only from media that are physically located in capital cities. New York state government, for example, gets a lot more attention from the Albany media than from the Buffalo, Rochester, Syracuse, or New York City media.

Not surprisingly, citizens are more likely to contact their representatives in Washington and local government than their representatives in state government. "Out of sight and out of mind" is a fairly apt description of many people's awareness of state officials, except for the governor. The irony is that the policies of state governments have more impact on people's daily lives than do those of either the national government or local governments. Schools, roadways, and hospitals are among the areas governed largely through state policies. State governments are deserving of your attention, even if news coverage in many locations makes that a difficult task.

bounds of the U.S. constitution (for example, in upholding the rights of the accused).

The workload of the state court system is enormous. State courts handle more than 100 million cases annually. Though many of these cases involve minor infractions, more than ten million have potentially serious consequences for at least one party in the case, including imprisonment, financial deprivation, or personal loss (as in the case of a parent who loses a child custody dispute).

The application of justice in the state court systems is relatively uneven. To say that the state courts are riddled with incompetence and favoritism would be unfair to the many skilled and conscientious jurists who work within them. But it is accurate to say that the state courts do not have enough resources to handle adequately the staggering load of cases thrust on them. Long delays are commonplace, placing pressure on these systems to reduce the caseload through plea bargains and other mechanisms that increase the likelihood of arbitrary outcomes. Many judges, particularly those who operate in the lower courts, are poorly informed about the laws they are asked to apply. And a few are downright incompetent, having acquired their positions simply because they had political connections or the name recognition to win a judicial election.

Most states have made efforts in recent decades to raise the performance level of their court systems. Administrative and legal procedures have been changed, for example, to expedite the handling of cases. In the past, the pursuit of justice in many state courts was slow and procedurally arbitrary. Delays and procedural injustices still occur, but they are less prevalent today as a result of federally imposed standards and state-initiated reforms, such as those that require law enforcement officials to dismiss a case unless it is presented to a judge or grand jury within a specified period of time. States have also established disciplinary boards to identify and remove or reprimand incompetent or biased judges.

Citizens, Parties, and Elections

When the Framers wrote the U.S. Constitution, they allowed for only minimal popular participation. The House of Representatives was the only popularly elected institution and the only one with a short term of office, two years. The democratic spirit of the Revolution of 1776 was more apparent at the state level. Every state but South Carolina held an annual legislative election, and several states chose their governors through annual election by the people.

Today, the states hold elections less frequently, but they have stayed ahead of the federal government in their emphasis on elections as a means of popular influence and control. As noted previously, most states elect their treasurer, attorney general, and secretary of state by popular ballot. Many states also choose their judges by direct election. No federal judges are chosen by this means.

Citizens as Legislators

State voters also have the opportunity to vote directly on issues of policy. In all states except Delaware, amendments to the state constitution require the approval of the electorate. In addition, more than a third of the states give popular majorities the power of the **initiative,** which allows citizens through signature petitions to place legislative measures on the ballot. If such a measure receives a majority vote, it becomes law, just as if it had been enacted by the state's legislature. A related measure is the **referendum,** which permits the legislature to submit proposals to the voters for approval or rejection. The initiative and referendum were introduced around 1900 as Progressive reforms. The Progressives also sought to protect the public from wayward state and local officials through the **recall,** in which citizens can petition for the removal from office of an elected official before the scheduled completion of his or her term. The state of California recalled its governor, Gray Davis, in the 2003 election that installed Arnold Schwarzenegger as the state's new chief executive.

Of these mechanisms, the initiative has been the most important. Increasingly, it has become an instrument of group politics.[7] The average citizen does not have the time or money to organize a statewide petition drive. Many groups do, however, and they have increasingly recognized the initiative as an alternative to the traditional method of lobbying the state legislature. Not only are their chances of success often greater, but they also get the opportunity to decide exactly how the measure will be worded. Once the initiative is placed on the ballot, a group can use its financial resources to mount a statewide advertising campaign to urge its passage. An irony is that the initiative was devised by the Progressives to protect citizens against the hold that powerful groups had acquired over state legislatures. The initiative was to be a means by which

initiative The process by which citizens can place legislative measures on the ballot through signature petitions, and if the measure receives a majority vote it becomes law.

referendum The process through which the legislature may submit proposals to the voters for approval or rejection.

recall The process by which citizens can petition for the removal from office of an elected official before the scheduled completion of his or her term.

Elections are a hallmark of American government at all levels. Over the course of an average year, citizens in many locations could easily vote in three or four different elections. In most states, citizens can also vote directly on issues of public policy through the referendum or initiative.

citizens could bypass the legislature and thus overcome the power of entrenched interests. Oregon is among the states in which restrictions on the use of the initiative by organized groups is under debate.

Voter Registration and Turnout

Although the states have been electoral innovators, their history also includes attempts to restrict access to the ballot. The clearest example is that of southern states after the Civil War. The Fifteenth Amendment, ratified in 1870, prohibited states from using race as the basis for denial of suffrage. Southern states responded with a number of devices designed to keep African Americans from voting. Through poll taxes, the grandfather clause, whites-only primary elections, and rigged literacy tests as a qualification for registration to vote, blacks in many areas of the South effectively were disenfranchised.

Action by the national government was necessary to bring a halt to state efforts to disenfranchise large groups of voters (see Chapter 5). Major steps included a Supreme Court decision outlawing whites-only primaries, a constitutional amendment barring poll taxes, and the Voting Rights Act of 1965, which forbids discrimination in voting and registration. However, the legacy of a century of state-supported efforts to keep blacks and poor whites from voting in the South is still evident. The region has the lowest voter turnout rate in the nation. By comparison, states like Minnesota, Wisconsin, and Idaho, which have pioneered methods—such as election-day registration—designed to encourage voting, are among the leaders in voter turnout.

The decline in voter turnout in presidential and congressional elections in recent decades (see Chapter 7) has also been a characteristic of state elections.[8] The average turnout in gubernatorial elections that do not coincide with a presidential election, for example, is less than 40 percent—a drop of several percentage points since the early 1960s.

Historical Background

Dillon's rule The term used to describe relations between state and local governments; it holds that local governments are creatures of the state, which in theory even has the power to abolish them.

THE STRUCTURE OF LOCAL GOVERNMENT

If the significance of a level of government were determined strictly on the basis of numbers, the local level would win handily. The United States has one national government and fifty state governments, but it has more than eighty thousand local governments, including counties, municipalities, school districts, and special districts such as water, sewage, and conservation districts.

Local governments, however, do not have sovereignty—that is, they do not have final authority within their governing spheres. Their authority derives from that of the state within which they are located. The general principle that describes the relationship between state power and localities is called **Dillon's rule.**

It holds that local governments are creatures of their states, which in theory even have the power to abolish them. The rule gets its name from judge John F. Dillon, who propounded it in a nineteenth-century treatise on municipal governments. These governments, he wrote, possess only those powers that are "expressly granted" them by their state or are "necessarily . . . implied in or incident to" these powers.[9]

The most important aspect of Dillon's rule is that local governments must act within constraints placed on them by the state. The state's power extends even to the issue of whether a local unit of government will provide a particular service. The state of Wisconsin, for example, requires each of its cities to have a solid-waste disposal facility.

States differ markedly in the degree of freedom they grant their local units. The states that grant the highest degree of autonomy to local units, and those that grant the least, are found in all regions of the country. For example, Oregon, North Carolina, and Connecticut rank high on local autonomy, while Idaho, Mississippi, and Massachusetts rank low.

The chief instrument by which a state governs its local units is the **charter.** No local government can exist without a charter, which is issued by the state and defines the limits within which a local unit must operate. By tradition, local charters are restrictive. They spell out in considerable detail what a local government can and cannot do. A typical charter, for example, specifies the types and limits of taxation that a local government may impose on its residents. The charters of some types of local government include a grant of lawmaking power. These governments can issue **ordinances,** or local laws. A locality might, for example, pass an ordinance requiring dog owners to leash their pets or an ordinance specifying a curfew for teenagers.

There are limits to a state's ability to control its local units. A state government does not have the time, the money, or the staff to make all the decisions concerning its many local units, nor can a state expect the same restrictions to work equally well for all local units. A charter that is suited to a city of a million inhabitants probably would not be suited to a village of several hundred people. Accordingly, all states give their local units some discretionary authority and make allowance for differences among them. In most cases, the charters for cities are different from those for towns, which in turn differ from those for villages.

Home rule is a device that is designed to give local governments more leeway in their policies. It developed out of a protest movement that sought to free local government from meddlesome interference by the states. Its guiding principle was the so-called **Cooley's rule,** articulated in an 1871 ruling by Michigan judge Thomas Cooley, who boldly declared that cities should be self-governing.[10] Home rule, first tried in 1875 in Missouri, allows a local government to design and amend its own charter, subject to the laws and constitution of the state and also subject to veto by the state.

The long-term trend in the states has been toward home rule and other means of granting localities a larger measure of independence. The issue is partly philosophical: Americans are accustomed to a substantial degree of local autonomy and expect their state governments to refrain from interfering too deeply in local affairs. It is also practical: states lack the capacity to make the everyday decisions of their local governments.

charter The chief instrument by which a state governs its local units; it spells out in detail what a local government can and cannot do.

ordinances Laws issued by a local government under authority granted by the state government.

home rule A device designed to give local governments more leeway in their policies; it allows a local government to design and amend its own charter, subject to the laws and constitution of the state and also subject to veto by the state.

Cooley's rule The term used to describe the idea that cities should be self-governing, articulated in an 1871 ruling by Michigan judge Thomas Cooley.

Police and firefighters are among the most visible symbols of local government. Their courageous actions in New York City on September 11, 2001, cost hundreds of them their lives and serve as a tragic reminder of the indispensable role they play in America's communities.

Local government is the source of most public employment. While there are fewer than three million federal workers and four million state employees, more than ten million people work in local government. Local government workers are one of the most heavily unionized groups in the country. Schoolteachers are represented through the American Federation of Teachers (AFT) and the National Education Association (NEA), and other local public employees are represented through such unions as the International Association of Fire Fighters (IAFF) and the American Federation of State, County, and Municipal Employees (AFSCME). These unions, with more than three million members, have been quite successful in obtaining better working conditions and job benefits for their members.

Types of Local Government

There is wide variation within and among states in the structure and responsibilities of local government. A full description of the various types could fill several books. The following sections highlight some of the major types.

County Government

The oldest form of local government in the United States is the county. It remains a top local governing unit in rural areas and in those few states, such as New York, where the county has broad responsibility for providing government services. The county is governed through an elected county commission (which, in some states, is called a county legislature or board of supervisors). Most states also have elected county sheriffs and county attorneys, and a few states have elected chief county executives.

Liberty, Equality & Self-Government

What's Your Opinion?

The Fourteenth Amendment

Originally, the Bill of Rights had a limitation: it applied only to actions of the national government. Thus, for example, the First Amendment prohibited Congress from abridging freedom of speech but did not restrict the state or local governments from doing so. Ratification of the Fourteenth Amendment in 1968 provided a basis for protecting the liberties established in the Bill of Rights from actions of the state and local governments. The Fourteenth Amendment says that no state shall "deprive any person of life, liberty, or property, without due process of law." Although a significant period of time elapsed before the Supreme Court interpreted the Fourteenth Amendment as a substantial limitation on state and local governments, it eventually did so. Free-expression rights, such as freedom of speech, were pro-tected through a set of court rulings in the 1920s and 1930s, while fair-trial rights, such as the right to counsel, were protected through a set of court rulings in the 1960s (see Chapter 4).

Do you think that Americans today, regardless of the state or community in which they live, would have roughly the same rights they have now if the Supreme Court had not extended the protections of the Bill of Rights to actions by the state and local governments? Would these governments, by now and on their own, have provided these protections to *all* their residents? How, if at all, does your answer relate to your view about the proper balance of national and state power in America's federal system of government? How, if at all, does your answer relate to what you know of your own state or community?

Counties are subdivisions of a state. They blanket the state in the sense that it is divided completely into county units. The shape and number of these county units, however, varies markedly. Texas is divided into 254 counties. Alaska, though larger in area, has only 16 county units. In most states, the county functions as an administrative subdivision of the state. The county's responsibility is to carry out programs, such as highway maintenance or welfare services, that are established by the state. Some analysts believe that the county will increase in importance in upcoming years because of the prominence of issues, such as waste disposal, that cannot be addressed adequately at the municipal level but instead require a regional response.

County government illustrates the variation that exists in local governmental structures. Two states, Louisiana and Alaska, call their counties by another name (parishes in Louisiana, boroughs in Alaska). Moreover, the role of the county is not always the same even within a particular state. The county is typically a more visible unit of government in rural areas (where, for example, the county sheriff is often the most widely known public official) than in urban areas (where, for example, residents may not even know where their county offices are located). Also, counties vary greatly in population. They range from some urban counties with more than a million inhabitants to some rural counties with only a few thousand residents. The largest county is Los Angeles County in California, with a population of roughly eight million.

TABLE 18–1	Common Forms of Municipal Government

Strong Mayor–Council System

An elected mayor has veto power over an elected council and has substantial authority over the budget and other policies.

Weak Mayor–Council System

An elected mayor does not have veto power and generally is weak relative to the elected council.

Commission System

Executive and legislative power is vested in an elected commission whose members each have a specified policy role, such as police commissioner.

City Manager System

An appointed chief executive administers programs and can be fired by the elected council.

Municipal Government

In most parts of the United States, the major unit of local government is the municipality, which can be a city, town, or village. While municipalities exist partly to carry out activities of the state government, they exist primarily to serve the needs of their residents. Most Americans depend on their municipal governments for law enforcement, water, and sanitation services.

Municipalities are legal entities that operate under a charter granted by the state. As indicated previously, a charter defines the limits within which a local governing unit must operate. Over the years, and consistent with the philosophy of local autonomy, municipal charters have become less restrictive. Moreover, rather than drafting separate charters for each municipality, states have developed more general charters that apply to all municipalities within a category (such as "small city" or "medium-size city," as defined by population). Of course, some municipalities are in a class by themselves and require a specific charter. New York City, for example, has taxing and other powers not granted to other municipalities in New York State.

The traditional and most common form of municipal government is the mayor-council system, which includes the mayor as the chief executive and the local council as the legislative body (see Table 18–1). The mayor-council system takes one of two forms. The more common form is the **strong mayor–council system,** in which the mayor has veto power and direct responsibility for budgetary and other policy actions. The mayor, rather than the council, is the more powerful policymaker. The alternative form is the **weak mayor–council system,** in which the mayor's policymaking powers are less substantial than those of the council. The mayor has no power to veto the council's actions and often has no formal role in activities such as budget making.

A different type of municipal government entirely is the **commission system.** This form invests executive and legislative authority in a commission, with each commissioner serving as a member of the local council but also having a specified executive role, such as police commissioner or public works

strong mayor–council system Most common form of municipal government, consisting of the mayor as chief executive and the local council as the legislative body, in which the mayor has veto power and a prescribed responsibility for budgetary and other policy actions.

weak mayor–council system Form of municipal government in which the mayor's policymaking powers are less substantial than the council's; the mayor has no power to veto the council's actions and often has no formal role in activities such as budget making.

commission system Form of municipal government that invests executive and legislative authority in a commission, with each commissioner serving as a member of the local council but also having a specified executive role, such as police commissioner or public works commissioner.

commissioner. The commission system has lost considerable favor in recent decades. Its major weakness is that it has no chief executive with the power and responsibility to set the local government's overall direction. Today only about 100 U.S. communities employ this governing system. Fargo, North Dakota, is one of the cities in this group.

A final type of municipal government is the **city manager system,** which was pioneered in Ohio during the Progressive era as a reaction against inefficiency and partisan corruption in many of the nation's cities. The system entrusts the executive role to a professionally trained manager, who is chosen—and can be fired—by the city council. This arrangement ensures that the manager will be at least somewhat responsive to political and popular pressures. Most city managers have specialized university training in the operation of municipal government. The typical form of this education is the master of public administration (MPA), which includes courses in areas such as public finance, budgeting, and organization. However, city managers are usually "outsiders" who did not grow up in the community they administer and who typically lack the political support necessary to exert strong leadership. Most of the larger cities that installed the city manager system have since reverted to the mayor-council system, but the city manager form is the most common type of government in smaller cities. California is one state where the city manager system has been widely adopted. San Jose is among the California cities with this form of local government.

A local chief executive, whether a mayor or a city manager, is, above all, an administrator whose main responsibility is to oversee the work of the component units of local government—the police, fire, sanitation, and other departments. Increasingly, local chief executives are also expected to provide economic leadership by fostering a business climate that will keep old firms in the community and attract new ones. In many cities, including Baltimore, San Antonio, and Minneapolis, mayors have played key roles in the revitalization of downtown areas. Of course, not all chief executives accomplish much, or even get the opportunity. In smaller towns and villages particularly, the position of mayor is often more honorary than active; it is a part-time position held by a trusted member of the community.

city manager system Form of municipal government that entrusts the executive role to a professionally trained manager, who is chosen—and can be fired—by the city council.

Towns and Townships

The word *town* is used in reference to a municipality that is smaller than a city and larger than a village. In most areas of New England, however, a town more often refers to a governing unit that functions as both a municipality and a county. In these areas, the county is often nothing more than a geographical entity—the town encompasses one or more communities and also their contiguous rural areas. The town has responsibility for both community streets and rural roads as well as other local services. The fabled town meetings that once governed New England towns still exist, but now they seldom attract many people. The towns effectively are governed by a town council of elected officials, who, in the larger towns, usually entrust day-to-day operations to a full-time town manager.

In several Midwestern states and a few states elsewhere, townships are an important governing unit. They are subdivisions of counties and, in rural areas

Members of the Metro Dade police departments recite the Pledge of Allegiance during a public ceremony. Miami and surrounding communities in south Florida have a metropolitan government. It provides police, sanitation, and other services to the area's residents. In most U.S. metropolitan areas, such services are provided separately by each community.

particularly, have key policy responsibilities, including roadways and other public services. They resemble New England towns in that they were created as geographical units and vary widely in their population density. Thus, they are unlike municipalities where, for the most part, residents live closely together. Townships also differ from municipalities in that, as subunits of the county, they do not have lawmaking power. They carry out county policy; they do not make policy of their own.

School Districts

The tradition of local public schools is deeply embedded in the American political experience. Unlike Europe, where private schools and national educational standards have historically been more important, the United States has emphasized public education and local control. This control is exercised through local school boards. In a few places, the school board is subordinate to the municipal government, but elsewhere it is an independent body. School policy is established by the local board rather than by the local mayor or council. The chief executive of the local public school system is a specially trained professional, the superintendent of schools. The superintendent is hired—and can be fired—by the local school board.

Some states have recently authorized charter schools as an alternative to traditional public schools. Such schools are granted a charter (much as local governments have a charter) within which they must operate. Charter schools have greater freedom than other public schools in selecting their admission, curriculum, and other policies.

Special Districts and Metropolitan Government

Another form of municipal government, and one of increasing importance, is the special district. As society has become more complex and interdependent, a need has arisen for local governing institutions that are responsive to the resulting policy needs. Special districts that deal with policy areas such as water supply, soil conservation, and waste disposal are an answer. These districts also provide an answer to the problem of coordinating the efforts of independent municipal governments. Issues such as pollution control are not easily addressed within a single community. Special districts bring municipalities together. The typical form of governance of these districts is a board that includes a member from each municipality within the district's boundaries. The day-to-day operation of these districts, however, is typically entrusted to trained administrators who often have specialized educations, such as the waste-management engineers who oversee municipal sewage systems.

Special districts ordinarily have responsibility for a specific policy activity, such as solid-waste management or soil conservation. In some urban areas, however, local governments have joined to create a **metropolitan government** that is given responsibility for a broader range of activities. An example is the Dade County (Florida) Metropolitan Government, which includes Miami and surrounding communities. Each community is represented on the Dade County Commission, which has responsibility for providing most local services. A metropolitan government is designed to reduce the waste and duplication that result when every locality in a densely populated area has its own police force, its own sanitation department, its own planning board, and so on. Although a metropolitan government is more efficient, the tradition of strong local autonomy makes it an unappealing option to many Americans.

> **metropolitan government**
> Form of local government created when local governments join together and assign it responsibility for a range of activities, such as police and sanitation, so as to reduce the waste and duplication that result when every locality in a densely populated area provides its own services.

Local Elections and Participation

The principle of elective office dominates local government. In addition to an elected mayor, most communities have an elected town or city council. The office of county commissioner is also an elective office throughout the country. Except in a few eastern states, local officials are chosen in nonpartisan elections. No party labels appear on the ballot.

Perhaps no local institution symbolizes the nature of American democracy better than the public schools. School board members are elected, and in many communities the voters even have the opportunity to approve or reject school budgets and bond proposals. In contrast, school officials in European countries typically are appointed to their positions, and school budgets are set primarily by national governments.

Voting in local elections is subject to state registration laws. However, as noted in Chapter 7, many local governments have tried to weaken the link between their level of government and the state and national levels by scheduling local elections for odd-numbered years rather than the even-numbered years during which all federal and most state elections are held. A predictable effect of this scheduling is that voter turnout is somewhat lower at each level than would be the case if national, state, and local elections were held simultaneously. The average turnout in local elections in most states is very low—30 percent or less. Turnout figures can be deceptive. There are countless instances of extraordinary turnout in local elections when a contentious issue is on the ballot. School bond issues, for example, often produce a high turnout and increasingly have pitted families with children in the public schools against the growing number of elderly Americans who, on the whole, are less supportive of school spending proposals.[11]

Local elections embody many of the conflicts that are found, in one form or another, throughout U.S. politics. Many communities, for example, use at-large (community-wide) districts to elect members of the local council. At-large council members presumably will act on behalf of the whole community and not sections of it, as might be the case if they were elected from separate districts within the community. However, at-large districts tend to result in the election of council members who are demographically similar to the majority of voters. Black and Hispanic candidates have fared poorly in these systems, creating pressures to change at-large districts to separate-district systems.

Elections, however, are only one form of citizen influence on local government. Although the opportunities for ordinary citizens to direct state and national officials are confined mostly to periodic elections, additional opportunities are available in local settings. As seen in Chapter 7, group participation is relatively high in the United States, and many groups are involved in community-oriented activities. A few cities, including St. Paul, Minnesota, have even delegated authority to neighborhood councils, which may have responsibility, for example, for creating and operating community centers or playgrounds.

The news media are also influential in local politics. Local newspapers and television stations sometimes take the lead in highlighting local issues and exposing inept or unethical officials. In any case, most local officials are wary of antagonizing the local media. On the state level, the media are less powerful because a state's boundaries rarely coincide with a news organization's market. Thus, state officials and policy actions receive less scrutiny from the press.

It would be a mistake to conclude, however, that local officials are highly responsive to local residents as a whole. Studies have found that in some locations officials are attentive primarily to the community's economic and social leaders. These citizens constitute a local power elite that, even more than the public officials themselves, decides community policies.[12]

 ## STATE AND LOCAL FINANCE

The federal government raises more tax revenues than do all fifty states and the thousands of local governments combined. Although states and localities have a substantial tax base, they are in an inherently competitive situation. People and businesses faced with state or local tax increases can move to another state or locality where taxes are lower. Between the 1960s and 1980s, there was a substantial movement of business firms from the northeast and midwest to the south and southwest. These firms were lured by the cheaper labor and lower energy costs of the sunbelt and also by the lower tax rates of southern states.

Local governments are also in a relatively weak tax position. They compete with one another for the jobs and income that business firms represent. Every sizable city in the United States offers tax breaks or other incentives to companies that might relocate there. The predatory nature of the competition makes it difficult for any locality to raise its tax rate substantially and virtually forces localities to give tax breaks to firms that could well afford to pay more.

A community may even find that it has to pay a business to remain in that community. An obvious example, but not the only one, is the sports franchise that threatens to move its team unless the host city builds an expensive new stadium or arena. San Francisco, Houston, and Miami are among the cities that decided it was in the community's interest to comply with such a demand. Los Angeles is among those that refused the demand and lost a professional sports team as a result.

States and localities are denied a form of taxation available to the federal government—tariffs. Congress has the power to levy taxes on goods shipped to the United States from abroad. The U.S. Constitution prohibits states from placing a duty on goods that cross their borders because such action would disrupt interstate commerce.

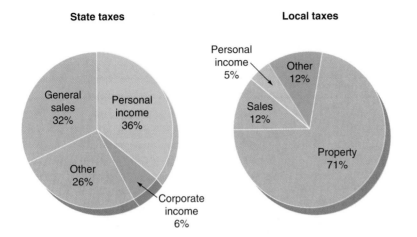

State taxes

General sales 32%

Personal income 36%

Other 26%

Corporate income 6%

Local taxes

Personal income 5%

Other 12%

Sales 12%

Property 71%

Figure 18–2

State and Local Government Taxes

States rely on sales and personal income taxes for most of their revenue. Localities depend heavily on property taxes.

Source: U.S. Bureau of the Census, 2004.

Sources of Revenue

The major sources of state revenue are sales taxes, personal income taxes, corporate income taxes, and user fees such as motor vehicle license fees (see Figure 18–2). However, there are substantial variations in the taxing policies of the states. A few states have no personal income tax. South Dakota is one of these states and also has no corporate income tax. Not surprisingly, South Dakota has one of the lowest levels of public services in the nation. Its neighbor Minnesota, for example, spends about 30 percent more per capita on public education than does South Dakota.

Income Taxes

Although a few states do not levy an income tax, it is a major revenue source, accounting for roughly a third of all state tax revenue. The competitive nature of state tax policy, however, serves to hold down income tax rates. The highest marginal rate on personal income on federal tax returns is 35 percent. At the state level, the highest rate averages about 5 percent. A few localities—New York City among them—raise revenue through income taxes. These taxes enable a local government to tax individuals who work in the community and use its services but who live elsewhere, usually in a nearby suburb.

Sales Tax

The *general sales tax* is a chief source of revenue for the states, accounting for a third of all the taxes they raise. The sales tax is a flat-rate tax on consumer goods and thus places a relatively heavy burden on lower-income individuals, who spend a higher proportion of their income on consumer goods than do upper-income persons. The regressive nature of the sales tax has been a source of criticism, and some states exempt food and medicine from sales tax in order to relieve somewhat the burden it places on lower-income people. Nevertheless, the sales tax is a reliable method of raising large sums of money.

States are in an inherently competitive situation with regard to taxation. A state cannot raise taxes very high without losing firms and residents to a state where taxes are lower. This situation has led states to develop alternative sources of revenue. One of the most common is a state lottery. The payout to lottery winners and vendors is typically about two-thirds the amount taken in. The remainder is used by governments to subsidize valuable programs such as education, parks, and recreation.

Reprinted by permission of California State Lottery.

In many states local governments also obtain revenue from the sales tax, and in some states the local share varies by location. In New York, for example, the state's sales tax is four cents on the dollar, while the local tax varies from two cents to four cents. Another form of sales tax is the *excise tax*, which is applied only to selected items, such as gasoline and jewelry. It is sometimes called the "sin tax" because liquor and cigarettes are among the items subject to such tax.

Lotteries and Fees

Although sales and income taxes account for a very large share of state revenues, they are not the only significant revenue sources. Lotteries, for example, account for a small but increasing percentage of revenue. Lotteries were banned by Congress as a form of illegal gambling until a few decades ago, but today more than two-thirds of the states run a lottery. The major complaint today about state lotteries is that many of the regular players are low-income Americans who cannot afford to play but who dream of striking it rich. In their lottery advertising, states play up this dream but rarely mention that the odds of winning the biggest jackpots are roughly those of being hit, not once but twice, by lightning. States also do not publicize the fact that they retain more than half the money spent to purchase lottery tickets.

License and user fees are a fourth source of state revenue. The most important are the license fees that states charge for vehicle registration and drivers' licenses. But there are also, for example, license fees charged to doctors and lawyers that allow them to practice in a state and license fees charged to stores and restaurants that sell or dispense liquor. A few states also derive substantial revenue from severance taxes that are imposed on those who extract natural resources, such as oil, coal, or bauxite, from the state's soil.

Texas is one of many states that depend heavily on federal spending for their economic vitality. Shown here is a scene from the army base at Fort Hood, one of many military installations in Texas.

Property Taxes

As Figure 18–2 indicates, local governments rely primarily on the property tax for their revenues. This form of taxation accounts for nearly three-fourths of all revenues raised directly by local government, but it has drawbacks. It is paid, for example, in a lump sum, which heightens taxpayers' awareness of its cost and leads them to resist any increase. Few actions are more likely to result in the defeat of a local official in the next election than a steep increase in property taxes. Accordingly, localities have turned increasingly to sales taxes (shared with the state and collected with the state's permission) and local income taxes (collected with the state's permission). The revenues from these sources increase automatically when the economy expands, providing localities with increased revenues without a raise in the tax rate.

Government Grants

States and localities also depend on revenues provided by other governments. More than 15 percent of state revenues are provided by federal grants-in-aid programs, while local governments get about 30 percent of their revenues from the state and 5 percent from Washington. States and localities would face hardships without these grants, but the money has a drawback—it comes with strings attached. As Chapter 3 explained, grants are provided for specific uses only.

The states and localities also benefit from federal spending. The states of the South and West, particularly, owe many of their jobs to federal programs. In Hawaii, for example, thirty thousand active U.S. military personnel are stationed at bases that include Pearl Harbor (Navy), Schofield Barracks (Army), and Hickam Field (Air Force).

Federal grants-in-aid and other federal policies tend to reduce somewhat the importance of state-to-state differences in wealth as a factor in state and local policies. Federal assistance is targeted disproportionately at less affluent states and communities. However, the leveling effect of this federal policy is not very great, and states differ enormously in their economic wealth. The level of public services in all areas—education, welfare, health, and so on—is higher in wealthier states. Compared to the ten poorest states, the ten wealthiest states spend over $1,000 per pupil more on public education each year.

Borrowing

A final source of revenue is borrowing. States and localities issue bonds for purchase by investors. Although borrowing is sometimes necessary, state and local governments try to hold it to a minimum because the funds at some point will have to be repaid, with interest.

The Ups and Downs of State and Local Finance

Some analysts have concluded that economics, not politics, is the chief determinant of a state's public policies. Whether that observation is literally true, there is no question that the wealth of a state greatly influences its policies. In the mid-1990s, the states were beneficiaries of a sharp upturn in the national economy. As corporate and personal incomes rose, so did the tax revenues flowing into the state treasuries. Policy initiatives flowed from the states, which seemed especially adept at combining programs designed to stimulate economic development with programs designed to tighten fiscal responsibility.

By 2002, however, the states were in financial trouble. A downturn in the national economy had sharply reduced their tax revenues. Nearly every state was forced to cut services in order to balance its budget. Some states also raised taxes as a means of offsetting the revenue decline.

Local governments also found themselves in a pinch. Their sales tax revenues declined, and their grants from the federal and state governments were cut back. Faced with a shortfall, thousands of local governments raised their property tax rate, prompting an angry outcry from homeowners.

This pattern of boom and bust results because the states and localities, unlike the federal government, have only a limited capacity to borrow money. The U.S. Constitution denies them the authority to print their own currency, which means that in hard times they have little choice but to either cut services or raise taxes.

police power A term that refers to the broad power of government to regulate the health, safety, and morals of the citizenry.

STATE AND LOCAL POLICY

Through the Tenth Amendment, the states possess what is sometimes called the **police power,** a term that refers to the broad power of government to regulate

Should Congress Exempt the Internet from Sales Taxes?

Before 2004, Congress had twice placed a moratorium on state and local taxes on e-commerce. The ban extended to the federal government. Proponents said that the Internet should be a tariff-free zone to allow it to grow as a commercial marketplace. When Congress began to reconsider the issue in 2004, there was a substantial division of opinion both within and outside the institution. Advocates of the exemption said that the Internet was still developing commercially and that its tax-free status was offset by the shipping costs associated with Internet transactions. Opponents said that a tax-free Internet was unfair to the mail-order and walk-in retailers whose goods and services were subject to taxation; they also claimed that state and local government services were being adversely affected by the loss of sales tax revenues.

Debating the Issues

Yes: When the economic evidence [against a sales tax on Internet transactions] becomes too overwhelming to ignore, the Internet tax proponents usually turn to the "fairness" issue—even though it has been as thoroughly debunked as the economic argument. That's right, our selfless [public officials] are simply attempting to level the playing field for small "mom and pop" and "brick-front" stores that must collect sales taxes while Internet companies currently do not. This argument holds that small hardware stores across the nation will go under—thrusting their salt-of-the-earth proprietors into the cold—because the "Big Hardware" Internet site is not forced to collect taxes and therefore has an unfair competitive advantage. . . . This line of reasoning has been debunked numerous times, but for the sake of argument let's briefly review its more blatant fallacies. The same argument was made about catalogue sales with no such dire consequences for local merchants. . . . Shipping and handling costs often offset any price advantage enjoyed by Internet retailers thanks to the absence of sales taxes. . . . This is hardly an exhaustive list. . . . Suffice it to say, the case against Internet sales taxes is solid and well known.

—*National Taxpayers Union*

No: We must be sensitive to issues of basic competitive fairness and the negative effect our action or inaction can have on brick-and-mortar retailers. . . . I understand the importance of protecting and promoting the growth of Internet commerce because of its potential economic benefits. It is a valuable resource because it provides access on demand. In addition, it is estimated that the growth of online businesses will create millions of new jobs nationwide in the coming years. . . . I do, however, have concerns about using the Internet as a sales tax loophole. Sales taxes go directly to state and local governments and I am very leery of any federal legislation that bypasses their traditional ability to raise revenue to perform needed services such as school funding, road repair and law enforcement. . . . While those who advocate a permanent loophole on the collection of a sales tax over the Internet claim to represent the principles of tax reduction, they are actually advocating a tax increase. Simply put, if . . . sales over the Internet go untaxed . . . revenues to state and local governments will fall and property taxes will have to be increased to offset lost revenue or states who do not have or believe in state income taxes will be forced to start one.

—*Mike Enzi, U.S. senator (R-Wyo.)*

the health, safety, and morals of the citizenry. Possession of this power has meant that the American states carry out many of the policy responsibilities that in other countries are dealt with at the national level. Law enforcement, public education, public health, and roads are among the policy areas that in America are defined largely by the state and local governments.

Although the policies enacted by Congress get more attention from the press, the acts of state legislatures have more influence on the day-to-day lives of most Americans. For example, most crimes are defined by state law, most

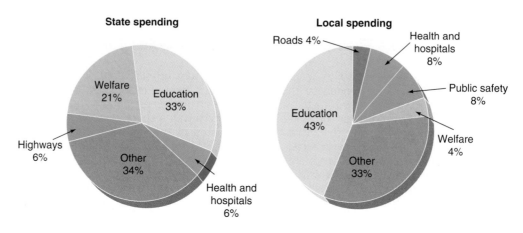

Figure 18–3

Spending Priorities of State and Local Governments
Education is the major spending category for both state and local governments.
Source: U.S. Bureau of the Census, 2004.

criminal acts are investigated by authorities operating under state law, most trials take place under state law, and most prisoners are held in penitentiaries and jails that operate under laws enacted by state legislatures.

Policy Priorities

One way to see how the states use their power is to rank policy areas by level of spending (see Figure 18–3). The top spending category for the states is public education, followed by public welfare, health and hospitals, and highways. These four areas are by far the most significant components of state spending.

The policy priorities of local governments are less easily described (see Figure 18–3). Some local units, such as school boards, operate in only one policy area. Municipalities vary in size from the largest cities to the smallest villages, and their policies differ accordingly. Despite such differences, a few patterns to local spending are discernible. Far and away the biggest expense for local governments is public education, which accounts for over 40 percent of all spending at the local level. Public safety (police, fire, corrections) and health and hospitals are next in line. Welfare and roads are among the other top spending categories.

Public Policy Patterns

A brief description of some of the policy activities of state and local governments, and where they get the money to pay for these activities, will provide a broader perspective on the role of states and localities in the American system.

Education

Public education—including primary schools, secondary schools, and colleges and universities—accounts for the largest share of combined state and local spending, about a third of the total. Education spending by state and local governments dwarfs that by the federal government—more than 90 percent of the money for public schools is provided by states and localities. Even higher education is mainly a state and local responsibility. Thus, the greatest share of the country's investment in the technical research and personnel that underpin the economy is provided by subnational governments, which also make the key substantive policy decisions in the education area, from curriculum to performance standards to length of schooling.

Of the many issues affecting public education in the states, two have stood out in recent years. One is the disparity in spending among school districts, which, in most instances, reflects differences in communities' wealth. Suburban schools, for example, typically are better funded and have better facilities than the inner-city schools in the same metropolitan area. Should such differences be allowed? In a 1973 Texas case, the Supreme Court concluded that a state has no obligation to provide students with an equal education; rather, its obligation is "to provide an 'adequate' education for all children."[13] Nevertheless, state financial contributions to local schools are typically designed to help poorer districts more than wealthier ones. This tendency, however, does not begin to offset the disparity in the quality of schools between a state's poorest communities and its richest ones.

In recent years, pressures have intensified to reduce disparities in school spending. In 1998, for example, New Jersey's highest court settled a years-long battle over school funding by ordering Governor Christine Todd Whitman to develop a plan to equalize spending in the state's public schools. Courts in about twenty states have ruled against inequitable school financing systems, although they have not gone as far as New Jersey's top court in ordering an equalization plan.[14]

A second major education issue is the quality of American schools. U.S. students perform poorly on standardized tests in comparison with students of other advanced industrialized nations. Twelfth-grade American students are not even among the top ten in subjects, such as science and math, where cross-national comparisons can reliably be made.[15] This situation has contributed to debates over merit pay for teachers, national tests for all U.S. students, and parent-student choice of schools. Some analysts claim that American public schools are simply not providing the quality of education found in other Western democracies and that alternative approaches must be found. Other analysts say that the schools are not the problem, or at least not the major problem. They claim that both the diversity of American society and the absence of a strong intellectual tradition limit the schools' ability to educate students at the highest level.

Welfare Assistance

The most expensive social welfare program in the United States is entirely a national one—social security for retirees. However, the states are vitally involved

With passage of the 1996 Welfare Reform Act, the states assumed primary responsibility for welfare and employment policy.

in the provision of welfare services, particularly public assistance programs for the needy. Programs such as TANF, Medicaid, and food stamps operate within federal guidelines, but the states have discretionary authority over benefit and eligibility levels. These programs are funded jointly by the state and national governments and are administered primarily by the state governments. The states have the local offices necessary for administering need-based welfare programs, which require regular contacts between caseworkers and welfare recipients.

Welfare programs account for about a sixth of all state and local spending. This spending and the American tradition of self-reliance make welfare a contentious political issue. The states have devised various ways of holding down spending. In response to the rapid increase in Medicaid costs, for example, the state of Oregon conducted a systematic study of medical procedures in order to identify and make ineligible for Medicaid reimbursement those procedures that physicians apply electively. Medicaid, however, is sure to remain a central issue. It is a joint federal-state program, but the high costs of medical care have made Medicaid the single largest item in state budgets. Health care costs are certain to rise in the future. Just as certain is the continuing need of poorer Americans for medical care. At some point, these fiscal and medical realities are sure to collide.

Health and Hospitals

More than 5 percent of state and local expenditures are in the health and hospitals policy area. All states and many localities operate public hospitals, and most of the laws and regulations affecting medical practices are established by state governments. In addition, states and localities offer public health programs such as immunization campaigns, mobile x-ray units, and health inspections of motels and restaurants.

Highways

Until the 1950s, the roadways of America were built almost entirely with state and local funds. The interstate highway system, begun in the 1950s, was funded largely by the national government. Today, Washington provides about a third of the total spending on highways, and states and localities contribute the rest. State and local governments set most policies governing use of highways, including traffic infractions and shipping methods. Highway spending accounts for about 5 percent of state and local expenditures.

Police and Prisons

While some democracies have a large national police force, the United States does not. Its law enforcement is entrusted almost entirely to local and state police forces. They enforce state laws and local ordinances, which collectively govern most aspects of crime and punishment. The state police include the highway patrol, game wardens, prison guards, and liquor control officers, and they are generally well trained and highly professional. Local police are less specialized, are more uneven in their training and professionalism, and are required to do most of the "dirty" work of law enforcement—crime control and the maintenance of public order. More than 5 percent of state and local spending is for public-safety activities.

States and localities in recent years have invested heavily in prisons and other correctional facilities. As indicated in Chapter 4, the United States on a per capita basis is rivaled only by Russia in the number of its people who are imprisoned. The large prison population in the United States reflects a policy of lengthened and mandatory sentencing that developed in the past two decades largely around drug-related crime. Many prisoners are in jail for possession or purchase of relatively small quantities of illegal drugs. As the fiscal and human costs of this policy have increased, some state and local officials have sought alternatives, including giving judges more discretion in the sentencing of nonviolent first-time offenders.

Homeland Security

An increasing share of state and local budgets is being spent on homeland security. Before September 11, 2001, homeland security was not even a part of the vocabulary of state and local officials. As the events of that day tragically revealed, however, states and localities are in the domestic forefront of the terrorist threat. Four hundred New York City firefighters and police officers lost their lives on September 11 as they rushed to assist people trapped in the twin towers of the World Trade Center.

State and local public employees are the "first providers" in the war on terrorism. Besides being the first on the scene in the event of a terrorist attack, they have responsibility for monitoring domestic sites that might be terrorist targets and with training citizens and public employees to respond to such attacks.

The federal government assists state and local governments in funding these and other activities related to the war on terrorism, but so far the funds have been insufficient to meet the costs. In 2004, the U.S. Conference of Mayors

The environment has become an important issue of state and local politics as a result of the public's growing awareness of the damage caused by pollution. Here, a bucket of oysters was dumped into New York harbor as part of an effort to restock oyster beds destroyed by contaminated wastes.

complained that an "unfunded local mandate" had been placed on cities as a result of their direct responsibility for the defense of their residents and infrastructure. The fiscal year 2005 budget did not provide the relief they sought. Washington officials explained that the federal deficit precluded full funding of first-responder programs. As a result, many of these programs have not reached the level of readiness that officials agree is necessary. Homeland security and its funding are sure to be central issues of state and local politics for years to come.

The Environment

The environment is a relatively small part of state and local budgets, but money alone is not a reliable indicator of policy effort in the environmental area. Much of it is directed at regulatory activities that impose costs on firms and consumers.

Most states and localities were complacent about environmental protection until the federal government in the 1960s and 1970s greatly broadened the scope of its activities. Today, states and localities are active participants in the effort to protect the environment. For example, they routinely require environmental impact statements for major development projects and have acted to protect their land and water resources from pollutants. In addition, conservation through the preservation of parks, natural resources, and wildlife has increasingly been a focus of state policy. New York, for example, has taken steps to purchase and otherwise protect tens of thousands of acres of undeveloped land in its Adirondack mountains.

Sewage and garbage disposal is a special problem for local governments. As environmental standards have increased, it has become an increasingly costly

In 2004, Massachusetts became the first state to legalize same-sex marriage. The policy was adopted after Massachusetts' highest court ruled that denial of marriage to same-sex couples violated the state's constitution. The ruling sparked a national debate that carried over into the 2004 presidential race between George W. Bush and John Kerry.

activity, ranking only behind schools, roadways, and public safety as an expenditure category for cities. It has also become increasingly contentious because neighborhoods nearly always resist the nearby placement of a new sewage treatment plant, garbage incinerator, or landfill. This opposition is so predictable that it has acquired an acronym—NIMBY, for "Not In My Back Yard." Public resistance has forced many communities into costly solutions, such as the shipping of garbage to distant landfills.

Civil Rights and Liberties

Civil rights and liberties also comprise a small part of state and local budgets, but, like the environment, they are of substantial importance. For a long period in U.S. history, civil rights and liberties were defined largely in the context of state and local politics. The Bill of Rights applied only to action by the national government, and states were more or less free to decide for themselves the free expression and fair trial rights their residents would enjoy. During the 1900s, however, federal courts, largely through the vehicle of the Fourteenth Amendment, assumed the power to compel states and localities to uphold certain individual rights (see Chapter 4). An example is the requirement that states and localities provide legal assistance to the criminally accused who are too poor to afford their own lawyer.

Nevertheless, states retain discretionary authority in many areas of civil rights and liberties. Although racial, ethnic, sexual, or religious discrimination is not permitted, states can decide, for example, the age-discrimination and disability-discrimination standards that will apply to their own employees (see Chapter 5).

Political Culture

One People Out of Many

America's Political Subcultures

Although Americans share a common political heritage that is built around principles such as liberty, equality, and self-government, distinctive regional subcultures persist. These subcultures, as political scientist Daniel Elazar noted in *American Federalism*, reflect differences in ethnic settlement patterns, historical episodes, economic conditions, and other influences.

The states in the northern tier of the nation have what Elazar describes as a *moralistic subculture*. It is characterized by an emphasis on "good government" (the public interest) and "clean government" (honesty). The states that share this subculture were populated primarily by northern Europeans, including the English, Germans, and Scandinavians. Minnesota is an example of a moralistic state. Minnesota has one of the highest rates of voter turnout in the country and one of the lowest rates of political corruption. Political competition in this subculture tends to focus on issues rather than on personalities, and activist government is accepted. Taxes are relatively high, but so is the level of public services. States in this region spend more heavily than other states in areas such as public education, and their students tend to score higher on standardized tests than do students in other regions.

The middle part of the United States—from Massachusetts to Maryland and then westward through Illinois and Missouri to southwestern states such as Arizona—is described by Elazar as having an *individualistic subculture*. This subculture is oriented toward private life and economic gain, and politics is largely an extension of this perspective. Political conflict is rough-and-tumble, political power is closely guarded, and public policy is often narrowly applied. Compared with states that have a moralistic subculture, those with an individualistic subculture tend to spend less per capita on public services. They place greater emphasis on self-sufficiency.

A *traditionalistic subculture*, in Elazar's terms, typifies the states of the old Confederacy and a few states bordering on it, such as West Virginia. This subculture reflects the stratified plantation society out of which it grew: it is conservative in its focus and elitist in its leadership. Government is likely to be a topic of considerable interest in a traditionalistic state, but not because government is activist. In fact, traditionalists prefer a government that reinforces the existing economic, social, and political structure.

These subcultures do not coincide exactly with state borders, and elements of each subculture are found in every region of the country. Other subcultures also exist. The South, for example, has a populist heritage that runs counter to its dominant traditionalist subculture. Several of the South's best-known politicians, including Alabama's George Wallace and Louisiana's Huey Long, rose to prominence by attacking entrenched power structures in their own states. Nevertheless, Elazar's typology illustrates the important point that the American states are politically diverse. They operate within the framework of a common federal government and a larger political culture, but they have distinctive features that make and mold their politics and policies.

No civil rights issue at the state and local levels has received more attention recently than the legal status of gays and lesbians. Although civil unions and same-sex marriages have received the most attention (see Chapter 5), other issues, including job and housing discrimination, have also come under scrutiny. A decade or two ago, almost no state or locality had a law that banned discrimination based on sexual orientation. Today, about half the U.S. population resides in a state or locality with such a law, although the scope of these laws varies greatly.[16] Only a few state and local governments, for example, require public and private employers to extend health benefits to the same-sex partner of an employee if such benefits are provided to the opposite-sex spouse of an employee.

The Politics of State and Local Policy

As mentioned previously, the general economic conditions of a state have a substantial impact on its policies. Richer states are simply in a stronger position to provide more and better services than poorer states are. West Virginia, with a per capita income only two-thirds that of Massachusetts, can hardly be expected to have schools, hospitals, roadways, and other facilities that match those of the Bay State.

Wealth alone, however, cannot fully explain state-to-state differences. Public policies also reflect variations in state politics, as the following discussion indicates.

Party Competition

The fifty states vary significantly in their support for one major party or the other. Where the Republicans are stronger, as in the mountain states, taxes and the level of public services tend to be lower. Where Democrats are stronger, as in the northeast, the reverse situation tends to hold.

The intensity of party competition has a somewhat less obvious, but no less important, relationship to public policy.[17] In states where party competition is weak, politics tends to be somewhat exclusive: a sizable share of the population, usually the poorest groups, will be more or less ignored by government. The dominant party has gained control without the help of these groups, and the minority party could not gain control even with their help. In other words, neither party has a strong incentive to seek their vote. The classic case of a neglected public was the black community in the South in the period before the modern civil rights movement of the 1950s and 1960s. African Americans were politically powerless. Neither the white Democrats who ran the south nor the white Republicans who offered token opposition had a real interest in bringing black people into their coalition.

Where party competition is more intense, any sizable group in a state is likely to receive the attention of one party or the other and thus to be in a position to influence public policy. In the modern South, which is increasingly competitive between the parties, black voters are a growing force and have tipped the balance in some elections; they are also more likely than at any time in the past to have policy influence.

The state party systems have become more competitive by some indicators and less competitive by others. Compared with the 1960s, there are fewer states today in which one party controls the governor's seat and both chambers of the state legislature (see "States in the Nation"). However, the number of state legislative races in which the incumbent has no or only token opposition has increased.[18] Faced with a well-funded and popular incumbent, the opposing party increasingly has conceded the election. The professionalization of state legislatures has had an effect similar to that of the professionalization of

STATES IN THE NATION

Party Control of State Government

The strength of the major parties varies substantially among states. An indicator of party dominance is whether one party controls all elected institutions—the governor's seat and the two legislative chambers (except in Nebraska, which has a unicameral, nonpartisan legislature). As of 2004, the Republican party had an edge on the Democrats, although control in most states was divided between the parties.

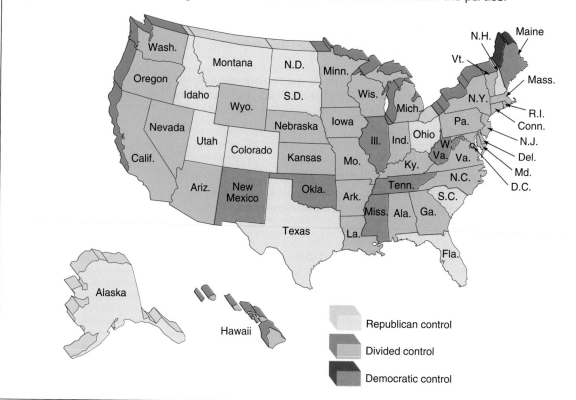

Congress: legislators have used their positions to solidify public support and dominate campaign contributions, thereby discouraging election challengers.

Group Competition

Interest-group systems can be looked at in a similar way.[19] In those states where interest groups are many in number and somewhat evenly balanced in their political resources, public policy tends to serve a broad range of interests. An example is the state of New York, which has many competing factions—including, for example, business and labor, the upstate and downstate areas, and environmentalists and developers. Almost any legislation that makes it through the New York state legislature requires negotiation among numerous groups.

In states where a particular group or interest is dominant, however, government tends to serve that group or interest above all others. A classic example was the Anaconda Copper Company in Montana, which, during the period when it accounted for nearly all the state's mining and manufacturing, nearly ran the state. A more recent example is the influence of the Church of Jesus Christ of Latter-day Saints in Utah. A majority of the state's residents are Mormons, and a policy alternative that is actively opposed by the church has almost no chance of becoming law. For example, the church for years opposed the sale of hard liquor in Utah, and such sales were prohibited by law. The law was modified in 1990, but only after Mormon leaders agreed not to oppose the change, which was prompted by the state's desire to improve its ability to attract tourists and conventions. Utah even succeeded in winning the bid to host the 2002 Winter Olympics.

Utah is a state where political alternatives are substantially shaped by a dominant interest. Policy proposals that are actively opposed by the Church of Jesus Christ of Latter-day Saints have little chance of becoming law. Shown here is a winter picture with holiday lights of the Mormon Temple in Salt Lake City. In 2002, Salt Lake City was host to the Winter Olympics.

Utah, with its Mormon population, is one of the most distinctive states in the union, but every state has its special characteristics. California is no more like Mississippi than Mississippi is like Rhode Island. Yet, as this chapter has shown, the American states also have many aspects in common. The differences and similarities among the states are testimony to the enduring nature of the American governing experiment. The states are different enough to provide their residents with a special identity and a special political experience; yet they are alike enough to allow the triumph of the national union that the Framers so keenly envisioned over two hundred years ago.

THE GREAT BALANCING ACT: LOCALISM IN A LARGE NATION

The structure of U.S. government—federalism and localism—was established when the nation was founded over two centuries ago. The seven million Americans of the time lived closer together, and yet farther apart, than Americans of today. They were crowded along the eastern seaboard, but travel from Savannah in the south to Boston in the north could take weeks. Communication was equally slow: news traveled no faster than people and ships could carry it. Today, the United States has nearly 300 million people spread across a continent, reaching even into Alaska and Hawaii. Yet communication is instantaneous, and an airplane can span the distance between Boston and Los Angeles in a few hours.

Is the constitutional structure that was created over two hundred years ago suited to modern needs? This is a question that scholars and policymakers sometimes ask. Yet none have concluded that the nation would be better off without its three relatively distinctive levels of government. They accept the essential wisdom of James Madison's argument extolling the strength of "a compound republic."[20]

The arguments today are confined to issues of the relative balance of power among the three levels. If conservatives are more inclined than liberals to stress localism, each side embraces the alternative position when doing so furthers its policy goals.

Accordingly, the relative balance among the levels has shifted from time to time. Throughout most of the twentieth century, power shifted upward toward the federal government as society became ever more complex and interdependent. The demand for greater efficiency and equality could be met only through a stronger national response. The U.S. economy had to be transformed into a national economy, and demands by disadvantaged Americans for equal treatment had to be addressed nationally if they were to be met.

More recent years have seen a flow of power back to the states and localities. The trend can be explained in part by the discovery that national solutions to certain policy problems are less effective than their original advocates envisioned. It is also attributable to Americans' respect for local differences and their willingness to experiment with new approaches. The federal social welfare programs that were established in the 1960s were not failures—they succeeded in lifting millions of Americans out of poverty. But they were not unbridled successes—they fostered welfare dependency and fueled taxpayer resentment. The welfare reform legislation enacted in 1996 sought a new balance, one that would preserve a safety net for low-income Americans yet empower the states to require able-bodied adults to enter the work force or lose their welfare benefits. Few analysts believe that the 1996 act is the final answer to Americans' welfare needs. But it is the current answer and will remain operative until an emerging problem generates political pressure for something different. Whether that "something" will enlarge or diminish the federal, state, or local role cannot be predicted. The response will depend on the nature of the problem and the political outlook of the moment. As historian Daniel Boorstin observed, pragmatism rather than orthodoxy is the defining characteristic of American politics.[21]

If anything, Americans' pragmatism will be even more evident in the years to come. They will become more, not less, interdependent as a result of expected changes in communication, computer technology, and the global economy. An effect of interdependency, as noted in Chapter 3, is an increase in the demands on government at all levels. The examples are countless. Homeland security, for instance, was barely an issue until the terrorist attacks on the World Trade Center and the Pentagon in 2001 forced Americans to take notice. Once they did, they turned to all levels of government for answers. As the national, state, and local governments responded, it became apparent to officials at each level that effective solutions would require cooperation among them. The federal government took the lead, particularly on overseas terrorist threats, but state and local officials in law enforcement and other areas were deeply involved in the effort to heighten Americans' security.

The writers of the U.S. Constitution could not possibly have envisioned life in twenty-first-century America. Theirs was a world of horse-drawn carriages and candlelight, not of jet airplanes and computers. But they did envision a governing system flexible enough to respond to changing needs during changing times.[22] The persistence of this system across more than two centuries is testimony to their vision and to the willingness of succeeding generations of Americans to find a combination of national, state, and local authority that could meet their governing needs.

Self-Test
www.mhhe.com/pattersontad7

Summary

Although developments in the twentieth century have narrowed the differences among the American states, they—and the localities that govern under their authority—remain distinctive and vital systems of government.

All states apply the constitutional principle of separate branches sharing power, but the structure of the state governments differs in some respects from that of the federal government. An example is the more widespread use of elections at the state level. Most states elect by popular vote their judges and a number of executives, including an attorney general and treasurer in addition to a governor. Through the initiative or the referendum, nearly all states also allow their residents to vote directly on policy issues.

Local governments are chartered by the state. They are not sovereign governments, but most states have chosen to grant local units a considerable level of policymaking discretion. Local governments include counties, municipalities, school districts, and special districts. Of these, the independent school district is the most distinctively American institution. The municipality is the primary governing unit. Municipalities are governed by one of four types of system: the strong mayor–council system, the weak mayor–council system, the commission system, or the city manager system.

The states and localities have primary responsibility for most of the public policies that directly touch Americans' daily lives. For example, the major share of legislation devoted to public education and more than 90 percent of the funding for it are provided by the states and localities. Public welfare, public health, roads, and police are other policy areas dominated by these subnational governments. They do not, however, have the amount of revenue that is available to the federal government. Competition between the states and localities holds down their taxing capacity. Their policies are also conditioned by the wealth of the state or locality and by the structure of its party and interest-group systems.

STUDY CORNER

Key Terms

bicameral legislatures *(p. 587)*

charter *(p. 593)*

city manager system *(p. 597)*

commission system *(p. 596)*

constitutional initiative *(p. 585)*

Cooley's rule *(p. 593)*

Dillon's rule *(p. 592)*

home rule *(p. 593)*

initiative *(p. 591)*

metropolitan government *(p. 599)*

ordinances *(p. 593)*

police power *(p. 604)*

recall *(p. 591)*

referendum *(p. 591)*

state constitutional
    convention *(p. 585)*

strong mayor–council system *(p. 596)*

weak mayor–council system *(p. 596)*

Self-Test

1. Which of the following statements about state governors is true?
   a. Nearly all power in state governments is vested in the office of governor.
   b. Only a few states give the governor a line-item veto.
   c. Most governors are mere figureheads; they have no significant political power.
   d. The large majority of governors share executive power with other elected executive officials.

2. The largest share of local government spending is for:
   a. policy and fire protection.
   b. roadways.
   c. education.
   d. welfare.

3. The largest share of state government spending is for:
   a. policy and fire protection.
   b. roadways.
   c. education.
   d. welfare.

4. The two major sources of revenue for state governments are:
   a. personal income and general sales taxes.
   b. personal income and property taxes.
   c. property and general sales taxes.
   d. personal income and corporate income taxes.

5. About the relationship of local governments to their respective state government, it is accurate to say that:
   a. local governments are not sovereign; their power derives from that of the state.
   b. the long-term trend in most states has been to grant more autonomy to local governments.
   c. local governments depend on state government for some of their revenues.
   d. all of the above are true.

6. The type of municipal government that is now used by only a few localities is:
   a. the strong–mayor system.
   b. the weak–mayor system.
   c. the city manager system.
   d. the commission system.

7. The property tax is by far the most important revenue source for local governments. (T/F)

8. The condition of the national economy has almost no impact on state and local tax revenues. (T/F)

9. Most of the state constitutions are shorter and contain fewer amendments than the U.S. Constitution. (T/F)

10. In most states, judges are nominated for office by the governor. (T/F)

Critical Thinking

What are the general limits on the capacity of states and localities to raise the revenues they need to provide services to their residents through taxes? What is the impact of a state or locality's wealth on its revenue-raising capacity? What is the impact of economic growth? Of an economic downturn?

Suggested Readings

Beyle, Thad L. *State and Local Government*. Washington, D.C.: Congressional Quarterly Press, 2003. An edited volume of articles on recent developments in state and local government.

Broder, David. *Democracy Derailed*. San Diego: Harcourt, 2000. An analysis of how powerful groups have captured the initiative process.

Henig, Jeffrey R., and Wilbur C. Rich. *Mayors in the Middle*. Princeton, N.J.: Princeton University Press, 2004. An edited volume on mayoral takeovers of troubled schools.

Hero, Rodney. *Faces of Inequality*. New York: Oxford University Press, 2000. An assessment of how states' politics and policies are shaped by their racial and ethnic composition.

Hunter, Kenneth G. *Interest Groups and State Economic Development Policies*. Westport, Conn.: Praeger, 1999. A look at the influence of groups on state policy decisions.

Jewell, Malcolm E., and Sarah M. Morehouse. *Political Parties and Elections in American States,* 4th ed. Washington, D.C.: Congressional Quarterly Press, 2000. A state-by-state comparison of parties and elections.

Morehouse, Sarah McCally. *The Governor as Party Leader*. Ann Arbor: University of Michigan Press, 1998. An examination of how governors campaign and govern.

Tarr, G. Alan. *Understanding State Constitutions*. Princeton, N.J.: Princeton University Press, 1998. A thorough assessment of state constitutions and how they differ from the U.S. Constitution.

List of Websites

http://www.nga.org/

The website of the National Governors Association.

http://www.nyc.gov/

The website for New York City's government. Most cities and towns have their own website.

http://www.state.tx.us

The website for the state of Texas. Every state government has a website.

http://www.usmayors.org/

The website for the U.S. Conference of Mayors.

Participate!

Local government offers many opportunities for participation and observation. Consider contacting a local official to arrange an internship in local government. If your time is limited, you might attend a local council meeting or school-board meeting to see firsthand how government in your community is conducted.

Extra Credit

For up-to-the-minute *New York Times* articles, interactive simulations, graphics, study tools, and more links and quizzes, visit the text's Online Learning Center at www.mhhe.com/pattersontad7.

(Self-Test Answers: 1. d   2. c   3. c   4. a   5. d   6. d   7. T   8. F   9. F   10. F)

APPENDIXES

THE DECLARATION OF INDEPENDENCE

IN CONGRESS, JULY 4, 1776

The Unanimous Declaration of the Thirteen United States of America

When, in the course of human events, it becomes necessary for one people to dissolve the political bands which have connected them with another, and to assume, among the powers of the earth, the separate and equal station to which the laws of nature and of nature's God entitle them, a decent respect to the opinions of mankind requires that they should declare the causes which impel them to the separation.

We hold these truths to be self-evident, that all men are created equal; that they are endowed by their Creator with certain unalienable rights; that among these, are life, liberty, and the pursuit of happiness. That, to secure these rights, governments are instituted among men, deriving their just powers from the consent of the governed; that, whenever any form of government becomes destructive of these ends, it is the right of the people to alter or to abolish it, and to institute a new government, laying its foundation on such principles, and organizing its powers in such form, as to them shall seem most likely to effect their safety and happiness. Prudence, indeed, will dictate that governments long established, should not be changed for light and transient causes; and, accordingly, all experience hath shown, that mankind are more disposed to suffer, while evils are sufferable, than to right themselves by abolishing the forms to which they are accustomed. But, when a long train of abuses and usurpations, pursuing invariably the same object, evinces a design to reduce them under absolute despotism, it is their right, it is their duty, to throw off such government and to provide new guards for their future security. Such has been the patient sufferance of these colonies, and such is now the necessity which constrains them to alter their former systems of government. The history of the present King of Great Britain is a history of repeated injuries and usurpations, all having, in direct object, the establishment of an absolute tyranny over these States. To prove this, let facts be submitted to a candid world:

He has refused his assent to laws the most wholesome and necessary for the public good.

He has forbidden his governors to pass laws of immediate and pressing importance, unless suspended in their operation till his assent should be obtained; and, when so suspended, he has utterly neglected to attend to them.

He has refused to pass other laws for the accommodation of large districts of people, unless those people would relinquish the right of representation in the legislature; a right inestimable to them, and formidable to tyrants only.

He has called together legislative bodies at places unusual, uncomfortable, and distant from the depository of their public records, for the sole purpose of fatiguing them into compliance with his measures.

He has dissolved representative houses repeatedly for opposing, with manly firmness, his invasions on the rights of the people.

He has refused, for a long time after such dissolutions, to cause others to be elected; whereby the legislative powers, incapable of annihilation, have returned to the people at large for their exercise; the state remaining, in the meantime, exposed to all the danger of invasion from without, and convulsions within.

He has endeavored to prevent the population of these States; for that purpose, obstructing the laws for naturalization of foreigners, refusing to pass others to encourage their migration hither, and raising the conditions of new appropriations of lands.

He has obstructed the administration of justice, by refusing his assent to laws for establishing judiciary powers.

He has made judges dependent on his will alone, for the tenure of their offices, and the amount and payment of their salaries.

He has erected a multitude of new offices, and sent hither swarms of officers to harass our people, and eat out their substance.

He has kept among us, in time of peace, standing armies, without the consent of our legislatures.

He has affected to render the military independent of, and superior to, the civil power.

He has combined, with others, to subject us to a jurisdiction foreign to our Constitution, and unacknowledged by our laws; giving his assent to their acts of pretended legislation:

For quartering large bodies of armed troops among us:

For protecting them by a mock trial, from punishment, for any murders which they should commit on the inhabitants of these States:

For cutting off our trade with all parts of the world:

For imposing taxes on us without our consent:

For depriving us, in many cases, of the benefit of trial by jury:

For transporting us beyond seas to be tried for pretended offences:

For abolishing the free system of English laws in a neighboring province, establishing therein an arbitrary government, and enlarging its boundaries, so as to render it at once an example and fit instrument for introducing the same absolute rule into these colonies:

For taking away our charters, abolishing our most valuable laws, and altering, fundamentally, the powers of our governments:

For suspending our own legislatures, and declaring themselves invested with power to legislate for us in all cases whatsoever.

He has abdicated government here, by declaring us out of his protection, and waging war against us.

He has plundered our seas, ravaged our coasts, burnt our towns, and destroyed the lives of our people.

He is, at this time, transporting large armies of foreign mercenaries to complete the works of death, desolation, and tyranny, already begun, with circumstances of cruelty and perfidy scarcely paralleled in the most barbarous ages, and totally unworthy of the head of a civilized nation.

He has constrained our fellow citizens, taken captive on the high seas, to bear arms against their country, to become the executioners of their friends, and brethren, or to fall themselves by their hands.

He has excited domestic insurrections amongst us, and has endeavored to bring on the inhabitants of our frontiers, the merciless Indian savages, whose known rule of warfare is an undistinguished destruction of all ages, sexes, and conditions.

In every stage of these oppressions, we have petitioned for redress, in the most humble terms; our repeated petitions have been answered only by repeated injury. A prince, whose character is thus marked by every act which may define a tyrant, is unfit to be the ruler of a free people.

Nor have we been wanting in attention to our British brethren. We have warned them, from time to time, of attempts made by their legislature to extend an unwarrantable jurisdiction over us. We have reminded them of the circumstances of our emigration and settlement here. We have appealed to their native justice and magnanimity, and we have conjured them, by the ties of our common kindred, to disavow these usurpations, which would inevitably interrupt our connections and correspondence. They, too, have been deaf to the voice of justice and of consanguinity. We must, therefore, acquiesce in the necessity which denounces our separation, and hold them as we hold the rest of mankind, enemies in war, in peace, friends.

We, therefore, the representatives of the United States of America, in general Congress assembled, appealing to the Supreme Judge of the world for the rectitude of our intentions, do, in the name, and by the authority of the good people of these colonies, solemnly publish and declare, that these united colonies are, and of right ought to be, free and independent states: that they are absolved from all allegiance to the British Crown, and that all political connection between them and the state of Great Britain is, and ought to be, totally dissolved; and that, as free and independent states, they have full power to levy war, conclude peace, contract alliances, establish commerce, and to do all other acts and things which independent states may of right do. And, for the support of this declaration, with a firm reliance on the protection of Divine Providence, we mutually pledge to each other our lives, our fortunes, and our sacred honor.

The foregoing Declaration was, by order of Congress, engrossed, and signed by the following members:

John Hancock

New Hampshire
Josiah Bartlett
William Whipple
Matthew Thornton

Massachusetts Bay
Samuel Adams
John Adams
Robert Treat Paine
Elbridge Gerry

Rhode Island
Stephen Hopkins
William Ellery

Connecticut
Roger Sherman
Samuel Huntington
William Williams
Oliver Wolcott

New York
William Floyd
Philip Livingston
Francis Lewis
Lewis Morris

New Jersey
Richard Stockton
John Witherspoon
Francis Hopkinson
John Hart
Abraham Clark

Pennsylvania
Robert Morris
Benjamin Rush
Benjamin Franklin
John Morton
George Clymer
James Smith
George Taylor
James Wilson
George Ross

Delaware
Caesar Rodney
George Reed
Thomas M'Kean

Maryland
Samuel Chase
William Paca
Thomas Stone
Charles Carroll, of Carrollton

Virginia
George Wythe
Richard Henry Lee
Thomas Jefferson
Benjamin Harrison
Thomas Nelson, Jr.
Francis Lightfoot Lee
Carter Braxton

North Carolina
William Hooper
Joseph Hewes
John Penn

South Carolina
Edward Rutledge
Thomas Heyward, Jr.
Thomas Lynch, Jr.
Arthur Middleton

Georgia
Button Gwinnett
Lyman Hall
George Walton

Resolved, That copies of the Declaration be sent to the several assemblies, conventions, and committees, or councils of safety, and to the several commanding officers of the continental troops; that it be proclaimed in each of the United States, at the head of the army.

THE CONSTITUTION OF THE UNITED STATES OF AMERICA[1]

We the People of the United States, in Order to form a more perfect Union, establish Justice, insure domestic Tranquility, provide for the common defence, promote the general Welfare, and secure the Blessings of Liberty to ourselves and our Posterity, do ordain and establish this CONSTITUTION for the United States of America.

ARTICLE I

SECTION 1

All legislative Powers herein granted shall be vested in a Congress of the United States, which shall consist of a Senate and House of Representatives.

SECTION 2

The House of Representatives shall be composed of Members chosen every second Year by the People of the several States, and the Electors in each State shall have the Qualifications requisite for Electors of the most numerous Branch of the State Legislature.

No Person shall be a Representative who shall not have attained to the Age of twenty-five Years, and been seven Years a Citizen of the United States, and who shall not, when elected, be an Inhabitant of that State in which he shall be chosen.

[Representatives and direct Taxes[2] shall be apportioned among the several States which may be included within this Union, according to their respective Numbers, which shall be determined by adding to the whole Number of free Persons, including those bound to Service for a Term of Years, and excluding Indians not taxed, three fifths of all other Persons.][3] The actual Enumeration shall be made within three Years after the first Meeting of the Congress of the United States, and within every subsequent Term of ten Years, in such Manner as they shall by Law direct. The Number of Representatives shall not exceed one for every thirty Thousand, but each State shall have at Least one Representative; and until such enumeration shall be made, the State of New Hampshire shall be entitled to chuse three, Massachusetts eight, Rhode-Island and Providence Plantations one, Connecticut five, New York six, New Jersey four, Pennsylvania eight, Delaware one, Maryland six, Virginia ten, North Carolina five, South Carolina five, and Georgia three.

When vacancies happen in the Representation from any State, the Executive Authority thereof shall issue Writs of Election to fill such Vacancies.

The House of Representatives shall chuse their Speaker and other Officers; and shall have the sole Power of Impeachment.

SECTION 3

The Senate of the United States shall be composed of two Senators from each State, chosen by the Legislature thereof, for six Years; and each Senator shall have one Vote.

Immediately after they shall be assembled in Consequence of the first Election, they shall be divided as equally as may be into three Classes. The Seats of the Senators of the first Class shall be vacated at the Expiration of the second Year, of the second Class at the Expiration of the fourth Year, and of the third Class at the Expiration of the sixth Year, so that one-third may be chosen every second Year; and if Vacancies happen by Resignation, or otherwise, during the Recess of the Legislature of any

---

[1] This version, which follows the original Constitution in capitalization and spelling, was published by the United States Department of the Interior, Office of Education, in 1935.
[2] Altered by the Sixteenth Amendment.

[3] Negated by the Fourteenth Amendment.

State, the Executive thereof may make temporary Appointments until the next Meeting of the Legislature, which shall then fill such Vacancies.

No Person shall be a Senator who shall not have attained to the Age of thirty Years, and been nine Years a Citizen of the United States, and who shall not, when elected, be an Inhabitant of that State for which he shall be chosen.

The Vice President of the United States shall be President of the Senate, but shall have no vote, unless they be equally divided.

The Senate shall chuse their other Officers, and also a President pro tempore, in the absence of the Vice President, or when he shall exercise the Office of President of the United States.

The Senate shall have the sole Power to try all Impeachments. When sitting for that purpose they shall be on Oath or Affirmation. When the President of the United States is tried, the Chief Justice shall preside: And no person shall be convicted without the Concurrence of two thirds of the Members present.

Judgment in Cases of Impeachment shall not extend further than to removal from Office, and disqualification to hold and enjoy any Office of honor, Trust, or Profit under the United States: but the Party convicted shall nevertheless be liable and subject to Indictment, Trial, Judgment and Punishment, according to Law.

SECTION 4

The Times, Place and Manner of holding Elections for Senators and Representatives, shall be prescribed in each State by the Legislature thereof; but the Congress may at any time by Law make or alter such Regulations, except as to the Places of Chusing Senators.

The Congress shall assemble at least once in every Year, and such Meeting shall be on the first Monday in December, unless they shall by Law appoint a different Day.

SECTION 5

Each House shall be the Judge of the Elections, Returns and Qualifications of its own Members, and a Majority of each shall constitute a Quorum to do Business; but a smaller number may adjourn from day to day, and may be authorized to compel the Attendance of absent Members, in such Manner, and under such Penalties, as each House may provide.

Each House may determine the Rules of its Proceedings, punish its Members for disorderly Behaviour, and, with the Concurrence of two thirds, expel a Member.

Each House shall keep a Journal of its Proceedings, and from time to time publish the same, excepting such Parts as may in their Judgment require Secrecy; and the Yeas and Nays of the Members of either House on any question shall, at the Desire of one fifth of those Present, be entered on the Journal.

Neither House, during the Session of Congress, shall, without the Consent of the other, adjourn for more than three days, nor to any other Place than that in which the two Houses shall be sitting.

SECTION 6

The Senators and Representatives shall receive a Compensation for their Services, to be ascertained by Law, and paid out of the Treasury of the United States. They shall in all Cases, except Treason, Felony, and Breach of the Peace, be privileged from Arrest during their Attendance at the Session of their respective Houses, and in going to and returning from the same; and for any Speech or Debate in either House, they shall not be questioned in any other Place.

No Senator or Representative shall, during the Time for which he was elected, be appointed to any civil Office under the Authority of the United States, which shall have been created, or the Emoluments whereof shall have been increased, during such time; and no Person holding any Office under the United States shall be a Member of either House during his continuance in Office.

SECTION 7

All Bills for raising Revenue shall originate in the House of Representatives; but the Senate may propose or concur with Amendments as on other bills.

Every Bill which shall have passed the House of Representatives and the Senate, shall, before it becomes a Law, be presented to the President of the United States; if he approve he shall sign it, but if not he shall return it, with his Objections, to that House in which it shall have originated, who shall enter the Objections at large on their Journal, and proceed to reconsider it. If after such Reconsideration two thirds of that House shall agree to pass the bill, it shall be sent, together with the objections, to the other House, by which it shall likewise be reconsidered, and if approved by two thirds of that House, it shall become a Law. But in all such Cases the Votes of both Houses shall be determined by Yeas and Nays, and the Names of the Persons voting for and against the Bill shall be entered on the Journal of each House respectively. If any Bill shall not be returned by the President within ten Days (Sundays excepted) after it shall have been presented to him, the Same shall be a Law, in like Manner as if he had signed it, unless the Congress by their Adjournment prevent its Return, in which Case it shall not be a Law.

Every Order, Resolution, or Vote to which the Concurrence of the Senate and House of Representatives may be necessary (except on a question of Adjournment) shall be presented to the President of the United States; and before the Same shall take Effect, shall be approved by him, or being disapproved by him, shall be repassed by two thirds of the Senate and House of Representatives, according to the Rules and Limitations prescribed in the Case of a Bill.

SECTION 8

The Congress shall have Power To lay and collect Taxes, Duties, Imposts and Excises, to pay the Debts and provide for the common Defence and general Welfare of the United States; but all Duties, Imposts and Excises shall be uniform throughout the United States;

To borrow money on the credit of the United States;

To regulate Commerce with foreign Nations, and among the several States, and with the Indian Tribes;

To establish a uniform rule of Naturalization, and uniform Laws on the subject of Bankruptcies throughout the United States;

To coin Money, regulate the Value thereof, and of foreign Coin, and fix the Standard of Weights and Measures;

To provide for the Punishment of counterfeiting the Securities and current Coin of the United States;

To establish Post Offices and post Roads;

To promote the Progress of Science and useful Arts, by securing for limited Times to Authors and Inventors the exclusive Right to their respective Writings and Discoveries;

To constitute Tribunals inferior to the Supreme Court;

To define and punish Piracies and Felonies committed on the high Seas, and Offenses against the Law of Nations;

To declare War, grant Letters of Marque and Reprisal, and make Rules concerning Captures on Land and Water;

To raise and support Armies, but no Appropriation of Money to that Use shall be for a longer Term than two Years;

To provide and maintain a Navy;

To make Rules for the Government and Regulation of the land and naval forces;

To provide for calling forth the Militia to execute the Laws of the Union, suppress Insurrections and repel Invasions;

To provide for organizing, arming, and disciplining the Militia, and for governing such Part of them as may be employed in the Service of the United States, reserving to the States respectively, the Appointment of the Officers, and the Authority of training the Militia according to the discipline prescribed by Congress;

To exercise exclusive Legislation in all Cases whatsoever, over such District (not exceeding ten Miles square) as may, by Cession of particular States, and the acceptance of Congress, become the Seat of the Government of the United States, and to exercise like Authority over all Places purchased by the Consent of the Legislature of the State in which the Same shall be, for the Erection of Forts, Magazines, Arsenals, Dock-yards, and other needful Buildings;—And

To make all Laws which shall be necessary and proper for carrying into Execution the foregoing Powers, and all other Powers vested by this Constitution in the Government of the United States, or in any Department or Officer thereof.

SECTION 9

The Migration or Importation of such Persons as any of the States now existing shall think proper to admit, shall not be prohibited by the Congress prior The Constitution of the United States of America to the Year one thousand eight hundred and eight, but a tax or duty may be imposed on such Importation, not exceeding ten dollars for each Person.

The privilege of the Writ of Habeas Corpus shall not be suspended, unless when in Cases of Rebellion or Invasion the public Safety may require it.

No bill of Attainder or ex post facto Law shall be passed.

No capitation, or other direct, Tax shall be laid unless in Proportion to the Census or Enumeration herein before directed to be taken.

No Tax or Duty shall be laid on Articles exported from any State.

No Preference shall be given by any Regulation of Commerce or Revenue to the Ports of one State over those of another: nor shall Vessels bound to, or from, one State, be obliged to enter, clear, or pay Duties in another.

No Money shall be drawn from the Treasury, but in Consequence of Appropriations made by Law; and a regular Statement and Account of the Receipts and Expenditures of all public Money shall be published from time to time.

No Title of Nobility shall be granted by the United States: And no Person holding any Office of Profit or Trust under them, shall, without the Consent of the Congress, accept of any present, Emolument, Office, or Title, of any kind whatever, from any King, Prince, or foreign State.

SECTION 10

No State shall enter into any Treaty, Alliance, or Confederation; grant Letters of Marque and Reprisal; coin Money; emit Bills of Credit; make any Thing but gold and silver Coin a Tender in Payment of Debts; pass any Bill of Attainder, ex post facto Law, or Law impairing the Obligation of Contracts, or grant any Title of Nobility.

No State shall, without the Consent of the Congress, lay any Imposts or Duties on Imports or Exports, except what may be absolutely necessary for executing its inspection Laws; and the net Produce of all Duties and Imposts, laid by any State on Imports or Exports, shall be for the use of the Treasury of the United States; and all such Laws shall be subject to the Revision and Control of the Congress.

No state shall, without the Consent of Congress, lay any duty of Tonnage, keep Troops, or Ships of War in time of Peace, enter into any Agreement or Compact with another State, or with a foreign Power, or engage in War, unless actually invaded, or in such imminent Danger as will not admit of delay.

ARTICLE II

SECTION 1

The executive Power shall be vested in a President of the United States of America. He shall hold his Office during the Term of four years, and, together with the Vice President, chosen for the same Term, be elected, as follows:

Each State shall appoint, in such Manner as the Legislature thereof may direct, a Number of Electors, equal to the whole Number of Senators and Representatives to which the State may be entitled in the Congress: but no Senator or Representative, or Person holding an Office of Trust or Profit under the United States, shall be appointed an Elector.

[The Electors shall meet in their respective States, and vote by Ballot for two persons, of whom one at least shall not be an Inhabitant of the same State with themselves. And they shall make a List of all the Persons voted for, and of the Number of Votes for each; which List they shall sign and certify, and transmit sealed to the Seat of the Government of the United States, directed to the President of the Senate. The President of the Senate shall, in the Presence of the Senate and House of Representatives, open all the Certificates, and the Votes shall then be counted. The Person having the greatest Number of Votes shall be the President, if such Number be a Majority of the whole Number of Electors appointed; and if there be more than one who have such Majority, and have an equal Number of Votes, then the House of Representatives shall immediately chuse by Ballot one of them for

President; and if no Person have a Majority, then from the five highest on the List the said House shall in like Manner chuse the President. But in chusing the President, the Votes shall be taken by States, the Representation from each State having one Vote; a quorum for this Purpose shall consist of a Member or Members from two-thirds of the States, and a Majority of all the States shall be necessary to a Choice. In every Case, after the Choice of the President, the Person having the greatest Number of Votes of the Electors shall be the Vice President. But if there should remain two or more who have equal votes, the Senate shall chuse from them by Ballot the Vice President.][4]

The Congress may determine the Time of chusing the Electors, and the Day on which they shall give their Votes; which Day shall be the same throughout the United States.

No person except a natural-born Citizen, or a Citizen of the United States, at the time of the Adoption of this Constitution, shall be eligible to the Office of President; neither shall any Person be eligible to that Office who shall not have attained to the Age of thirty-five years, and been fourteen Years a Resident within the United States.

In Case of the Removal of the President from Office, or of his Death, Resignation, or Inability to discharge the Powers and Duties of the said Office, the same shall devolve on the Vice President, and the Congress may by Law provide for the Case of Removal, Death, Resignation, or Inability, both of the President and Vice President, declaring what Officer shall then act as President, and such Officer shall act accordingly, until the disability be removed, or a President shall be elected.

The President shall, at stated Times, receive for his Services a Compensation, which shall neither be increased nor diminished during the Period for which he shall have been elected, and he shall not receive within that Period any other Emolument from the United States, or any of them.

Before he enter on the execution of his Office, he shall take the following Oath or Affirmation:—"I do solemnly swear (or affirm) that I will faithfully execute the Office of President of the United States, and will, to the best of my Ability, preserve, protect, and defend the Constitution of the United States."

SECTION 2

The President shall be Commander in Chief of the Army and Navy of the United States, and of the Militia of the several States, when called into the actual Service of the United States; he may require the Opinion, in writing, of the principal Officer in each of the executive Departments, upon any subject relating to the Duties of their respective Offices, and he shall have Power to Grant Reprieves and Pardons for Offenses against the United States, except in Cases of Impeachment.

He shall have Power, by and with the Advice and Consent of the Senate, to make Treaties, provided two-thirds of the Senators present concur; and he shall nominate, and by and with the Advice and Consent of the Senate, shall appoint Ambassadors, other public Ministers and Consuls, Judges of the supreme Court, and all other Officers of the United States, whose Appointments are not herein otherwise provided for, and which shall be established by Law: but the Congress may by Law vest the Appointment of such inferior Officers, as they think proper, in the President alone, in the Courts of Law, or in the Heads of Departments.

The President shall have Power to fill up all Vacancies that may happen during the Recess of the Senate, by granting Commissions which shall expire at the End of their next Session.

SECTION 3

He shall from time to time give to the Congress Information of the State of the Union, and recommend to their Consideration such Measures as he shall judge necessary and expedient; he may, on extraordinary occasions, convene both Houses, or either of them, and in Case of Disagreement between them, with respect to the Time of Adjournment, he may adjourn them to such Time as he shall think proper; he shall receive Ambassadors and other public Ministers; he shall take care that the Laws be faithfully executed, and shall Commission all the Officers of the United States.

[4.] Revised by the Twelfth Amendment.

SECTION 4

The President, Vice President and all civil Officers of the United States, shall be removed from Office on Impeachment for, and Conviction of, Treason, Bribery, or other high Crimes and Misdemeanors.

ARTICLE III

SECTION 1

The judicial Power of the United States, shall be vested in one supreme Court, and in such inferior Courts as the Congress may from time to time ordain and establish. The Judges, both of the supreme and inferior Courts, shall hold their Offices during good Behaviour, and shall, at stated Times, receive for their Services, a Compensation, which shall not be diminished during their Continuance in Office.

SECTION 2

The judicial Power shall extend to all Cases, in Law and Equity, arising under this Constitution, the Laws of the United States, and Treaties made, or which shall be made, under their Authority;—to all Cases affecting ambassadors, other public ministers and consuls;—to all cases of admiralty and maritime Jurisdiction;—to Controversies to which the United States shall be a Party;—to Controversies between two or more states;—between a State and Citizens of another State;[5]—between Citizens of different States—between Citizens of the same State claiming Lands under Grants of different States, and between a State, or the Citizens thereof, and foreign States, Citizens, or Subjects.

In all Cases affecting Ambassadors, other public Ministers and Consuls, and those in which a State shall be Party, the supreme Court shall have original Jurisdiction. In all the other Cases before mentioned, the supreme Court shall have appellate Jurisdiction, both as to Law and Fact, with such Exceptions, and under such Regulations as the Congress shall make.

The trial of all Crimes, except in Cases of Impeachment, shall be by Jury; and such Trial shall be held in the State where the said Crimes shall have been committed; but when not committed within any State, the Trial shall be at such Place or Places as the Congress may by Law have directed.

SECTION 3

Treason against the United States, shall consist only in levying War against them, or in adhering to their Enemies, giving them Aid and Comfort. No Person shall be convicted of Treason unless on the Testimony of two Witnesses to the same overt Act, or on Confession in open Court.

The Congress shall have power to declare the Punishment of Treason, but no Attainder of Treason shall work Corruption of Blood, or Forfeiture except during the Life of the Person attainted.

ARTICLE IV

SECTION 1

Full Faith and Credit shall be given in each State to the public Acts, Records, and judicial Proceedings of every other State. And the Congress may by general Laws prescribe the Manner in which such Acts, Records and Proceedings shall be proved, and the Effect thereof.

SECTION 2

The Citizens of each State shall be entitled to all Privileges and Immunities of Citizens in the several States.

A Person charged in any State with Treason, Felony, or other Crime, who shall flee from Justice, and be found in another State, shall on demand of the executive Authority of the State from which he fled, be delivered up, to be removed to the State having Jurisdiction of the crime.

No Person held to Service or Labour in one State, under the Laws thereof, escaping into another, shall, in Consequence of any Law or Regulation therein, be discharged from such Service or Labour, but shall be delivered up on Claim of the Party to whom such Service or Labour may be due.

[5.] Qualified by the Eleventh Amendment.

SECTION 3

New States may be admitted by the Congress into this Union; but no new State shall be formed or erected within the Jurisdiction of any other State; nor any State be formed by the Junction of two or more States, or parts of States, without the Consent of the Legislatures of the States concerned as well as of the Congress.

The Congress shall have Power to dispose of and make all needful Rules and Regulations respecting the Territory or other Property belonging to the United States; and nothing in this Constitution shall be so construed as to Prejudice any Claims of the United States, or of any particular State.

SECTION 4

The United States shall guarantee to every State in this Union a Republican Form of Government, and shall protect each of them against Invasion; and on Application of the Legislature, or of the Executive (when the Legislature cannot be convened) against domestic Violence.

ARTICLE V

The Congress, whenever two-thirds of both Houses shall deem it necessary, shall propose Amendments to this Constitution, or, on the Application of the Legislatures of two-thirds of the several States, shall call a Convention for proposing Amendments, which, in either Case, shall be valid to all Intents and Purposes, as part of this Constitution, when ratified by the Legislatures of three-fourths of the several States, or by Conventions in three-fourths thereof, as the one or the other Mode of Ratification may be proposed by the Congress; Provided that no Amendment which may be made prior to the Year One thousand eight hundred and eight shall in any Manner affect the first and fourth Clauses in the Ninth Section of the first Article; and that no State, without its Consent, shall be deprived of its equal Suffrage in the Senate.

ARTICLE VI

All Debts contracted and Engagements entered into, before the Adoption of this Constitution, shall be as valid against the United States under this Constitution, as under the Confederation.

This Constitution, and the Laws of the United States which shall be made in Pursuance thereof; and all Treaties made, or which shall be made, under the Authority of the United States, shall be the supreme Law of the Land; and the Judges in every State shall be bound thereby, any Thing in the Constitution or Laws of any State to the Contrary notwithstanding.

The Senators and Representatives before mentioned, and the Members of the several State Legislatures, and all executive and judicial Officers, both of the United States and of the several States, shall be bound by Oath or Affirmation to support this Constitution; but no religious Tests shall ever be required as a qualification to any Office or public Trust under the United States.

ARTICLE VII

The Ratification of the Conventions of nine States shall be sufficient for the Establishment of this Constitution between the States so ratifying the same.

Done in Convention by the Unanimous Consent of the States present the Seventeenth Day of September in the Year of our Lord one thousand seven hundred and Eighty seven, and of the Independence of the United States of America the Twelfth. In Witness whereof We have hereunto subscribed our Names.[6]

George Washington
President and deputy from Virginia

New Hampshire
John Langdon
Nicholas Gilman

Massachusetts
Nathaniel Gorham
Rufus King

Connecticut
William Samuel Johnson
Roger Sherman

New York
Alexander Hamilton

New Jersey
William Livingston
David Brearley
William Paterson
Jonathan Dayton

[6.] These are the full names of the signers, which in some cases are not the signatures on the document.

Pennsylvania
Benjamin Franklin
Thomas Mifflin
Robert Morris
George Clymer
Thomas FitzSimmons
Jared Ingersoll
James Wilson
Gouverneur Morris

Delaware
George Read
Gunning Bedford, Jr.
John Dickinson
Richard Bassett
Jacob Broom

Maryland
James McHenry
Daniel of St. Thomas
  Jenifer
Daniel Carroll

Virginia
John Blair
James Madison, Jr.

North Carolina
William Blount
Richard Dobbs Spaight
Hugh Williamson

South Carolina
John Rutledge
Charles Cotesworth
  Pinckney
Charles Pinckney
Pierce Butler

Georgia
William Few
Abraham Baldwin

Articles in Addition to, and Amendment of, the Constitution of the United States of America, Proposed by Congress, and Ratified by the Legislatures of the Several States, Pursuant to the Fifth Article of the Original Constitution[7]

AMENDMENT I

Congress shall make no law respecting an establishment of religion, or prohibiting the free exercise thereof; or abridging the freedom of speech, or of the press; or the right of the people peaceably to assemble, and to petition the Government for a redress of grievances.

AMENDMENT II

A well regulated Militia, being necessary to the security of a free State, the right of the people to keep and bear Arms shall not be infringed.

[7.] This heading appears only in the joint resolution submitting the first ten amendments, which are collectively known as the Bill of Rights. They were ratified on December 15, 1791.

AMENDMENT III

No Soldier shall, in time of peace, be quartered in any house, without the consent of the Owner, nor in time of war, but in a manner to be prescribed by law.

AMENDMENT IV

The right of the people to be secure in their persons, houses, papers, and effects, against unreasonable searches and seizures, shall not be violated, and no Warrants shall issue, but upon probable cause, supported by Oath or affirmation, and particularly describing the place to be searched, and the persons or things to be seized.

AMENDMENT V

No person shall be held to answer for a capital or otherwise infamous crime, unless on a presentment or indictment of a Grand Jury, except in cases arising in the land or naval forces, or in the Militia, when in actual service in time of War or public danger; nor shall any person be subject for the same offence to be twice put in jeopardy of life or limb; nor shall be compelled in any criminal case to be a witness against himself, nor be deprived of life, liberty, or property, without due process of law; nor shall private property be taken for public use, without just compensation.

AMENDMENT VI

In all criminal prosecutions, the accused shall enjoy the right to a speedy and public trial, by an impartial jury of the State and district wherein the crime shall have been committed, which district shall have been previously ascertained by law, and to be informed of the nature and cause of the accusation; to be confronted with the witnesses against him; to have compulsory process for obtaining witnesses in his favour, and to have the Assistance of Counsel for his defence.

AMENDMENT VII

In suits at common law, where the value in controversy shall exceed twenty dollars, the right of trial by jury shall be preserved, and no fact tried by a jury, shall be otherwise reexamined in any Court of the United States, than according to the rules of the common law.

AMENDMENT VIII

Excessive bail shall not be required, nor excessive fines imposed, nor cruel and unusual punishments inflicted.

AMENDMENT IX

The enumeration of the Constitution, of certain rights, shall not be construed to deny or disparage others retained by the people.

AMENDMENT X

The powers not delegated to the United States by the Constitution, nor prohibited by it to the States, are reserved to the States respectively, or to the people.

AMENDMENT XI [1795]

The Judicial power of the United States shall not be construed to extend to any suit in law or equity, commenced or prosecuted against one of the United States by Citizens of another State, or by Citizens or Subjects of any Foreign State.

AMENDMENT XII [1804]

The Electors shall meet in their respective States and vote by ballot for President and Vice-President, one of whom, at least, shall not be an inhabitant of the same State with themselves; they shall name in their ballots the person voted for as President, and in distinct ballots the person voted for as Vice-President, and they shall make distinct lists of all persons voted for as President, and of all persons voted for as Vice-President, and of the number of votes for each, which lists they shall sign and certify, and transmit sealed to the seat of the government of the United States, directed to the President of the Senate;—The President of the Senate shall, in the presence of the Senate and House of Representatives, open all the certificates and the votes shall then be counted;—The person having the greatest number of votes for President, shall be the President, if such number be a majority of the whole number of Electors appointed; and if no person have such majority, then from the persons having the highest numbers not exceeding three on the list of those voted for as President, the House of Representatives shall choose immediately, by ballot, the President. But in choosing the President, the votes shall be taken by states, the representation from each state having one vote; a quorum for this purpose shall consist of a member or members from two-thirds of the states, and a majority of all the states shall be necessary to a choice. And if the House of Representatives shall not choose a President whenever the right of choice shall devolve upon them, before the fourth day of March next following, then the Vice-President shall act as President, as in the case of the death or other constitutional disability of the President.—The person having the greatest number of votes as Vice-President, shall be the Vice-President, if such number be a majority of the whole number of Electors appointed, and if no person have a majority, then from the two highest numbers on the list, the Senate shall choose the Vice-President; a quorum for the purpose shall consist of two-thirds of the whole number of Senators, and majority of the whole number shall be necessary to a choice. But no person constitutionally ineligible to the office of President shall be eligible to that of Vice-President of the United States.

AMENDMENT XIII [1865]
SECTION 1

Neither slavery nor involuntary servitude, except as a punishment for crime whereof the party shall have been duly convicted, shall exist within the United States, or any place subject to their jurisdiction.

SECTION 2

Congress shall have power to enforce this article by appropriate legislation.

AMENDMENT XIV [1868]

SECTION 1

All persons born or naturalized in the United States, and subject to the jurisdiction thereof, are citizens of the United States and of the State wherein they reside. No State shall abridge the privileges or immunities of citizens of the United States; nor shall any State deprive any person of life, liberty, or property, without due process of law; nor deny to any person within its jurisdiction the equal protection of the laws.

SECTION 2

Representatives shall be apportioned among the several States according to their respective numbers, counting the whole number of persons in each State, excluding Indians not taxed. But when the right to vote at any election for the choice of electors for President and Vice-President of the United States, Representatives in Congress, the Executive and Judicial officers of a State, or the members of the Legislature thereof, is denied to any of the male inhabitants of such State, being twenty-one years of age, and citizens of the United States, or in any way abridged, except for participation in rebellion, or other crime, the basis of representation therein shall be reduced in the proportion which the number of such male citizens shall bear to the whole number of male citizens twenty-one years of age in such State.

SECTION 3

No person shall be a Senator or Representative in Congress, or elector of President and Vice-President, or hold any office, civil or military, under the United States, or under any State, who, having previously taken an oath, as a member of Congress, or as an officer of the United States, or as a member of any State legislature, or as an executive or judicial officer of any State, to support the Constitution of the United States, shall have engaged in insurrection or rebellion against the same, or given aid or comfort to the enemies thereof. But Congress may by a vote of two-thirds of each House, remove such disability.

SECTION 4

The validity of the public debt of the United States, authorized by law, including debts incurred for payment of pensions and bounties for services in suppressing insurrection or rebellion, shall not be questioned. But neither the United States nor any State shall assume or pay any debts or obligation incurred in aid of insurrection or rebellion against the United States, or any claim for the loss or emancipation of any slave; but all such debts, obligations, and claims shall be held illegal and void.

SECTION 5

The Congress shall have the power to enforce, by appropriate legislation, the provisions of this article.

AMENDMENT XV [1870]

SECTION 1

The right of citizens of the United States to vote shall not be denied or abridged by the United States or by any State on account of race, color, or previous condition of servitude.

SECTION 2

The Congress shall have power to enforce this article by appropriate legislation.

AMENDMENT XVI [1913]

The Congress shall have power to lay and collect taxes on incomes, from whatever source derived, without apportionment among the several States, and without regard to any census or enumeration.

AMENDMENT XVII [1913]

The Senate of the United States shall be composed of two Senators from each State, elected by the people thereof, for six years; and each Senator shall have one vote. The electors in each State shall have the qualifications requisite for electors of the most numerous branch of the State legislatures.

When vacancies happen in the representation of any State in the Senate, the executive authority of such State shall issue writs of election to fill such vacancies: *Provided,* That the legislature of any State may empower the executive thereof to make temporary appointments until the people fill the vacancies by election as the legislature may direct.

This amendment shall not be so construed as to affect the election or term of any Senator chosen before it becomes valid as part of the Constitution.

AMENDMENT XVIII [1919]

SECTION 1

After one year from the ratification of this article the manufacture, sale, or transportation of intoxicating liquors within, the importation thereof into, or the exportation thereof from the United States and all territory subject to the jurisdiction thereof for beverage purposes is hereby prohibited.

SECTION 2

The Congress and the several States shall have concurrent power to enforce this article by appropriate legislation.

SECTION 3

This article shall be inoperative unless it shall have been ratified as an amendment to the Constitution by the legislatures of the several States, as provided in the Constitution, within seven years from the date of the submission hereof to the States by the Congress.

AMENDMENT XIX [1920]

The right of citizens of the United States to vote shall not be denied or abridged by the United States or by any State on account of sex.

Congress shall have power to enforce this article by appropriate legislation.

AMENDMENT XX [1933]

SECTION 1

The terms of the President and Vice-President shall end at noon on the 20th day of January, and the terms of Senators and Representatives at noon on the 3d day of January, of the years in which such terms would have ended if this article had not been ratified; and the terms of their successors shall then begin.

SECTION 2

The Congress shall assemble at least once in every year, and such meeting shall begin at noon on the 3d day of January, unless they shall by law appoint a different day.

SECTION 3

If, at the time fixed for the beginning of the term of the President, the President elect shall have died, the Vice-President elect shall become President. If a President shall not have been chosen before the time fixed for the beginning of his term or if the President elect shall have failed to qualify, then the Vice-President elect shall act as President until a President shall have qualified; and the Congress may by law provide for the case wherein neither a President elect nor a Vice-President elect shall have qualified, declaring who shall then act as President, or the manner in which one who is to act shall be selected, and such person shall act accordingly until a President or Vice-President shall have qualified.

SECTION 4

The Congress may by law provide for the case of the death of any of the persons from whom the House of Representatives may choose a President whenever the right of choice shall have devolved upon them, and for the case of the death of any of the persons from whom the Senate may choose a Vice-President whenever the right of choice shall have devolved upon them.

SECTION 5

Sections 1 and 2 shall take effect on the 15th day of October following the ratification of this article.

SECTION 6

This article shall be inoperative unless it shall have been ratified as an amendment to the Constitution by the legislatures of three-fourths of the several States within seven years from the date of its submission.

AMENDMENT XXI [1933]

SECTION 1

The eighteenth article of amendment to the Constitution of the United States is hereby repealed.

SECTION 2

The transportation or importation into any State, Territory, or possession of the United States for delivery or use therein of intoxicating liquors, in violation of the laws thereof, is hereby prohibited.

SECTION 3

This article shall be inoperative unless it shall have been ratified as an amendment to the Constitution by conventions in the several States, as provided in the Constitution, within seven years from the date of the submission hereof to the States by the Congress.

AMENDMENT XXII [1951]

No person shall be elected to the office of the President more than twice, and no person who has held the office of President, or acted as President, for more than two years of a term to which some other person was elected President shall be elected to the office of the President more than once.

But this Article shall not apply to any person holding the office of President when this Article was proposed by the Congress, and shall not prevent any person who may be holding the office of President, or acting as President, during the term within which this Article becomes operative from holding the office of President or acting as President during the remainder of such term.

This article shall be inoperative unless it shall have been ratified as an amendment to the Constitution by the legislatures of three-fourths of the several states within seven years from the date of its submission to the states by the Congress.

AMENDMENT XXIII [1961]

SECTION 1

The District constituting the seat of Government of the United States shall appoint in such manner as the Congress may direct:

A number of electors of President and Vice-President equal to the whole number of Senators and Representatives in Congress to which the District would be entitled if it were a State, but in no event more than the least populous State; they shall be in addition to those appointed by the States, but they shall be considered, for the purposes of the election of President and Vice-President, to be electors appointed by a State; and they shall meet in the District and perform such duties as provided by the twelfth article of amendment.

SECTION 2

The Congress shall have power to enforce this article by appropriate legislation.

AMENDMENT XXIV [1964]

SECTION 1

The right of citizens of the United States to vote in any primary or other election for President or Vice President, for electors for President or Vice President, or for Senator or Representative in Congress, shall not be denied or abridged by the United States or any state by reason of failure to pay any poll tax or other tax.

SECTION 2

The Congress shall have the power to enforce this article by appropriate legislation.

AMENDMENT XXV [1967]

SECTION 1

In case of the removal of the President from office or of his death or resignation, the Vice President shall become President.

SECTION 2

Whenever there is a vacancy in the office of the Vice President, the President shall nominate a Vice President who shall take office upon confirmation by a majority vote of both Houses of Congress.

SECTION 3

Whenever the President transmits to the President Pro Tempore of the Senate and the Speaker of the House of Representatives his written declaration that he is unable to discharge the powers and duties of his office, and until he transmits to them a written declaration to the contrary, such powers and duties shall be discharged by the Vice President as Acting President.

SECTION 4

Whenever the Vice President and a majority of either the principal officers of the executive departments or of such other body as Congress may by law provide, transmit to the President Pro Tempore of the Senate and the Speaker of the House of Representatives their written declaration that the President is unable to discharge the powers and duties of his office, the Vice President shall immediately assume the powers and duties of the office as Acting President.

Thereafter, when the President transmits to the President Pro Tempore of the Senate and the Speaker of the House of Representatives his written declaration that no inability exists, he shall resume the powers and duties of his office unless the Vice President and a majority of either the principal officers of the executive departments or of such other body as Congress may by law provide, transmit within four days to the President Pro Tempore of the Senate and the Speaker of the House of Representatives their written declaration that the President is unable to discharge the powers and duties of his office. Thereupon Congress shall decide the issue, assembling within forty-eight hours for that purpose if not in session. If the Congress, within twenty-one days after receipt of the latter written declaration, or, if Congress is not in session, within twenty-one days after Congress is required to assemble, determines by two-thirds vote of both Houses that the President is unable to discharge the powers and duties of his office, the Vice President shall continue to discharge the same as Acting President; otherwise, the President shall resume the powers and duties of his office.

AMENDMENT XXVI [1971]

SECTION 1

The right of citizens of the United States, who are eighteen years of age or older, to vote shall not be denied or abridged by the United States or by any State on account of age.

SECTION 2

The Congress shall have the power to enforce this article by appropriate legislation.

AMENDMENT XXVII [1992]

No law varying the compensation for the service of Senators and Representatives shall take effect until an election of Representatives shall have intervened.

FEDERALIST NO. 10
(JAMES MADISON)

Among the numerous advantages promised by a well-constructed union, none deserves to be more accurately developed than its tendency to break and control the violence of faction. The friend of popular governments never finds himself so much alarmed for their character and fate as when he contemplates their propensity to this dangerous vice. He will not fail, therefore, to set a due value on any plan which, without violating the principles to which he is attached, provides a proper cure for it. The instability, injustice, and confusion introduced into the public councils have, in truth, been the mortal diseases under which popular governments have everywhere perished, as they continue to be the favorite and fruitful topics from which the adversaries to liberty derive their most specious declamations. The valuable improvements made by the American constitutions on the popular models, both ancient and modern, cannot certainly be too much admired; but it would be an unwarrantable partiality to contend that they have as effectually obviated the danger on this side, as was wished and expected. Complaints are everywhere heard from our most considerate and virtuous citizens, equally the friends of public and private faith and of public and personal liberty, that our governments are too unstable, that the public good is disregarded in the conflicts of rival parties, and that measures are too often decided, not according to the rules of justice and the rights of the minor party, but by the superior force of an interested and overbearing majority. However anxiously we may wish that these complaints had no foundation, the evidence of known facts will not permit us to deny that they are in some degree true. It will be found, indeed, on a candid review of our situation, that some of the distresses under which we labor have been erroneously charged on the operation of our governments; but it will be found, at the same time, that other causes will not alone account for many of our heaviest misfortunes; and, particularly, for that prevailing and increasing distrust of public engagements and alarm for private rights which are echoed from one end of the continent to the other. These must be chiefly, if not wholly, effects of the unsteadiness and injustice with which a factious spirit has tainted our public administration.

By a faction I understand a number of citizens, whether amounting to a majority or minority of the whole, who are united and actuated by some common impulse of passion, or of interest, adverse to the rights of other citizens, or to the permanent and aggregate interests of the community.

There are two methods of curing the mischiefs of faction: the one, by removing its causes; the other, by controlling its effects.

There are again two methods of removing the causes of faction: the one, by destroying the liberty which is essential to its existence; the other, by giving to every citizen the same opinions, the same passions, and the same interests.

It could never be more truly said than of the first remedy that it was worse than the disease. Liberty is to faction what air is to fire, an aliment without which it instantly expires. But it could not be a less folly to abolish liberty, which is essential to political life, because it nourishes faction than it would be to wish the annihilation of air, which is essential to animal life, because it imparts to fire its destructive agency.

The second expedient is as impracticable as the first would be unwise. As long as the reason of man continues fallible, and he is at liberty to exercise it, different opinions will be formed. As long as the connection subsists between his reason and his self-love, his opinions and his passions will have a reciprocal influence on each other; and the former will be objects to which the latter will attach themselves. The diversity in the faculties of men, from which the rights of property originate, is not less an insuperable obstacle to a uniformity of interest. The protection of these faculties is the first object of government. From the protection of different and unequal faculties of acquiring property, the possession of different degrees and kinds of property immediately results; and from the influence of these on the sentiments and views of the respective proprietors ensues a division of the society into different interests and parties.

The latent causes of faction are thus sown in the nature of man; and we see them everywhere brought into different degrees of activity, according to the different circumstances of civil society. A zeal for different opinions concerning religion, concerning government, and many other points, as well of speculation as of practice; an attachment to different leaders ambitiously contending for pre-eminence and power; or to persons of other descriptions whose fortunes have been interesting to the human passions, have, in turn, divided mankind into parties, inflamed them with mutual animosity, and rendered them much more disposed to vex and oppress each other than to co-operate for their common good. So strong is this propensity of mankind to fall into mutual animosities that where no substantial occasion presents itself the most frivolous and fanciful distinctions have been sufficient to kindle their unfriendly passions and excite their most violent conflicts. But the most common and durable source of factions has been the various and unequal distribution of property. Those who hold and those who are without property have ever formed distinct interests in society. Those who are creditors, and those who are debtors, fall under a like discrimination. A landed interest, a manufacturing interest, a mercantile interest, a moneyed interest, with many lesser interests, grow up of necessity in civilized nations, and divide them into different classes, actuated by different sentiments and views. The regulation of these various and interfering interests forms the principal task of modern legislation and involves the spirit of party and faction in the necessary and ordinary operations of government.

No man is allowed to be a judge in his own cause, because his interest would certainly bias his judgment, and, not improbably, corrupt his integrity. With equal, nay with greater reason, a body of men are unfit to be both judges and parties at the same time; yet what are many of the most important acts of legislation but so many judicial determinations, not indeed concerning the rights of single persons, but concerning the rights of large bodies of citizens? And what are the different classes of legislators but advocates and parties to the causes which they determine? Is a law proposed concerning private debts? It is a question to which the creditors are parties on one side and the debtors on the other. Justice ought to hold the balance between them. Yet the parties are, and must be, themselves the judges; and the most numerous party, or in other words, the most powerful faction must be expected to prevail. Shall domestic manufacturers be encouraged, and in what degree, by restrictions on foreign manufacturers? [These] are questions which would be differently decided by the landed and the manufacturing classes, and probably by neither with a sole regard to justice and the public good. The apportionment of taxes on the various descriptions of property is an act which seems to require the most exact impartiality; yet there is, perhaps, no legislative act in which greater opportunity and temptation are given to a predominant party to trample on the rules of justice. Every shilling with which they overburden the inferior number is a shilling saved to their own pockets.

It is in vain to say that enlightened statesmen will be able to adjust these clashing interests and render them all subservient to the public good. Enlightened statesmen will not always be at the helm. Nor, in many cases, can such an adjustment be made at all without taking into view indirect and remote considerations, which will rarely prevail over the immediate interest which one party may find in disregarding the rights of another or the good of the whole.

The inference to which we are brought is that the *causes* of faction cannot be removed and that relief is only to be sought in the means of controlling its *effects*.

If a faction consists of less than a majority, relief is supplied by the republican principle, which enables the majority to defeat its sinister views by regular vote. It may clog the administration, it may convulse the society; but it will be unable to execute and mask its violence under the forms of the Constitution. When a majority is included in a faction, the form of popular government, on the other hand, enables it to sacrifice to its ruling passion or interest both the public good and the rights of other citizens. To secure the public good and private rights against the danger of such a faction, and at the same time to preserve the spirit and the form of popular government, is then the great object to which our inquiries are directed. Let me add that it is the great desideratum by which alone this form of government can be rescued from the opprobrium under which it has so long labored and be recommended to the esteem and adoption of mankind.

By what means is this object attainable? Evidently by one of two only. Either the existence of the same passion or interest in a majority at the same time must be prevented, or the majority, having such coexistent passion or interest, must be rendered, by their number and local situation, unable to concert and carry into effect schemes of oppression. If the impulse and the opportunity be suffered to coincide, we well know that neither moral nor religious motives can be relied on as an adequate control. They are not found to be such on the injustice and violence of individuals, and lose their efficacy in proportion to the number combined together, that is, in proportion as their efficacy becomes needful.

From this view of the subject it may be concluded that a pure democracy, by which I mean a society consisting of a small number of citizens, who assemble and administer the government in person, can admit of no cure for the mischiefs of faction. A common passion or interest will, in almost every case, be felt by a majority of the whole, a communication and concert result from the form of government itself; and there is nothing to check the inducements to sacrifice the weaker party or an obnoxious individual. Hence it is that such democracies have ever been spectacles of turbulence and contention; have ever been found incompatible with personal security or the rights of property; and have in general been as short in their lives as they have been violent in their deaths. Theoretic politicians, who have patronized this species of government, have erroneously supposed that by reducing mankind to a perfect equality in their political rights, they would at the same time be perfectly equalized and assimilated in their possessions, their opinions, and their passions.

A republic, by which I mean a government in which the scheme of representation takes place, opens a different prospect and promises the cure for which we are seeking. Let us examine the points in which it varies from pure democracy, and we shall comprehend both the nature of the cure and the efficacy which it must derive from the Union.

The two great points of difference between a democracy and a republic are: first, the delegation of the government, in the latter, to a small number of citizens elected by the rest; secondly, the greater number of citizens and greater sphere of country over which the latter may be extended.

The effect of the first difference is, on the one hand, to refine and enlarge the public views by passing them through the medium of a chosen body of citizens, whose wisdom may best discern the true interest of their country and whose patriotism and love of justice will be least likely to sacrifice it to temporary or partial considerations. Under such a regulation it may well happen that the public voice, pronounced by the representatives of the people, will be more consonant to the public good than if pronounced by the people themselves, convened for the purpose. On the other hand, the effect may be inverted. Men of factious tempers, of local prejudices, or of sinister designs, may, by intrigue, by corruption, or by other means, first obtain the suffrages, and then betray the interests of the people. The question resulting is, whether small or extensive republics are most favorable to the election of proper guardians of the public weal; and it is clearly decided in favor of the latter by two obvious considerations.

In the first place it is to be remarked that however small the republic may be the representatives must be raised to a certain number in order to guard against the cabals of a few; and that however large it may be they must be limited to a certain number in order to guard against the confusion of a multitude. Hence, the number of representatives in the two cases not being in proportion to that of the constituents, and being proportionally greatest in the small republic, it follows that if the proportion of fit characters be not less in the large than in the small republic, the former will present a greater option, and consequently a greater probability of a fit choice.

In the next place, as each representative will be chosen by a greater number of citizens in the large than in the small republic, it will be more difficult for unworthy candidates to practice with success the vicious arts by which elections are too often carried; and the suffrages of the people being more free, will be more likely to center on men who possess the most attractive merit and the most diffusive and established characters.

It must be confessed that in this, as in most other cases, there is a mean, on both sides of which inconveniencies will be found to lie. By enlarging too much the number of electors, you render the representative too little acquainted with all their local circumstances and lesser interests; as by reducing it too much, you render him unduly attached to these, and too little fit to comprehend and pursue great and national objects. The federal Constitution forms a happy combination in this respect; the great and aggregate interests being referred to the national, the local and particular to the State legislatures.

The other point of difference is the greater number of citizens and extent of territory which may be brought within the compass of republican than of democratic government; and it is this circumstance principally which renders factious combinations less to be dreaded in the former than in the latter. The smaller the society, the fewer probably will be the distinct parties and interests composing it; the fewer the distinct parties and interests, the more frequently will a majority be found of the same party; and the smaller the number of individuals composing a majority, and the smaller the compass within which they are placed, the more easily will they concert and execute their plans of oppression. Extend the sphere and you take in a greater variety of parties and interests; you make it less probable that a majority of the whole will have a common motive to invade the rights of other citizens; or if such a common motive exists, it will be more difficult for all who feel it to discover their own strength and to act in unison with each other. Besides other impediments, it may be remarked that, where there is a consciousness of unjust or dishonorable purposes, communication is always checked by distrust in proportion to the number whose concurrence is necessary.

Hence, it clearly appears that the same advantage which a republic has over a democracy in controlling the effects of faction is enjoyed by a large over a small republic—is enjoyed by the Union over the States composing it. Does this advantage consist in the substitution of representatives whose enlightened views and virtuous sentiments render them superior to local prejudices and to schemes of injustice? It will not be denied that the representation of the Union will be most likely to possess these requisite endowments. Does it consist in the greater security afforded by a greater variety of parties, against the event of any one party being able to outnumber and oppress the rest? In an equal degree does the increased variety of parties comprised within the Union increase this security. Does it, in fine, consist in the greater obstacles opposed to the concert and accomplishment of the secret wishes of an unjust and interested majority? Here again the extent of the Union gives it the most palpable advantage.

The influence of factious leaders may kindle a flame within their particular States but will be unable to spread a general conflagration through the other States. A religious sect may degenerate into a political faction in a part of the Confederacy; but the variety of sects dispersed over the entire face of it must secure the national councils against any danger from that source. A rage for paper money, for an abolition of debts, for an equal division of property, or for any other improper or wicked project, will be less apt to pervade the whole body of the Union than a particular member of it, in the same proportion as such a malady is more likely to taint a particular county or district than an entire State.

In the extent and proper structure of the Union, therefore, we behold a republican remedy for the diseases most incident to republican government. And according to the degree of pleasure and pride we feel in being republicans ought to be our zeal in cherishing the spirit and supporting the character of Federalists.

FEDERALIST NO. 51
(JAMES MADISON)

To what expedient, then, shall we finally resort, for maintaining in practice the necessary partition of power among the several departments as laid down in the Constitution? The only answer that can be given is that as all these exterior provisions are found to be inadequate, the defect must be supplied, by so contriving the interior structure of the government as that its several constituent parts may, by their mutual relations, be the means of keeping each other in their proper places. Without presuming to undertake a full development of this important idea I will hazard a few general observations which may perhaps place it in a clearer light, and enable us to form a more correct judgment of the principles and structure of the government planned by the convention.

In order to lay a due foundation for that separate and distinct exercise of the different powers of government, which to a certain extent is admitted on all hands to be essential to the preservation of liberty, it is evident that each department should have a will of its own; and consequently should be so constituted that the members of each should have as little agency as possible in the appointment of the members of the others. Were this principle rigorously adhered to, it would require that all the appointments for the supreme executive, legislative, and judiciary magistracies should be drawn from the same fountain of authority, the people, through channels having no communication whatever with one another. Perhaps such a plan of constructing the several departments would be less difficult in practice than it may be in contemplation appear. Some difficulties, however, and some additional expense would attend the execution of it. Some deviations, therefore, from the principle must be admitted. In the constitution of the judiciary department in particular, it might be inexpedient to insist rigorously on the principle; first, because peculiar qualifications being essential in the members, the primary consideration ought to be to select that mode of choice which best secures these qualifications; second, because the permanent tenure by which the appointments are held in that department must soon destroy all sense of dependence on the authority conferring them.

It is equally evident that the members of each department should be as little dependent as possible on those of the others for the emoluments annexed to their offices. Were the executive magistrate, or the judges, not independent of the legislature in this particular, their independence in every other would be merely nominal.

But the great security against a gradual concentration of the several powers in the same department consists in giving to those who administer each department the necessary constitutional means and personal motives to resist encroachments of the others. The provision for defense must in this, as in all other cases, be made commensurate to the danger of attack. Ambition must be made to counteract ambition. The interest of the man must be connected with the constitutional rights of the place. It may be a reflection on human nature that such devices should be necessary to control the abuses of government. But what is government itself but the greatest of all reflections on human nature? If men were angels no government would be necessary. If angels were to govern men, neither external nor internal controls on government would be necessary. In framing a government which is to be administered by men over men, the great difficulty lies in this: you must first enable the government to control the governed; and in the next place oblige it to control itself. A dependence on the people is, no doubt, the primary control on the government; but experience has taught mankind the necessity of auxiliary precautions.

This policy of supplying, by opposite and rival interests, the defect of better motives, might be traced through the whole system of human affairs, private as well as public. We see it particularly displayed in all the subordinate distributions of power, where the constant aim is to divide and arrange the several offices in such a manner as that each may be a check on the other—that the private interest of every individual may be a sentinel over the public rights. These inventions of prudence cannot be less requisite in the distribution of the supreme powers of the State.

But it is not possible to give to each department an equal power of self-defense. In republican government, the legislative authority necessarily predominates. The remedy for this inconveniency is to divide the legislature into different branches; and to render them, by different modes of election and different principles of action, as little connected with each other as the nature of their common functions and their common dependence on the society will admit. It may even be necessary to guard against dangerous encroachments by still further precautions. As the weight of the legislative authority requires that it should be thus divided, the weakness of the executive may require, on the other hand, that it should be fortified. An absolute negative on the legislature appears, at first view, to be the natural defense with which the executive magistrate should be armed. But perhaps it would be neither altogether safe nor alone sufficient. On ordinary occasions it might not be exerted with the requisite firmness, and on extraordinary occasions it might be perfidiously abused. May not this defect of an absolute negative be supplied by some qualified connection between this weaker department and the weaker branch of the stronger department, by which the latter may be led to support the constitutional rights of the former, without being too much detached from the rights of its own department?

If the principles on which these observations are founded be just, as I persuade myself they are, and they be applied as a criterion to the several State constitutions, and to the federal Constitution, it will be found that if the latter does not perfectly correspond with them, the former are infinitely less able to bear such a test.

There are, moreover, two considerations particularly applicable to the federal system of America, which place that system in a very interesting point of view.

First. In a single republic, all the power surrendered by the people is submitted to the administration of a single government; and the usurpations are guarded against by a division of the government into distinct and separate departments. In the compound republic of America, the power surrendered by the people is first divided between two distinct governments, and then the portion allotted to each subdivided among distinct and separate departments. Hence a double security arises to the rights of the people. The different governments will control each other, at the same time that each will be controlled by itself.

Second. It is of great importance in a republic not only to guard the society against the oppression of its rulers, but to guard one part of the society against the injustice of the other part. Different interests necessarily exist in different classes of citizens. If a majority be united by a common interest, the rights of the minority will be insecure. There are but two methods of providing against this evil: the one by creating a will in the community independent of the majority—that is, of the society itself; the other, by comprehending in the society so many separate descriptions of citizens as will render an unjust combination of a majority of the whole very improbable, if not impracticable. The first method prevails in all governments possessing an hereditary or self-appointed authority. This, at best, is but a precarious security; because a power independent of the society may as well espouse the unjust views of the major as the rightful interests of the minor party, and may possibly be turned against both parties. The second method will be exemplified in the federal republic of the United States. Whilst all authority in it will be derived from and dependent on the society, the society itself will be broken into so many parts, interests and classes of citizens, that the rights of individuals, or of the minority, will be in little danger from interested combinations of the majority. In a free government the security for civil rights must be the same as that for religious rights. It consists in the one case in the multiplicity of interests, and in the other in the multiplicity of sects. The degree of security in both cases will depend on the number of interests and sects; and this may be presumed to depend on the extent of country and number of people comprehended under the same government. This view of the subject must particularly recommend a proper federal system to all the sincere and considerate friends of republican government, since it shows that in exact proportion as the territory of the Union may be formed into more circumscribed Confederacies, or States, oppressive combinations of a majority will be facilitated; the best security, under the republican forms, for the rights of every class of citizen, will be diminished; and consequently the stability and independence of some member of the government, the only other security, must be proportionately increased. Justice is the end of government. It is the end of civil society. It ever has been and ever will be pursued until it be obtained, or until liberty be lost in the pursuit. In a society under the forms of which the stronger faction can readily unite and oppress the weaker, anarchy may as truly be said to reign as in a state of nature, where the weaker individual is not secured against the violence of the stronger; and as, in the latter state, even the stronger individuals are prompted, by the uncertainty of their condition, to submit to a government which may protect the weak as well as themselves; so, in the former state, will the more powerful factions or parties be gradually induced, by a like motive, to wish for a government which will protect all parties, the weaker as well as the more powerful. It can be little doubted that if the State of Rhode Island was separated from the Confederacy and left to itself, the insecurity of rights under the popular form of government within such narrow limits would be displayed by such reiterated oppressions of factious majorities that some power altogether independent of the people would soon be called for by the voice of the very factions whose misrule had proved the necessity of it. In the extended republic of the United States, and among the great variety of interests, parties, and sects which it embraces, a coalition of a majority of the whole society could seldom take place on any other principles than those of justice and the general good; whilst there being thus less danger to a minor from the will of a major party, there must be less pretext, also, to provide for the security of the former, by introducing into the government a will not dependent on the latter, or, in other words, a will independent of the society itself. It is no less certain than it is important, notwithstanding the contrary opinions which have been entertained, that the larger the society, provided it lie within a practicable sphere, the more duly capable it will be of self-government. And happily for the *republican cause*, the practicable sphere may be carried to a very great extent by a judicious modification and mixture of the federal principle.

GLOSSARY

affirmative action A term that refers to programs designed to ensure that women, minorities, and other traditionally disadvantaged groups have full and equal opportunities in employment, education, and other areas of life.

age-cohort tendency The tendency for a significant break in the pattern of political socialization to occur among younger citizens, usually as the result of a major event or development that disrupts preexisting beliefs.

agency point of view The tendency of bureaucrats to place the interests of their agency ahead of other interests and ahead of the priorities sought by the president or Congress.

agenda setting The power of the media through news coverage to focus the public's attention and concern on particular events, problems, issues, personalities, and so on.

agents of socialization Those agents, such as the family and the media, that have significant impact on citizens' political socialization.

air wars A term that refers to the fact that modern campaigns are often a battle of opposing televised advertising campaigns.

alienation A feeling of personal powerlessness that includes the notion that government does not care about the opinions of people like oneself.

Anti-Federalists A term used to describe opponents of the Constitution during the debate over ratification.

apathy A feeling of personal noninterest or unconcern with politics.

appellate jurisdiction The authority of a given court to review cases that have already been tried in lower courts and are appealed to it by the losing party; such a court is called an appeals court or appellate court. (See also **original jurisdiction.**)

authoritarian government A form of government in which leaders, though they admit to no limits on their powers, are effectively limited by other centers of power in the society.

authority The recognized right of an individual or institution to exercise power. (See also **power.**)

autocracy A form of government in which absolute control rests with a single person.

balanced budget When the government's tax revenues for the year are roughly equal to its expenditures.

bicameral legislatures Legislatures having two chambers.

bill A proposed law (legislative act) within Congress or another legislature. (See also **law.**)

Bill of Rights The first ten amendments to the Constitution. They include such rights as freedom of speech and trial by jury.

bipolar (power structure) A power structure dominated by two powers only, as in the case of the United States and the Soviet Union during the cold war.

block grants Federal grants-in-aid that permit state and local officials to decide how the money will be spent within a general area, such as education or health. (See also **categorical grants.**)

brief A written statement by a party in a court case that details its argument.

budget deficit When the government's expenditures exceed its tax revenues.

budget surplus When the government's tax and other revenues exceed its expenditures.

bureaucracy A system of organization and control based on the principles of hierarchical authority, job specialization, and formalized rules. (See also **formalized rules; hierarchical authority; job specialization.**)

bureaucratic accountability The degree to which bureaucrats are held accountable for the power they exercise.

bureaucratic rule The tendency of large-scale organizations to develop into the bureaucratic form, with the effect that administrators make key policy decisions.

cabinet A group consisting of the heads of the (cabinet) executive departments, who are appointed by the president, subject to confirmation by the Senate. The cabinet was once the main advisory body to the president but no longer plays this role. (See also **cabinet departments.**)

cabinet (executive) departments The major administrative organizations within the federal executive bureaucracy, each of which is headed by a secretary (cabinet officer) and has responsibility for a major function of the federal government, such as defense, agriculture, or justice. (See also **cabinet; independent agencies.**)

candidate-centered politics Election campaigns and other political processes in which candidates, not political parties, have most of the initiative and influence. (See also **party-centered politics.**)

capital-gains tax Tax that individuals pay on money gained from the sale of a capital asset, such as property or stocks.

capitalism An economic system based on the idea that government should interfere with economic transactions as little as possible. Free enterprise and self-reliance are the collective and individual principles that underpin capitalism.

categorical grants Federal grants-in-aid to states and localities that can be used only for designated projects. (See also **block grants.**)

charter The chief instrument by which a state governs its local units; it spells out in detail what a local government can and cannot do.

checks and balances The elaborate system of divided spheres of authority provided by the U.S. Constitution as a means of controlling the power of government. The separation of powers among the branches of the national government, federalism, and the different methods of selecting national officers are all part of this system.

citizens' (noneconomic) groups Organized interests formed by individuals drawn together by opportunities to promote a cause in which they believe but that does not provide them significant individual economic benefits. (See also **economic groups; interest group.**)

city manager system Form of municipal government that entrusts the executive role to a professionally trained manager, who is chosen, and can be fired, by the city council.

civic duty The belief of an individual that civic and political participation is a responsibility of citizenship.

civil law cases Disputes between parties where no criminal act is alleged and where the parties are making conflicting claims, as in a property dispute.

civil liberties The fundamental individual rights of a free society, such as freedom of speech and the right to a jury trial, which in the United States are protected by the Bill of Rights.

civil rights (equal rights) The right of every person to equal protection under the laws and equal access to society's opportunities and public facilities.

civil service system See **merit system.**

clear-and-present-danger test A test devised by the Supreme Court in 1919 to define the limits of free speech in the context of national security. According to the test, government cannot abridge political expression unless it presents a clear and present danger to the nation's security.

clientele groups Special-interest groups that benefit directly from the activities of a particular bureaucratic agency and are therefore strong advocates of the agency.

cloture A parliamentary maneuver that, if a three-fifths majority votes for it, limits Senate debate to thirty hours and has the effect of defeating a filibuster. (See also **filibuster.**)

cold war The lengthy period after World War II when the United States and the USSR were not engaged in actual combat (a "hot war") but were nonetheless locked in a state of deep-seated hostility.

collective (public) goods Benefits that are offered by groups (usually citizens' groups) as an incentive for membership but that are nondivisible (e.g., a clean environment) and therefore are available to nonmembers as well as members of the particular group. (See also **free-rider problem; private goods.**)

commerce clause The clause of the Constitution (Article I, Section 8) that empowers the federal government to regulate commerce among the states and with other nations.

commission system Form of municipal government that invests executive and legislative authority in a commission, with each commissioner serving as a member of the local council but also having a specified executive role, such as police commissioner or public works commissioner.

common-carrier role The media's function as an open channel through which political leaders can communicate with the public. (See also **public-representative role; signaler role; watchdog role.**)

communism An economic system in which government owns most or all major industries and also takes responsibility for overall management of the economy.

compliance The issue of whether a court's decisions will be respected and obeyed.

concurring opinion A separate opinion written by a Supreme Court justice who votes with the majority in the decision on a case but who disagrees with their reasoning. (See also **dissenting opinion; majority opinion; plurality opinion.**)

confederacy A governmental system in which sovereignty is vested entirely in subnational (state) governments. (See also **federalism; unitary system.**)

conference committees Temporary committees that are formed to bargain over the differences in the House and Senate versions of a bill. The committee's members are usually appointed from the House and Senate standing committees that originally worked on the bill.

conservatives Those who believe government does too many things that should be left to firms and individuals but look to government to uphold traditional social values. (See also **liberals; libertarians; populists.**)

constituency The individuals who live within the geographical area represented by an elected official. More narrowly, the body of citizens eligible to vote for a particular representative.

constitution The fundamental law that defines how a government will legitimately operate.

constitutional democracy A government that is democratic in its provisions for majority influence through elections and constitutional in its provisions for minority rights and rule by law.

constitutional initiative The process by which a citizen or group can petition to place a proposed amendment on the ballot at the next election by obtaining the signatures of a certain number of registered voters, and if the amendment gets majority support, it becomes part of the constitution.

constitutionalism The idea that there are definable limits on the rightful power of a government over its citizens.

containment A doctrine, developed after World War II, based on the assumptions that the Soviet Union was an aggressor nation and that only a determined United States could block Soviet territorial ambitions.

Cooley's rule The term used to describe the idea that cities should be self-governing, articulated in an 1871 ruling by Michigan judge Thomas Cooley.

cooperative federalism The situation in which the national, state, and local levels work together to solve problems.

criminal law cases Disputes in which an individual is charged by government with engaging in an act that is prohibited by law.

de facto discrimination Discrimination on the basis of race, sex, religion, ethnicity, and the like that results from social, economic, and cultural biases and conditions. (See also **de jure discrimination.**)

de jure discrimination Discrimination on the basis of race, sex, religion, ethnicity, and the like that results from a law. (See also **de facto discrimination.**)

decision A vote of the Supreme Court in a particular case that indicates which party the justices side with and by how large a margin.

deficit spending When the government spends more than it collects in taxes and other revenues.

delegates Elected representatives whose obligation is to act in accordance with the expressed wishes of the people whom they represent. (See also **trustees.**)

demand-side economics A form of fiscal policy that emphasizes "demand" (consumer spending). Government can use increased spending or tax cuts to place more money in consumers' hands and thereby increase demand. (See also **fiscal policy; supply-side economics.**)

democracy A form of government in which the people govern, either directly or through elected representatives.

demographic representativeness The idea that the bureaucracy will be more responsive to the public if its employees at all levels are demographically representative of the population as a whole.

denials of power A constitutional means of limiting governmental action by listing those powers that government is expressly prohibited from using.

deregulation The rescinding of excessive government regulations for the purpose of improving economic efficiency.

descriptive reporting The style of reporting that aims to describe what is taking place or has occurred.

détente A French word meaning "a relaxing" and used to refer to an era of improved relations between the United States and the Soviet Union that began in the early 1970s.

deterrence The idea that nuclear war can be discouraged if each side in a conflict has the capacity to destroy the other with nuclear weapons.

devolution The passing down of authority from the national government to states and localities.

Dillon's rule The term used to describe relations between state and local government; it holds that local governments are creatures of the state, which in theory even has the power to abolish them.

direct primary See **primary election.**

dissenting opinion The opinion of a justice in a Supreme Court case that explains his or her reasons for disagreeing with the majority's decision. (See also **concurring opin-**

ion; majority opinion; plurality opinion.)

diversity The principle that individual and group differences should be respected and are a source of national strength.

dual federalism A doctrine based on the idea that a precise separation of national power and state power is both possible and desirable.

due process clause (of the Fourteenth Amendment) The clause of the Constitution that has been used by the judiciary to apply the Bill of Rights to the actions of state governments.

economic depression A very severe and sustained economic downturn. Depressions are rare in the United States: the last one was in the 1930s.

economic globalization The increased interdependence of nations' economies. The change is a result of technological, transportation, and communication advances that have enabled firms to deploy their resources across the globe.

economic groups Interest groups that are organized primarily for economic reasons but that engage in political activity in order to seek favorable policies from government. (See also **citizens' groups; interest group.**)

economic recession A moderate but sustained downturn in the economy. Recessions are part of the economy's normal cycle of ups and downs.

economy A system of production and consumption of goods and services that are allocated through exchange among producers and consumers.

effective tax rate The actual percentage of a person's income that is spent to pay taxes.

efficiency An economic principle that holds that firms should fulfill as many of society's needs as possible while using as few of its resources as possible. The greater the output (production) for a given input (for example, an hour of labor), the more efficient the process.

elastic clause See "**necessary and proper**" **clause.**

Electoral College An unofficial term that refers to the electors who cast the states' electoral votes.

electoral votes The method of voting that is used to choose the U.S. president. Each state has the same number of electoral votes as it has members in Congress (House and Senate combined). By tradition, electoral voting is tied to a state's popular voting; thus, the presidential candidate with the most popular votes overall has usually also had the most electoral votes.

elitism The view that the United States is essentially run by a tiny elite (composed of wealthy or well-connected individuals) who control public policy through both direct and indirect means.

entitlement program Any of a number of individual benefit programs, such as social security, that require government to provide a designated benefit to any person who meets the legally defined criteria for eligibility.

enumerated (expressed) powers The seventeen powers granted to the national government under Article I, Section 8 of the Constitution. These powers include taxation and the regulation of commerce as well as the authority to provide for the national defense.

equal-protection clause A clause of the Fourteenth Amendment that forbids any state to deny equal protection of the laws to any individual within its jurisdiction.

equal rights See **civil rights.**

equality The notion that all individuals are equal in their moral worth, in their treatment under the law, and in their political voice.

equality of opportunity The idea that all individuals should be given an equal chance to succeed on their own.

equality of result The objective of policies intended to reduce or eliminate the effects of discrimination so that members of traditionally disadvantaged groups will have

the same benefits of society as do members of advantaged groups.

equity (in relation to economic policy) The situation in which the outcome of an economic transaction is fair to each party. An outcome can usually be considered fair if each party enters into a transaction freely and is not knowingly at a disadvantage.

establishment clause The First Amendment provision that government may not favor one religion over another or favor religion over no religion, and that prohibits Congress from passing laws respecting the establishment of religion.

exclusionary rule The legal principle that government is prohibited from using in trials evidence that was obtained by unconstitutional means (for example, illegal search and seizure).

executive departments See **cabinet departments.**

executive leadership system An approach to managing the bureaucracy that is based on presidential leadership and presidential management tools, such as the president's annual budget proposal. (See also **merit system; patronage system.**)

expressed powers See **enumerated powers.**

externalities Burdens that society incurs when firms fail to pay the full cost of resources used in production. An example of an externality is the pollution that results when corporations dump industrial wastes into lakes and rivers.

facts (of a court case) The relevant circumstances of a legal dispute or offense as determined by a trial court. The facts of a case are crucial because they help determine which law or laws are applicable in the case.

federalism A governmental system in which authority is divided between two sovereign levels of government: national and regional. (See also **confederacy; unitary system.**)

Federalists A term used to describe supporters of the Constitution during the debate over ratification.

filibuster A procedural tactic in the U.S. Senate whereby a minority of legislators prevents a bill from coming to a vote by holding the floor and talking until the majority gives in and the bill is withdrawn from consideration. (See also **cloture.**)

fiscal federalism A term that refers to the expenditure of federal funds on programs run in part through states and localities.

fiscal policy A tool of economic management by which government attempts to maintain a stable economy through its taxing and spending decisions. (See also **demand-side economics; monetary policy; supply-side economics.**)

formalized rules A basic principle of bureaucracy that refers to the standardized procedures and established regulations by which a bureaucracy conducts its operations. (See also **bureaucracy.**)

free-exercise clause A First Amendment provision that prohibits the government from interfering with the practice of religion or prohibiting the free exercise of religion.

free-rider problem The situation in which the benefits offered by a group to its members are also available to nonmembers. The incentive to join the group and to promote its cause is reduced because nonmembers (free riders) receive the benefits (e.g., a cleaner environment) without having to pay any of the group's costs. (See also **collective goods.**)

free-trade position The view that the long-term economic interests of all countries are advanced when tariffs and other trade barriers are kept to a minimum. (See also **protectionism.**)

freedom of expression Americans' freedom to communicate their views, the foundation of which is the First Amendment rights of freedom of conscience, speech, press, assembly, and petition.

gender gap The tendency of women and men to differ in their political attitudes and voting preferences.

gerrymandering The process by which the party in power draws election district boundaries in a way that advantages its candidates.

government corporations Bodies, such as the U.S. Postal Service and Amtrak, that are similar to private corporations in that they charge for their services, but different in that they receive federal funding to help defray expenses. Their directors are appointed by the president with Senate approval.

graduated personal income tax A tax on personal income in which the tax rate increases as income increases; in other words, the tax rate is higher for higher income levels.

grants-in-aid Federal cash payments to states and localities for programs they administer.

grants of power The method of limiting the U.S. government by confining its scope of authority to those powers expressly granted in the Constitution.

grassroots lobbying A form of lobbying designed to persuade officials that a group's policy position has strong constituent support.

grassroots party A political party organized at the level of the voters and dependent on their support for its strength.

Great Compromise The agreement of the constitutional convention to create a two-chamber Congress with the House apportioned by population and the Senate apportioned equally by state.

hard money Campaign funds given directly to candidates to spend as they choose.

hierarchical authority A basic principle of bureaucracy that refers to the chain of command within an organization whereby officials and units have control over those below them. (See also **bureaucracy**.)

hired guns The professional consultants who run campaigns for high office.

home rule A device designed to give local governments more leeway in their policies; it allows a local government to design and amend its own charter, subject to the laws and constitution of the state and also subject to veto by the state.

honeymoon period The president's first months in office, a time when Congress, the press, and the public are more inclined than usual to support presidential initiatives.

ideology A consistent pattern of opinion on particular issues that stems from a core belief or set of beliefs.

imminent lawless action test A legal test that says government cannot lawfully suppress advocacy that promotes lawless action unless such advocacy is aimed at producing, and is likely to produce, imminent lawless action.

implied powers The federal government's constitutional authority (through the "necessary and proper" clause) to take action that is not expressly authorized by the Constitution but that supports actions that are so authorized. (See also **"necessary and proper" clause**.)

in-kind benefit A government benefit that is a cash equivalent, such as food stamps or rent vouchers. This form of benefit ensures that recipients will use public assistance in a specified way.

inalienable (natural) rights Those rights that persons theoretically possessed in the state of nature, prior to the formation of governments. These rights, including those of life, liberty, and property, are considered inherent and as such are inalienable. Since government is established by people, government has the responsibility to preserve these rights.

independent agencies Bureaucratic agencies that are similar to cabinet departments but usually have a narrower area of responsibility. Each such agency is headed by a presidential appointee who is not a cabinet member. An example is the

National Aeronautics and Space Administration. (See also **cabinet departments**.)

individual goods See **private goods**.

individualism The idea that people should take the initiative, be self-sufficient, and accumulate the material advantages necessary for their well-being.

inflation A general increase in the average level of prices of goods and services.

initiative The process by which citizens can place legislative measures on the ballot through signature petitions, and if the measure receives a majority vote, it becomes law.

inside lobbying Direct communication between organized interests and policymakers, which is based on the assumed value of close ("inside") contacts with policymakers.

insurgency A type of military conflict in which irregular soldiers rise up against an established regime.

interest group A set of individuals who are organized to promote a shared political interest. (See also **citizens' groups; economic groups**.)

interest-group liberalism The tendency of public officials to support the policy demands of self-interested groups (as opposed to judging policy demands according to whether they serve a larger conception of "the public interest").

intermediate-scrutiny test A test applied by courts to laws that attempt a gender classification. In effect, the test eliminates gender as a legal classification unless it serves an important objective and is substantially related to the objective's achievement.

internationalist A person who holds the view that the country should involve itself deeply in world affairs. (See also **isolationist**.)

interpretive reporting The style of reporting that aims to explain *why* something is taking place or has occurred.

iron triangle A small and informal but relatively stable group of well-positioned legislators, executives, and lobbyists who seek to promote policies beneficial to a particular interest. (See also **issue network.**)

isolationist A person who holds the view that the country should deliberately avoid a large role in world affairs and, instead, concentrate on domestic concerns. (See **also internationalist.**)

issue network An informal network of public officials and lobbyists who have a common interest and expertise in a given area and who are brought together temporarily by a proposed policy in that area. (See also **iron triangle.**)

job specialization A basic principle of bureaucracy that holds that the responsibilities of each job position should be explicitly defined and that a precise division of labor within the organization should be maintained. (See also **bureaucracy.**)

judicial activism The doctrine that the courts should develop new legal principles when judges see a compelling need, even if this action places them in conflict with the policy decisions of elected officials. (See also **judicial restraint.**)

judicial conference A closed meeting of the justices of the U.S. Supreme Court to discuss and vote on the cases before them; the justices are not supposed to discuss conference proceedings with outsiders.

judicial restraint The doctrine that the judiciary should be highly respectful of precedent and should defer to the judgment of legislatures. The doctrine claims that the job of judges is to work within the confines of laws set down by tradition and lawmaking majorities. (See also **judicial activism.**)

judicial review The power of courts to decide whether a governmental institution has acted within its constitutional powers and, if not, to declare its action null and void.

jurisdiction (of a congressional committee) The policy area in which a particular congressional committee is authorized to act.

jurisdiction (of a court) A given court's authority to hear cases of a particular kind. Jurisdiction may be original or appellate.

laissez-faire doctrine A classic economic philosophy that holds that owners of businesses should be allowed to make their own production and distribution decisions without government regulation or control.

large-state plan See **Virginia Plan.**

law (as enacted by Congress) A legislative proposal, or bill, that is passed by both the House and Senate and is either signed or not vetoed by the president. (See also **bill.**)

lawmaking function The authority (of a legislature) to make the laws necessary to carry out the government's powers. (See also **oversight function; representation function.**)

laws (of a court case) The constitutional provisions, legislative statutes, or judicial precedents that apply to a court case.

legitimacy (of election) The idea that the selection of officeholders should be based on the will of the people as reflected through their votes.

legitimacy (of judicial power) The issue of the proper limits of judicial authority in a political system based in part on the principle of majority rule.

libel Publication of material that falsely damages a person's reputation.

liberals Those who believe government should do more to solve the nation's problems but reject the notion that government should favor a particular set of social values. (See also **conservatives; libertarians; populists.**)

libertarians Those who believe government tries to do too many things that should be left to firms and individuals and who oppose government as an instrument of traditional values. (See also **conservatives; liberals; populists.**)

liberty The principle that individuals should be free to act and think as they choose, provided they do not infringe unreasonably on the rights and freedoms of others.

limited government A government that is subject to strict limits on its lawful uses of powers and hence on its ability to deprive people of their liberty.

lobbying The process by which interest-group members or lobbyists attempt to influence public policy through contacts with public officials.

logrolling The trading of votes between legislators so that each gets what he or she most wants.

majoritarianism The idea that the majority prevails not only in elections but also in determining policy.

majority opinion A Supreme Court opinion that results when a majority of the justices is in agreement on the legal basis of the decision. (See also **concurring opinion; dissenting opinion; plurality opinion.**)

material incentive An economic or other tangible benefit that is used to attract group members.

means test The requirement that applicants for public assistance must demonstrate they are poor in order to be eligible for the assistance. (See also **public assistance.**)

merit (civil service) system An approach to managing the bureaucracy whereby people are appointed to government positions on the basis of either competitive examinations or special qualifications, such as professional training. (See also **executive leadership system; patronage system.**)

metropolitan government Form of local government created when local governments join together and assign it responsibility for a range of activities, such as police and sanitation, so as to reduce the waste and duplication that results when every locality in a densely populated area provides its own services.

military-industrial complex The three components (the military establishment, the industries that manufacture weapons, and the members of Congress from states and districts that depend heavily on the arms industry) that mutually benefit from a high level of defense spending.

momentum A strong showing by a candidate in early presidential nominating contests, which leads to a buildup of public support for the candidate.

monetary policy A tool of economic management, available to government, based on manipulation of the amount of money in circulation. (See also **fiscal policy.**)

money chase A term used to describe the fact that U.S. campaigns are very expensive and that candidates must spend a great amount of time raising funds in order to compete successfully.

multilateralism The situation in which nations act together in response to problems and crises.

multinational corporations Business firms with major operations in more than one country.

multiparty system A system in which three or more political parties have the capacity to gain control of government separately or in coalition.

national debt The total cumulative amount that the U.S. government owes to creditors.

natural rights See **inalienable rights.**

"necessary and proper" clause (elastic clause) The authority granted Congress in Article I, Section 8 of the Constitution "to make all laws which shall be necessary and proper" for the implementation of its enumerated powers. (See also **implied powers.**)

negative government The philosophical belief that government governs best by staying out of people's lives, thus giving individuals as much freedom as possible to determine their own pursuits. (See also **positive government.**)

neutral competence The administrative objective of a merit-based bureaucracy. Such a bureaucracy should be "competent" in the sense

that its employees are hired and retained on the basis of their expertise and "neutral" in the sense that it operates by objective standards rather than partisan ones.

New Jersey (small-state) Plan A constitutional proposal for a strengthened Congress but one in which each state would have a single vote, thus granting a small state the same legislative power as a larger state.

news The news media's version of reality, usually with an emphasis on timely, dramatic, and compelling events and developments.

news media See **press.**

nomination The designation of a particular individual to run as a political party's candidate (its "nominee") in the general election.

noneconomic groups See **citizens' groups.**

North-South Compromise The agreement over economic and slavery issues that enabled northern and southern states to settle differences that threatened to defeat the effort to draft a new constitution.

objective journalism A model of news reporting that is based on the communication of "facts" rather than opinions and that is "fair" in that it presents all sides of partisan debate. (See also **partisan press.**)

oligarchy Government in which control rests with a few persons.

open party caucuses Meetings at which a party's candidates for nomination are voted on and that are open to all the party's rank-and-file voters who want to attend.

open-seat election An election in which there is no incumbent in the race.

opinion (of a court) A court's written explanation of its decision, which serves to inform others of the legal basis for the decision. Supreme Court opinions are expected to guide the decisions of other courts. (See also **concurring opinion; dissenting opinion; majority opinion; plurality opinion.**)

ordinances Laws issued by a local government under authority granted by the state government.

original jurisdiction The authority of a given court to be the first court to hear a case. (See also **appellate jurisdiction.**)

outside lobbying A form of lobbying in which an interest group seeks to use public pressure as a means of influencing officials.

oversight function A supervisory activity of Congress that centers on its constitutional responsibility to see that the executive carries out the laws faithfully and spends appropriations properly. (See also **lawmaking function; representation function.**)

packaging (of a candidate) A term of modern campaigning that refers to the process of recasting a candidate's record into an appealing image.

partisan press Newspapers and other communication media that openly support a political party and whose news in significant part follows the party line. (See also **objective journalism.**)

party caucus A group that consists of a party's members in the House or Senate and that serves to elect the party's leadership, set policy goals, and determine party strategy.

party-centered politics Election campaigns and other political processes in which political parties, not individual candidates, hold most of the initiative and influence. (See also **candidate-centered politics.**)

party coalition The groups and interests that support a political party.

party competition A process in which conflict over society's goals is transformed by political parties into electoral competition in which the winner gains the power to govern.

party discipline The willingness of a party's House or Senate members to act together as a cohesive group and thus exert collective control over legislative action.

party identification The personal sense of loyalty that an individual may feel toward a particular political party. (See also **party realignment.**)

party leaders Members of the House and Senate who are chosen by the Democratic or Republican caucus in each chamber to represent the party's interests in that chamber and who give some central direction to the chamber's deliberations.

party organizations The party organizational units at national, state, and local levels; their influence has decreased over time because of many factors. (See also **candidate-centered politics; party-centered politics; primary election.**)

party realignment An election or set of elections in which the electorate responds strongly to an extraordinarily powerful issue that has disrupted the established political order. A realignment has a lasting impact on public policy, popular support for the parties, and the composition of the party coalitions. (See also **party identification.**)

patronage system An approach to managing the bureaucracy whereby people are appointed to important government positions as a reward for political services they have rendered and because of their partisan loyalty. (See also **executive leadership system; merit system; spoils system.**)

pluralism A theory of American politics that holds that society's interests are substantially represented through the activities of groups.

plurality opinion A court opinion that results when a majority of justices agree on a decision in a case but do not agree on the legal basis for the decision. In this instance, the legal position held by most of the justices on the winning side is called a plurality opinion. (See also **concurring opinion; dissenting opinion; majority opinion.**)

police power A term that refers to the broad power of government to regulate the health, safety, and morals of the citizenry.

policy Generally, any broad course of governmental action; more narrowly, a specific government program or initiative.

policy implementation The primary function of the bureaucracy; it refers to the process of carrying out the authoritative decisions of Congress, the president, and the courts.

policy process The interplay of actors and institutions that leads to the adoption, modification, or rejection of public policy proposals.

political action committee (PAC) The organization through which an interest group raises and distributes funds for election purposes. By law, the funds must be raised through voluntary contributions.

political culture The characteristic and deep-seated beliefs of a particular people.

political movements See **social movements.**

political participation Involvement in activities intended to influence public policy and leadership, such as voting, joining political parties and interest groups, writing to elected officials, demonstrating for political causes, and giving money to political candidates.

political party An ongoing coalition of interests joined together to try to get their candidates for public office elected under a common label.

political socialization The learning process by which people acquire their political opinions, beliefs, and values.

political system The various components of American government. The parts are separate, but they connect with each other, affecting how each performs.

politics The process through which society makes its governing decisions.

population In a public opinion poll, the people (for example, the citizens of a nation) whose opinions are being estimated through interviews with a sample of these people.

populists Those who believe government should do more to solve the nation's problems and who look to it to uphold traditional values. (See also **conservatives; liberals; libertarians.**)

pork-barrel projects Legislative acts whose tangible benefits are targeted at a particular legislator's constituency.

positive government The philosophical belief that government intervention is necessary in order to enhance personal liberty when individuals are buffeted by economic and social forces beyond their control. (See also **negative government.**)

poverty line As defined by the federal government, the annual cost of a thrifty food budget for an urban family of four, multiplied by three to allow also for the cost of housing, clothes, and other expenses. Families below the poverty line are considered poor and are eligible for certain forms of public assistance.

power The ability of persons or institutions to control policy. (See also **authority.**)

precedent A judicial decision in a given case that serves as a rule of thumb for settling subsequent cases of a similar nature; courts are generally expected to follow precedent.

preemptive war doctrine The idea, espoused by president George W. Bush, that the United States could attack a potentially threatening nation even if the threat had not yet reached a serious and immediate level.

presidential approval ratings A measure of the degree to which the public approves or disapproves of the president's performance in office.

presidential commissions Organizations within the bureaucracy that are headed by commissioners appointed by the president. An example is the Commission on Civil Rights.

press (news media) Those print and broadcast organizations that are in the news-reporting business.

primary election (direct primary) A form of election in which voters choose a party's nominees for public office. In most states, eligibility to vote in a primary election is limited to voters who designated themselves as party members when they registered to vote. A primary is direct when it results directly in the choice of a nominee; it is indirect (as in the case of presidential primaries) when it results in the selection of delegates who then choose the nominee.

prior restraint Government prohibition of speech or publication before the fact, which is presumed by the courts to be unconstitutional unless the justification for it is overwhelming.

private (individual) goods Benefits that a group (most often an economic group) can grant directly and exclusively to the individual members of the group. (See also **collective goods.**)

probability sample A sample for a poll in which each individual in the population has a known probability of being selected randomly for inclusion in the sample. (See also **public opinion poll.**)

procedural due process The constitutional requirement that government must follow proper legal procedures before a person can be legitimately punished for an alleged offense.

proportional representation A form of representation in which seats in the legislature are allocated proportionally according to each political party's share of the popular vote. This system enables smaller parties to compete successfully for seats. (See also **single-member districts.**)

prospective voting A form of electoral judgment in which voters choose the candidate whose policy promises most closely match their own preferences. (See also **retrospective voting.**)

protectionism The view that the immediate interests of domestic producers should have a higher priority (through, for example, protective tariffs) than should free trade between nations. (See also **free-trade position.**)

public assistance A term that refers to social welfare programs funded through general tax revenues and available only to the financially needy. Eligibility for such a program is established by a means test. (See also **means test; social insurance.**)

public goods See **collective goods.**

public opinion The politically relevant opinions held by ordinary citizens that they express openly.

public opinion poll A device for measuring public opinion whereby a relatively small number of individuals (the sample) is interviewed for the purpose of estimating the opinions of a whole community (the population). (See also **probability sample.**)

public policy A decision of government to pursue a course of action designed to produce an intended outcome.

public-representative role A role whereby the media attempt to act as the public's representatives. (See also **common-carrier role; signaler role; watchdog role.**)

purposive incentive An incentive to group participation based on the cause (purpose) that the group seeks to promote.

realignment See **party realignment.**

reapportionment The reallocation of House seats among states after each census as a result of population changes.

reasonable-basis test A test applied by courts to laws that treat individuals unequally. Such a law may be deemed constitutional if its purpose is held to be "reasonably" related to a legitimate government interest.

recall The process by which citizens can petition for the removal from office of an elected official before the scheduled completion of his or her term.

redistricting The process of altering election districts in order to make them as nearly equal in population as possible. Redistricting takes place every ten years, after each population census.

referendum The process through which the legislature may submit proposals to the voters for approval or rejection.

registration The practice of placing citizens' names on an official list of voters before they are eligible to exercise their right to vote.

regulation Government restrictions on the economic practices of private firms.

regulatory agencies Administrative units, such as the Federal Communications Commission and the Environmental Protection Agency, that have responsibility for the monitoring and regulation of ongoing economic activities.

representation function The responsibility of a legislature to represent various interests in society. (See also **lawmaking function; oversight function.**)

representative democracy A system in which the people participate in the decision-making process of government not directly but indirectly, through the election of officials to represent their interests.

republic Historically, the form of government in which representative officials met to decide on policy issues. These representatives were expected to serve the public interest but were not subject to the people's immediate control. Today, the term *republic* is used interchangeably with *democracy.*

reserved powers The powers granted to the states under the Tenth Amendment to the Constitution.

retrospective voting A form of electoral judgment in which voters support the incumbent candidate or party when their policies are judged to have succeeded and oppose the candidate or party when their policies are judged to have failed. (See also **prospective voting.**)

rider An amendment to a bill that deals with an issue unrelated to the content of the bill. Riders are permitted in the Senate but not in the House.

sample In a public opinion poll, the relatively small number of individuals interviewed for the purpose of estimating the opinions of an entire population. (See also **public opinion poll.**)

sampling error A measure of the accuracy of a public opinion poll. It is mainly a function of sample size and is usually expressed in percentage terms. (See also **probability sample.**)

selective incorporation The absorption of certain provisions of the Bill of Rights (for example, freedom of speech) into the Fourteenth Amendment so that these rights are protected from infringement by the states.

self-government The principle that the people are the ultimate source and proper beneficiary of governing authority; in practice, a government based on majority rule.

senatorial courtesy The tradition that a U.S. senator from the state in which a federal judicial vacancy has arisen should have a say in the president's nomination of the new judge if the senator is of the same party as the president.

seniority A member of Congress's consecutive years of service on a particular committee.

separated institutions sharing power The principle that, as a way to limit government, its powers should be divided among separate branches, each of which also shares in the power of the others as a means of checking and balancing them. The result is that no one branch can exercise power decisively without the support or acquiescence of the others.

separation of powers The division of the powers of government among separate institutions or branches.

service relationship The situation where party organizations assist candidates for office but have no power to require them to accept or

campaign on the party's main policy positions.

service strategy Use of personal staff by members of Congress to perform services for constituents in order to gain their support in future elections.

signaler role The accepted responsibility of the media to alert the public to important developments as soon as possible after they happen or are discovered. (See also **common-carrier role; public representative role; watchdog role.**)

single-issue politics The situation in which separate groups are organized around nearly every conceivable policy issue and press their demands and influence to the utmost.

single-member districts The form of representation in which only the candidate who gets the most votes in a district wins office. (See also **proportional representation.**)

slander Spoken words that falsely damage a person's reputation.

small-state plan See **New Jersey Plan.**

social capital The sum of face-to-face interactions among citizens in a society.

social contract A voluntary agreement by individuals to form a government, which is then obligated to work within the confines of that agreement.

social insurance Social welfare programs based on the "insurance" concept, so that individuals must pay into the program in order to be eligible to receive funds from it. An example is social security for retired people. (See also **public assistance.**)

social (political) movements Active and sustained efforts to achieve social and political change by groups of people who feel that government has not been properly responsive to their concerns.

socialism An economic system in which government owns and controls many of the major industries.

soft money Campaign contributions that are not subject to legal limits

and are given to parties rather than directly to candidates.

solicitor general The high-ranking Justice Department official who serves as the government's lawyer in Supreme Court cases.

sovereignty The ultimate authority to govern within a certain geographical area.

split ticket The pattern of voting in which the individual voter in a given election casts a ballot for one or more candidates of each major party.

spoils system The practice of granting public office to individuals in return for political favors they have rendered. (See also **patronage system.**)

standing committees Permanent congressional committees with responsibility for a particular area of public policy. An example is the Senate Foreign Relations Committee.

state constitutional convention A state convention convened to amend the state constitution or draft a new one.

stewardship theory A theory that argues for a strong, assertive presidential role, with presidential authority limited only at points specifically prohibited by law. (See also **Whig theory.**)

strict-scrutiny test A test applied by courts to laws that attempt a racial or ethnic classification. In effect, the strict scrutiny test eliminates race or ethnicity as legal classification when it places minority group members at a disadvantage. (See also **suspect classifications.**)

strong mayor–council system Most common form of municipal government, consisting of the mayor as chief executive and the local council as the legislative body, in which the mayor has veto power and a prescribed responsibility for budgetary and other policy actions.

suffrage The right to vote.

sunset law A law containing a provision that fixes a date on which a program will end unless the program's life is extended by Congress.

supply-side economics A form of fiscal policy that emphasizes "supply" (production). An example of supply-side economics would be a tax cut for business. (See also **demand-side economics; fiscal policy.**)

supremacy clause Article VI of the Constitution, which makes national law supreme over state law when the national government is acting within its constitutional limits.

suspect classifications Legal classifications, such as race and national origin, that have invidious discrimination as their purpose and are therefore unconstitutional. (See also **strict-scrutiny test.**)

symbolic speech Action (for example, the waving or burning of a flag) for the purpose of expressing a political opinion.

totalitarian government A form of government in which the leaders claim complete dominance of all individuals and institutions.

transfer payment A government benefit that is given directly to an individual, as in the case of social security payments to a retiree.

trustees Elected representatives whose obligation is to act in accordance with their own consciences as to what policies are in the best interests of the public. (See also **delegates.**)

two-party system A system in which only two political parties have a real chance of acquiring control of the government.

tyranny of the majority The potential of a majority to monopolize power for its own gain and to the detriment of minority rights and interests.

unipolar (power structure) A power structure dominated by a single powerful actor, as in the case of the United States after the collapse of the Soviet Union.

unitary system A governmental system in which the national government alone has sovereign (ultimate) authority. (See also **confederacy; federalism.**)

unit rule The rule that grants all of a state's electoral votes to the candidate who receives most of the popular votes in the state.

unity The principle that Americans are one people and form an indivisible union.

veto The president's rejection of a bill, thereby keeping it from becoming law unless Congress overrides the veto.

Virginia (large-state) Plan A constitutional proposal for a strong Congress with two chambers, both of which would be based on numerical representation, thus granting more power to the larger states.

voter turnout The proportion of persons of voting age who actually vote in a given election.

watchdog role The accepted responsibility of the media to protect the public from deceitful, careless, incompetent, and corrupt officials by standing ready to expose any official who violates accepted legal, ethical, or performance standards. (See also **common-carrier role; public-representative role; signaler role.**)

weak mayor–council system Form of municipal government in which the mayor's policymaking powers are less substantial than the council's; the mayor has no power to veto the council's actions and often has no formal role in such activities as budget making.

Whig theory A theory that prevailed in the nineteenth century and held that the presidency was a limited or restrained office whose occupant was confined to expressly granted constitutional authority. (See also **stewardship theory.**)

whistle-blowing An internal check on the bureaucracy whereby individual bureaucrats report instances of mismanagement that they observe.

writ of certiorari Permission granted by a higher court to allow a losing party in a legal case to bring the case before it for a ruling; when such a writ is requested of the U.S. Supreme Court, four of the Court's nine justices must agree to accept the case before it is granted certiorari.

NOTES

CHAPTER ONE

[1]Alexis de Tocqueville, *Democracy in America (1835–1840),* ed. J. P. Mayer and A. P. Kerr (Garden City , N.Y.: Doubleday/Anchor, 1969), 640 .

[2]See John Harmon McElroy, *American Beliefs: What Keeps a Big Country and a Diverse People United* (Chicago: I. R. Dee, 1999).

[3]Clinton Rossiter, *Conservativism in America* (New York: Vintage, 1962), 67.

[4]Tocqueville, *Democracy in America,* 310.

[5]James Bryce, *The American Commonwealth,* vol. 2 (New York: Macmillan, 1960), 247–54. First published in 1900.

[6]Ralph Barton Perry, *Puritanism and Democracy* (New York: Vanguard, 1944), 124–25; see also Peter D. Salins, *Assimilation, American Style* (New York: Basic Books, 1996); Philip L. Fetzer , *The Ethnic Moment* (Armonk, N.Y.: M. E. Sharpe, 1996).

[7]See Gabriel Almond and Sidney Verba, *The Civic Culture* (Boston: Little, Brown, 1965); Richard Merelman, *Making Something of Ourselves: On Culture and Politics in the United States* (Berkeley: University of California Press, 1984).

[8]Paul Gagnon, "Why Study History?" *Atlantic Monthly,* November 1988, 47.

[9]Louis Hartz, *The Liberal Tradition in America* (New York: Harcourt, Brace, 1953), 12; see also Jeffrey Stout, *Democracy and Tradition* (Princeton, N.J.: Princeton University Press, 2004).

[10]James Bryce, *The American Commonwealth,* vol. 2 (Indianapolis, Ind.: Liberty Fund, 1995), 1419.

[11]The Pew Research Center for the People and the Press's Global Attitudes survey, 2002.

[12]See Douglas Muzzio and Richard Behn, "Thinking About Welfare," *The Public Perspective,* February/ March 1995, 35–38; Stanley Feldman and John Zaller, "The Political Culture of Ambivalence: Ideological Responses to the Welfare State," *American Journal of Political Science* 36 (1992): 268–307.

[13]See Seymour Martin Lipset, *American Exceptionalism: A Double-Edged Sword* (New York: Norton, 1996); Claude Levi-Strauss, *Structural Anthropology* (Chicago: University of Chicago Press, 1983); Clifford Geertz, *Myth, Symbol, and Culture* (New York: Norton, 1974).

[14]U.S. Census Bureau figures.

[15]Quoted in Ralph Volney Harlow, *The Growth of the United States,* vol. 2 (New York: Henry Holt, 1943), 497.

[16]Survey of American Political Culture, James Davison Hunter and Carol Bowman, directors, University of Virginia, 1996; Debra L. DeLaet, *U.S. Immigration Policy in an Age of Rights* (Westport, Conn.: Praeger Publishers, 2000).

[17]Harold D. Lasswell, *Politics: Who Gets What, When, How* (New York: McGraw-Hill, 1938).

[18]See Charles H. McIlwain, *Constitutionalism: Ancient and Modern* (Ithaca, N.Y.: Cornell University Press, 1983).

[19]Alan S. Rosenbaum, ed., *Constitutionalism: The Philosophical Dimension* (Westport, Conn.: Greenwood, 1988), 4.

[20]Tocqueville, *Democracy in America,* ch. 6.

[21]Harold D. Lasswell and Abraham Kaplan, *Power and Society* (New Haven, Conn.: Yale University Press, 1950), 75–77.

[22]Benjamin I. Page and Robert Shapiro, "Effects of Public Opinion on Policy," *American Political Science Review* 77 (March 1983): 178; see also Urie Bronfenbrenner, Peter McClelland, Stephen Leci, Phyllis Moen, and Elaine Wethington, *The State of Americans* (New York: Free Press, 1996).

[23]See Robert Dahl, *Democracy and Its Critics* (New Haven, Conn.: Yale University Press, 1989).

[24]C. Wright Mills, *The Power Elite* (New York: Oxford University Press, 1965).

[25]G. William Domhoff, *Who Rules America?* (Mountain View, Calif.: Mayfield Publishing, 1998).

[26]See, for example, Robert Dahl, *On Democracy* (New Haven, Conn.: Yale University Press, 1998).

[27]See H. H. Gerth and C. Wright Mills, eds., *From Max Weber: Essays in Sociology* (New York: Oxford University Press, 1958).

[28]Roberto Michels, *Political Parties* (New York: Collier Books, 1962). First published in 1911.

[29]David Easton, *The Political System* (New York: Knopf, 1965), 97.

[30]E. E. Schattschneider, *Two Hundred Million Americans in Search of a Government* (New York: Holt, Rinehart & Winston, 1969), 42.

CHAPTER TWO

[1] Quoted in Charles S. Hyneman, "Republican Government in America," in George J. Graham Jr. and Scarlett G. Graham, eds., *Founding Principles of American Government*, rev. ed. (Chatham, N.J.: Chatham House, 1984), 19.

[2] See Russell Hardin, *Liberalism, Constitutionalism, and Democracy* (New York: Oxford University Press, 1999); A. John Simmons, *The Lockean Theory of Rights* (Princeton, N.J.: Princeton University Press, 1994).

[3] George Bancroft, *History of the Formation of the Constitution of the United States of America*, 3d ed., vol. 1 (New York: D. Appleton, 1883), 166.

[4] Catherine Drinker Bowen, *Miracle at Philadelphia* (Boston: Little, Brown, 1986), 10.

[5] Alfred H. Kelly, Winifred A. Harbison, and Herman Belz, *The American Constitution*, 7th ed. (New York: Norton, 1991), 122.

[6] Quoted in "The Constitution and Slavery," Digital History Website, December 1, 2003.

[7] Gaillard Hunt, ed., *The Writings of James Madison* (New York: Putnam, 1904), 274; see also Garret Ward Sheldon, *The Political Philosophy of James Madison* (Baltimore: Johns Hopkins University Press, 2000).

[8] *Federalist* No. 47.

[9] See *Federalist* Nos. 47 and 48.

[10] Richard Neustadt, *Presidential Power* (New York: Macmillan, 1986), 33.

[11] Henry J. Abraham, *The Judicial Process*, 6th ed. (New York: Oxford University Press, 1993), 320–22.

[12] *Marbury v. Madison*, 1 Cranch 137 (1803).

[13] Martin Diamond, *The Founding of the Democratic Republic* (Itasca, Ill.: Peacock, 1981), 62–71.

[14] *Federalist* No. 10.

[15] Leslie F. Goldstein, "Judicial Review and Democratic Theory: Guardian Democracy vs. Representative Democracy," *Western Political Quarterly* 40 (1987): 391–412.

[16] Benjamin Ginsberg, *The Consequences of Consent* (New York: Random House, 1982), 22.

[17] Robert Dahl, *Pluralist Democracy in the United States* (Chicago: Rand McNally, 1967), 92.

[18] This interpretation is taken from Walter Lippmann, *Public Opinion* (New York: Free Press, 1965), 178–79; for a general discussion of the uncertain meaning of the Constitution, see Lawrence H. Tribe and Michael C. Dorf, *On Reading the Constitution* (Cambridge, Mass.: Harvard University Press, 1991).

[19] Charles S. Beard, *An Economic Interpretation of the Constitution* (New York, Macmillan, 1941). First published in 1913.

[20] See Randall G. Holcombe, *From Liberty to Democracy* (Ann Arbor: University of Michigan Press, 2002).

CHAPTER THREE

[1] Woodrow Wilson, *Constitutional Government in the United States* (New York: Columbia University Press, 1908), 173.

[2] See Samuel Beer, *To Make a Nation: The Rediscovery of American Federalism* (Cambridge, Mass.: The Belknap Press of Harvard University, 1993).

[3] *Federalist* No. 2; for the Anti-Federalist view, see Saul Cornell, *The Other Founders* (Chapel Hill: University of North Carolina Press, 1999).

[4] *McCulloch v. Maryland*, 4 Wheaton 316 (1819).

[5] *Gibbons v. Ogden*, 22 Wheaton 1 (1824).

[6] Oliver Wendell Holmes Jr., *Collected Legal Papers* (New York: Harcourt, Brace, 1920), 295–96.

[7] See John C. Calhoun, *The Works of John C. Calhoun* (New York: Russell & Russell, 1968).

[8] See *Cooley v. Board of Wardens of the Port of Philadelphia*, 53 Howard 299 (1851).

[9] *Dred Scott v. Sanford*, 19 Howard 393 (1857).

[10] *U.S. v. Cruikshank*, 92 U.S. 452 (1876).

[11] Edward S. Corwin, *The Constitution and What It Means Today*, 12th ed. (Princeton, N.J.: Princeton University Press, 1958), 248.

[12] *Slaughter-House Cases*, 16 Wallace 36 (1873); *Civil Rights Cases*, 109 U.S. 3 (1883).

[13] *Plessy v. Ferguson*, 163 U.S. 537 (1896).

[14] *Santa Clara County v. Southern Pacific Railroad Co.*, 118 U.S. 394 (1886).

[15] *U.S. v. E. C. Knight Co.*, 156 U.S. 1 (1895).

[16] *Hammer v. Dagenhart*, 247 U.S. 251 (1918).

[17] *Lochner v. New York*, 198 U.S. 25 (1905).

[18] Alfred H. Kelly, Winifred A. Harbison, and Herman Belz, *The American Constitution*, 7th ed. (New York: Norton, 1991), 529.

[19] James E. Anderson, *The Emergence of the Modern Regulatory State* (Washington, D.C.: Public Affairs Press, 1962), 2–3.

[20] *Schechter Poultry Co. v. United States*, 295 U.S. 495 (1935).

[21] *NLRB v. Jones and Laughlin Steel*, 301 U.S. 1 (1937).

[22] *American Power and Light v. Securities and Exchange Commission*, 329 U.S. 90 (1946); see also Richard A. Maidment, *The Judicial Response to the New Deal: The U.S. Supreme Court and Economic Regulation* (New York: Manchester University Press, 1992).

[23] Louis Fisher, *American Constitutional Law* (New York: McGraw-Hill, 1990), 384.

[24] See Maidment, *Judicial Response to the New Deal*.

[25] *Brown v. Board of Education*, 347 U.S. 483 (1954).

[26] *Miranda v. Arizona*, 384 U.S. 436 (1966).

[27] See Thomas Anton, *American Federalism and Public Policy* (Philadelphia: Temple University Press, 1989).

[28] Morton Grodzins, *The American System: A New View of Government in the United States* (Chicago: Rand McNally, 1966).

[29]See Paul A. Peterson, *The Price of Federalism* (Washington, D.C.: The Brookings Institution, 1995).

[30]Rosella Levaggi, *Fiscal Federalism and Grants-in-Aid* (Brookfield, Vt.: Avebury, 1991).

[31]Richard Nathan and Fred Doolittle, *Reagan and the States* (Princeton, N.J.: Princeton University Press, 1987); Timothy J. Conlan, *From New Federalism to Devolution* (Washington, D.C.: Brookings Institution, 1998).

[32]*Garcia v. San Antonio Authority*, 469 U.S. 528 (1985).

[33]*United States v. Lopez*, 514 U.S. 549 (1995).

[34]*Printz v. United States*, 521 U.S. 98 (1997).

[35]*Kimel v. Florida Board of Regents*, 528 U.S. 62 (2000).

[36]*Board of Trustees of the University of Alabama v. Garrett*, 531 U.S. 356 (2002).

[37]See Tinsley E. Yarbrough, *The Rehnquist Court and the Constitution* (New York: Oxford University Press, 2000).

[38]*Nevada Department of Human Resources v. Hibbs*, No. 01-1368 (2003).

[39]*Reno v. Condon*, 528 U.S. 141 (2000).

[40]See Robert F. Nagel, *The Implosion of American Federalism* (New York: Oxford University Press, 2001).

[41]Andrew W. Dobelstein, *Politics, Economics, and Public Welfare* (Englewood Cliffs, N.J.: Prentice-Hall, 1980), 5.

[42]Lloyd A. Free and Hadley Cantril, *The Political Beliefs of Americans* (New York: Simon & Schuster , 1968), 21; see also William Lunch, *The Nationalization of American Politics* (Berkeley: University of California Press, 1987).

[43]Survey for the Times Mirror Center for the People and the Press by Princeton Survey Research Associates, July 12–27, 1994; see also Tommy Thompson, *Power to the People* (New York: HarperCollins, 1996).

[44]Daniel J. Boorstin, *The Americans: The Democratic Experience* (New York: Vintage Books, 1974).

CHAPTER FOUR

[1]Julian P. Boyd, ed., *The Papers of Thomas Jefferson*, vol. 12 (Princeton, N.J.: Princeton University Press, 1955), 440.

[2]*Anderson v. Creighton*, 483 U.S. 635 (1987).

[3]*Bose Corp. v. Consumers Union of the United States*, 466 U.S. 485 (1984).

[4]*Schenck v. United States*, 249 U.S. 47 (1919).

[5]*Dennis v. United States*, 341 U.S. 494 (1951).

[6]See, for example, *Yates v. United States*, 354 U.S. 298 (1957); *Noto v. United States*, 367 U.S. 290 (1961); *Scales v. United States*, 367 U.S. 203 (1961).

[7]*United States v. Carolene Products Co.*, 304 U.S. 144 (1938).

[8]*United States v. O'Brien*, 391 U.S. 367 (1968).

[9]*Texas v. Johnson*, 109 S. Ct. 2544 (1989).

[10]*United States v. Eichman*, 496 U.S. 310 (1990).

[11]*New York Times Co. v. United States*, 403 U.S. 713 (1971).

[12]*Nebraska Press Assn. v. Stuart*, 427 U.S. 539 (1976).

[13]*Barron v. Baltimore*, 7 Peters 243 (1833).

[14]*Gitlow v. New York*, 268 U.S. 652 (1925).

[15]*Fiske v. Kansas*, 274 U.S. 30 (1927); *Near v. Minnesota*, 283 U.S. 697 (1931); *Hamilton v. Regents, U. of California*, 293 U.S. 245 (1934); *DeJonge v. Oregon*, 299 U.S. 253 (1937).

[16]*Near v. Minnesota*, 283 U.S. 697 (1931).

[17]*Brandenburg v. Ohio*, 395 U.S. 444 (1969).

[18]*R.A.V. v. St. Paul*, No. 90-7675 (1992).

[19]*Wisconsin v. Mitchell*, No. 92-515 (1993).

[20]*National Socialist Party v. Skokie*, 432 U.S. 43 (1977).

[21]*Forsyth County v. Nationalist Movement*, No. 91-538 (1992).

[22]*New York Times Co. v. Sullivan*, 376 U.S. 254 (1964).

[23]*Milkovich v. Lorain Journal*, 497 U.S. 1 (1990); see also *Masson v. The New Yorker*, No. 89-1799 (1991).

[24]*Roth v. United States*, 354 U.S. 476 (1957).

[25]*Miller v. California*, 413 U.S. 15 (1973).

[26]*Barnes v. Glen Theatre*, No. 90-26 (1991).

[27]*Stanley v. Georgia*, 394 U.S. 557 (1969).

[28]*Osborne v. Ohio*, 495 U.S. 103 (1990).

[29]*Ashcroft v. Free Speech Coalition*, No. 00-795 (2002).

[30]*Denver Area Consortium v. Federal Communications Commission*, No. 95-124 (1996).

[31]*Reno v. American Civil Liberties Union*, No. 96-511 (1997).

[32]*Ashcroft v. ACLU*, No. 03-0218 (2004).

[33]See Michael J. Perry, *Religion in Politics* (New York: Oxford University Press, 1997).

[34]*Board of Regents v. Allen*, 392 U.S. 236 (1968).

[35]*Lemon v. Kurtzman*, 403 U.S. 602 (1971).

[36]Ibid.

[37]*Mitchell v. Helms*, No. 98-1648 (2000).

[38]*Zelman v. Simmons-Harris*, No. 00-1751 (2002); *Locke v. Davey*, No. 02-1315 (2004).

[39]*Engel v. Vitale*, 370 U.S. 421 (1962).

[40]*Abington School District v. Schempp*, 374 U.S. 203 (1963).

[41]*Wallace v. Jaffree*, 472 U.S. 38 (1985).

[42]*Santa Fe Independent School District v. Does*, No. 99-62 (2000).

[43]*Wisconsin v. Yoder*, 406 U.S. 295 (1972); see also *Church of the Lukumi Babalu Aye v. City of Hialeah*, No. 91-948 (1993).

[44]*Edwards v. Aguillard*, 487 U.S. 578 (1987).

[45]*Griswold v. Connecticut*, 381 U.S. 479 (1965).

[46]*Roe v. Wade*, 401 U.S. 113 (1973).

[47]*Webster v. Reproductive Health Services*, 492 U.S. 490 (1989); see also *Rust v. Sullivan*, No. 89-1391 (1991).

[48]*Planned Parenthood v. Casey*, No. 91-744 (1992).

[49]*Stenberg v. Carhart*, No. 99-830 (2000).

[50]*Bowers v. Hardwick*, 478 U.S. 186 (1986).

[51]*Lawrence and Garner v. Texas*, No. 02-102 (2003).

[52]*Vacco v. Quill*, 117 S.C. 36 (1996); *Washington v. Glucksberg*, No. 96-110 (1997).

[53]*Gregg v. United States*, No. 00-939 (2001).

[54]*Powell v. Alabama*, 287 U.S. 45 (1932).

[55]*Palko v. Connecticut*, 302 U.S. 319 (1937).

[56]*Mapp v. Ohio*, 367 U.S. 643 (1961).

[57]*Gideon v. Wainwright*, 372 U.S. 335 (1963).

[58]*Malloy v. Hogan*, 378 U.S. 1 (1964).

[59]*Miranda v. Arizona*, 384 U.S. 436 (1966); see also *Escobedo v. Illinois*, 378 U.S. 478 (1964).

[60]*Pointer v. Texas*, 380 U.S. 400 (1965).

[61]*Klopfer v. North Carolina*, 386 U.S. 213 (1967).

[62]*Duncan v. Louisiana*, 391 U.S. 145 (1968).

[63]*Benton v. Maryland*, 395 U.S. 784 (1969).

[64]*Dickerson v. United States*, No. 99-5525 (2000). *Missouri v. Siebert*, No. 02-1371 (2004).

[65]*Michigan v. Sitz*, No. 88-1897 (1990).

[66]*Indianapolis v. Edmund*, No. 99-1030 (2001).

[67]*Kyllo v. United States*, No. 99-8508 (2001).

[68]*Ferguson v. Charleston*, No. 99-936 (2001).

[69]*Board of Education of Independent School District No. 92 of Pottawatomie County v. Earls*, No. 01-332 (2002).

[70]*Weeks v. United States*, 232 U.S. 383 (1914).

[71]*Nix v. Williams*, 467 U.S. 431 (1984); see also *United States v. Leon*, 468 U.S. 897 (1984).

[72]*Whren v. United States*, 517 U.S. 806 (1996).

[73]*U.S. v. Drayton et al.*, No. 01-631 (2002).

[74]*Townsend v. Sain*, 372 U.S. 293 (1963).

[75]*Keeney v. Tamaya-Reyes*, No. 90-1859 (1992); see also *Coleman v. Thompson*, No. 89-7662 (1991).

[76]*Brecht v. Abrahamson*, No. 91-7358 (1993); see also *McCleskey v. Zant*, No. 89-7024 (1991).

[77]*Felker v. Turpin*, No. 95-8836 (1996); but see *Stewart v. Martinez- Villareal*, No. 97-300 (1998).

[78]*Miller-El v. Cockrell*, No. 01-7662 (2003); *Wiggins v. Smith*, No. 02-311 (2003).

[79]*Williams v. Taylor*, No. 99-6615 (2000).

[80]Kurt Heine, "Philadelphia Cops Beat One of Their Own," *Syracuse Herald-American*, January 15, 1995, A13.

[81]Richard Sobel, "Anti-Terror Campaign Has Wide Support, Even at Expense of Cherished Rights," *Chicago Tribune*, November 4, 2001, Internet copy.

[82]*Wilson v. Seiter*, No. 89-7376 (1991).

[83]*Harmelin v. Michigan*, No. 89-7272 (1991).

[84]*Lockyre v. Andrade*, No. 01-1127 (2003); see also *Ewing v. California*, No. 01-6978 (2003).

[85]*Atkins v. Virginia*, No. 01-8452 (2002); see also Roger Hood, *The Death Penalty: A Worldwide Perspective* (New York: Oxford University Press, 2003).

[86]*Ring v. Arizona*, No. 01-488 (2002). *Blakley v. Washington*, No. 02-1632 (2004).

[87]*Korematsu v. United States*, 323 U.S. 214 (1944).

[88]Cases cited in Charles Lane, "In Terror War, 2nd Track for Suspects," *Washington Post*, December 1, 2001, A1.

[89]Bill Mears, "Supreme Court Rejects Appeal over Secret 9/11 Detentions," *Washington Post*, January 12, 2004. Internet copy.

[90]*Rasul v. Bush*, No. 03-334 (2004); *al-Odah v. United States*, No. 03-343 (2004).

[91]*Hamdi v. Rumsfeld*, No. 03-6696 (2004); *Rumsfeld v. Padilla*, No. 03-1027 (2004).

[92]Quoted in "Feds Get Wide Wiretap Authority," CBSNEWS.com, November 18, 2002.

[93]See "Ashcroft to Appear Before House Panel on Patriot Act," CNN.com, May 22, 2003.

[94]Lane, "In Terror War, 2nd Track for Suspects," A1.

[95]Sobel, "Anti-Terror Campaign."

[96]See Alpheus T. Mason, *The Supreme Court: Palladium of Freedom* (Ann Arbor: University of Michigan Press, 1962); see also Henry J. Abraham, *Freedom and the Court* (New York: Oxford University Press, 1998).

CHAPTER FIVE

[1]Speech of Martin Luther King Jr. in Washington, D.C., August 2, 1963.

[2]*Washington Post* wire story, May 14, 1991.

[3]"African-American Health," amednews.com (online newspaper of the American Medical Association), May 1, 2000.

[4]Robert Nisbet, "Public Opinion Versus Popular Opinion," *Public Interest* 41 (1975): 171.

[5]See, for example, John R. Howard, *The Shifting Wind* (Albany: State University of New York Press, 1999).

[6]The classic analysis of this system of legalized segregation is C. Vann Woodward, *The Strange Career of Jim Crow*, 3d rev. ed. (New York: Oxford University Press, 1974).

[7]*Plessy v. Ferguson*, 163 U.S. 537 (1896).

[8]See, for example, *Missouri ex rel. Gaines v. Canada*, 305 U.S. 57 (1938).

[9]*Brown v. Board of Education of Topeka*, 347 U.S. 483 (1954).

[10]See Sar Levitan, William Johnson, and Robert Taggert, *Still a Dream* (Cambridge, Mass.: Harvard University Press, 1975).

[11]Data from National Office of Drug Control Policy, 1997.

[12]See Keith Reeves, *Voting Hopes or Fears?* (New York: Oxford University Press, 1997); Tali Mendelberg, *The Race Card* (Princeton, N.J.: Princeton University Press, 2001).

[13]See Glenna Matthews, *The Rise of Public Women* (New York: Oxford University Press, 1994).

[14]*Tinker v. Colwell*, 193 U.S. 473 (1904).

[15]See Ellen Carol DuBois, *Feminism and Suffrage: The Emergence of an Independent Women's Movement in America, 1848–1869* (Ithaca, N.Y.: Cornell University Press, 1978).

[16]See Jane Mansbridge, *Why We Lost the ERA* (Chicago: University of Chicago Press, 1986).

[17]See Kathleen Hall Jamieson, *Beyond the Double Bind* (New York: Oxford University Press, 1995).

[18]Linda Witt, Karen M. Paget, and Glenna Matthews, *Running as a Woman* (New York: Free Press, 1994).

[19]Timothy Bledsoe and Mary Herring, "Victims of Circumstance: Women in Pursuit of Political Office," *American Political Science Review* 84 (1990): 213–24.

[20]See, however, Sara M. Evans and Barbara Nelson, *Wage Justice* (Chicago: University of Chicago Press, 1989).

[21]*County of Washington v. Gunther*, No. 80-429 (1981).

[22]*Faragher v. City of Boca Raton*, No. 97-282 (1998); *Pennsylvania State Police v. Suders*, No. 03-95 (2004).

[23]See Joane Nagel, *American Indian Ethnic Renewal* (New York: Oxford University Press, 1996).

[24]*De Canas v. Bica*, 424 U.S. 351 (1976).

[25]Ron Hutcheson and Dave Montgomery, "Bush's Guest Worker Proposal," *Detroit Free Press*, January 8, 2004, web download.

[26]See Rudulfo O. de la Garza, Louis DeSipio, F. Chris Garcia, John Garcia, and Angelo Falcon, *Latino Voices* (Boulder, Colo.: Westview Press, 1992).

[27]James G. Gimpel, "Latinos and the 2002 Election: Republicans Do Well When Latinos Stay Home," Center for Immigration Studies, University of Maryland, January 2003, web download; see also Louis DeSipio, *Counting on the Latino Vote* (Charlottesville: University of Virginia Press, 1996).

[28]James Truslow Adams, *The March of Democracy*, vol. 4 (New York: Scribner's, 1933), 284–85; see also Charles McClain, *In Search of Equality* (Berkeley: University of California Press, 1994).

[29]*Lau v. Nichols*, 414 U.S. 563 (1974).

[30]See Gordon Chang, ed., *Asian Americans and Politics* (Stanford, Calif.: Stanford University Press, 2001).

[31]*Kimel v. Florida Board of Regents*, No. 98-791 (2000).

[32]*Board of Trustees of the University of Alabama v. Garrett*, No. 99-1240 (2002). *Tennessee v. Lane*, No. 02-1667 (2004).

[33]*Boy Scouts of America v. Dale*, No. 99-699 (2000).

[34]Examples from Sean Cahill, "Public Policy Issues Affecting Gay, Lesbian, Bisexual and Transgender People," unpublished paper, August 2003, p. 4.

[35]*Romer v. Evans*, 517 U.S. 620 (1996).

[36]*Lawrence v. Texas*, No. 02-102 (2003).

[37]Cahill, "Public Policy Issues," p. 2.

[38]Gallup poll, May 2003.

[39]Kaiser Family Foundation poll, 2001.

[40]*Craig v. Boren*, 429 U.S. 190 (1976).

[41]*Rostker v. Goldberg*, 453 U.S. 57 (1980).

[42]*United States v. Virginia*, No. 94-1941 (1996).

[43]Survey by Federal Financial Institutions Examination Council, 1998.

[44]U.S. Conference of Mayors Report, 1998.

[45]V. O. Key Jr., *Southern Politics* (New York: Knopf, 1949), 495.

[46]*Smith v. Allwright*, 321 U.S. 649 (1944).

[47]See Bernard Grofman, Lisa Handley, and Richard Niemi, *Minority Representation and the Quest for Voting Equality* (New York: Cambridge University Press, 1992); David Lublin, *The Paradox of Representation* (Princeton, N.J.: Princeton University Press, 1997); Fred Pincus, *Reverse Discrimination: Dismantling the Myth* (Boulder, Colo.: Lynne Reiner, 2003).

[48]*Muller v. Johnson*, No. 94-631 (1995); *Bush v. Verg*, No. 94-805 (1996); *Shaw v. Hunt*, No. 94-923 (1996).

[49]*Easley v. Cromartie*, No. 99-1864 (2001).

[50]See Terry Eastland, *Ending Affirmative Action* (New York: Basic Books, 1997); but see also Barbara A. Bergmann, *In Defense of Affirmative Action* (New York: Basic Books, 1997).

[51]*University of California Regents v. Bakke*, 438 U.S. 265 (1978).

[52]*Steelworkers v. Weber*, 443 U.S. 193 (1979); *Fullilove v. Klutnick*, 448 U.S. 448 (1980).

[53]*Local No. 28, Sheet Metal Workers v. Equal Employment Opportunity Commission*, 478 U.S. 421 (1986); see also *Local No. 93, International Association of Firefighters v. Cleveland*, 478 U.S. 501 (1986); *Firefighters v. Stotts*, 459 U.S. 969 (1984); *Wygant v. Jackson*, 476 U.S. 238 (1986).

[54]See *Wards Cove Packing v. Antonio*, 490 U.S. 642 (1989).

[55]*Adarand v. Pena*, No. 94-310 (1995).

[56]Jodi Wilgoren, "New Law in Texas Preserves Racial Mix in State's Colleges," *New York Times*, November 24, 1999, A1.

[57]*Gratz v. Bollinger*, No. 02-516 (2003).

[58]*Grutter v. Bollinger*, No. 02-241 (2003).

[59]*Swann v. Charlotte-Mecklenburg County Board of Education*, 402 U.S. 1 (1971).

[60]*Milliken v. Bradley*, 418 U.S. 717 (1974).

[61]Christopher Jencks and Meredith Phillips, eds., *The Black-White Test Score Gap* (Washington, D.C.: Brookings Institution Press, 1998).

[62]Quoted in Megan Twohey, "Desegregation Is Dead," *National Journal* 31, no. 38 (September 18, 1999), 2614.

[63]*Board of Education of Oklahoma City v. Dowell*, 498 U.S. 237 (1991).

[64]*Sheff v. O'Neill*, No. 95-2071 (1996).

[65]Twohey, "Desegregation Is Dead." See also David J. Armor, *Forced Justice: School Desegregation and the Law* (New York: Oxford University Press, 1995).

[66]Linda Darling-Hammond, "Black America: Progress and Prospects," Brookings Institution, 1998.

[67]Gunnar Myrdal, *An American Dilemma: The Negro Problem and Modern Democracy* (New York: Harper, 1944).

CHAPTER SIX

[1]V. O. Key Jr., *Public Opinion and American Democracy* (New York: Knopf, 1961), 8.

[2]See Jeremy Bentham, *An Introduction to the Principles of Morals and Legislation* (Oxford, England: Clarendon Press, 1996; originally published in 1789).

[3]Jerry L. Yeric and John R. Todd, *Public Opinion*, 3d ed. (Itasca, Ill.: Peacock, 1996), 3.

[4]Elisabeth Noelle-Neumann, *The Spiral of Silence*, 2d ed. (Chicago: University of Chicago Press, 1993), ch. 1.

[5]"Study Finds Widespread Misperceptions on Iraq Highly Related to Support for War," web release of the Program on International Policy Attitudes, School of

Public Affairs, University of Maryland, October 2, 2003.

[6]Times-Mirror Center for the People and the Press survey, 1994.

[7]Survey of students of the eight Ivy League schools by Luntz & Weber Research and Strategic Services, for the University of Pennsylvania's Ivy League Study, November 13–December 1, 1992.

[8]See R. Michael Alvarez and John Brehm, *Hard Choices, Easy Answers* (Princeton, N.J.: Princeton University Press, 2002); see also Samuel L. Popkin, *The Reasoning Voter* (Chicago: University of Chicago Press, 1991).

[9]Sidney Verba and Norman H. Nie, *Participation in America: Political Democracy and Social Equality* (New York: Harper & Row , 1972), 281–84.

[10]See Herbert Asher, *Polling and the Public*, 6th ed. (Washington, D.C.: Congressional Quarterly Press, 2004).

[11]Example from Adam Clymer, "Wrong Number: The Unbearable Lightness of Public Opinion Polls," *New York Times,* July 22, 2001. Internet copy.

[12]M. Kent Jennings and Richard G. Niemi, *Generations and Politics* (Princeton, N.J.: Princeton University Press, 1981); David Easton and Jack Dennis, *Children in the Political System* (New York: McGraw-Hill, 1969).

[13]See Robert D. Hess and Judith V. Torney, *The Development of Political Attitudes in Children* (Chicago: Aldine, 1967), 219; Orit Ichilov, *Political Socialization, Citizenship Education, and Democracy* (New York: Teachers College Press, 1990).

[14]Thomas E. Patterson, *Out of Order* (New York: Vintage, 1994), ch. 2.

[15]Noelle-Neumann, *Spiral of Silence.*

[16]See, however, Dietram A. Scheufele, Matthew C. Nisbet, and Dominique Brossard, "Pathways to Political Participation: Religion, Communication Contexts, and Mass Media," *International Journal of Public Opinion Research* 15 (Autumn 2003): 300–324.

[17]See E. J. Dionne, *Why Americans Hate Politics* (New York: Simon & Schuster, 1992); E. J. Dionne, *They Only Look Dead* (New York: Simon & Schuster, 1996); David Frum, *What's Right?* (New York: Basic Books, 1996).

[18]John L. Sullivan, James E. Pierson, and George E. Marcus, "Ideological Constraint in the Mass Public," *American Journal of Political Science* 22 (May 1978): 233–49.

[19]CNN/USA Today poll conducted by the Gallup Organization, 1997.

[20]Philip Converse, "The Nature of Belief Systems in Mass Publics," in David Apter, ed., *Ideology and Discontent* (New York: Free Press, 1965), 206.

[21]"The Gender Story," *The Public Perspective,* August/September 1996, 1–33; Sue Tolleson Rinehart, *Gender Consciousness and Politics* (New York: Routledge, 1992).

[22]Susan A. MacManus, *Young v. Old: Generational Combat in the Twenty-first Century* (Boulder, Colo.: Westview Press, 1996).

[23]See Angus Campbell, Philip Converse, Warren Miller, and Donald Stokes, *The American Voter* (New York: Wiley, 1960), chs. 3 and 4.

[24]Martin P. Wattenberg, *The Decline of American Political Parties, 1952–1996* (Cambridge, Mass.: Harvard University Press, 1998).

[25]Donald Green, Bradley Palmquist, and Eric Schickler, *Partisan Hearts and Minds* (New Haven, Conn.: Yale University Press, 2002).

[26]See E. E. Schattschneider, *The Semisovereign People* (New York: Holt, Rinehart & Winston, 1980), ch. 8.

[27]See William Domhoff, *The Power Elite and the State* (New York: Aldine de Gruyter, 1990).

[28]Benjamin I. Page and Robert Y. Shapiro, "Effects of Public Opinion on Policy," *American Political Science Review* 77 (March 1983): 178; see also Richard Sobel, *The Impact of Public Opinion on U.S. Foreign Policy* (New York: Oxford University Press, 2001).

[29]See Benjamin Ginsberg, *The Consequences of Consent* (New York: Random House, 1982).

[30]Lawrence R. Jacobs and Robert Y. Shapiro, *Politicians Don't Pander* (Chicago: University of Chicago Press, 2000).

[31]See Paul Brace and Barbara Hinckley, *Follow the Leader: Opinion Polls and Modern Presidents* (New York: Basic Books, 1992).

CHAPTER SEVEN

[1]Walter Lippmann, *Public Opinion* (New York: Free Press, 1965), 36.

[2]Quoted in Ralph Volney Harlow, *The Growth of the United States* (New York: Henry Holt, 1943), 312.

[3]See William H. Flanigan and Nancy Zingale, *The Political Behavior of the American Electorate,* 10th ed. (Washington, D.C.: Congressional Quarterly Press, 2002), 24–26.

[4]Example from Gus Tyler, "One Cheer for the Democrats," *New Leader,* November 3, 1986, 6.

[5]Turnout figures provided by Washington, D.C., embassies of the respective countries, 2000.

[6]Thomas E. Patterson, *The Vanishing Voter* (New York: Knopf, 2002), 134.

[7]Ivor Crewe, "Electoral Participation," in David Butler, Howard R. Penniman, and Austin Ranney, eds., *Democracy at the Polls* (Washington, D.C.: American Enterprise Institute, 1981), 251–53.

[8]Malcom Jewell and David Olson, *American State Politics and Elections* (Homewood, Ill.: Irwin Press, 1978), 50.

[9]A. Karnig and B. Walter, "Municipal Elections," in *Municipal Yearbook, 1977* (Washington, D.C.: International City Management Assn., 1977).

[10]Richard Boyd, "Decline of U.S. Voter Turnout," *American Politics Quarterly* 9 (April 1981): 142.

[11]G. Bingham Powell, "Voting Turnout in Thirty Democracies," in Richard Rose, ed., *Electoral Participation: A Comparative Analysis* (Beverly Hills, Calif.: Sage, 1980), 6.

[12]See Joseph Nye, David King, and Philip Zelikow, *Why People Don't Trust Government* (Cambridge, Mass.: Harvard University Press, 1997).

[13]John M. Strate, Charles J. Parrish, Charles D. Elder, and Coit Ford III, "Life Span Civic Development and Voting Participation," *American Political Science Review* 83 (June 1989): 443–65.

[14]M. Margaret Conway, *Political Participation in the United States*, 3d ed. (Washington, D.C.: Congressional Quarterly Press, 2000), 23–25.

[15]Sidney Verba, Kay Schlozman, and Henry Brady, *Voice and Equality* (Cambridge, Mass.: Harvard University Press, 1995); Jan Leighley, *Strength in Numbers* (Princeton, N.J.: Princeton University Press, 2001).

[16]But see Jeffrey Stonecash, *Class and Party in American Politics* (Boulder, Colo.: Westview Press, 2000).

[17]Vanishing Voter Survey, 2000.

[18]Michael Delli Carpini and Scott Keeter, *What Americans Know About Politics* (New Haven, Conn.: Yale University Press, 1996).

[19]Thomas E. Patterson, *The Mass Media Election* (New York: Praeger, 1980), chs. 7–10.

[20]Patterson, *Vanishing Voter*, ch. 4.

[21]Gallup Reports, 1936–2000.

[22]V. O. Key Jr., *The Responsible Electorate* (Cambridge, Mass.: Belknap Press of Harvard University Press, 1966), ch. 1.

[23]W. Russell Neuman, *The Paradox of Mass Politics* (Cambridge, Mass.: Harvard University Press, 1986), 176.

[24]Samuel H. Barnes et al., eds., *Political Action* (Beverly Hills, Calif.: Sage, 1979), 541–42.

[25]Russell J. Dalton, *Citizen Politics in Western Democracies*, 3d ed. (Chatham, N.J.: Chatham House, 1996), 43.

[26]Robert Putnam, *Bowling Alone* (New York: Simon & Schuster , 2000).

[27]For example, interest group membership has risen.

[28]Theda Skocpol, *Diminished Democracy: From Membership to Management in American Civic Life* (Norman: University of Oklahoma Press, 2003).

[29]Patterson, *Vanishing Voter*, chs. 1, 4.

[30]Ibid., 21.

[31]See Bruce Bimber and Richard Davis, *Campaigning Online* (New York: Oxford University Press, 2003); Bruce Bimber, *Information and American Democracy* (New York: Cambridge University Press, 2003).

[32]See Benjamin Ginsberg, *The Consequences of Consent* (New York: Random House, 1982), ch. 2.

[33]See Laura R. Woliver, *From Outrage to Action* (Urbana: University of Illinois Press, 1993).

[34]ABC News/Washington Post poll, March 23, 2003.

[35]Dalton, *Citizen Politics in Western Democracies*, 38.

[36]Ibid., 68.

[37]Ronald Inglehart, "Post-Materialism in an Environment of Insecurity," *American Political Science Review* 75 (1981): 880–900; Edward N. Mueller and Mitchell A. Seligson, "Inequality and Insurgency," *American Political Science Review* 81 (1987): 425–51.

[38]Gallup poll, January 2003.

[39]William Watts and Lloyd A. Free, eds., *The State of the Nation* (New York: University Books, Potomac Associates, 1967), 97.

[40]Robert E. Lane, "Market Justice, Political Justice," *American Political Science Review* 80 (1986): 383; see also Jennifer Nedelsky, *Private Property and the Limits of American Constitutionalism* (New York: Oxford University Press, 1990).

[41]Sidney Verba and Norman Nie, *Participation in America* (New York: Harper & Row, 1972), 131.

[42]See Verba and Nie, *Participation in America*, 332; V. O. Key Jr., *Southern Politics* (New York: Vintage Books, 1949), 527; Lawrence Jacobs and Robert Shapiro, *Politicians Don't Pander* (Chicago: University of Chicago Press, 2000).

CHAPTER EIGHT

[1]E. E. Schattschneider, *Party Government* (New York: Rinehart, 1942), 1.

[2]See John Aldrich, *Why Parties? The Origin and Transformation of Political Parties in America* (Chicago: University of Chicago Press, 1995); L. Sandy Maisel, *Parties and Elections in America*, 3d ed. (Latham, Md.: Rowman and Littlefield, 1999), 27.

[3]E. E. Schattschneider, *The Semisovereign People: A Realist's View of Democracy in America* (New York: Holt, Rinehart & Winston, 1961), 140.

[4]Thomas E. Patterson, *The Vanishing Voter* (New York: Knopf, 2002), ch. 2.

[5]See Richard P. McCormick, *The Second American Party System: Party Formation in the Jacksonian Era* (Chapel Hill: University of North Carolina Press, 1966).

[6]Alexis de Tocqueville, *Democracy in America (1835–1840)*, ed. J. P. Mayer and A. P. Kerr (Garden City , N.Y.: Doubleday/Anchor, 1969), 60.

[7]Aldrich, *Why Parties?* 151.

[8]See Kristi Andersen, *The Creation of a Democratic Majority, 1928–1936* (Chicago: University of Chicago Press, 1979).

[9]See Kevin Phillips, *The Emerging Republican Majority* (New Rochelle, N.Y.: Arlington House, 1969).

[10]See Harold W. Stanley, "Southern Partisan Changes: Dealignment, Realignment or Both?" *Journal of Politics* 50 (1988): 64–88; Earl Black and Merle Black, *Politics and Society in the South* (Cambridge, Mass.: Harvard

University Press, 1987); Robert H. Swansbrough and David M. Brodsky, eds., *The South's New Politics: Realignment and Dealignment* (Columbia: University of South Carolina Press, 1988); Dewey L. Grantham, *The Life and Death of the Solid South* (Lexington: University of Kentucky Press, 1988).

[11]Gallup Organization, January 2004.

[12]William H. Flanigan and Nancy Zingale, *Political Behavior of the American Electorate*, 9th ed. (Washington, D.C.: Congressional Quarterly Press, 1998), 58–63.

[13]See Lewis L. Gould, *Grand Old Party* (New York: Random House, 2003).

[14]See John B. Judis and Ruy Teixeira, *The Emerging Democratic Majority* (New York: Scribner, 2002).

[15]The classic account of the relationship of electoral and party systems is Maurice Duverger, *Political Parties* (New York: Wiley, 1954), bk. 2, ch. 1; see also Arend Lijphardt, *Electoral Systems and Party Systems* (New York: Oxford University Press, 1994).

[16]Clinton Rossiter, *Parties and Politics in America* (Ithaca, N.Y.: Cornell University Press, 1960), 11.

[17]Nancy Gibbs and Michael Duffy, "Fall of the House of Newt," *Time*, November 16, 1998, 47.

[18]Gerald M. Pomper, *Passions and Interests: Political Party Concepts of American Democracy* (Lawrence: University Press of Kansas, 1992), ch. 1.

[19]John F. Bibby, *Politics, Parties, and Elections in America*, 5th ed. (Belmont, Calif.: Wadsworth, 2002), 275–83.

[20]Steven J. Rosenstone, Roy L. Behr, and Edward H. Lazarus, *Third Parties in America*, 2d ed. (Princeton, N.J.: Princeton University Press, 1996).

[21]Daniel A. Mazmanian, *Third Parties in Presidential Elections* (Washington, D.C.: Brookings Institution, 1984), 143–44.

[22]See Lawrence Goodwyn, *The Populist Movement* (New York: Oxford University Press, 1978).

[23]Anthony King, *Running Scared* (New York: Free Press, 1997).

[24]See Alan Ehrenhalt, *The United States of Ambition* (New York: Times Books, 1991).

[25]See Paul S. Herrnson and John C. Green, eds., *Responsible Partisanship* (Lawrence: University Press of Kansas, 2003).

[26]See Sarah McCally Morehouse, "Money Versus Party Effort," *American Journal of Political Science* 34 (1990): 706–24.

[27]David Adamany, "Political Parties in the 1980s," in Michael J. Malbin, ed., *Money and Politics in the United States* (Chatham, N.J.: Chatham House, 1984), 114.

[28]*Senator Mitch McConnell et al. v. Federal Election Commission et al.*, No. 02-1674 (2003).

[29]Joseph Napolitan, *The Election Game and How to Win It* (New York: Doubleday, 1972).

[30]Federal Elections Commission data, 2004.

[31]David B. Magleby and Candice J. Nelson, *The Money Chase: Congressional Campaign Finance Reform* (Washington, D.C.: Brookings Institution, 1990).

[32]David Chagall, *The New King-Makers* (New York: Harcourt Brace Jovanovich, 1981).

[33]Michael W. Traugott and Paul J. Lavrakas, *The Voters' Guide to Election Polls* (Chatham, N.J.: Chatham House, 1996).

[34]Kiku Adatto, "Sound Bite Democracy," Joan Shorenstein Center on the Press, Politics, and Public Policy, Research Paper R-2, Harvard University, Cambridge, Mass., June 1990.

[35]Darrell M. West, *Air Wars: Television Advertising in Election Campaigns, 1952–2000* (Washington, D.C.: Congressional Quarterly Press, 2001), 140–46.

[36]Ibid.

[37]Stephen Ansolabehere and Shanto Iyengar, *Going Negative* (New York: Free Press, 1995), ch. 5.

[38]West, *Air Wars*, 12.

CHAPTER NINE

[1]E. E. Schattschneider, *The Semisovereign People: A Realist's View of Democracy in America* (New York: Holt, Rinehart & Winston, 1960), 35.

[2]Alexis de Tocqueville, *Democracy in America (1835–1840)*, ed. J. P. Mayer and A. P. Kerr (Garden City , N.Y.: Doubleday/Anchor, 1969), bk. 2, ch. 4.

[3]Mancur Olson, *The Logic of Collective Action*, rev. ed. (Cambridge, Mass.: Harvard University Press, 1971), 147; see also Theda Skocpol, *Diminished Democracy* (Norman: University of Oklahoma Press, 2003).

[4]See Jack L. Walker, *Mobilizing Interest Groups in America* (Ann Arbor: University of Michigan Press, 1991).

[5]See Lawrence Rothenberg, *Linking Citizens to Government: Interest Group Politics at Common Cause* (New York: Cambridge University Press, 1992); Jeffrey M. Berry, *The New Liberalism: The Rising Power of Citizen Groups* (Washington, D.C.: Brookings Institution Press, 1999).

[6]Olson, *Logic of Collective Action*, 64.

[7]Christopher J. Bosso, "The Color of Money: Environmental Groups and the Pathologies of Fund Raising," in Allan J. Cigler and Burdett Loomis, *Interest Group Politics*, 4th ed. (Washington, D.C.: Congressional Quarterly Press, 1995), 101–3.

[8]Kay Lehman Schlozman and John T. Tierney, *Organized Interests and American Democracy* (New York: Harper & Row , 1986), 54; see also Ronald J. Hrebenar and Ruth K. Scott, *Interest Group Politics in America* (Englewood Cliffs, N.J.: Prentice-Hall, 1990), 167.

[9]See Beverly A. Cigler, "Not Just Another Special Interest: Intergovernmental Representation," in Cigler and Loomis, *Interest Group Politics*, 4th ed., 131–53.

[10]Norman J. Ornstein and Shirley Elder, *Interest Groups, Lobbying, and Policymaking* (Washington, D.C.: Congressional Quarterly Press, 1978), 82–86.

[11]See John Mark Hansen, *Gaining Access* (Chicago: Chicago University Press, 1991); Bruce Wolpe and Bertram Levine, *Lobbying Congress* (Washington, D.C.: Congressional Quarterly Press, 1996).

[12]Robert H. Salisbury and Paul Johnson, "Who You Know Versus What You Know," *American Journal of Political Science* 33 (February 1989): 175–95; see also William P. Browne, *Cultivating Congress* (Lawrence: University Press of Kansas, 1995).

[13]Ornstein and Elder, *Interest Groups, Lobbying, and Policymaking*, 70.

[14]Quoted in ibid., 77.

[15]Paul J. Quirk, *Industry Influence in Federal Regulatory Agencies* (Princeton, N.J.: Princeton University Press, 1981).

[16]John E. Chubb, *Interest Groups and the Bureaucracy: The Politics of Energy* (Stanford, Calif.: Stanford University Press, 1983), 200–201.

[17]Charles T. Goodsell, *The Case for Bureaucracy*, 3d ed. (Chatham, N.J.: Chatham House, 1994), 55–60.

[18]Lee Epstein and C. K. Rowland, "Interest Groups in the Courts," *American Political Science Review* 85 (1991): 205–17.

[19]See Hansen, *Gaining Access;* but see Browne, *Cultivating Congress.*

[20]Hugh Heclo, "Issue Networks and the Executive Establishment," in Anthony King, ed., *The New American Political System* (Washington, D.C.: American Enterprise Institute, 1978), 87–124.

[21]Ornstein and Elder, *Interest Groups, Lobbying, and Policymaking*, 88–93.

[22]Ernest Wittenberg and Elisabeth Wittenberg, *How to Win in Washington* (Cambridge, Mass.: Blackwell, 1989), 81.

[23]Quoted in Mark Green, "Political PAC-Man," *The New Republic*, December 13, 1982, 20; see also Frank J. Sorauf, *Inside Campaign Finance* (New Haven, Conn.: Yale University Press, 1992).

[24]Quoted in Larry Sabato, *PAC Power: Inside the World of Political Action Committees* (New York: Norton, 1984), 72.

[25]Federal Elections Commission data, 2004.

[26]See Michael J. Malbin, "Of Mountains and Molehills," in Michael J. Malbin, *Parties, Interest Groups, and Campaign Finance Laws* (Washington, D.C.: American Enterprise Institute, 1981), 157–77.

[27]See Dan Clawson, Alan Neustadtl, and Denise Scott, *Money Talks* (New York: Basic Books, 1992); Thomas L. Gatz, *Improper Influence* (Ann Arbor: University of Michigan Press, 1996); Gene M. Grossman and Elhanan Helpman, *Interest Groups and Trade Policy* (Princeton, N.J.: Princeton University Press, 2002).

[28]See Robert Dahl, *Who Governs?* (New Haven, Conn.: Yale University Press, 1961).

[29]Walker, *Mobilizing Interest Groups in America*, 112.

[30]Theodore J. Lowi, *The End of Liberalism: The Second Republic of the United States* (New York: Norton, 1979).

[31]See Rothenberg, *Linking Citizens to Government.*

CHAPTER TEN

[1]Theodore H. White, *The Making of the President, 1972* (New York: Bantam Books, 1973), 327.

[2]See Richard Davis, *The Press and American Politics*, 2d ed. (Upper Saddle River, N.J.: Prentice-Hall, 1996), 24–27.

[3]Comment at the annual meeting of the American Association of Political Consultants, Washington, D.C., 1977.

[4]Frank Luther Mott, *American Journalism, a History: 1690–1960* (New York: Macmillan, 1962), 114–15.

[5]Culver H. Smith, *The Press, Politics, and Patronage* (Athens: University of Georgia Press, 1977), 163–68.

[6]Doris A. Graber, *Mass Media and American Politics*, 6th ed. (Washington, D.C.: Congressional Quarterly Press, 2001), 36; Mark Wahlgren Summers, *The Press Gang* (Chapel Hill: University of North Carolina Press, 1994).

[7]Mott, *American Journalism*, 122–23, 220–27.

[8]Ibid., 220–27, 241, 243.

[9]Edwin Emery, *The Press and America: An Interpretive History of the Mass Media* (Englewood Cliffs, N.J.: Prentice-Hall, 1977), 350.

[10]Quoted in Mott, *American Journalism*, 529.

[11]See Dean Alger, *The Media and Politics*, 2d ed. (Belmont, Calif.: Wadsworth, 1996), 122–23.

[12]Quoted in David Halberstam, *The Powers That Be* (New York: Knopf, 1979), 208–9.

[13]Quoted in Michael Robinson and Margaret Sheehan, *Over the Wire and on TV* (New York: Russell Sage Foundation, 1983), 226.

[14]William Cole, ed., *The Most of A. J. Liebling* (New York: Simon, 1963), 7.

[15]Figures from *Standard Rate and Data Service and Electronic Media*, various dates.

[16]Ibid.

[17]Graber, *Mass Media and American Politics*, 36.

[18]See Ben Bagdikian, *The Media Monopoly*, 6th ed. (Boston: Beacon Press, 2000).

[19]See Kathleen Hall Jamieson and Paul Waldman, *The Press Effect* (New York: Oxford University Press, 2002).

[20]See Timothy E. Cook, *Governing with the News* (Chicago: University of Chicago Press, 1997); Bartholomew Sparrow, *Uncertain Guardians* (Baltimore: Johns Hopkins University Press, 1999).

[21]Dean Alger, *Megamedia* (Lanham, Md.: Rowman & Littlefield, 1998).

22Ibid., 13–14; see also Leonard Downie Jr. and Robert G. Kaiser, *The News About the News: American Journalism in Peril* (New York: Knopf, 2002).

23James T. Hamilton, *All the News That's Fit to Sell* (Princeton, N.J.: Princeton University Press, 2004).

24Study for Committee of Concerned Journalists, 2000.

25Walter Lippmann, *Public Opinion* (New York: Free Press, 1965), 214. First published in 1922.

26See Kenneth T. Walsh, *Feeding the Beast* (New York: Free Press, 1996).

27Donald Shaw and Maxwell McCombs, *The Emergence of American Political Issues: The Agenda-Setting Function of the Press* (St. Paul, Minn.: West Publishing, 1977).

28Bernard C. Cohen, *The Press and Foreign Policy* (Princeton, N.J.: Princeton University Press, 1963), 13.

29Kiku Adatto, "Sound Bite Democracy," Joan Shorenstein Center on the Press, Politics, and Public Policy, Research Paper R-2, Harvard University, Cambridge, Mass., June 1990.

30Thomas E. Patterson, *Out of Order* (New York: Vintage, 1994), ch. 3.

31Thomas E. Patterson, "Bad News, Bad Governance," *ANNALS* 546 (July 1996): 97–108; Larry J. Sabato, Mark Stencel, and S. Robert Lichter, *Peep Show: Media and Politics in the Age of Scandal* (Lanham, Md.: Rowman & Littlefield, 2000).

32Data from Center for Media and Public Affairs, Washington, D.C., 1996.

33Quoted in Doreen Carvajal, "For News Media, Some Introspection," *The New York Times*, April 5, 1998, 28.

34Quoted in Max Kampelman, "The Power of the Press," *Policy Review* 6 (1978): 19.

35James Reston, "End of the Tunnel," *The New York Times*, April 30, 1975, 41.

36Quoted in Edward J. Epstein, *News from Nowhere* (New York: Random House, 1973), ix.

37See Matthew Baum, *Soft News Goes to War* (Princeton, N.J.: Princeton University Press, 2003).

38"Study Finds Widespread Misperceptions on Iraq," Program on International Policy Attitudes, University of Maryland, October 2, 2003.

39Lippmann, *Public Opinion*, 221.

40Bill Kovach and Tom Rosensteil, *Warp Speed* (New York: The Century Foundation Press, 1999).

CHAPTER ELEVEN

1Roger H. Davidson and Walter J. Oleszek, *Congress and Its Members*, 9th ed. (Washington, D.C.: Congressional Quarterly Press, 2004), 4.

2See Paul S. Herrnson, *Congressional Elections: Campaigning at Home and in Washington*, 4th ed. (Washington, D.C.: Congressional Quarterly Press, 2003).

3See Gary C. Jacobson, *The Politics of Congressional Elections*, 5th ed. (New York: Longman, 2001).

4See Jonathan S. Krasno, *Challenges, Competition, and Reelection* (New Haven, Conn.: Yale University Press, 1995).

5Bruce Cain, John Ferejohn, and Morris P. Fiorina, *The Personal Vote* (Cambridge, Mass.: Harvard University Press, 1987).

6Information provided by Clerk of the House.

7Harold W. Stanley and Richard G. Niemi, *Vital Statistics on American Politics*, 5th ed. (Washington, D.C.: Congressional Quarterly Press, 1995), 217.

8*Congressional Quarterly Guide to Congress*, 3d ed. (Washington, D.C.: Congressional Quarterly Press, 1982), 666; see also Frank J. Sorauf, *Inside Campaign Finance* (New Haven, Conn.: Yale University Press, 1992), 67, 86; Edward Sidlow, *Challenging the Incumbent: An Underdog's Undertaking* (Washington, D.C.: Congressional Quarterly Press, 2003).

9Jennifer Babson and Kelly St. John, "Momentum Helps GOP Collect Record Amounts from PACs," *Congressional Quarterly Weekly Report*, December 3, 1994, 3456.

10Quoted in "A Tale of Myths and Measures: Who Is Truly Vulnerable?" *Congressional Quarterly Weekly Report*, December 4, 1993, 7; see also Dennis F. Thompson, *Ethics in Congress* (Washington, D.C.: Brookings Institution Press, 1995).

11James E. Campbell, *The Presidential Pulse of Congressional Elections* (Lexington: University Press of Kentucky, 1993).

12Linda L. Fowler and Robert D. McClure, *Political Ambition* (New Haven, Conn.: Yale University Press, 1989); see also Jonathan S. Krasno and Donald Philip Green, "Preempting Quality Challengers in House Elections," *Journal of Politics* 50 (November 1988): 878.

13Keith R. Poole and Howard Rosenthal, "Patterns of Congressional Voting," *American Journal of Political Science*, 35 (February 1991): 228.

14See Linda L. Fowler, *Candidates, Congress, and the American Democracy* (Ann Arbor: University of Michigan Press, 1994).

15*Congressional Quarterly Weekly Report*, various dates.

16Linda Witt, Karen M. Paget, and Glenna Matthews, *Running as a Woman: Gender and Power in American Politics* (New York: Free Press, 1993); Sue Thomas, *How Women Legislate* (New York: Oxford University Press, 1994); Tali Mendelberg, *The Race Card* (Princeton, N.J.: Princeton University Press, 2001).

17See Barbara Sinclair, *Legislators, Leaders, and Lawmaking* (Baltimore, Md.: Johns Hopkins University Press, 1995); Ronald M. Peters Jr., *The American Speakership* (Baltimore: Johns Hopkins University Press, 1990).

18Fred R. Harris, *Deadlock or Decision: The U.S. Senate and the Rise of National Politics* (New York: Oxford University Press, 1993), 182.

[19]Barbara Sinclair, *Majority Leadership in the U.S. House* (Baltimore, Md.: Johns Hopkins University Press, 1983).

[20]See, for example, Donald Matthews, *U.S. Senators and Their World* (Chapel Hill: University of North Carolina Press, 1960).

[21]See Steven H. Haeberle, "The Institutionalization of the Subcommittee in the United States House of Representatives," *Journal of Politics* 40 (November 1978): 1054–65.

[22]See Christopher J. Deering and Steven S. Smith, *Committees in Congress*, 3d ed. (Washington, D.C.: Congressional Quarterly Press, 1997).

[23]See Stephen E. Frantzich and Steven E. Schier, *Congress: Games and Strategies* (Dubuque, Iowa: Brown & Benchmark, 1995), 127.

[24]See Gerald S. Strom, *The Logic of Lawmaking* (Baltimore, Md.: Johns Hopkins University Press, 1990).

[25]See Barbara Sinclair, *Unorthodox Lawmaking: New Legislative Processes in the U.S. Congress* (Washington, D.C.: Congressional Quarterly Press, 1997).

[26]See Robert Spitzer, *President and Congress* (New York: McGraw-Hill, 1993); but see also Jon R. Bond and Richard Fleisher, eds., *Polarized Politics: Congress and the President in a Partisan Era* (Washington, D.C.: Congressional Quarterly Press, 2000).

[27]See Gary Orfield, *Congressional Power: Congress and Social Change* (New York: Harcourt Brace Jovanovich, 1975).

[28]James L. Sundquist, "Congress and the President: Enemies or Partners?" in Lawrence C. Dodd and Bruce I. Oppenheimer, eds., *Congress Reconsidered* (New York: Praeger, 1977), 240.

[29]See Paul C. Light, *Forging Legislation* (New York: Norton, 1992).

[30]Christopher J. Deering and Steven S. Smith, *Committees in Congress*, 3d ed. (Washington, D.C.: Congressional Quarterly Press, 1997), 74.

[31]Keith Krehbiel, "Are Congressional Committees Composed of Preference Outliers?" *American Political Science Review* 84 (1990): 149–64; Richard L. Hall and Bernard Grofman, "The Committee Assignment Process and the Conditional Nature of Committee Bias," *American Political Science Review* 84 (1990): 1149–66.

[32]See Gary W. Cox and Mathew D. McCubbins, *Legislative Leviathan* (Berkeley: University of California Press, 1993).

[33]Eric M. Uslaner, *The Decline of Comity in Congress* (Ann Arbor: University of Michigan Press, 1994).

[34]Joel A. Aberbach, *Keeping a Watchful Eye* (Washington, D.C.: Brookings Institution, 1990); William T. Gormley, *Taming the Bureaucracy* (Princeton, N.J.: Princeton University Press, 1989).

[35]Davidson and Oleszek, *Congress and Its Members*, 2d ed., 7.

CHAPTER TWELVE

[1]Woodrow Wilson, *Constitutional Government in the United States* (New York: Columbia University Press, 1908), 67.

[2]Sidney Milkis and Michael Nelson, *The American Presidency: Origins and Development, 1790–2002*, 4th ed. (Washington, D.C.: Congressional Quarterly Press, 2003).

[3]James W. Davis, *The American Presidency* (New York: Harper & Row , 1987), 13.

[4]See Barry M. Blechman and Stephen S. Kaplan, *Force Without War* (Washington, D.C.: Brookings Institution, 1978).

[5]*United States v. Belmont*, 57 U.S. 758 (1937).

[6]Robert DiClerico, *The American President*, 4th ed. (Englewood Cliffs, N.J.: Prentice-Hall, 1995), 47.

[7]Quoted in Wilfred E. Binkley, *President and Congress*, 3d ed. (New York: Vintage, 1962), 142.

[8]Theodore Roosevelt, *An Autobiography* (New York: Scribner's, 1931), 383.

[9]See Richard M. Pious, *The American Presidency* (New York: Basic Books, 1979), 83.

[10]Harry S Truman, *Years of Trial and Hope* (New York: Signet, 1956), 535.

[11]See Joseph A. Pika and John Anthony Maltese, *The Politics of the Presidency*, 6th ed. (Washington, D.C.: Congressional Quarterly Press, 2004).

[12]James Bryce, *The American Commonwealth* (New York: Commonwealth Edition, 1908), 230.

[13]Hugh Heclo, "Introduction: The Presidential Illusion," in Hugh Heclo and Lester M. Salamon, eds., *The Illusion of Presidential Government* (Boulder, Colo.: Westview Press, 1981), 6.

[14]Thomas R. Marshall, *Presidential Nominations in a Reform Age* (New York: Praeger, 1981); James W . Ceaser, *Presidential Selection: Theory and Development* (Princeton, N.J.: Princeton University Press, 1979).

[15]Thomas E. Patterson, *The Vanishing Voter* (New York: Vintage, 2003); John S. Jackson and William J. Crotty, *The Politics of Presidential Selection* (New York: Longman, 2001).

[16]Sidney Kraus, ed., *The Great Debates* (Bloomington: Indiana University Press, 1962), 190.

[17]John P. Burke, *The Institutionalized Presidency* (Baltimore: Johns Hopkins University Press, 1992); Charles E. Walcott and Karen M. Hult, *Governing the White House* (Lawrence: University Press of Kansas, 1995).

[18]Quoted in Stephen J. Wayne, *Road to the White House, 1992* (New York: St. Martin's Press, 1992), 143; see also Timothy Welch, ed., *At the President's Side* (Columbia: University of Missouri Press, 1997).

[19]See Shirley Anne Warshaw, *Powersharing: White House–Cabinet Relations in the Modern Presidency* (Albany: State University of New York Press, 1995).

[20]See Jeffrey E. Cohen, *The Politics of the United States Cabinet* (Pittsburgh: University of Pittsburgh Press, 1988).

[21]James Pfiffner, *The Modern Presidency* (New York: St. Martin's Press, 1994), 123.

[22]Quoted in James MacGregor Burns, "Our Super-Government—Can We Control It?" *The New York Times*, April 24, 1949, 32.

[23]See Paul C. Light, *Thickening Government: Federal Hierarchy and the Diffusion of Accountability* (Washington, D.C.: Brookings Institution, 1995).

[24]James Pfiffner, "The President's Chief of Staff: Lessons Learned," *Presidential Studies Quarterly* 22 (Winter 1993): 77–102.

[25]Erwin Hargrove, *The Power of the Modern Presidency* (New York: Knopf, 1974); see also John H. Kessel, *Presidents, the Presidency, and the Political Environment* (Washington, D.C.: Congressional Quarterly Press, 2001).

[26]James P. Pfiffner, *The Strategic Presidency: Hitting the Ground Running*, 2d ed. (Chicago: Dorsey Press, 1996).

[27]Aaron Wildavsky, "The Two Presidencies," *Trans-Action*, December 1966, 7.

[28]Pfiffner, *The Modern Presidency*, ch. 6.

[29]Thomas P. (Tip) O'Neill, with William Novak, *Man of the House: The Life and Political Memoirs of Speaker Tip O'Neill* (New York: Random House, 1987), 297.

[30]Fred I. Greenstein, ed., *Leadership in the Modern Presidency* (Cambridge, Mass.: Harvard University Press, 1988), ch. 10.

[31]Robert J. Spitzer, *The Presidential Veto: Touchstone of the American Presidency* (Albany: State University of New York Press, 1988).

[32]Richard E. Neustadt, *Presidential Power and the Modern Presidents* (New York: Free Press, 1990), 71–72.

[33]Ibid., 33.

[34]Mary E. Stuckey, *The President as Interpreter-in-Chief* (Chatham, N.J.: Chatham House, 1991).

[35]Harvey G. Zeidenstein, "Presidents' Popularity and Their Wins and Losses on Major Issues: Does One Have a Greater Influence over the Other?" *Presidential Studies Quarterly*, Spring 1985, 287–300; see also Richard Brody, *Assessing the President* (Stanford, Calif.: Stanford University Press, 1991).

[36]John E. Mueller, "Presidential Popularity from Truman to Johnson," *American Political Science Review* 64 (March 1970): 18–34; Kathleen Frankovic, "Public Opinion in the 1992 Campaign," in Gerald M. Pomper, ed., *The Election of 1992* (Chatham, N.J.: Chatham House, 1993).

[37]See John Anthony Maltese, *Spin Control* (Chapel Hill: University of North Carolina Press, 1994); Howard Kurtz, *Spin Cycle* (New York: Basic Books, 1998).

[38]Samuel Kernell, *Going Public: New Strategies of Presidential Leadership*, 3d ed. (Washington, D.C.: Congressional Quarterly Press, 1997), 1; see also Robert M. Eisinger, *The Evolution of Presidential Polling* (New York: Cambridge University Press, 2003).

[39]Jeffrey Tulis, *The Rhetorical Presidency* (Princeton, N.J.: Princeton University Press, 1987); Craig Allen Smith, *The White House Speaks* (Westport, Conn.: Greenwood, 1994); but see also Kenneth Walsh, *Feeding the Beast* (New York: Random House, 1996).

[40]Heclo, "Introduction: The Presidential Illusion," 2.

[41]Theodore J. Lowi, *The "Personal" Presidency: Power Invested, Promise Unfulfilled* (Ithaca, N.Y.: Cornell University Press, 1985); see also Jeffrey E. Cohen, *Presidential Responsiveness and Public Policymaking* (Ann Arbor: University of Michigan Press, 1997).

CHAPTER THIRTEEN

[1]Norman Thomas, *Rule 9: Politics, Administration, and Civil Rights* (New York: Random House, 1966), 6.

[2]James P. Pfiffner, "The National Performance Review in Perspective," working paper 94-4, Institute of Public Policy, George Mason University, 1994, 2.

[3]Ibid., 12.

[4]Max Weber, *Economy and Society,* trans. Guenther Roth and Claus Wittich (New York: Bedminster Press, 1968), 23.

[5]See Cornelius M. Kerwin, *Rulemaking*, 3d ed. (Washington, D.C.: Congressional Quarterly Press, 2003).

[6]Michael Lipsky, *Street-Level Bureaucracy* (New York: Russell Sage Foundation, 1980); see also George Serra, "Citizen-Initiated Contact and Satisfaction with Bureaucracy," *Journal of Public Administration* 5 (April 1995): 175–88.

[7]Paul Van Riper, *History of the United States Civil Service* (Evanston, Ill.: Peterson, 1958), 36.

[8]David H. Rosenbloom, *Federal Service and the Constitution* (Ithaca, N.Y.: Cornell University Press, 1971), 83.

[9]Herbert Kaufman, "Emerging Conflicts in the Doctrine of Public Administration," *American Political Science Review* 50 (December 1956): 1060.

[10]Ibid., 1062.

[11]Quoted in Hugh Heclo, *A Government of Strangers* (Washington, D.C.: Brookings Institution, 1977), 225.

[12]Norton E. Long, "Power and Administration," *Public Administration Review* 10 (Autumn 1949): 269; Joel D. Aberbach and Bert A. Rockman, *In the Web of Politics* (Washington, D.C.: Brookings Institution Press, 2000).

[13]See Heclo, *A Government of Strangers,* 117–18.

[14]Quoted in Aaron Wildavsky, *The Politics of the Budgetary Process*, 4th ed. (Boston: Little, Brown, 1984), 19.

[15]Joel D. Aberbach and Bert A. Rockman, "Clashing Beliefs Within the Executive Branch," *American Political Science Review* 70 (June 1976): 461.

[16]See B. Dan Wood and Richard W. Waterman, *Bureaucratic Dynamics* (Boulder, Colo.: Westview Press, 1994).

[17]See John Brehm and Scott Gates, *Working, Shirking, and Sabotage* (Ann Arbor: University of Michigan Press, 1996).

[18]Long, "Power and Administration," 269; see also John Mark Hansen, *Gaining Access* (Chicago: University of Chicago Press, 1991).

[19]See B. Guy Peters, *The Politics of Bureaucracy*, 5th ed. (New York: Routledge, 2001).

[20]William T. Gormley Jr. and Steven J. Balla, *Bureaucracy and Democracy* (Washington, D.C.: Congressional Quarterly Press, 2003).

[21]See Paul Light, *Thickening Government* (Washington, D.C.: Brookings Institution, 1995).

[22]James G. March and Johan P. Olson, "Organizing Political Life: What Administrative Reorganization Tells Us About Government," *American Political Science Review* 77 (June 1983): 281–96.

[23]Kenneth J. Meier, *Regulation* (New York: St. Martin's Press, 1985), 110–11.

[24]See Heclo, *A Government of Strangers.*

[25]See Donald Kettl, *Deficit Politics* (New York: Macmillan, 1992).

[26]See Joel D. Aberbach, *Keeping a Watchful Eye* (Washington, D.C.: Brookings Institution, 1990).

[27]David Rosenbloom, "The Evolution of the Administrative State, and Transformations of Administrative Law," in David Rosenbloom and Richard Schwartz, eds., *Handbook of Regulation and Administrative Law* (New York: Marcel Dekker, 1994), 3–36.

[28]See *Vermont Yankee Nuclear Power Corp. v. National Resources Defense Council, Inc.*, 435 U.S. 519 (1978); *Chevron v. National Resources Defense Council*, 467 U.S. 837 (1984); *Heckler v. Chaney*, 470 U.S. 821 (1985); but see *FDA v. Brown & Williamson Tobacco Co.* (2000).

[29]*Pigeford v. Veneman*, U.S. District Court for the District of Columbia, Civil Action No. 97-1978 (1999).

[30]"Clark: Bush Didn't See Terrorism as 'Urgent,'" *CNN.com*, March 25, 2004.

[31]See Brian J. Cook, *Bureaucracy and Self-Government* (Baltimore, Md.: Johns Hopkins University Press, 1996).

[32]Ibid.

[33]David Osborne and Ted Gaebler, *Reinventing Government: How the Entrepreneurial Spirit Is Transforming the Public Sector* (New York: Addison-Wesley, 1992); see also Michael Barzelay and Babak J. Armajani, *Breaking Through Bureaucracy* (Berkeley: University of California Press, 1992); Robert D. Behn, *Leadership Counts* (Cambridge, Mass.: Harvard University Press, 1991).

[34]Pfiffner, "The National Performance Review in Perspective," 7.

[35]Ronald C. Moe, "The 'Reinventing Government' Exercise: Misinterpreting the Problem, Misjudging the Results," *Public Administration Review*, March/April 1994, 125–36.

CHAPTER FOURTEEN

[1]*Marbury v. Madison*, 5 U.S. 137 (1803).

[2]*Bush v. Gore*, No. 00-949 (2000).

[3]Rebecca Mae Salokar, *The Solicitor General: The Politics of Law* (Philadelphia: Temple University Press, 1992); see also Cornell W. Clayton, *The Politics of Justice: The Attorney General and the Making of Legal Policy* (Armonk, N.Y.: Sharpe, 1992).

[4]See Bernard Schwartz, *Decision: How the Supreme Court Decides Cases* (New York: Oxford University Press, 1996).

[5]Henry Glick, *Courts, Politics, and Justice*, 3d ed. (New York: McGraw-Hill, 1993), 214.

[6]Lawrence Baum, *The Supreme Court*, 8th ed. (Washington, D.C.: Congressional Quarterly Press, 2003), 120.

[7]*Gideon v. Wainwright*, 372 U.S. 335 (1963).

[8]From a letter to the author by Frank Schwartz of Beaver College; this section reflects substantially Professor Schwartz's recommendations to the author, as does the later section that addresses the federal court myth. See also Robert A. Carp, *The Federal Courts*, 3d ed. (Washington, D.C.: Congressional Quarterly Press, 1998).

[9]*Hutto v. Davis*, 370 U.S. 256 (1982).

[10]*Lawrence v. Texas*, No. 02-102 (2003).

[11]*Bowers v. Hardwick*, 478 U.S. 186 (1986).

[12]See George L. Watson and John Alan Stookey, *Shaping America: The Politics of Supreme Court Appointments* (New York: Longman, 1995).

[13]Stephen L. Wasby, *The Supreme Court in the Federal Judicial System*, 4th ed. (Chicago: Nelson-Hall, 1993), 75; Henry J. Abraham, *The Judicial Process*, 7th ed. (New York: Oxford University Press, 1998), 24–26.

[14]Robert Scigliano, *The Supreme Court and the Presidency* (New York: Free Press, 1971), 146; see also Lee Epstein and Jack Knight, *The Choices Justices Make* (Washington, D.C.: Congressional Quarterly Press, 1998).

[15]Quoted in Baum, *The Supreme Court*, 37.

[16]See John C. Hughes, *The Federal Courts, Politics, and the Rule of Law* (New York: Longman, 1995).

[17]John Gottschall, "Reagan's Appointments to the U.S. Courts of Appeals," 70 *Judicature* 48 (1986): 54.

[18]Carp, *The Federal Courts.*

[19]Joseph B. Harris, *The Advice and Consent of the Senate* (Berkeley: University of California Press, 1953), 313.

[20]Quoted in Louis Fisher, *American Constitutional Law* (New York: McGraw-Hill, 1990), 5.

[21]Quoted in Charles P. Curtis, *Law and Large as Life* (New York: Simon & Schuster, 1959), 156–57.

[22]See Lee Epstein and Jack Knight, *The Choices Justices Make* (New York: Longman, 1995).

[23]*Faragher v. City of Boca Raton*, No. 97-282 (1998).

[24]Wasby, *The Supreme Court in the Federal Judicial System*, 53.

[25]Linda Greenhouse, "Sure Justices Legislate. They Have To," *The New York Times*, July 5, 1998, sect. 4, p. 1.

[26]John Schmidhauser, *The Supreme Court* (New York: Holt, Rinehart & Winston, 1964), 6.

[27]Linda Greenhouse, "In a Momentous Term, Justices Remake the Law, and the Court," *The New York Times*, July 1, 2003, A1.

[28]*Bush v. Gore*, No. 00-949 (2000).

[29]See, however, James L. Gibson, Gregory A. Caldeira, and Lester Kenyatta Spence, "The Supreme Court and the U.S. Presidential Election of 2000," *British Journal of Political Science* 33 (2003): 535–56.

[30]David M. O'Brien, *Storm Center: The Supreme Court in American Politics,* 5th ed. (New York: Norton, 2000), 14–15.

[31]Ross Sandler and David Schoenbrod, *Democracy by Decree* (New Haven, Conn.: Yale University Press, 2003).

[32]Some of the references cited in the following sections are taken from Henry J. Abraham, "The Judicial Function Under the Constitution," *News for Teachers of Political Science* 41 (Spring 1984): 12–14; see also Louis Michael Seidman, *Our Unsettled Constitution* (New Haven, Conn.: Yale University Press, 2002).

[33]Abraham, "The Judicial Function," 14.

[34]Alexander M. Bickel, *The Supreme Court and the Idea of Progress* (New Haven, Conn.: Yale University Press, 1978), 173–81; see also Antonin Scalia, *A Matter of Interpretation* (Princeton, N.J.: Princeton University Press, 1997).

[35]Louis Lusky, *By What Right? A Commentary on the Supreme Court's Power to Revise the Constitution* (Charlottesville, Va.: Michie, 1975), 214–16.

[36]*Romer v. Evans*, No. 94-1039 (1996).

[37]*Lawrence v. Texas*, No. 02-102 (2003).

[38]Abraham, "The Judicial Function," 13.

[39]"Good for the Left, Now Good for the Right," *Newsweek*, July 8, 1991, 22.

[40]Linda Greenhouse, "The Justices Decide Who's in Charge," *The New York Times*, June 27, 1999, sect. 4, p. 1.

[41]Quoted in ibid.

CHAPTER FIFTEEN

[1]The section titled "Efficiency Through Government Intervention" relies substantially on Alan Stone, *Regulation and Its Alternatives* (Washington, D.C.: Congressional Quarterly Press, 1982).

[2]See Marc Allen Eisner, *Regulatory Politics in Transition* (Baltimore: Johns Hopkins University Press, 1993).

[3]Paul Portney, "Beware of the Killer Clauses Inside the GOP's 'Contract,'" *The Washington Post National Weekly Edition,* January 23–29, 1995, 21.

[4]See Richard A. Harris and Sidney M. Milkis, *The Politics of Regulatory Change* (New York: Oxford University Press, 1996).

[5]Lawrence E. Mitchell, *Corporate Irresponsibility* (New Haven, Conn.: Yale University Press, 2003).

[6]H. Peyton Young, *Equity: In Theory and Practice* (Princeton, N.J.: Princeton University Press, 1995).

[7]"Hill Foes of New Clean Air Rules Unite Behind Moratorium Bill," *Congressional Quarterly Weekly Report*, Spring 1998 (Washington, D.C.: Congressional Quarterly Press, 1998), 61.

[8]See Thomas Streeter, *Selling the Air* (Chicago: University of Chicago Press, 1996); Robert McChesney, *The Problem of the Media* (New York: Monthly Review Press, 2004).

[9]See Kenneth Gould, Allan Schnaiberg, and Adam Weinberg, *Local Environmental Struggles* (New York: Cambridge University Press, 1996).

[10]Rachel Carson, *The Silent Spring* (Boston: Houghton Mifflin, 1962).

[11]Robert B. Keiter, *Keeping Faith with Nature* (New Haven, Conn.: Yale University Press, 2003).

[12]*U.S. News & World Report,* June 30, 1975, 25.

[13]*Whitman v. American Trucking Association,* No. 99-1257 (2001).

[14]See Walter A. Rosenbaum, *Environmental Politics and Policy,* 5th ed. (Washington, D.C.: Congressional Quarterly Press, 2002); Norman J. Vig and Michael E. Kraft, eds., *Environmental Policy: New Directions for the Twenty-First Century* (Washington, D.C.: Congressional Quarterly Press, 2003).

[15]See Robert Lekachman, *The Age of Keynes* (New York: Random House, 1966).

[16]See Bruce Bartlett, *Reaganomics: Supply-Side Economics* (Westport, Conn.: Arlington House, 1981).

[17]Aaron Wildavsky, *The New Politics of the Budgetary Process* (New York: Harper-Collins, 1992); Allen Schick, *The Federal Budget,* rev. ed. (Washington, D.C.: Brookings Institution Press, 2000).

[18]U.S. Senate clerk, 2002.

[19]Martin Mayer, *FED: The Inside Story of How the World's Most Powerful Financial Institution Drives the Markets* (New York: Free Press, 2001).

CHAPTER SIXTEEN

[1]Quoted in E. J. Dionne Jr., "Reflecting on 'Reform,'" *Washington Post,* web download, February 15, 2004.

[2]Press releases of House Committee on Ways and Means and National Conference of State Legislatures, September 19 and June 26, 2002, respectively.

[3]Michael Harrington, *The Other America: Poverty in the United States* (New York: Macmillan, 1962); see also Sheldon H. Danziger, Gary D. Sandefur, and Daniel H. Weinberg, eds., *Confronting Poverty* (Cambridge, Mass.: Harvard University Press, 1994); James T. Patterson, *America's Struggle Against Poverty in the Twentieth Century* (Cambridge, Mass.: Harvard University Press, 2000).

[4]Charles Murray, *Losing Ground: American Social Policy, 1950–1980* (New York: Basic Books, 1984).

[5]*Five Thousand American Families* (Ann Arbor: University of Michigan Institute for Social Research, 1977); see also William Julius Wilson, *When Work Disappears* (New York: Knopf, 1996).

[6]See Katherine S. Newman, *No Shame in My Game* (New York: Alfred A. Knopf and Russell Sage Foundation, 1999), 41.

[7]Everett Carll Ladd, *American Political Parties* (New York: Norton, 1970), 205.

[8]Institute on Taxation and Economic Policy data, 2002; see also Paul Krugman, "Hey, Lucky Duckies," *The New York Times,* December 3, 2002, A31.

[9]V. O. Key Jr., *The Responsible Electorate* (Cambridge, Mass.: Belknap Press of Harvard University, 1966), 43.

[10]Fay Lomax Cook and Edith J. Barrett, *Support for the American Welfare State* (New York: Columbia University Press, 1992).

[11]For a general overview of 1950s and 1960s policy disputes, see James Sundquist, *Politics and Policy* (Washington, D.C.: Brookings Institution, 1968).

[12]Hobart Rowan, "The Budget: Fact and Fiction," *The Washington Post National Weekly Edition,* January 16–22, 1995, 5.

[13]"Welfare: Myths, Reality," Knight-Ridder News Service story, *Syracuse Post-Standard,* December 5, 1994, A1, A6.

[14]Quoted in Malcolm Gladwell, "The Medicaid Muddle," *The Washington Post National Weekly Edition,* January 16–22, 1995, 31.

[15]Based on Organization for Economic Cooperation and Development (OECD) data, 2004; see Douglas S. Reed, *On Equal Terms: The Constitutional Politics of Educational Opportunity* (Princeton, N.J.: Princeton University Press, 2003).

[16]See Paul E. Peterson, "Ticket to Nowhere," *Education Next* 3 (Spring 2003): 39–46.

[17]See John E. Chubb and Terry M. Moe, *Politics, Markets, and America's Schools* (Washington, D.C.: Brookings Institution, 1990); Tony Wagner and Thomas Vander Ark, *Making the Grade* (New York: Routledge, 2001).

[18]See Jeffrey R. Henig, *Rethinking School Choice* (Princeton, N.J.: Princeton University Press, 1995).

[19]See Emily Van Dunk and Anneliese M. Dickman, *School Choice and the Question of Accountability: The Milwaukee Experience* (New Haven, Conn.: Yale University Press, 2003).

[20]*Zelman v. Simmons-Harris,* No. 00-1751 (2002).

[21]Press release, Congressman John Boehner, January 4, 2003.

CHAPTER SEVENTEEN

[1]See Peter B. Kenen, ed., *Understanding Interdependence: The Macroeconomics of the Open Economy* (Princeton, N.J.: Princeton University Press, 1995).

[2]American Assembly Report (co-sponsored by the Council on Foreign Relations), *Rethinking America's Security* (New York: Harriman, 1991), 8.

[3]For an overview of Soviet policy, see Alvin Z. Rubenstein, *Soviet Foreign Policy Since World War II,* 4th ed. (New York: HarperCollins, 1992); for an assessment of U.S. policy, see Robert Dallek, *The American Style of Foreign Policy* (New York: Oxford University Press, 1990); see also Mr. X. (George Kennan), "The Sources of Soviet Conduct," *Foreign Affairs* 25 (July 1947): 566–82.

[4]David M. Barrett, *Uncertain Warriors: Lyndon Johnson and His Vietnam Advisors* (Lawrence: University Press of Kansas, 1993); see also Stanley Karnow, *Vietnam: A History* (New York: Penguin, 1983).

[5]See Keith L. Nelson, *The Making of Détente* (Baltimore, Md.: Johns Hopkins University Press, 1995).

[6]For a general view of this world role, see Kenneth A. Oye, Robert J. Lieber, and Donald Rothchild, *Eagle in a New World: American Grand Strategy in the Post–Cold War Era* (New York: HarperCollins, 1992).

[7]State of the Union Address, January 29, 2002.

[8]West Point speech, June 1, 2002.

[9]PIPA-Knowledge Network survey, October 29–November 10, 2003.

[10]State of the Union Address, January 20, 2004.

[11]Address to the Council on Foreign Relations, New York City, December 3, 2003.

[12]Loch K. Johnson, *Secret Agencies* (New Haven, Conn.: Yale University Press, 1996); William E. Odom, *Fixing Intelligence* (New Haven, Conn.: Yale University Press, 2003).

[13]Ole Holsti, *Public Opinion and American Foreign Policy* (Ann Arbor: University of Michigan Press, 1996); Richard Sobel, *The Impact of Public Opinion on U.S. Foreign Policy Since Vietnam* (New York: Oxford University Press, 2001).

[14]George C. Wilson, *This War Really Matters: Inside the Fight for Defense Dollars* (Washington, D.C.: Congressional Quarterly Press, 2000).

[15]"The B-1: A Flight Through Adversity," *Los Angeles Times,* reprinted in *Syracuse Post-Standard,* July 29, 1983, A7.

[16]U.S. government data, various agencies, 2004.

[17]*The World Competitiveness Yearbook* (Lausanne, Switzerland: International Institute for Management Development, 2004).

[18]American Assembly Report, *Rethinking America's Security,* 9; see also Robert O. Keohane, Joseph S. Nye, and Stanley Hoffmann, eds., *After the Cold War* (Cambridge, Mass.: Harvard University Press, 1993).

[19]Manfred B. Steger, *Globalism: The New Market Philosophy* (New York: Rowman & Littlefield, 2002).

[20]See, for example, The Pew Research Center for the People and the Press surveys, multiple dates.

[21]PIPA-Knowledge Network survey, January 2004.

[22]Tom Masland, "Going Down the Aid 'Rathole'?" *Newsweek*, December 5, 1994, 39.

[23]Hobart Rowen, "The Budget: Fact and Fiction," *The Washington Post National Weekly Edition*, January 16–22, 1995, 5.

[24]Philip Gordon, "September 11 and American Foreign Policy," website of the Brookings Institution, downloaded on June 21, 2002. The chapter's last section is based substantially on Gordon's observations.

CHAPTER EIGHTEEN

[1]*Reno v. Condon*, No. 98-1464 (2000).

[2]*Kimel v. Florida Board of Regents*, No. 98-791 (2000).

[3]Paul Burka, "What a Texas Record Can't Tell," *The New York Times*, April 28, 2000, A23.

[4]Thad Beyle, "Governors: The Middlemen and Women in Our Political System," in Virginia Gray and Herbert Jacobs, *Politics in the American States: A Comparative Analysis* (Washington, D.C.: Congressional Quarterly Press, 1996), 237; see also Sarah McCally Morehouse, *The Governor as Party Leader* (Ann Arbor: University of Michigan Press, 1998).

[5]Amy Pyle, "California and the West," *Los Angeles Times*, October 24, 1999, A30.

[6]Advisory Commission on Intergovernmental Relations (ACIR), *The Question of State Government Capability* (Washington, D.C.: ACIR, 1985), 123.

[7]David Broder, *Democracy Derailed* (San Diego: Harcourt, 2000).

[8]Thomas E. Patterson, *The Vanishing Voter* (New York: Vintage, 2003), 10.

[9]John F. Dillon, *Commentaries on the Law of Municipal Corporations*, 5th ed. (Boston: Little, Brown, 1911), vol. 1, sec. 237.

[10]*People v. Hurlbut*, 24 Michigan 44 (1871).

[11]Susan MacManus, *Young v. Old: Generational Combat in the Twenty-first Century* (Boulder, Colo.: Westview Press, 1996).

[12]See, for example, G. William Domhoff, *Who Rules America?* 4th ed. (New York: McGraw-Hill, 2001).

[13]*San Antonio Independent School District v. Rodriquez*, 411 U.S. 1 (1973).

[14]Abby Goodnough, "Major Court Challenge on How State Allocates School Funds," *The New York Times*, October 12, 1999, B1.

[15]Diana Jean Schemo, "Worldwide Survey Finds U.S. Students Are Not Keeping Up," *The New York Times*, December 6, 2000. Web download.

[16]Gay and Lesbian Task Force data, 2003.

[17]See Malcolm E. Jewell and Sarah M. Morehouse, *Political Parties and Elections in American States*, 4th ed. (Washington, D.C.: Congressional Quarterly Press, 2000).

[18]Thomas R. Dye, *Politics in States and Communities*, 8th ed. (Englewood Cliffs, N.J.: Prentice-Hall, 1994), 162.

[19]Alan Rosenthal, *The Third House: Lobbyists and Lobbying in the States*, 2d ed. (Washington, D.C.: Congressional Quarterly Press, 2001).

[20]*Federalist* No. 10.

[21]Daniel J. Boorstin, *The Americans: The Democratic Experience* (New York: Vintage Books, 1974).

[22]See articles in Thad Beyle, ed., *State and Local Government 2003–2004* (Washington, D.C.: Congressional Quarterly Press, 2003).

CREDITS

DaimlerChrysler Corporation; p. 282 top right: Used by permission from General Motors.; p. 284: Library of Congress; p. 285: © Noah Berger/AP/Wide World Photos; p. 286: AP/Wide World Photos; p. 287: © Wally McNamee/Corbis; p. 289: © Tom McCarthy/PhotoEdit; p. 294: Frederic Neema/Corbis Sygma; p. 295: © Dennis Cook/AP/Wide World Photos; p. 297: © Greg Smith/Corbis Saba; p. 301: Davis Barber/PhotoEdit

Chapter 10

p. 308: © AP/Wide World Photos; p. 310: © Stock Montage; p. 311: © Brown Brothers; p. 313 left: U.S. House of Representatives; p. 313 right: U.S. Senate; p. 317: © Jeff Greenberg/PhotoEdit; p. 321: © Thorne Anderson/Corbis Sygma; p. 325: © AFP/Getty Images; p. 326: © EPA/David Maxwell/Wide World Photos; p. 327: © Allan Tannenbaum

Chapter 11

p. 336: © Vanessa Vick/Photo Researchers; p. 341: © Wide World Photos; p. 342: © Corbis-Bettmann; p. 347: © Dennis Cook/AP/Wide World Photos; p. 350: © Douglas Graham/Corbis Images; p. 353: © Jonathan Nourok/PhotoEdit; p. 357: © Ron Sachs/Corbis Images; p. 359: © Bob Daemmrich/Corbis/Sygma; p. 361: © Bettmann/CORBIS; p. 363: © John Van Hasselt/Corbis/Sygma; p. 368: © US Senate/AP/Wide World Photos

Chapter 12

p. 374: © Pablo Martinez Monsivais/APWide World Photos; p. 379: © UPI/Corbis-Bettmann; p. 380: © James P. Blair/Getty Images; p. 384: © Spencer Platt/Getty Images; p. 390: © Andrew Gombert/AP/Wide World Photos; p. 392: © UPI/Corbis-Bettmann; p. 394: © AP/Wide World Photos; p. 398: © Rene Burri/Magnum Photos; p. 402: © Corbis/Saba; p. 406: Library of Congress, Prints & Photographs Division, [LC-USZ62-13037]; p. 408: © AP/Wide World Photos

Chapter 13

p. 414: © AP/Wide World Photos; p. 421: © Bob Daemmrich/Stock Boston; p. 422: © Corbis/Vol. 70; p. 424: © Corbis-Bettmann; p. 429: © Don Perdue/Gamma Liaison/Getty Images; p. 434: Wally McNamee/Woodfin Camp & Assoc.; p. 437: © Mark Wilson/Getty Images

Chapter 14

p. 446: AP/Wide World Photos; p. 450: © Corbis; p. 453: © Billy Barnes/Stock Boston; p. 456: © AP/Wide World Photos; p. 457: © Ken Heinen/AP/Wide World Photos; p. 458: © AP/Wide World Photos; p. 465: © Michael C. York/AP/Wide World Photos; p. 470: © Byrce Flynn; p. 472: © AP/Wide World Photos; p. 550: Bettmann/Corbis

Chapter 15

p. 482: © AP/Wide World Photos; p. 484: By courtesy of the National Portrait Gallery, London.; p. 486: © Najlah Feanny/Corbis; p. 489: © Reed Saxon/AP/Wide World Photos; p. 493: © John M. Roberts/Corbis Stock Market; p. 494: © Jim Pickerell/Stock Boston; p. 497: © Damian Dovarganes/Wide World Photos; p. 500: © Hulton-Deutsch Collection/Corbis; p. 506: © AP/Wide World Photos; p. 509: © Bill Nation/Corbis Sygma

Chapter 16

p. 520: © Michael Newman/PhotoEdit; p. 521: © Stephen Jaffe/Reuters/Archive Photos/Getty Images; p. 523: © Bob Daemmrich/Stock Boston; p. 527: Library of Congress, Prints & Photographs Division, [LC-USZ62-117121]; p. 528: © William Johnson/Stock Boston; p. 532: © Dana Fineman-Appel/Corbis Sygma; p. 533: © Mary Steinbacher/PhotoEdit; p. 538: Bob Daemmrich/The Image Works; p. 539 left: © Sally Weigand /Index Stock Imagery; p. 539 right: © Glenn Kulbako/Index Stock Imagery

Chapter 17

p. 548: © AP/Wide World Photos; p. 549: © Michael Barson Collection/Past Perfect; p. 552: © AP/Wide World Photos; p. 553: © Robert Nickelsberg/Getty Images; p. 558: © Sam Sargent/Getty Images; p. 561: © AP/Wide World Photos; p. 565: StaffSgt. Jeremy T. Lock/U.S. Air Force; p. 570: © Wolfgang Kaehler/Corbis Images; p. 573: © Spencer Platt/Getty Images; p. 576: Photo Courtesy of U.S. Army

Chapter 18

p. 583 © Larry Kolvoord/Image Works; p. 586: © Stephan Savoia/AP/Wide World Photos; p. 588: © Sandra Baker/Liaison Agency/Getty Images; p. 592: © John Elderfield/Gamma Liaison/Getty Images; p. 594: © Matthew McDermott/Corbis Sygma; p. 598: © Lunne Sladky/AP/Wide World Photos; p. 602: Reprinted with permission of the California State Lottery; p. 603: © Jana Birchum/Getty Images; p. 608: © Andy Sacks/Stone/Getty Images; p. 610: © Mike Derer/AP/Wide World Photos; p. 611: © Elise Amendola/AP/Wide World Photos; p. 615: © Craig J. Brown/Gamma Liaison/Getty Images

INDEX